REGIONAL DEVELOPMENT AND PLANNING

A Reader

REGIONAL DEVELOPMENT AND PLANNING

A Reader

Edited by

JOHN FRIEDMANN

and

WILLIAM ALONSO

THE M.I.T. PRESS

Massachusetts Institute of Technology

Cambridge, Massachusetts

Second printing, June 1965
Third printing, December 1967

Library of Congress Catalog Card Number 64-25214
Printed in the United States of America

For Walter Isard

Acknowledgments

CHAPTER 1 Reprinted from the *Quarterly Journal of Economics,* Vol. 64, No. 1 (February 1950), pp. 89–104, with permission of the author and Harvard University Press.

CHAPTER 2 Reprinted from Carl J. Friedrich and Seymour E. Harris, eds., *Public Policy,* A Yearbook of the Harvard University Graduate School of Public Administration, Vol. 12 (1963), pp. 141–162, with permission of the author and Harvard University Press.

CHAPTER 3 Reprinted from the *Journal of the American Institute of Planners,* Vol. 29, No. 3 (August 1963), pp. 168–175, with permission of the editor.

CHAPTER 5 Reprinted from the *Southern Economic Journal,* Vol. 5, No. 1 (July 1938), pp. 71–78, with permission of the editor.

CHAPTER 6 Paper presented at the Annual Meeting of the Regional Science Association, Chicago, December 1963. Printed with permission of the author and the editor of the *Papers and Proceedings of the Regional Science Association.*

CHAPTER 7 Reprinted from *Economic Development and Cultural Change,* Vol. 9, No. 4 (July 1961), Part I, pp. 573–587, with permission of the author and the University of Chicago Press.

CHAPTER 8 Reprinted from *Papers and Proceedings of the Regional Science Association,* Vol. 4 (1958), pp. 179–198, with permission of the author and the editor.

CHAPTER 9 Reprinted from the *Annals of the Association of American Geographers,* Vol. 53, No. 1 (March 1963), pp. 1–14, with permission of the author and the editor.

CHAPTER 10 Reprinted from the *Annals of the Association of American Geographers,* Vol. 52, No. 1 (March 1962), pp. 1–20, with permission of the authors and the editor.

CHAPTER 11 Reprinted from Joseph J. Spengler, ed., *Natural Resources and Economic Growth,* Washington, D. C., Resources for the Future, Inc., 1961, pp. 191–212, with permission of the authors and Resources for the Future, Inc.

CHAPTER 12 Reprinted from the *Journal of Political Economy,* Vol. 63, No. 3 (June 1955), pp. 243–258, with permission of the author and the University of Chicago Press.

CHAPTER 13 Reprinted from the *Journal of Political Economy,* Vol. 64, No. 2 (April 1956), pp. 160–169, with permission of the authors and the University of Chicago Press.

CHAPTER 14 Reprinted from the *Manchester School of Economics and Social Studies,* Vol. 24, No. 2 (May 1956), pp. 161–179, with permission of the author and the editor.

CHAPTER 15 Reprinted from *Economic Development and Cultural Change,* Vol. 11, No. 2 (January 1963), Part I, pp. 134–151, with permission of the author and the University of Chicago Press.

CHAPTER 16 Reprinted from *Economic Development and Cultural Change,* Vol. 9, No. 2 (January 1961), pp. 128–143, with permission of the authors and the University of Chicago Press.

CHAPTER 17 Reprinted from *Economic Development and Cultural Change,* Vol. 3, No. 2 (January 1955), pp. 81–102, with permission of the author and the University of Chicago Press. Omitted sections include (5) The Economic History of Urban-Industrial Growth, (6) Neo-technic Urbanization: the System of Cities, and (7) Some "Lessons" for Underdeveloped Countries.

CHAPTER 18 Reprinted from *Comparative Studies in Society and History,* Vol. 4, No. 1 (November 1961), pp. 86–103, with permission of the editor.

CHAPTER 19 Reprinted from *Comparative Studies in Society and History,* Vol. 4, No. 4 (July 1962), pp. 473–493, with permission of the author and editor.

CHAPTER 20 Reprinted from Roy Turner, ed., *India's Urban Future,* Berkeley, University of California Press, 1962, pp. 192–212, with permission of the author and the University of California Press.

CHAPTER 21 Reprinted from United Nations, Department of Economic and Social Affairs, *Economic Survey of Europe, 1954,* Geneva, 1955, pp. 136–160, with permission of the United Nations. Tables 70–76 have been eliminated from this re-edition.

CHAPTER 22 Reprinted from the *Journal of Political Economy,* Vol. 69, No. 4 (August 1961), pp. 319–340, with permission of the author and the University of Chicago Press.

CHAPTER 23 Reprinted from the *Southern Economic Journal,* Vol. 26, No. 3 (January 1960), pp. 187–198, with permission of the author and editor.

CHAPTER 24 Reprinted from the *American Economic Review,* Vol. 49, No. 2 (May 1960), pp. 379–391, with permission of the author and editor.

CHAPTER 25 Reprinted from United Nations, Economic and Social Council, Working Paper No. 12 (E/CN.11/RP/L.14), June 25, 1958, pp. 1–6, with permission of the United Nations, and from *Land Economics,* Vol. 32, No. 1 (February 1956), pp. 1–13, with permission of the editor.

CHAPTER 26 Reprinted with permission of the author and publisher from *Area and Power: A Theory of Local Government* by Arthur Maass, editor, copyright 1959 by The Free Press, A Corporation, pp. 27–49.

CHAPTER 27 Reprinted from the *American Political Science Review,* Vol. 55, No. 4 (December 1961), pp. 831–842, with permission of the authors and the American Political Science Association.

CHAPTER 28 Reprinted from the *American Political Science Review,* Vol. 44, No. 3 (September 1950), pp. 607–630, with permission of the author and the American Political Science Association.

CHAPTER 29 Reprinted from the *Journal of the American Institute of Planners,* Vol. 30, No. 2 (May 1964), with permission of the author and editor.

CHAPTER 30 Reprinted from the *American Economic Review,* Vol. 45, No. 2 (May 1955), pp. 120–132, with permission of the author and editor.

CHAPTER 31 Reprinted from Werner Hochwald, ed., *Design of Regional Accounts,* Published for Resources for the Future, Inc., Baltimore, The Johns Hopkins Press, 1961, pp. 253–261, with permission of the authors and the Johns Hopkins Press. The selection is taken from the complete essay entitled "The Role of Accounts in the Economic Study of the Pittsburgh Metropolitan Region."

CHAPTER 32 Reprinted from Albert O. Hirschman, *The Strategy of Economic Development,* New Haven, Yale University Press, 1958, pp. 183–201, with permission of the author and Yale University Press.

CHAPTER 33 Reprinted from Paul Rosenstein-Rodan, ed., *Pricing and Fiscal Policies: A Study in Method,* Cambridge, Mass., The M.I.T. Press, 1964, pp. 18–29.

CHAPTER 34 Reprinted from the *Quarterly Journal of Economics,* Vol. 77, No. 1 (February 1963), pp. 26–39, with permission of the author and Harvard University Press.

CHAPTER 35 Reprinted from the *Quarterly Journal of Economics,* Vol. 76, No. 4 (November 1962), pp. 515–548, with permission of the author and Harvard University Press.

Contributors

WILLIAM ALONSO, Acting Director, Center for Urban Studies, and Associate Professor, Harvard University, Cambridge, Massachusetts.

ROBERT E. BALDWIN, Professor of Economics, University of Wisconsin, Madison, Wisconsin.

BRIAN J. L. BERRY, Associate Professor of Geography, The University of Chicago, Chicago, Illinois.

MARION A. BUCK, Associate Professor, and Acting Director, Business Research Center, Syracuse University, Syracuse, New York.

HOLLIS B. CHENERY, Assistant Administrator for Program, Agency for International Development, Department of State, Washington, D. C.

BENJAMIN CHINITZ, Chairman, Department of Economics, Professor of Economics, and Associate Director, Center for Regional Economic Research, University of Pittsburgh, Pittsburgh, Pennsylvania.

JOHN FRIEDMANN, Associate Professor of Regional Planning, Department of City and Regional Planning, Massachusetts Institute of Technology, Cambridge, Massachusetts.

PETER R. GOULD, Assistant Professor of Geography, The Pennsylvania State University, State College, Pennsylvania.

DALE E. HATHAWAY, Professor of Economics, Department of Agricultural Economics, Michigan State University, East Lansing, Michigan.

ALBERT O. HIRSCHMAN, Professor of International Economic Relations, Department of Economics, Columbia University, New York, New York.

EDGAR M. HOOVER, Director, Center for Regional Economic Research, and Professor of Economics, University of Pittsburgh, Pittsburgh, Pennsylvania.

JOHN V. KRUTILLA, Associate Director, Water Resources Program, Resources for the Future, Inc., Washington, D. C.

ERIC E. LAMPARD, Professor of History, University of Wisconsin, Madison, Wisconsin.

LOUIS LEFEBER, Associate Professor of Economics, Massachusetts Institute of Technology, Cambridge, Massachusetts.

CHARLES LEVEN, Associate Director, Center for Regional Economic Research, and Associate Professor of Economics, University of Pittsburgh, Pittsburgh, Pennsylvania.

AUGUST LÖSCH, died 1945. Author of *The Economics of Location.* (New Haven: Yale University Press, 1954).

CHARLES MCKINLEY, Professor of Political Science, Portland State College, Portland, Oregon.

RICHARD L. MORRILL, Assistant Professor of Geography, University of Washington, Seattle, Washington.

RICHARD M. MORSE, Chairman, Department of History, and Professor of History, Yale University, New Haven, Connecticut.

WILLIAM H. NICHOLLS, Consulting Economist, Getúlio Vargas Foundation, Rio de Janeiro, Brazil, and Professor of Economics, Vanderbilt University, Nashville, Tennessee.

DOUGLASS C. NORTH, Director, Institute for Economic Research and Professor of Economics, University of Washington, Seattle, Washington.

BERNARD OKUN, Associate Professor of Economics, Queens College, City University of New York, Flushing, New York.

VINCENT OSTROM, Editor, *Public Administration Review,* and Professor of Political Science, University of California, Los Angeles, California.

HARVEY S. PERLOFF, Member, "Committee of Nine," Alliance for Progress, and Director of Regional Studies, Resources for the Future, Inc., Washington, D. C.

FRANÇOIS PERROUX, Director, Institute de Science Économique Appliquée, Paris, France.

RICHARD L. PFISTER, Associate Professor of Economics, Dartmouth College, Hanover, New Hampshire.

M. A. RAHMAN, Reader in Economics, University of Dacca, Dacca, Pakistan.

RICHARD W. RICHARDSON, Deputy Chief (Program), International Division, Bureau of the Budget, Washington, D. C.

LLOYD RODWIN, Chairman of the Faculty, M.I.T.–Harvard Joint Center for Urban Studies and Professor of Land Economics, Department of City and Regional Planning, Massachusetts Institute of Technology, Cambridge, Massachusetts.

SIDNEY C. SUFRIN, Professor of Economics and Business Administration, Syracuse University, Syracuse, New York.

SHANTI TANGRI, Associate Professor of Economics, Wayne State University, Detroit, Michigan.

JOHN H. THOMPSON, Professor of Geography, Syracuse University, Syracuse, New York.

CHARLES M. TIEBOUT, Professor of Economics, University of Washington, Seattle, Washington.

EDWARD L. ULLMAN, Professor of Geography, University of Washington, Seattle, Washington.

ROBERT WARREN, Assistant Professor of Political Science, University of Washington, Seattle, Washington.

LOWDON WINGO, JR., Research Associate in Regional Studies and Secretary of the Committee of Urban Economics, Resources for the Future, Inc., Washington, D. C.

PAUL YLVISAKER, Director, Public Affairs Program, Ford Foundation, New York, New York.

Contents

Part III
THEORY OF REGIONAL DEVELOPMENT

Part IV
NATIONAL POLICY FOR REGIONAL DEVELOPMENT

Part V
A GUIDE TO THE LITERATURE

Introduction

John Friedmann and William Alonso

REGIONAL DEVELOPMENT AS A POLICY ISSUE

In the few years that nations have sought economic development as an explicit goal it has become clear that the arithmetic of macroeconomics has need of and is made more powerful by the geometry of regional considerations. Not only must decisions be made on how much of a scarce resource shall be allocated to a given purpose but also on where investments shall take place. Regions and space are a neglected but necessary dimension of the theory and the practice of economic development. Without the spatial point of view, the analysis is incomplete, somewhat like a two-dimensional projection of a three-dimensional object. A nation has an economic landscape, akin to a physiographic one, with peaks and valleys, with areas which teem with life and areas which are deserted. The decision of *where* to locate a new project is as important as the decision to invest in it. The questions of social justice in the distributions of the fruits of economic development are as important and as difficult in terms of regions as in terms of social classes.

Public policy has thus become concerned with the manner and pace of economic development of subnational areas, and space and distance are increasingly considered explicitly in the determination of national policies. But the conceptual structure necessary for the intelligent making of policy is in its infancy. The social sciences, principally economics and sociology, have been laggard in taking notice of space; while geography, which has always dealt with space, has lacked analytic power. The readings in this volume are therefore symptomatic of the state of our knowledge, which is eclectic. Having evolved rapidly from an ancestry of many disciplines, they reflect substantial insights but are deficient in integration. If our knowledge were more advanced, we could write a textbook, epitomizing and codifying principles in ordered cadences. The time may come, in a decade or two, when this can be done; but the topic is an urgent one, both for the technician and for those charged with responsibility for making decisions. It is thus our intention to make available in one place a sampling of some of the thinking of those concerned with the regional aspects of development, to show both the underlying threads and the varieties of style. When the time comes for a textbook to be written, students of regions will be more confident of their art; for the moment, however, the time is filled with the excitement of discovery.

Human activities are distributed over the national territory in certain rhythms and patterns that are neither arbitrary nor the workings of chance. They result rather from the interdependencies that give form to economic space. Spatial patterns will change with shifts in the structure of demand and of production, in the level of technology, and in the social and political organization of the nation. The economic and social development of the nation is reflected in its patterns of settlement; its systems of flow and exchange of commodities, money, and information; its patterns of commuting and migration; and its reticulation of areas of urban influence. And if there is a spatial pattern corresponding to each "stage" of economic development, it may be further suggested that there is an optimal strategy for spatial transformation from one stage to the next. In the early period of development, marginal returns to the factors of production differ greatly among regions. With economic advancement, economic functions become more differentiated in space, and the relevant scale of many functions will increase. At an advanced stage of development, the national economy will appear as a fully integrated hierarchy of functional areas, with most of the population and activities polarized in metropolitan areas and, in effect, with national markets for labor, capital, and commodities.

Two concerns of public policy for spatial organization may, therefore, be distinguished. Where economic development occurs unequally across the nation's territory, regional differences in the level of welfare may become an urgent political issue. And where the manner in which economic space is organized affects the pace and structure of economic growth, national policy must turn to strategies of spatial evolution to further the general development objectives of the economy.

These policy issues must eventually be reduced to the specific programmatic questions of the priority and location of activities. Often these questions are treated within a microanalytic framework whereby specific projects, such as a new steel mill, a hospital, or even a new national capital, are located in terms of what is best for the project itself. For example, profit-making enterprises may be located to maximize expected returns to investment. But these decisions may also be taken within the context of a national program for regional development in which the decision maker must balance the optimizing considerations of the project with consideration of the best over-all strategy for sustained national development. Thus, the balance sheet for a given project may show the largest "private" gain at one location, *A*, but considerations of multiplier effects or economies of agglomeration may indicate another location, *B*, as being the most beneficial to the national economy as a whole.

In transitional societies, the regional problem thrusts itself on policy-makers during the period of early industrialization when, for a variety of reasons, activities come to be concentrated in one or a few centers. These centers not only grow so rapidly as to create problems of an entirely new order, but they also act as suction pumps, pulling in the more dynamic elements from the more static regions. The remainder of the country is thus relegated to a second-class, peripheral position. It is placed in a quasi-colonial relationship to the center, experiencing net outflows of people, capital, and resources, most of which redound to the advantage of the center where economic growth will tend to be rapid, sustained, and cumulative. As a result, income differences between center and periphery tend to widen. But the periphery frequently includes what during the preindustrial era were important settlements and producing regions, and may account for a major portion of the national population. It is therefore likely to hold considerable political power which may be used to persuade the national government to adopt an aggressive policy for extending the scope of economic development beyond the narrow confines of the initial growth regions.

Although basic, the center-periphery dichotomy is too crude to serve as a meaningful policy framework for regional development. The fourfold classification of development areas below may be more suitable for this purpose.

1. *Metropolitan regions.* Sometimes called "core regions" or "growth poles," they are large urban centers of industry, commerce, and administration that, together with their immediate region of influence, possess high potentialities for further economic expansion.

2. *Development axes.* These are elongated corridors along principal transport routes linking two or more metropolitan regions. Their prospects for development may be said to be roughly proportional to the size of the centers they link and inversely proportional to some function of the distance separating them.

3. *Frontier regions.* New technologies, population pressures, or new national objectives sometime suggest the occupation of virgin territory. Frontiers contiguous to the older developed regions may expand more or less spontaneously along a broad front, often springing from urban settlements. Noncontiguous frontiers are

usually associated with large-scale resources development, and take the form of relatively isolated enclaves, frequently having an urban focus, but at a considerable distance from existing metropolitan regions.

4. *Depressed regions.* The remainder of the effectively settled parts of the nation tend to consist of areas of declining or stagnant economy. They offer only modest development prospects, and provide most of the workers and a good portion of the capital to the major growth regions.

Metropolitan and depressed regions represent, in essence, center and periphery. Development axes are an extension of metropolitan regions and an embryonic form of what, in developed nations, has recently been baptized megalopolis. Frontier regions are the growing areas of the periphery and may contain the seeds of future metropolitan centers. A national policy of regional development must therefore recognize not only that the problems and methods of development will differ within each region, but also that economic changes across all regional categories are to a marked degree interdependent. That is to say, it must be *comprehensive* by considering the national economy in its spatial dimensions and regional economies as subsystems having internal balances and external flows.

Transitional societies too often view the spatial aspect of regional development as involving a choice between mutually exclusive alternatives: either a dispersal of investments so that every region will receive its "fair share" (this usually means favoring the depressed regions), or concentration of investment resources at existing growth poles. This dilemma is commonly regarded as a choice between social equity and growth in production. So formulated, the choice is obviously an extremely difficult one, even on technical grounds, and is complicated in reality by the political pressures that the periphery exerts upon the center. A further complication arises from the fact that dispersion and concentration also have a bearing on the temporal choice between present benefits and greater but more distant ones. By following the strategy of selective concentration, enjoyment of the fruits of the economy is postponed, whereas dispersion may lead to early payoffs in terms of politics and economic egalitarianism.

No simple formula will yield an answer to the problem of the choice of region. It is clear, however, that the real options are not bracketed by extreme formulations in terms of either welfare or efficiency, present time or future. Rather, the choice of regions for development must be considered in light of their potential contribution to the nation's development objectives. And here, the fundamental goal of most transitional societies is their economic and social integration *in space*. Large underdeveloped nations, such as Indonesia and India, generally find that their regional elements are insufficiently interrelated, that they are nations composed largely of regional "islands." The struggle is to achieve a common ethos and a closely interdependent national economic system. Such countries look upon their development as a process leading to the progressive internal integration of their national territories. At the same time, developing nations may discover that the new activities created in process of development require market areas exceeding the national boundaries. As a result, movements are now afoot in South America, Asia, and Africa in furtherance of multinational economic regions.

In deciding upon the allocation of resources among regions, welfare and the present must be weighed against economic growth and the future; and the clear immediate considerations of particular project decisions must be weighed against general strategies that involve balances among sectors within regions as well as balances among regions.

It may be helpful to formulate these general considerations as a set of criteria for testing the consequences of specific policy proposals. The first of these is the objective of national integration. Accordingly, it is held that one of the fundamental purposes of economic development is the creation of a national economic space articulated by an interdependent system of cities, areal functional specialization, and national markets. A second criterion demands that efficiency considerations be taken into account in the location of new activities. At a minimum this means that projects should be located so as not to require to operate effectively or where private and social interests diverge. In sustained subsidies for survival. Third, regional investment allocation should be guided by the criterion of maximizing opportunities for the further growth of the national economy. For it is clear that subnational areas cannot themselves make progress if the nation as a whole should stagnate: sustained national economic growth must always be a first consideration in regional investment choices. Finally, a certain interregional balance in levels of living must be maintained, at least sufficient to preserve political stability in support of the drive to national growth.

It is evident that, in any application, each of these criteria will be assigned different weights, depending on the situation. To attain one set of values, others must be sacrificed. Nevertheless, the criteria are useful in deciding on regional investment allocation, if only because they call to mind the major considerations relevant to societies transitional to an industrial order.

As a country approaches mature industrialization, policy interest in regional problems will noticeably decline. This may be ascribed to certain consequences of the development process itself. Regional differences become blurred as markets are unified, resources more fully utilized, and differences in the costs of location attenuated. With growing urbanization and improved transport-communication networks, intense regionalism will gradually yield as an ideological expression to a pervasive cosmopolitanism. Relations will be more among cities—as a system of cities extends its influence over the entire country—than among regions. The urban focus, in fact, will come to predominate, as increasing numbers of the population come to live within metropolitan areas. Welfare differences among regions are likely to be reduced significantly from what they were during the early period of industrialization—though pockets of backwardness may remain here and there—and consequently lose a good deal of their potency as a prime political issue. To some degree, public policy may still be addressed to the problem of lagging regions, but this will be regarded as a welfare problem stemming from the immobility of human resources rather than as a key issue for national economic growth.

Economic development will also bring with it an improvement in private decision-making. As the economy matures, there will be more entrepreneurs, and they will act upon better and more comprehensive information about alternative investment opportunities. The capital market, too, will be improved, extending for all practical purposes across the nation. As a result, investors will respond more readily to small incentives, and few opportunities will long go unexploited. This will reduce the number of situations where "automatic" processes fail to operate effectively or where private and social interests diverge. In short, many regional development problems which, during earlier periods, required purposeful government action, are attenuated through the normal functioning of the market. This observation applies to socialist countries as well, through the increase of the quality as well as the numbers of bureaucratic entrepreneurs.

In economically advanced countries, therefore, the regional problem will appear in forms different from those prevailing in transitional societies. The predominant effort in spatial planning will be shifted to problems of location and land use internal to the structure of metropolitan areas. In addition, national policy will sometimes become concerned—as in England and France—with what is presumed to be an excessive concentration of population and activities around the national capital. In such cases the argument, although unproved, appears to be that the agglomerative decision of the entrepreneur may show profit from his point of view, but that the societal diseconomies are greater from the point of view of the economy as a whole. Or it may be that the depressed conditions of rural or mining areas call for special efforts to stimulate their economies, although the emphasis will be mainly on welfare rather than efficiency considerations. Occasionally, comprehensive river basin development may be undertaken as a regional project. All these problems involve the national government to some degree, but, except for the organization of urban-metropolitan space, may be regarded as "mopping-up" operations rather than as activities critical to the national development process itself.

There is one situation however, in which regional policy may become crucial even in advanced economies. It has been commonplace, since Adam Smith and his pin factory, that development and functional specialization go hand in hand. Such specialization is always localized, and the articulation of areal and functional differences into a single economic system constitutes what we have called the integration of the space economy. As economic development progresses, economies of scale in production call for larger markets, while rapid growth in demand calls for an increasing variety of goods and services, some of which must often come from great distances. Technology permits the size of economic regions to grow larger, to the point where the regional problem is shifted unto a less bounded stage in which nations are transformed into economic subregions of a larger entity, such as a "common market." As a result, new political instrumentalities are called into being to deal with issues already familiar: dispersal versus the polarization of growth; the balancing of individual project returns and regional considerations; and the spatial integration of the new multinational economy in terms of labor, capital, and goods. Moreover, the changes in activity location which result from an expansion of markets to countries joining in an economic union will set up requirements for adaptation to both growth and decline on a regional basis which will clearly involve spatial considerations. An example is the gradual depopulation of former agricultural regions and their conversion to less intensive uses, such as recreation. Matters of national pride and history, as well as politics, will always constrain the ability of planners to decide on a "best" strategy. But the recent tendencies toward creating more comprehensive spatial and economic unities appear to be the beginning of a new cycle of economic growth in which regional issues will once again loom as a highly significant concern for public policy. Western Europe is the outstanding instance of this trend.

TOWARD AN UNDERSTANDING OF REGIONAL DEVELOPMENT

Academic concern with regional development stems from the policy issues discussed. We have seen how these issues differ in transitional and economically advanced countries and how they arise from two main sources: the desire to attain a range of national objectives and the need to adapt effectively to the growth and decline of subnational economies.

The mainstream of the literature on economic development, however, has not dealt adequately with the regional problem. Typically, the focus has been the nation construed, in effect, as a point devoid of spatial dimension. This slighting of space is not surprising, for considering the factor of spatial differentiation greatly complicates the analytical problem. The impetus for a fuller recognition of the regional problem has come chiefly from politicians, administrators, economists, and city planners who are engaged at close quarters with the practical demands of development policy. These men, having to make concrete decisions in which the question of *where* had to be answered, have turned to the academicians in search of a rational basis for choice.

The urgency of regional problems has led, in most cases, to approaches which are not so much interdisciplinary as mindless of the traditional boundaries among academic disciplines. In considering problems of urbanization, depressed regions, and interregional migration, the subject matter of diverse social sciences becomes so thoroughly intertwined that its separation into "pure" disciplinary strands is nothing but a sterile exercise. Urbanization, for example, is studied by the geographer with a view to discovering the reasons for city location, by the regional scientist for evidence of the systemic arrangements of cities within a country, by the sociologist with a concern for patterns of urban social structure and their influence on regional integration, by the economist with a view to discovering the bases of urban economy and the pattern of emerging growth poles, and by the city planner with an eye to the requirements for investment in urban infrastructure and the optimal arrangements of urban land-use patterns. None of these approaches can be ignored if a full understanding of the role of cities in regional development is sought.

From a theoretical standpoint, two questions assume importance: (1) How is economic growth spatially differentiated, and, (2) what accounts for differential patterns and sequences of growth?

The first question has been inadequately explored, so that we know, in fact, relatively little either about spatial activity patterns at different periods in the economic development of nations or about typical growth sequences in space. One surmise is that a space economy normally evolves from a number of small and relatively closed regional economies into a fully integrated national economy in which the significance of locational differences is sharply reduced. Another hypothesis is that modern economic development occurs typically at only a few points in space and that development proceeds from there to incorporate successively larger portions of the national periphery.

In studying the spatial structure of economic development, both physical and activity patterns must be considered as two aspects of the same reality. The first refers to the arrangement in space of human settlements, productive facilities, transport routes, land uses, and the like. Activity patterns consist of the flows of capital, labor, commodities, and communications which link the physical elements in space. While the former have a direct significance for calculating investment requirements, the latter are chiefly responsible for energizing the development process itself. Large urban concentrations, for example, continue to expand for as long as they offer substantial cost advantages to interpersonal communications. As soon as these advantages are reduced by being spread more evenly across a larger territory such as a metropolitan region or belts of continuous urbanization, activity patterns will be dispersed. As a result, economic growth may reach into areas that heretofore had lagged behind the general drive towards greater productivity.

The spatial structure of an economy comes into being from the interaction of physical and activity patterns. It may be described and studied with reference to such phenomena as growth poles, development axes, functional urban hierarchies, trade areas, and intermetropolitan peripheries. And it will stand in some logical relation to the technology and productivity levels of the economy. As these change, the spatial structure of activities is likely to be changed, although historical patterns will continue to exert their initial influence. The second question, then, concerns the reasons for differential spatial patterns and sequences of spatial transformation. Here, two approaches are equally valid. In the first, the interest is chiefly historical and the focus a given region. The problem is to explain the region's past development and to carry projections into the future. In this case, the rest of the nation is treated as a noncontrollable, exogenous variable.

Given the behavior of the larger economy, how has the study area responded and what are its possibilities? This is a legitimate question, but little of a general nature can be inferred from an answer. No two "regions" are alike, and their histories will differ as do those of nations. No universal pattern will emerge.

In the second approach, attention focuses on the nation whose territory is regarded as a differentiated continuum. The question is therefore not why a given area, arbitrarily defined, has fared in a certain way, but why particular patterns and sequences of spatial organization have accompanied the evolution of the national economy. Boundaries are not regarded as fixed. Regional delimitations will be valid only for limited periods of time. In a sense, the problem is to explain these temporal shifts in the boundaries and lines of interdependence by which the space economy is historically defined.

Economists and others concerned with this issue have sought an explanation along several lines. One obvious approach was through location theory and a consideration of natural resources (as a spatially immobile factor) in the context of interregional trade. It is noteworthy in this connection that spatial immobilities tend to exert a strong influence early in the development process, but gradually yield to the attractions of local, regional, and even national markets. In general, the development process leads to increased locational freedom.

The surplus yielded by interregional trade and prompted by some resource advantage may be invested locally and ultimately lead to cumulative growth. But much depends on the institutional structure of the area and who profits. In many cases, such as plantation economies, regional exports do not lead to sustained investment and growth. Instead, the profits are spent on the increased consumption of goods and services produced outside the region.

Location analysis in terms of transport costs must be related to urbanization economies arising chiefly from reductions in the costs of communications. This provides the intellectual bridge for introducing urban theory as a second level of explanation. The questions here resolve into such problems as the minimum critical mass required to push an urban economy into self-sustaining growth, the changing urban social structure and its influence on surrounding areas, and the institutional bases for national integration. Students of cities sometimes distinguish "generative" from "parasitic" cities—between cities that fulfill a creative, civilizing role and those that exist largely by virtue of the exploitation of rural areas.

A final link in explaining the spatial patterning of the national economy is found in the analysis of internal migration. Migration tends to adjust imbalances in welfare at the same time that it allows a more rational exploitation of resources, both in regions of substantial emigration (as a result of possible adjustments in land use and in production techniques) and in frontier regions. Without migration, economic growth would come to a halt. But it can also be a disturbing element, as where the number of inbound migrants greatly exceeds the available job opportunities at specified locations or where, because of its magnitude and selective character, it leaves rural communities abandoned to their own incompetence. In any event, no explanation of regional economic growth can be complete without full attention to this aspect of the problem.

All three approaches are treated at some length in the present volume. In conclusion, therefore, a word is due in explanation of the selections made.

ORGANIZATION OF SELECTIONS

At the outset, it may be well to state what this volume does *not* include. It is silent, for instance, on questions of analytical method. Problems in the application of social income accounting, regional input-output analysis, industrial complex analysis, and linear and nonlinear programing—to cite only a few of the relevant techniques—are expertly discussed in a recent compendium by Walter Isard.[1] Most of the pertinent literature up to that time is reviewed critically there, and the student of regional development will find the volume an indispensable guide through the entanglements of methodology and regional theory.

In general, we have also avoided material predating 1955, since almost all of this has been superseded or stated more incisively in more current writings. For a similar reason, we have not undertaken to translate material not already available in English; most of it is duplicated in one form or another in American studies. East European literature, however, presents a problem of a different order. Its institutional assumptions depart so radically from ours that their applicability to

[1] Walter Isard, in association with others, *Methods of Regional Analysis: an Introduction to Regional Science,* New York and London, The Technology Press of the Massachusetts Institute of Technology and John Wiley & Sons, Inc., 1960.

Western problems and experience is probably not very great.[2] Neither have we included the writings on regionalism, a form of cultural philosophy which flourished in the 1930's but is now widely regarded as an oddity, at least in the United States with its exceptionally fluid social patterns. In any event, little has been added to the subject since the excellent symposium edited by Jensen in 1951.[3] Finally, we decided to exclude case studies of regional development. Few studies of article length are such that the reader may draw valid inferences from them. Although many of the selections make use of concrete examples, and areas as widely separated as Italy's Mezzogiorno and the American Pacific Northwest are discussed at length, we have been guided in our choice by a desire to include only those articles which make a substantive contribution to knowledge beyond their immediate area of reference.

This exclusion of case studies was prompted by yet another concern. We wished to emphasize *national* approaches to regional development. Our first section, therefore, introduces the principal regional policy issues that arise at the national level. It deals with concepts of space and planning, elaborating on the differences between physical and socioeconomic space and between the study of planning and its practice. The second section is devoted to the anatomy of space, and is meant to serve as an introduction to the organization of regions. The third section deals with the theory of regional development and with the various explanations that have been advanced to account for growth or retardation of subnational economies. The first part of this section concentrates on the role of natural resources, external trade, and migrations; the second part on the role of cities in development; and the third on the problems of backward areas. A fourth section deals with national policy for regional development. The issue of how to define optimal planning regions is discussed, followed by essays on the definition of regional objectives and the evalution of regional economic progress. The final part of this section is devoted to a review of national strategies which have been proposed for regional development.

The readings collected in this volume attempt to furnish a foundation for realistic thinking about the regional problem. Selections are drawn from many of the relevant fields of investigation. Specialists in

[2] Volumes on Polish and Yugoslav experiences with regional and city planning are being edited by Dr. Jack C. Fischer of Cornell University and are to be published soon.

[3] Merrill Jensen, ed., *Regionalism in America,* Madison, University of Wisconsin Press, 1951.

one discipline may be delighted to discover materials from another that are pertinent to their own set of problems. The general reader, on the other hand, is given an opportunity to synthesize in his own mind, and with the help of the brief commentary provided, the dimensions of a new specialization focused on regional development, policy, and planning. The readings are arranged in order to facilitate this task.

PART I
Space and Planning

Introductory Note

In the three essays which follow, the reader will be introduced to the central concepts and problems with which this book is concerned: space, development, and planning. These three terms are seldom thought of as being related. While the link between space and planning is as familiar to urbanists as the link between planning and development is to the economist, the joining of "space" to development is only now coming to be acknowledged as a significant extension of traditional ways of thinking. One result of this is the appearance of a new goal dimension: spatial planners are made aware of economic objectives such as productivity growth, full employment, and financial stability, while economic planners are discovering objectives for the organization of economic space.

A study of economic development as a dynamic system of spatial relations can, in fact, yield deep insights. Locations and spatial interaction patterns not only define this system but strongly influence its performance characteristics as measured by the usual criteria. It is thus that Lloyd Rodwin can pose the choice of regions—that is, the choice of a gross location pattern for investment—as one of the basic problems for transitional societies to solve. Much in the same vein, John Friedmann attempts to trace the outlines and core interests of regional planning as a new field of academic study. He draws a sharp distinction between the practice and the study of regional planning, defining the latter as a specialized form of spatial planning concerned principally with the normative ordering of activities in economic space for areas larger than a single city.

But what is the nature of these relations? What, indeed, is the basic concept of space which is used here as a common thread, relating the several parts of this book to each other? It is this question which François Perroux addresses directly in his Harvard lecture of fifteen years ago.

The traditional concept of space (which Perroux calls *banal*) is defined by studying the extent, density, and sequence of physical phenomena on the earth's surface. It obeys conventional Euclidian geometry or, in some cases, the geometry of the surface of a sphere. It is the space of traditional geographic inquiry, though geographers are beginning to advance beyond the earlier physical models. In a rather simplified form, it is the space we mean when we say that Iceland has 38,900 square miles, or that Karachi lies approximately 700 miles southwest of New Delhi. But this concept of space is rudimentary and allows one to make only a small number of inferences. As a scientific concept, it is not very productive, and as a concept in planning it is practically worthless. A more useful reading is obtained if the physical distance between New Delhi and Karachi is modified according to the mode of travel used, the degree of social and political compatibility between India and Pakistan, Hindus and Moslems, and the cost of shipping commodities across an international frontier. The space so defined and measured is more varied and complex than purely physical space. It also constitutes the basis for any further work in spatial analysis.

It is difficult to grasp the concept that the form and properties of space vary with the functional meaning of the interrelation being considered. Sometimes it is disturbing to leave the comfortable common sense of every day, where two cities are always a fixed number of miles apart. But there is no mystery here. Imagine a map of a country showing the location of its principal cities. One may lay a scale between any two cities and read the distance from one to the other. Imagine now a map in which the straight-line distance between two cities represents the time it takes a train to travel from one to the other. It will be a very different map, in that some trains are fast, others slow, some travel over direct routes, others zigzag. Some cities connected by fast, direct trains, will appear close to each other. Others, perhaps only a few miles apart, may require indirect routes on slow trains and be far apart on the map. In fact, the very shape of the nation will be changed.

Intuitively, the concept presents no difficulty. In fact, it is very unlikely that such a map could be drawn. A map drawn on a sheet of paper must obey the dictates of Euclidean geometry, and the proportions among any three cities would have to conform to the laws of trigonometry. Such consistency is most improbable, and we would be forced to adopt a new type of "map": a variety of railroad timetable, with all the cities listed on the top and on the side, and each box showing the time it took to reach one city from another. In this fashion there would not be any difficulty in handling even a case (not infrequent) in which it takes longer to reach city A from city B than to make the reverse trip.

This timetable, or matrix of railroad time-distances, would be a strange sort of map, but it would function as one. It would be a map at a higher level of abstraction. Should we want to map more complex relationships, such as balance of payments among cities, the probability of migration, or the contribution of diverse possible locations of a project to national economic development, our maps might take the form of sets of mathematical equations, or even a discursive article. In any case we shall use the symbolic instrumentality that best represents the interrelations which interest us.

In this sense space is shaped by the functional interrelations being considered, and there will be as many varieties of space as fundamental relations. It is possible to think of a superspace in which there would be in addition to time and the three dimensions of geometric space, as many additional dimensions as there are modes of interrelation. Any one specialized space, such as that of the railroad time-distances, would be a particular aspect of that superspace, abstracted from the whole, much as in considering how a child grows tall we may abstract the dimensions of height and time.

Needless to say, the formulation of such a superspace is only a distant dream. It would require the discovery and definition of the fundamental variables and their organization into a taxonomy which classified them into discrete, nonoverlapping elements. Yet the very concept of such a superspace makes clear that any partial space is a selective simplification, implying a purpose in including some things and excluding others. When that purpose is a cognitive one, the space will include those elements necessary to explain or describe the phenomena that interest us. When the purpose is normative, the space must be formulated with a view to the effectiveness of action upon it. Thus the very definition of region will vary with our purpose. A region defined for water control will be very different from one for the integration of the iron and steel industry or from one for the measurement of the multiplier effects of an investment. For some purposes our region may be an area, while for others, such as urban renewal, it may consist of points which are not joined. In short, the nature of the space in any case will depend both on the type of interrelations being considered and on the purpose in mind.

Implicit in the discussion has been the issue of levels of abstraction. That is to say, the concept of socioeconomic space is at a higher level of generality than the concept of geographic space. This is necessary not only for more sophisticated understanding, but also for the process of policy planning. Policy is no mere collection of decisions, but a series of generalized, related statements meant to guide the flow of current decisions. It involves prediction, and therefore the type of generalization that says that one thing is like another in some respects and that certain parallels in their behavior may be expected. This is the essential ingredient of rationality and the only basis for faith in the possibility of planning. Therefore our conceptualization must be expressed at the level of abstraction necessary to capture the relevant similarities of distinctions.

The search for the proper level of abstraction underlies much of the work being done in this field, as the reader will find reflected in the selections. Sometimes too abstract a position is taken, and our very imperfect understanding makes it easy to lose one's way. Sometimes too low a level is used, so that no synthesizing is possible and the only result is the cumulation of case materials. The issue is to find that level which will be most fruitful, granting the intellectual leverage of abstraction while firmly holding in focus the specific questions that must be answered, such as where to put a new factory, how many migrants must be housed in a particular locality, or whether barley or rice should be planted in a certain region.

Finally, a comment may be appropriate in explanation of the claim advanced that the problem of regional development can be reduced to one in spatial organization. Regional development concerns the incidence of economic growth. It is ultimately the result of the location of economic activities in response to differential regional attractions. Shifts in the location pattern have direct repercussions on income, employment, and welfare. Since spatial organization is a function of activity and interaction patterns, regional development is simply an expression of these patterns. And regional *planning* consequently endeavors to improve the organization of economic space in accordance with indicated criteria or goals.

1. Economic Space: Theory and Applications[1*]

FRANÇOIS PERROUX

I have no intention of playing the easy and hardly glorious role of a European who comes to criticize Europe in America. But having spoken and written in this vein a number of times in Europe, I probably retain the right to say here and now that the hard trials we have undergone have caused an increase, amongst our élite and our masses, of a certain number of *pathological complexes* which make a reasonable international policy very difficult.

I will cite four of these complexes: (*a*) that of the "small nation," (*b*) that of encirclement (*Einkreisung*), (*c*) that of people without space (*Volk ohne Raum*), and of vital space, and (*d*) that of "natural frontiers" and of historical frontiers.

Each of these topics has clearly a real foundation. If the facts which gave them birth were interpreted in cold blood, there would not be any reason to use the big words "complexes" and "pathology." But around a kernel of reality there develops a double process of *interpretation* and of *dramatization*. It is the result of more or less spontaneous reactions of the masses; it is also stimulated and maintained by political leaders.

The great inequality of nations and of economic resources amongst nations is a fact. The interpretation and dramatization begin when, without investigation or qualification, the opinion is formed that the small country is condemned to impotence, dependence and exploitation.

It is also a fact that any nation or group of nations does not cover the surface of the entire world. From the point of view of cartography, there is no nation that is not in some degree encircled. From these acknowledged facts, the interpretation and dramatization give rise to a "besieged castle" mentality.

1. This article was delivered as a lecture at Harvard University on November 2, 1949. For the translation into English, I am indebted to Y. Mainguy, Director of the London branch of the I. S. E. A. (Institute of Applied Economic Science), G. Rottier, assistant to the Director, and Mrs. Copp, technical secretary; and I wish to express to them my sincere thanks.

* Reprinted from the *Quarterly Journal of Economics,* Vol. 64 (Feb. 1950).

Population pressures are unequal amongst nations. But it is by no means necessary to attribute to them proletarianization, the vital necessity of war, or the doctrine of "need as the source of right."

Geography proposes themes to history, and history is *one* of the raw materials for the statesman. The earth cannot be remodelled entirely and without delay, the past cannot be effaced. But there is nothing in all that to lay the foundations of venomous and interminable quarrels about historical frontiers and natural frontiers.

I observe that this pathological deformation of some indisputable data is only possible through the aid of a *common and inexact notion of space.* A banal sense of space location creates the illusion of the coincidence of political space with economic and human space. More precisely, we go on depicting to ourselves the relations between different nations as consisting exclusively in men and things in *one* space, conceiving them as *material* objects *contained* in a *container.* Thus it comes about that the pathological doctrines which have just been mentioned present themselves as supported by the admitted facts of a sound "common sense." The men and objects contained in a containing national space appear in effect to be threatened if the nation is small, if it is surrounded, if it is not economically well provided for, if it has not the outline to which it believes it has a claim by virtue of geographical configurations or historical tradition. This central conception of "container" and "contained" is contradicted on all sides by modern life, especially in its economic aspects. The concept remains tyrannical however, and a sort of disciplined intellectual effort is indispensable when we wish to remove it from intellectual analysis and from concrete policy. If international policy fails, one may certainly accuse interests and passions, but one should principally accuse everyday concepts. We shall risk losing the construction of a new world and of a new economy if we persist in thinking of them in terms borrowed from the old world and the old economy.

In this connection, I will try to demonstrate three propositions.

1. The extension to economic science of the notion of abstract space defined by modern mathematics and physics has not yet been made, even in its most rudimentary form.

2. Even in its most rudimentary and most provisional forms, this extension is a remedy for the pathological complexes, which I have denounced. It results in freedom from the obsession with "contained" and "containing." It allows a description of real economic relations which this obsession conceals or at least obscures. It opens the way to an understanding of the world economy other than by addition or combination of national areas.

3. This extension is necessary for the radical transformation of some of our fundamental economic theories. Since it is necessary eventually to make a choice, this last point will be illustrated by some examples concerning, on the one hand, a specific kind of economic activity, that is, monetary space, and on the other hand complex sets of economic activities — the economic space of a nation and the economic space of a group of nations, for example, the so-called "European" economic space.

I. The Idea of Abstract Space and Economic Analysis

Mathematics has long used and still uses space defined by two or three dimensions, in which points, lines and volumes can be located by their coordinates. Rigid shapes, in Euclidean geometry, are situated in this "containing" space; they are contained within it.

Modern mathematics, following recognized work to which the French have contributed, had become accustomed to consider the abstract relations which define mathematical beings, and so to give the name "spaces" to these structures of abstract relations. There exist therefore as many spaces as there are structures of abstract relations which define an object. These *abstract spaces*, some of which are known to be extremely complicated, are sets of relations which respond to questions without involving directly the location of a point or a shape by two or three coordinates.

By pure and simple transposition of this distinction between Euclidean and abstract space, we may distinguish in our discipline as many economic spaces as there are constituent structures of abstract relations which define each object of economic science. Since, mathematically, an abstract space is entirely expressed only by a constituent structure or by a mathematical system of relations, and since we do not possess either the inventory or the symbolization of relations which characterize either all the objects of economic science or even the more important of them, we have the impression of being blocked at the start and of being unable to get from our distinction anything other than regret and nostalgia. This, I think, is a false impression. Abstract spaces have been accurately defined in mathematics and physics by way of particular and specialized investigations, and such investigations will be necessary to define abstract space in economics. At least we can organize the necessary researches and experiments, and to do this, the distinction in question is of great help. Formulated with the sole resources of logic and ordinary language, it already greatly aids us to interpret the innumerable acts of *delocalization* of economic activity in the contemporary world.

This delocalization appears in relatively simple form in relation to the classical dispute on national income. Leaving aside all the difficulties of the definition of income, shall we calculate the income *in* the nation, or the income *of* the nation? The income *in* the nation is the sum of net services obtained within the national territory by nationals and residents (not nationals). The national territory is, in this case, considered as a container; men and objects are contained therein. The observer determines for a period the flow of net services which issues from the whole. This brings us back to defining the space from which the national income is obtained and to confusing it with the territorial area surrounded by political frontiers.

The income *of* the nation is another thing; it includes in principle the net services obtained by the nationals whether or not resident in the nation. (The social accounting does not keep rigorously to the exigencies of logic and does not refuse to submit to considerations of pure convenience.) There is no longer any need to determine the contents of a container; one acts *as if* an entity had drawn up *a* plan of employment for the goods and services which periodically deliver a net global revenue. From banal space we have passed into an economic space characterized by a *hypothetical* plan of employment for the national entity.

This example, chosen because it is known, has the object only of establishing a rigorous distinction between *geonomic* space and *economic* spaces. While the latter are, by definition, the proper fields of our discipline, they are also those which have been the least directly and deeply studied. Space has probably given rise to technical literature less precise and less extensive than time; however, our science possesses numbers of mathematically developed studies on the localization of an economic unit or activity considered with respect to cost and price, in so far as they are dependent on space. But it does not possess, to my knowledge, a central study on the *illusions of localization*, which shows clearly that localization in banal space from the point of view of cost and of price is only one aspect of the difficulties of our analyses and policies. Another aspect, not less important, arises from the fact that economic units or activities *cannot be localized;* a concrete economic policy must never forget that.

Geonomic space — a term which we will use as synonymous with "banal" space, is defined by the geonomic relations between points, lines and volumes. Men and groups of men, objects and groups of objects, economically characterized in other respects, find a place here; they can be treated by geonomic localizations which give rise to resulting economic consequences.

SYNOPTICAL TABLE OF ECONOMIC SPACES[1]

Space	Relations	Unit		Localization
		Simple	Complex	
I Geonomic Space (E_o)	Geonomic relations between: points, lines, surfaces, volumes	Men Things	Groups of men Groups of things	Geonomic
II Economic Space (E_a)	Economic relations	Micro-units of production	Macro-units of production	Economic
(1) Space as defined by a plan (Ea_1)	Relations defining the plan of a unit Relations defining the plans of the other units in the same set	Micro-quantities Prices of micro-quantities	Macro-quantities Prices of macro-quantities	
(2) Space as a field of forces (Ea_2)	Forces arising from a unit Forces acting on a unit	Micro-units of consumption		
(3) Space as a homogeneous aggregate (Ea_3)	Relations of homogeneity, relative to the units, relative to relations between these units			

[1] Every set of relations designated by Ea_1, Ea_2, and Ea_3 can be considered as an *abstract space*. This concept, used by the French mathematician Fréchet, can be specified following the nature of the abstract spaces which have been submitted to a process of mathematization (*e.g.*, vectorial space, topographical space, etc.). One suspects — although the certainty will be given only by the mathematization itself — that Ea_1, Ea_2, and Ea_3 present us with very different difficulties when we try to submit them to a process of mathematical formalization.

But the spaces which directly concern us are *economic spaces.* They are defined by the *economic* relations which exist between economic elements. These economic spaces conveniently reduce to three: (1) economic space *as defined by a plan;* (2) economic space *as a field of forces;* and (3) economic space *as a homogeneous aggregate* (see table on page 93).[2]

The meaning and the fruitfulness of these categories can be judged by reference to the firm, taken as an elementary unit of production and considered, according to the accustomed definition, as a set of material means and manpower subject to the same economic authority.

The banal space of the firm is that in which the material means and manpower of the firm are situated when it is functioning: the buildings, machines, raw materials, and workmen. It is not easy to locate, except under several conditions: the enterprise and the establishment must be one and the same thing, it must be built on one spot only, and one must have a material and possibly over-simple view of the economic resources which are utilized. This space is technical rather than economic. The number of square metres necessary for the installation and functioning of a firm is doubtless a function of the organization, but the economy of space cannot be carried on indefinitely; so that the determining factors are finally technical data such as the nature of the material to store, to stock, to transform; the machines and engines to use; the space required for the necessities of the work and for its preparation. Under these determinate conditions, an optimum technical spatial arrangement exists for a given unit of industrial work.

As soon as we eliminate the simplifications which make our job easy, it is no longer possible to situate the firm in banal space. It is often composed of establishments geographically dispersed, amongst which are formed bonds of organization of varying strength. The same establishment is possibly composed of parts which are not contiguous. The means of production comprise machines and materials, and also electric current and money in the bank. These difficulties of everyday localization do not interest us; the essential point is to recognize that economic analyses centred around *this* localization or

2. My colleague, W. Isard of Harvard University, during the discussion of this lecture, made me aware of the fact that some of the points expressed here have been mentioned by August Lösch in his book, *Die räumliche Ordnung der Wirtschaft* (Jena: G. Fischer, 1944). I agree, with the reservations that Lösch's fundamental visual angle differs from my own, and that the generalization in terms of "abstract spaces" is alien to his important contribution.

connected with it, engender serious illusions which dissipate the notion of *economic* space which we have proposed.

The firm has, in the first place, a space defined by a plan. This plan is the set of relations which exist between the firm and, on the one hand, the suppliers of *input* (raw materials, labor, power, capital) and, on the other hand, the buyers of the *output* (both intermediary and final). The economic distance measured in monetary terms, that is to say in terms of prices and costs, is determined by factors outside the plan; it depends on the structure and arrangement of the plan of the firm, as well as on the structure and arrangement of the plans of groups in relation to the firm. The economic space envisaged therefore escapes all cartography, and even any *single* table of characteristics; a rough expression would be given to it for a period, by some *alternative* tables of characteristics, within the framework of possible combinations. The head of the firm, to a certain extent, gives himself his own economic distances over a period. But, in the event of expansion, the plan in any one period does not contain only quantities for the next period. The development plan itself is situated within the framework of an economic *horizon*, meaning in this case the whole of the elements taken into consideration for drawing up a plan. In this new respect, economic distances can be molded by the initiative of the head of the firm. We must go still further.

The network of property rights is as misleading as the space delimited by physical boundaries or geographic outlines. In these latter spaces, the head of the firm meets the plans of the state, of labor and of competitors. These interferences upset his calculations of economic distances worked out from everyday localization, and it is these that he must overcome, as well as the results of physical distance, in order to achieve his goal. The economic space of the firm is thus in the first place a structure of relations defining the plan of this very unit and the plan of other units; it is largely independent of banal space.

In a second aspect, the firm has a space defined as a field *of forces.* As a field of forces, economic space consists of centres (or poles or foci) from which centrifugal forces emanate and to which centripetal forces are attracted. Each centre being a centre of attraction and repulsion, has its proper field, which is set in the fields of other centres. Any banal space whatever, in this respect, is a collection of centres and a place of passage for forces.

The firm considered as a centre releases centrifugal and centripetal forces. It attracts men and objects (personal and material aggregations around the firm) into its banal space, or it removes them (diverting tourist activities, land reserved for further expansion, etc.). It attracts economic elements, supplies and demands, into the space of its plan, or it removes them.

Through this process, the economic zone of influence, whether or not it is linked to the topographical one, is determined. The topographical zone of influence of Michelin in France is inscribed in a region, but its economic zone of influence, like that of all large firms, defies cartography.

The firm, in a third aspect, has a space defined as a *homogeneous aggregate*. The relations of homogeneity which define economic space in this respect are relative to the units and to their structure, or relative to the relations between these units.

The firm has, or has not, a structure more or less homogeneous with those of other firms which are its neighbors topographically or economically — it belongs to a space where, roughly speaking, one price reigns. To speak more exactly, each firm has its price. Even in a régime approximating to competition, each firm does not have exactly the same conditions of production, or sale, or cost, as the next firm. But it happens that various firms are placed in approximately the same conditions and set approximately the same price, for a clientèle situated at the same physical distance. Alternatively, firms placed in very unequal conditions regarding cost, can offer the same price for clients situated at very different physical distances. These firms are in the same economic space, whatever their coordinates in everyday space.

I think this analysis is sufficient to show to what extent, in spite of centuries of economic teaching, the present conceptions which inspire our decisions are rough and inadequate. It is not an exaggeration to say that we are still obsessed by *everyday space* and *everyday localization*. This obsession results in troublesome and even tragic consequences; it maintains and aggravates disputes of a territorial nature at a time when evolution itself demands that nations and classes should *devaluate their frontiers* and, in so far as possible, harmonize those plans of employment of economic and human resources which *delocalize* not only the progress of our technique, but also the progress of our scientific conceptions of the world. The moment has arrived to provoke consciously *a change of visual angle*, to run systematically, knowing well what we do, counter to economic analysis which tries to determine the *place* and the *causes of the place* of an economic unit in everyday space.

I shall make a beginning towards this objective by examining some concrete applications of the distinction between the three economic spaces: (1) space as defined by a plan, (2) space as a field of forces, (3) space as a homogeneous aggregate.

II. Some Applications of the Distinction Between the Three Types of Economic Space

The spheres of application are innumerable and the choice of some of them, for brief explanation, is of necessity arbitrary. I do not think, however, that I can be reproached for having neglected the most serious and present difficulties if, as a test for my basic distinctions, I concentrate attention on two economic spaces: (1) *monetary space*, and (2) *national space.*

(1) The notion of monetary space, which of course must be understood for its own sake, also deserves to be scrutinized and analyzed because the effort clarifies such obscure and indeterminate notions as national money, supranational money, and world money.

Before 1913, when the gold standard was in force, the different national gold coins were not customarily used in the same regions of the world. The pound sterling moved about very generally. The American eagle and double eagle circulated in the Pacific regions or elsewhere with the trade of the United States. The Louis and the Napoleon, outside France, were encountered especially in the nations to which France gave loans. The places of actual use of gold coins were perfectly distinct from the places of *possible* use under the régime of the gold standard. Today the actual use of the check in Europe has spread but little into the countryside. The hoarding of notes and gold has different degrees and forms in the town and in the country, according to the period. The localization of monetary flow and monetary stocks in slow circulation or at rest, operate with reference to banal space. Their delocalization, which is the essential thing, is understood, realized and measured in quite other spaces.

In the first place let us look at a monetary space as defined by a *plan.* In this sense, the monetary space of a unit is formed by the relations which constitute the plan for employment of money by this unit. There are plans for employment of money by individuals, by monetary centres and by states. Money is internationalized or delocalized according to the extent to which the various plans of employment are compatible; and they are rendered so to a practicable extent by conscious organization and not by the mechanical moving of metal in banal space. The monetary space which is nationally or imperially self-sufficient is the work of a state which arbitrates in its proper interest, that is to say by reference to its proper plan, the plans for employment of money by individuals and groups on which it exercises its authority. The monetary space of a monetary union or of a monetary agreement is the work of states which in principle leave to contractual laws the task of easing the compatibility of their own plans for employment of money with those of their subjects; in fact dominant plans exercise their partially irreversible influence over dominated plans. The monetary space of the gold standard itself, in its heyday, resulted from the action of dominating monetary powers and from their rules of the game.

A single plan of organization for the employment of money was supposed to reign over the whole of the planet. The moneys exchanged with one another on the basis of their metal content. This all took place as if a world central bank with national branches compelled the parties to accept convertibility and multilateralism. In fact, as is well known, it was very much otherwise, and the practical functioning of the gold standard was conditioned by the action of monetary powers unequally dominating and dominated — so much so that the monetary space of the gold standard was always in some degree that of one or of several dominant economies. The delocalization of money is all relative for this main reason, that in an economy based on the competition of individuals and of groups, the plans of monetary employment cannot be made entirely compatible, either by the application of the rules of the game or by the pressure of a *de facto* immovable sovereignty. It would be useless to repeat this, if one did not still find economists who have confidence, or pretend to have confidence, in the application of out-of-date rules of the game or in the effect of a *de facto* authority for the long-term internationalization of money.

Monetary space as a *field of forces* is not easily understood if one is in the path of the forces; it is seen more easily in terms of a "network" (in the mathematical sense) of payments, or by means of the description of monetary flows. A centre (or pole) has then to be chosen, from which one draws the "network" of payments towards or from other centres; or from which emanate, and to which come, monetary flows. The most significant of these "centres" are complex aggregates of monetary and financial organisms — the "places." The monetary flows attracted towards or issuing from one of these financial "places" of the nineteenth or twentieth centuries, the variations of their direction, their composition and their volume, actualize a monetary space which is not totally independent of the one described as defined by a plan, but which cannot be approximated or reduced to it.

The history of the sterling area — at one time unofficial, at another time armed with official and authoritative institutions — illustrates well the interference of monetary plans of organization with the proper powers of attraction of a financial place. Money can be delocalized for a large number of transactions, either because one place exercises in regard to the world a role centralizing the supply and demand of currency and the collection and redistribution of the means of settlement, or because several financial centres play this role, each in a sphere and with the means to form a relatively harmonious aggregate. In an economy which is based on the competition of individuals and groups (nations) it is vain to hope, in this respect also, that there should be a perfect delocalization of money. None the less, our method reveals the ambiguity of the idea of international monetary space and international money. International currency is, in one case, a dominant national currency, and in another, a currency dealt with by a number of places of comparable power and harmonizing policies. The discussion on the key currencies and the "modest" success of Bretton Woods in the control of devaluation has very likely some relation to this sort of interpretation.

Finally monetary space conceived as a *homogeneous aggregate* suggests an almost perfect international currency market and an approximate unity in exchange rates. Theoretically this would be the monetary space of a gold standard functioning without resistance or friction. Actually, we see areas where currencies exchange for each other under market conditions which are not too imperfect, and where the price of one currency in relation to another is relatively uniform. History has recorded in this respect only international monetary spaces insufficiently homogenized.

The distinction between the various economic spaces dissipates the illusion of an effective and complete internationalization of money, but indicates how a *practicable* internationalization can be obtained: by making compatible the plans of monetary employment and harmonizing the influences of dominant monetary centres. It also allows one to judge rightly autarchical spaces which do not venture to give their real names, but which hide under the label, as ambiguous as it is out-of-date, of "European Federation."

(2) The outlook is broadened when *national space* is submitted to analysis, that is to say when one attacks, by the means which it offers us, the ambiguous concept of nation, with its doctrinal and practical errors, in the world economy.

By its actual growth, and by the states of mind which it has encouraged or even created, the nation has given rise to, and kept in being, the *illusion that the various human and economic spaces are superimposable.*

The French example is typical. For many of our countrymen, France is a political space which coincides more or less with a cultural space and with an economic space. French men and French objects are *contained* in a *container*, of which the contours are the frontiers. Some nationalists become excited at the idea of this picture. They go into ecstasies over the hexagon, lauding its proportions, its unity, rejoicing in the "equilibrium" of the continental and sea borders, the beauty of mountainous swellings and navigational arteries. Within the hexagon a political system reigns; its limits are those of "liberty." A "balanced" economy is supposed to exist there, with suitable proportions between agricultural and industrial sectors, heavy industries and industries for consumption goods, etc. The frontier becomes the limit of a sort of masterpiece, too perfect to be anything other than static. The celebrants of this cult of the bounded field, full of piety for the object which they are embracing, are unaware of the impiety they show to the objects they forget. Thousands of Frenchmen live and have died outside of France: the "ashes of the dead" which "have created the country" are not concentrated in a basement. The space where French ideas, traditions and feelings are present, overflows in all directions the metropolitan space. The French economy, to the extent that it maintains its health and vitality, is outside France, as well as in France. Banal localization obscures the unforgettable pronouncement of Renan that a nation is a "spiritual principle."

But, let us close the parenthesis. Let us return quickly to the purely economic analysis. In all its forms, even the most modern, analysis has interpreted the nation as a fact of *localization* in banal space. It has been powerless to put in evidence the phenomena of *delocalization,* which do not appear except by examination of the economic spaces which we have distinguished. It has, by doing so, aggravated the tyrannies of localistic interpretation to which we are so spontaneously inclined, instead of freeing our minds and enabling us to see the error of the views according to which a national economy is contained in a place. Only liberalism, in the vigor of its development, understood the fruitfulness of the delocalization of economic activities. But it has not taken the whole advantage of its intuition, and has left to the free play of prices the task of harmonizing the plans of both individuals and groups, whereas conscious decisions are necessary to harmonize the plans of groups, especially national groups. Of course, the economy appears as a matter of localization if one choses to interpret it by reference to banal space. It is then easy to say what is "within" and "without," "domestic" and "external." This way of looking at it will be made into a more or less elegant concept, and, no doubt, one would surprise many of the most up-to-date theoreticians of international trade by telling them that they have not been able to break completely with the naivetés of organicism. Nevertheless it seems to be so. For, to organicism of all forms, the nation is essentially a "big individual," a collective entity which takes up a certain space. Thus there is installed in economic thought an unconfessed autarchy, close to the very concept of the nation. Even though one should go on to observe that any of the functions of this organism (defence, production, consumption) are not formed with reference to men and objects assembled and organized in a territory, the vice of the original thought would not thereby be eliminated. The collective indifference curves (isosatisfactions and isocosts) drawn for a whole nation, about which a literature is accumulating, refer to a "big individual" who has an aggregate of tastes, disposes of a stock of goods, indulges in productive plans and sometimes possesses bargaining power against other "big individuals."

In addition, recent analyses treat the nation as a local complex of factors of production, of which the contents are determined by the relative supplies of these factors contributed by the various nations. National space in all these cases is treated as "contents" which have a "container." The customary analysis binds its conclusions to a banal space, bounded by political frontiers, thus *accepting fundamentally the very limits which ought to be devaluated.*

The analysis which I am suggesting develops in the opposite way. The economic spaces with which it is concerned give the nation an image which cannot be given by any cartography because the relations which compose them are largely independent of banal localization.

The space of the national economy is not the national territory but the domain covered by the economic plans of the government and of individuals. (Note that we do not speak of *the* economic plan of the nation, which would bring us back inopportunely to a "big individual.") These economic plans, even under a liberal régime, are variously dominant and dominated and usually incompatible one with another. The internationalization of these spaces does not consist, then, in a redistribution of resources amongst national spaces, nor in an addition or combination of national spaces. It consists in making the plans of governments and of individuals compatible so far as possible. This effort raises all the real difficulties; it indicates also all the real results. The difficulties exist, whatever the outlines of frontiers; *theoretically*, the results can be attained between countries which accept the essentials of the market economy, without alteration of frontiers.

Economic space being in other respects *a field of forces*, the nation is presented either as a place of passage for these forces, or as a set of centres or poles from which emanate, or to which go, certain of these forces. According to the domain of the concrete economy, the nature of the activities considered, and the period, national spaces take an *essentially variable* meaning, which can never be made precise by their outline or by their container.

Finally economic space as a *homogeneous aggregate* allows the measurement of the effect of the expression "national market," or "national level of prices." The nation creates by its growth and by its policy relatively effective conditions of the market and of the formation of prices. But, except in the case of integral planning, national space is an inextricably woven network of national and international markets by categories of products and services, of prices fixed by data given by national space, and of prices determined by elements external to the national space and to spaces of the economic plans of the Government and of its nationals.

If one applies the analysis here outlined to a group of nations (why not Europe?) one is radically cured of the seduction of European economic space, of the great nation of Europe, and of the great European market and even of the "liberal bloc." One distinctly perceives the difference between an economic cooperation which *devaluates* frontiers and one which pretends only to move them back; between a helpful empiricism which frees trade in and *around* the nations of Europe and a so-called federalist doctrine which only lowers the obstacles to trade inside by transferring them to the circumference.[3]

The European economy like all other economies is not localizable and the policies which forget this truth are harmful.

The extension of abstract spaces to economic science will probably react upon its further development; it will also make its previous development clearer. It will act on the future, it will give new color to the past, it will develop effects downstream as well as upstream.

3. In order to make the ideas on this point precise, the table (page 103) shows the contrast between two very different groups of associated decisions, which, unfortunately, are evoked by one and the same expression, that of European Federalism (or European Union).

Amongst the upstream effects might be indicated the relatively new understanding, and the generalization, of some of the classical propositions of liberalism. How I wish that a short history of liberalism would be written from the angle of the dissociation of economic and human space, or if you prefer, the *delocalization of units and economic relations!* Perhaps one would draw from it the conclusion that the most remarkable and essential contribution of liberalism is found neither in the emancipation of the individual nor in cosmopolitanism, as is often said, but *in a truly decisive intuition* concerning *abstract spaces in an epoch when their mathematical theory had not been initiated.*

The distinction between (1) spaces of political sovereignty, (2) spaces of judicial ownership, and (3) spaces of power of economic utilization, is the intellectual weapon by which liberalism has attacked the trickery and duplicity of economic policy founded on banal localization. It has understood that the "normal nation," or more widely the "normal economic unit," is not that which is "self-sufficient," but better that which, if it happened to disappear, would make the

"European Union"

A. As an enlarged nation	**B. As a devaluating of frontiers**
In the economic field	
(1) Europe is bounded by customs barriers or by preferential tariffs.	(1) The nations of Europe reduce protection amongst themselves and also to extra-European nations.
(2) Europe is composed of complementary parts, or of parts becoming complementary.	(2) The complementarities, valued on a world scale, can be revised, and are plastic; they are not fixed in any institutional structure.
(3) Europe allows the free movement of men, goods and capital within its borders but regulates it to the rest of the world.	(3) The nations of Europe progressively give up the regulation of these movements amongst themselves and to the rest of the world.
(4) Europe has *one* network of transport, *one* currency, *one* army, etc.	(4) The nations of Europe use a world money, intercontinental networks; they participate in a world army.
(5) The economy of the great European nation carries out communal services, enlarged markets, concerted measures for the improvement of productivity in the same way as does a great enterprise.	(5) The economies of large scale are realized through groups of activities and not by groups of nations.
In the political field	
(1) Europe becomes a third "Big Power."	(1) The European nations propose to make bargaining power useless in the international order or at least to restrict its importance.
(2) Europe hopes or pretends to think that it is in a situation to "arbitrate" the possible conflicts between the other Great Powers.	(2) European nations take the political decisions necessary to ensure the maintenance of peace and the defence, in peace or war, of the values of civilization.
In the spiritual field	
(1) Europe has a table of European values; it strengthens the feeling of "European" values; it is a "European nation."	(1) The European nations have a table of "human" values, they affirm that the cultural problems of the twentieth century cannot be posed or treated on a European scale; they refuse to add to the nationalism which rends the world, one more nationalism.
(2) Europe thinks or pretends to think that nationalism with an enlarged base loses its virulence.	(2) The European nations know that large nations are not less dangerous to the peace of the world than small ones.

others "inadequate." It has, facing the difficulties of its time, traced the route by which we can pose and resolve *the* problem of our time, that is to say, *transcending the nation and the national economy.* It has done this by means of a theory, more or less implicit, of economic spaces and human spaces which must now be revised and developed with the intellectual tools of the science of the twentieth century.

2. Choosing Regions for Development*†

LLOYD RODWIN

I LIKE sometimes to define an expert as someone who knows what he doesn't know. This definition has its advantages. Aside from its teasing ambiguities, it is a reassuring foil for anyone who presumes to discuss a problem which appears insoluable; and that, for better or worse, is what I propose to do.

The problem involves the criteria or the rules for selecting regions for development in underdeveloped countries given specified goals such as a minimum rate of increase of per capita income, to take the simplest case. Certain modern research strategies may be suggestive in examining the problem; but at present, it can't be theoretically "solved", at least not through mathematical or quantitative analysis. We can best explain the reasons by turning to the existing literature on the subject. The most relevant ideas may be divided into two broad categories: 1) the contributions of the theorists, particularly those associated with the doctrines of comparative advantage, economic growth, decision rules and programming, and space and location theory; 2) the empirical contributions, such as the studies of urban hierarchy and rank size relationships plus a number of miscellaneous investigations of urban history, migration patterns and urbanization effects.

Before we proceed, however, let me explain how I first became interested in this problem.

NATIONAL POLICY AND REGIONAL DEVELOPMENT

About a decade ago (prompted largely by John Gaus) I was in Great Britain looking into the New Towns policy. My interest then in investment criteria and regional development was only incidental to the subject I was studying. The British embarked on this novel experiment partly to encourage a more rational organization of new development at the periphery of the London region, partly as a device for slowing down the rate of

* This paper is a revised version of a lecture delivered in the Spring of 1961 at the Case Institute of Technology under the sponsorship of the Program in Planning and Policy Sciences.

† Reprinted from Carl J. Friedrich and Seymour R. Harris, eds., *Public Policy,* Vol. 12 (1963).

growth in the London region relative to the rate of development in other regions of Great Britain; and partly as a model of how relatively self-contained communities could be comprehensively planned in terms of their economic, social and physical development. In the past, it was taken for granted that, save for an occasional exception, the national pattern of urban development would be set by the decisions of families and firms, guided largely by market price and private interest. The New Towns policy was a radical departure, in theory at least, because, for the first time in contemporary western history, the pattern of urban and regional development was explicity considered a variable, subject to control or manipulation from the vantage of national policy. While I admired many of the British planners' accomplishments, certain aspects of their program appeared to me then to be hampered by some fairly serious inconsistencies or badly thought out details of execution. One of these problems was the number and location of the New Towns. Why fifteen, instead of one, two or four? Why eight in the London region, three in Scotland, one in Wales, two in the Northeast, and one in the Midlands and none for Liverpool, Birmingham or Manchester? There were a number of practical and intuitive reasons behind the decisions, but it would be easy to question them if intra-metropolitan and inter-regional decentralization were, indeed, the high priority goals of the program.[1]

I knew that it was not easy to say what factors should be taken into account in deciding how many towns should be built, and where. There was, as a matter of fact, a good deal of conflict in Great Britain between the economic and physical planners on these issues. The economic planners weren't sure the New Towns made any sense at all; and in any case they were trying to encourage both export activities (which would not necessarily be located in the New Towns), and the so-called "Development Areas" where serious problems of structural unemployment were encountered. On the other hand, the physical planners were relatively less interested in inter-regional than intra-metropolitan development problems, and gave, in effect,

[1] L. Rodwin, *The British New Towns Policy* (Cambridge, 1956); and P. Self, *Cities in Flood* (London, 1957).

highest priority to the London region where the problems were most serious. In the end, the New Towns tended to have no significant effect on the inter-regional pattern; and even on the intra-regional pattern, the towns made only a very modest contribution because of the picayune proportion that New Towns represented of the total development undertaken in the region.

Of course, one could maintain that the New Towns only constituted a better technical solution for the building that was going to occur in these regions under any circumstances. That view may be correct; but it implies a decided toning down of objectives. What is more, the argument doesn't face squarely the basic, underlying issue and it makes assumptions which the policy makers themselves appeared inclined to question. That issue is: what pattern of regional development most contributes to the welfare of Great Britain, as defined by the effects of these patterns on increased per capita income, minimum unemployment, or by whatever other criteria considered appropriate. The British Socialists and Conservatives didn't believe that the existing pattern growing out of the unfettered market mechanism solved these problems adequately. Both parties favored economic assistance for the so-called "depressed" or "Development Areas." But, analytically speaking, there was no adequate explicit justification for the location of the New Towns from the national point of view; and there was no clear national policy for regional development, though from the programs actually undertaken it might be possible to derive an implicit one.

That was roughly as far as I pursued this aspect of the question while I was in Great Britain. In the next few years, I worked in a number of underdeveloped countries including Puerto Rico, Venezuela and Turkey; and I visited many others. Originally, I was vaguely aware, and then grew more intensely aware, of the fact that these countries faced problems very similar to, although much more exacerbated, than those of Great Britain. Most of these countries were close to or had reached the "take off stage" of economic development. Typically, they have a few giant metropolitan areas experiencing formidable "growing pains." These are the principal foci of economic activity. Typically, too, all of these countries have an extremely primitive hinterland of lagging regions and a far less mature urban complex. One might contend, of course, that there are lagging regions even in most economically advanced countries: indeed, these regions even exercise enough of a drag on the economy to become serious political issues, as is evident from the British experience, not to mention the current debate about depressed areas and structural unemployment now being carried on in the United States. The difference in the underdeveloped countries, however, is that their lagging regions are dominant elements, partly because of their magnitude and partly because some of these regions may have extraordinary growth potentials. It should not be surprising, therefore, to find that this deep seated disequilibrium in the national pattern of regions complicates and exacerbates the claims for the spatial allocation of the meager capital and skills available for development. In the giant cities there are the pressures to do something about the monstrous slums, traffic congestion and shortages of essential services (water, power, drainage and sewerage facilities, etc.); and in the hinterland, there are the pressures to create investment opportunities, to exploit the country's resources with more drive and balance, and perhaps equally important, to establish new "growing points" and reception areas for migrants, if the problems of the big cities are not to become utterly unmanageable.

Despite these pressures, the crux of the problem was and on the whole still is, in my judgment, being fundamentally neglected both by the physical planners and the economists. In part, this is because the physical planners (architects, engineers, city planners) have tended historically to operate at the local and regional level. With rare exceptions, they are not at all *au courant* of or knowledgeable about national economic development policies and programs. The economic planners, also, with infrequent exceptions, wear a different set of blinders. They tend to conduct their analyses and programs on an aggregative and sector basis. The emphasis is on national accounts, including national income, savings and investments plus related magnitudes, such as population trends, problems of exchange, industrial production, labor force, productivity, etc. They may also examine investment needs and possibilities in particular sectors such as agriculture, industry, transportation, education.

Both approaches have their uses, of course; but they are too general to permit understanding, evaluation or encouragement of inter-sectoral or inter-regional relationships.

These failings are all the more astonishing on purely practical grounds. Considering that some 50- to 70 per cent of the public funds available for investment goes into overhead capital, an extremely critical question is where to put that investment.[2] To suggest that the decision ought to be made by the market makes even less sense in the underdeveloped countries because most of them don't have a vigorous market economy, and because the public development decisions, albeit permissive, will have a strong influence on where the private sector of the economy is able to function. So once again, from the point of view of a national economic development program, it seems that the question of where growth should be encouraged, and on what scale, must be explicitly faced.

Suppose we turn now to the existing professional literature for a better understanding of the analytical problems these issues involve and the leads they might furnish in formulating a national policy for regional development, given the present state of our knowledge.

The Contributions of the Theorists

If development policy were to be guided by the principle of comparative advantage, regions, like countries, would import the things they could buy more cheaply and sell what they could produce at a lower cost up to the point where price equals cost. Under these circumstances, one might argue that there is no need for criteria or decision rules for regional development. Presumably, the optimum pattern would emerge from traditional market behavior. But this rule wouldn't be of much help in deciding where to invest overhead capital unless one assumed that these public decisions were to be made after the private investment decisions occurred, which after all would be equivalent to following the dictates of the market.

The relevance of comparative advantage has been questioned

[2] For references and more detailed discussion of these problems, see L. Rodwin, "Metropolitan Policy for Developing Areas," in L. Rodwin, ed., *The Future Metropolis* (N. Y., George Braziller, 1961), pp. 171-189.

because of its equilibrium assumptions where market prices equal opportunity costs. Indeed they do under perfect competition, but not in the actual market and certainly not in the underdeveloped countries, where we know that factors and commodities, such as labor and foreign exchange, are incorrectly priced and produce serious problems of disequilibria. The doctrine also takes no account of internal or external economies of scale, of changes in cost, efficiency, and demand as production increases and new activities burgeon. Moreover, many countries are reluctant to depend on the pattern of prices and fluctuations of international "primary" markets. Where possible, a more diversified economy is preferred, one amply enough served with basic overhead capital and services so that it can more readily assume other functions should changing trade conditions make this necessary. Unfortunately, as Chenery and others have noted, modification of the comparative advantage thesis to take account of these objections would rob the doctrine of much of its practical value. In effect one would have to make "an explicit analysis of the growth process itself before it is possible to determine, even theortically, where comparative advantage lies; market prices and current opportunity costs are no longer sufficient."[3]

Because of the difficulties inherent in the doctrine of comparative advantage, the growth economists relax equilibrium assumptions, allow for internal and external economies of scale, and for changes in the quantity and quality of production over time. To obtain a pattern of production and trade which maximizes income over time, they favor the encouragement of economic activities oriented to "leading sectors." These leading sectors have varied and naturally will vary for different countries. Typical examples cited are the timber industry in Sweden, oil in Venezuela, cotton textiles in Great Britain, and railroads in the United States, France, Germany, Canada, and Russia. Investment prospects, they argue, will

[3] H. Chenery, "Comparative Advantage and Development Policy," *The American Economic Review,* Vol. LI, No. 1, March 1961, p. 20. It may be, however, that the potential gains from comparative advantage tend today to be neglected. Despite the greater realism of the approach of the growth economists, Chenery thinks they under-rate the risk in ignoring comparative advantage both for countries with a shortage of capital and foreign exchange and for smaller countries with a limited range of production possibilities.

hinge on the effects of the expansion of the leading sectors on complementary or related sectors, and of the sequences in which the patterns of expansion occur over time. The policy recommendations of the growth economists diverge at this point and they may be roughly divided into two major groups:[4] those assuming an elastic supply of capital and labor, who stress "balanced growth," or the simultaneous expansion of a number of interrelated sectors; and those, assuming inelasticities of capital, managerial ability, technological innovations, etc., who argue in favor of concentrated and sequential growth patterns to achieve economies of scale and significant initial breakthroughs which will induce further development.

The insights of the growth economists have definite, although limited applications for the decision maker interested in encouraging more satisfactory patterns of regional development. True, with the exception perhaps of Hirschman[5] and one or two others, most of these growth economists view these issues in terms of sectors rather than regions. But the same considerations apply: thus it would appear to be effective strategy to promote development in a few "leading regions" and to push those programs which would stimulate leading sectors within the regions. By the same token, "balance" would imply simultaneous development of some related sectors within the region; and imbalance, or what I prefer to call concentrated decentralization, would mean that some regional and sector development would be stopped, curtailed, or not encouraged until some later stage, because of scarcities of capital, managerial and administrative talent, and markets.

If we examine the more specific kinds of rules or criteria that are being used today in national planning to guide investment decisions, we run into a serious impasse. The criteria are generally formulated for "projects." The basic choices are whether to produce a given product or products and the best technique to employ to produce this output. There are a num-

[4] H. Chenery, *op. cit.*, pp. 20-22. See also R. E. Caves, *Trade and Economic Structure* (Cambridge, 1960); R. Nurske, *Problems of Capital Formation in Underdeveloped Countries* (Oxford, 1953); A. O. Hirschman, *The Strategy of Economic Development* (New Haven, 1958), and W. W. Rostow, *The Stages of Economic Growth* (Cambridge, 1960).

[5] A. O. Hirschman, *op. cit.*, Ch. 10.

ber of measures to guide such decisions, and their merits vary depending on the use to which they are put.[6] Summarized in reverse order of versatility and of demands on skill and data, they are: the minimum capital output ratio, which stresses the production of items using less capital and the import of items requiring more capital; the capital labor ratio which favors activities with low capital labor ratios; the marginal productivity criteria which try to measure the contribution of specific projects to national product and to rank projects on the basis of this contribution; the marginal growth criteria which adjusts the marginal product criteria by taking into account future project effects, especially on savings and reinvestments; and, finally, most versatile of all and most difficult to apply, are the programming techniques.[7] These attempt, on the basis of specified goals, to develop a consistent and optimum allocation of resources among a number of feasible economic activities, with due allowance for the expected demand for goods and services, resource limitations, and the probable repercussion effects of the new investments on the economy.

The simpler ratios are often employed when data are not available, which is often the case; but they can hardly be used with much confidence since they rely on a number of erroneous assumptions, e.g., that capital is the only scarce resource and that there are no variations in efficiency by sector. From our point of view, another objection to the use of these ratios for selecting development regions is that they make the choice of regions grow out of the specific project investment analyses; and the decision maker may often have to select regions in advance of such project analyses.

On the other hand, the programming techniques, which add a powerful tool to the economists' analytical techniques, have

[6] H. Chenery, *op. cit.*, pp. 25-46. Incidentally, on this point as well as the others on which Chenery is cited, this paper leans heavily on Chenery's perceptive article cited above.

[7] The programming techniques can accommodate other constraints besides capital, such as labor, foreign exchange and the supply of particular factors and commodities. They can also handle certain sequential effects including the impact on import prices of investment in supplying sectors and the revision of initial calculations of opportunity costs, of labor, capital and foreign exchange. In addition, the techniques can take into account different processes of production as well as the effects of those indirect benefits and costs which can be specified in quantitative form. *Ibid.*

some serious limitations. Quite aside from the assumption of linear relationships (which eventually perhaps may not be indispensable), or the empirical difficulties in estimating economies of scale, training effects, external economies, etc., the programming model cannot handle intangibles or non-quantitative relationships. An example, noted by Hirschman[8] and acknowledged by Chenery, is the preference for one type of growth sequence rather than another because it economizes on managerial ability or can spur political action. Unfortunately, all of these knotty problems crop up in attempting to estimate the effects of specific overhead capital investment projects; and the problems would appear to be all the more intractable since the estimates would be required for linked projects in different regions.

However, one encouraging prospect held out by the programming criteria is that a particular regional pattern could be established as a constraint within which a solution could be sought, or so Chenery believes.[9] If so, there would appear to be some likelihood of specifying several regional development possibilities for a set of investment programs. That might provide a basis some day, assuming we ever refine our data sufficiently, for estimating optimum resource allocations for varying regional patterns; and, if successful, it would be no mean accomplishment. But it would not disclose which regional pattern was the optimum, as defined.

Turning to the spatial theorists is a disappointing experience since the assistance furnished by them on this topic is relatively meager whereas one might have expected them to be the most helpful. To begin with, the traditional approach of location theory, with few exceptions, has been largely from the point of view of equilibrium theory with extensions to take account of transportation and trade variables. This aspect of location theory is, therefore, subject to all the strictures of the growth economists about equilibrium theory and comparative advantage, which I touched on earlier. How serious these limitations are is best illustrated by citing Isard on this subject. In his major work on location theory he specifically poses the questions,

[8] A. O. Hirschman, *op. cit.*, Chs. 2 and 4; and H. Chenery, *op. cit.*, p. 40.
[9] H. Chenery, *op cit.*, p. 33.

which prompted this review, to wit: "What is the optimum spatial distribution and hierarchy of cities of different size?" And a little later Isard asks: "Given a network of cities and corresponding patterns of land use, along what channels should changes in the structure of this network and these patterns be fostered in order to attain a situation closer to optimum?"[10] After a brief discussion he concludes "that agglomeration analysis, particularly that of the substitutional variety, has little to say beyond the obvious; units are attracted to or repelled from cities according to a simple comparison of advantages and disadvantages generated by these cities."[11]

Perhaps inter-regional input-output models may hold some promise in the future. Stevens suggests that these models

> . . . are basically . . . identical in form to the non-spatial models of Leontief except that the interindustry matrix is expanded by the inclusion of interregional relationships; each input is specified as coming, not just from a particular industry, but from a particular industry in a specific region. As is usual in input-output, the coefficients in the matrix are assumed constant. Thus, fixed proportions of each good are assumed drawn from each region no matter what the pattern of outputs. This, coupled with the usual condition that there be fixed factor proportions in the production of any good—makes an interregional input-output system completely determinate. Once a bill of goods is specified there is no choice mechanism for optimizing shipment patterns or substituting factors to achieve a more efficient allocation of available resources.[12]

If these interregional matrices were easier to construct, more realistic and relatively reliable, they might be of considerable value not only in depicting the existing economic relationships within and between regions but also in tracing the national and interregional effects of specified investments in particular regions. However, the neglect of price effects, the difficulty of getting data for these models, the vastly increased computational problems which regional breakdowns entail coupled with the egregious simplifications of industry categories and the unrealistic linearity assumptions makes one skeptical of the im-

[10] W. Isard, *Location and Space Economy* (N. Y., 1956), p. 183.
[11] *Ibid.*
[12] B. Stevens, "Interregional Linear Programming," *Journal of Regional Science*, Vol. I, No. 1, Summer 1958.

mediate, not to mention the long term usefulness of this instrument.

Interregional linear programming involves problems even more serious than those previously discussed. These prescriptive models provide a mechanism for choosing optimum shipment patterns and a "means for determining efficient resource allocations among the various productions and shipments . . . based on linear homogenous production functions with constant coefficients."[13]

Lefeber and Stevens have been among the first to apply programming methods to the analysis of interregional spatial equilibrium. Both have developed linear models where location and transportation costs are allowed to vary, and where transportation is included in the productive system as a consumer of factors."[14] Lefeber believes the method is promising, but recognizes that "because of the complexity of spatial adjustment, investigations which involve a large number of locations, goods and factors result in a prohibitively large number of choice variables; hence an investigation of spatial allocation embracing many details cannot be undertaken without suitable simplifications."[15] Stevens is even more optimistic. He expects his interregional model to be helpful in comparing existing regional patterns with some optimum, as defined; and he also thinks his model can enable the analyst to trace the differential

[13] *Ibid.*

[14] L. Lefeber, *Allocation in Space, Production, Transport and Industrial Location* (Amsterdam, 1958), p. 134; B. Stevens, *op. cit.*, pp. 60-98; see also W. Isard, *Methods of Regional Science* (N. Y., 1960), Ch. 10; and L. H. Moses, "General Equilibrium Model of Production, Interregional Trade and Location of Industry," *The Review of Economics and Statistics*, Vol. 42, No. 4, Nov. 1960, pp. 373-396. Roughly the same limitations noted for Lefeber's and Stevens' papers apply to Moses' stimulating paper too.

[15] Lefeber suggests that "in a detailed analysis of larger areas, a fruitful approach might be to work out a skeleton system based on the main flows of prime materials. Then, as a second step, one may work out the allocation patterns in the different regions, with suitable aggregation, taking the skeleton system as given. By considering several feasible skeleton systems and their corresponding regional adjustments, one may approximate that overall pattern for spatial allocation that yields the highest level of welfare.

"The empirical investigation of spatial general equilibrium adjustment presents difficulties which should not be underestimated. The insufficiency of basic data, the problem of aggregating flows, and the limitations of existing forecasting methods may prove to be the most difficult obstacles to overcome. Nevertheless, it is believed that the analytical approach developed in this work is a step in the right direction." P. 134.

effects of locational decisions, for example, the building of major public works or the development of some new private installation, such as a steel plant.[16] Perhaps so, but Stevens spells out no details. In any case, on the main point that concerns us, Stevens, like Chenery, assumes an existing spatial or regional pattern. Even if, somehow, new regional concentrations or additions were hypothetically introduced in the model, they would only provide a more refined basis for optimizing resource allocations for various regions by taking transportation variables into account. But Stevens' model, like Chenery's, would not disclose which regional pattern was the optimum. More specifically, it would not indicate how, or where, new regional concentrations or significant new overhead additions to existing concentrations should be developed; and so his work, too, is of limited value for our purposes, even if we overlook the problems inherent in his model, such as data handling and the severe restrictive assumptions (linearity, the advance specification of prices, the neglect of household behavior, etc.).

The Empirical Contributions

Christaller, Lösch, and others have shown how one could derive an order or hierarchy of cities based on the market areas or hinterland within a defined territory; and "corresponding to each order there is both a definite number of functions which each city of that order performs and a population size typical for each city of that order."[17] A number of empirical studies have furnished some statistical evidence of such hierarchical patterns. These relationships may be coupled with another apparent empirical uniformity relating urban size and rank. Generally referred to as the rank size rule, it suggests that the population of cities in an array of cities by size within a defined territory is inversely proportional to its rank, such that the second largest city is one half the largest, the third largest is one third, the fourth largest is one fourth, and so on.[18]

We know something about the common factors in this re-

[16] B. Stevens, *op. cit.*, pp. 89-90.
[17] W. Isard, *Methods of Regional Science*, *op. cit.*
[18] E. M. Hoover, "The Concept of a System of Cities: A Comment on Rutledge Vining's Paper," *Economic Development and Cultural Change*, Vol. 3, No. 2,

lationship. Christaller's urban hierarchy constitutes one type of skewed distribution. The rank size formula represents another. There are several reasons why one should expect these relationships, though not necessarily one conforming to the rank size rule. Herbert Simon has shown that a class of skewed distributions may emerge if net urban growth is proportional to the size of the urban population.[19] Changes in the specific type of such distributions would occur via changes in growth rates and migration. However, the factors influencing migration flows likewise produces skewed distributions. Briefly summarized, this result occurs because most urban areas perform simple service, manufacturing, marketing and government functions. Only a very few cities have special advantages in terms of resource endowment; and these advantages, reinforced by economies of scale and agglomeration, favor the growth within these cities of export activities which serve national and international markets, plus a wide range of market and service oriented activities.

The significance of the rank size rule is that it formulates a precise hypothesis as to the specific form of this skewed distribution. If this rule accurately depicted urban size relationships, it might be employed either for purposes of projection or as an important factor to take into account in framing urban development policy. Actually, the evidence in support of the rule, as formulated, can be questioned. At best, it seems to apply very

---

Jan. 1955, p. 196. The rank size rule conforms to a Pareto distribution with an exponent greater than one. The function has the form

$$y.x^a = b$$

Where y is the number of cities greater than a specified size a; and x is the size of a specified city. a and b are constants; or alternatively expressed, y is the rank and x is the size of a given city and b may be the population of the largest city. See also, W. Stolper, "Spatial Order and the Economic Growth of Cities: A Comment on Lampard's Paper," *Ibid.*, Vol. 3, No. 2, pp. 137-146; and M. Beckman, "Some Reflections on Losch's Theory of Location," *Regional Papers and Proceedings,* Vol. I, 1955, pp. Ni-N8; and "City Hierarchies and the Distribution of City Size," *Economic Development and Cultural Change,* 1958, pp. 243-248. Beckman multiplies the rank of the city in the midpoint of its class and its population, and concludes that "After a fair number of such multiplications, the product itself will show a distribution pattern . . . [in which] the steps in the rank size diagram are thus smoothed out, the distinctness of the size classes is lost, and [the rank size rule] applies in effect throughout the size classes." p. 245.

[19] H. Simon, "On a Class of Skew Distribution Functions," *Biometrika,* Vol. 52, 1955, pp. 425-40. This proposition requires other questionable assumptions, such as a net increase of urban population by natural increase, which we can ignore for the purposes of this discussion.

roughly to the United States and Canada,[20] and the fit appears particularly poor for many underdeveloped countries.[21]

It is possible, however, that we could modify the rank size formula by computing an exponent that gives the best fit. Whether such a revised version could prove serviceable for projections is an open question. In any case, it would still be subject to some of the same limitations of the original formulation. In part, this is because the basis for the definition of the territory is unclear. Neither central place theory nor the modified version of the rule provide adequate guidance on this matter. As Hoover remarks, "the ascending series of orders of places could be carried on up to the largest city in the world or else arbitrarily chopped off at any given smaller size or confined to a smaller area."[22] Another limitation is that these ideas, at best, only describe an equilibrium model. They presuppose an interrelated urban system in which the growth rates of cities in relation to each other do not change. But over time the rank sizes or relative growth rates of cities do change. Even more serious, the critical determinants of the rank size relationships and growth rates are unclear.

Despite the ambiguities, however, the hierarchical pattern of cities does suggest that any effort in underdeveloped countries to equalize urban scale must reverse powerful trends and is likely to encounter serious resistance. A more feasible alternative might be to try to convert a few significant growing points into large cities of varying sizes and thus achieve a somewhat more balanced urban hierarchy. In these countries there are less big cities, partly because of the size of the market, and partly perhaps because of the deficiency of heavy industries, which tend to be more raw material oriented and which tend

[20] F. T. Moore, "A Note on City Size Distributions," *Economic Development and Cultural Change,* Vol. 7, No. 4, pp. 465-6; G. R. Allen, "The 'Courbe Des' Populations," *Bulletin of the Oxford Institute of Statistics,* Vol. 16, May and June, 1954; B. J. L. Berry and W. L. Garrison, "Alternate Explanations of Urban Rank Size Relationships," *Annals of the Association of American Geographers,* Vol. 48, March 1958; and C. H. Madden, "On Some Indication of Stability in the Growth of Cities in the United States," *Economic Development and Cultural Change,* Vol. IV, No. 3; C. H. Madden, "Some Spatial Aspects of Urban Growth in the United States," *ibid.,* Vol. IV, No. 4.

[21] This estimate is based on the author's inspection of data assembled in student reports for Puerto Rico, Mexico, Venezuela, Turkey, Indonesia, India, Japan, Pakistan and Israel.

[22] E. M. Hoover, *op. cit.,* p. 198.

also for a variety of reasons to avoid the very largest cities.[23] Transportation and other services might be planned so as to reverse what appears to be theoretically ideal urban stages, i.e., the emergence of lower and then higher order communities which could eventually perform their specialized functions. By fostering a very few large urban concentrations one could maximize external economies,[24] encourage more heavy as well as market oriented industries and thereby magnify multiplier effects and cultural influences. This might be all the more feasible if these cities were selected in part on the basis of the capacity to supply them with the most efficient transportation linkages to a large and potentially rich hinterland slated for further accelerated development.

Still other suggestive hints may be gleaned from a number of historical studies of the patterns of urban and regional development. For lack of space I shall be cavalier in picking illustrations for comment.

Consider, for instance, Gras' analysis of settlement patterns. His distinctions between the collectional, the nomadic, the settled village, the town and the metropolitan economy are not of particular usefulness for us. In fact, only the last two stages are directly relevant. But Gras' insistence that the metropolis, besides possessing a healthful and an efficient location between consumers and producers "must possess a *hinterland,* a tributary of adjacent territory, rich in natural resources, occupied by a productive population and accessible by means of transportation,"[25] links neatly into the central place studies and also into Hoselitz's distinction between "generative" and "parasitic" cities. The generative cities, in Hoselitz's sense, perform functions for themselves and for their hinterlands on which they

[23] I am indebted for this point to Mr. R. S. Rodd who is working on a dissertation on aspects of this topic.

[24] Dynamic external economies is used by Scitovsky to indicate the effect of investment in one sector on the probability of investment in another sector via increased demand or reduced costs. These economies are particularly induced by urbanization, i.e., improved infrastructure, demand increases in other sectors, economies of scale, better financial services, education, formal and in-serve training, etc. These economies cannot be gauged through sector by sector analysis. See T. Scitovsky, "The Concepts of External Economies," *Journal of Political Economy,* April 1954, Vol. 62, pp. 143-151; and H. Chenery, *op. cit.,* pp. 20-21 and 24-25.

[25] N. S. B. Gras, *An Introduction to Economic History* (N. Y. and London, 1922), p. 185.

depend for supplies and markets; but the physical hinterland of the parasitic cities is neither their market nor their supply areas.[26] An aspect of this relationship, stressed by Stolper, is that every consumer has more or less access to the market area of each good in the developed countries but such access is remote or non-existent for much of the hinterland of underdeveloped countries.[27] Providing such access through improvements in transportation and communication would help to open the hinterland as a supply and market area. It is also likely to raise the productivity of the surrounding agricultural regions and provide a channel for the out-migration of redundant farm labor, not to mention the flow of capital into agriculture, and the flow of capital from the more successful agricultural enterprises into local trade and manufactures.[28] However, a number of studies emphasize that reliance on migration alone to shift labor and other resources to areas of higher returns, while important, appears unlikely to reduce population growth and to transform the economy of the lagging areas.[29] Moreover, these effects are apt to be significantly retarded if relatively large distances separate them from the large cities.[30]

These crude observations, culled from a variety of sources, reinforce our previous, tentative, suspicion that a critical factor

[26] B. F. Hoselitz, "Generative and Parasitic Cities," *Economic Development and Cultural Change,* Vol. 3, No. 3, pp. 278-294.

[27] W. F. Stolper, *Ibid,* Vol. 3, No. 2, Jan. 1955, pp. 141-2.

[28] E. E. Lampard, "The History of Cities in the Economically Advanced Areas," *Ibid.,* pp. 131-2; W. H. Nicholls, "Research on Agriculture and Economic Development," *American Economic Review,* Vol. 50, No. 2, 1960, pp. 629-635; "Accommodating Economic Change in Underdeveloped Countries," Vol. 49, No. 2, May 1959, pp. 156-168; B. F. Hoselitz, "The Role of Cities in the Economic Growth of Underdeveloped Countries," *The Journal of Political Economy,* Vol. 61, No. 3, June 1953, pp. 195-208. See also the articles in *Economic Development and Cultural Change,* Vol. 3, No. 1, 1954, pp. 3-77, and especially R. Redfield and M. B. Singer ("The Cultural Role of Cities," *Ibid.,* pp. 53-73) for some qualifications of the points raised above; D. C. North, "The Spatial and Interregional Framework of the U.S. Economy: An Historical Perspective," *Papers and Proceedings of the Regional Science Association,* Vol. II, 1956, pp. 13-1—13-9; and T. W. Schulz, *The Economic Organization of Agriculture* (New York), Chs. 9 and 10.

[29] H. S. Perloff, E. S. Dunn, Jr., E. E. Lampard and R. F. Muth, *Regions, Resources and Economic Growth* (Baltimore, 1960), pp. 600-607; and G. H. Borts, "The Equalization of Returns and Regional Economic Growth," *The American Economic Review,* Vol. 50, No. 3, pp. 318-347.

[30] S. A. Stouffer, "Intervening Opportunities: A Theory Relating Mobility and Distance," *American Sociological Review,* Vol. 5, Dec. 1940, pp. 845-867; and W. Isard, *Location and Space Economy, op. cit.,* pp. 64-65, footnote 13.

for our decision maker might be the range and significance of the effects of any proposed regional development program over the presently inaccessible hinterland. What we need to get, however, from future historical studies, is better evidence on possible or more effective sequences or stages by which growth and urban development spreads to lagging regions, and on the types of urban pattern which exert the maximum influence over the lagging hinterlands.

Policy Implications

While we may not have learned much in this quest for clues, perhaps at the very least we know a little better what it is that we don't know. Moreover, at the risk of convicting myself as an incorrigible optimist, I think the survey has not been altogether fruitless. Let me try to summarize some of the possible tentative inferences.

The growth and comparative advantage doctrines suggest the desirability of accelerating the development of a few "leading regions." These regions will often be identified with or associated with leading sectors. In these regions, consideration would be given to those activities which might enjoy comparative advantage, if not now, then "for a specified set of production levels in supplying and using sectors"[31] in the future. Within these same regions one might press for more simultaneous development of the more important related sectors. The aim, one must stress, is not to equalize growth rates in all regions or in all sectors of a region; nor, to put the matter paradoxically, can the aim even be to achieve theoretically optimum growth rates simply because, given our present state of knowledge, we don't know how to define or to translate such optimum rates into meaningful or reliable operational specifications. Rather the pragmatic aim would be to reach some roughly gauged estimates of "critical size" for a few selected urban regions, which, in turn, might induce a wide range of internal and external economies plus training and multiplier effects. Because of the constraints, i.e., the critical shortage of capital, markets, and managerial and administrative talent, develop-

[31] H. B. Chenery, *op. cit.*

ment in other regions and sectors would be arrested at some point approximating a politically acceptable minimum. The decision rules are not particularly helpful for our purposes except that one could at the very least specify alternative regional development possibilities in attempting to approximate what is judged to be superior resource allocations. However, the studies of market areas, urban hierarchy and metropolitan hinterlands do suggest one possible strategy for urban selection and development. An essential condition might be to select urban growth complexes, which, with relative economy, could improve their access to large hinterlands; and both, the urban growth complexes and their hinterlands, must be judged to be susceptible to measures encouraging their further growth and development.

Perhaps one should also emphasize that any extensive development planned for selected regions will take a number of years to promote. Therefore, while tentative programs may be started based on existing knowledge and judgement, more detailed studies can be gotten underway. Then at some later stage, these programs and their planned sequences could be reviewed, stepped up or contracted, as one gets a better sense and feel of the development prospects. Assuming there was agreement on this approach, what would it be wise to start examining to facilitate this subsequent review?

To begin with, the country's basic goals ought to be as clearly specified as possible. For most of these countries the immediate objectives are to maximize the increase in per capita income. This general goal, however, is subject to a variety of qualifications or constraints,[32] of which some of the more important are minimum levels of consumption and implicit discount rates of future returns; desired distribution, or rate of change in the distribution, of income by class and region; and minimum acceptable levels, or rate of decrease, of the levels of unemployment by class and region. Other restrictions will emerge from projected defense requirements and from the need for internal consistency in resource allocations, such as specified

[32] The difference between goals and constraints is often moot or meaningless. See R. Dorfman, "Operations Research," *American Economic Review,* Vol. 50, No. 4, 1960, p. 609; and J. Margolis, "The Evaluation of Water Resources Development," *Ibid.,* Vol. 49, No. 1, 1959, pp. 99-100.

exchange balances and execution of programs within available or potentially available resources of capital and of managerial and administrative ability. Clearly one may add new goals, weight them differently, specify less or additional constraints, or spell out the implications more or less precisely. The task is difficult and is easily slighted; but ideally, the more important of the country's objectives should be examined to see how they might affect the choice and scale of sector and regional programs that might be undertaken.

In addition, if there is to be any closer evaluation of regions for development, the leading regions under consideration have to be at least roughly defined. This job is a treacherous one and likely to beget friction and difference of opinion. My guess is that some rough ad hoc internal demarcations of the leading development regions will have to suffice for the decision makers' purposes. The nucleus would be some existing or potentially important urban complex; the outer limits of the boundaries might be roughly mapped on the basis of the hinterland which appears likely now or in the future to come within the market and influence zone of this complex; and the actual boundaries should conform as closely to these limits as data gathering opportunities permit.

Some comparative analysis of the long-term prospects for the leading regions is also essential. This would involve projections of trends in the principal economic activities, in population, income, investment and consumption, and the demand and supply implications for related activities in the "leading regions." It would be indiscreet, but probably indispensable, to hazard some rough estimates of the probable effects of existing national development policies on sectors within particular regions, not to mention the need to evaluate those "backward and forward linkages"[33] and multiplier effects which would give us some basis for gauging the impact and relative strength of the induced effects of the regions' development on the national economy. Where data and circumstances permit, even the presently inadequate and unrealistic inter-regional input-output matrices and programming methods might be employed, if

[33] A. O. Hirschman, *op. cit.*, pp. 98-104.

used mainly to direct attention to possibly significant relationships and implications which might otherwise be overlooked.

Inexorable short-term considerations, such as serious disproportions in the use and availability of productive factors, might have to warp these evaluations. The foreign exchange problem or serious unemployment areas are examples; and in selecting regions as well as in determining the pattern of their development, the capacity to contribute solutions to these problems may well become the prime requisite of any effective strategy of regional priorities and development. Thus, priority for development programs might be given to regions depending on their estimated capacity to respond effectively to direct or indirect efforts. It goes without saying that the form of the response might vary from the exploitation of the regions' export potential of raw materials or agricultural products, the stimulation of import substitution activities, the attraction of labor oriented industries, the encouragement of "tourism," the minimum use of overhead capital, etc.[34]

There is also the question of how to knit the lagging regions of the non-monetized hinterland of the country into a single unified economy, culture and urban system. If, as Rostow and others have suggested, one of the essential roles of the state for these underdeveloped countries is to create a national market, the regional programming of infra-structure is one of the essential steps through which the national market can be created. Such programs can become the innovation seedbed for new development regions, indeed one of the key mechanisms for achieving spread effects as well as "dynamic external economies for the agricultural, manufacturing and service sectors." Hence, efforts might be made to estimate the probable social and cultural effects of the proposed development in different regions, especially the number of families affected and the likely changes in consumption, expenditure and savings patterns, and in social and power relationships. Most of these changes could not

[34] Chenery points out that "leading sectors are likely to be industries in which import substitution becomes profitable as markets expand and capital and skills are acquired. Even in Japan, the most successful of the low income countries in increasing exports, import substitution accounted for nearly 40% of the rise of industry (from 23% of GNP to 33% between 1914 and 1954) as compared to less than 10% for exports." H. B. Chenery, "Patterns of Industrial Growth," *The American Economic Review,* Vol. 50, No. 4, 1960, p. 651.

be traced with precision; but if an essential aim is to transform traditional attitudes and values, some effort might be made to gauge how effectively different regional developments would serve this end.

A closely related, but even less tangible consideration is the effect of different regional development programs on general public attitudes. Have the schemes the possibility of changing the citizen's, not to mention the decision maker's image of himself and of his country? Can it arouse the public's imagination sufficiently to set in train a whole new level of aspiration? It would be folly to neglect these possibilities; yet who but the greatest political leaders can fathom their significance? This is one of the reasons why need as well as effects have to be taken into account. Investment in a particular region may well yield poor returns, yet warrant high priority. A region—such as southern Italy or the Negev in Israel—may be so backward, neglected or difficult to develop—that it acquires symbolic value. It is as though a nation should stubbornly choose to pit its energies and will against insuperable odds. Or it may consciously prefer a slower rate of development. Such programs, of necessity, must be unique exceptions—but it is worth remarking that over the long run, they may speed up rather than retard the development effort.

What about those regions which are not selected for large-scale development programs? They cannot be entirely neglected; and yet they cannot be adequately served. To begin with, the effects of regional development elsewhere may perhaps be exploited—or at least underscored. Certain programs involving a *minimum* commitment of resources may also be undertaken to allay discontent. A few self-help and technical assistance programs may be initiated including information and educational programs of benefit to migrants from the region. Some uneconomic investments and tax benefits may be inescapable but not especially underscored. In short, token efforts and consummate political skill will be essential. The measure of sucess will hinge on the balance struck between economic progress, social welfare and relative sensitivity to those repercussion effects that may upset a theoretically rational development calculus.

It seems almost hopeless to assign weights to the factors just discussed, partly because many of them are intangible and interact. All that one seems able to say at present is that the decision makers must somehow ponder and estimate the relative significance of these considerations in their countries in arriving intuitively at some final judgment.

Once a decision has been made, however, and a firm set of regional development goals and a program agreed upon, then what next? There is a need to orient the thinking of the key officials in the agencies engaged in sector development to relate their own program to the national objectives for both regional and sector development. As the program gets under way, better linkages and coordinating and feedback mechanisms will be required to deal with problems and errors before they become too serious. To influence the contours of the region's development programs and to project overhead capital and land use requirements, detailed cost and industry feasibility studies will be required. Training and education measures to support these programs must be pushed; and effective tax, incentive programs and other credit measures may be needed to spur the momentum of development in the designated regions. All of these things are important; but something more is needed if these and other hard, but essential, staff activities are to achieve disproportionate effect. The regional development goals, like the other goals in the national development plan, need to be spelled out, enlarged, dramatized, made more visible. For many countries the goal of transformation of the hinterland can play a powerful role in propelling a nation forward. Even if the programs were limited to one or a few areas, the idea has tremendous ignition potentials which might spark unsuspected energies. "Manifest Destiny," the development of Russia beyond the Urals, the Turkish move to Ankara, are some examples, perhaps not too far-fetched. Today if proposed, they would be labelled show-piece psychology; and yet we know there is a difference—because they actually worked.

3. Regional Planning as a Field of Study*†

John Friedmann

Regional planning as an academic discipline is characterized by a concern with the clarification of social objectives in the ordering of activities in supra-urban space. This concept is used to identify the principal issues of public policy that may challenge the professional competence of regional planners. Although regional planning is most appropriate for societies in transition to a mature industrial economy, continuing preoccupation with developing areas suggests the desirability of establishing regional planning as a field of specialization within leading planning schools in the United States. A curriculum is proposed.

The field of regional planning has always been something of an intruder among the planning fraternity. Although city planners have for some time now been recognized professionally in the United States, professionalization has been slower among those whose primary concern in planning is the "region." Despite this lack of professional dignity, regional planning is fast becoming a subject of serious public concern. In the United States, activities in metropolitan planning and area redevelopment are expanding; outstanding state legislation for land use and resources planning has been passed in Alaska and Hawaii; there is an upsurge of interest in regional transportation studies. In many of the newly developing countries, interest in regional planning is even more articulate, with an emphasis on the problems of depressed regions, the development of new resource complexes, and the region-

* Reprinted from the *Journal of the American Institute of Planners*, Vol. 29 (Aug. 1963).

† An earlier version of this paper was presented at the meeting of the Southeast Section of the Regional Science Association in Atlanta, Georgia, November 9, 1962. I wish to take this opportunity to express my gratitude to Bernard Frieden, my colleague at M.I.T., for the unstinting gift of his time in discussing, criticizing, and contributing to this essay. At the same time, I wish to absolve him in advance of any guilt-by-association: final responsibility rests with the author.

alization of national economic programs. In response to this continuing demand, a number of American planning schools have been offering subjects in regional planning, and a recent publication of the OECD is to a large extent devoted to problems in the teaching of that subject.[1] The wide and uncertain scope of regional planning activities has made it difficult, however, to devise an academic course of study that would lead to specialization in the field.

"Regional planning" is often used as a phrase to describe a congeries of more or less unrelated activities. Some of this diversity of meanings is brought out in a recent publication of the United Nations.[2] Reporting on a seminar sponsored by that organization a few years ago, C. V. Narasimhan, Executive Secretary of the U.N. Economic Commission for Asia and the Far East, writes: "The Seminar considered that regional planning would provide the most suitable frame of reference for a balanced integration of development projects of national significance and those based on local initiative. Such comprehensive regional planning would apply to the development of metropolitan areas, to areas in which natural resources are being developed, as well as to rural reconstruction programs and to the location of industries."[3]

In this attempt to circumscribe the field of regional planning, three separate meanings can be distinguished. Regional planning is made synonymous with regional development policy at the national level ("balanced integration"); with a process of decision-making and design in the elaboration of investment projects at the regional level; and with economic development programs for sub-national areas. There is, in addition, an intimation that regional planning has something to do with metropolitan development, resources management, and agricultural and community improvement.

It is questionable whether any or all of these connotations are useful for delimiting regional planning as a field of study. Narasimhan refers to practical activities of public agencies and not to a field of professional specialization. In fact, no one person could be expected to be equally competent in the great complexity of tasks which he cites as being involved in regional policy, planning, and development. Such undertakings normally require large staffs on which trained regional planners, where they participate at all, will have to share responsibility with other specialists. An example may help to make this clear.

The Venezuelan government has undertaken a large-scale effort at regional development in Guayana, an area that has its focus at the confluence of the Caroni and Orinoco Rivers. The project is conceived on a grand and comprehensive scale, including investments in hydroelectric facilities, heavy industry, a "new town," agriculture, transportation, and so forth. An autonomous development agency, the Corporacion Venezolana de Guayana, is responsible for all phases of the project. Although there can be no doubt that the Corporacion is engaged in regional planning, "regional planners" are not among its staff. Instead, it employs economists, engineers, architects, urban designers, public administrators, lawyers, city planners, statisticians, geologists, agronomists, resource analysts, and anthropologists in various capacities. It would indeed be folly to imagine that the tasks of all these specialists could be performed as well or better by a team of professional regional planners; it would be equally in error to suppose that a trained regional planner, as a specialist in his own right, would be qualified to coordinate the efforts of all others. Coordination on a large and complex project such as Guayana depends far less on the substantive knowledge that a professional generalist might contribute than on competent leadership. Such leadership may be entrusted to a planner, but it could as reasonably be placed in the hands of a lawyer, economist, or engineer. Administrative ability, leadership, and political aptitude are important; the professional degree is not. The specialist in regional planning will have to take his place alongside other experts in the organization.

If this is granted, what specialized contribution could a trained regional planner be expected to make? How shall his competence be defined? Does there, in fact, exist a core of theory and method which may be taught to prospective regional planners? Where should the boundaries of regional planning as a field of study be drawn?

THE CORE OF REGIONAL PLANNING STUDY

Before proceeding to answer these questions, attention must turn to the concept of planning itself. Planning inevitably appears modified by adjectives such as regional, city, economic, or industrial. These varied usages suggest the existence of a certain unity of approach in all forms of planning endeavor. A general theory of planning as a mode of human action has not as yet been written, but some common elements have been identified and are widely accepted as describing the essential nature of the planning process.[4] Primarily a *way of thinking* about social and economic problems, planning is oriented predominantly toward the future, is deeply concerned with the relation of goals to collective decisions, and strives for comprehensiveness in policy and program.[5] Wherever these modes of thought are applied, there is a presumption that planning is being done.

This formulation is helpful insofar as it points to certain elements of action which underlie not only regional but also other forms of planning. It does not answer the question of a substantive core for a specialization in regional planning. Pursuing this question further, one is led to those academic disciplines which have made regional studies their special concern. Perhaps it is in geography and the economics of location that one can discover an adequate theoretical foundation for planning on a scale that is larger than the city.

Two interesting conclusions emerge from an examination of the pertinent literature: first, that the concept of the region as a "natural" unit capable of being defined unambiguously in space has been abandoned;[6] second, that as the concept of "region" has receded into the background of academic discussion, its place has been taken by the more neutral concept of "space." Intensive work has been done in spatial theory within the last eight or ten years, both in this country and abroad.[7] The theoretical achievements of these efforts, however, are still meager, perhaps because more emphasis has been given to developing empirical data and the tools for their analysis than to the formulation of new concepts and hypotheses. Nevertheless, it is now possible to assert a few simple, empirical generalizations whose validity has been established reasonably well. Although these generalizations do not constitute a systematic body of theoretical propositions, they strongly suggest that there is a certain regularity and order in the structure of space as it is shaped by human activities. The following may serve for illustration.[8]

1. The structure of human settlements can be defined as a system of nodes and functional linkages.
2. Nodes are arranged into a loose hierarchical structure which is internally differentiated by function.
3. Surrounding each node is a "density field" of functional interaction, the densities declining with increasing distance from the center.
4. The cost of overcoming distance exerts a pervasive influence on the distribution of activities in space as well as on the level of activity at any given location.

These propositions are capable of mathematical formulation; moreover, the results of any density distribution can be mapped.[9] It is worthwhile to note, however, that all quantitative results will be historically contingent: the peculiarities of spatial structure appear as a function of both time and place. They will vary with changes in technology, economic and social development, cultural values, and geography. Nevertheless, the mere fact that it has become possible to assert *some* general propositions concerning spatial structure indicates that activity distributions cannot be wholly arbitrary but must, in some sense, be considered "lawful." Attempts to explain these empirical regularities have not met with complete success. A number of hypotheses have been put forward, such as the principle of "least effort" (Zipf), distance inputs (Isard), agglomeration economies (Weber), intervening opportunities (Stouffer), social gravity laws (Stewart), and stochastic processes (Vining). But even though no completely convincing explanation has been given, the observed regularities of spatial structure remain. This fact, it would seem, offers the possibility for an approach to regional planning that is both grounded in theory and, in the broadest sense, scientific.

But regional planning must be thought of as a scientific undertaking of a special kind. Primarily oriented to the future, it looks to the relation between social purposes and spatial arrangements. This insight yields a first and proximate definition of the field of regional planning as an academic discipline: *regional planning is concerned with the ordering of human activities in supra-urban space*—that is, in any area which is larger than a single city.

This as yet preliminary definition provides a convenient link to city planning. Common to both city and regional planning study is a central concern with the organization of space. Regional planning focuses attention on supra-urban space, while intra-urban space is, of course, of primary importance in city planning. The two approaches touch in the border areas of metropolis and megalopolis, where perhaps new specializations are emerging.

The continuity referred to is important, but there are persuasive reasons for keeping the two areas of planning study distinct from one another. The obvious distinction of scale is there, but in itself this would be an insufficient argument. A more valid criterion for differentiation arises from differences in the institutional setting for city and regional planning. The means available for implementing public policy will influence the perception and definition of relevant problems in the organization of space. At the regional level, therefore, much of the emphasis will be on the economic problem of resource allocation and development, whereas physical land use and design problems will tend to predominate at the city scale. But an even more fundamental discontinuity is due to differences in the theoretical approaches to spatial organization. Regional planning theory has evolved out of special theories in economics (location) and geography (central places); city planning theory is based on human ecology, land economics, and the aesthetics of urban form.[10] Preliminary efforts to extend central place theory to the internal structure of cities have not been successful in developing an adequate theoretical framework for spatial organization at all scales.[11] One result of this divergence has been that students of regional planning use a substantially different vocabulary and a different set of concepts from urbanists. At the same time, theoretical considerations lead them to identify problems in a different way, quite aside from any institutional considerations.

But the field of regional planning study must now be defined with greater precision. The process of planning may, in general, be regarded as one which leads to the formulation and clarification of goals and to their ultimate reduction to specific courses of action, programs, and projects.[12] Thus, our earlier definition may be extended to say that *regional planning is the process of formulating and clarifying social objectives in the ordering of activities in supra-urban space.* The basic question, therefore, is: "How are activities to be distributed in space so as to meet social objectives? Alternatively, what are the proper social objectives in accordance with which activities are to be allocated in space? This formulation links regional planning to its basis in the pure theory of location without, however, achieving an identity.[13]

THE SPECTRUM OF SPATIAL PLANNING ACTIVITIES

The better to understand what the professionally trained regional planner might be asked to do in a specific situation, and to show the relation of regional planning to planning at city and national levels, we shall consider the total spectrum of co-ordinated spatial planning activities that might be brought into existence in a hypothetical society. In this fashion, it will be possible to show the extent to which regional planning as a field of study may be usefully distinguished from other forms of spatial planning.

To begin with, general policy issues would predominate at the *national* level. What principles should guide the geographic allocation of resources within the country? To the extent to which there is national planning—and budgeting may be considered as a limiting case of such planning—there will inevitably be spatial implications of any set of resource allocations. The problem of spatial resource allocation may, of course, be treated entirely on a short-term, political basis; but if it is to be guided by foresight, a review of the available alternatives, and a clear vision of the public interest, the problem is essentially one for planning. In policy planning, the technical, economic, and political elements are closely interwined.

Regional policy for the nation would accompany policies for the over-all development of its resources. Specifically, it would add the dimension of *space* to other considerations. Modern economic development—the transition from one form of social order to another—leads necessarily to shifts in the organization of the space economy. In the simplest and most schematic case, where an economy is moving out of an agrarian past into an industrial future, spatial reorganization involves primarily a process of concentrating people and economic activities in cities. Further shifts take place as development proceeds into the post-industrial phase. These shifts pose serious problems for the society: Where should concentrations be encouraged? How may areas of emigration—the traditional economic regions of the country—be helped to adapt to the new requirements of the economy? What should be done with areas that fail to adapt to the changed conditions. What may be done to assist the process of concentrated development?

The spatial shifts which are implicit in economic development necessarily create regional inequities: while economic development makes rapid strides forward at the "center," the "periphery" threatens to collapse. These inequities may lead to serious political consequences where the traditional economic areas are densely populated, and where opportunities at the center are insufficient to absorb into regular employment all newcomers in the labor force. Social and political unrest resulting from increasing impoverishment on the periphery may ultimately undermine developments at the center itself. Countervailing measures to maintain minimum inter-regional balances in the major indices of welfare may therefore have to be undertaken.

But the rationale for regional policy does not derive solely from inequities on the periphery. Regional policy should be thought of as a tool for comprehensive national development in which all parts of the country contribute in their own ways to the attainment of national objectives.

A national urban policy must be approached by way of broader regional considerations: the implications for urban planning on a national scale become evident only when prior attention has been given to the regional problem, and the basic allocation decisions have been made. Goals, priorities, and standards must be defined; the national interest must be rendered specific, and decisions must be made where, in what manner, and with what resources the national government is to support such urban activities as public housing, mass transit, sanitary works, and metropolitan highways. On the other hand, regional choices cannot be made independently of considering the urban problem. Indeed, the urban problem will often be decisive, for regional space is structured primarily through a hierarchy of urban places and through the fields of interaction which relate them. The very closest co-ordination of city and regional policy planning is therefore essential.[14]

At the *regional,* as contrasted with the national level, an even greater diversity of problems is pressed upon the attention of our hypothetical planner. In part, this diversity reflects the underlying spatial structure which consists of urban nodes, nodal regions, and the channels of transport and communications which connect them. Since attention at the regional level is focussed on spatial units larger than the city, the first problem of spatial organization emerges on the level of the metropolitan region.

The historic city is turning obsolete. As Lewis Mumford has aptly put it, it has burst its container. The concept of the city as a physical artifact is being replaced by one in which interaction and relation are emphasized. The new city may be identified as a density configuration that is measured by the flows of interaction within a given "matrix." This matrix, however, has no firm boundaries but represents a continuum of densities of interaction where the actual lines of division become more or less arbitrary symbols put down for convenience. The metropolitan region is the new, etherealized city.

What are its chief characteristics? To begin with, it has one or more cores, or control centers. Second, it provides a complete and year-round habitat for man, a place for work and residence and the pursuit of leisure. Third, it generally includes areas in which some forms of intensive agriculture will be carried on chiefly to supply the region. Fourth, it represents a suitable unit area (location matrix) with respect to which investment decisions will be made. Planning for this new form of human settlement must be related to its several cores and proceed outward from these centers to a line where densities of interaction fall below a certain threshold level. At this invisible boundary, one metropolitan region may run into another (megalopolis) or yield to a rural periphery which is not yet fully integrated with any metropolitan center.

City and regional planning approaches meet and merge in the metropolitan region. The task of the regional planner will be to state the ordering of control centers within the area, to identify the functions to be performed by each center, and to study the inter-regional effects of the expansion of metropolitan economies.

A related area of concern is the pattern of functional linkages which connect metropolitan regions in a more comprehensive spatial framework. Transportation of people and commodities is perhaps the most important of these, but power grids, communication networks, and water supply channels must also be considered.

Finally, the regional planner may be called upon to deal with problems of areas that do not fall within the control spans of metropolitan regions—the so-called peripheral areas. From an economic standpoint, many of these areas will have become locationally obsolescent, even though they may include potentially valuable resource complexes. One possible solution would be to attempt to achieve a more perfect integration of these areas with existing metropolitan centers; another, to plan for their adjustment to a lower economic equilibrium through planned out-migration and suitable changes in land use; a third, to stimulate local development efforts and to create new location matrices within them. In broad terms, however, the problem of peripheral areas is primarily one of resource management. The regional planner's contribution to the development of peripheral areas can be only a limited one; he will have to work with many other specialists in a comprehensive endeavor.

At the *urban* level, finally, tradition, scale, and institutional setting suggest a somewhat different approach to spatial planning. Here, the distinctions put forward in a recent paper by Perloff and Wingo may help to refine the nature of the planning function.[15] In their formulation, elements that enter into planning at the supra-metropolitan, metropolitan, and intra-metropolitan levels are the assets appropriate for development: human and natural resources, private and public capital, and organizational endowments. At the intra-metropolitan or urban level, some elements are identical with those significant for regional planning —industry, residences, transportation—but the difference in scale emphasizes more immediate spatial relationships among these activities. Still other elements enter solely into what is traditionally called city planning: schools below the college level, local utilities, and neighborhood parks.

The planning function, however, is limited still more clearly by organizational considerations. The content of urban planning reflects to a large extent the powers of local government, while regional planning is more closely a reflection of the functions of state governments and specially constituted public authorities, such as the Guayana Development Corporation in Venezuela or the TVA. City governments in the United States exercise power over the spatial arrangement of activities by means of zoning laws, capital investment programs for municipal facilities, tax and assessment policies, subdivision controls over vacant land, building and occupancy codes, and urban renewal and public housing programs. City planning, therefore, concerns itself primarily with activities which fall broadly within this sphere of influence and regulation: the juxtaposition and patterning of land uses, provision of public services, creation and management of the housing stock. Decisions in this sphere of planning may have implications at the regional and even the national level. Renewal and housing policies that call for reductions of central city density, for example, will exert powerful influences in shaping the settlement pattern of the metropolitan area, since the overspill of population will usually locate elsewhere in the larger community.

Conceptually, city planning shares with regional planning a concern for the large-scale arrangement of activities in space. But city planning has a separate focus in its additional concern with the quality of the micro-environment. Questions of "neighborhood" character and services, the social and economic implications of different residential densities and patterns, the juxtaposition of industry and housing, and the staging of small-scale changes in land use—all these fall particularly within the province of city planning. In operational language, these concerns call for action to stimulate investment at selected locations, to provide local services to keep pace with changing demands and shifts in activities, and to accommodate change by special programs involving new development and the relocation of old activities.

EDUCATION FOR REGIONAL PLANNING

The hierarchy of planning concerns that has just been described delimits a range of problems to whose solution regional planners could usefully contribute. At the core of regional planning lies an interest in the relation between the spatial arrangement of activities and social values. This interest can be explored at the level of national policy, where it comes to focus chiefly on the formulation of regional development strategies, the allocation of resources in space, the location of productive facilities, and the arrangement of settlement patterns. It can be pursued at the regional level, where attention is drawn not only to the order of settlement and possible improvement in man's physical environment, but also to the effective integration into the national space economy of structurally remote peripheral areas. Finally, it can be brought into focus at the urban level where city and regional planning skills meet in solving the many-faceted problems of an expanding metropolis.

In emphasizing these functions of regional planning, however, it must be recognized that they are time-bound and intimately caught up with the flow of economic and social events. Regional planning, as a separate field of academic study, is most appropriate during the transition of a society to industrialism. Strong pressures for a regional approach to planning are coming from countries whose economies are less well integrated than is that of the United States and where, as a result, there are emphatic regional differences in production, welfare, and cultural development.[16] National policy for regional development, settlement policy, and planning for inter-regional networks are among the truly vital issues confronting these countries, and must be dealt with from a vantage point that is altogether different from that of traditional city planning. Once the stage of self-sustaining cumulative growth has been attained, however, and a reasonable measure of inter-regional integration has been achieved, the spectrum of problems will inevitably shift to the metropolis, where a vast majority of the population will be residing. At that point, regional planning will imperceptibly fuse with metropolitan planning. In the United States today—except for relatively remote areas such as Alaska and Hawaii—spatial planning occurs predominantly in a metropolitan context.[17] The great emerging need in the United States is not for regional or city, but for *spatial* planners who will be competent to deal with problems of metropolitan development and organization on all the relevant scales, from local site to megalopolis.

Confusion about the nature of regional planning can be traced to the fact that of its historical contingency. The traditional distinction between city and regional planning belongs to an earlier day in the history of the United States; both are today obsolete as meaningful designations for spatial planning in a post-industrial society. If interest in the education of U.S. planners were to fit them solely for the great national tasks at home, the claim for both city and regional planning as distinctive fields of study would have to be abandoned in favor of an approach to comprehensive spatial planning with a focus on metropolitan development. But the responsibilities of the United States go further in the present generation. Not only will many Americans be called upon to render service and advice to the newly developing countries, but students from these countries are coming in growing numbers to study in the United States. To teach these students a tradition of planning that is suited primarily to the present needs of the United States would be, I think, a grievous error. In transitional societies, the distinction between city and regional planning is still a meaningful, and indeed, an essential one.

The principal need in American planning education today is for a program of comprehensive spatial planning in which consideration of the metropolis will be central. But it would seem to be enlightened policy for leading planning schools in the country to include a specialization in regional planning within such a program. What would be required to acquire mastery in this field? To begin with, all spatial (including regional) planners should be held responsible for a common core of knowledge that would include, as a minimum, elements of planning theory, theories of spatial organization, methods of urban and regional analysis, urban social structure and change, and planning law. In addition, it would be desirable for all planning students to participate, toward the end of their formal education, in a co-ordinative studio or workshop problem in which problems of spatial organization are dealt with simultaneously at all the relevant scales: national, sub-national, and local.

Beyond this common foundation, however, specialization ought to occur. In addition to regional planning, courses leading to expertise in urban design, metropolitan planning, and methematical techniques of planning analysis might be offered. Other areas of specialization may eventually be added.

The student who opts for regional planning should build a curriculum, adapted to his personal interests and inclinations, from subject offerings in the following areas of study: *one,* economic location theory; *two,* central place studies; *three,* analysis of metropolitan and inter-metropolitan ecological structure; *four,* regional economic development; *five,* urbanization processes and the role of cities in the historical development of regions; *six,* theory of resource use; and *seven,* the spatial structure of decisions and political authority—the last two being the least developed of all the topics at the present time.

Ultimately, a good deal of freedom ought to be given the student in the choice of subject matter, although reasonable competence in areas *one* through *four* should probably be required of every candidate for a degree. The present two-year graduate curricula in planning do not allow for adequate preparation along the lines suggested. It may well be that a course of study in regional planning is best devised at the doctoral level, with the master's degree acquired but in passing. In this way, a high level of professional competence could be assured.

NOTES

[1] *Aspects of Training in Economic Development,* "Problems of Development" series, Organization for Economic Cooperation and Development, January, 1962.

[2] United Nations, *Housing, Building, and Planning,* Nos. 12 and 13, "Regional Planning," New York: U.N. Department of Economic and Social Affairs, 1959.

[3] *Ibid.,* p. 1.

[4] See, for instance, the works of Karl Mannheim, Rexford Tugwell, Robert Dahl, Charles E. Lindblom, Edward Banfield, and Herbert Simon. For recent statements of this viewpoint, see John Friedmann, "Introduction to the Study and Practice of Planning," *International Social Science Journal,* IX (1959), 327–340, and Paul Davidoff and Thomas A. Reiner, "A Choice Theory of Planning," *Journal of the American Institute of Planners,* XXVIII (May, 1962), 103–115.

[5] John Friedmann, "Urbanismo como Vocação," *Binário,* No. 47 (Lisbon, August, 1962), 526–533.

[6] Derwent Whittlesey, "The Regional Concept and the Regional Method," in James E. Preston and Clarence F. Jones, ed., *American Geography: Inventory and Prospects* (Syracuse: Syracuse University Press, 1954). A concept of shifting regional boundaries is applied in Harvey S. Perloff *et al., Regions, Resources, and Economic Growth* (Baltimore: Johns Hopkins Press, 1960). However, a plea for a single "true" set of regions is made by Walter Isard, "Regional Science, The Concept of Region, and Regional Structure," Regional Science Association, *Papers and Proceedings,* II (1956), 13–26.

[7] See, for example, Brian J. L. Berry and Allen Pred, *Central Place Studies: A Bibliography of Theory and Applications* (Philadelphia: Regional Science Research Institute, 1961). Outstanding contributions have been made by Walter Isard, Otis D. Duncan, Rutledge Vining, J. Q. Stewart, Carl H. Madden, W. L. Garrison, Brian Berry, Arthur Maass, Harvey S. Perloff, William H. Nicholls, and Edwin von Böventer, among others.

[8] Some of the evidence is presented by Rutledge Vining in "A Description of Certain Spatial Aspects of an Economic System," *Economic Development and Cultural Change,* III (1955), 147–95, and "On Describing the Structure and Development of a Human Population System," *Journal of Farm Economics,* XLI (1959), 922–42. See also Walter Isard *et al., Methods of Regional Analysis* (New York: J. Wiley, 1960), *passim.*

[9] For a recent example, see John H. Thompson *et al.,* "Toward a Geography of Economic Health: The Case of New York State," *Annals of the Association of American Geographers,* LII (1962), 1–20.

[10] The problem of urban and metropolitan structure has been approached from a number of different directions, but so far no synthesis has been achieved. The best general summary is still found in E. M. Hoover, *The Location of Economic Activity* (New York: McGraw-Hill, 1948). Since that time, however, important studies have been published by Amos Hawley, Donald J. Bogue, Otis and Beverly Duncan, Leo Schnore, Robert Mitchell and Chester Rapkin, William Alonso, Bernard Frieden, and others.

[11] For instance, Brian Berry, "Ribbon Development in Urban Business Patterns," *Annals of the Association of American Geographers,* XLIX (1959), 145–55; Hans Carol, "The Hierarchy of Central Functions Within the City," *Annals*

of the Association of American Geographers, L (1960), 419–38; and G. J. Foster and H. J. Nelson, *Ventura Boulevard: A String-Type Shopping Street* (Los Angeles: Real Estate Research Program, University of California, 1958).

[12] Martin Meyerson and Edward C. Banfield, *Politics, Planning, and the Public Interest* (Glencoe, Ill.: The Free Press, 1955), pp. 312–22.

[13] E. M. Hoover, *op. cit.,* provides a good summary of the classical approach. For recent advances, see Walter Isard, *Location and Space Economy* (New York: J. Wiley, 1956), and Louis Lefeber, *Allocation in Space* (Amsterdam: North Holland Publishing Co., 1958).

[14] Very little attention has so far been given in the professional literature to the problems of regional and urban policy at the national level. Noteworthy exceptions include writings of François Perroux, Albert Hirschman, Gunnar Myrdal, Harvey Perloff, and Lloyd Rodwin. Virtually all contributions, however, have been written with the problems of newly developing countries in mind. For a recent statement, see John Friedmann, "Regional Policy for Developing Areas," Regional Science Association, *Papers and Proceedings,* XI (1962), forthcoming.

[15] Harvey S. Perloff and Lowdon Wingo, Jr., "Planning and Development in Metropolitan Areas," *Journal of the American Institute of Planners,* XXVIII (May, 1962), 67–90.

[16] See John Friedmann, "Cities in Social Transformation," *Comparative Studies in Society and History,* IV (1961), 86–103.

[17] See Britton Harris, "Some Problems in the Theory of Intra-Urban Location," *Journal of Operations Research,* IX (September–October 1961), 695–721. Harris' paper exemplifies the new trend in American planning in which the traditional distinctions along areal lines are disappearing. Much of what passes for state planning in the United States is concerned with little more than industrial promotion. The possibilities of comprehensive spatial planning at the national scale are brilliantly explored in *Die Raumordnung der Bundesrepublik Deutschland* (Stuttgart: Kohlhammer, 1962).

PART II

Location and Spatial Organization

Introductory Note

A knowledge of the theories and principles of economic location must underlie sound regional planning. Classical location theory, as summarized by William Alonso in this volume, deals primarily with the location of the individual producing unit in a world in which nearly everything else is fixed, including the location of other competing and complementary activities. Going beyond the individual unit to systems of firms in their analysis of the location problem, economists finally succeeded in formulating spatial models for the pattern of economic relationships which extend over the physical landscape but are not isomorphic with it. Foremost among them was August Lösch, whose article reprinted here provides a glimpse into his crowning achievement, *The Economics of Location.* With the theory of the firm as his principal point of departure, Lösch develops his analysis of the region with remarkable force of vision. Although much of his analysis is flawed by inconsistencies, the power of his insight into economic space has proved seminal for many subsequent studies.

Lösch's work was extended and generalized by Walter Isard, who also founded the Regional Science Association early in the 1950's as a meeting ground for scholars interested in the study of spatial relations chiefly by the use of mathematical models. At about the same time, geographers began to collect the empirical materials with which the hypotheses of Lösch, Isard, and other regional scientists could be tested. Geography thus changed its focus from the honored tradition of the analysis of place-bound structures, emphasizing the uniqueness of man-environment relationships, to the recurring regularities of economic phenomena in space.

As the evidence accumulated, it became apparent that patterns of spatial relations could be ordered cross-regionally, and that certain relations remained stable despite significant regional variations in other respects. Empirical regularities, such as the spatial sequence and orderly pattern of magnitudes of concentrations, the hierarchical arrangement of trade relationships, and the regular decline of the density of interaction as a simple function of distance, have fascinated the scholar and posed challenging questions to the policy planner about the pattern of "normality" and the possibilities of its change. These regularities have supported earlier theoretical findings, such as the hierarchy of market areas; but the full force of location theory still lacks an explanation of many of their features as well as their general form.

The empirical study of the organization of space is represented in this volume by two articles by Brian Berry, and essays by Edward Ullman, Richard Morrill, and John Thompson and collaborators. Berry's first piece is an extended review and evaluation of recent literature in the field; his second is a study of the relations between city-size distributions and economic development. Edward Ullman analyzes the spatial patterns of economic concentration in the United States, a pattern that is typical for many countries, and gauges the prospects for the development of the national fringe areas of periphery. Richard Morrill's original attempt at simulating Swedish settlement patterns in their historical evolution is of particular interest as an instance of the use of stochastic processes. And, finally, the careful measurement and mapping of Thompson and his co-workers identifies the structuring influence of urban fields upon the pattern of regional development. The reader may be interested in comparing their conclusions with William Nicholl's on the influence of urbanization on agricultural development, which are reported in Part III of this volume.

All this analytical material, whether empirical or theoretical, is of great import to the regional planner. The purpose of regional planning is to seek changes in the spatial organization of an economy through an improved ordering of economic relations. But interference with existing patterns requires an understanding of the laws that underlie their structure.

The meaning of this approach to regional development and planning may be clarified by reference to the well-known problem of depressed areas. By definition, a depressed area is one in which economic growth has lagged and in which the population enjoys a level of welfare substantially lower than that in other regions. The reason for the region's backwardness is that rapid growth has located elsewhere. Opportunities in other regions draw off its resources, including capital and labor; and its relative inaccessibility prevents its being integrated more effectively with the focal points of new growth, which are typically metropolitan areas.

As the causes for the economic depression of the region are locational, so are the policy solutions for its problems. If substantial undeveloped resources exist within the region, additional investment may create attractive locations for further growth at strategic points. Alternatively, growth poles along the margins of the depressed region may be favored so that they may extend their vitalizing influence into it and improve its general accessibility. Finally, in an attempt to make the levels of welfare more nearly equal among regions, transfer payments may be made into the region from other parts of the nation. In all these solutions, the key decisions are locational, and the problem is one of altering the existing pattern of spatial organization. "The real duty of the economist," writes August Lösch, "is not to explain our sorry reality but to improve it. The question of the best location is far more dignified than the determination of the actual one." But, he might have added, it is also essential to understand the forces that have determined actual locations.

The example of a depressed area points to one of the central methodological problems of spatial analysis. Economic space is continuous and unbounded, except for rare cases of extreme political or natural barriers. Yet, for purposes of administration, planning, and measurement, it must usually be divided and treated as if it were, in fact, discontinuous. The very term "region" refers to areas that are differentiated within a more comprehensive national space. Working with such a discrete space, the analyst finds it easier to trace out complex networks of internal relationships and their evolution through time. Continuous space is theoretically valid, but our intellectual tools permit us at present to carry out the analysis of only very simple structures in such space. In this way, the problem of space is akin to that of time, in which the analyst is usually faced with the choice between a deep static structural analysis within a discrete period and a dynamic analysis in continuous time that requires great simplifications of structural relations. In general the term "locational" has been used for analyses in continuous space, and "regional" for analyses in discontinuous space. Insofar as project decisions usually are made for the single element, they tend to be locational; insofar as economic development depends on complex structural relationships, its theory has tended to be regional.

4. Location Theory

WILLIAM ALONSO

INTRODUCTION

This article tries to acquaint the reader with the theory of the location of the firm. The formal theory originated in the work of Alfred Weber and, through the contributions of later writers, developed rapidly until the 1950's, when further additions to its elegant structure seemed to bring increasing costs in terms of complexity of form and decreasing marginal returns in terms of new insights. At this time Walter Isard demonstrated its unity with the classical economics of substitution analysis, and an awareness developed of other problems of location and regions beyond the scope of this theory. Consequently scholars have turned elsewhere, and significant contributions to location theory have become rare.

In these pages are presented some of the principal insights of this branch of economic theory as it stands today. The first part of the article tries to synthesize the work of many scholars. To trace the intellectual ancestry of the various parts would be a laborious exercise; rather, a brief bibliographic note has been appended pointing to seminal and representative works. The second part seeks to clarify some of the deficiencies and limitations of this type of theory, and in doing this it points to some areas where further work would be fruitful. In particular, the theory of market areas seems to be the key to future developments. It was, in a sense, the culmination of the theory of the firm. But it was also the beginning of the theory of August Lösch, as represented by his article in this volume, and, in the form of central place theory, it constitutes the principal tool for understanding the empirical regularities that concern Brian Berry, among others. The theory of market areas is implicit too in the modern theories of regional development such as Perroux's growth poles. Thus, in a way as yet unrealized, it may be said to be the fulcrum on which turn the various spokes of the understanding of regional structure and development.

The theory of the location of the firm has been developed in the context of a free market. In recent years, however, concern has turned to national regional development. Increasingly the question of the location of a factory is being considered as a "project" by a government agency rather than as a profit-making venture by a private corporation. It is clear that, as long as the decision turns on the project maximizing its own returns, there is little difference whether those making the decision serve a public or a private body. But the theory has little force in considering the costs and benefits accruing outside the books of the particular enterprise. Regional economics is concerned with these external or multiplicative effects within the region, and national regional planning with these effects among regions. In this sense, the theory of the location of the firm extends to project planning but antecedes regional and national spatial planning.

Because of the variety of backgrounds of those interested in regional development, and at the risk of irritating the knowledgeable, I have explained the technical terms in this article. Moreover, to avoid awkwardness of language, I have based most of the analysis on the businessman as protagonist rather than the project planner.

In essence, the firm wishes to maximize its profits. If the businessman can state clearly what factors are involved and what relations bind them, his problem is one of manipulating these variables to get the largest profits. In reality these variables are many, and some cannot be quantified. Here we shall begin with very simple problems, paring the problem down to a few essentials, and introducing complications gradually to make the theory more realistic; but some considerations will remain outside the formal theory. We shall call attention to some of these, but they are potentially infinite. For instance, a study of the New England region found a manufacturing firm in Worcester which would clearly have been better off in Boston. The reason for its location, it was discovered, was that the manufacturer's mother-in-law lived in Worcester, and his wife insisted on living in the same city. No amount of formal theory would have unearthed this reason, but formal theory could tell the manufacturer how much this cost him.

THE PRINCIPLE OF MEDIAN LOCATION

Let us begin by considering the location of a firm which, let us say, makes and delivers bakery products. Neither the cost of making these products nor the volume of business will vary with the location of the firm. The only variable in this case is the delivery costs, so that maximizing profits is identical with minimizing delivery costs. The customers, *A, B, . . . , G,* each take one delivery a day, and are distributed along a road as shown in Figure 1. The bakery sends out a boy who can carry only one customer's order at a time, so that he has to make one trip per customer. Where then to locate the bakery to minimize the boy's trips? The almost automatic answer would be the "average," center of gravity, or mean location. This is easily found by summing the distances from either end and dividing by the number of customers. In this case, summing from *A*, it would be $0 + 1 + 2 + 4 + 6 + 14 + 15 = 42$; dividing by the number of customers or trips (7), the mean is 6 blocks to the right of *A*, at the same location as *E*. *But this*

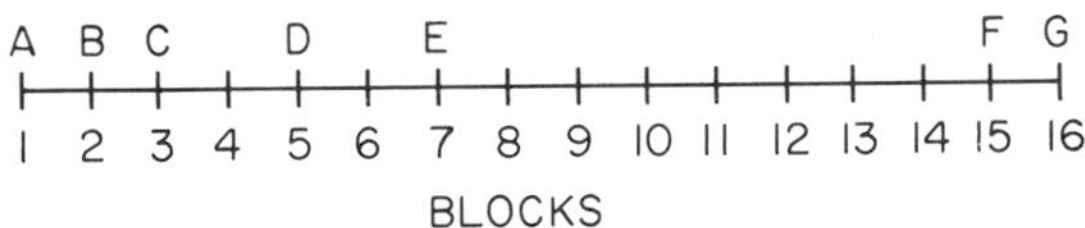

FIG. 1. Distribution of the bakery's customers.

is the wrong solution. Examine Table 1. The total distance is less if the bakery locates at *D* than if it locates at *E*. If we had gone about the problem in a systematic fashion, we should have asked: Which location minimizes the sum of the distances from the bakery to its customers? This can readily be solved by elementary calculus. In fact, however, we might have recognized that the point on a distribution along a line at which the total distance to all other points is minimized

TABLE I
TOTAL TRIPS ACCORDING TO LOCATION OF THE BAKERY AT E OR D IN FIGURE 1

Customer	*Distance from location at* E	*Distance from location at* D
A	6	4
B	5	3
C	4	2
D	2	0
E	0	2
F	8	10
G	9	11
Total Distance	34	32

is the median (that is to say, the point at which there are as many points to one side as to the other). The median in this case is *D*. The mean or center of gravity, on the other hand, minimizes the sum of the squares of the distances, and therefore is irrelevant for our purposes.

This simple example is a very enlightening one. We would not often meet a bakery in these precise conditions, but the logic often applies to other enterprises. For instance, a factory which has shipping costs proportional to the weight of the shipments and the distance shipped would benefit from locating at the median location unless there were strong reasons to the contrary. Thus, a firm selling 200 units in one city, 300 in a second, and 550 in a third would have its median location in the third city. Since the median of the distribution of customers will tend to be in large cities, this is one of the reasons why big cities tend to grow bigger.

COMPETITION ALONG A LINE

It is a truism that what may be good for someone may be disadvantageous for another, but this is often forgotten. It is important, therefore, to make clear whose point of view we are considering when we say that a location is optimal.

Imagine a long beach, with people evenly distributed along its length. Each person on the beach buys one ice-cream cone, and will walk as far as necessary to get it, though he will naturally prefer to walk the shortest possible distance. If there is a single vendor of ice cream, he will not care where he locates since every customer on the beach will walk as far as necessary to buy his cone. Every customer, however, would prefer to minimize his walk by having the vendor as near to him as possible. A third point of view might be that of a public official who wants to minimize the total amount of walking for the general benefit. As shown in our first example, this total will be minimized at the median location, in this case the midpoint of the beach.

Consider now the same problem with two vendors, *A* and *B,* who are at two locations as in the first stage of Figure 2. Vendor *A* will sell to all the customers to his left, and Vendor *B* to all those to his own right; of the customers between the two, the left half will go to *A* and the right to *B*. But *A,* after examining the situation, decides that by moving to the right he can take away many of *B*'s customers without losing any of his own (second stage). Vendor *B* then decides to hop over to the left of *A* (third stage). It can easily be seen that the final stage will have both *A* and *B* together at the center of the beach, each selling to half the customers. Neither *A* nor *B* will then be able to increase the number of his customers by moving, and the situation will be stable.

Free competition in this case will result in both vendors joining at the middle of the beach. Since people are evenly distributed along the length of the beach, the average distance walked will be one fourth of the length. A public official might point out, however, that this average distance is unnecessarily high. If the two vendors were located at the quarter points, as in the "planned location" of Figure 2, the average

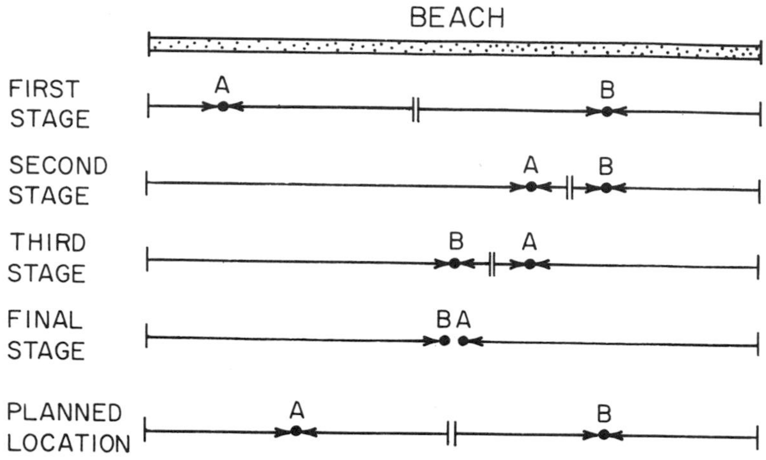

FIG. 2. Locations of vendors on the beach.

distance walked would be reduced by half, while both vendors would still enjoy the same sales. To obtain the benefits of this solution it is only necessary to assure each vendor that the other will not start moving in on him.

There are two lessons to be learned from this. On the one hand, we have seen once again a tendency toward concentration, which may be interpreted as another indication of the reasons for the development of centers of human activity. On the other, we have seen that the solution of free competition may differ from that of the public interest. This is not to say that the results of private initiative need be in conflict with the interests of the community. In fact, it will be seen that theory indicates they usually coincide. But this coincidence of interests is something to be proved in each case, rather than something to be taken for granted.

THE FIRM WITH ONE MARKET AND ONE RAW MATERIAL

Let us consider an activity that uses only one material and sells all of its product at one market. Such a firm might use sheets of steel from a steel plant at *M* in Figure 3 as its raw material, and bend them into boxes which it sells in a city at *C*. For simplicity say that the costs of production are the same everywhere, so that the firm's only consideration will be to minimize its *total transport costs*. These consist of *assembly costs* of bringing the steel from *M* to the factory, and *distribution costs* of sending the boxes from the factory to *C*. Let *T* be the

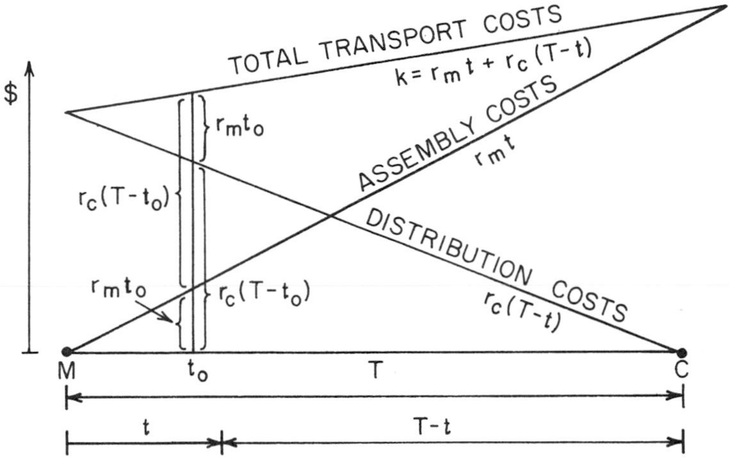

FIG. 3. Transport costs of a firm with a single market and a single material; transport costs proportional to distance.

distance from *M* to *C*, and *t* the distance from *M* to the box factory. The distance from the factory to *C* is the remainder of *T*, or $(T - t)$. Now, if the cost per mile of carrying enough steel to build one box is r_m, assembly costs per unit will be $r_m t$; and if the cost of carrying one box is r_c per mile, distribution costs per unit will be $r_c(T - t)$. The total transport costs, which we represent by *k*, are the sum of these:

$$k = r_m t + r_c(T - t) \tag{1}$$

The firm will locate at that value of *t* that minimizes *k*.

Examine Figure 3, where assembly, distribution, and transport costs are shown for one case. The curve of total transport costs is the sum of the other two, as illustrated for location t_0. In the case illustrated it can be seen that transport costs will be least when the box factory is at *M*, where $t = 0$. As the diagram is drawn, the curve of assembly costs is steeper than that of distribution costs, meaning that it is more expensive to move steel than boxes; or, to put it another way, that the transport rate for steel (r_m) is greater than that for boxes (r_c). We may rewrite Equation 1 as $k = (r_m - r_c)t + r_cT$ without changing its meaning. From this form of the equation it can be seen that when r_m is greater than r_c, as in Figure 3, the firm will want to keep t as small as possible (that is, locate at M, where $t = 0$). But when r_c is greater, the coefficient of t will be negative, and the firm will want to locate at the maximum t (that is, at C, where $t = T$). Finally, if the costs of moving boxes or steel are equal, so that $r_m = r_c$, the coefficient of t will be zero and transport costs will be r_cT wherever the plant locates. The plant may then locate at M, at C, or at any point in between.

THE STRUCTURE OF TRANSPORT COSTS

Although the costs of transportation do increase with distance, it is not accurate to say, as we have been saying, that they increase in direct proportion. In the first place, there are terminal costs: the costs of putting things on a truck or train, and of taking them off, the costs of packaging and certain paper work. These in general will not vary with distance. Therefore, transport costs are better represented by an expression such as $s_m + r_mt$, where s_m are the terminal costs, r_m is the rate per mile, and t the number of miles. Thus, above we used the expression r_mt, which results in a straight line passing through the origin, such as A in Figure 4. Introducing terminal costs will add s_m all

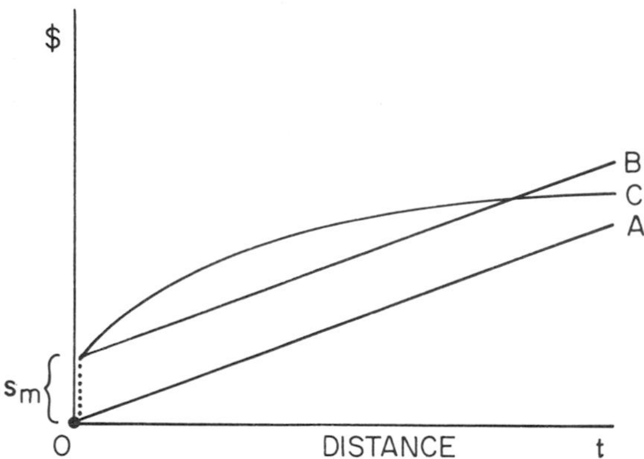

FIG. 4. Transport costs: (A) proportional to distance, (B) considering terminal costs, (C) considering decreasing marginal costs.

along to line A, resulting in line B. Of course, at $t = 0$ nothing has been moved and costs will be zero. This is indicated by the dot at the origin in Figure 4.

Another realistic refinement considers that the rate per mile is lower for longer hauls. This is common practice in the transportation industry as in most others: costs are lower when buying in bulk, it is cheaper to rent by the month than by the week, and so on. This results in a flattening of the slope of the curve of transport costs with increasing distance, reflecting the lower rates. In practical terms, it is cheaper to make one 1000-mile shipment than two 500-mile ones. The curvature of the curve of transport costs is increased by the variety of carriers: ship, train, truck, pipe, and so on. Usually trucks have lower terminal costs but higher per-mile costs than trains, as do trains with respect to ships. Figure 5 shows the relation of transport costs to distance when alternative carriers are considered. The shipper will choose the carrier with the lowest costs for a particular distance, so that his effective curve of transport costs will be the heavy line in Figure 5, which is more curved than that of any one carrier.

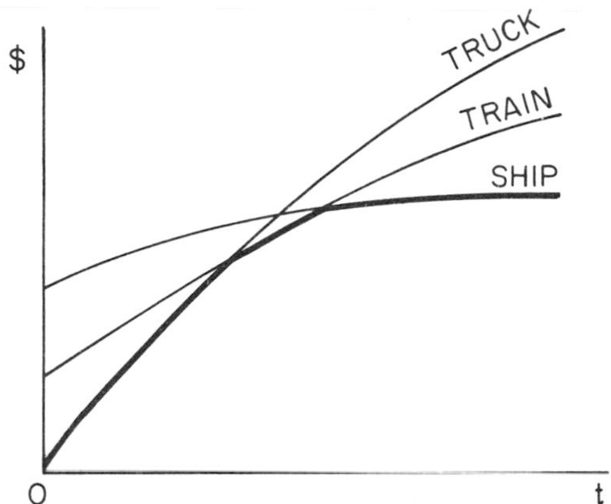

FIG. 5. Transport costs considering alternative carriers.

Terminal costs and the curvature of transport costs reinforce the attractiveness of end-point locations, such as *M* or *C* in the example of Figure 3. In Figure 6 the case of identical transport costs for steel and boxes is re-examined under this more realistic structure of transport costs. When we considered the case without regard for terminal costs or the economies of longer hauls, we concluded that when the rates are the same for assembly and distribution costs the firm would locate at *M* or *C* or at any intermediate point. But now, the curvature of the curves of assembly and distribution costs leads to a curvature of the curve of total transport costs, with the midway point the costliest although assembly and distribution costs are symmetrical. The economy of long hauls points to location at either end since the continuous curve of total costs reaches as low as *OY*. But by locating at either *M* or *C* the firm can save the terminal costs on either steel or boxes, and have only *OX* transport costs. Even without considering the curvature, the

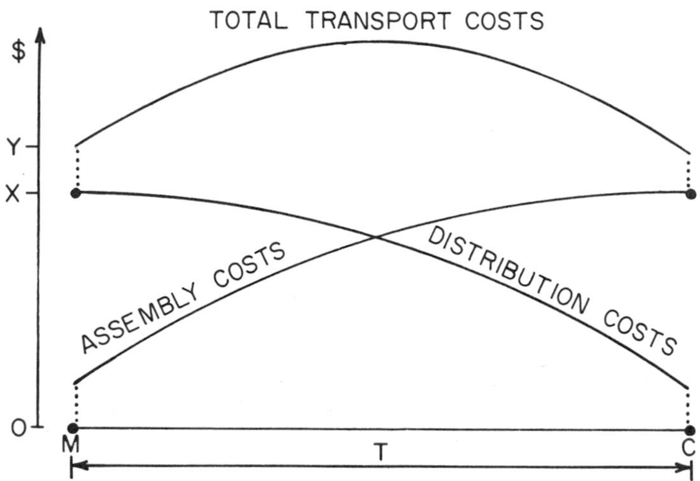

FIG. 6. Transport costs of a firm with a single market and a single material, considering terminal costs and decreasing marginal costs.

elimination of one set of terminal costs would lead to location either at the source of the material or at the market. Although the conclusion requires some reservations, this is part of the explanation for the spatial concentration as opposed to the dispersion of industry.

TRANSSHIPMENT POINTS: THE IMPORTANCE OF PORTS

One special case deserves attention since it accounts in large measure for the existence of many great cities of the world such as New York, London, and Buenos Aires. This is the case of points of transshipment, of which a seaport is a prime example. At these points things brought in by water must be taken off ships and put on trucks or railroads, and vice versa. This provides an excellent opportunity to process materials as they are being taken off one carrier and before they are put onto another. For instance, the American Midwest ships wheat to Buffalo by water. There it is taken off the ships, milled into flour, and the flour shipped by train to the bakeries of the Eastern markets. Or petroleum is brought by ship to New York, there refined, and the petroleum products are sent to other cities. Or cattle is brought from the interior by rail to Buenos Aires, there slaughtered, tinned or frozen, and shipped to foreign markets.

A diagrammatic analysis of the advantages of a transshipment point is presented in Figure 7 for a one-material, one-market concern such as our steel-box manufacturer. Let us say that steel is produced at *M*, which is separated by a sea from *B*, from which there is rail connection

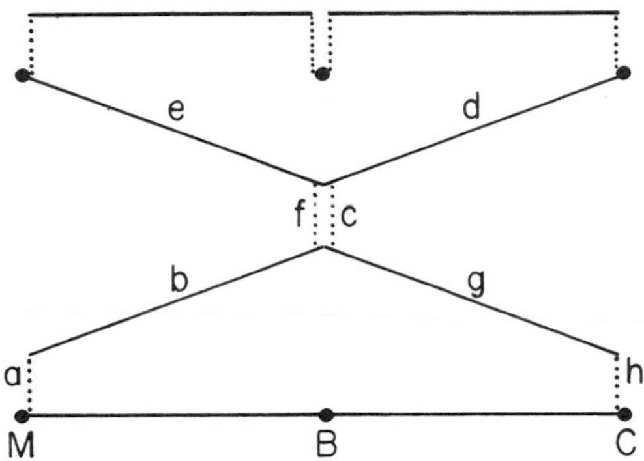

FIG. 7. Transport costs involving a transshipment point.

to the market at *C*. The curve of assembly costs is $a - b - c - d$, where *a* indicates the costs of putting the steel on a ship and taking it off, *b* the costs of moving the steel across the sea from *M* to *B*, *c* the costs of putting it on and taking it off the train, and *d* the costs of moving it from *B* to *C*. The curve of distribution costs is $e - f - g - h$, where *e* are the costs of moving the boxes from *M* to *B* across the sea, *f* are the costs of putting them on and taking them off the ship, *g* are the costs of moving them from *B* to *C*, and *h* the costs of putting them on and taking them off the train. The top curve represents the total costs of transportation, and is the sum of the other two curves. Because of terminal and transshipment costs it has three low points: if the plant is located at *M*, the costs will be $e + f + g + h$; if it is located at *B*, the costs will be $a + b + g + h$; and if it is located at *C*, they will be $a + b + c + d$. In Figure 7 all three are shown as having the same total transport costs, but which will be best will depend on the particular values of the components in each case. Ports owe their growth to the fact that they often turn out to be the best location.

The existence of a transshipment point clearly depends on the technology and development of transportation. Thus, some believe that the development of the St. Lawrence Seaway, which permits direct shipment by water from the Midwest to world markets, may affect adversely cities such as Buffalo and Montreal, which have been transshipment points. There have been instructive instances of artificial transshipment points at locations where railroads of different gauges meet, or where two railroad networks serving a city have purposely refused to interconnect. Even such trivial breaks in transportation can bring about local development. Within cities, commuter railroad and subway stations represent transshipment points for those who use them, and generally foster development of local centers of activity. Looking into the future, one may well speculate the possible effects of the development of craft that travel on a cushion of air, able to move indifferently over land or water. It would seem that should such craft prove to be economical, they would seriously threaten the age-old pre-eminence of ports.

LOCATION OF INDUSTRY WITH MANY RAW MATERIALS

In the analysis of the location of firms with one market and one source of raw material we used diagrams (such as that in Figure 3) of only two dimensions: the horizontal for the distance, and the vertical for the costs of transportation. But when we consider distances between three or more locations, a one-dimensional straight line is not enough and we need a map, which uses up the two dimensions available on a page. Now the costs of transportation require a third dimension. Although difficult, it would be possible to work with three-dimensional models to analyze these cases; there is, however, a simpler way of handling them. In the upper part of Figure 8 the transport costs from some point *A* are shown much as in Figure 6, except that we are considering the possibility of movement in both directions from *A*. In reality we have in mind movement in every direction from *A*, so that the transport costs would look like a windblown umbrella as shown in the side-diagram, where the stem represents the terminal costs, and the umbrella itself the movement costs. The lower part of Figure 8 shows the costs seen from above as in a map. The $2 level of transport costs would be a circle around *A*, the $3 level a larger concentric circle, and so forth. The meaning of each circle is that one unit of whatever is being shipped from *A* can be carried to any point in the circle at that cost. At *A* itself, of course, the transport costs are zero.

Consider now the location of a firm which uses two raw materials, M_1 and M_2, and sells its products at a city *C*. It is necessary to stand-

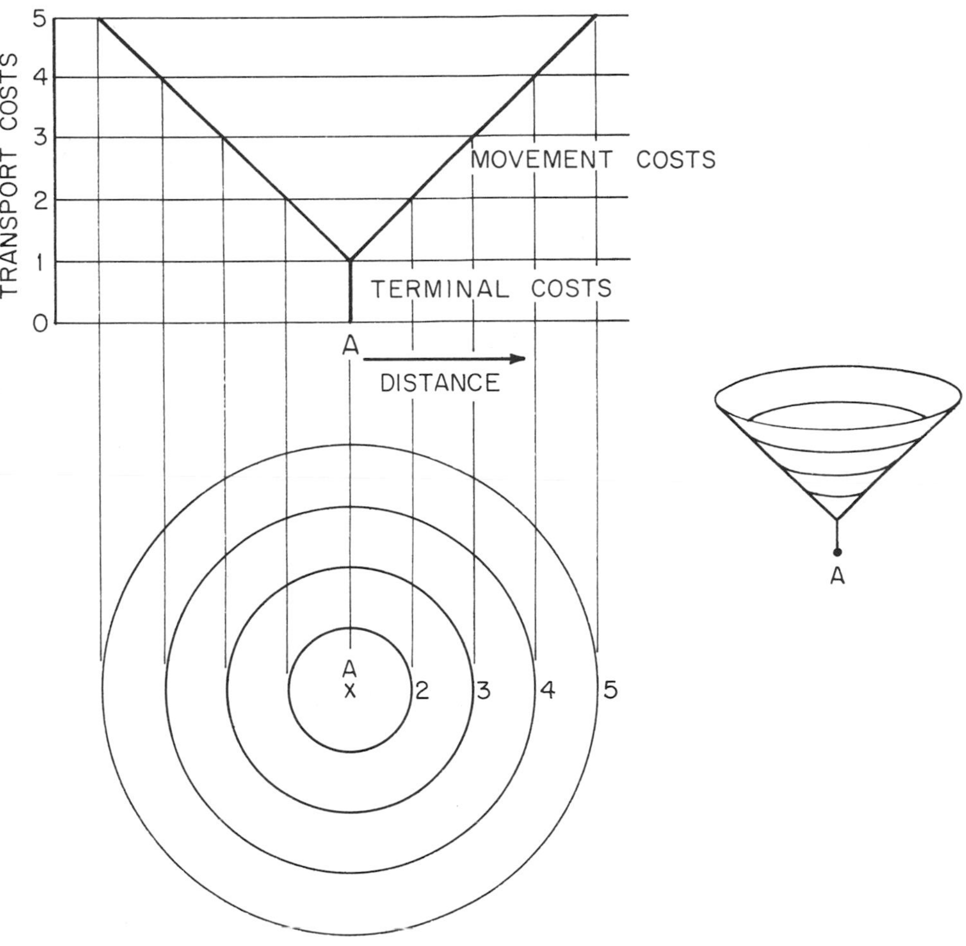

FIG. 8. Transport costs: three diagrammatic representations.

ardize the quantities per unit of product; let us say that for one unit of product we need two tons of M_1 and one of M_2. We find that terminal costs per ton are \$1.00 for M_1 and for M_2, so that terminal costs *per unit of product* are \$2 for M_1 and \$1 for M_2. Movement costs per ton are \$0.67 per hundred miles for M_1 and \$1 for M_2. Movement costs per unit of product, therefore, will be \$1.34 for M_1 and \$1 for M_2. The terminal costs for the product are \$3, and the movement costs \$1 per hundred miles.

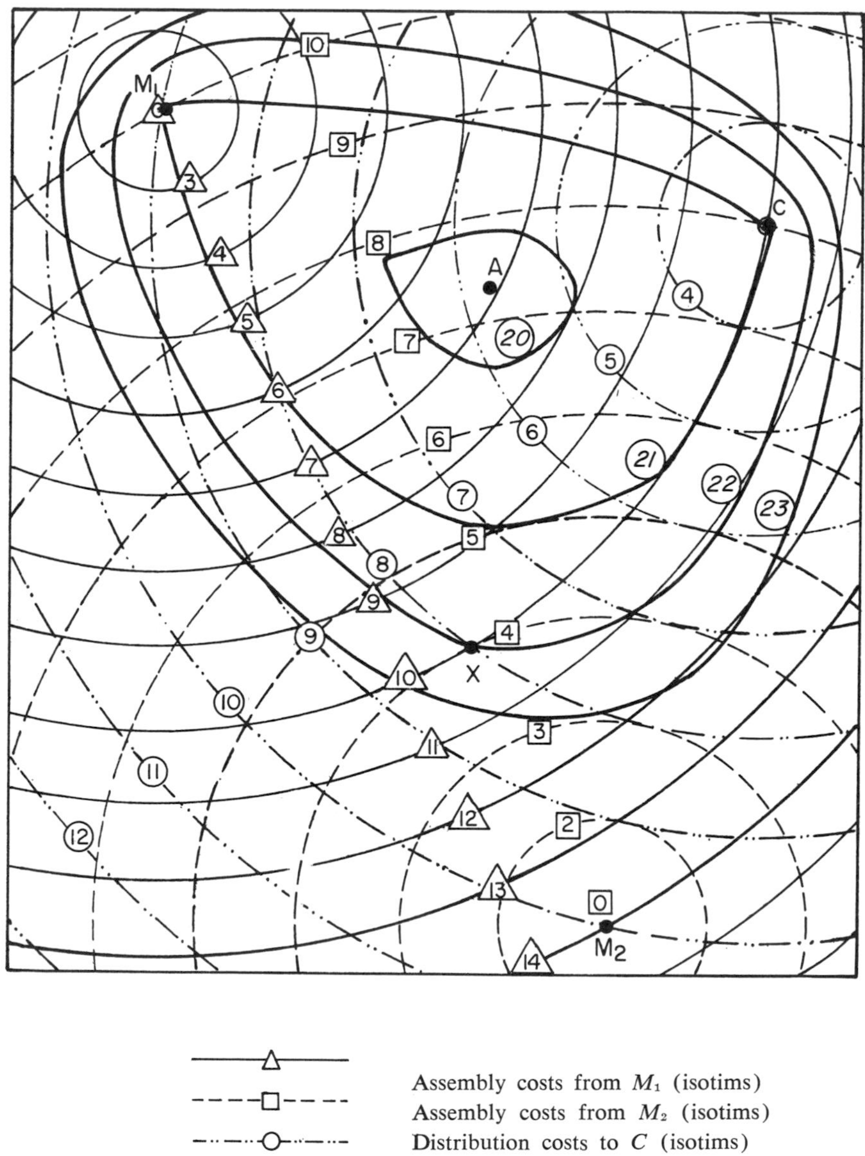

FIG. 9. Isotims and isodapanes for a firm with two materials and one market.

We may now carry out the analysis as in Figure 9. We draw around M_1 the transport costs for the two tons needed per unit of product, shown by the thin continuous lines in Figure 9. These curves are called *isotims.* Similarly, we draw the transport costs of moving the necessary quantity of M_2, shown by the dashed circles. And finally, we draw the isotims for the product, centered around the market at C, shown by the dot-and-dash lines. The total transport costs at any point will be the sum of the isotims; for instance, at point X the costs of bringing two tons of M_1 are \$10, the cost of bringing one ton of M_2 are \$4, and the cost of delivering the product to C is \$8. Total transport costs, then, are $10 + 4 + 8 = 22$. As total transport costs are calculated over the map, points with the same total costs may be joined. The resulting lines, shown by the heavy solid curves in Figure 9 are called *isodapanes,* and constitute a mapping of total transport costs.

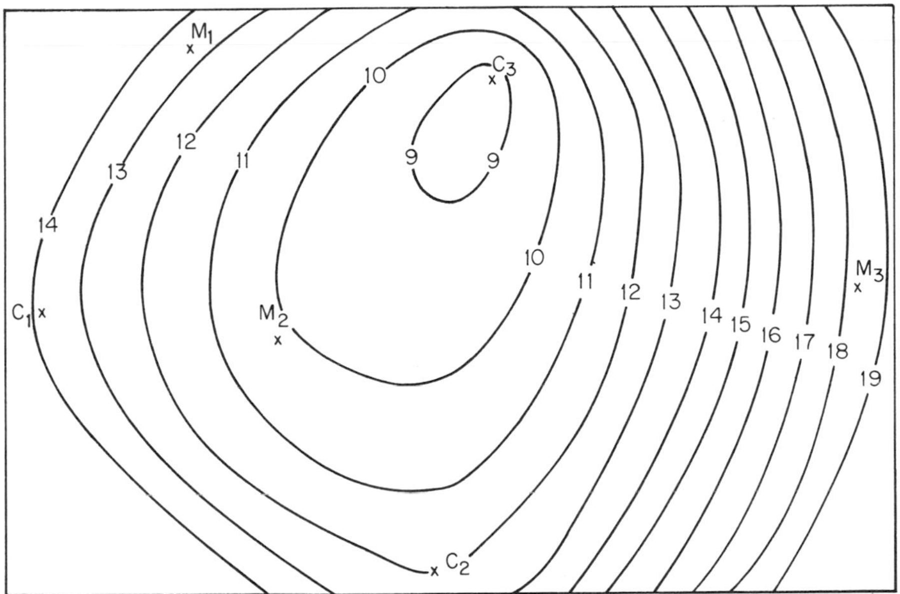

FIG. 10. Isotims of combined distribution costs.

To locate the plant, we want to find the point of least transport costs. The isodapanes in Figure 9 show a low point in transport costs at point A within the \$20 isodapane. In many cases the true minimum may be at such an intermediate point; that is to say, at a point which is neither one of the sources of materials nor the market. In this case, however, the intermediate location A is only a relative minimum. Location at

M_1 results in only \$19 transport costs (\$10 from M_2 and \$9 to C); and location at C in \$18 total costs (\$10 from M_1 and \$8 from M_2). The best location, therefore, would be at C. The minimum found by isodapane mapping should be checked against location at the sources of materials or at the markets to insure that the true minimum is found.

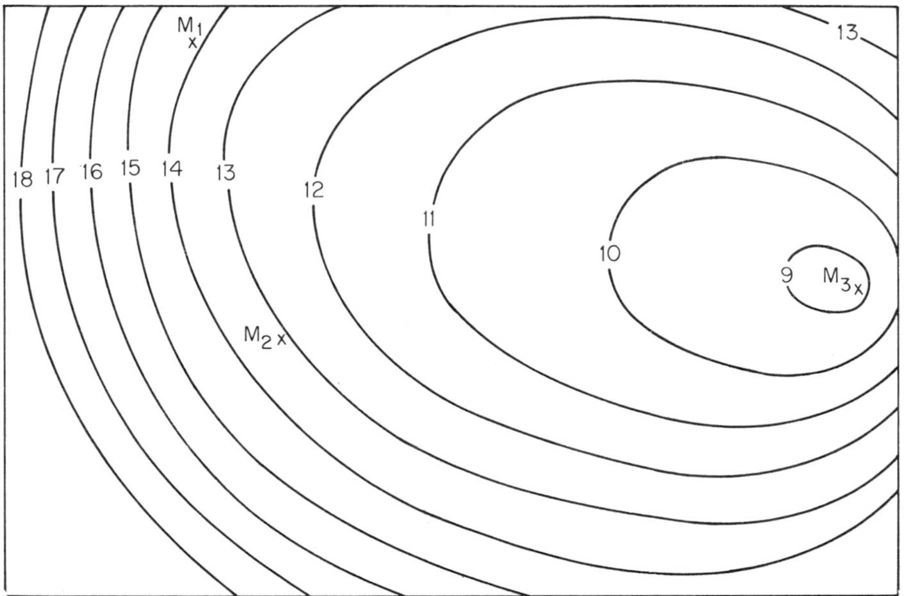

FIG. 11. Isotims of combined assembly costs.

By this method we may consider a problem involving any number of points. Figures 10, 11, and 12 deal with an industry with three markets, C_1, C_2, and C_3, and three sources of materials, M_1, M_2, and M_3. For simplicity, let us say that terminal costs are insignificant, although they could be considered just as they were in the discussion of Figures 4, 6, and 7.

The firm sells 20 per cent of its products at C_1, 30 per cent at C_2, and 50 per cent at C_3. In this case we may observe in advance, from the rule of median location, that the minimum of these distribution costs must be at C_3. However, a full mapping of the isotims of distribution costs will be necessary to combine with the assembly costs to find total transport costs. Since the proportions shipped to each market are known, we may draw a set of isotims for each market. If the transport rate per unit of product is \$4 per hundred miles, we may consider that 0.20 of that unit will be shipped to C_1, at a cost of \$0.80 per hundred miles; that 0.30 units will be shipped to C_2 at a cost of \$1.20

per hundred miles, and 0.50 units to C_3 at a cost of \$2.00 per hundred miles. If we were considering terminal costs, they too would be divided proportionally. On this basis a set of isotims may be drawn around each

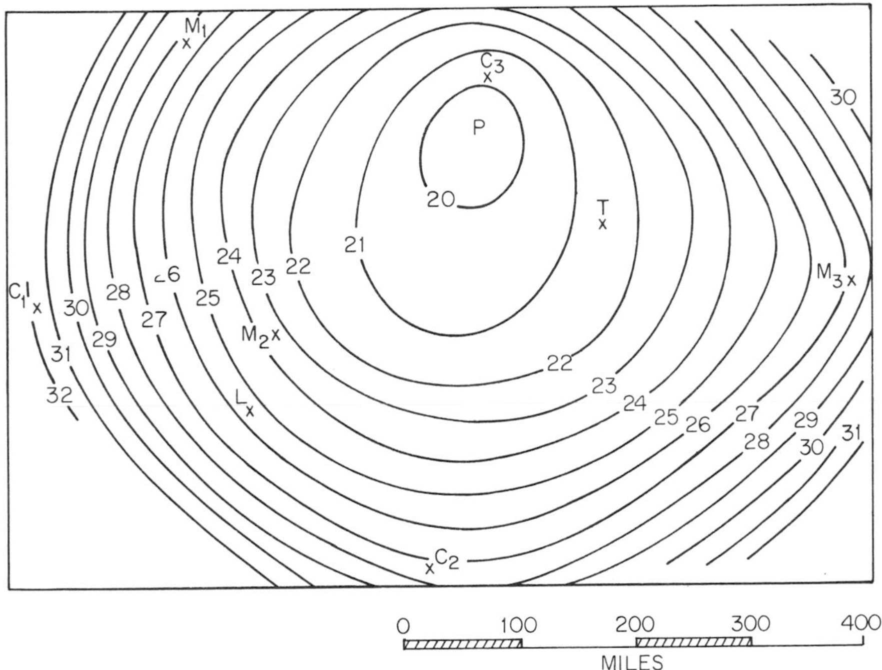

Fig. 12. Isodapanes: sum of isotims in Figures 10 and 11.

of the markets, and they may be summed (in the same way as in Figure 9) to obtain a set of distribution costs isotims. The resulting distribution costs isotims are shown in Figure 10. Note that the lowest point is indeed at C_3, where distribution costs are \$8.65 per unit.

Similarly, we may draw the isotims for each of the raw materials and sum them to obtain an isotim mapping of assembly costs, as has been done in Figure 11. The basis of this mapping is as follows:

	M_1	M_2	M_3
Units of material per unit of product	2	1	1
Rate per unit of material per 100 miles	\$0.50	0.50	2.00
Rate per units of material necessary per unit of product	\$1.00	0.50	2.00

Now, total transport costs (isodapane mapping) may be obtained by summing the isotims of distribution costs (Figure 10) to the isotims of assembly costs (Figure 11). The result is Figure 12. Minimum total transport costs will be at point *P*, where they will be $19.70 per unit of product, and the firm would locate there. Clearly, this minimum must always be within the polygon whose vertices are the locations of the markets and materials.

It would have been possible, of course, to have added the six sets of isotims (from M_1, M_2, M_3, to C_1, C_2, C_3) at the same time, but having so many lines in one map is confusing, and it is easier to do it by parts.

PRODUCTION COST DIFFERENTIALS

Suppose that at point *L* in Figure 12 there is a city with surplus labor, so that wages are lower than elsewhere. The manufacturer wants to know if he should locate there rather than at *P*. He would calculate the savings per unit of product that cheaper labor would imply, considering both the wage rates and the efficiency of that labor. If the saving is, let us say, $10, *L* would be the best location, since total transport costs at *L* are shown in the isodopane mapping as $25.50, as compared with $19.70 at *P*. The extra transport costs, then, are $5.80, leaving a net savings of $4.20. We could consider, similarly, another point such as *T*, where there is a tax saving of $1 per unit of product (would *T* be better than *P*?, better than *L*?), or any other point at which special conditions obtain, such as special climatic conditions, association with other activities, and so on.

MARKET AREAS

If a firm needs a certain raw material that may come from either of two sources, the choice of one source or the other will depend on the location of the firm. But to decide the location of the firm we must know which of the two sets of isotims to consider. To do this we delimit the areas best supplied by each of the alternative sources, and consider only the isotims of the preferred source within its market area. In other words, we construct an isotim mapping for the material, rather than for the sources as such.

In Figure 13 two alternative sources *M* and *M′* of one material are considered. In the upper part of the figure are shown the delivered costs from each of the two sources. The stems are the production costs for the material plus the terminal costs, while the gradients are the costs of moving the material over space. It can be seen that to the left of *A*, *M* can deliver more cheaply, while to the right of *A*, *M′* has the advantage. In the bottom part of the figure, the analysis is carried out by curves similar to isotims except that the cost of production as

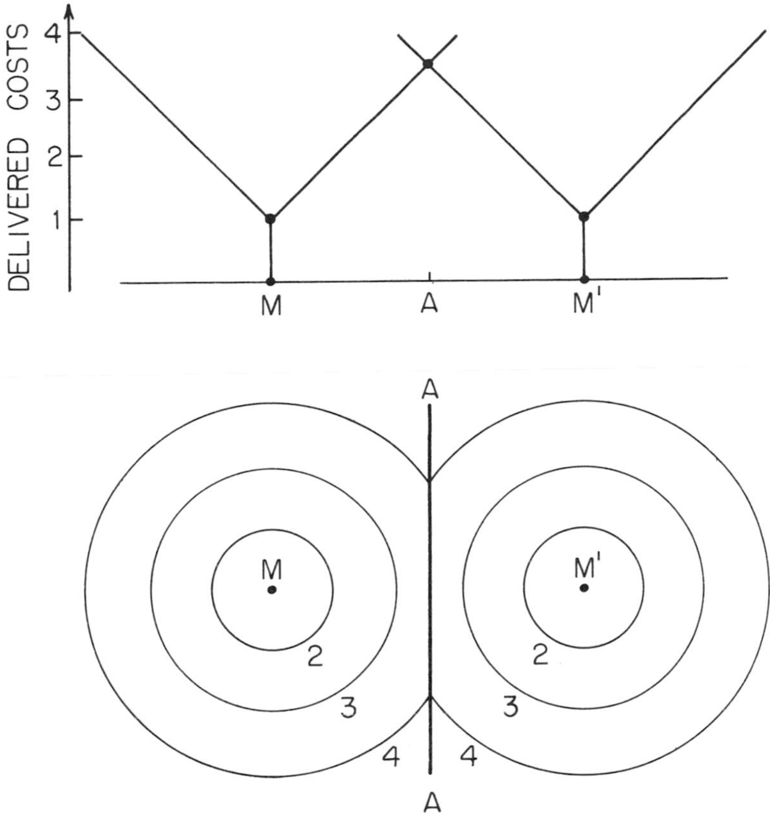

FIG. 13. Market areas: identical production and transport costs.

well as that of transportation is considered at every point. The line *A–A* (the perpendicular bisector of the line *M–M′*) is the market boundary between *M* and *M′*. In constructing the isodapane mapping we would use isotims centered about *M* to the left of *A–A*, and isotims centered about *M′* to the right of it.

In Figure 14 another case is considered, where production costs are greater at *M′* than at *M*, but transport rates are the same. The resulting market boundary is an open hypercircle *A–A* (similar to a hyperbola), as shown in the figure. In Figure 15 a case is shown for which transport rates are higher for *M′* than for *M*. The market area of *M′* will be that bounded by the closed hypercircle *A–A*. This situation might arise, for instance, if we were considering coal mines, and

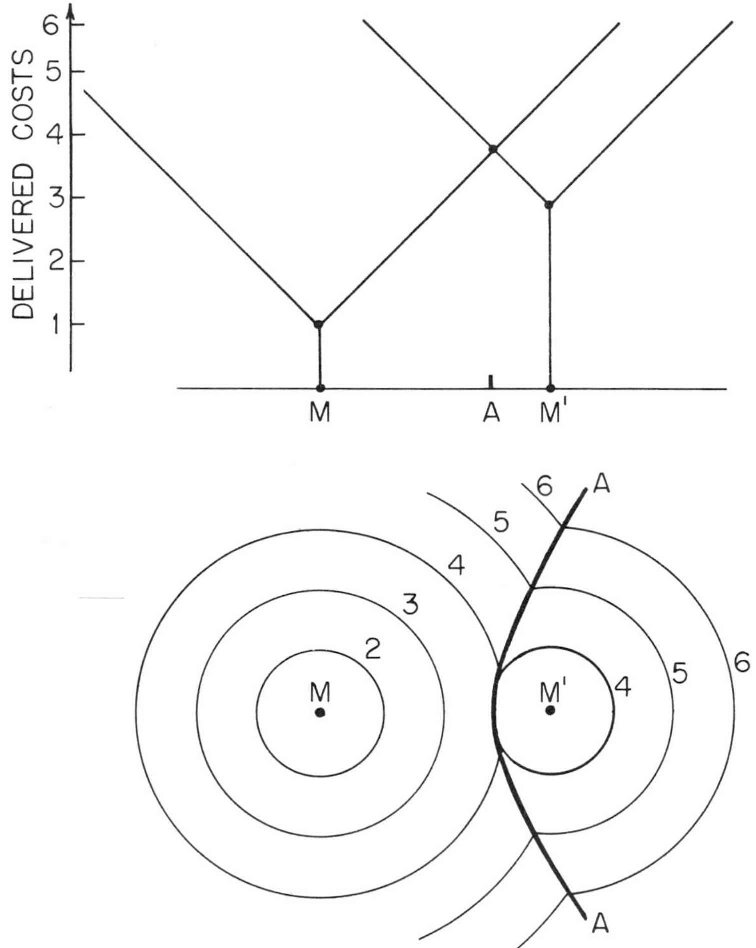

FIG. 14. Market areas: different production costs and identical transport rates.

the coal produced at *M′* were of inferior quality, so that greater quantities per unit of product are necessary.

This analysis holds as well for determination of the markets of firms of known location if their pricing policy is such that the customer bears the transport costs. However, if the producers charge the same "list" price everywhere, their markets could not be determined in this way. It would depend on the policy of the producer with respect to how far

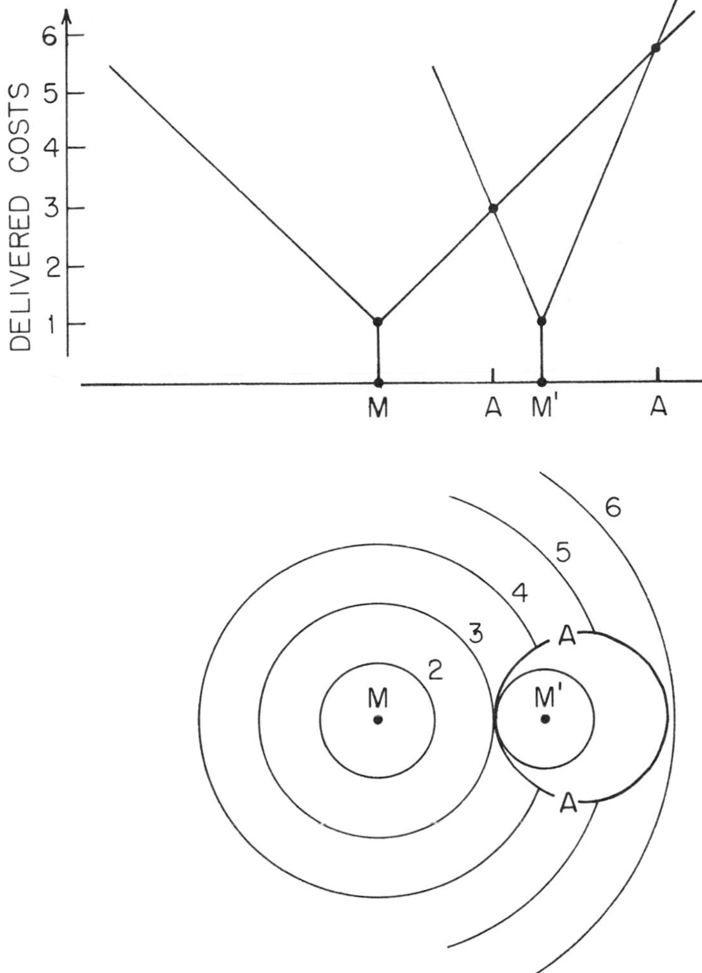

FIG. 15. Market areas: different transport rates.

he would be willing to ship his products when he himself absorbs the transport costs. Moreover, in some cases firms may engage in quite elaborate price wars to capture certain markets, or may be able to sell in certain areas even at higher prices because of advertising.

SOME REALISTIC COMPLICATIONS

In the preceding illustrations isotims have been shown as evenly spaced concentric circles. The economies of longer hauls, which were reflected in a curvature of the transport gradient in Figure 4, will be reflected in increasingly wider spacing of isotims with increasing distance from the source.

There are other realistic features that may be considered by the use of isotims. We have been assuming that transportation is equally possible in all directions. But if we realize that there exist roads and railroads only in some directions, we see that, rather than perfect circles, isotims will take forms more similar to starfish, with arms extending along the transport routes, as in Figure 16, where *A–A* and

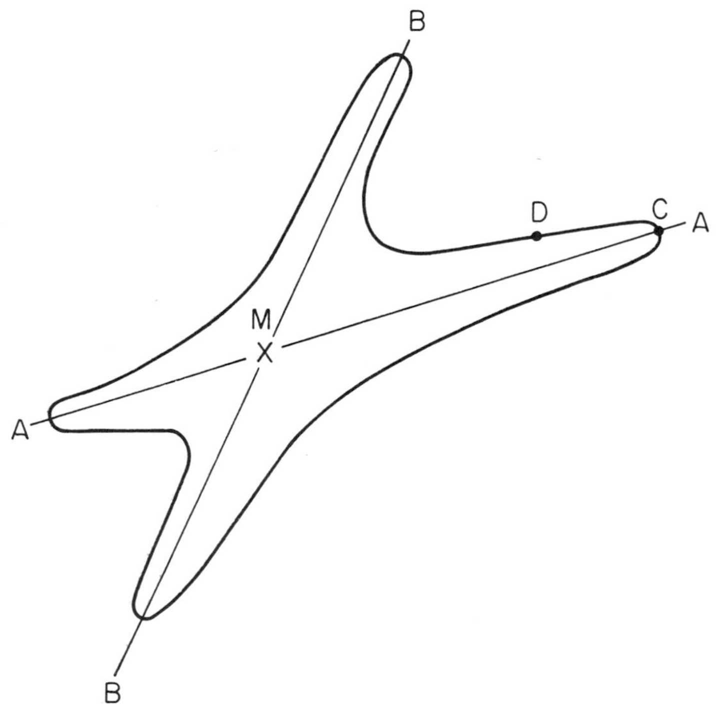

FIG. 16. Isotim considering transport network.

B–B are highways or railroads and a single isotim is shown. Although point *D* is nearer than *C* to *M*, it is as expensive to reach, since part of the travel must be over routes inferior to *A–A*. Similarly, we could consider the effects of intervening seas or lakes, mountains, or tariff barriers, routes with fixed stops that may require some backtracking to reach certain points, and so on. All of these will complicate the geometry of the isotims, but not their logic: an isotim is a curve over a map that joins points of equal transport costs.

SOME TERMS AND SHORTCUTS

The analysis thus far could to some extent be paralleled by a device of strings, pulleys, and weights where, disregarding terminal costs, the weight at each material or market point is proportional to the weight per unit of product times the relevant transport rate, and all the strings are tied together at one knot. This knot will come to rest at the optimal transport location. More formally, the pull at each point is $w_i r_i$, where w_i is the amount of i necessary per unit of product, and r_i is the cost of moving one unit of i a given distance. For the product itself, w_i is unity if there is only one market, and the proper fraction if there is more than one market. The quantity $w_i r_i$ is called the *ideal weight.* Clearly, if one of these ideal weights is greater than the sum of all the others, it will pull the knot right to its pulley. Such an ideal weight is called a *dominant weight;* represented formally, $w_j r_j$ is the dominant weight when $w_j r_j \geqslant \sum_i w_i r_i,\ i \neq j$. The significance of the dominant weight is that if there is a location with the least transport costs, it will be at the source of the dominant material (or at the destination, in the case of the product). Therefore, it is not necessary to do the isotim-isodopane analysis, since we know the answer. It will be noted, of course, that this is no more than the principle of median location in another form.

But what if there is no dominant weight? If we disregard terminal costs, this means that the point with least transport costs will be within the polygon formed by drawing the lines between the various sources of materials and markets, but not at either a source or a market. In other words, the full analysis must be carried out, and because of terminal costs the low point of transport costs within the polygon must be compared with the costs at the various sources and markets. Thus, the best location may, after all, be at one of the terminal points.

In the production of some goods, much of the materials is wasted or expended: dirt is washed from ore, material is cut into shape, chemicals are used up. In such cases, of course, the product will weigh less than the materials that go into it. Such industries are called *weight-losing* and are often *material-oriented.* The classical example of this type was the iron and steel industry, which burned great quantities of coal per ton of product, and therefore was usually found in coal-producing regions. Modern technology, however, has greatly reduced the quantities of coal used, and reduced the material-orientation of the industry.

Conversely, there are cases in which the product weighs more than the materials that go into it. This strange-seeming phenomenon is quite frequent, and may stem from either of two sources. The freight rate of the product may be very high, because of refrigeration, fragility, great bulk, or other reasons, so that the ideal weight of the product is very high. This is the case with some glass products and precision machinery. The other common reason is the use of an ubiquitous material, such as water or air, which is available everywhere and thus does not need to be transported. Such ubiquitous materials do not enter into the calculations of dominant weights, and this type of industry is called weight-gaining and often is market-oriented. A prime example of this type of industry is beer production, which locates its plants at the major markets. But calling an industry material-orientated or market-orientated only tells us of a tendency. These terms are verbal shortcuts, similar to the concept of dominant weight, but less precise. For any particular firm, it is necessary to do a full analysis to be certain of its best location.

We have been considering industries which find transportation costs of paramount importance in selecting a location, that is, *transport-oriented industries.* Typically these are industries with a high bulk-to-value ratio for materials or products; or to be more precise, with high ideal weight-to-value ratios. For other industries, especially those with a high value-to-bulk ratio, other considerations may be more important. Thus, textiles are usually attracted to places with abundant cheap labor and are called *labor-oriented,* and aluminum is attracted to cheap electricity and is called *power-oriented.* Another type of orientation is emerging that might be called *amenity-orientation.* Research industries, such as electronics, have small transport costs but need very specialized scientists and engineers. To attract them these firms often locate where there are climatic or cultural advantages. The Worcester manufacturer mentioned at the beginning of this chapter was, in a sense, amenity-oriented. It will be noted, however, that these various orientations are really instances of the production cost differentials, and that they can be integrated with the analysis of transport costs.

Industries that have no strong locational preferences, and particularly industries that are not transport-oriented, are often called *foot-loose,* and there is good reason to believe that technical developments are making more industries foot-loose. In the first place, in the long run, transportation tends to become cheaper, quicker, and more efficient, lessening transport-orientation. Second, production processes tend to become more efficient, requiring less materials per unit of product, thus reducing total transport costs, and, incidentally, increasing market orientation. Finally, products themselves are improved and made more efficient, so that they do more of a job per unit of weight.

CONCENTRATION AND DISPERSION OF INDUSTRY

Does increasing foot-looseness mean that industrial activities will become increasingly dispersed? Probably not. Foot-looseness simply means that transport costs are relatively less important, not that one place is as good as any other. Industries may now be attracted to areas of good weather, either because it is important to their operations (as in the case of the aircraft industry), or because it will be attractive to their workers (as in the case of some research industries). Or they may be attracted to special site advantages, or to cheap labor, or, perhaps most important, to contacts. These contacts are infinitely varied in their forms. They may be managerial exchanges, where vital information is exchanged casually over lunch, or close supplier-customer coordination, or the chance remark that discloses an unsuspected opportunity, or the shoptalk of technical people that stimulates new ideas. The importance of contacts will probably increase the attraction of large urban centers for many industries, and lead to further concentration.

Concentration in cities does not necessarily mean concentration in downtown. We are using the word city in its technical sense of the geographic extent of the area of homes and work places of an urban concentration. Thus, by "city" we may mean a metropolitan area, central city and suburbs. Since World War II, much of the industry in metropolitan areas in the United States has moved to the suburbs. The principal reason for this movement is that plants need more land because one-story buildings are better suited to today's production processes and because vast areas are needed for workers' parking. Since much more land is needed, plants go to the suburbs, where it is cheaper. The increasing shift from railroads to trucks has helped to make this possible, since trucks are more versatile and can better service industry dispersed over a metropolitan area. This dispersion or decentralization *within* metropolitan areas has sometimes been confused with a national dispersion.

Although it is hard to generalize about industrial location patterns within cities (both because we know little about it and because much of what we know requires very cumbersome technical description), one frequent pattern or life cycle of industries has become relatively recognizable. It is similar to the cycle of residential migration for American families: young couples or those recently arrived from rural areas live at first in small apartments near the center of the city. As the families grow or the rural immigrants become adapted, they tend to move to newer houses in the suburbs. Similarly, many new industries get their start in the old buildings near the center of the city, where they can rent space relatively inexpensively. When the firm becomes successful and needs more space, it frequently builds its new plant in the suburbs. In our sense of the word, this is a move to another part of the city, but not a movement out of the city.

HOW IS IT DONE IN PRACTICE?

We have been discussing the logic of the location of industries. But the question may be raised whether businessmen or project planners do in fact follow the methods outlined here. Many, of course, do not. In many cases the decision is made almost by whim: the businessman may simply operate his business in the town in which he was born and raised, or in a city that has persuaded him with a clever promotional campaign. However, irrational decisions in a competitive economy usually pay a heavy penalty. The "survival of the fittest" will mean that, however the decision is made, it will be those industries which are well located that will survive and become important. A planned economy would suffer similarly from inefficient locations, although the cost of the inefficiency may be dispersed throughout the economic system. The reader is reminded, however, that here we are considering the point of view of the firm or, in the planned case, that of the project. As discussed in the introduction to this volume, regional considerations may in some cases justify higher costs from the point of view of the project in pursuing such goals as the development of a depressed region.

The majority of businessmen do not consciously go through the analysis in the form presented here. They are familiar with the operations of their industry, they know where their markets are and where their raw materials come from, and from this general knowledge can pick the likeliest spots and investigate them further. The businessman will then, if he is prudent, do a careful comparative examination of these alternatives. He will check transport costs, frequency of schedules, labor availability, rates, quality, and organization, power costs, local taxes and prospects, available sites, climate, the housing situation, educational opportunities, availability of finance and cost of borrowing, local regulations, and any other factors of importance to his operation. This type of analysis is quite difficult, however, and most businessmen do not have within their staffs people with the training and experience to do such investigations. Consequently, businessmen are increasingly turning to location consultants to help them make a decision. These consultants do follow the logic that has been outlined, although often with differences of style.

LIMITATIONS OF THIS ANALYSIS

We have been examining the underlying logic of the location decision from the point of view of the firm or of the project, but, of course, only in outline. We have concentrated on transport costs because these vary in a patterned way over space, and only touched on such things as labor costs and taxes, which vary in no regular way. For these, all that is necessary is to compare the savings per unit among alternatives, setting off a savings here against an extra expense there to arrive at the total localization economies. Certainly there is no theoretical difficulty here. But the theory has little to say on some important topics which remain matters of judgment rather than of scientific analysis. I shall briefly discuss some of these.

Demand has been taken for granted: we have been saying that we know where the markets are and how many units they want. This, of course, is not always a cut-and-dried matter. The demand may vary for many reasons, price often being the most important. Therefore, when a producer may sell in several markets, the delivered price of the product and the quantities sold at each of these markets may depend on the location of the plant. At the same time, the scale of operations of the plant affects the unit costs of production. Thus, it is quite possible that a plant may choose a location where transport costs are somewhat higher per unit than the minimum possible, so that it may sell its products to a city that would otherwise be outside its market area, and thus obtain a volume of production sufficient to reduce the unit production costs. And, of course, very often decisions are made in the face of competition. There may already be a firm producing the same thing at the point of minimum transport costs, so that if the new plant located there, it would be fighting for the same customers. It may be better to locate at some point with higher transport costs, but where the firm can have to itself some customers that are now distant from the existing plants. Further, when a firm makes a decision it must keep in mind how its competitors are likely to react. And finally, many firms do not make just one product. A shoe factory makes many sizes and styles, and perhaps wallets and luggage. A chemical plant can turn out thousands of different combinations of products by slight changes in the processes it uses. Therefore when the firm considers alternative locations, it must also consider variations of its "product mix." The combination that may be best at one location may not be best at another.

All of these are in essence complications of the basic theory, and although the analysis may be long and difficult, fairly good answers should be possible. But there are problems of another type, involving things that are hard to quantify. Perhaps the principal one is that of *external economies*. These are the advantages or disadvantages that arise from the close proximity of the plant to other activities. For instance, a group of plants may use a machine-repair shop jointly, rather than each having its own. Among the disadvantages, higher rents and insurance rates are often mentioned. However, many of these advantages and disadvantages are very hard to measure. How much is it worth to have access to a good tax lawyer, or to be able to visit a supplier or a customer in person, or to have a first-rate printer to do a report, or to be able to receive some supplies within minutes of ordering? On the other hand, how much does it cost to fight congested traffic? It is not only hard to measure these advantages and disadvantages, it is often difficult to identify them. For instance, one large office that moved out of the city into the country was forced to return when it discovered that it could not get girls to work so far away from marriageable men. On the other hand, one research concern moved from a big city to a small town in order to keep competitors from raiding its technical personnel.

Further, and most difficult of all, are the problems of uncertainty and of time. The future is usually uncertain: tastes may change, there may be a technological revolution, tax laws and customs duties may be revised. In short, when decisions are made, it is only rarely that one can be sure of the exact results. Some interesting new work is being done in location theory to take uncertainty into account in the location decision, but so far only a small beginning has been made. In general terms, the new theory tries to estimate the costs and benefits of alternative decisions in the light of the probabilities of different things happening. This, of course, is what businessmen themselves try to do. For instance, an American businessman will be attracted by a 10 per cent return on investment in the United States, but he will not be interested in a similar investment in an unstable foreign country unless it pays 30 per cent or more because of the danger of revolution, expropriation, severe restrictions, and so on. Thus far one of the most interesting conclusions of these investigations is that there often is no single best strategy for the businessman. He may choose to act boldly for big gains or losses, or conservatively for smaller ones, both being rational possibilities with the choice depending on the goals and attitudes of the businessman.

Uncertainty aside, the question of time itself is not sufficiently considered in the existing location theory. The decision that is best in the light of today's situation may not be best at some future time: production methods will change, and transport routes and costs, as well as the tastes, location, and resources of customers and the nature of the competition. Even when these changes can be predicted with certainty, we do not have a fully spelled-out method of making a decision that will be best over a period of time rather than at a moment in time. Such a theory would seem to be possible—in fact, not particularly difficult to develop—if we are willing to grant that all the relevant changes can be predicted with some accuracy. To combine time and uncertainty in a meaningful method of analysis will be much more difficult, but may be possible. It is clear, however, that there may be no single best answer, but that the choice would depend to a large degree on "time preference": whether to try for early profits or for larger later ones. Both may be rational choices.

BIBLIOGRAPHIC NOTE

The seminal book in this field is Alfred Weber's *Theory of the Location of Industries,* first published in German in 1909, and edited and translated into English by C. J. Friedrich in 1928, (Chicago, University of Chicago Press). Edgar M. Hoover, in *The Location of Economic Activity,* (New York, McGraw-Hill Book Co., Inc., 1948), improved on many aspects of the analysis and introduced a greater measure of reality. Walter Isard in *Location and Space-Economy* (New York: The Technology Press and John Wiley & Sons, Inc., 1956), generalized and extended the theory. The works of Melvin Greenhut, such as *Microeconomics and the Space Economy* (Chicago, Scott Foresman and Co., 1963) and *Plant Location in Theory and Practice* (Chapel Hill, University of North Carolina Press, 1956) continue to explore this topic.

The reader interested in the practitioner's views may refer to L. C. Yaseen, *Plant Location* (New York, American Research Council, 1960) for the private firm; and for government projects, to the *Manual on Economic Development Projects,* (New York, United Nations, 1958).

The example of the ice-cream vendors on the beach is based on H. Hotelling, "Stability in Competition," *Economic Journal,* Vol. 39 (March 1929), pp. 41–57. For an attempt to consider probabilities in the location decision, see W. Isard and T. A. Reiner, "Aspects of Decision-Making Theory and Regional Science," *Papers and Proceedings of the Regional Science Association,* Vol. 9 (1962).

5. The Nature of Economic Regions*

AUGUST LÖSCH

Impressed by the accidental way in which states are created and smashed, we are looking out for a more natural and lasting spatial order of things. Geographical and cultural regions, however, are from an economic point of view just as artificial units of reference as states are. True enough, they all are of some economic relevance, but this does not alter their essentially non-economic nature. Important as their balance of payments, their price levels, their barter terms of trade may be for them, to *us* these averages and aggregates are entirely arbitrary and accidental. It is independent economic regions that we here discuss, regions not derived from but equivalent to those political, cultural, geographical units.

Even if we already knew the characteristics of economic regions—which we do not—their counterparts in the world of reality would be likely to differ more from each other than from an ideal picture. Hence studying the ideal region is both the only way to learn about the *essential*, and the first step towards investigating the *actual* structure of any real economic region. So we shall deal first with the theoretical nature of such regions, and second with their actual existence.

I

Let us start from very radical assumptions in order to prevent any spatial differences of an uneconomic origin from hiding in our starting points. We assume a vast plain with an equal distribution of raw materials, and a complete absence of any other inequalities, either political or geographical. We further assume that nothing but self-sufficient farmyards are regularly dispersed over that plain. How can any spatial differences possibly result from this initial situation?

* Reprinted from the *Southern Economic Journal,* Vol. 29 (Aug. 1963).

Supposing one of those farmers tries to produce a certain commodity beyond his needs, will he be able to sell the surplus? He will be helped by the economies of large scale production, and handicapped by costs of transportation. Will the balance be in his favor? If his neighbors all have a similar way of living, the demand curve of one of them will be typical for the others as well. Let us assume *d* in Figure 1 to be such an individual demand curve for beer. *OP* being the price at the center of production *P*, the demand of the people living there will be *PQ*. *PR* being the freight from *P* to *R*, the demand of each of the people living in *R* is *RS*. Farther out, at *F*, where the freight is *PF*, no more beer will be sold. Hence *PF* is the maximum shipping radius for beer, and the total demand within that radius is equal to the volume of the cone which we get by rotating the triangle *PQF* around *PQ* as axis. Figure 2 shows that cone. To repeat: its volume, corrected for the density of population, is equal to the total possible demand if the price at the factory is *OP*. For other prices at the mill we get other cones of demand, and as a final result the curve Δ of Figure 3, that represents the total demand as a function of the price at the mill. π of Figure 3 is a so-called "planning curve," showing the minimum costs at which a given output could be produced if a new factory had to be built for that purpose. Only if the planning curve π intersects or is to the left of the total demand curve Δ, is it possible for our farmer to run a brewery. Otherwise he would produce at a loss.

The shape of a trading area, however, is not a circle, as we have so far assumed. For even if the whole country were filled up with such circular areas that are close enough to just touch each other, a number of people could still successfully try to enter the brewing business. For all the black corners in Figure 4 are left unused, and moreover, as has been shown by Chamberlin,[1] the size of the

[1] For those not acquainted with Chamberlin's theory it may be worth while to point out that his argument is based mainly on two facts: (1) Due to product differentiation, of which differentiation of the seller's location is just a special case, the demand curve facing the individual seller is not horizontal (as in pure competition where the product is perfectly uniform) but has a negative slope. If e.g. the seller raises his price, not all his customers will buy from his competitors as in a perfect market. To a number of them the special advantages (e.g. of convenient location) offered by him will be worth the higher price. (2) As long as the demand curve is to the right of the cost curve the extra profits thus possible

individual firm will be reduced from *MN* to *M'N'* (in Figure 3) without rendering it unprofitable. The way to make use of the corners is to change the shape of the area into a regular hexagon. This will shift the curve Δ slightly to the left, as the hexagon is somewhat smaller than the circle that circumscribes it. Moreover, by Chamberlin's operation the size of the hexagon will be reduced until it is so small that the corresponding demand curve Δ' just touches the offer curve in *N'*. Now apparently no more people can enter the brewing business.[2] As the largest possible shipping radius results in a total demand *MN*, so the necessary minimum radius must yield the demand *M'N'*. Figure 4 shows the development from the largest to the smallest possible shipping range.

Two other possibilities of avoiding black corners are conceivable, namely the square and the triangle. But it can be shown[3] that the hexagon has an economic advantage over both: it affords the larger demand per square mile, provided the total area is the same in all cases. *The hexagon is, therefore, the most economical shape for trading areas.* For every commodity, a trading area in the form of a hexagon with a characteristic inner radius ρ is necessary and sufficient to render the production of this commodity profitable.

The trading areas of the various products look like nets of such hexagons, from very small ones to very large ones, depending upon the product. We can throw these nets over our plain at random. In spite of the resulting disorder, every place on the plain would have access to every product. Several considerations, however, which can only be mentioned here, suggest a more orderly and at the same time more economical arrangement. In the first place, we lay our nets in such a way that all of them have one center of

---

will attract new competitors. They will sell products slightly different from those already in the market, or, as in our case, locate their businesses at places more convenient for part of the buyers. This will shift the demand curves of the old establishments to the left until they just touch the cost curves and all extra profits are wiped out. (See E. Chamberlin, *The Theory of Monopolistic Competition.*)

[2] We disregard here the possibility of reducing the area even more through spatial price discrimination.

[3] Whilst a more accurate and detailed proof is too lengthy for this short paper, the plausibility of our assertion can readily be seen from the fact that the regular hexagon has the advantage over the circle of using up all the territory, without departing as far from the ideal circular shape as either square or triangle.

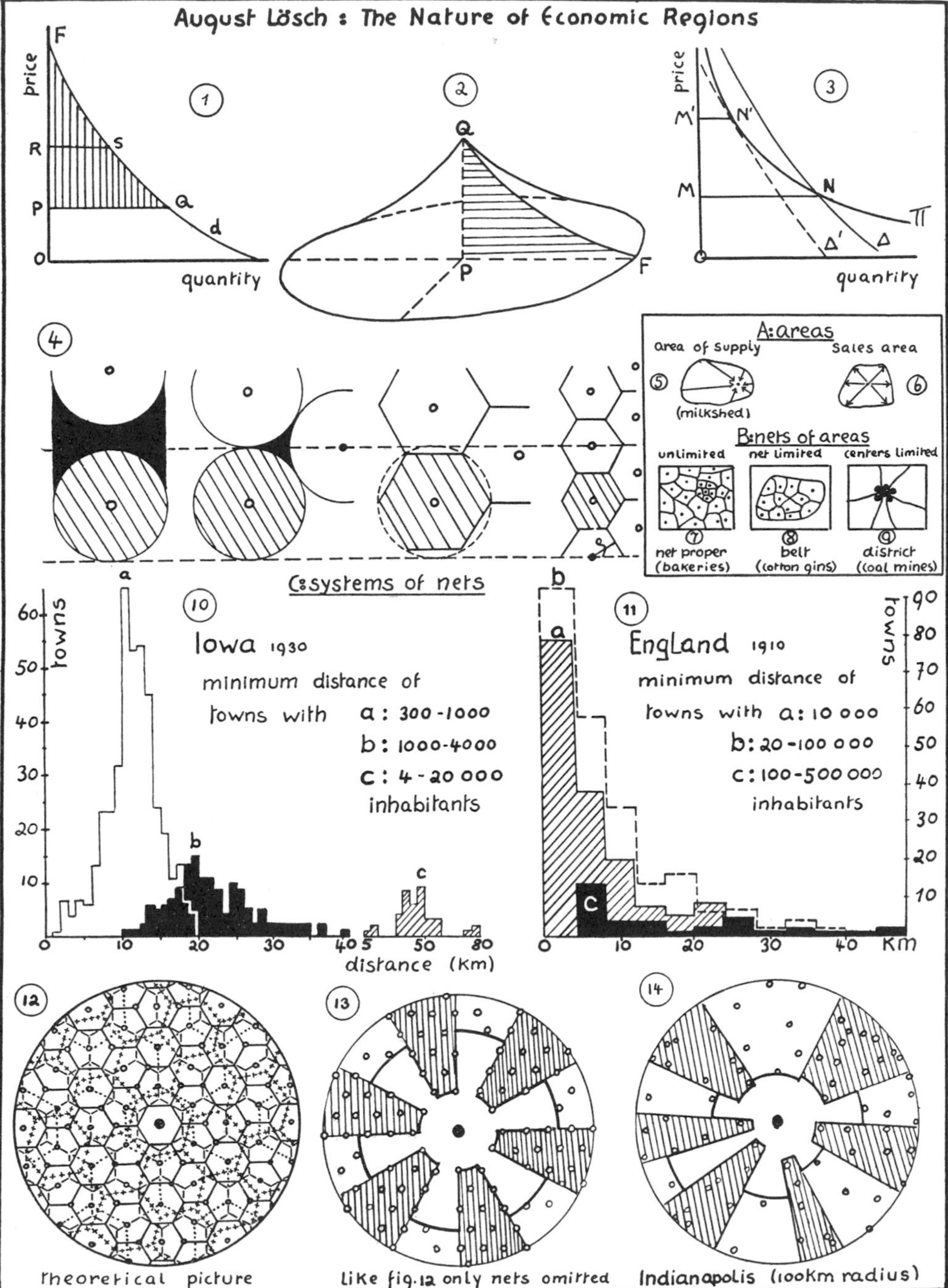
August Lösch : The Nature of Economic Regions
price
quantity
price
quantity
A: areas
area of supply
sales area
(milkshed)
B: nets of areas
unlimited
net limited
centers limited
net proper (bakeries)
belt (cotton gins)
district (coal mines)
C: systems of nets
Iowa 1930
minimum distance of towns with a : 300-1000 b : 1000-4000 c : 4-20 000 inhabitants
towns
distance (km)
England 1910
minimum distance of towns with a: 10 000 b: 20-100 000 c: 100-500 000 inhabitants
theoretical picture
like fig. 12 only nets omitted
Indianapolis (100 km radius)

production in common. This point will enjoy all the advantages of a large local demand. Secondly, we turn the nets around this center so that we get six sectors where centers of production are frequent, and six others where they are scarce, as is shown on Figures 12 and 13. This arrangement does not deprive any place of its access to every product, and at the same time provides for the best lines of transportation. It can be shown that the aggregate of freights is a minimum,[4] and the final result is a complicated but orderly system of market areas. How many of these self-sufficient systems will come into existence on our plain depends merely upon the commodity which has the largest necessary shipping radius, as long as there are no economic limits to the size of the central city.

More striking about our result than any particulars is the fact that we suddenly have crowds of economic areas on a plain which we deprived of all spatial inequalities at the outset. We first have the hexagonal market area surrounding every center of production or consumption. Second, we have a net of such areas for every commodity. And third, we have a systematic arrangement of the nets of market areas of the various commodities. It is the latter, the self-sufficient system of market areas as shown in Figure 12, that I should like to call the ideal economic region. How much of it we find in reality will be discussed in the second part of the paper.

II

As soon as we drop the assumption of a uniform plain, the size and shape of our market areas evidently become irregular. Moreover, if we no longer stick to the supposition of a uniform product, the individual areas for the same line of production overlap, and may consequently be full of holes particularly near the periphery. Yet there are numerous instances left where our assumptions are roughly fulfilled and where our results, therefore, must hold true without much modification, as factual investigations indeed seem to indicate.

[4] As more centers of production coincide more consumers are able to buy from local mills than under any other arrangement of the nets. Not only the mileage of transports but the mileage of lines of transportation as well is reduced.

Actually it is not quite accurate to compare the numerous market areas of a commodity to a net. Due to the overlapping just mentioned they often rather resemble fish scales or an irregular layer of slabs of slate. In spite of this modification the essential characteristics of a net are mostly retained, and as a matter of fact most of the maps showing trading areas that were prepared either by scholars or by business men do not give any consideration to the overlapping at all. Far more important than this modification of the structure of our nets are the changes in their extension. In some instances, for which bakeries may serve as an example (Figure 7), the nets still cover the whole territory under consideration. In fact, a survey made by the author of about half the American industry[5] would seem to indicate that the importance of this type of production is rather underrated. Nevertheless, the very nets or at least their centers are often compressed on a relatively small space, and we may speak then of belts and districts respectively. The former case may be exemplified by the net of the areas of supply of the cotton gins that is naturally limited by the cotton belt. And an illustration of the concentration of the centers of production only are the mines in a coal district (see Figures 8 and 9 respectively). Instead of tracing out the areas, which is a very difficult task, we can show their character just as clearly by measuring the minimum distance of their centers from each other. This is done in Figures 10 and 11, not for centers of a single production but for towns of a supposedly similar economic function. In Iowa, with its rather equal distribution of production, the distances between towns increase with their size, just as in our theoretical picture based on assumptions approximately fulfilled in Iowa. In England, on the other hand, the cities cluster in the coal districts and show the same distance from each other irrespective of size. Such concentrations of the nets or their centers may have purely economic reasons such as the advantages due to the proximity of many establishments of the same branch. But it may also be a reflection of the limited geographical extension of factors of economic consequence although not of economic nature. It is worth noting, however, that these non-economic

[5] It will be included in a forthcoming book on the laws of location.

factors and their economic reflections are not co-extensive. For instance, the area where cotton *could* be grown is larger than the actual cotton belt.

In addition to the limited size of the nets, and the overlapping of the individual market areas, a third deviation from the ideal pattern is worth mentioning. In our theoretical deduction we had to cope with the problem of how the various nets should be located, while the distribution of the centers of production within a net was conspicuous for its regularity. Actually this too is a problem, and a very difficult one at that. Neither of the two traditional instruments of determining the geographical distribution of production can solve it: the theory of location proper cannot because it is applicable only to a single establishment, not to a whole industry; and the theory of comparative costs fails because it is applicable only to trade between men, not between countries. The only adequate solution of the location of all the interdependent centers of production is a system of locational equations which the author hopes to present later.

The systems of nets come off worse in the real world than either the nets or the individual market areas. It is simply impossible to arrange all the irregular nets in such a way that they have at least one point in common. There exists nowhere either a city with a complete set of industries or a self-sufficient region. But this is not the worst. We could at least imagine and probably find a few actual cases where regions trade their specialties with each other through their central cities, and through them alone. In such an instance a systematic arrangement of towns as in our ideal region would still be conceivable. Actually, however, small places which in every other respect entirely depend upon neighboring cities are the centers of large market areas. As far as their particular products are concerned, even metropolitan cities or the whole nation may be tributary to those little places, the industries of which neither need nor attract a large local market. Furthermore, while the regional system of nets of market areas centers in a large city, not every big city dominates such a system. Many mining towns, for instance, have not much of an economic function towards their hinterland. In contrast with such specialized cities, a regional center is characterized by a variety of production and trade that links it to the surrounding country. If, now, we disregard all the market areas of the type just described, a substructure of economic regions is left. They *differ* from the ideal pattern in the important respect that there are not self-sufficient; they *correspond* to the ideal inasmuch as they too are based (1) on the advantages of a large local concentration of production, consumption or trade; (2) on the most economical layout of lines of communication.

This regional substructure can be discovered almost everywhere but it is not everywhere of equal importance. Its importance can be measured by comparison with those market areas that have to be eliminated from a regional analysis as was just pointed out. To give some examples: regionalism prevails in southern Germany.[6] The distribution of the undisputed regional centers: Frankfurt, Nürnberg, München, Zürich, Strassburg, with Stuttgart in the middle is very regular. There should be one more center to the south of München but the Alps make this obviously impossible. The rise of München over Augsburg that had the advantage of an earlier start is worth noting. München has the better location from the point of view of our theory. It is right in the middle of the region, and at the proper distance from the neighboring centers. The German Ruhr district, on the other hand, hardly displays any regional pattern whatever. According as the systematic or the chaotic distribution of the nets of market areas prevails in a given case, we may stress or disregard the regional substructure. From this it follows that while the regional concept will be most realistic with respect to some parts of a country, it would be difficult and not very useful to divide a state up into its regions.

Finally, as to the relation between economic and other regions, it is essential for the regional system of market areas to have a center. In rare and particularly fortunate cases these economic centers are the same time cultural and political ones, thus becoming the true heart of their region, as Paris is for France.

[6] This has very ably been shown by Walter Christaller, *Die zentralen Orte in Süddeutschland.*

III

To summarize, we found three main types of economic areas: simple market areas, nets of such areas, and systems of nets. Or, if we want to give a popular name to each, we may speak of markets, belts, and regions. In this sequence they become more complex, more self-sufficient, and unfortunately less real. On the one end there are the individual market areas, most simple, most real, and most dependent upon trade. The systems of market areas, or regions, on the other hand, are very complex; in an ideal case quite self-sufficient, but harder to find in reality. Many commodities are produced and traded outside of any system. And whatever systems we do find, overlap even more than the market areas of a single commodity. A clear economic region is a fortunate accident rather than a natural subdivision of states. Still, beneath a sphere of irregular market areas, we find a regional substructure of varying importance almost everywhere. Between the simple area of sale or supply and the full regional system is the net. The geographical extension of these nets or of their centers is often small. In this case these belts or districts of production or consumption are very conspicuous, but should still be distinguished from regions. A region is a system of *various* areas, an organism rather than just an organ.

6. Cities as Systems Within Systems of Cities*

BRIAN J. L. BERRY

INTRODUCTION

This paper examines some of the ways in which understanding of cities and sets of cities has been advanced during the first decade of Regional Science. Originally, I was asked to prepare a paper that reviews the entire range of urban models, but for several reasons decided to take a more limited view. The Social Science Research Council's Committee on Urbanization has recently completed a comprehensive review of urban studies, to be published shortly as *The Study of Urbanization,*[1] and to attempt to duplicate this work in a short paper would be as foolhardy as the result would be superficial. Other papers to be presented at these meetings will deal with certain kinds of urban models (for example those related to metropolitan transportation studies, or those involving study of the urban economic base via input-output matrices) and we will not attempt to duplicate what they have to say.

What, then, is the scope of this paper? Three channels that lead toward development of sound urban models are explored and relevant implications drawn. By models we mean *symbolic* models, not those of the *iconic* or *analogue* kinds.[2] Further, the symbolic models of interest are those that provide idealized representations of properly formulated and verified scientific theories relating to cities and sets of cities perceived as spatial systems. Any scientific theory logically comprises two parts:

(*a*) Simple inductive generalizations drawn from observable facts about the world.
(*b*) Abstract logical constructs.

It is the coincidence of deductions drawn from the logical constructs and inductive generalizations drawn from fact that makes for a valid

* Paper presented at the Annual Meeting of the Regional Science Association, Dec. 1963.

scientific theory. Ten years ago urban studies were in an either/or situation; either inductive generalizations or logical constructs existed, the former as likely as not produced by urban geographers and the latter by urban economists. As the word model became fashionable, both called their products models, but neither had models of theories in the strict sense.

The importance of the last decade has been that the twain *have* met through the medium of Regional Science. Moreover, the meeting came just when quantitative methods of analysis, facilitated by rapid developments in computer technology, began a technological revolution that has wrought havoc throughout the sciences. What more shattering change could there be than one which facilitates the large-scale studies that lead to specification of strength of belief in inductive generalizations, allow objective testing of the degree of coincidence between inductive generalizations and deductions from logical constructs, and ease replication? The technological advance has meant more, however: virtual elimination of the once lengthy gap between problem formulation and evaluation of results; sharpening of the questions asked; initiation and completion of experiments of a size unthinkable under earlier technical conditions; and many more.

The meeting, then, was timely. Inductive generalizations could be eased toward theory; logical constructs could be faced with the ultimate test of reality and new kinds of empiricism and experimentation could be developed. These are the three channels discussed in this paper. Examples are presented in an expository rather than a rigorous manner, since each has been elaborated elsewhere. The conclusions of the paper are that urban models are the same kinds of models as appear in other kinds of systems inquiry. Urban theory therefore may be viewed as one aspect of General Systems Theory. Viable avenues for future urban research might therefore be identified by looking at those other aspects of General Systems Theory that are relatively well advanced, to see how they reached this more developed position.

INDUCTIVE GENERALIZATIONS IN SEARCH OF A THEORY

Two of the better-known generalizations concerning cities are the rank-size relationship for sets of cities and the inverse-distance relationship for population densities within cities. Both had been observed many times when they were formalized as empirical "rules" a decade or so ago, the former as the *rank-size rule* by G. K. Zipf and the latter as the *negative exponential density distance relationship* by Colin Clark.

Yet as Isard noted in 1956, "How much validity and universality should be attributed to the rank-size rule is, at this stage, a matter of individual opinion and judgment."[3] Further, although Clark argued that the negative exponential "appears to be true for all times and places studied," he provided no theoretical rationale for his observations, only specified that they might have something to do with transport costs.[4] During the past decade both inductive generalizations have been brought closer to the status of scientific models, with the range of their validity carefully specified.

Distribution of City Sizes[5]

The rank-size rule says that for a group of cities, usually the cities exceeding some size in a particular country

$$P_r{}^q = P_1/r \tag{1}$$

where

P_1 is the population of the largest or first-ranking city
P_r is the population of the city of rank r

and

q is a constant.[6]

Whence it follows that

$$\text{Log } r = \log P_1 - q \cdot \log P_r \tag{2}$$

so that a plot of rank against size on double logarithmic paper should give a straight line with a slope of $-q$.

Another way of expressing the foregoing is that the frequency distribution of cities by size seems to be highly skewed in the shape of a reversed-*J*. A whole series of probability distributions, among them the lognormal and the Yule, have a similar reversed-*J* shape, each bearing a general family resemblance through their skewness. Each is, in fact, the steady-state distribution of the same simple stochastic process. Could it be that rank-size regularities of city sizes also result from such a stochastic process? The tenor of arguments provided in the past decade is that stochastic processes do indeed provide such a framework, and both the Yule distribution and the lognormal have been proposed as the basis of rank-size regularities.[7] The two are in fact so similar that each could obtain when the cumulative distribution of cities by size forms a straight line on lognormal probability paper, and which is applicable to the particular case depends upon whether a closed or an expanding system of cities is being considered.

Consider the transition matrix of a stochastic process in which the rows and columns are specified by city-size groups. If the probability density function of each size-class of cities is approximately the same,[8] then the steady state of the stochastic process will be lognormal if the set of cities existing at the beginning of the process is the same as the set achieving the steady state at the end. If, however, the smallest size class is augmented by new cities at a fairly steady rate throughout the process, the steady state is that of the Yule distribution. If growth of cities within the set can be said to occur in small independent increments, with probabilities of growth the same for each size class (growth is the result of "many factors operating in many ways" and occurs such that if city sizes for time period 1 are plotted against sizes for time period *n* the resulting scatter of points is homoscedastic with a slope of —1), then the basic conditions of such a stochastic process can be said to have been met. One or another constraint leads to the lognormal or the Yule; in the former case a closed system of cities must exist, whereas in the latter the system must go on growing at a steady rate by addition of cities at the lowest level.

A recent study shows that the rank-size regularity applies throughout the world for countries which are highly developed with high degrees of urbanization, for large countries, and for countries such as India and China which in addition to being large also have long urban traditions; conversely, "primate cities" or some stated degree of primacy obtains if a country is very small, or has a "dual economy."[9] Moreover, additional studies have recently shown that many distributions with some degree of primacy take on more of a rank-size form as level of development and degree of urbanization increase.[10] By virtue of size and complexity, then, countries with rank-size distributions appear to satisfy the condition of "many factors operating in many ways" and increasing complexity of a space economy certainly brings the city-size distribution closer to rank-size. A rank-size regularity is not found when few factors mold the urban system in a few simple ways: in small countries, where economies of scale accrue in a single "primate city"; or in "dual economies," where one or a few exogenous, colonial cities of great size are superimposed upon an indigenous urban system of smaller places. In such cases, growth patterns cannot be summarized in the form of a stochastic process of the simple kind just outlined.[11] For all large, complex systems of cities which exist in the world, however, aggregate growth patterns do conform to such a stochastic process, so that one macroscopic feature of these systems is a rank-size regularity of city sizes. The regularity may, in turn, be "explained"[12] by the stochastic process.

URBAN POPULATION DENSITIES[13]

No city has yet been studied for which a statistically significant fit of the expression

$$d_x = d_0 e^{-bx} \tag{3}$$

does not obtain. In this equation, which was derived empirically by Colin Clark,

d_x is population density d at distance x from the city center
d_0 is central density, as extrapolated into the city's central business district

and

b is the density gradient, so that, of course

$$\text{Ln } d_x = \ln d_0 - bx \tag{4}$$

Muth and Alonso have provided a satisfactory "explanation"[14] of the observed regularity recently in terms of the rent-transport cost trade-off of individuals in different stages of the family cycle at different income levels and at different distances from the city center.[15] Apparently, the bid-rent function is steeper for the poorer of any pair of households with identical tastes in the American city, so the poor live toward the city center on expensive land consuming little of it and the rich at the periphery consuming much.[16] The negative exponential shape of the decline stems from the nature of the production function for housing and the shape of the price-distance function.[17] Expression 3 is thus an equation of some generality that can be derived as a logical implication of the theory of the urban land market.

This being so, a variety of conclusions may be drawn. For example, the population residing at distance m from the city center is

$$P_m = \int_0^m d_0 e^{-bx}(\pi 2x)\, dx \tag{5}$$

which becomes

$$P_m = 2d_0\pi b^{-2}[1 - e^{-bm}(1 + bm)] \tag{6}$$

This implies that the population pattern of an urban area can be described by two parameters alone, b and d_0. Winsborough has called the former a measure of the *concentration* of the city's population and the latter an index of its *congestion*.[18]

Now for any set of cities and for any particular city through time, another empirical expression holds:[19]

$$b = aP^{-c} \tag{7}$$

Thus, b is in turn a function of city size, and a is the intercept. Central density d_0 is, on the other hand, apparently a function of the form of the city as established at the particular stage at which it grew, and is thus directly related to the city's age.[20] Knowing the population of a city and its age, it is possible to predict fairly closely the pattern of population densities within it.

In any system of cities for which the rank-size regularity obtains, the population P of a city of rank r, P_r, is a function of only P_1 and q (Equation 1). Hence, b must likewise be a function of P_1 and q (Equations 1 and 7). The distribution of population within cities is a function of the position of these cities within the entire system of cities, and age. If the larger system is Yule in form, age is simply the generation of the underlying stochastic process at which the city entered the system, so that congestion d_0 as well as concentration b is given within the framework of the larger system. The preceding statement can thus be modified to read: the distribution of population within cities is a function of the position of these cities within the entire system of cities at some point in time, and of the period of time for which they have been within the system.

LOGICAL CONSTRUCTS IN SEARCH OF A TEST: CENTRAL PLACE THEORY[21]

The preceding two models account for the size and the distributional characteristics of urban populations, but they say nothing of the locations of the cities concerned. Three sets of reasons for cities have been advanced, each with locational parameters more or less explicit: cities as strategic locations on transport routes; cities as the outcome of local concentrations of specialized economic activities; and cities as "central places" performing retail and service functions for surrounding areas. Only the latter is of interest here.

Central place theory was formulated by Walter Christaller as a "general purely deductive theory" designed "to explain the size, number and distribution of towns" for reasons that also made it "the theory of urban trades and institutions."[22] A decade ago this theory was perhaps the only one concerning systems of cities that was at all well developed.[23] At that time, although many empirical studies of central places had been completed, the fact that no satisfactory test of the theory had been made largely reflects the fact that investigators looked for examples of theoretical implications drawn simply for exemplification by Christaller under the assumption of an isotropic plain. There was a lively debate as to whether certain of the most fundamental theoretical implications—for example, that of a hierarchy of central places—had any empirical validity. It has only been during the last decade that such questions have been settled. A thorough review of most aspects of the topic is to be found in *Central Place Studies: A Bibliography of Theory and Applications,* the first of the Regional Science Research Institute's Bibliography Series, and so will not be repeated here.[24] Subsequent to the Bibliography, the various postulates of the theory were drawn together in a model, however, and since the model appears to have some generality (implications drawn from the model have been verified independently, for example) it will be presented here.[25]

The model applies to systems of central places in which the elements are viewed aggregatively. A set of inequalities supplements the model, however, and these empirically derived expressions link aggregate patterns to local arrangements of central places under specified conditions of population density by specifying expectations as to the steps of the central place hierarchy. Random variations from ideal steplike patterns of central places in a series of local areas, combined with logical changes in location of the steps according to population density, interact to produce the regularities which may be observed in the aggregate. The definitions, identities, structural equations, and implications of the model follow without lengthy comment.

Definitions:

- P_t the total population served by a central place
- P_c population of the central place
- P_r rural population and population of lower level centers served by the central place
- A area of the trade area
- Q_t population density of the area served
- Q_r population density of those parts of the area served lying outside the central place
- T number of central functions performed by the center, and since central functions enter in a regular progression and can be ranked

from 1 · · · T in decreasing order of ubiquity, also the highest level central function performed by the center

E number of establishments providing the T types of business

D_m maximum distance consumers will travel to a central place of size T, *or* the range of good T

Identities:

$$P_t = P_c + P_r \tag{8}$$

$$P_t = AQ_t \tag{9}$$

$$P_r = AQ_r \tag{10}$$

$$A = kD_m{}^q \tag{11}$$

Figure 1*a* shows identity (9) in five distinct study areas in the United States.[26] In each case total population and total area served slope upwards to the right on double logarithmic paper with a slope of +1. Differences between study areas are simply a function of population densities.

Structural Equations:[27]

$$\text{Log } P_c = a_1 + b_1 T \tag{12}$$

$$\text{Log } D_m = a_2 + b_2 T \tag{13}$$

$$\text{Log } E = a_3 + b_3 \log P_t \tag{14}$$

These structural equations hold in any study area (that is, at any level of density), and relate, by means of the intercept a and regression coefficient b, the population of a market center to the variety of central functions performed for surrounding areas, the drawing power of the center to its offerings, and the number of separate establishments performing the T functions (E exceeds T for all except the smallest villages and hamlets) to the total population served to account for nonbasic demands for goods and services from the population P_c as well as basic demands generated by the population of the area served P_r.

Implications:

$$P_c = P_t^s w^{-s} Q_t^{-s} \tag{15}$$

where

$$w = k\{\log^{-1} [qb_1^{-1}(a_2 - a_1 b_2)]\}$$

and

$$s = (b_1)/(qb_2)$$

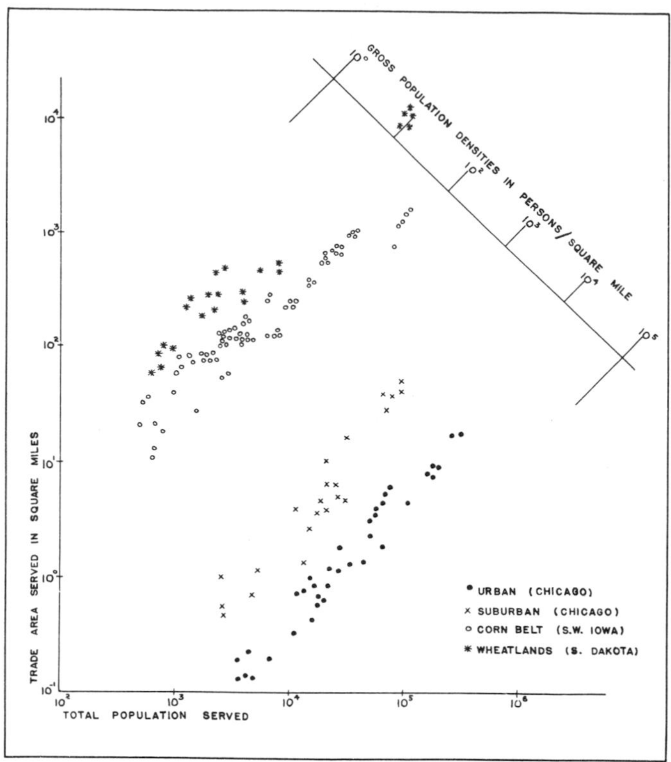

FIG. 1*a*. Relationships between population and area served at different levels of population density.

As total population served increases, the central population comes to assume an increasing proportion of the total, but this tendency varies inversely with population densities.

$$A = wP_c^{\,x} \tag{16}$$

where

$$x = s^{-1}$$

Area served increases exponentially with size of center.

$$E = mQ_t^{\,b_3}P_c^{\,b_3} \tag{17}$$

where

$$\text{Log}\, m = a_3 + b_3 \log w$$

Total number of establishments varies exponentially with both size of center and total population densities.

These and similar structural equations and implications have now been verified in several studies[28] and appear to be a reasonable summary of many of the aggregate features of central place systems. Each has particular implications within the framework of central place theory as well, particularly as it has been generalized. However, a set of inequalities is needed in combination with Figure 1*a* to lay out the steps of the central place hierarchy as it is found in local areas at different levels of density. These inequalities were established empirically by factor analyses of the functional structure of central places in each of several study areas, to determine the hierarchy individually within each of those areas, and then by discovering, unexpectedly, that limits to each of the levels varied consistently across the set of study areas as population density varied. With the second subscripts v referring to villages, t to towns, and c to cities, these inequalities are

$$\text{Log}\, A_{tv} < 10.4 - 2.67 \log P_t \tag{18}$$

$$\text{Log}\, A_{tt} < 9.3 - 2.067 \log P_t \tag{19}$$

$$\text{Log}\, A_{tc} < 22.25 - 4.75 \log P_t \tag{20}$$

They are inserted into Figure 1*b*, and in the case of the corn belt study area the individual observations are identified as they were classified in the factor analysis.[29]

INNOVATION UNDER TECHNICAL IMPETUS: SOCIAL AREA ANALYSIS

The decade has seen a variety of innovations, most of them facilitated by rapid developments in computer technology, making possible kinds of research that could never have been contemplated prior to the developments. Beginnings are to be seen in the construction of urban simulators that will facilitate study of cities and sets of cities in laboratory-type experimental situations.[30] The most successful attempts so far have been those of Chapin in studies of land development[31] and Morrill in analyses of changing central place patterns,[32] although this statement is not intended to denigrate attempts along these lines in current urban transportation and economic studies. Out of these studies, particularly those undertaken in Chicago, Pittsburgh, and the Penn-Jersey region, and also those of the RAND Corporation and Resources for the Future Inc., will surely emerge models of some predictive power and experi-

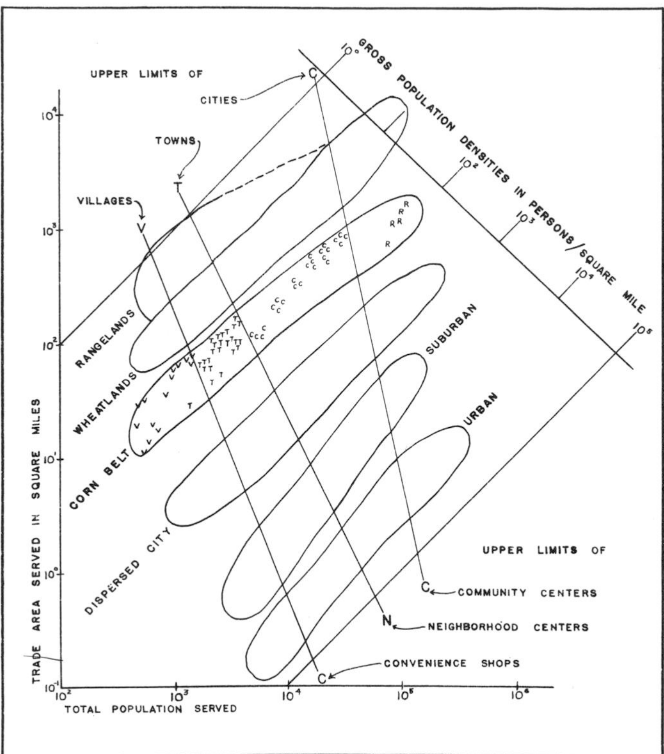

FIG. 1*b*. Consistent upper limits have been identified for successive levels of central place at different levels of population density.

mental capability. Another paper at these meetings considers this topic, however, recognizing what may be the most significant new dimension to urban research added during the past decade. We will concentrate here on another topic, the new empiricism of the decade, stimulated by advancing computer technology and consequent diffusion of multivariate analysis throughout the social sciences. We focus here on one form of multivariate analysis, *factor analysis,* and briefly review how, in the form of *social area analysis,* it has facilitated studies of the internal structure of cities.

Social area analysis is one approach to the classic problem of urban ecology,[33] the succinct description of the location of residential areas by type within cities in terms meaningful to persons interested in social differentiation and stratification. Over the years several constructs have been developed in this context:[34] Hurd's concept of urban growth proceeding according to two patterns, central growth and axial growth; Burgess' concentric zone hypothesis of the location of residential areas by type, stemming from the nature of a growth process that proceeds outwards from the city center, accompanied by waves of residential invasion and succession; Hoyt's emphasis upon the axial growth of higher income neighborhoods outward from the city center along some sector; and Harris and Ullmans' notions of the multiple nucleation of the city. Both the social area analysts and their critics[35] have emphasized the difficulty of testing these hypotheses with the wide variety of socioeconomic data available, for example, from censuses. Which variables should be used in the test? Will the story told by different but presumedly related variables be the same? What in fact are the stories told about the structure and differentiation of urban neighborhoods by the wide range of census data available?

Factor analysis can provide answers to questions of the latter kinds. Let us review the basic features of the method. Consider a data matrix ${}_nX_m$ in which are recorded the data for n observations (say, census tracts) over m variables (census variables). If the column vectors of X are normalized and standardized to yield ${}_nZ_m$, then $n^{-1}Z^TZ = {}_mR_m$, which is, of course, the correlation matrix of the m variables. Since the column vectors of X were standardized, R is the variance-covariance matrix of Z, and the trace of R, equaling m, is the total variance of the m variables.

Now assume that each of the m variables is regressed in turn upon the $m - 1$ remaining. For each is then available a coefficient of determination expressing how much of its variance is held in common with the $m - 1$ other variables; in factor analysis these coefficients of determination are called communalities, and denoted h^2. For each variable, then, in its standardized form $1.0 - h^2 = u^2$ is the proportion of variance unique to the variable. A diagonal matrix U^2 can thus be formed with individual u^2's along the diagonal. It follows that $[R - U^2]$ has communalities on its diagonal, and the trace of $[R - U^2]$ is the total common variance of the m variables. This total common variance plus the trace of U^2 equals m, the total variance.

Principal axes factor analysis provides a procedure whereby a matrix ${}_mA_r$ may be found such that

$$[R - U^2] = AA^T \tag{21}$$

$$A^TA = \Lambda \tag{22}$$

The dot product of each row vector of A yields one of the communalities, and the inner product of any pair of row vectors reproduces a correlation. The array Λ is a diagonal matrix, which implies that inner products of pairs of column vectors of A are zero. Such vectors are thus orthogonal (uncorrelated). The dot product of each column vector yields an eigenvalue λ. Since the sum of the eigenvalues must equal the sum of the communalities, these eigenvalues represent another way of parceling up the total common variance, the one (communalities) relating to the amount of the total common variance contributed by the association of any one variable with all other variables, the other (eigenvalues) to that part of the total attributable to one of the column vectors of A. These independent column vectors are the factors of factor analysis, the principal dimensions of variation underlying the original body of variables m.

Individual elements of A are factor loadings, the correlation coefficients between the original variables and each of the underlying common dimensions. The property of orthogonality of the dimensions is useful, because it means that each of the dimensions accounts for a different slice of the common variance, which slices are additive in any reconstitution of the whole; such additivity was not a property of the original intercorrelated m variables. Each dimension summarizes, then, one pattern of variation—one story told by—the original m variables. A further step which is useful is to form

$$ {}_nS_r = [(A^TA)^{-1}A^TZ^T]^T \tag{23} $$

In the matrix S, the individual s_{ij} are factor scores of the original observations on each of the new dimensions formed by the analysis. The matrix S expresses all associations and common patterns found in X, but in a simpler form.

Factor analysis of census data for a whole series of U.S. cities by social area analysts has led to the conclusion that three dimensions are all that are required to summarize the stories told by the characteristics recorded for census tracts by the census. Study of the correlations between the original variables and the three dimensions has also revealed remarkably stable patterns from one city to another. One factor was consistently highly correlated with income, education, occupation, and wealth. A second was related to family structure, fertility, type of household, and position of women in the labor force. Finally, a third was associated with ethnic and racial structure of the population, age and sex composition, and measures of deterioration and blight. Speculation about the meaning of these regularities led social area analysts to identify the first as depicting variations in the *social rank* of individuals and families, the second as representing variations in the *urbanization* or *family status* of neighborhoods, and the third as resulting from *segregation.* The factor scores of tracts on these three dimensions could be used to characterize neighborhoods, since the three dimensions appear to be those responsible for the basic features of urban differentiation and stratification.

If the latter statement is true, then the three dimensions should enable research workers to test some of the classical constructs concerning such urban differentiation and stratification. A first study along these lines has revealed that factor scores of tracts with respect to social rank are differentiated in a sectoral fashion, as they should be if Hoyt's concepts apply, and that factor scores on urbanization and family status are differentiated in a concentric fashion, as they should be if Burgess's ideas are valid.[36] However, spatial variations in segregation show no regularity, but are specific to each case. As Hurd had speculated much earlier, then, concentric and axial patterns are additive and independent sources of urban differentiation from city to city, with spatial variations specific to each city added by the third dimension of segregation.

It is clear that although social area analysts began simply in a "look-see" manner, with later work facilitated by advancing computer technology, their work has now laid the bases for a spatial model of the internal socioeconomic pattern of cities in which the relevance and role of the traditional concepts is clear. [37,38]

A SYSTEMS FRAMEWORK

The previous findings point in one direction: that cities and sets of cities are *systems* susceptible of the same kinds of analysis as other systems and characterized by the same generalizations, constructs, and models. *General Systems Theory* provides a framework for such inquiry into the nature of systems; indeed Boulding calls it the skeleton of science. Further, *Information Theory* has come to the fore as one of the foundations of general systems theory, contributing the two complementary ideas of *entropy* and *information* to the vocabulary of general systems research.[39] Entropy is achieved in the steady state of a stochastic process and is at its maximum if this process is unconstrained. Information is a measure of the order present if some systematic pressures for organization constrain the operation of the stochastic process.

Curry[40] has shown that given Z settlements, with Z_i having a population i, the numbers of ways people can be distributed among settlements is

$$P = Z!/\prod_{i=0}^{n} Z! \qquad (0 \leqslant i \leqslant n) \tag{24}$$

and in a large system the entropy E is given by

$$E_{\text{def}} = \log P = Z \log Z - \Sigma Z_i \log Z_i \tag{25}$$

E is maximized when

$$Z_i = (Z/N)e^{-(i/N)} \tag{26}$$

in which equation N is the mean population per settlement, or $N = n/Z$. Now if S is the size of the largest city,

$$Z_{i \leq S} = S(1 - e^{-(i/N)}) \tag{27}$$

in which case

$$E_{\max} = Z \log (eN) \tag{28}$$

and the most probable state of the system (that is, the state in which maximum entropy is found) is one in which, given the size of the largest city, the probability of the $(q + 1)$st city having a population that is a given ratio of the qth city is a constant. Under these conditions the sum of the logarithms is a maximum, and of course it is the conditions satisfied when the rank-size rule for cities obtains. If a system of cities assumes rank-size, then, entropy has been maximized and it has assumed its most probable steady state.[41]

On the other hand, organization exists due to pressures for order in central place systems. If the per cent change in establishments in central places is constant with each addition of new business types, then[42]

$$dE/E\,dT = k \tag{29}$$

Integrating yields

$$\text{Log } E = k_1 T + c_1 \tag{30}$$

If similar percentage ratios exist for the sizes of central places P_c then

$$\text{Log } P_c = k_2 T + c_2 \tag{31}$$

From equations 30 and 31

$$T = K_1 \log E - C_1 \tag{32}$$

$$T = K_2 \log P_c - C_2 \tag{33}$$

Now the equation

$$I = K \log \text{(number of states)} \tag{34}$$

has been identified as one measure of macroscopic negentropy, the inverse of entropy. It follows that the number of business types T is an index of the amount of information present in a set of establishments located in central places, or of the population of those places. This is consistent with the use of types of functions to identify and classify the central place hierarchy. Many attempts have been made to assess the "centrality" of central places. It would seem that number of types of business—information content—provides such an index. In southwestern Iowa, very strong fits to Equations 32 and 33 are found:

$$T = 55.56 \log E - 58 \qquad (r^2 = 0.96) \tag{35}$$

$$T = 50.00 \log P_c - 105 \qquad (r^2 = 0.91) \tag{36}$$

indicating that where urban centers are almost exclusively central places, necessary empirical bases for these arguments are to be found. It will be apparent that the above equations are compatible with those presented earlier for central place systems in the third section. Lösch and Christaller postulate such constant percentage relationships also with the addition of *levels* to the regular hierarchy ($k = 3$, $k = 4$, $k = 7$ networks and their implications); related measures of information should therefore exist for the order maintained by the steplike nature of the hierarchy.

It is not difficult to extend similar arguments to the situation within cities.[43] For example, urban population densities settle down to a most probable state in which densities are ranked with distance from the city center. Conversely, the model of central place systems also applies, indicating that certain aspects of urban life are constrained from reaching their most probable state.

Maruyama[44] has speculated about an apparent contradiction of the second law of thermodynamics in social phenomena, including those of cities. According to the second law, an isolated system will most probably trend to its most probable state, even if it begins in an inhomogeneous state. He points out that Cybernetics, the study of equilibrating systems, considers many cases of self-regulation such that deviations are counteracted and the system is brought back towards its equilibrium, usually a most-probable state under constraint. But many instances can be cited in which feedback does not lead to self-correction toward some preset equilibrium (morphostasis). Rather, progressively greater contrasts appear, as between Myrdal's "rich lands and poor" or with progressively greater centralization of urban functions in fewer larger cities, or when the "growth of a city increases the internal structuredness of the city itself" (Maruyama's words). These are all examples of deviation *amplifying* processes (morphogenesis), which run counter to the second law.

Whether or not a system trends toward maximum entropy because processes working are deviation-correcting, or toward maximum information because the processes are deviation- and therefore structure-amplifying apparently depends upon the nature of the causal relationships at work, and of their feedback characteristics. Maruyama concludes that any system, together with the subsystems into which it may be partitioned, contains many examples of both deviation-correcting and deviation-amplifying processes. One subsystem may be becoming more highly organized, another may be approximating its most probable state. To understand the system as a whole demands that each of the subsystems be understood, as well as the relationships between them.[45]

So be it in the urban field. It is clear that cities may be considered as systems—entities comprising interacting, interdependent parts. They may be studied at a variety of levels—structural, functional, and dynamic—and they may be partitioned into a variety of subsystems. The most immediate part of the environment of any city is other cities, and sets of cities also constitute systems to which all the preceding statements apply. For systems of cities the most immediate environment is the socioeconomy of which they are a part, and so forth.

CONCLUSIONS

Whereas progress has been made in understanding various facets of these systems and subsystems, for other facets we stand much as we did a decade ago. In a systems framework we should no longer worry about apparent contradictions between the kinds of conclusions reached for different subsystems, that is, between the distribution of city sizes and the functional arrangement of market centers in a hierarchy, however, for the difference is understood to be one of the relative balance of entropy-approximating or order-generating processes in various parts of the system. In contradistinction, however, we have very little understanding of how to put these different patterns together in more general models that are broad in scope. Sound models of partial kinds are providing the building blocks, but maximum progress during the next decade awaits the architectural systematizer.

FOOTNOTES

[1] This volume [33] includes review papers by historians, geographers, political scientists, sociologists, economists, and the like.

Throughout this article, bracketed numbers refer to the list of references at the end of the article.

[2] Ackoff [1] elaborates these terms.

[3] See Isard [34] in connection with a discussion of empirical regularities.

[4] See [12] for review comments.

[5] Berry [8] lists the relevant literature in some detail. Subsequent contributions include those of Bell [5], Friedmann [29], and Ward [51].

[6] If the entire population were urban, then $P_t = P_1 \Sigma r^{-q}$. See Weiss [52].

[7] Simon [48], Berry and Garrison [7], Thomas [49], Dacey [25], and Ward [51].

[8] That is, so that the "law of proportionate effect" holds.

[9] Berry [8].

[10] Bell [5], Friedmann [29].

[11] Unless the process works, for example, to a random power of size, as with the log-lognormal, see Thomas [49].

[12] Nagel [42] discusses the various modes of scientific explanation, and the role of explanation in science.

[13] Berry [12] lists the relevant literature. Also see Winsborough [54].

[14] See [2] and [41], also footnote 12.

[15] *Ibid.*

[16] Alonso.

[17] Muth.

[18] Winsborough [54].

[19] Berry [12], Weiss [52], Newling [43].

[20] Winsborough.

[21] Berry and Pred [9]. Later studies include [10], [11], [13], [22]. See also the parallel speculations of Rashevsky [46], [47].

[22] Christaller [21].

[23] Berry and Pred [9].

[24] *Ibid.*

[25] See [10] and [14].

[26] See [10] or [11] for details.

[27] Only a sample of the structural equations necessary to facilitate the present discussion is given here.

[28] See [10], also subsequent studies as yet unpublished by Karaska, Pitts, Murdie, and others.

[29] The factor analytic results are presented in [14] and [10].

[30] Garrison [30] has one of the first presentations.

[31] See [20].

[32] See [38] and [39].

[33] Bell [6] has an excellent review.

[34] See the review by Anderson [3].

[35] The Duncans write "students of urban structure have lived for some time with the uncomfortable realization that their theories, or rather their abstract, schematic descriptions of urban growth and form are not very susceptible to empirical testing." [26].

[36] Anderson [3].

[37] This, in spite of criticism [26], has been the *accumulative* result.

[38] It is worthwhile to note some of the other contributions made possible by factor analysis: (*a*) more general urban typologies [40]; (*b*) clear-cut evidence of the hierarchy of central places as an additive class system [10], [14]; (*c*) multivariate regionalization [31]; (*d*) metropolitan structure [32].

[39] Bertalanffy [16], [17], Boulding [19], Beer [4].

[40] Curry [23]. Other cases he examines are the spacing of nearest neighbors (see also Dacey [24]), the spacing of nearest neighbors of the same size, and the percentage manufacturing in an urban labor force.

[41] Curry points out that entropy in the same system, constrained such that persons had to be allocated in threes, as families, would be $H' = Z \log (eN/3)$. Hence, a measure of order is $R = 1 - H'/E_{\max}$.

[42] Odum [44], Berry [11].

[43] Meier [37].

[44] Reference [35] is a review statement of Maruyama's ideas, and contains other references of interest.

[45] Maruyama provides an example of the operation of deviation amplifying mutual causal processes in a two-dimensional spatial distribution, and his discussion of systems, subsystems, and feedback is phrased in terms of cities.

REFERENCES

1. Ackoff, R. L., *Scientific Method. Optimizing Applied Research Decisions,* New York, John Wiley & Sons, Inc., 1961.

2. Alonso, W., "A Theory of the Urban Land Market," *Papers and Proceedings of the Regional Science Association,* Vol. 6 (1960), pp. 149–158.

3. Anderson, T. R., and J. E. Egeland, "Spatial Aspects of Social Area Analysis," *American Sociological Review,* Vol. 26 (1961), pp. 392–398.

4. Beer, S., "Below the Twilight Arch—A Mythology of Systems," in D. F. Eckman, ed., *Systems: Research and Design,* New York, John Wiley & Sons, Inc., 1961.

5. Bell, G., "Change in City Size Distribution in Israel," *Ekistics,* Vol. 13 (1962), p. 98.

6. Bell, W., "Social Areas: Typology of Urban Neighborhoods," in M. B. Sussman, ed., *Community Structure and Analysis,* Riverside, N. J., Crowell-Collier Press, 1959.

7. Berry, B. J. L., and W. L. Garrison, "Alternate Explanations of Urban Rank-Size Relationships," *Annals,* Association of American Geographers, Vol. 48 (1958), pp. 83–91.

8. ———, "City Size Distributions and Economic Development," *Economic Development and Cultural Change,* Vol. 9 (1961), pp. 573–588.

9. Berry, B. J. L., and A. Pred, *Central Place Studies: A Bibliography of Theory and Applications,* Philadelphia, Regional Science Research Institute, 1961.

10. ———, "Comparative Studies of Central Place Systems," final report of project NONR 2121-18, Office of Naval Research, Geography Branch, U.S. Department of the Navy, 1961.

11. ———, H. G. Barnum, and R. J. Tennant, "Retail Location and Consumer Behavior," *Papers and Proceedings of the Regional Science Association,* Vol. 9 (1962), pp. 65–106.

12. ———, J. W. Simmons, and R. J. Tennant, "Urban Population Densities, Structure and Change," *The Geographical Review,* Vol. 53 (1963), pp. 389–405.

13. ———, *Commercial Structure and Commercial Blight,* Department of Geography Research Paper No. 85, University of Chicago, 1963.

14. ———, and H. G. Barnum, "Aggregate Patterns and Elemental Components of Central Place Systems," *Journal of Regional Science,* Vol. 4 (1963).

15. ———, "Research Frontiers in Urban Geography," in P. Hauser and L. Schnore, eds., *The Study of Urbanization,* Social Science Research Council, 1964, in press.

16. Bertalanffy, L. von, "General System Theory: A New Approach to the Unity of Science," *Human Biology,* Vol. 23 (1951), pp. 303–361.

17. ———, "General System Theory," *General Systems,* Vol. 1 (1956).

18. ———, "General System Theory: A Critical Review," *General Systems,* Vol. 7 (1962).

19. Boulding, K., "General Systems Theory—The Skeleton of Science," *Management Science,* Vol. 2 (1956), pp. 197–208.

20. Chapin, F. S., and S. F. Weiss, *Factors Influencing Land Development,* Chapel Hill, University of North Carolina Press, 1962.

21. Christaller, W., *Die zentralen Orte in Süddeutschland,* Jena, Gustav Fischer, 1933.

22. Claval, P., *Géographie Générale des Marches,* Besançon, 1962.

23. Curry, L., "Explorations in Settlement Theory: The Random Spatial Economy, Part I," *Annals,* Association of American Geographers, Vol. 54 (1964), pp. 138–146.

24. Dacey, M. F., and T. H. Tung, "The Identification of Point Patterns, I," *Journal of Regional Science,* Vol. 4 (1963).

25. ———, "Another Explanation for Rank-Size Regularity," Philadelphia, 1962.

26. Duncan, B., and O. D. Duncan, "The Measurement of Intra-city Locational and Residential Patterns," *Journal of Regional Science,* Vol. 2 (1960), pp. 37–54.

27. ———, "Variables in Urban Morphology," in E. W. Burgess and D. J. Bogue, eds., *Research Contributions to Urban Sociology,* Chicago, University of Chicago Press, 1963.

28. Friedmann, J. R. P., *The Spatial Structure of Economic Development in the Tennessee Valley,* Department of Geography Research Paper No. 39, University of Chicago, 1955.

29. ———, "Economic Growth and Urban Structure in Venezuela," *Cuadernos de la Sociedad Venezolana de Planificacion,* special issue, 1963.

30. Garrison, W. L., "Toward a Simulation Model of Urban Growth and

Development," *Proceedings of the IGU Symposium in Urban Geography, Lund, 1960,* Lund, Gleerup, 1962.

31. Ginsburg, N., *An Atlas of Economic Development,* Chicago, University of Chicago Press, 1961.

32. Hattori, K., K. Kagaya, and S. Inanaga, "The Regional Structure of Surrounding Areas of Tokyo," *Chirigaku Hyoron,* 1960.

33. Hauser, P., and L. F. Schnore, eds., *The Study of Urbanization,* New York, Social Science Research Council, 1964, in press.

34. Isard, W., *Location and Space Economy,* New York, The Technology Press of the Massachusetts Institute of Technology and John Wiley & Sons, Inc., 1956.

35. Maruyama, M., "The Second Cybernetics: Deviation Amplifying Mutual Causal Processes," *American Scientist,* Vol. 51 (1963), pp. 164–179.

36. McIntosh, R., "Ecosystems, Evolution and Relational Patterns of Living Organisms," *American Scientist,* Vol. 51 (1963), pp. 246–267.

37. Meier, R. L., *A Communications Theory of Urban Growth,* Cambridge, Mass., The M.I.T. Press, 1962.

38. Morrill, R. L., "Simulation of Central Place Patterns over Time," *Proceedings of the IGU Symposium in Urban Geography, Lund, 1960,* Lund, Gleerup, 1962.

39. ———, "The Development of Spatial Distributions of Towns in Sweden: An Historical-Predictive Approach," *Annals,* Association of American Geographers, Vol. 53 (1963), pp. 1–14.

40. Moser, C. A., and W. Scott, *British Towns: A Statistical Study of their Social and Economic Differences,* Edinburgh, Oliver and Boyd, 1961.

41. Muth, R. F., "The Spatial Structure of the Housing Market," *Papers and Proceedings of the Regional Science Association,* Vol. 7 (1961), pp. 207–220.

42. Nagel, E., *The Structure of Science,* New York, Harcourt, Brace and World, Inc., 1961.

43. Newling, B., *The Growth and Spatial Structure of Kingston, Jamaica,* Ph.D. dissertation, Northwestern University, 1962.

44. Odum, H. T., J. E. Cantlon, and L. S. Kornicker, "An Organizational Hierarchy Postulate for the Interpretation of Species—Individual Distributions, Species Entropy, Ecosystem Evolution, and the Meaning of the Species—Variety Index," *Ecology,* Vol. 41 (1960), pp. 395–399.

45. Pierce, J. R., *Symbols, Signals and Noise,* New York, Harper and Row, Publishers, 1961.

46. Rashevsky, N., "Outline of a Mathematical Approach to History," *Bulletin of Mathematical Biophysics* (1953).

47. ———, "Some Quantitative Aspects of History," *Bulletin of Mathematical Biophysics* (1953).

48. Simon, H. A., "On a Class of Skew Distribution Functions," *Biometrika,* Vol. 42 (1955), pp. 425–440.

49. Thomas, E. N., "Additional Comments on Population-Size Relationships for Sets of Cities," in W. L. Garrison, ed., *Quantitative Geography,* New York, Atherton Press, in press.

50. Van Ardsol, M. D., S. F. Camilleri, and C. F. Schmid, "The Generality of Urban Social Area Indexes," *American Sociological Review,* Vol. 23 (1958), pp. 277–284.

51. Ward, B., *Greek Regional Development,* Athens, Center for Economic Research, 1962.

52. Weiss, H. K., "The Distribution of Urban Population and an Application to a Servicing Problem," *Operations Research,* Vol. 9 (1961), pp. 860–874.

53. Wingo, L., *Transportation and Urban Land,* Resources for the Future, Inc., 1961.

54. Winsborough, H. H., "City Growth and City Structure," *Journal of Regional Science,* Vol. 4 (1963).

7. City Size Distributions and Economic Development*†

BRIAN J. L. BERRY

Students of urbanization have recognized two kinds of city size distributions: rank-size,[1] according to which the distribution of cities by population size class within countries is truncated lognormal;[2] and primate, whereby a stratum of small towns and cities is dominated by one or more very large cities and there are deficiencies in numbers of cities of intermediate sizes.[3] Rank-size regularities have been associated with the existence of integrated systems of cities in economically advanced countries,[4] whereas primate cities have been associated

---

* This paper is designed in part as an example of the potential uses of the data brought together in the Atlas of Economic Development (Chicago, 1961). The author wishes to thank its author, Norton Ginsburg, for his constructive criticisms.

1. John Q. Stewart, "Empirical Mathematical Rules concerning the Distribution and Equilibrium of Population," The Geographical Review, Vol. 37 (1947), pp. 461-485; George Kingsley Zipf, National Unity and Disunity (Bloomington, 1941); and the same author's Human Behavior and the Principle of Least Effort (Cambridge, 1949).

2. A statement which is valid when a variable exponent is allowed. See Martin J. Beckmann, "City Hierarchies and the Distribution of City Size," Economic Development and Cultural Change, Vol. 6 (1958), 243-248; Brian J. L. Berry and William L. Garrison, "Alternate Explanations of Urban Rank-Size Relationships," Annals, Association of American Geographers, Vol. 48 (1958), 83-91; Herbert A. Simon, "On a Class of Skew Distribution Functions," Biometrika, Vol. 42 (1955), pp. 425-440; and J. Aitchison and J. A. C. Brown, The Lognormal Distribution (Cambridge, 1957). The truncated lognormal is used here rather than the Yule distribution because both are similar in form and because subsequent analysis is facilitated by use of lognormal probability paper. See also the discussion of E. N. Thomas, "Additional Comments on Population-Size Relationships for Sets of Cities," paper read to Symposium on Quantitative Methods in Geographic Research, Chicago, 1960, and to be published in the Proceedings.

3. Mark Jefferson, "The Law of the Primate City," The Geographical Review, Vol. 29 (1939), 226-232. Here we use the term "primate" in a sense somewhat different from that of Jefferson, but in accord with the discussion in UNESCO, "Report by the Director-General on the Joint UN/UNESCO Seminar on Urbanization in the ECAFE Region," Paris (1956), for example.

4. Zipf, National Unity... and Human Behavior..., op. cit.; Brian J. L. Berry, "An Inductive Approach to the Regionalization of Economic Development," in Norton Ginsburg, ed., Essays on Geography and Economic Development, Department of Geography, University of Chicago, Research Paper Number 62 (Chicago, 1960), pp. 78-107; and UNESCO, op. cit. See also the studies of Beckmann, op. cit., and Berry and Garrison, op. cit., both of which argue for compatibility of Christaller-Lösch type hierarchies and rank-size distributions of city sizes.

† Reprinted from *Economic Development and Cultural Change,* Vol. 9 (July 1961).

with overurbanization and superimposed colonial economies in underdeveloped countries or with political-administrative controls in indigenous subsistence and peasant societies.[5] Questions as to the empirical reality of rank-size distributions have been raised, however.[6] Likewise, the idea of a primate city was not developed with Asian dual economies in mind.[7] There seems to be a need for detailed investigation of the whole question of the relations of city size distributions and economic development. Such an investigation is the purpose of this paper. The study will draw upon previous theoretical investigations of rank-size,[8] and upon a detailed analysis of the relative economic development of countries.[9] It will not be concerned with systems of cities defined in terms of functional characteristics,[10] but simply with the distribution of cities by size within countries and with the economic development of these countries as ascertained in a principal components analysis of multiple indices to economic development.

The plan of the paper is as follows: (a) to describe the city size distributions of as many countries as seem necessary for purposes of this analysis and to compare them with indices of urbanization and primacy included in the Atlas of Economic Development;[11] (b) to describe the relative economic development of these countries; and (c) to compare the materials presented in the first two sections in an attempt to test the hypothesized relationship between city size distributions and economic development. A model of city size distributions is formulated.

---

5. UNESCO, *op. cit.*, refers to the over-urbanization of Asian economies because of (1) excessive in-migration, and (2) superimposition of limited economic development of a colonial or semi-colonial type, creating dual economies and primate cities which contrast with systems of cities in the west. It was reported that primate cities have paralytic effects upon the development of smaller urban places and tend to be parasitic in relation to the remainder of the national economy.

6. C. Stewart, "The Size and Spacing of Cities," *The Geographical Review*, Vol. 48 (1958), 222-245, argues that there are marked divergences from Zipf's rank-size rule that in any country the nth ranking city has a population of $1/n^{th}$ that of the largest city because (i) for 72 countries in the world and (ii) for major political divisions within the six largest countries the theoretical 1.0: 0.5: 0.33: 0.25: 0.20 ratios of the sizes of the five largest cities are not found. Using Sweden and Denmark as his examples, and four time periods for each, he argues that there is, instead, an S-shaped distribution of towns by size (pp. 230 and 231). The comments of F. T. Moore, "A Note on City Size Distributions," *Economic Development and Cultural Change*, Vol. 7 (1959), 465-466, on Zipf's limiting case are also germane.

7. Jefferson, *op. cit.*

8. Beckmann, *op. cit.*; Berry and Garrison, *op. cit.*; Simon, *op. cit.*; C. Stewart, *op. cit.*; and Thomas, *op. cit.*

9. Berry, *op. cit.*

10. The paper is not concerned with central place systems and the like in the sense of Walter Christaller, *Die zentralen Orte in Süddeutschland* (Jena, 1933); and August Losch, *Die raumliche Ordnung der Wirtschaft* (Jena, 1944), trans. W. H. Woglom and W. F. Stolper, *The Economics of Location* (New Haven, 1954); or in the sense of rural-urban relationships as discussed by N. Rashevsky, *Mathematical Theory of Human Relations* (Bloomington, 1947).

11. Norton Ginsburg, *Atlas of Economic Development* (Chicago, 1961), Part 8, "A Statistical Analysis," by Brian J. L. Berry.

The City Size Distributions

Figures 1-6 contain best-fitting curves to 38 city size distributions. These 38 were selected simply on the basis of convenience of access to data. In each the plot is of cumulative frequencies on lognormal probability paper, so that if a city size distribution is lognormal it assumes the form of a straight line. Data are listed in Appendix A. The cumulative frequencies obtained were for cities with populations exceeding 20,000 and the cumulation proceeded over six size classes: 20,000-50,000; 50,000-100,000; 100,000-250,000; 250,000-500,000; 500,000-1,000,000; and over 1,000,000 to 100 percent at the population of the largest city. As the list of countries in Appendix A suggests, all world regions except Africa are well-represented; under-representation in that continent results because very few African countries have many cities with populations exceeding 20,000. Since we only have comparable urbanized area statistics for cities exceeding 100,000 in population (see Appendix note), the statistics used refer to "city proper" populations.

Thirteen of the 38 countries have lognormally-distributed city sizes (Figures 1 and 2). The higher one of the thirteen curves appears in the graph, the greater the percentage of small cities in the country concerned. The steeper the slope of a curve, the smaller is the largest city. Among the thirteen are both very large countries such as China and very small countries such as Switzerland. The smaller the country, the steeper is the curve. The thirteen also include both highly developed countries like the United States and underdeveloped countries like Korea. The lower the degree of economic development, the steeper is the curve and the greater the percentage of large cities in the country concerned. It is noticeable that countries with long urban traditions such as India and China and highly developed countries such as the United States and West Germany have very similar city size distributions.

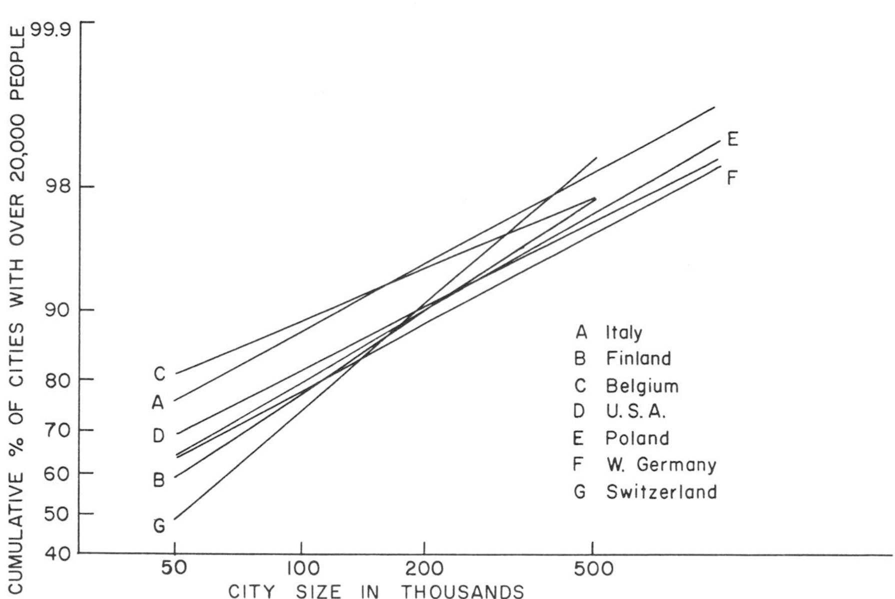

Figure 1. Seven lognormal (rank-size) distributions.

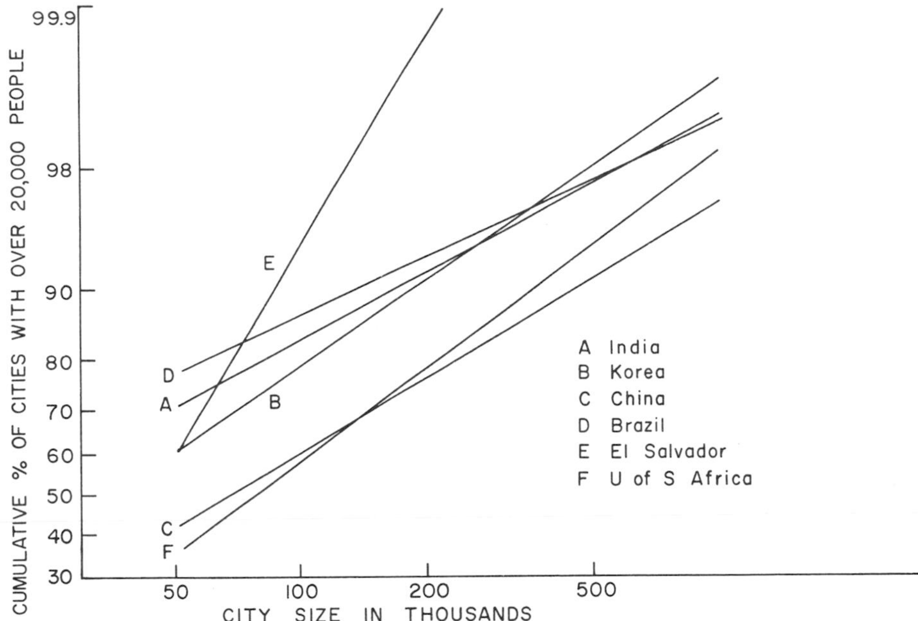

Figure 2. Lesser developed countries may also have lognormal city size distributions

There are fifteen countries with primate city size distributions (Figures 3 and 4). Note the shape of the curves: lognormally-distributed lesser city sizes are followed by a gap because cities of intermediate size are absent, and then by a rapid cumulation to a primate city or to several primate cities. Mexico, for example, has lognormally-distributed city sizes up to an urban population of 250,000, and then a considerable gap followed by a primate capital city of over a million people. In the case of Ceylon the gap comes earlier, and the capital is smaller. In Japan the gap comes later and indicates absence of cities in the size bracket 500,000 to 1,000,000; in this case there are several larger cities. The gap need not be a void, but a considerable deficiency of cities of intermediate size, as in the examples of Spain and Sweden. Thailand and Guatemala are limiting cases in which the lower lognormal distribution is absent; instead, a few cities with between 20,000 and 50,000 people are followed by a considerable gap and a single large primate city. All fifteen countries are small, and they range from underdeveloped Thailand through countries with dual and peasant economies to Denmark and the Netherlands, with highly specialized agricultural economies.

Nine countries have city size distributions intermediate between lognormal and primate (Figures 5 and 6). All display some primacy, but none are without cities of intermediate size. Some, such as Norway and Canada, approach lognormal. Others are almost primate, for example, Malaya and Pakistan. In the cases of Australia and New Zealand the deficiency is not in cities of middling size, but in smaller cities. Figure 6 also includes the special case of England and Wales, with primate cities grafted on top of a complete lower lognormal distribution. These intermediate cases again include countries of a variety of sizes and at a variety of levels of development.

What do these differences in city size distributions mean? We can begin to make sense out of them--and to refute some myths--if we compare them with two indices of the nature and degree of urban development, an index of urbanization and an index of primacy.

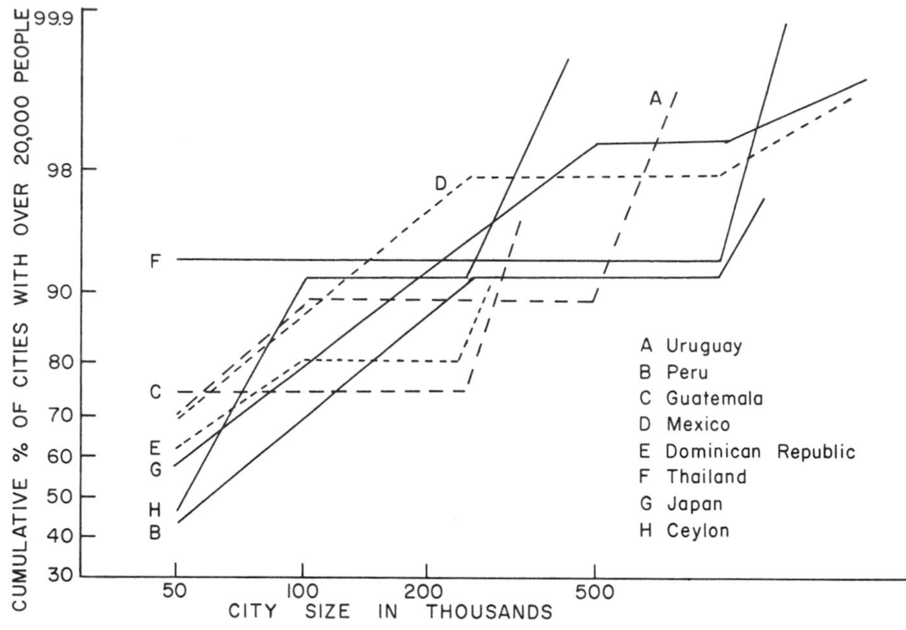

Figure 3. Eight primate distributions

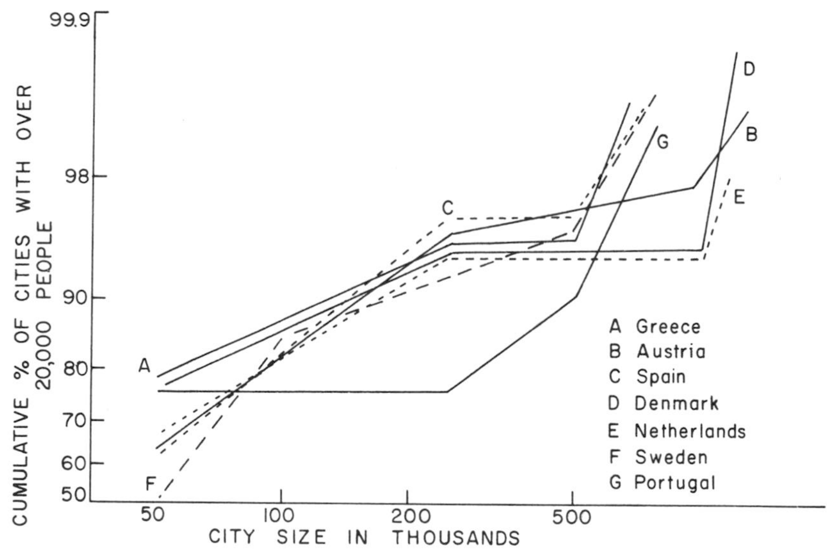

Figure 4. More developed countries may have primate distributions

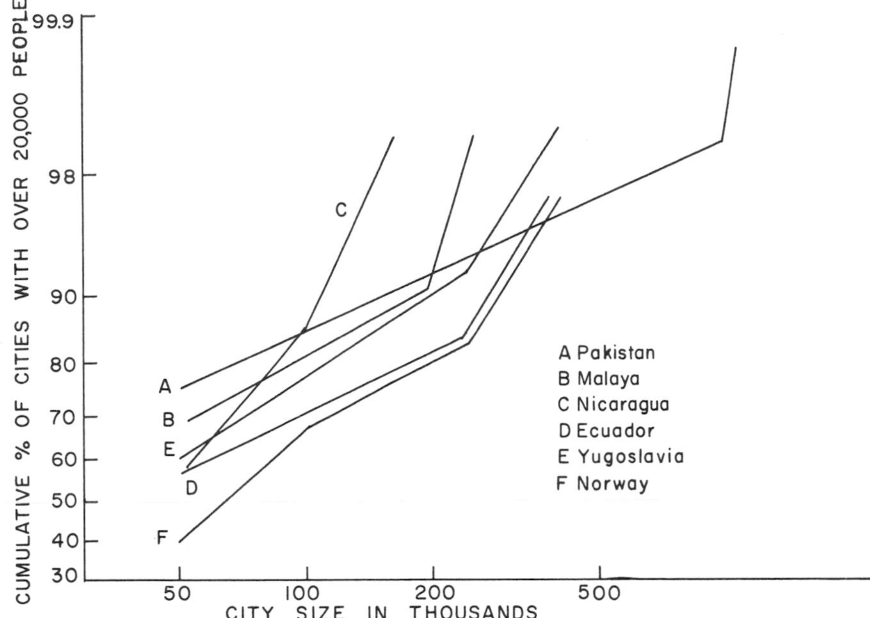

Figure 5. Six distributions intermediate between lognormal and primate

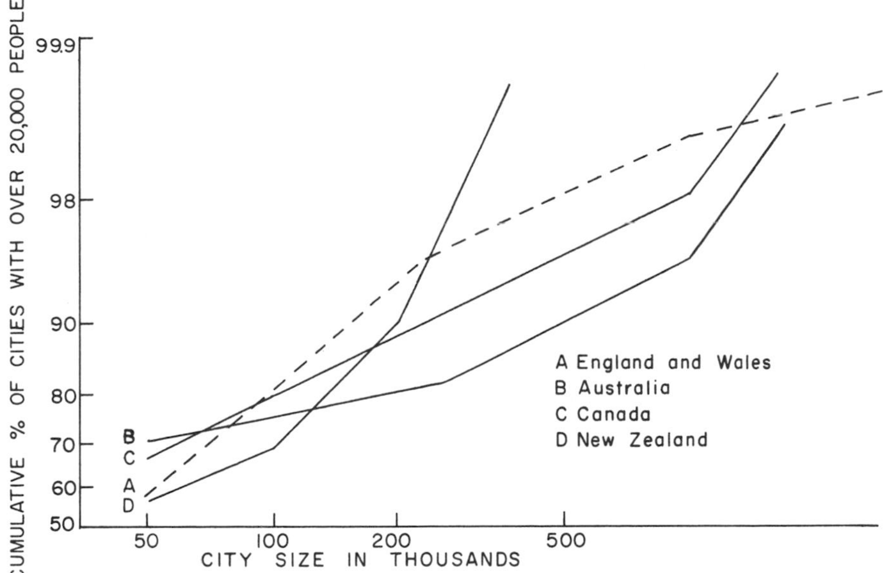

Figure 6. Three additional intermediate distributions, plus the special case of England and Wales

Relationship to Degree of Urbanization

The Atlas of Economic Development[12] includes a map showing the world pattern of urbanization (Figure 7). Countries are shaded in this map according to the percent of their population in cities of 20,000 and more people, and are divided into six classes of urbanization for convenience of mapping. In Table 1 we cross-classify 37 countries according to these six categories of urbanization and the three categories of city size distribution.

Table 1. Urbanization and City Size Distributions

Degree of urbanization	City Size Distribution		
	Rank size	Intermediate	Primate
Most	4	2	5
2	2	2	1
3	1	2	3
4	4	2	3
5	2	1	3
Least	-	-	-

None of the 37 countries falls within the "least urbanized" category because in this group very few countries possess more than a couple of cities with populations exceeding 20,000. A chi-square test shows the arrangement of countries in the cross classification to be not significantly different from an arrangement which could have arisen at random. Therefore we conclude that there is no relationship between type of city size distribution and the degree to which a country is urbanized. Countries with lognormal city sizes and low urbanization include China, India, Korea, Poland, and Brazil, whereas countries with primate cities and high degrees of urbanization include Spain, the Netherlands, Denmark, Sweden, Japan, and Uruguay. Australia and New Zealand are the most urbanized of the intermediate cases. All of these countries deviate from the commonly hypothesized but nonexistent relationship between urbanization and rank-size regularities.

Relationship to an Index of Primacy

The Atlas[13] also includes an index of primacy which is very similar to that used by Jefferson,[14] namely, the ratio of the population of the largest city in a country to the combined population of the first four cities (Figure 8). In Table 2 we cross classify 37 countries according to city size distribution and six classes of this primacy index. There is an obvious relationship: countries with the lowest primacy indices have rank-size city sizes, and countries with the highest have primate city size distributions. But there are also anomalies: Spain, the Netherlands, Sweden, and Japan have primate distributions yet low primacy indices, because they have more than one large city above the intermediate city size gap; countries which combine a high primacy index and a primate distribution have only one large primate city. This anomaly reflects a deficiency of the Atlas index: it only indicates primacy when a country has a single primate city. Intermediate Australia, New Zealand, Canada, and Yugoslavia also have low primacy indices because they have more than one large city, yet all display some primacy if their entire city size distributions are studied.

---

12. Ginsburg, Atlas..., op. cit.

13. Ibid.

14. Jefferson, op. cit.

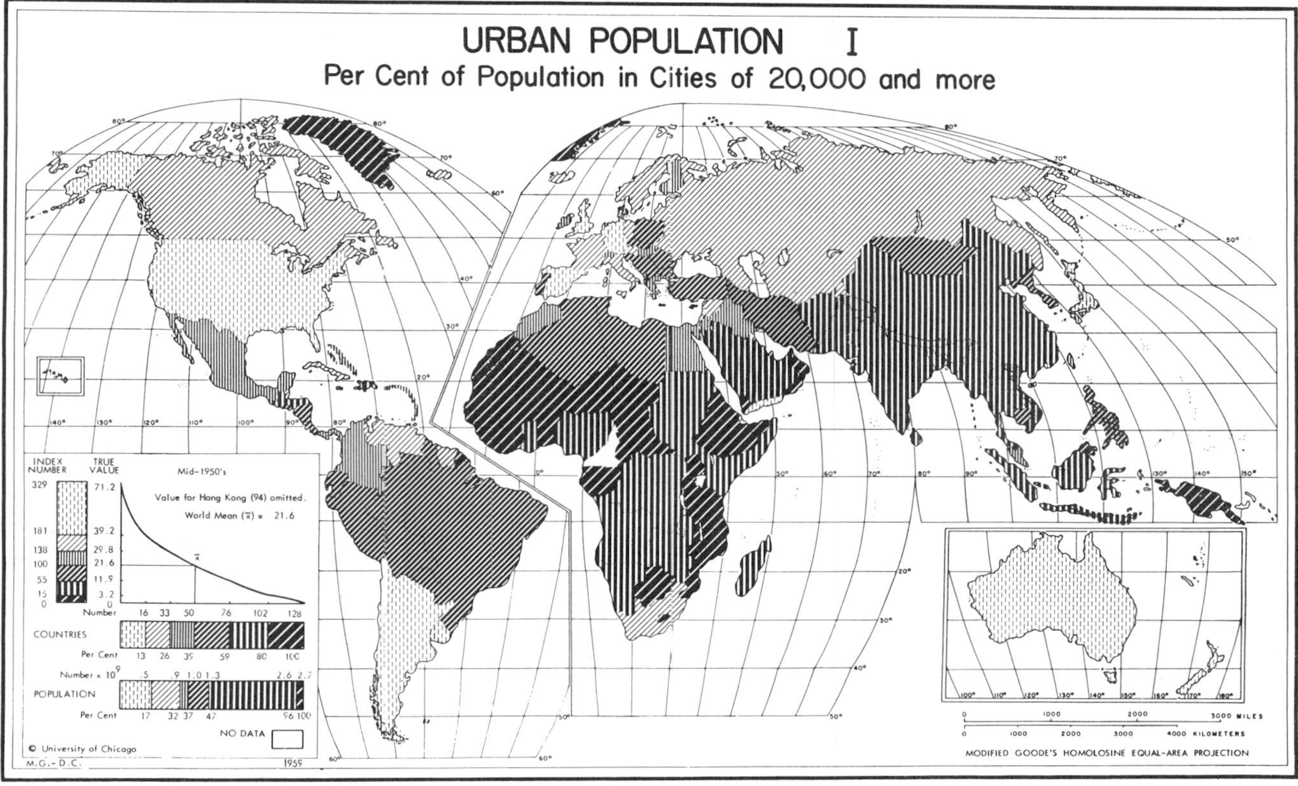
URBAN POPULATION I
Per Cent of Population in Cities of 20,000 and more
Mid-1950's
Value for Hong Kong (94) omitted.
World Mean (x̄) = 21.6
INDEX NUMBER
TRUE VALUE
329 71.2
181 39.2
138 29.8
100 21.6
55 11.9
15 3.2
0 0
Number 16 33 50 76 102 128
COUNTRIES
Per Cent 13 26 39 59 80 100
Number x 10^9 .5 .9 1.0 1.3 2.6 2.7
POPULATION
Per Cent 17 32 37 47 96 100
NO DATA
© University of Chicago
M.G.-D.C.
1959
0 1000 2000 3000 MILES
0 1000 2000 3000 4000 KILOMETERS
MODIFIED GOODE'S HOMOLOSINE EQUAL-AREA PROJECTION

Figure 7.

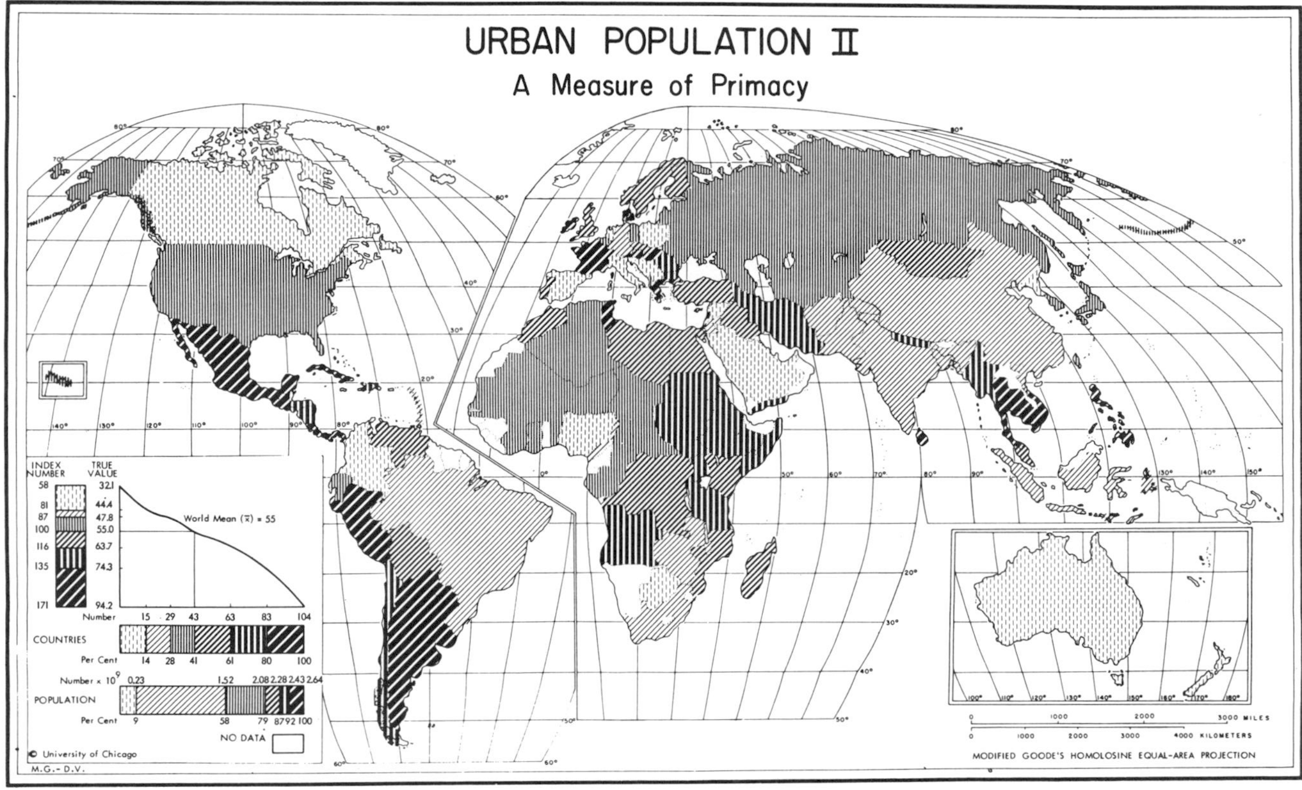
URBAN POPULATION II
A Measure of Primacy
INDEX NUMBER
TRUE VALUE
58 32.1
81 44.4
87 47.8
100 55.0
116 63.7
135 74.3
171 94.2
World Mean (x̄) = 55
Number 15 29 43 63 83 104
COUNTRIES
Per Cent 14 28 41 61 80 100
Number × 10^9 0.23 1.52 2.08 2.28 2.43 2.64
POPULATION
Per Cent 9 58 79 87 92 100
NO DATA
© University of Chicago
M.G.-D.V.
0 1000 2000 3000 MILES
0 1000 2000 3000 4000 KILOMETERS
MODIFIED GOODE'S HOMOLOSINE EQUAL-AREA PROJECTION

Figure 8.

Table 2. Primacy and City Size Distributions

Degree of primacy	City Size Distribution		
	Rank size	Intermediate	Primate
Most			8
2	1	1	2
3	1	2	1
4	1		2
5	6	2	
Least	4	4	2

If the deficiencies of the primacy index are taken into account in an interpretation of Figure 8, however, the map throws light on the differentiation of city size distributions we have exposed. Countries which have until recently been politically and/or economically dependent on some outside country tend to have primate cities, which are the national capitals, cultural and economic centers, often the chief port, and the focus of national consciousness and feeling. Small countries which once had extensive empires also have primate cities which are on the one hand "empire capitals" (Vienna, Madrid, Lisbon, etc.) and on the other hand centers in which such economies of scale may be achieved that cities of intermediate size are not called for. Countries with more than one large city are either, like Canada, Australia, and New Zealand, effectively partitioned into several city-regions dominated by very similar primate cities or, like Sweden, Spain, the Netherlands, and Japan, have several large specialized cities which are complementary rather than duplicative. Countries with the lowest degrees of primacy, and therefore with lognormally distributed city sizes, include many of those with considerable industrialization, but also those with long urban traditions and histories of urbanization.

A Model of City Size Distributions

Given the above evidence, a simple graphic model may be proposed which places the several types of city size distributions on a scale between the limiting cases of primacy (e. g., Thailand) and lognormality (e. g., the United States). The model is presented in Figure 9.

A rationale for the model comes from the work of Simon,[15] who showed that lognormal distributions are produced as limiting cases by stochastic growth processes. Berry and Garrison[16] argued that, as a limiting case, a lognormal distribution is a condition of entropy, defined as a circumstance in which the forces affecting the distribution are many and act randomly. This contrasts with other distributions which are simpler in that they are produced by fewer forces.

We assume that primacy is the simplest city size distribution, affected by but few simple strong forces. Thus, primate cities are either orthogenetic political and administrative capitals, heterogenetic capitals of the emerging nations, or empire capitals (we use the terms orthogenetic and heterogenetic in the original sense of Redfield and Singer, realizing that they are subject to debate).

At the other extreme, rank-size distributions are found when, because of complexity of economic and political life and/or age of the system of cities many forces affect the urban pattern in many ways.

---

15. Simon, op. cit.

16. Berry and Garrison, op. cit.

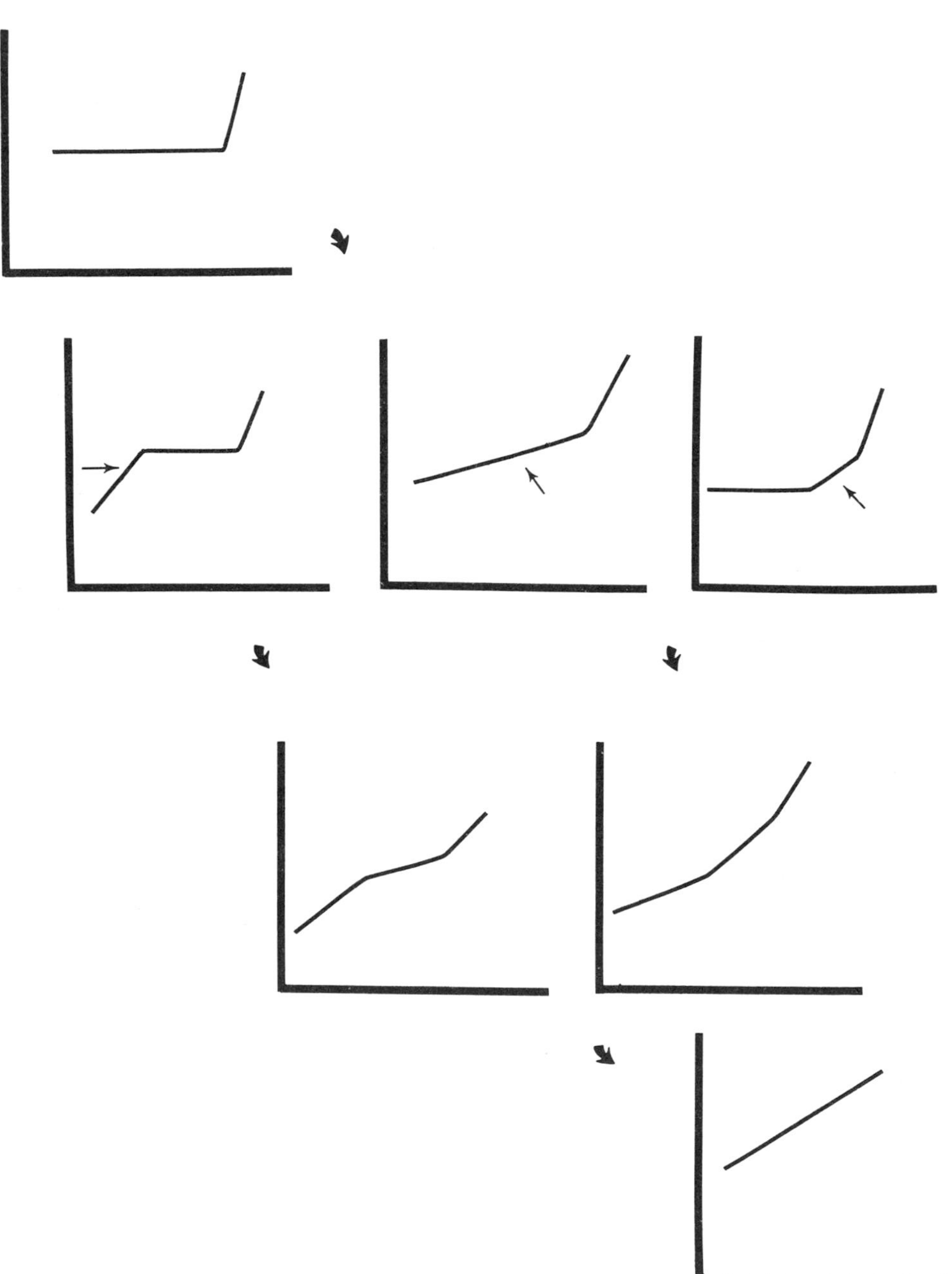

Figure 9. A developmental model city size distributions (for explanation see text)

Intermediate distributions are arranged on the assumed scale from primacy to lognormality. Three intermediate sub-categories are evident: those with more small cities than the primate, those with more medium-sized cities, and those with more large cities. In addition, two stages in the intermediate progression from primate to rank-size are pictured.

The model in effect proposes a major hypothesis: increasing entropy is accompanied by a closer approximation of a city size distribution to lognormality. Common sense leads to several sub-hypotheses: fewer forces will affect the urban structure of a country (a) the smaller is that country, (b) the shorter is the history of urbanization in the country, and (c) the simpler is the economic and political life of the country and the lower its degree of economic development. The converse of each sub-hypothesis also follows.

In the simple orderly cases most cities perform essentially the same set of functions, whether political and/or concerned with rudimentary economic activities. As complexity increases so do urban functions--political, as centers on transport routes, as specialized centers of primary or secondary economic activities, or as central places performing tertiary economic functions. At the highest levels of development a country will contain many specialized cities performing one or the other or several of these functions, and viewed in the aggregate, a condition of entropy will obtain.

The limited data available from the previous discussion seem to bear out several of the sub-hypotheses. Countries with rank-size distributions include urban-industrial economies (Belgium, United States), larger countries (Brazil), and countries with long histories of urbanization (India and China). Intermediate distributions nearest rank-size characterize countries which are larger (Canada) and have both primary and secondary commercial specialities (Australia and New Zealand), or at least have considerable commercialization in their economies. The more primate of the two intermediate stages is found in small countries engaged in primary production of relatively few commodities (Austria, Sweden, Netherlands, Denmark) or with some commercialization superimposed on a subsistence or peasant agricultural system in dual economies (Ceylon, Mexico, Dominican Republic). Primacy characterizes small countries with simple subsistence economies (Thailand), or is associated with the presence of an empire capital (Portugal).

What of the relationship to degree of economic development, the major topic of this paper? This is explored in the following section.

Relative Economic Development of 95 Countries

The author recently completed a principal components analysis of a data matrix comprising the ranks of 95 countries on each of 43 proposed indices to economic development.[17] The results of this analysis are available elsewhere, and hence will be reviewed only briefly here. Principal components analysis reduced the dimensions of variation of the data matrix and revealed an extremely simple structure comprising only four basic patterns that differentiated among countries just as well as the original 43 indices and accounted for 92.8 percent of the sum of squares of the data matrix. The analysis also produced scores for each country on each basic pattern.[18]

---

17. Berry, _op. cit._; and Ginsburg, _Atlas..._, _op. cit._

18. _Ibid._

The First Pattern

Indices of accessibility, transportation, trade, industrialization, urbanization, and national product differentiated among countries in the same way. Thus, when redundancies were eliminated by the statistical analysis, these indices collapsed to form the first basic pattern accounting for 84.2 percent of the total sum of squares. This pattern was identified as a technological scale. The urbanization index used was the index pictured in Figure 7. Thus Figure 7 provides an approximate map of the world pattern of countries on the composite technological scale.

The Second Pattern

A second basic pattern was produced by collapse of indices relating to the population of countries to the demographic scale. These indices included birth, death, infant mortality, and population growth rates, population densities, and so forth.

The Third Pattern

In the third pattern countries with considerable external relations but low national income (e.g., countries located in Latin America, or colonial territories) were contrasted with countries with the converse (e.g., the Soviet bloc).

The Fourth Pattern

A fourth pattern pointed out a group of large countries with persistently high per capita indices and low per unit area indices, and a group of small countries with the opposite. Canada, the United States, and the USSR were included among those in the first group, while Hong Kong, Lebanon, Israel were included in the second.

A Scale of Economic-Demographic Development

The first two patterns are of most interest here. If they are used as the abscissa and ordinate of a graph and the scores of countries on each are used to locate countries in this graph, a scale of economic-demographic development of countries results. Figure 10 presents this as scale A. Note the linearity of the distribution, the continuum of countries (i.e., there are no groups of countries on the basis of economic development), and the inversion of technological and demographic scores such that a "developed" country ranks high in terms of technology (high national product, etc.) and low on the basis of demographic characteristics (low infant mortality rates, etc.).

City Sizes and Economic Development

Thirty-seven city size distributions have been classified on the basis of the four stages in the model pictured in Figure 9. Using a different symbol for each of the four stages, the 37 countries have been plotted on the scale of economic-demographic development. Results are shown in Figure 10 part B. If type of city size distribution is related to economic development the symbols representing a particular kind of city size distribution should cluster in this graph. It is readily apparent that no clusters occur; therefore it may be concluded that different city size distributions are in no way related to the relative economic development of countries. Rank size is not the culmination of a process in which national unity[19] is expressed in a system of cities. Primacy is not confined to lesser developed countries. We do not find in economic

---

19. Zipf, National Unity... and Human Behavior..., op. cit.

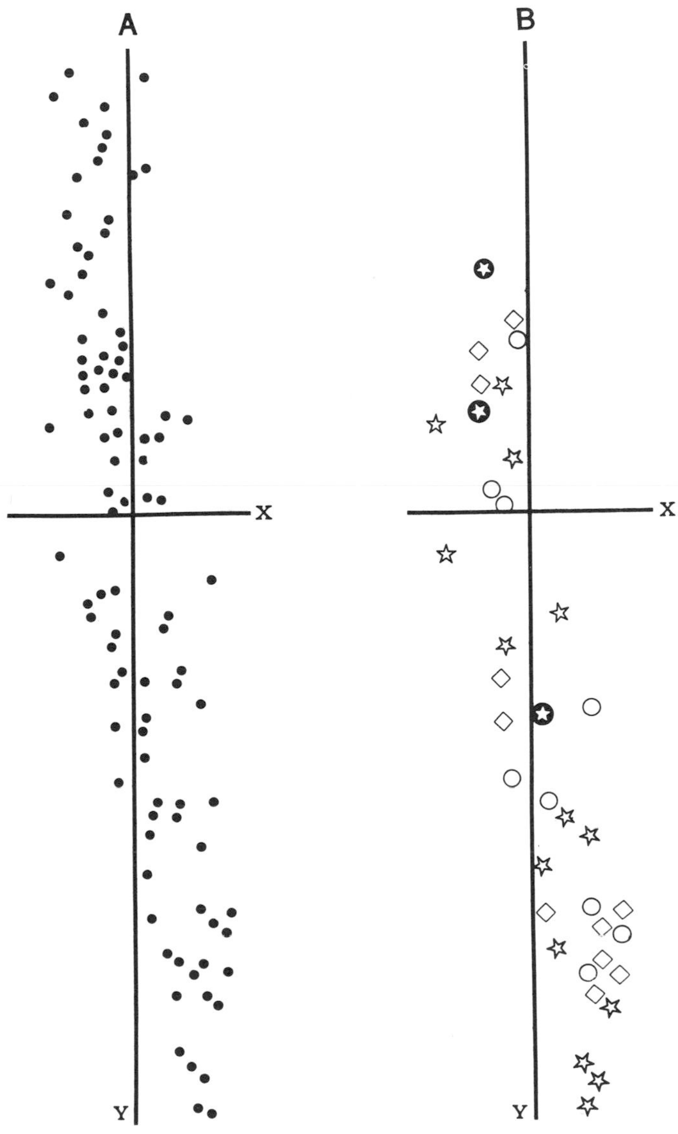

Figure 10.

A. Distribution of 95 countries on a scale of economic-demographic development. Ordinate is a technological scale, abscissa is a demographic scale. Countries with the highest level of development are at bottom right and least developed countries are at top left (see text for explanation).

B. Countries classified by city size distribution. Star is lognormal, star in black circle is primate, diamond and circle are intermediate, former nearer lognormal, latter nearer primate.

development a ready explanation of variations in city size distributions on a scale from simple structure (primacy) to entropy (lognormality).

Conclusions

There are no relationships between type of city size distribution and either relative economic development or the degree of urbanization of countries, although urbanization and economic development are highly associated. It appears that there is a scale from primate to lognormal distributions which is somehow tied to the number and complexity of forces affecting the urban structure of countries, such that when few strong forces obtain primacy results, and when many forces act in many ways with none predominant a lognormal city size distribution is found. Simplicity was associated with indigenous political and administrative controls exercised from orthogenetic primate cities, with dual or multiple colonial economies and controls exercised from heterogenetic primate cities, and with empire capitals, in all cases also combined with small countries. Note that in most instances of primacy these statements apply only to the primate cities themselves, for the system of smaller urban centers is generally distributed lognormally. Complexity was associated with specialized economies, but also with countries which have strong urban traditions and long histories of urbanization, and was found in countries of every size.

8. Regional Development and the Geography of Concentration*

EDWARD L. ULLMAN

THE CONCENTRATION OF DEVELOPMENT, especially industrial, in a few parts of the world, notably the United States and Western Europe, is widely recognized. The contrast in development is just as pronounced in the internal structure of countries, whether it be Northern Italy *vs.* Southern Italy, or Central Japan *vs.* Northern Japan. Equally notable is the disparity within the United States, where, in the northeast, about 7% of the U.S. area has about 70% of the nation's industrial employment; the rest of the country fights for the remainder in a manner not unlike a pack of hungry dogs fighting over a dry bone. The major policy and research problem therefore is created by the other side of the coin - underdevelopment elsewhere.

Our main concern will be the extent of the concentration, particularly in the U.S., and its effect on development of the fringe areas. As to reasons for the concentration it must be conceded that most of the core areas have or had remarkably better natural endowments particularly in productive plains areas than the fringes. Even economists would concede that in Canada, for example, the contrast between southern Ontario and the vast cold northern stretches and the rocky Laurentian Shield provides necessary and sufficient conditions for relative non-development in the latter sections. Australia, Switzerland, the United States and many other countries provide somewhat similar examples of extreme natural differences.

In relating non-development to lack of resources one explains the phenomenon in terms of itself, but such is the nature of resources; they are not resources unless man's technology can use them. It was a fortunate coincidence that the Industrial Revolution, in that important

* Reprinted from *Papers and Proceedings of the Regional Science Association,* Vol. 4 (1958).

phase of its evolution which used coal for generation of steam and manufacture of steel, occurred close to the coal fields of western Europe and eastern United States. In this case precisely what is cause and what is effect is difficult to determine.

Equally important, once the concentration gets started, is the self generating momentum of the concentration itself. The concentration becomes the important geographical fact.[1] A host of complementary activities and services is established, each helping the other in pyramiding the productive process; the largest market in the country is created, in which transport costs dictate location of much industry if national distribution is desired to take advantage of scale economies. For the fringe areas to develop in the face of this formidable competition poses an almost insuperable obstacle.

This is not entirely correct, since the market of the core area is also generally the principal market for the corner area. However, if every part of the world or of a country were equally developed or undeveloped, by definition there would be no underdeveloped areas. By the same token if undeveloped areas develop at an even slower rate than developed areas, as is often the case, they remain relatively undeveloped. The contrast poses the problem.

Even in most non-industrialized countries there is a remarkable concentration of settlement in one portion; this concentration cannot be explained solely by resource endowment. The better areas are crowded beyond reasonable capacity and the remoter areas, many with reasonably good natural endowments, are relatively empty. Reasons for this are obscure, but probably include difficulty of shifting lowland farming techniques to uplands or vice-versa,[2] lack of access roads, and generally a reluctance, apparently, to move away from neighbors and the amenities associated even with a modest level of social overhead.

The problem of concentration thus is world wide. Let us now examine the American situation in detail.

[1]*Cf.* C. D. Harris, "The Market as a Factor in the Localization of Industry in the United States," *Annals of the Association of American Geographers*, XLIV, 1954, p. 315. See also Gunnar Myrdal, *Rich Lands and Poor Lands*, New York, 1957, Ch. III.

[2]Institute of Pacific Relations, *The Development of Upland Areas in the Far East*, New York, 1951; Pierre Gourou, "The Quality of Land Use of Tropical Cultivators," *Man's Role in Changing the Face of the Earth* (Wm. Thomas, ed., Chicago, University of Chicago Press, 1956), pp. 336-49.

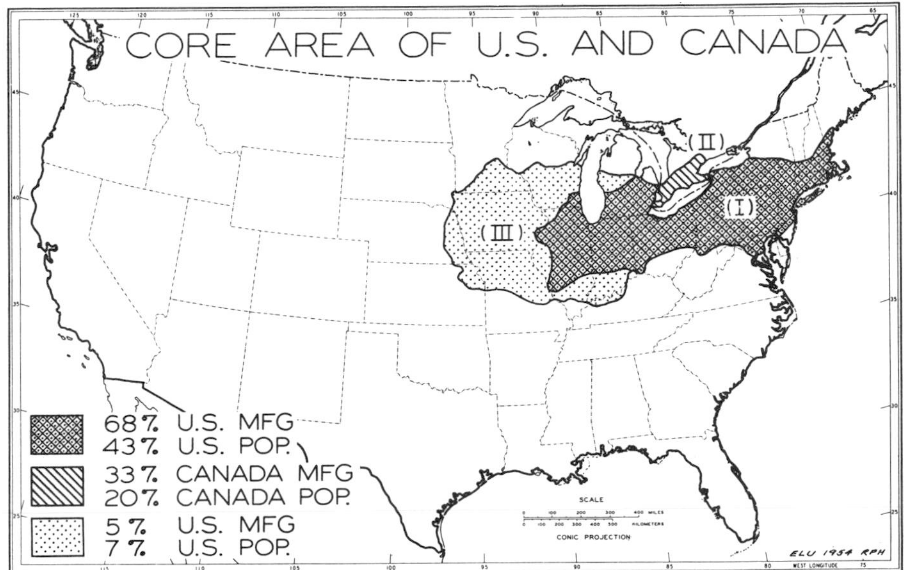

MAP 1. **Core Areas of the United States and Canada. Additional data. Area I (% U.S.): 7.7% area, 52% income, 70% persons listed in *Who's Who*. Area III (% U.S.): 6.9% area, 7.3% income. Areas I & III combined (% U.S.): 14.6% area, 50.3% population, 59% income, 73.3% industrial employment. Area II (% Canada): .4% area, 19.8% population, 33% industrial employment. Areas I & II combined (% U.S. + Canada): 3.7% area, 41.2% population, 65.9% industrial employment. Areas I, II & III combined (% U.S. + Canada): 6.9% area, 47.7% population, 70.8% industrial employment. (For sources see footnotes 3 and 4.)**

CORE AREA OF AMERICA

Map I shows the concentration area in the United States, about 7% of total U.S. area, generally called the industrial belt, since in addition to concentration of population (43% of U.S. total) and income (52% of U.S. total), it is the center of industry with almost 70% of the U. S. total.[3] It has similar or even higher percentages of still

[3]U.S. population calculated from county data in *Census of Population, 1950;* manufacturing employment from county data in *Census of Manufactures, 1947;* income from county figures in U.S. Bureau of the Census, *County and City Data Book, 1949* (A Statistical Abstract supplement, U.S. Government Printing Office, Washington, D. C. 1952). Canadian data from *Census of Canada:* 1951 Vol. IV, Labor Force, Occupations and Manufactures. (Dominion Bureau of Statistics, Ottawa). Note also C. D. Harris' calculation that the belt contains 50% of U.S. retail sales (*op. cit.*, p. 319).

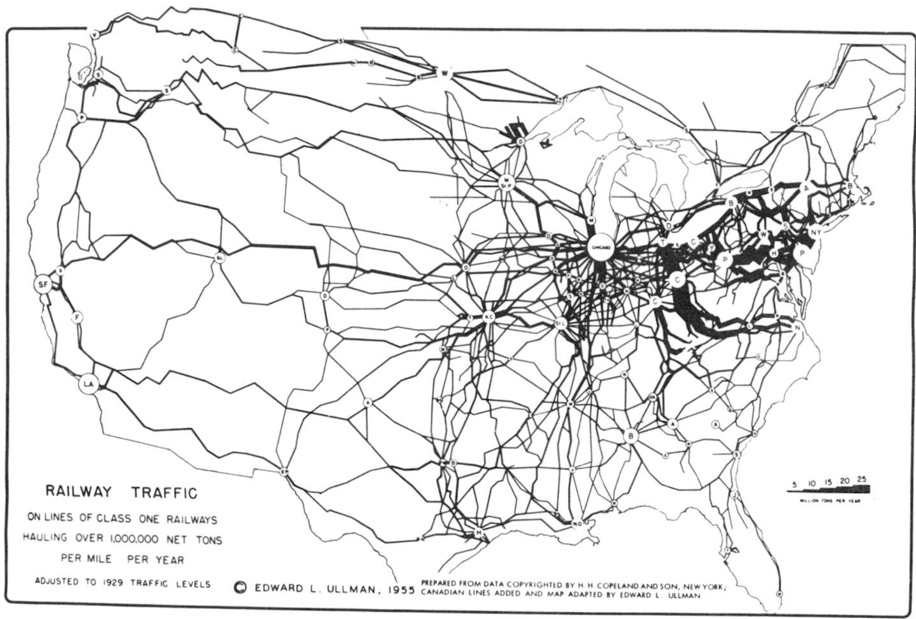

MAP 2. **Railway Traffic in the United States and Canada on Lines of Class One Railways Hauling Over 1,000,000 Net Tons Per Mile Per Year. Widths of lines are proportionate to volume (of short tons of 2,000 lbs.)**

other activities; to name but one example, about 70% of those listed in *Who's Who*.[4] Altogether this is a remarkable concentration, although, as noted earlier, characteristic of the internal areal structure of most countries of the world. Map 2 (R.R. Traffic) also shows the transport net focussing remarkably on the industrial belt; the same would be true of natural gas and petroleum pipe lines. The core area clearly aligns the major flows in the American economy.[5] Map 3, showing shipments of animals and products from the state of Iowa, the leading animal producer, indicates the shipment of the products to the industrial belt and secondarily to California the southern half of

[4]Calculated from locality data in "Geographical Index-Non Current Listings-Necrology, etc.", supplement to *Who's Who in America* (Vol. 28, 1954-55, Chicago, 1954).

[5]*Cf.* Edward L. Ullman, *American Commodity Flow*, University of Washington Press, Seattle, 1957.

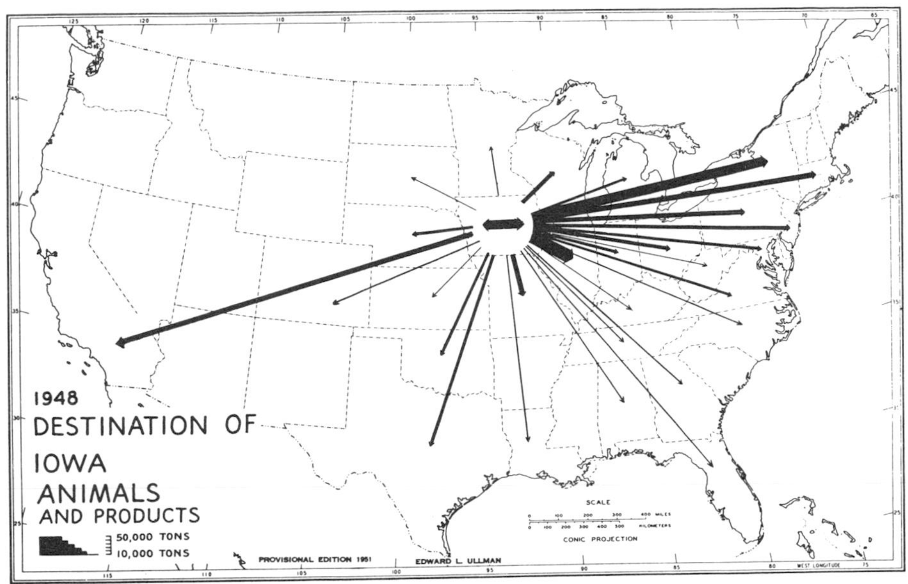

MAP 3. **Destination, by States, of Animals and Products Shipped out of Iowa by Rail, 1948.**
Widths of lines are proportionate to volume (of short tons of 2,000 lbs.)

which has, expecially since the war, developed into a subsidiary and smaller industrial concentration.[6]

INADEQUACY OF STATE DATA TO INDICATE DEGREE OF CONCENTRATION

The map (Map 1) showing the industrial belt was constructed on a county basis. In this manner it was possible to show the really significant concentration better than by using states as building blocks.[7] Furthermore in the process of making the map it was discovered that most of the states of the United States are set up on a "long lot" basis--one

[6]Map 3 prepared from Interstate Commerce Commission's one percent sample of rail traffic reported in *Carload Waybill Analyses*, 1948, Washington, D.C. (statements: 4838, October 1948; 492, January 1949; 498, March 1949; 4920, June 1949).

[7]*Cf.* also Harvey S. Perloff, "Problems of Assessing Regional Progress," *Regional Income, Studies in Income and Wealth*, Vol. 21, National Bureau of Economic Research, N.Y., Princeton, 1957, p. 39.

similar to the classic examples in French Louisiana and Quebec where land holdings are laid down at right angles to the major rivers or foci. The same pattern is followed by many minor civil divisions and counties, most notably some in southern California with their nodes in the coastal oasis and their vast extent stretching out into the empty desert. This long lot characteristic is notable for most of the major states of the industrial belt; New York, Michigan and Wisconsin extend up into the relatively empty Adirondacks or the sterile glacial outwash plains and ice scoured rocks of the north. Illinois, Indiana and Ohio in turn extend southward into relatively less fertile, non-glaciated terrain. To the West, the Great Plains states, from Dakota to Texas, exhibit remarkable long lot characteristics extending from their eastern Gateway nodes, in humid climate, into the semi-arid reaches of the western high plains. The Canadian Provinces also strikingly exhibit this characteristic with their long north-south extent. As a result using most state aggregates creates meaningless averages, masking significant differences and, for our purpose, biasing the results. Using most states and nations to show national averages thus builds in an error, an error for many purposes and places which might almost be more biased than using a world average, which at least has the merit of combining everything, and not just two diametrically opposite aggregates on which extreme long lot political units are based.

ASSEMBLY AND MARKET ADVANTAGES OF CORE AREA

To return to the industrial belt, the reasons for the concentration are similar to those in the rest of the world: a combination of resources, early start, type of settlement, and what is most important for our purposes, a self perpetuating momentum resulting from a pyramiding of complementary activities and services to produce notable external economies of scale and the largest market in the country. As a result most assembly and selling can be most economically done in this area. As just one example, 98% of the members of the American Machine Tool Builders Association, a critical industrial service, are located within the Industrial Belt.[8] Only four are outside; two in contiguous southern states and two in southern California. Chauncy Harris has demonstrated quantitatively and graphically the importance of the industrial belt as the market and place to locate to reach the greatest national customer potential. For the West alone the center of gravity

[8]Data furnished by the Association which includes about 200 of the approximately 300 concerns in the business; over 2/3 of the members are west of Pennsylvania.

is Los Angeles, so large is its population.[9] Finally, it should be emphasized that the market is becoming increasingly important as an industrial location factor because of increasing economies in consumption of fuels and raw materials and other factors. In 1900 each dollar of raw material yielded $4.20 in finished product; in 1950 $7.80, in constant value dollars.[10] Likewise it appears that economies in the shipment of bulky commodities in volume--coal, oil, ores--are increasing relatively to the handling costs of the finished packaged materials, further drawing industry to the market. However, the increasingly lower grade of many non-fuel mineral products may work in the opposite direction, although the main effect is merely to set up, near the ore, concentration plants which employ few, rather than fabricating establishments employing many.

PROSPECTS FOR THE FRINGE AREAS

In contrast to the core areas the prospects for the fringe or corner areas appear rather bleak, since they are remote from the center of the system and the self generating momentum of the center. Their best hope is to possess some special lure such as the present role of climate of California or Florida, or, in the past, superior trees in the Pacific Northwest. Only by such lures have the corner areas been able to overcome their remoteness from the Industrial Belt, as I have noted for amenities in papers published elsewhere.[11]

One special point that deserves attention in the peripheral areas of the United States is that only one part, the South, has markedly lower per capita income than the core area. The West (especially the Pacific Coast) has essentially the same or even higher incomes than the core, whereas the lowest income state in the South, Mississippi, has only about 1/3 the per capita income of the highest in the North, although states not so deep in the South are better off. This is essentially the same pattern as in Italy, where the lowest per capita incomes, in

[9]Chauncy D. Harris, "The Market as a Factor in the Localization of Industry in the United States." *Annals of the Association of American Geographers*, XLIV, 1954, pp. 315-48.

[10]Edw. S. Mason, *Economic Concentration and the Monopoly Problem*, Cambridge, Harvard University Press, 1957, p. 255.

[11]Edward L. Ullman, "Amenities as a Factor in Regional Growth" *Geographical Review*, XLIV, Jan. 1954, pp. 119-32; *Arizona Business and Economic Review*, Vol. 3, No. 4, April 1954 and "A New Force in Regional Growth," *Proceedings Western Area Development Conference*, Stanford Research Institute, Nov. 17, 1954, pp. 64-71.

the Southern provinces, are only about 1/3 those in the north.[12] Presumably somewhat similar disparities exist in other, older settled countries, whereas the newer West of the United States has migration into it controlled by real or psychic income available, rather than having filled up earlier on a low income level, or something like that (precisely what is not germane to our problem). In terms of national percentage of concentration, however, the West and the South are similar, except that the low per capita incomes of the South provide a special lure insofar as lower wage rates attract industry and lower living costs favor labor, although not true to the degree that a lower level of social overhead (schools, roads, etc.) is associated with the lower per capita income and this in turn affects development. Likewise a high labor cost area provides more incentives for innovations in labor saving devices and thus stays ahead of the procession to that degree.

Let us now consider the prospects of corner areas on a purely spatial basis. By definition a corner area would have less area and possibility for large market and concomitant thresholds for economies of scale than would a central location. This is a factor of some importance. If the 1,400,000 population of British Columbia and the 2,600,000 population of Washington were added together a larger market and greater development theoretically would result. In practice this happens for some goods and services which can cross the international border, notably the recently finished long distance natural gas and oil pipelines from the North, which the market of British Columbia alone could not have supported. For most industrial products however the boundary is a barrier, as absence of heavy rail traffic across the border shows (see Map 2). Southern California, and Mexico through remittances, however, also benefit from the flow of Mexican agricultural labor across the border. Miami serves somewhat as an air and resort center for neighboring Latin America, etc., and all corner locations on the ocean can attempt to develop sea trade, which opens up the markets of the world to them. Some leakages thus are available. However in actual practice, even without leakages, corner location need not be crippling because of the possibility of concentrated lures, as at Los Angeles.

A second aspect of the problem is that areas remote from the main market, and thus unable to compete nationally, do by the same token have a protected local market. Here the problem is to develop sufficient economies of scale; southern California appears to be crossing this threshold,

[12] *Cf.* Lloyd Saville, "Sectional Developments in Italy and the United States," *Southern Economic Journal,* XXIII, July 1956, pp. 39-53.

with many branch plants, although exactly how far this has gone is difficult to say.[13]

An institutional factor retarding regional development is the presence of national competition in the United States. This means that no one company gets all the business for one product in a region and hence the threshold of scale economies is not crossed and a local plant is not established. National competition in many lines forces industry to locate in the core and thus results in regional monopoly of the industrial belt, the center of gravity of the country. As a corollary, therefore, one might say that much of our anti-trust policy has worked for regional monopoly of the industrial belt; however, I do not mean to imply that this policy has been any more than a minor factor, or that it is necessarily wrong.

Protection from competition of the industrial belt can also produce advantages not related to scale economies. For example, a large aviation company in the Northwest, the only one in the area, feels that it has greater labor stability than other centers with many competitors because engineers and labor are not constantly shifting from company to company seeking better jobs; consequently, from management's viewpoint the benefits of isolation just about cancel out the drawbacks.

In general terms, however, it seems safe to say that a region in the commercial American economy cannot be expected to grow unless it has some ways of sharing in some aspects of the total national market or supply area--in other words, be nationally commercial or competitive. Something has to bring population into the area before local service can develop to serve it. This is the traditional pattern for development in the U.S., after the earliest subsistence era, as Douglas North has pointed out.[14]

One way to visualize this might be to speculate on what would happen if the United States were divided into a series of 3 to 4 truly independent countries. How would each unit fare? Each would have to compete on the world market, instead of enjoying free access to the national market, to the extent this is permitted today by transport costs and national competition. So many variables are present in terms of varying resource

[13]Edward L. Ullman, "A New Force" etc., p. 70. *Cf.* also the statement about the South, ". . . the new production represents in many instances a filling in of the local industrial structure.", by Glenn E. McLaughlin and Stefan Robock, *Why Industry Moves South,* National Planning Association, Wash., D.C., 1949, p. 125.

[14]Douglas North, "Locational Theory and Regional Economic Growth," *Journal of Political Economy,* LXIII, pp. 243-58.

endowments, scale thresholds, government policies, etc., that it would be difficult to make a definitive reply, but some general logical conclusion can be postulated.

Insight might be gained first by considering Canada. Canada does have branch plants behind her tariff wall, but can sell only non-competitive products freely across the wall into the United States. Canadian per capita income is lower than that of the United States and most of her consumer industrial products are higher priced, presumably because of smaller scale production. The result is a considerably lower real per capita income and, in the past, a net migration toward the United States. If there were no international boundary one might well postulate that Canadian population would be lower, but per capita real income higher, in spite of the fact that Canada would have less of some manufacturing and other activities traditionally associated with high incomes.[15] (However Canada also is a special case; the loss in branch plants would probably be more than compensated for by the spillover of American national industrial belt production into lower Ontario, which is in the heart of the American industrial belt.) Agricultural and competitive raw material prices also would be higher if Canada had free access to the U.S. market, although the terms of trade could be more readily controlled by an independent Canada in the future as U. S. demand for its resources mounts, than would be the case if it were part of the U.S. Canada's present refusal to permit reservoir construction to store water in British Columbia for generation of power downstream in the U.S. lowers Canadian income at present, but may raise it in the future. Likewise the St. Lawrence Seaway would not now be under construction if Canada were a part of the U.S. Urban development, metropolitan services and some transport within present Canada (outside the special case of lower Ontario, if it received national manufacturing) would be lower if it were a part of the U.S. and prices of industrial goods considerably lower.

The general principle at work is the old one that trade benefits both partners considered as a unit but not necessarily each individually, nor the various sectors equally. Thus, we might say that if the international boundary did not exist that population in much of the smaller country, Canada, would be smaller, but per capita incomes would be

[15] *Cf.* Stephen B. Jones' discussion of the draining of trade south down the valleys into the United States from British Columbia via branches of the Great Northern Railway and the counter move of the Canadian Pacific in building the Crowsnest Pass line from East to West to divert these flows to all-Canadian routes. ("The Cordilleran Section of the Canada-United States Borderland," *Geographical Journal*, LXXIX, 1937, pp. 439-50).

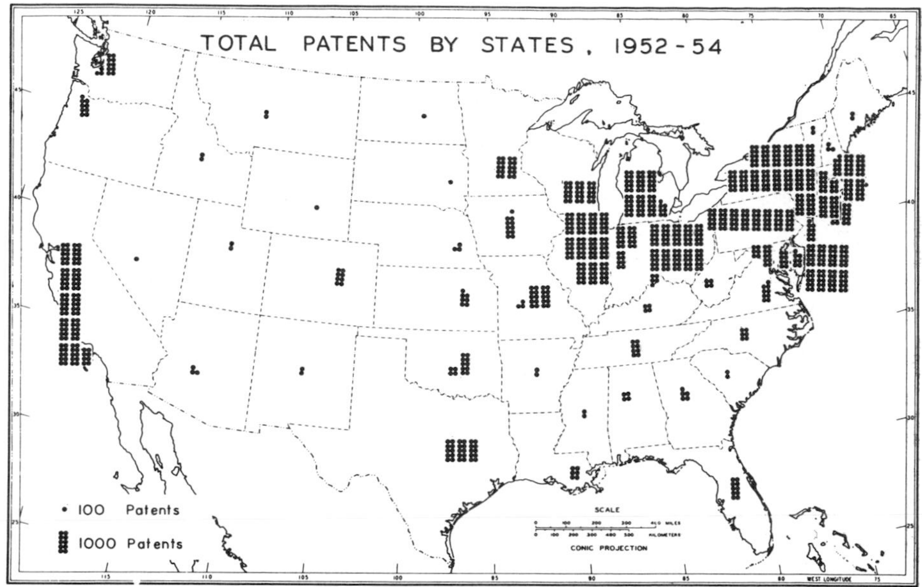

MAP 4. **Distribution of Patents in the United States, by States, 1953-54. (For sources see footnote 17.)**

higher because of fewer members and general spillover of American income levels and prices.[16]

For the reverse process, creation of several individual countries in the United States, the opposite should occur; incomes would drop all over but development might *increase* in the smaller units, but *decrease* in the present core area. In both cases equal relative mobility or immobility of all factors of production (goods, capital, labor, etc.) is assumed.

INNOVATION AND CENTERS OF CONTROL

If the prospects for the fringe areas are bleak, what are their chances of overcoming this disadvantage by innovation and local initiative, especially in developing superior footloose industries and activities

[16]Here we are talking of advanced countries, where Myrdal says "spread" effects operate. *Cf.* other aspects also as treated in Ch. III of Gunnar Myrdal, *Rich Lands and Poor*, N.Y., 1957.

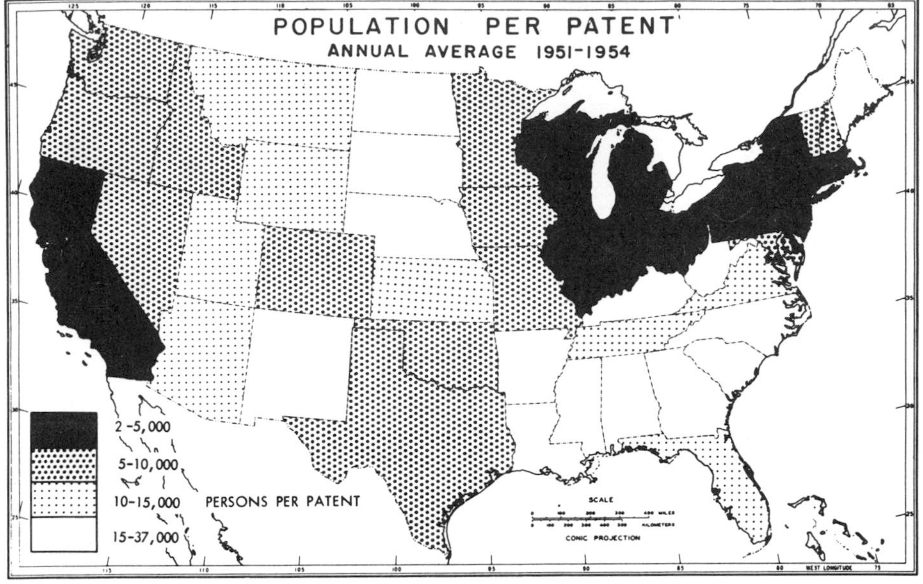

MAP 5. **United States Population Per Patent, by States, Annual Average 1952-54. (For sources see footnote 17.)**

which can enter the national market without undue transport penalty? Can or will they build a better mousetrap? In attempting to predict possibilities here I shall present two sets of findings, which are related to the problem but are by no means conclusive. They are new quantitative measures presented for speculation.

Innovation

Map 4 shows issuance of patents by states. The industrial belt, not surprisingly, has 70% of the patents issued in the country. On a per capita basis the industrial belt states and California rank highest. (Map 5). On a county basis the concentration would be even sharper, but data are not available.[17] Location of patents, of course, is not conclusive evidence of innovation, ability, or application. They may be used anywhere in the country, especially since many of them are

[17]Source of the maps are manuscript reports of the U.S. Patent Office from which a three year annual average, 1951-54, was computed.

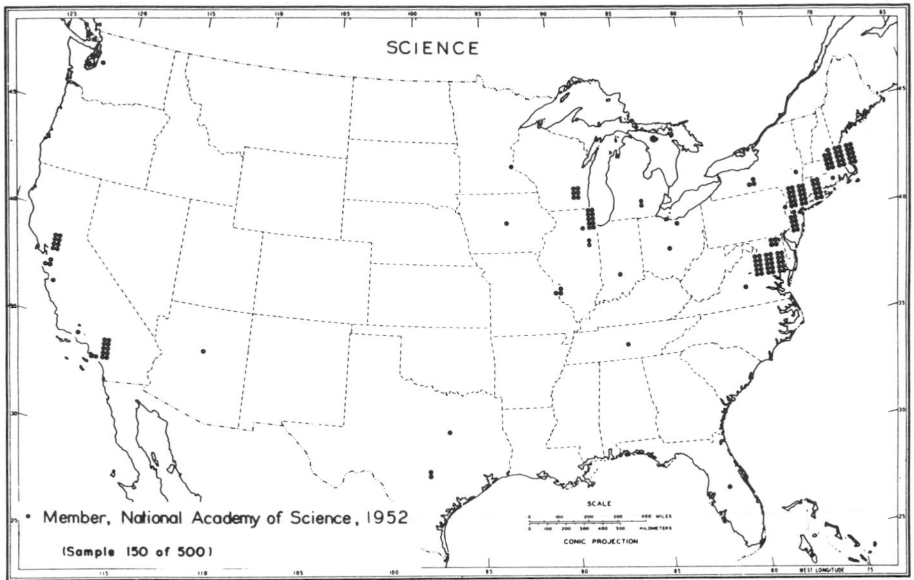

MAP 6. **Distribution of Members of the National Academy of Sciences, United States, 1952. (For sources see footnote 18.)**

granted to industries with nationwide plants. The situation is not the same today as it used to be when a local invention resulted in a local industry. Nevertheless localization of invention does create many localized industries even today, although exactly how many we do not know.

Turning to some other measures of possible innovation or superior technique, some further maps are presented whose bearing on the problem is probably even less direct, but which may at least be of interest for themselves. They are: location of leading scientists and scholars as represented by (1) members of National Academy of Sciences (top scientific honorary), and (2) directors of Social Science Research Council and directors and delegates of American Council of Learned Societies (humanities and social sciences). (See Maps 6 and 7)[18] Note that the concentration is strikingly similar to industry--in the industrial belt and California, except for relatively greater emphasis on the eastern, older half of the industrial belt. (Perhaps a small part of the concentration in the core area occurs because those close to the core are better known, simply because of more frequent contact).

[18]Compiled from rosters furnished by National Academy of Sciences, Social Science Research Council, and A.C.L.S.

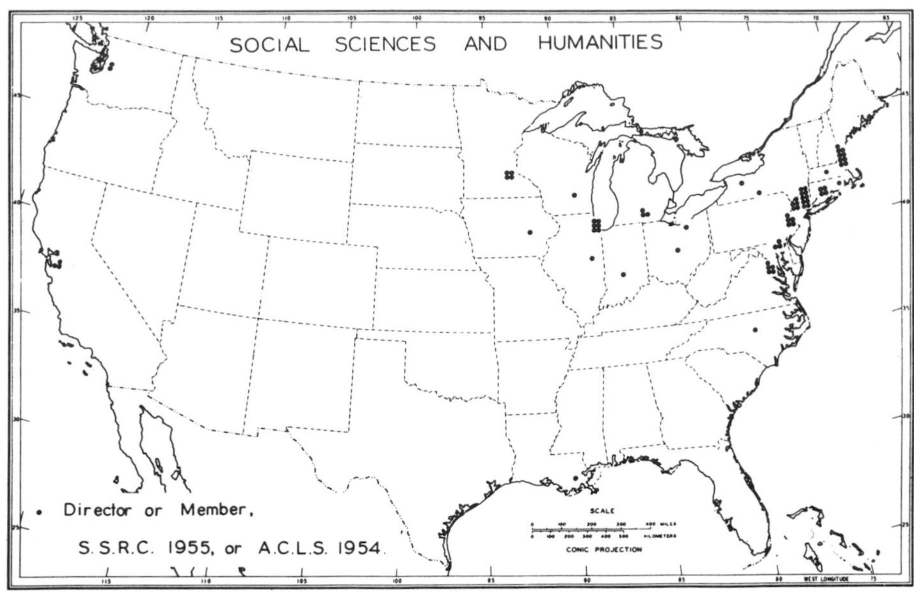

MAP 7. **Distribution of Directors of the U.S. Social Science Research Council, 1955, and of Directors and Delegates of the American Council of Learned Societies, 1954. (For sources see footnote 18.)**

Other maps prepared by the author but not included here show: (1) location of the members of the American Association of Universities and (2) the size and distribution of the 38 largest university libraries, a better measure of eminence. Again, the industrial belt - California orientation emerges. If the universities were ranked on quality, this orientation would be even more pronounced. A recent survey of 25 leading universities by the University of Pennsylvania shows, of the top 15 ranked, that 13 are in the industrial belt (or very close) and the other two in California. Distribution of other large libraries or top engineering schools and industrial-economic research institutes would exhibit similar patterns.

A last map in this series (Map 8), showing book publishing,[19] provides an extreme example of localization; almost all the publishing houses are in New York City. This also reminds us that since the invention of the printing press, ideas can circulate without personal contact, although there is a lag in publication.

[19]Data for year 1954, as reported by Publisher's Weekly, 1955.

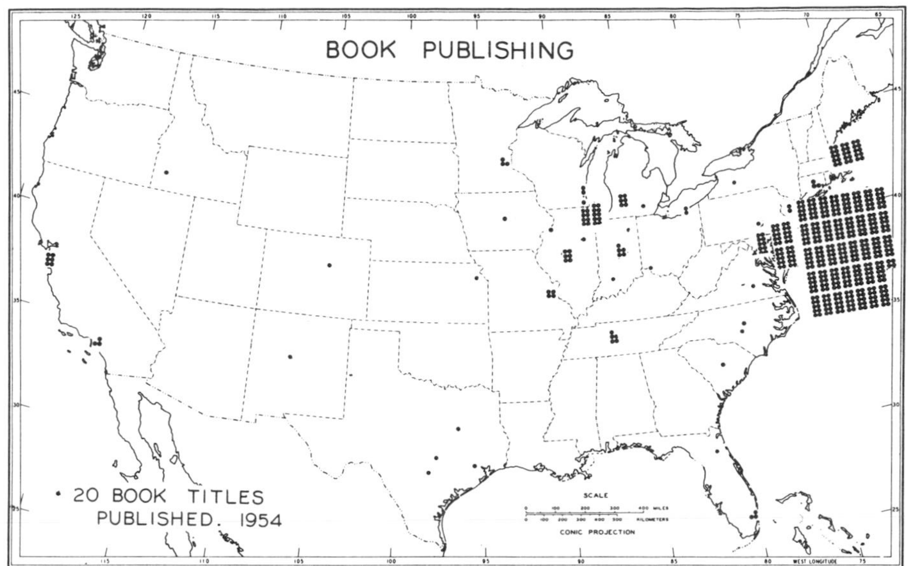

MAP 8. **Distribution of Book Titles Published in the United States, 1954. (For source see footnote 19.)**

How are we to interpret these data? Does the concentration of great minds affect the development of regions? Manifestly, we in the fringe areas today, especially in cities or large institutions, are not as badly off as the Georgia poet Sidney Lanier was in the late 19th century when he found in Baltimore what he missed in the South where there was "not enough attrition of mind on mind ... to... bring out any sparks from a man."[20] Nevertheless the competition and inspiration from association with superior minds does affect the performance of others. Good also tends to attract good. The concentration of brains therefore has some effect on the future localization of intelligence, a legitimate part of regional development. How much effect this in turn has on the general underpinnings of economic development would be more difficult to determine.[21]

[20] Van Wyck Brooks and Otto L. Bettman, *Our Literary Heritage*, New York, 1956, p. 134.

[21] Up to now it has not been the dominant regional influence within all of the U.S., as witness the relative decline of New England, in spite of concentration of certain skills and learning there, although strictly industrial research and development are probably not above the U.S. average. However, New England's initial rise, somewhat of a mystery, its subsequent failure to collapse utterly, and its future prospects, may owe something to local ingenuity and invention; research-based industries are developing and apparently will become more important (*cf.* Richard M. Alt, "Research Based Industries in New England," Arthur D. Little, Inc., Cambridge, Mass., June 22, 1955, especially pp. 8 and 16-22).

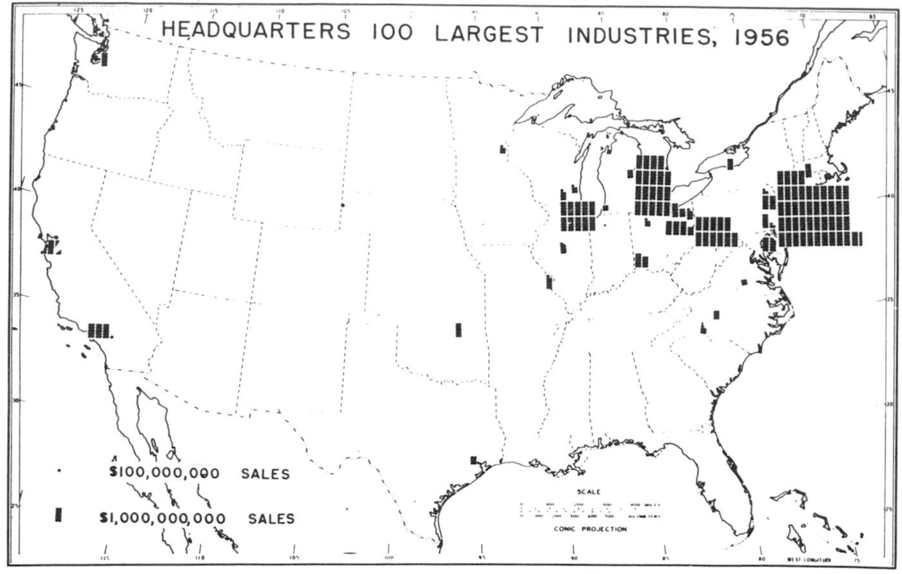

MAP 9. **Distribution of the Headquarters of the 100 Largest Industrial Corporations in the United States, Measured by Dollar Sales, 1956.**
(For sources see footnote 22.)

Centers of Decision Making

Maps showing the location of the 100 and 500 largest industrial corporations indicate that about 90% measured by value of production (or assets) are in the industrial belt, an even higher concentration than for other activities.[22] (See Map 9. The map of the 500 largest industries shows essentially the same distribution and is not included here.) This is natural, since most large industries are national in scope. The home office and principal plants however may not be in the same place, but in a majority of cases they are, except for many New York City headquarters. Even in this case, if home office and principal plants are separated, the principal plant is likely to be in the industrial belt. Maps showing the location of the 100 largest trade corporations show almost the same concentration in the industrial belt.

[22]Maps compiled from *The Fortune Directory of 500 Largest U.S. Industrial Corporations*, Supplement to *Fortune*, July 1957, with assistance from Thomas Directory of Manufactures. U.S. Steel and Pullman Company, for example, were credited to Pittsburgh and Chicago respectively, since these cities are their effective headquarters, even though *Fortune* lists New York as the legal headquarters.

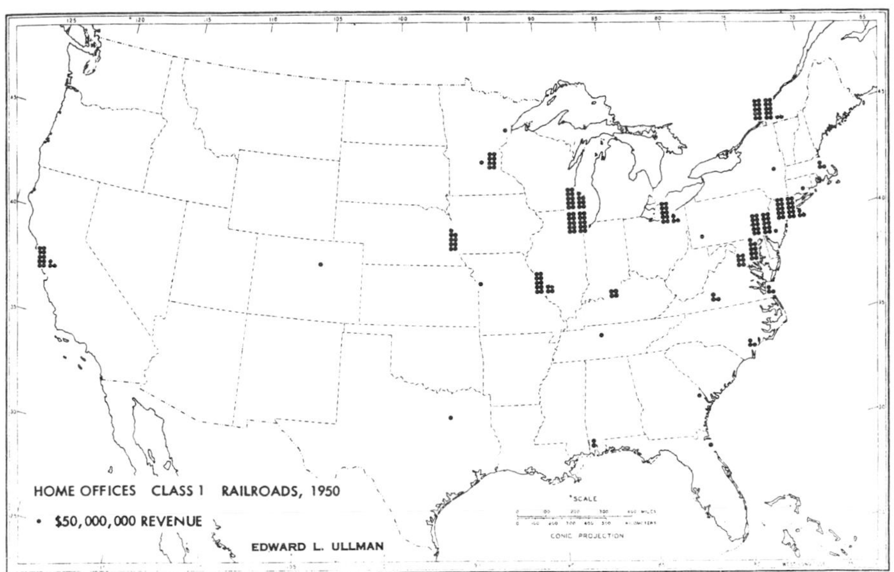

MAP 10. **Distribution of the Headquarters of Class One Railroads in the United States, by Dollar Revenue, 1950.**

The map of home offices of railroads, (Map 10) based on revenue, is especially interesting, inasmuch as it shows location on the margins of the industrial belt, at gateways to the rest of the country (except for Cleveland, a readily explainable special case based on real estate speculation). Major exceptions are port gateways elsewhere in the country.[23]

What does this concentration mean? As in patents, a decision to start something new or expand does not necessarily result in expansion at the headquarters of the company. Often, however, in the absence of compelling reasons, or even without reason, the expansion occurs at or close to headquarters. As one executive of a large company remarked to me "We would be less than human if we did not favor our own location." In any case the research and innovation center is apt to be near home base; furthermore, competing or complementary innovators are regularly spun off from the parent; they establish their own plants, generally on a shoestring, and therefore naturally in the same town. In periods of contraction a company would also be more disposed to close out branch

[23] *Cf.* Edward L. Ullman, ***American Commodity Flow***, University of Washington Press, Seattle, 1957, Ch. 2.

plants than headquarters, as many communities learned to their sorrow during the depression. Exceptions might occur where the branch plant is more modern, but generally fringe areas might be compared to minority groups; "First fired, last hired."

CONCLUSION

Concentration within countries is the rule. This fact may signal the operation of a general localization principle in man's use of the earth: initial location advantages at a critical stage of change become magnified in the course of development.[24] Geographical differentiation starts out as a matter of homeopathic doses of mild concentration and winds up as a system of massive localization based on a wide range of internal and external economies of scale. This direction continues until some radical new change is precipitated and indeed may persist, even though new competitors arise elsewhere, through several such changes including cataclysmic wars or development of new energy sources, as in the shift from wood to coal to petroleum and, in the future perhaps, even to nuclear energy. The really significant geography thus becomes the latter concentration of man himself, his works, his institutions, and his inventive momentum.

This concentration in practice takes the form of an area of concentration in many countries[25] as in the American industrial belt, rather than building up to one point, as Haig theoretically postulated some years ago.[26] Reasons are obscure, but are probably related to resource

[24]For a remarkably similar concept note Gunnar Myrdal, *Rich Lands and Poor*, in *World Perspectives*, Vol. 16, Ruth N. Anshen ed., New York, 1957, pp. 26-27. I discovered these statements after writing this paper. They read in part; "... play of the forces in the market normally tends to increase, rather than to decrease, the inequalities between regions," and "occasionally these favored localities and regions offer particularly good natural conditions for the economic activities concentrated there; in rather more cases they did so at a time when they started to gain a competitive advantage." Still other statements are similar, including noting of the hampering of industrial growth in southern Italy after unification removed tariff barriers (pp. 28-29).

How provision of transport routes and establishment of commodity rates alone accentuates and perpetuates initial areal differences is set forth in my "The Role of Transportation and the Bases for Interaction" in *Man's Role in Changing the Face of the Earth*, Wm. L.T. Thomas, ed., Chicago, 1956, p. 865.

[25]Except for the primate city in some countries and former Colonial areas.

[26]R. M. Haig, "Toward an Understanding of the Metropolis: Some Speculations Regarding the Economic Base of Urban Concentration," *Quarterly Journal of Economics*, XL, 1926, pp. 179-208.

distribution and processing requirements, as Haig implied, and to strategic values of different sites for different purposes. In practice, of course, the concentration is at points--cities--in an area.

The American industrial belt might also be considered as divided by the relatively less developed Appalachian barrier into two halves; seaboard, with New York as capital and central, with Chicago as largest city. Added to this would be a third, smaller node, southern California, protected by distance from the industrial belt competition, with Los Angeles as center of gravity. This arrangement superficially appears to coincide with a rank-size rule--New York, Chicago, Los Angeles, (especially if one considers Philadelphia an abberration!). However, the fit is too inexact, there is leakage in the system, especially through the port of New York and other ports and, most important, there are national functions in the two halves of the industrial belt. New York and Washington, however, are of a higher order on the hierarchy for many national services involving intangible flows, including finance and government; conversely, the western half is higher for many large scale industrial and distribution activities involving tangible flows. Part of the mischief is caused by the center, New York, being on the edge of the country and thus not advantageously located for national assembly and distribution of many products.[27]

Prospects for the corner of fringe areas to compete with the core area are bleak, as many have noted, because of transport costs to the market and lack of local economies of scale, together with the assembly advantages of the core area. The marked concentration of innovation and decision making in the core area also favors that area, insofar as an effect can be deduced.

Prospects for the fringe areas are not all hopeless. Room exists for use of ingenuity in discovering and promoting still more distinctive lures in the fringe regions; later generations of entrepreneurs in the core area may become complacent, or old plants less efficient as a result of inherited obsolescence. Even mere emptiness of a remote area can become a lure, as witness the establishment of the atomic bomb range in southern Nevada, the best site in the country for this purpose.[28] However, such advantages tend to be exceptions rather than the rule in the world today, in spite of exhaustion of many natural resources near the present centers.

[27]C.D. Harris, *op. cit.*

[28]Within urban areas emptiness may provoke spectacular growth in furnishing large blocks of vacant land for large scale subdivisions, shopping centers, or even airports located on swampy ground.

A final factor of great importance is direct government intervention to even the competition, whether it be on the international level with capital and technical assistance, or particularly on the national level as the Cassa per Mezzogiorno--Fund for the South--in Italy. In the United States the same occurs with reclamation projects, highway allocations, and the like. Fringe areas do have votes; in Italy they are numerous, since one poor vote is more or less equal to one rich vote; in the United States our built-in system of equal state representation in the senate gives added representation and political power to the West and South. To a degree this compensates for the unequal distribution of economic power, although I have no intention of pursuing the point. In any event the "early" stages of development often are subsidized by someone for welfare reasons, whether it be children by parents or schools, or new metals such as titanium and magnesium, or new weapons such as airplanes by the government. Fringe regions are no exception, with low income fringe regions in particular even receiving an extra measure of assistance for humane reasons.

The policy problem is to determine how far fringe assistance should go in terms of benefiting the total national welfare and not harming other sectors elsewhere. Internal country assistance tends to be greater than international, in spite of the fact that mobility of population and other factors are greater internally than internationally. At the same time that the negro moves North, the federal government builds super highways in the South and pressure mounts for increased federal aid to education. As a result of these twin forces of increased mobility and increased national subsidy, disparity of per capita development within countries, at the least, will be less than would be the case without the operation of these forces. If one postulates that these forces will be reasonably effective, then intranational disparity in concentration will be measured more in absolute terms of population density, industrial build-up and the like, and not so much in per capita income. On the world wide scene such a degree of anticipation is not so warranted, because of lack of either extensive mobility or sufficient extra-regional and world wide assistance. However, some developments work in this direction, as with the proposals for the European Common Market, which includes not only free exchange of goods and capital, but also of persons, within the six nations. Thus, Europe appears to be moving toward the pattern and scale of the United States.

9. The Development of Spatial Distributions of Towns in Sweden: An Historical-Predictive Approach[1]*

RICHARD L. MORRILL

THE city or town is now the home of the majority of the population of the more developed countries, but the rise of a modern urban culture has been rapid and rather recent. This phenomenon fascinates scholars in many fields. In geography, attention has centered on three aspects of urbanization: the general nature of urbanization,[2] the detailed analysis of cities, and, within the framework of central place theory,[3] explanation of the size and location of places.

This paper attempts a rather general approach to the development of the spatial distribution of towns. The approach recognizes that urbanization involves more than the location of central place activities; much urban support derives, of course, from activities that do not depend on a local hinterland. Furthermore, the development of urbanization takes place through time, and conditions are constantly changing. For this study an experimental model has been developed in which a pattern of town distribution gradually emerges. The predictive model, of course, rests upon such general knowledge about the process of urbanization as has been accumulated over the years. For verification, the model was applied to a study area in Sweden. The objective of the paper is to develop a theory out of the study of real patterns, the test of which is whether the actual patterns could have been reproduced by the suggested theory.

The discussion that follows is in four parts: first, a discussion of the major factors which must be taken into account in the study of urbanization; second, a tentative description of the process of urbanization; third, a review of the application of the model to a study area in Sweden; and finally, a summary of the suggested model of urban development.

THE PROBLEM OF URBANIZATION AND MIGRATION

The distribution of towns in any region (implying their location *and* size) is the result of a long and complex interplay of forces. At the very least, any study which proposes to explain the origins of such patterns must take into account these major factors: (1) the economic and social conditions which permit and/or encourage concentration of economic activities in towns and cities; (2) the spatial or geographic conditions which influence the spacing and size of towns; (3) the fact that such development takes place gradually over time; and (4) recognition that there is an element of uncertainty or indeterminancy in all behavior.

The economic aspects of urbanization have

[1] This paper is a partial report of research carried out at the University of Lund in Sweden under a grant from the National Science Foundation, Office of Social Sciences. Professor Torsten Hägerstrand was most generous in his aid to this research. A detailed presentation of methods, historical background, and findings is in preparation and will be published in *Series B, Lund Studies in Human Geography* (1963).

[2] A. E. Smailes, *The Geography of Towns* (London: Hutchinson's University Library, 1953), pp. 7–83. Harold M. Mayer and Clyde F. Kohn (eds.), *Readings in Urban Geography* (Chicago: University of Chicago Press, 1959): Kingsley Davis, "The Origin and Growth of Urbanization in the World," pp. 59–68, and Robert L. Dickinson, "The Growth of the Historical City," pp. 69–84. Paul K. Hatt and Albert J. Reiss, *Cities and Society* (Glencoe: Free Press, 1957), pp. 64–222.

[3] For an annotated summary of central place work, see Brian J. L. Berry and Allan Pred, *Central Place Studies,* Bibliography Series No. 1 (Philadelphia: Regional Science Research Institute, 1961).

*** Reprinted from *Annals of the Association of American Geographers,* Vol. 53 (March 1963).**

been actively studied and have yielded information concerning the rate and direction of economic expansion, economies of agglomeration for activities in cities, threshold conditions for successful entry of activities, and the importance of technological change on the utilization of resources, natural and human. These data influence the kinds, scale, and spatial extent and grouping of activities and hence play a major role in the location and sizes of towns.

The spatial analysis of distributions of towns comprises three aspects: central place theory asks how large an area is necessary to support towns, what is an efficient spacing of settlements, if there is an hierarchy of settlements. Central place activities can be considered as those which serve a local market. The underlying assumption is that man makes some effort at organizing his activities over space in an efficient manner. Central place theory seeks to ascertain what is the most efficient division of space, given an array of functions.

In contrast, industrial location theory treats the spatial distribution of activities which serve regional or national markets and which depend on a complex of resources, transport connections, labor supplies, etc. These are nevertheless of even greater importance than central place activities as support for urban populations. A realistic model of urbanization cannot ignore one or the other. An example of their mutual dependence is the emergence of an irregular central place net upon a mining-industrial complex or an agricultural base.

The spatial process of the development of rural land uses, especially in agricultural and forest locations, provides a close link between the natural environment and human settlement. However, for purposes of this study, the effects of rural land use are subsumed through the location of central place and other activities which the rural land uses and population support.

The growth of cities based upon the location and concentration of activities implies migration. Migration is the process in space through which the redistribution of population occurs. In the early stages of urbanization, almost the entire population of the new cities must have migrated from rural life. The pertinent spatial questions concern migration distances, types of migrants, and motivations of migrants.

These spatial processes of central place location, industrial location, rural land use, and migration give rise to the observed distribution of settlement—a scatter of towns, a few larger ones, many smaller ones, and a transportation network linking the towns and cities. Together they specify the spatial dimension of urbanization.

The important role of the element of time is suggested by the very word, development. It is not possible to study a spatial process in isolation.[4] The present settlement pattern is the result of a long interplay of forces. The historical dimension is of crucial importance to the study of urban development for three reasons: (1) technologies change; (2) the characteristics of the urban population and physical plant are constantly being modified; (3) locational decisions are made at a point in time, after which social and economic conditions may radically change. Established locations possess great inertia; once decided upon, removal is difficult. An efficient decision at one time may be rendered obsolete well within the lifetime of the facility. Previous locations, later seen as good or bad, must powerfully influence future locations. One must therefore ask whether the fact of growth in time supports or alters central place or industrial location conceptions as presently formulated.

Central place theory has undergone significant development in recent years. A contention of this paper is that a further improvement can be realized through consideration of time as well as space, that is by requiring the locational concepts of central place theory to operate in an historical context. The gradual unfolding of distributions of towns over a long period of changing economic and social conditions helps account for the discrepancies found between theoretical and observed patterns.[5]

One reason for developing a model which operates in time is that our evaluation of space

[4] See also J. M. Blaut, "Space and Process," *The Professional Geographer*, Vol. XII, No. 4 (1961), pp. 3–5.

[5] For other discussions of these discrepancies see *Papers and Proceedings*, Lund Symposium on Urban Geography, International Geographical Congress, Lund, 1960. (Lund: 1963).

changes with technological improvement, for example, with transportation innovation. However, even if this were not true, the fact that growth as such is a process of change requires an expanded central place theory. Places do not suddenly change functional level, but gradually add new activities. Hinterlands expand and contract. Commercialization and urbanization began in certain areas and slowly spread.[6] Under conditions of a moving frontier of settlement the effect of time is even more apparent.[7] The off-center gateway city is a case in point. Thus, at any one time the perfect equilibrium that static theory suggests can never exist in fact.

The development of spatial distributions of towns then, takes place over time within a changing economic and social setting and is subject to changing conditions influencing location. A theory or model could now be devised which would determine in a strict economic or geometric manner all locational decisions. Our knowledge of the real world, however, requires us to admit the operation of another dimension to the problem—randomness. In other words, locational decisions are subject to errors or uncertainties which we cannot specify or wish away. Human decisions are rarely perfect. People may not know a correct decision or be able to distinguish between almost equally good alternatives. Generally, in a period of time, there are many more possible locations for plants, or destinations for migrants, than plants to establish or persons to move. Some kind of random decision, like coin-tossing, is required to decide in the face of such uncertainty. Finally, theories are simplifications and usually deal only with the major variables. Many small forces, whose net effect may often be considered random, also exist. Real patterns of activities and towns will be approximations growing out of many less than perfect decisions. If real patterns are to be understood, theory must incorporate this uncertainty.

THE DEVELOPMENT OF DISTRIBUTIONS OF TOWNS

The development of an urban pattern is a growth process involving the location of central place activities, that is, those which serve a local hinterland, non-central place activities, for example much manufacturing and transportation which have a non-local market, and migration, which provides many of the people for the growing towns.

Central Place Activities

The basic notion in central place theory is that those activities which serve a surrounding population vary widely in the minimum population, purchasing power, or threshold, needed for their support.[8] Functional groupings of activities with similar thresholds, that is levels of urban function, are recognizable for a given time. A central place of the lowest level emerges, or an existing central place rises in importance, as it is able to satisfy these basic conditions: to dominate a hinterland with a population at least equal to the minimum needed, all parts of which are closer to the new central place than to any other existing central place. This becomes possible as density of population increases, or as increasing wealth (as from industrialization and commercialization) of the society enables the same population to support a greater volume and variety of activities. Locations midway between existing centers are most likely to become new centers, since they will be the first to be able to secure an adequate hinterland.[9] Under perfect conditions, an hexagonal pattern of places would emerge (if there were only central place activities.)

However, imagine an elongated area, which at a point in time is just able to support two central places. As wealth increases, the minimum threshold falls, and these two places enjoy "excess markets" until a new central place emerges.[10] Many specific locations can be expected to try to become a new center. There may exist one "best" location, but there may be several which satisfy the conditions of a

[6] Torsten Hägerstrand, *Innovationsförloppet ur korologisk synpunkt* (Lund: 1953). For a summary see "Propagation of Innovation Waves," *Lund Studies in Geography*, Series B, No. 4 (1952).

[7] In Richard L. Morrill, "Simulation of Central Place Patterns over Time," *op. cit.*, Lund Symposium in Urban Geography, 1960, this aspect is treated in some detail.

[8] B. J. L. Berry, and W. L. Garrison, "A Note on Central Place Theory and the Range of a Good," *Economic Geography*, Vol. 34 (1958), pp. 304–11.

[9] Sven Godlund, "The Function and Growth of Bus Traffic Within the Sphere of Urban Influence," *Lund Studies in Geography*, Series B, No. 18 (1956).

[10] B. J. L. Berry, and W. L. Garrison, *op. cit.*

sufficient hinterland. Which succeeds in winning out over its rivals is, in historical fact, found to depend on much more than geometry (a midway position). The presence or absence of manufacturing and mining activities and transportation facilities, entrepreneurial skill, and an element of chance, as well as the present population and its characteristics may be decisive, and these factors must be incorporated into an adequate theory.

Non-central Place Activities

Non-central place activities, typified by much manufacturing and by many transport routes, do not depend upon carving out local hinterlands. Many locations, whether a central place, or close or far from one, may compete for such activities. The probability of an area obtaining investments and employment varies with population (labor force) and its characteristics, size of existing settlements, the nature and extent of already existing activities (both urban and rural), transport position, and, of course, natural resources.

A complete theory would include an industrial location analysis for each possible addition of every type. Since the purpose of this study is to understand general distributions of towns and not specific industrial patterns, the location of manufacturers is treated at a secondary level. That is, if we take all the specific plant location decisions for a year, and look at them as a "set of plants or investments" to be allocated without concern for type, it is found that a random assignment (with restricted choice), taking into account the greater attraction of skilled labor pools, good transport, etc., will closely approximate the real pattern of location. A valuable simplification of model, a substitution of partial analysis, is thus permitted.

Migration

Migration is of fundamental importance to the development of the human landscape. Although it is a process in space, it has not been widely studied by geographers. International migration has been extensively studied, particularly by historians and demographers. Although there are often similarities in motivation between internal and international population movements, the latter involve political problems normally absent in more local movement. The displacement of persons as a result of political change has been reviewed recently by Velikonja.[11] Migration has been studied in three ways: (1) Migration to and from a state or country may be analyzed.[12] Such studies reveal factors which both encourage and restrict movements. Hence, they provide hypotheses to be tested for inclusion in a study of migration. (2) A common approach is a detailed socio-economic survey of regional or national migration or redistribution of population.[13] Such surveys often provide statistical tests of many notions about migration; for example, that there is a relation between migration volume and distance.[14] (3) Another group has provided models of migration.[15] Some of these are deterministic, that is, the

---

[11] Joseph Velikonja, "Postwar Population Movements in Europe," *Annals,* Association of American Geographers, Vol. 48 (December, 1958), pp. 458–71.

[12] For example, J. Fraser Hart, "Migration and Population Change in Indiana," *Proceedings,* Indiana Academy of Science (Indianapolis: 1957), pp. 195–203. Walter M. Kollmorgen, and George Jenks, "A Geographic Study of Population and Settlement Changes in Sherman County, Kansas," *Transactions* of the Kansas Academy of Science (Lawrence: 1951), pp. 449–94. Richard L. Morrill, "Regional Growth and Net Migration," *University of Washington Business Review,* Vol. 21 (1962), pp. 5–13. Warren S. Thompson, "Migration within Ohio, A Study of Redistribution of Population," *Scripps Foundation Studies in Population Distribution,* No. 3 (Oxford, Ohio: Scripps Foundation for Research in Population Problems, Miami University, 1951).

[13] Donald J. Bogue, et al., "Streams of Migration between Subregions," *Scripps Foundation Studies in Population Distribution,* No. 5 (Oxford, Ohio: Scripps Foundation for Research in Population Problems, Miami University, 1953). *Migration in Sweden,* A Symposium. Lund Studies in Human Geography, Series B, No. 13 (University of Lund, 1957). *Population Redistribution and Economic Growth,* Simon Kuznets and D. S. Thomas, eds. (Philadelphia: American Philosophical Society, 1959). Warren C. Thornthwaite, *Internal Migration in the United States,* Bulletin 1, Study of Population Redistribution (Philadelphia: University of Pennsylvania Press, 1934).

[14] Esse Lövgren, "The Geographic Mobility of Labor," *Geografiska Annaler,* Vol. 38 (1956), pp. 344–94. Phillip Nelson, "Migration, Real Income, and Information," *Journal of Regional Science,* Vol. 1, No. 2 (1959), pp. 43–74. Larry A. Sjaastad, "The Relationship between Migration and Income in the United States," *Papers of the Regional Science Association,* Vol. 6 (1960), pp. 37–64.

[15] For a summary of migration models see: Walter Isard, "Migration Estimation," Chapter 3, *Methods of Regional Analysis* (New York: John Wiley & Sons,

migrant's destination is determined by economic or distance conditions;[16] and others are probabilistic, that is, involve individual choice.[17] Recently the importance of individual social contact has been stressed.[18]

The migration involved in the development of town distributions is primarily an internal circulation between rural and rural, rural and urban, and urban and urban locations. Throughout the period of urbanization the net effect of such movements generally has been the transfer of rural population to urban locations. Migration is normally an individual or family movement which seems to depend on three major controls: (1) Distance between the origin and possible destinations. As the distance from his origin increases, an individual is likely to have contact with a smaller and smaller proportion of available opportunities. The effect of distance as a barrier to migration changes over time, primarily with improvements in transportation and communication. Intervening opportunities may modify the role of distance. (2) The differential attractiveness of areas, both those of present residence, and those of possible destinations. The most important attraction is the greater economic opportunity in more urban and/or wealthier areas, but climate and other amenities play an increasing role. (3) Information, in the sense that migrants must know about an opportunity in order to move to it. Frequently people migrate to areas to which friends and relatives have previously moved.

These factors are brought together into a "simulation" model, a kind of probability model. It is necessary to state here that simulation refers to an experimental procedure of restricted choice which identifies a process—here urbanization and migration—and generates patterns which are similar to actual ones. Before the model procedure is outlined, however, the application of the model to a study area in Sweden will be presented. The model can then be seen in terms of a practical example.

APPLICATION OF THE MODEL

In this study the simulation model takes as a starting point the population pattern at a particular time. Then, for a selected later time period, assigns, i.e., chooses by means of random numbers, locations for new transport links (out of many possible ones), assigns locations for manufacturing or other non-central place activities, and assigns locations for central place activities. Each stage depends on the previous stage. These assignments of activities change the attractiveness of areas; i.e., the anticipated urban population creates new opportunities. The model then assigns, or chooses paths for migrants, between all areas, in reflection of the altered opportunities. A new population structure results and the entire process is repeated in another time period. A flow-diagram illustrates this process.

Pattern at time 1 → Assign new transport links → Assign new manufactures → Assign new central places → Pattern at time 1 modified by urban population anticipated from above assignments

↓

repeat for next time period ← new pattern at time 2 ← assign migrants between areas

Data Sources

Sweden is a valuable area in which to conduct social studies, since rather accurate and detailed census statistics date from about 1750. These include most changes of property and residence. The Census of Population is complete from 1750 for very small areas which have remained extraordinarily stable over the entire period. Data on details of migration are available, although use of parish church records is required. Data on the industrial

1960). Richard L. Morrill, "The Development of Models of Migration and the Role of Electronic Processing Machines," International Symposium in the Human Sciences: The Measure of Human Displacement (Monaco, May 1962).

[16] Esse Lövgren, "Mutual Relations Between Migration Fields," in *Migration in Sweden, op. cit.* (1957), pp. 159–69. S. A. Stouffer, "Intervening Opportunities: A Theory Relating Mobility and Distance," *American Sociological Review*, Vol. 5 (1940). G. K. Zipf, *Human Behavior and the Principle of Least Effort* (Cambridge: Harvard University Press, 1949), pp. 386–415.

[17] T. Hägerstrand, "Migration and Area," *Migration in Sweden, op. cit.* (1957), pp. 126–52. R. Porter, "Approach to Migration Through its Mechanism" *Geografiska Annaler*, Vol. 38 (1956), pp. 317–43. Daniel Price, "A Mathematical Model of Migration Suitable for Simulation on an Electric Computer," *Proceedings*, International Population Conference (Wien: 1959), pp. 665–73.

[18] Hägerstrand, *op. cit.* (1957), pp. 27–158. Benjamin Luebke, and J. F. Hart, "Migration from a Southern Appalachian Community," *Land Economics*, Vol. 34 (1958), pp. 44–53.

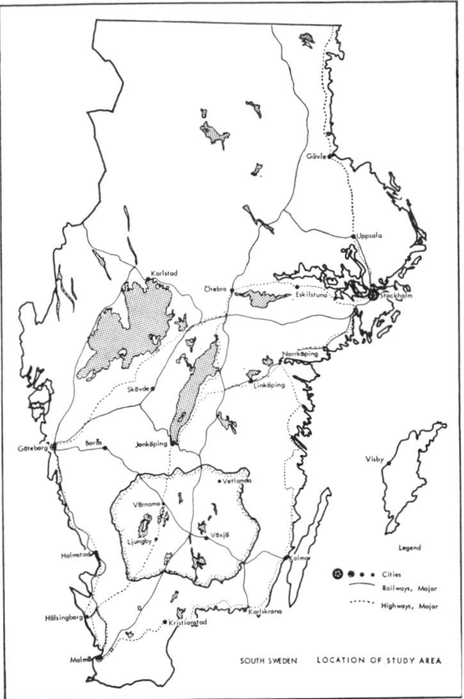

FIGURE 1

structure of places with a population as small as 50 are available.[19] The information on conditions in 1850 was taken from regional maps and histories of the period.

The Study Area

The particular study area was chosen for its simplicity and convenience. The boundaries generally enclose functional units. The area is restricted in size and population and contains no large cities or ports. Nevertheless it is a regional microcosm of the national urban pattern, and in fact of the urban pattern of any developed country. The same reasons for urbanization apply; the same kinds of economic activities are carried on; the same spatial forces which tend to produce an efficient pattern of towns are present. The distinctive geographic conditions of the area have contributed to a distinctive distribution of towns, to be sure, if one wishes to emphasize individuality.

Historical Survey

The study area, situated in southern Sweden, is traversed by the main north-south railway and highway (Fig. 1). The population of about 270,000 has a density of less than 50 per square mile, which is low by European standards. The area lacks much good farmland; most of the land is forested. Although the wood industry (in all forms) is the most important, the area is one of a great diversity of small industries. Industrialization did not begin until 1865 and was not really significant before 1880. By 1960, however, manufacturing supported over 40 per cent of the population, whereas agriculture and forestry supported but 30 per cent. In contrast to the United States, here one finds small factories scattered in towns and villages. Most famous are probably the glass factories, e.g., those at Orrefors and Kosta.

Figure 2 depicts the contemporary scene. Dominance of north-south transportation routes is evident. A fairly wide sprinkling of urban-type settlements occurs; their distribution closely reflects the railway pattern. The objective of this research was to trace the development of this distribution to discover the conditions which produced it, and to express them in a model which would produce a similar distribution.

As recently as 1850 urban development was extremely limited. Pressure on the land was great, and very large-scale migration to America was just beginning. Emigration reached its peak between 1870 and 1890. The distribution (about 1850) of parish churches, principal roads, inns, and mills is given in Figure 3. The population was rather evenly distributed. Only the local capital and three small regional towns provided a framework for the later urban development.

Construction of the main north-south railway (Stockholm-Malmö) by 1865 provided the impetus for beginning industrialization. The route chosen was a straightened version of an old high road, but it deliberately bypassed principal towns. However a connection was built to the local capital the next year. This first line has always maintained its domi-

[19] *Tätortsregister*: Jonköping och Kronobergs Del., ed. Sven Dahl. (Stockholm: Geografiska Institution vid Handekshögskolan [Community Register]).

nance; hence many of the station villages created in the construction period have become important small industrial and commercial centers. The central place pattern was distorted by the railway—i.e., attracted partially to it. By 1880, fifteen years after the first railway, about twenty non-agricultural villages had developed, and the earlier towns grew rapidly. Some of the manufacturing development was in anticipation of a railroad. Perhaps only eight of these villages had any significant central place functions. A large-scale movement of population had begun to the towns and new station villages from the overcrowded countryside.

The period 1880–1900 was one of net population loss from migration, but the towns and villages continued to gain population. These settlements frequently developed out of stations on the new railways. Village growth was at the expense of rural areas of their own and neighboring parishes (Fig. 4). By 1900 there were about thirty-five towns and villages, most of which were growing very rapidly. Many railway lines were built. The motivation for some seems to have been to connect the new towns to the main north-south railway, but for others the motivation was to connect more important outside places.

The urban situation in 1910 is shown in Figure 5. Although the population at this time could support about eighteen basic central places, only fourteen had developed.[20] This discrepancy was simply the result of the spacing of earlier centers, which at this point in time were far enough apart to give many of them excess markets, but not far enough to permit new centers between. (See also Figures 13a and b). Similarly, there could be six higher-level centers, but the location of the four original towns prevented the growth of additional centers. Here is one example, to be found again and again in this study, of how an earlier decision in time prevents the most efficient location patterns and why it is necessary to include the historical dimension in the theory.

From 1900 to 1940 the population remained stable. Gains by natural increase were offset by net migration loss out of the area. Within the area, industrialization and urbanization proceeded rapidly. From 1940 to 1960 the population increased slightly as better opportunities within the area slowed down migration losses to other parts of the country. The urban patterns had now proliferated to the many centers shown on Figure 2.

Several empirical "runs" of the model were made. Two trial simulations were made for 1810–1820 and 1820–1840. Since no urbanization was occurring, the model simply assigned internal migration between parishes. The results were adequate but suffered from lack of consideration of outside factors. Two other simulations using actual data were made. For the period 1860–1880 migration was simulated between parishes as before, but parishes through which the railway passed or in which it was known that some manufacturing was developing were weighted in accordance with employment anticipated by such investment. Differential growth of parishes was induced in the light of this predicted urbanization. For 1960–1980 a predictive simulation was made in which areas were weighted by their urban population. Some of the detailed migration from selected areas is shown in Figure 6. These results were quite satisfactory and correlate with recent events and expected changes.[21]

The main set of simulations, however, was a united series for 1860 to 1960. Each simulation located new activities, which in turn changed the attractiveness of areas and induced a pattern of population gains and losses from migration. Beginning with actual 1860 data and the presence of the four towns (Fig. 3), the only other outside information used was the net growth or loss of the region in twenty-year intervals,[22] the volume of activities that the population could support and the total demand for transportation, manufacturing, etc. All railways, manufacturing, and central place activities were randomly

[20] The number of places that could be supported by a population at a given level can be determined from marketing data. If these are unavailable, the ideal maximum number of places may be estimated from the actual distribution by measuring the amount of excess markets.

[21] Kunglige Arbetsmarknadsstyrelsen, *Lokaliseringutredning För Kronobergs Län* [Location analysis] (Stockholm: 1959).

[22] Shorter time periods would be preferable. The twenty-year interval was accepted for reasons of time and manpower.

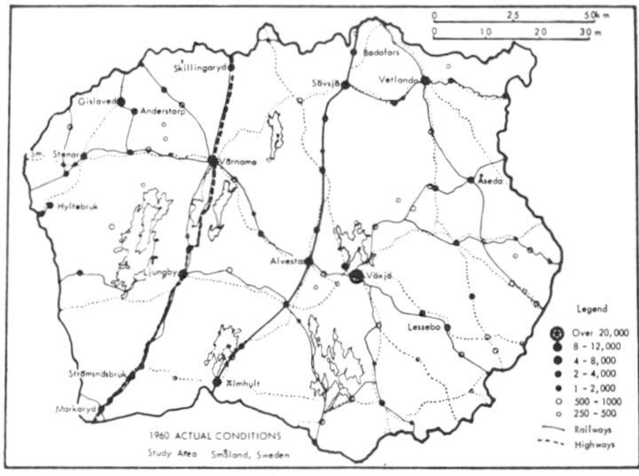

FIGURE 2

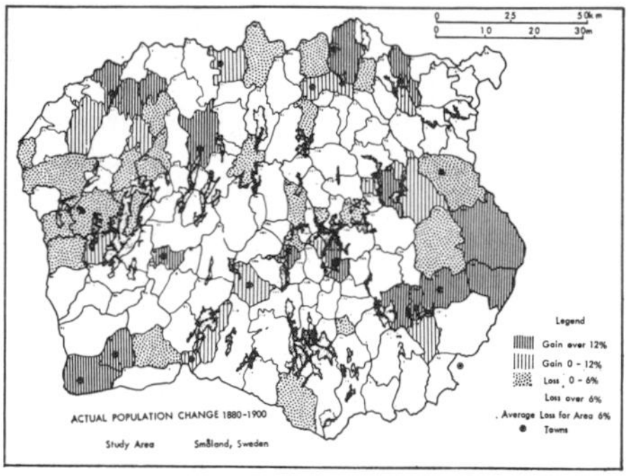

FIGURE 4

assigned. The location of the assigned centers often coincided with the actual ones. In some cases this was random coincidence. In other cases the coincidence reflected the strong advantage of the area relative to already existing centers or a favored transport position. The choice of location for railroads was often quite restricted, and in several cases the routes coincided, at least in part.

The one-hundred year simulation produced a dynamic distribution of urban places and currents of migration to support the urbanization. Distributions may be compared both from generation to generation and as end-products. Since it was not intended to try to reproduce the actual pattern, comparison must be more indirect. Some results are shown in Figures 6–9. The simulated and actual distributions for 1910 are shown on Figures 5 and 7. The distributions for 1960 are shown on Figures 2 and 8.

The objective of the study was to discover and utilize the major locational forces channeling urban development and migration. If this were achieved, the following characteristics of actual development should be matched by the simulated development: (1) The set of urban places should exhibit a certain range of sizes, yet maintain a spatial hierarchy. This was achieved very closely (e. g., Figs. 2 and 8). (2) The spatial distribution should have a certain set of distances between places. The distribution was close, but there was slight tendency for the simulated towns to be more regularly spaced. The actual distortion resulting from historical change and from locations of manufacturers and railways was even greater than predicted.

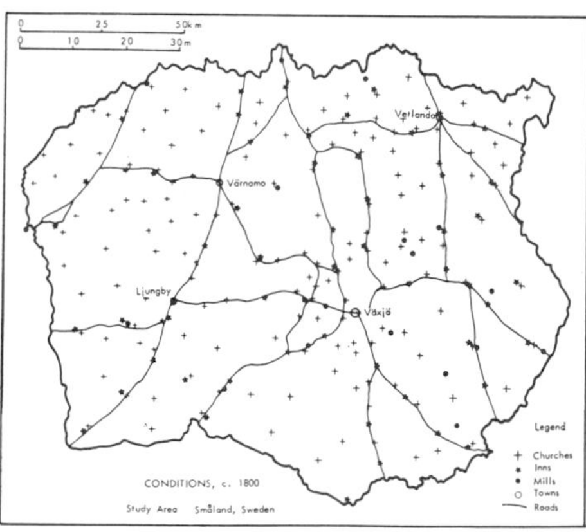

FIGURE 3

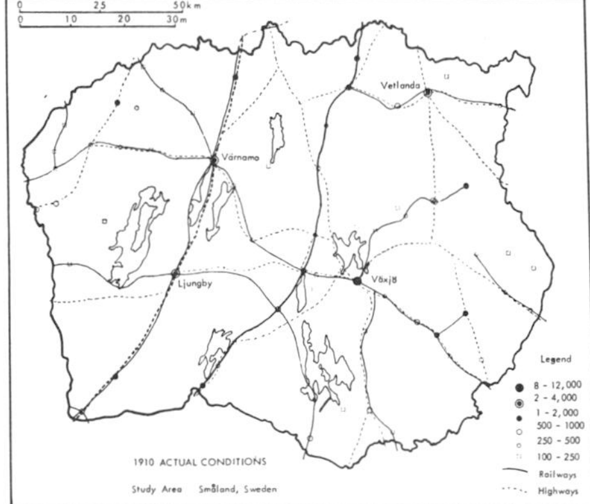

FIGURE 5

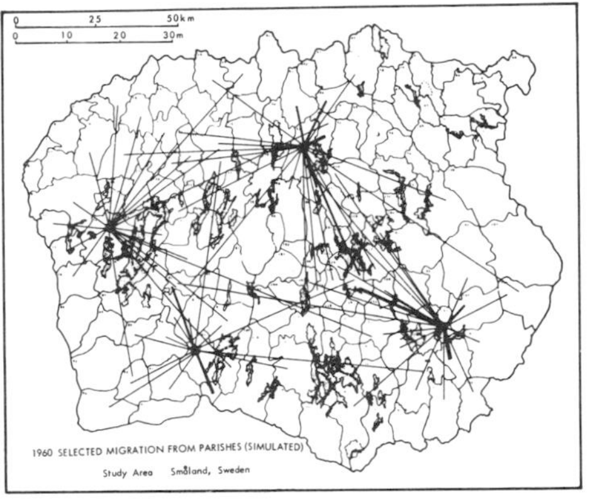

FIGURE 6

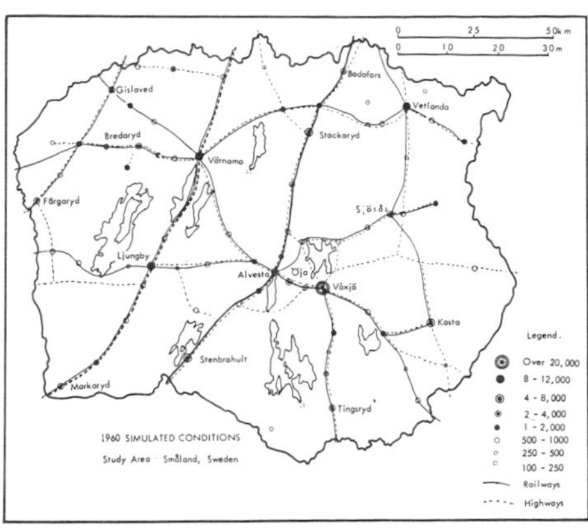

FIGURE 8

(3) Early location decisions, railways, towns, and manufactures, should have strong and lasting effects on later locations. The model reproduced this process well. The extent to which the original towns, both in reality and in the model, restricted and channeled the ultimate development of the current distribution was striking. Although there were great changes in the fortunes of places and much redistribution of population, such changes were not chaotic. The present distribution can be seen as the growth of the old distribution into new conditions. (4) Migration patterns should have a characteristic distribution of distances and directions. The simulation correctly matched the typical distance traveled by migrants, but the failure to take into account the strong dependence of migration on previous movements resulted in a more regular migration field over time than actually occurred. This failure can be easily corrected. (5) A net flow of migrants, of certain volumes and directions, from rural to urban locations should occur. This was achieved. (6) Certain numbers and kinds of areas should gain or lose and by similar volumes. Again the patterns are similar (Figs. 4 and 9), but the simulation is somewhat too regular. Too few parishes lost. The problem here seems to be the omission from the model of significant variations in local birth and death rates.

In sum, the model results can be considered realistic from the point of view of distribution, that is, similarity in spatial structure; and from the point of view of process, or a reasonable recognition and treatment of the pertinent

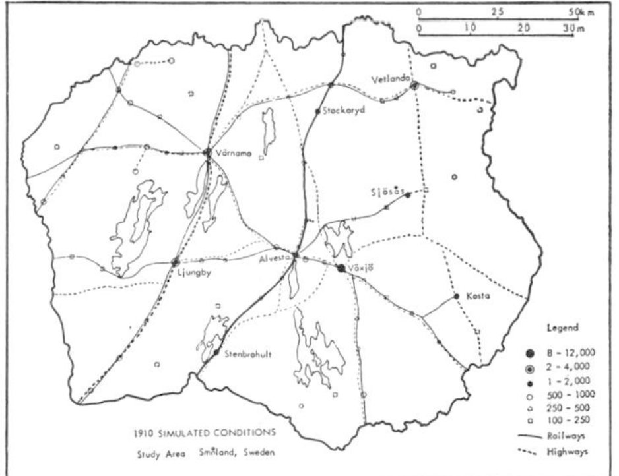

FIGURE 7

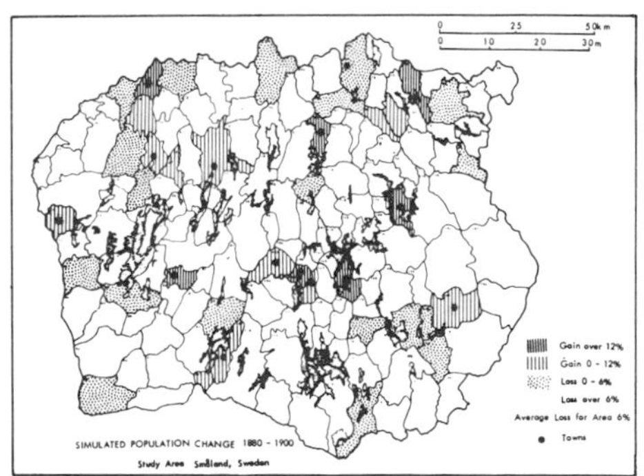

FIGURE 9

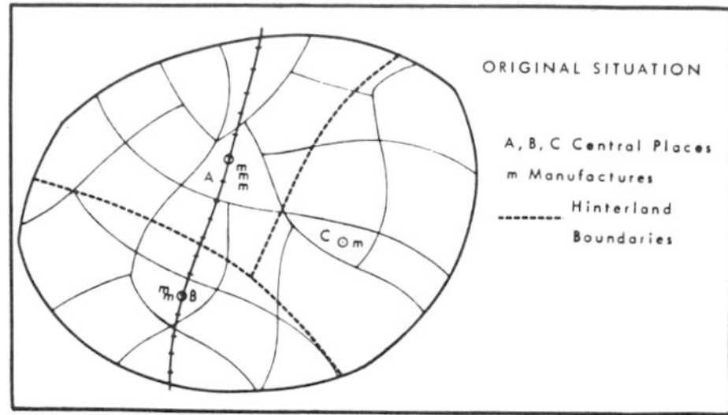

FIGURE 10

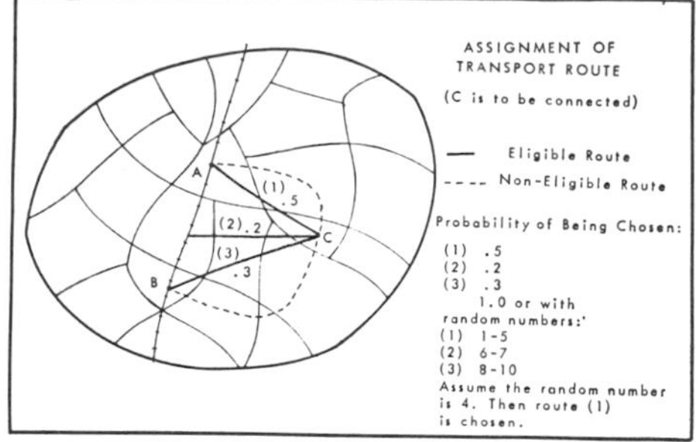

FIGURE 11

forces. Deviations resulted in the main from oversimplified assumptions rather than from a mistaken approach.

This example of the use of the simulation approach seems to indicate that the technique is applicable to a wide range of problems that involve the development of a spatial pattern over time. Their application to problems of innovation and the spread of techniques and ideas has been well demonstrated.[23] From culture to culture, area to area, and time to time, the exact nature of the forces to be built into a model may differ. In one kind of frontier settlement, for example, it may be best to locate as far as possible from another settler.[24] In another case grouping may be required for protection. Most of the controls over location and migration, however, are more universal. Distance is always a barrier and, when crossed by a route, an opportunity. Only the importance attached to it may vary. There seems to be much historical and predictive research that might utilize such methods: the spread of the frontier, the future development of urban patterns, and the spatial growth of the metropolis. The simulation technique, however, is not to be used for its own sake. It is useful only as its provides an operational framework for explanations of behavior in space.

THE SIMULATION MODEL

The preceding example indicated the general nature of the model—a model which operates as a process through time and which involves locational choice restricted by many regularizing forces. More formally, this simulation model is a system represented by a sampling procedure (random numbers) which satisfies the same probability laws (for example, the probability of migrating various distances).[25] Probability models are often used when it is necessary to evaluate an otherwise indeterminate solution. Rather than various factors converging to a unique solution, a range of possibilities occurs. Certain possibilities, for example locations for an activity, are more likely choices than others and can be given higher probabilities of being selected. The final choice is random, i.e., given by random numbers. The procedure is also called the "Monte Carlo" or "model sampling" method. In this technique, choice ultimately depends on previous decisions and their results. The growth of a distribution of urban centers and the migration to support such growth can logically be treated in such a model. There are only a limited number of new plants, stores, or migrants, but many places compete for them. In addition, an individual decision cannot be isolated from the historical stream of decisions.

A simulation model, however, does not abandon all to chance. Many forces tend to determine a solution, but there is always an element of choice. We cannot reproduce the real world exactly, but we may hope to generate distributions which resemble those of the real world.

Let us demarcate a study region, divide it

[23] Hägerstrand, *op. cit.* (1953). Professor F. Pitts, University of Oregon, is now completing a dual study of the spread of hand tractors and the disappearance of horses in Japan.

[24] Erik Bylund, *Kolonisering av Pite Lappmark* (Uppsala: Almqvist and Wiksell, 1959).

[25] C. W. Churchman, R. L. Ackoff, and E. L. Arnoff, *Introduction to Operations Research* (New York: John Wiley and Sons, 1957).

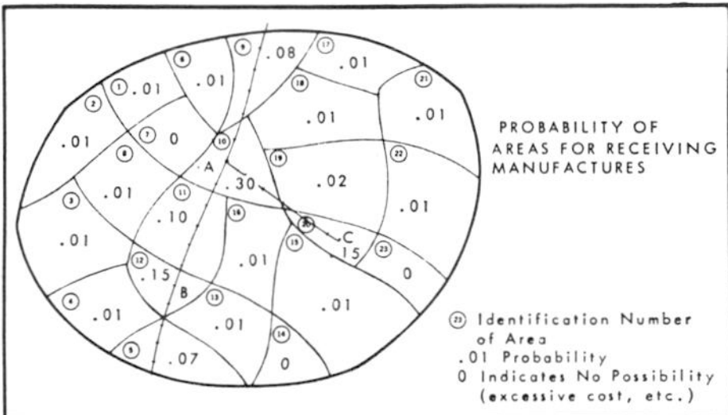

FIGURE 12a

into component areas, and choose time periods. Figure 10, for example, depicts a possible situation at the beginning of a simulation process. Necessary supporting information is collected: net growth rates for the chosen time period; the demand for new transportation; the amount of new economic activities of whatever sort that can be supported; and the propensity to migrate.

Step 1: Assignment of Transport Routes

a. Each demanded link (Fig. 11, the link to C) has several specific possible routes. These are to be evaluated. Eligibility requirements may be included, for example, a rule that a possible route may be only a certain degree longer than the shortest possible route.

b. To choose a particular route for a demanded link it is necessary to determine the probabilities of the various alternative routes. These probabilities will vary according to distance of the route, population (especially urban) of the areas traversed, and costs of construction.

c. A specific route is chosen by means of random numbers as shown in the example (Fig. 11). These probabilities may be taken to mean in this case the relative lobbying strength of the proponents of the three alternatives. Which group would prevail is uncertain. Resorting to a random number solves the problem, after the probabilities are summed in a form useful for matching against random numbers.

The assignment of transport routes is important to the process of urban development, both because of directly added non-agricultural employment, and because of the enhanced attractiveness of the served areas for other economic activities.

Step 2: Assignment of Non-Central Place Activities

a. The demand for new activities is a function of population, income, resources, etc. The number of new plants for the entire area and their contribution to urban support is given from economic analysis.

b. Eligibility of areas. All areas may be considered eligible, or restrictions may be imposed. For example, an activity may be able to locate in a place (area) if costs of assembling and/or processing do not exceed some maximum level, and if the local labor force equals at least some level. Many areas might be rejected at once owing to excess cost or lack of labor (Fig. 12a).

c. Probability of areas for receiving manufactures. Even if eligible, areas will vary widely in their attractiveness to industry. The probability of locating in a particular area will depend on characteristics of the local rural and urban population, on the transport facilities existing previously or just assigned (Step 1), on the cost of assembling materials and processing, and on the volume and kind of activities already present. This step is simply the application of industrial location concepts, but rather than a unique location being found, for every plant of each type, this model recognizes a choice for plants in general among several locations. The best locations, of course, have the highest probability of being chosen. Figure 12a shows how transport facilities and existing towns influence the probabilities.

d. Random assignment of plants: To assign a limited number of plants among many possible locations, random numbers may be used. To do this, it is necessary to convert the basic

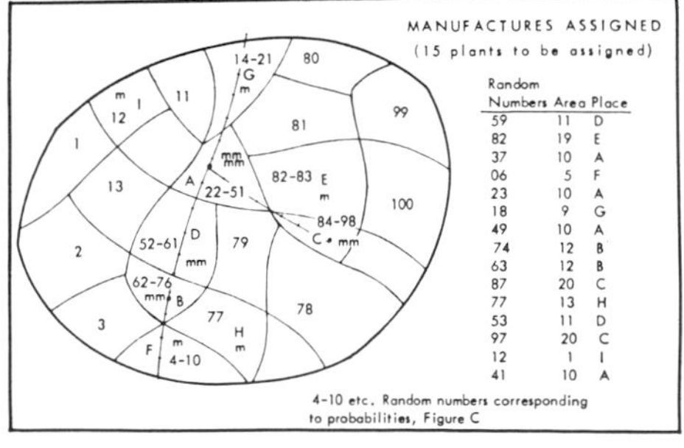

Random Numbers	Area	Place
59	11	D
82	19	E
37	10	A
06	5	F
23	10	A
18	9	G
49	10	A
74	12	B
63	12	B
87	20	C
77	13	H
53	11	D
97	20	C
12	1	I
41	10	A

FIGURE 12b

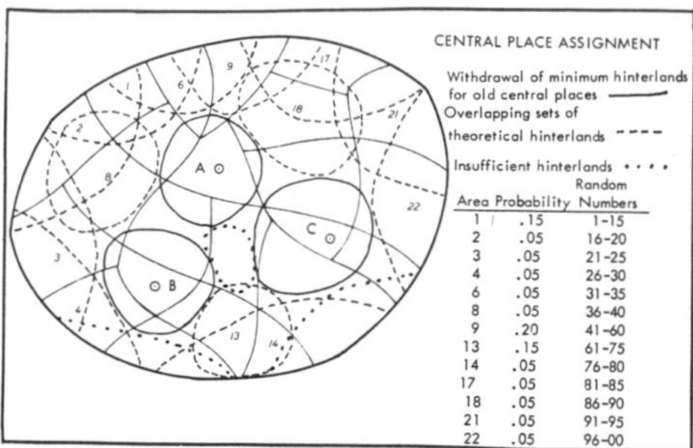

FIGURE 13a

probabilities (Fig. 12a) into useful form. In Figure 12b, the equivalent tally of numbers, to be matched against random numbers, replaces the basic probabilities. For example, the probability of area 5 to receive plants is .07. This is the range .04 through .10 if we add the probabilities cumulatively. The equivalent discrete numbers are 4–10. Then random numbers, as many as there are plants to be assigned, are matched against the tally. This process is illustrated in Figure 12b.

Step 3: Assignment of Central Place Activities

This process is one of determining which areas, out of many competing ones, will succeed in carving out a local hinterland, as the economy is able to support greater volume and more levels of activities. The probabilities of areas receiving central place activities (to become central places) depends also on present and anticipated transportation and manufacturing activities.

a. Find the maximum possible number of central places of a given level that could be supported by the population in the new time period. This is simply the total population divided by the minimum threshold needed.

b. Before any possible new central places can be evaluated, minimum hinterlands around already existing central places at that level must be withdrawn from eligibility (Fig. 13a).

c. Any hinterland, new or old, must satisfy these conditions: (1) The hinterland must contain at least the minimum threshold population. (2) The hinterland must contain no area which is actually closer to another existing center. (3) The hinterland must be "integral," that is contain no areas farther away than some closer available intervening areas. This does not imply a circular hinterland, since a hinterland may contain areas farther away in one direction than some areas which are closer to older central places in another direction; that is, the "gateway" hinterland may occur (Fig. 13a).

d. The sum of areas around the old central places (areas enclosed by solid lines, Fig. 13a) constitute the withdrawn territory. All the remaining territory from which the new central places and their hinterlands must come is obtained by subtraction.

e. All possible theoretical hinterlands are now found. These must come out of the eligible territory and satisfy the restrictions of c. However, since they are theoretical, not actual, their hinterlands may have many elements in common. In Figure 13a are marked thirteen such hinterlands, from which the actual ones will be chosen.

f. Relative attractiveness of possible central places. Some areas can be expected to have a better chance to succeed in becoming central places than do others. This evaluation depends upon population, especially any urban population resulting from earlier assignment of manufacturing activities, and on transport position. These probabilities are treated as before (Fig. 13a).

g. Which places actually become central places is determined by a priority given by random numbers. The first random number selects the first central place and minimum actual hinterland. When the first is selected, many others may be eliminated from consideration, since in contrast to theoretical hinterlands, actual hinterlands must be mutually exclusive. All the possible central places contained in the first chosen hinterland or which have elements in common with it are now eliminated. For example in Figure 13b, the first number, 92, selects area 21 (place J).

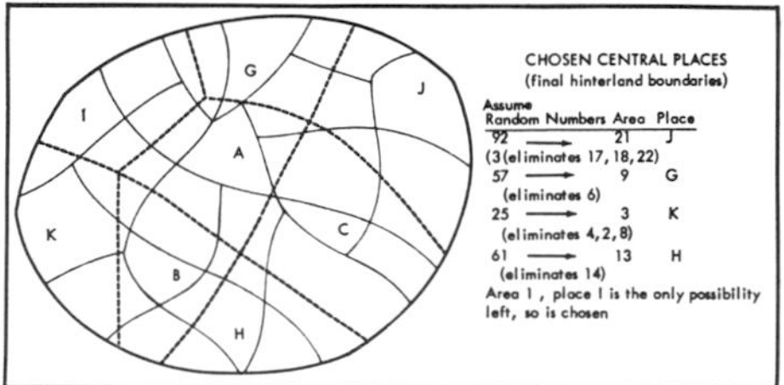

FIGURE 13b

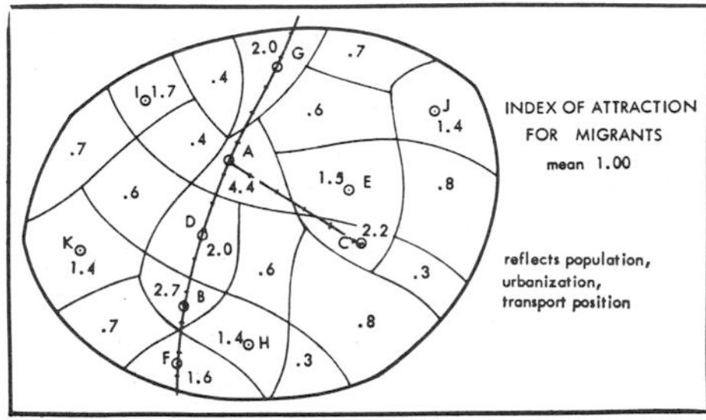

FIGURE 14a

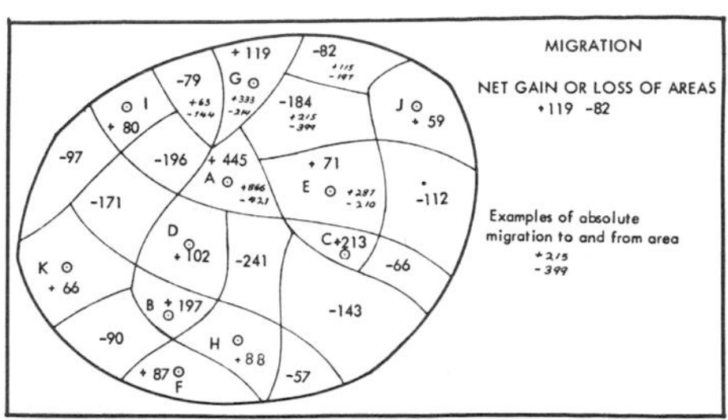

FIGURE 14c

This at once eliminates the possibility of central places in areas 17, 18, and 22.

h. In similar fashion new central places and hinterlands are chosen until there are no more possible hinterlands from which to choose.

i. There will now remain some areas, or parts thereof, which were not in the minimum hinterlands, but from which no additional hinterlands could be formed (for example, the space between the minimum hinterlands of the old central places, Fig. 13a). These are simply assigned to the nearest central place.

j. The process is repeated for higher levels of central places, except that, to be eligible, a place must already be a central place of the next lower order (as from a previous time period).

Step 4: Migration

While the underlying basis for population redistribution is the creation of differential opportunities (as assigned in the previous steps), the actual population shifts are brought about by migration. The model process is one of assigning migrants between areas.

a. The propensity to migrate, or expected volume of migration from each source area, is a function of population and its characteristics (such as rural and urban components, age structure, race, education), employment conditions, resource depletion, and normal rates of turnover in job, residence, etc.

b. The probability of migration between two areas: The most important factors affecting the destination of migrants from any one area to another are (1) the *distance* between areas, as a measure of the decreasing probability of contact, (2) the differential *attractiveness* of the area, and (3) previous migration (as a key to contacts via relatives and friends).

c. Relative attractiveness is an index which takes into account those factors tending toward regular net gains or losses. During the basic process of industrialization, commercialization, and urbanization which is studied here, this attractiveness is almost entirely a function of differential economic opportunities. Therefore, it is reasonable to weight

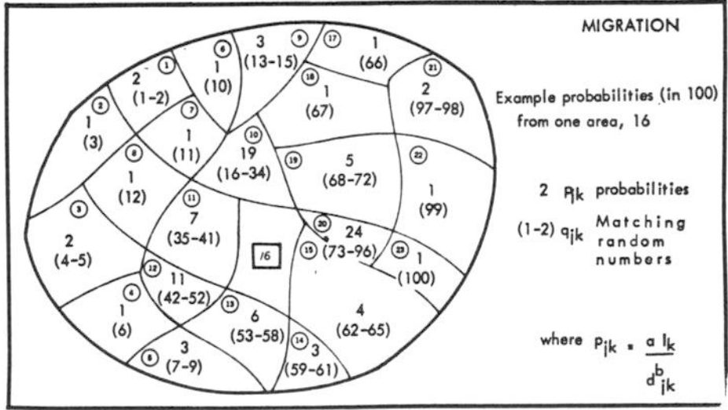

FIGURE 14b

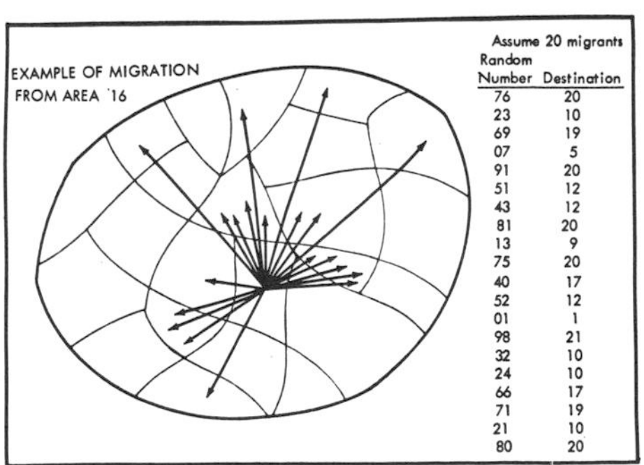

Random Number	Destination
76	20
23	10
69	19
07	5
91	20
51	12
43	12
81	20
13	9
75	20
40	17
52	12
01	1
98	21
32	10
24	10
66	17
71	19
21	10
80	20

FIGURE 14d

more heavily those areas with present or anticipated urban population (as a result of opportunities created in the assignment of activities above (see Fig. 14a). The correct weight for such opportunities must be empirically determined and statistically tested.

d. The basic migration relation between any two areas, that is the probability that a migrant will choose that path, is of the simple inverse distance type (Fig. 14b). The probability varies directly with relative attractiveness of the possible destination and inversely with some function of its distance. The relative strength of distance as a barrier is expected to vary with the state of technology at the time or in the area and perhaps for rural and urban migrants.

e. The sum of probabilities of migrating from one area to all its possible destinations is made to sum to 1 (for probability purposes) and converted into useful form as before. A typical pattern of such probabilities is shown in Figure 14b. There is such a set of probabilities for all source areas.

f. Random numbers, equal to the number of migrants from an area, are matched against its "migration probability field" (Fig. 14b). The random numbers select specific paths (Fig. 14d). The process is repeated for all other areas.

g. Results of migration assignment may be printed out (presumably from machine storage) in entirety (each migrant's source and destination) summarized into the total number of migrants from each area to every other area, or further summed into the total number of migrants to and from an area (Fig. 14c). From the latter, the net gain or loss due to internal migration is easily found.

h. At this point the results of the assignment of activities and of migrants can be summarized, and the net population, including its rural and urban components, can be totalled. This sets the stage for repetition of the entire process for another time period. The results of one simulation in a period of time at once alter the population structure and require the computation of whole new sets of probabilities. The computations become enormous. For migration alone, in the present study using 155 areas, there are 155×155 or 24,025, possible migration paths and probabilities, to be recomputed entirely for each time period. The entire migration process was therefore programmed for computer.

The above outline of a particular model illustrates two useful properties of the simulation technique: (1) the fact that no particular mathematical sophistication is required and; (2) the great flexibility of the model. Simulation is a sampling procedure. The "rules" of this sampling may be altered and realtered until the best possible results are obtained. For this present study, the evaluation suggests the inclusion of additional rules, e.g., for migration. In this experimental manner, it is possible gradually to expand and improve our understanding of spatial patterns.

10. Toward a Geography of Economic Health: The Case of New York State*

JOHN H. THOMPSON, SIDNEY C. SUFRIN, PETER R. GOULD AND MARION A. BUCK

SPATIAL variation in such phenomena as levels of living or unemployment, and wide ranges in regional and local economic growth produce an interesting and important geography of economic health. Unemployment in general, and the designation of certain parts of the country as distressed areas in particular,[1] have focused attention upon the need for action by local, state, and national government.

Three of the authors of this paper were retained by New York State to present a report on the economic status of Upstate New York.[2] The purpose here is to summarize some of the significant aspects of that report, and to present results of investigations carried out since its publication. Specifically, this paper considers the meaning of economic health by comparing its various facets, presents a statistical interpretation of the data used, and explores the possibility of making geographic reality out of the coarse grid of county statistical units. The final product is a map of economic health, using New York State as a case study.

[1] "Distress," as indicated by the United States Department of Labor, is a function of unemployment exclusively, involving both amount of unemployment and duration of unemployment at various levels.

[2] Sidney C. Sufrin, John H. Thompson, Marion A. Buck, and Arland E. Charlton, *The Economic Status of Upstate New York at Mid-Century, With Special Reference to Distressed Communities and Their Adjustments* (Syracuse University: Business Research Center, College of Business Administration, August, 1960), 158 pp. Departmental affiliations of authors of the present study are as follows: Thompson and Gould, Geography; Sufrin, Economics; and Buck, Business Research Center.

Reasonable indicators of economic health such as unemployment and per capita income, when considered separately, produce quite different results. It is suggested, therefore, that various indicators might be used advantageously. It is further suggested that these indicators should include measures of both level of economic activity and trend in economic growth. The problem of combining several significant indicators into a composite measure is not new,[3] nor is it easy to implement. This paper suggests that factor analysis produces useful results when several indicators are handled simultaneously, and provides a logical basis for presenting spatial variation in economic health. A chorographic county map, usually far from spatial reality, can be reconstituted into a relatively accurate isopleth map by subjective interpretation of relevant geographic patterns.

ECONOMIC HEALTH AND ITS INDICATORS

The expressions "economic health," "economic distress," "stagnation," and "underdevelopment" do not have universally agreed upon or rigid definitions. To a great extent they are generally understood, but in actuality are reflections of the opinions and expectations of individual observers. When the New York State study was begun there was no preconceived notion that one indicator of economic health was better than another. Rather, the question was raised as to whether dif-

[3] Experimentation along this line was carried out in John H. Thompson, "A New Method for Measuring Manufacturing," *Annals*, Association of American Geographers, Vol. 45 (1955), pp. 416–436.

* Reprinted from the *Annals of the Association of American Geographers,* Vol. 52 (March 1962).

TABLE 1.—RANK ORDER OF NEW YORK STATE COUNTIES FOR NINE INDICATORS OF ECONOMIC HEALTH[1]

	Increase in per capita income, 1950–1957	Per cent population growth, 1950–1956	Per cent population in 20–49 age group	Per cent growth employment, 1947–1956	Per capita income, 1958	Per cent growth retail sales, 1948–1958	Per cent average unemployment, 1948–1958	Per cent increase value added by manufacturing, 1947–1954	Increase average weekly earnings, 1950–1958
New York City (considered as one statistical unit)	5	58	1	45	2	53	19	51	31
Nassau	27	2	2	1	3	1	5	2	19
Rockland	12	6	6	8	8	4	2	4	10
Suffolk	54	1	14	2	5	2	25	1	4
Westchester	1	8	5	11	1	5	21	30	11
Broome	6	17	12	26	14	27	4	25	26
Chenango	41	36	51	22	43	9	26	12	31
Delaware	44	44	43	3	34	42	16	5	29
Otsego	51	40	47	29	38	43	52	27	50
Cattaraugus	33	42	31	35	37	51	14	49	44
Chautauqua	18	26	27	33	23	45	32	34	28
Erie	16	14	7	30	15	22	23	29	12
Niagara	3	7	9	15	9	17	8	23	5
Albany	24	32	10	25	10	34	3	43	25
Rensselaer	36	37	15	52	39	48	48	47	40
Saratoga	39	15	21	48	47	31	18	45	17
Schenectady	4	10	4	42	4	38	6	7	2
Schoharie	52	35	54	14	49	40	55	58	49
Warren	32	25	32	44	22	36	42	36	53
Washington	31	51	39	24	32	46	1	17	20
Alleghany	35	47	46	55	48	50	29	13	9
Chemung	22	9	19	41	29	41	22	18	27
Schuyler	43	28	56	28	51	58	30	37	33
Steuben	20	34	48	17	27	33	17	9	21
Tioga	37	19	50	31	42	24	15	24	1
Tompkins	9	3	3	20	18	32	7	41	23
Columbia	29	48	42	38	24	14	40	48	48
Dutchess	9	4	13	12	13	21	12	8	7
Greene	40	56	52	9	33	30	34	20	47
Orange	21	11	17	18	17	26	32	31	41
Putnam	13	5	20	16	7	16	28	3	34
Sullivan	26	43	24	48	21	23	20	19	55
Ulster	9	39	23	4	26	12	27	11	6
Fulton	49	46	34	54	46	55	56	57	54
Hamilton	57	57	35	57	58	8	n.a.	22	58
Herkimer	38	50	33	58	45	39	53	35	56
Montgomery	58	54	16	56	35	56	45	56	57
Oneida	2	24	18	40	11	29	36	39	16
Clinton	56	22	22	19	56	7	47	53	24
Essex	30	49	45	36	50	10	24	46	36
Franklin	53	55	53	51	55	52	57	15	53
Jefferson	25	53	49	34	30	44	39	38	37
Lewis	50	52	58	46	53	54	11	42	43
St. Lawrence	14	16	40	5	44	6	37	19	3
Genesee	17	38	30	27	19	11	33	26	30
Livingston	34	41	29	37	25	20	46	33	15
Monroe	7	18	11	39	6	25	9	16	8
Ontario	45	23	28	43	28	18	38	52	39
Orleans	28	29	44	7	41	13	51	10	35
Seneca	15	30	57	10	16	15	10	6	18
Wayne	19	21	38	6	21	3	44	28	38
Wyoming	23	45	25	14	31	28	54	44	22
Yates	48	27	55	21	54	57	50	32	46
Cayuga	42	32	26	49	36	47	41	55	42
Cortland	46	20	37	50	40	49	35	50	45
Madison	47	13	36	32	52	37	49	40	51
Onondaga	11	12	8	23	12	19	13	21	13
Oswego	55	33	41	53	57	35	43	54	32

[1] The counties in this table (and also Table 3) are listed in a regional rather than an alphabetical order. For example, the New York City suburban counties of Nassau, Rockland, and Westchester are grouped together, as are the Buffalo area counties of Cattaraugus, Chautauqua, Erie, and Niagara. This regional order is employed in statistical tables published by the New York State Department of Commerce, and is an attempt to group counties into what that Department considers to be "economic areas."

ferent indicators produced similar or quite different results.

Because of the wide variety of economic data available for countries, they are used as the statistical unit. The period of investigation is 1947–1958. The work is carried forth under the premise that level of economic conditions and trends in economic conditions are two different, but essential, elements in the concept of economic health. For example, increase in per capita income between 1950 and 1957 measures economic health, but in a different way than per capita income for any one time during that period. Based on this premise of the duality of economic health, per capita income, unemployment, and population in the 20–49 age group are used as indicators of *level* of economic health, whereas increase in per capita income, growth of population, growth in total employment, growth in retail sales, increase in value added by manufacture, and increase in earnings are used to show *trends* in economic health. No argument is presented here that these nine indicators are the best that could be devised, but they were selected as most appropriate from a larger

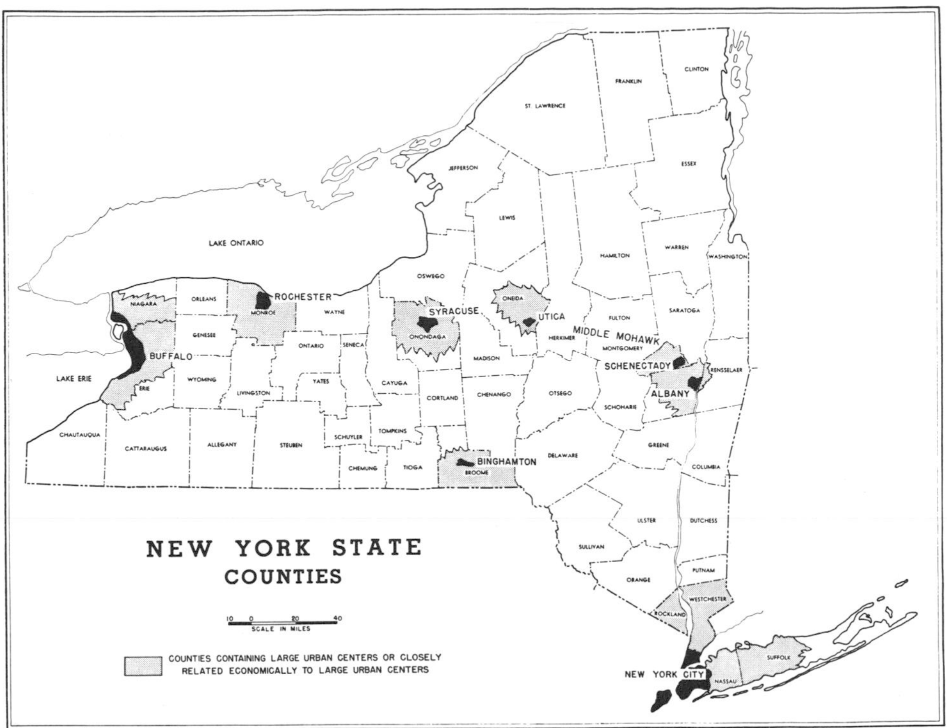

FIG. 1. New York State Counties. Those parts of urban counties which have experienced little or no urbanization are unshaded.

number representing the spread of available data.

Table 1 shows the rank order of counties for each of the nine indicators. There are 58 counties (counting New York City as one). A ranking of "1" is an expression of first place or highest level of economic health; "58" indicates last place or lowest level. It might be noted that New York City ranks first in per cent of population in the 20–49 age group, implying that there is an in-migration of people in this, the most vigorous age level. On the other hand, it ranks forty-fifth in per cent growth of employment. Nassau County, known for its recent rapid growth because of a peripheral location with respect to New York City, ranks first in per cent growth of employment, but twenty-seventh in increase in per capita income. These and most other variations in rank order among the indicators make sense when the situations are examined in detail. The important point is that a wide variation in rank order occurs. Table 2, which contains rank-order correlation coefficients, further illuminates the divergencies between the indicators. Table 3 shows the divergencies in actual figures, i.e. per capita income in dollars, population growth in per cent, and so forth.

Figures 2 through 10 also show data for the various indicators, but in addition exhibit, through map patterns, a quintile breakdown. In each case the lighter the pattern the greater the implied economic health.[4]

[4] Were other areas to be mapped and compared with New York State, the same dates and same numerical breaks between quintiles would have to be employed. In such a case, Pennsylvania, New England, or some other area might conceivably fall largely in two, or even one, of the categories based on the New York State quintiles.

TABLE 2.—RANK ORDER CORRELATION COEFFICIENTS FOR NEW YORK STATE COUNTIES

	Increase in per capita income, 1950–1957	Per cent population growth, 1950–1956	Per cent population in 20–49 age group	Per cent growth employment, 1947–1956	Per capita income, 1958	Per cent growth retail sales, 1948–1958	Per cent average unemployment, 1948–1958	Per cent increase value added by manufacturing, 1947–1954	Increase average weekly earnings, 1950–1958
Increase in Per Capita Income, 1950–1957	1.00	0.42	0.55	0.34	0.77	0.34	0.58	0.36	0.59
Per Cent of Population Growth, 1950–1956	0.42	1.00	0.53	0.43	0.51	0.42	0.43	0.29	0.47
Per Cent of Population in 20–49 Age Group, 1950	0.55	0.53	1.00	0.06	0.72	0.27	0.41	0.06	0.41
Per Cent Growth of Total Employment, 1947–1956	0.34	0.43	0.06	1.00	0.37	0.56	0.30	0.53	0.46
Per Capita Income, 1958	0.77	0.51	0.72	0.37	1.00	0.37	0.59	0.40	0.49
Per Cent Growth in Retail Sales, 1948–1958	0.34	0.42	0.27	0.56	0.37	1.00	0.17	0.43	0.43
Per Cent of Average Unemployment, 1949–1958	0.58	0.43	0.41	0.30	0.59	0.17	1.00	0.39	0.61
Per Cent Increase in Value Added by Manufacture, 1947–1954	0.36	0.29	0.06	0.53	0.40	0.43	0.39	1.00	0.48
Increase in Average Weekly Earnings, 1950–1958	0.59	0.47	0.41	0.46	0.49	0.43	0.61	0.48	1.00

TABLE 3.—STATUS OF NEW YORK STATE COUNTIES ACCORDING TO NINE INDICATORS OF ECONOMIC HEALTH

	Increase in per capita income, 1950–1957	Per cent population growth, 1950–1956	Per cent population in 20–49 age group	Per cent growth employment, 1947–1956	Per capita income, 1958	Per cent growth retail sales, 1948–1958	Per cent average unemployment, 1948–1958	Per cent increase value added by manufacturing, 1947–1954	Increase average weekly earnings, 1950–1958
New York State	662	9.00	45.93	8.92	2609	16.66	8.36	21.94	27.70
Upstate					2086	17.99	8.70	36.24	27.81
New York City	761	1.90	48.20	1.18	2906	1.26	8.33	1.63	27.95
Nassau	452	66.00	47.42	151.13	2811	136.32	5.82	300.14	26.69
Rockland	655	14.70	45.34	41.55	2406	61.46	4.76	116.56	29.98
Suffolk	310	70.30	43.48	150.10	2571	122.58	8.82	486.34	34.64
Westchester	818	13.54	45.61	36.64	3456	42.89	8.57	30.54	29.42
Broome	730	10.24	43.92	12.88	2202	17.13	5.25	39.95	24.75
Chenango	392	7.22	38.13	18.97	1650	36.24	8.99	54.32	22.97
Delaware	377	6.21	39.16	65.45	1731	8.11	7.75	110.54	24.10
Otsego	332	7.03	38.66	12.00	1697	8.03	17.11	39.02	17.84
Cattaraugus	425	6.34	40.47	7.48	1720	3.79	7.07	3.56	20.52
Chautauqua	538	8.42	40.96	10.88	1952	6.50	10.15	23.41	24.46
Erie	573	10.85	45.14	11.34	2188	21.83	8.66	34.30	29.03
Niagara	770	13.97	44.77	33.01	2401	25.08	6.14	42.73	33.01
Albany	472	7.79	44.40	13.67	2373	13.64	5.14	13.45	24.76
Rensselaer	419	7.21	43.07	–0.09	1695	4.80	15.49	8.22	21.57
Saratoga	394	10.77	41.87	–0.02	1616	14.39	8.21	10.93	26.78
Schenectady	762	12.83	46.32	4.13	2641	11.66	5.85	105.52	40.45
Schoharie	323	7.27	37.92	33.33	1586	9.28	19.03	–24.59	18.04
Warren	430	8.49	40.45	3.13	1965	11.89	14.16	17.73	17.76
Washington	434	3.80	39.78	15.63	1741	5.92	3.84	48.38	25.76
Alleghany	420	5.10	39.03	–0.15	1615	4.36	9.87	50.50	30.32
Chemung	482	13.07	42.45	4.48	1777	8.56	8.58	48.09	24.70
Schuyler	383	8.33	37.04	12.50	1523	–12.57	9.95	17.49	22.87

TABLE 3.—*Continued*

	Increase in per capita income, 1950–1957	Per cent population growth, 1950–1956	Per cent population in 20–49 age group	Per cent growth employment, 1947–1956	Per capita income, 1958	Per cent growth retail sales, 1948–1958	Per cent average unemployment, 1948–1958	Per cent increase value added by manufacturing, 1947–1954	Increase average weekly earnings, 1950–1958
Steuben	495	7.39	38.64	28.00	1815	13.75	7.83	67.25	25.64
Tioga	417	9.49	38.17	11.11	1667	19.61	7.33	42.54	46.51
Tompkins	676	19.76	46.54	19.81	2033	14.36	5.86	14.39	25.14
Columbia	447	5.08	39.31	7.14	1896	26.30	13.25	4.27	19.46
Dutchess	676	19.21	43.80	34.69	2325	22.64	6.94	80.82	32.38
Greene	393	2.81	38.[illegible]1	37.50	1737	15.06	11.30	45.10	19.75
Orange	492	12.37	42.62	22.47	2045	17.87	10.15	30.26	21.42
Putnam	621	15.51	42.09	28.57	2526	25.40	9.77	279.67	22.76
Sullivan	460	6.26	41.32	–0.02	1991	20.93	8.38	45.32	16.42
Ulster	676	7.17	41.33	63.80	1839	27.98	9.12	55.21	32.55
Fulton	337	5.22	40.38	–0.12	1618	–2.06	23.26	–24.01	17.09
Hamilton	248	2.60	40.17	–0.23	1263	37.64	n.a.	43.08	10.47
Herkimer	406	4.05	40.44	–0.24	1629	10.38	17.98	21.90	16.08
Montgomery	230	3.04	42.80	–0.22	1730	–9.11	14.41	–13.71	11.47
Oneida	784	8.58	42.60	4.81	2349	15.56	11.68	15.58	27.77
Clinton	289	8.71	41.64	21.21	1419	40.31	14.65	–0.88	24.86
Essex	440	4.07	39.10	7.44	1550	32.06	8.71	8.63	22.24
Franklin	313	2.82	37.98	–0.07	1438	3.46	27.68	49.27	17.76
Jefferson	469	3.32	38.46	7.50	1748	7.64	13.15	16.36	22.20
Lewis	336	3.34	36.68	0.00	1461	–1.36	6.84	14.22	20.55
St. Lawrence	604	10.74	39.72	55.78	1632	41.41	11.96	50.08	38.64
Genesee	551	2.81	40.48	12.62	2023	29.23	10.28	39.03	23.52
Livingston	424	6.63	40.61	7.27	1840	22.95	14.46	25.93	27.81
Monroe	682	9.91	44.04	6.71	2569	19.27	6.48	48.84	32.04
Ontario	372	8.56	40.63	3.88	1784	23.85	12.79	1.45	21.90
Orleans	451	7.91	39.15	43.90	1685	26.50	17.01	63.48	22.66
Seneca	583	7.80	36.97	37.14	2097	25.58	6.61	107.20	26.75
Wayne	536	8.72	39.79	49.43	1991	105.21	14.27	35.38	22.09
Wyoming	480	6.20	41.16	33.33	1747	17.11	18.78	11.08	25.19
Yates	354	8.40	37.20	19.05	1452	–12.12	16.16	26.90	19.97
Cayuga	390	7.79	41.03	–0.03	1725	5.19	13.73	–7.61	21.16
Cortland	369	9.15	39.91	–0.05	1693	4.70	11.64	1.88	20.19
Madison	357	10.88	39.94	10.91	1518	11.79	15.55	15.49	17.77
Onondaga	667	11.88	44.78	16.33	2330	23.12	7.02	44.76	28.74
Oswego	303	7.66	39.44	–0.10	1393	12.73	14.19	–7.01	22.93

COMBINING THE INDICATORS

Tables 1 through 3 and Figures 2 through 10 provide considerable evidence of spatial variation in economic health and clearly show that each indicator must measure a somewhat different facet. It follows that the question should be raised as to whether there is any rational basis for combining the indicators into a single measurement or ranking of economic health. Certainly it would be useful if this could be done.

Equal Weighting

When there appears to be no basis for saying that one indicator is better than any other, there is always an urge, and frequently some justification, for weighting the indicators equally. For Figure 11 the indicators within the level and trend categories are weighted equally to provide level and trend rankings. It is not surprising that on this map New York City exhibits a very high ranking (4th) among the fifty-eight counties in level of economic development, but a low one (46th) in trend; or that St. Lawrence County, a relatively poorly-developed county, which profited from construction of the St. Lawrence Seaway and Power projects during the 1950's, should rank low (43rd) in level but high (4th) in trend.

If the equal weighting procedure is carried one step further, all indicators, both level and trend, may be combined to produce a single ranking of economic health. In such a case the single ranking is derived by adding the

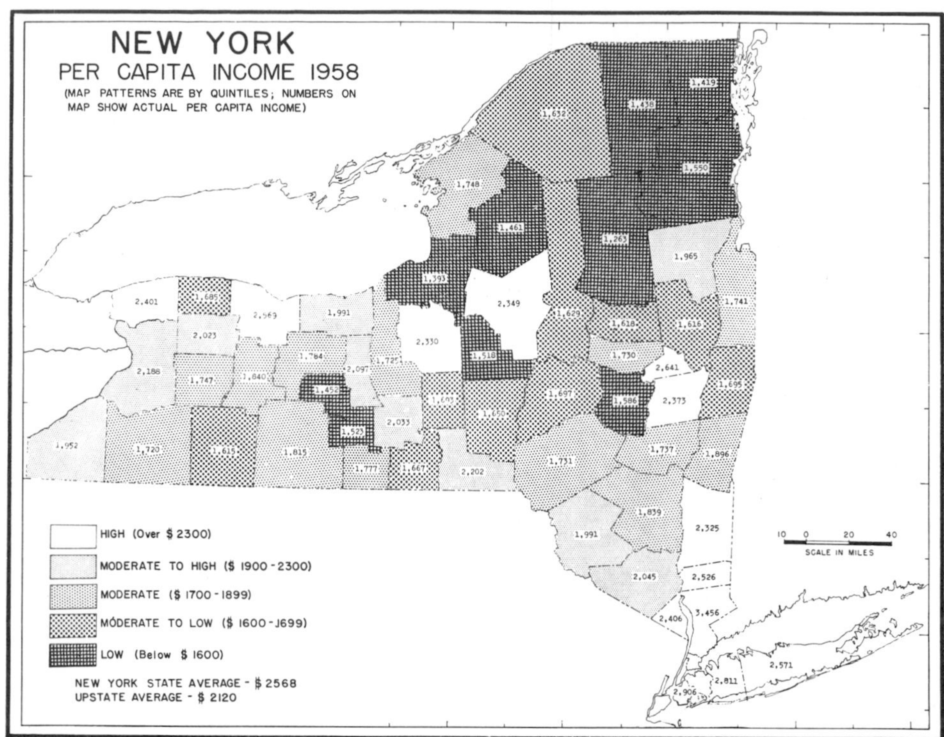

FIG. 2. Per capita income, 1958. Implication: the higher the per capita income, the better the economic health. The quintile patterns plus the actual values in dollars point up outstanding variations within the state. Counties dominated by large urban centers rank high compared to ones with smaller centers, or those which are largely rural.

TABLE 4.—FACTOR LOADINGS[1]

	Factors								
	Significant dimensions of economic health			Terms of uniqueness and error					
	I	II	III	IV	V	VI	VII	VIII	IX
Increase in Per Capita Income, 1950–1957	8015	–2528	–1554	–2919	0531	–2302	–1676	2972	–1100
Per Cent of Population Growth, 1950–1956	7068	–0535	3799	4952	–2215	0805	–1044	2014	0313
Per Cent of Population in 20–49 Age Group, 1950	6479	–5972	3165	–0678	0171	1571	–0139	–2566	–1662
Per Cent Growth of Total Employment, 1947–1956	6157	6091	0914	0686	–1490	–4042	–0324	–2133	–0690
Per Capita Income, 1958	8396	–3071	0156	–2770	–2277	–0566	0411	–0885	2435
Per Cent Growth in Retail Sales, 1948–1958	6038	4505	4700	–2114	2753	0980	2606	1157	0127
Per Cent of Average Unemployment, 1949–1958	7212	–1975	–4696	0263	0068	–0386	3838	0196	–0448
Per Cent Increase in Value Added by Manufacture, 1947–1954	6020	5226	–3193	–0161	–2470	4054	–0885	–0063	–0602
Increase in Average Weekly Earnings, 1950–1958	7848	0842	–2183	0195	4629	0598	–2281	–1129	0923

[1] Decimals omitted.

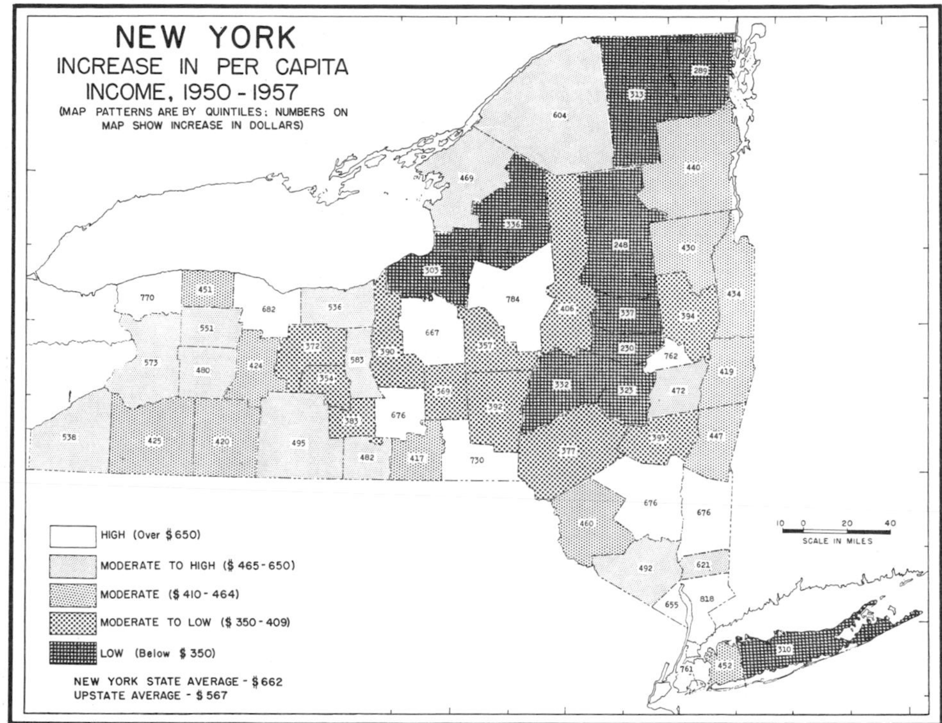

Fig. 3. Increase in per capita income, 1950–1957. Implication: the greater the increase in per capita income, the better the economic health. A comparison of this map with Figure 2 illustrates an appreciable difference in the two indicators. Counties on Long Island rank high in per capita income, but much lower in increase in per capita income. This can be explained by the extensive postwar migration of middle-income people into a relatively high income area. St. Lawrence County is a striking case of low per capita income (4th quintile on Fig. 2) but rapid growth (2nd quintile on Fig. 3). Construction of the St. Lawrence Seaway and Power projects during the 1950's undoubtedly explains the increase in income.

ranks of the individual indicators and re-ranking the totals. Such is the basis for Figure 12. The result shows Rockland County ranked first, and Fulton County in the distressed middle Mohawk region, ranked last (58th).

Factor Analysis

Subjective judgment based on knowledge of conditions within the state suggests that Figure 12 is reasonably accurate, yet it must be pointed out that in this case the equal weighting technique is without underlying mathematical logic. It is in just such a situation that statistical treatment can often be useful. When applied to this problem, factor analysis constructs a foundation of logic upon which the results presented can rest with some security.

Most of the pioneer work in factor analysis has been carried out by psychologists and has been developed, in part, to deal with problems similar to the one considered here; namely, to condense a number of measures into one or more independent factors.[5] Sheer computa-

[5] The basic work in the field is L. L. Thurstone, *Multiple Factor Analysis* (Chicago: University of Chicago Press, 1949). Another advanced work incorporating the latest techniques is Harry H. Harman, *Modern Factor Analysis* (Chicago: University of Chicago Press, 1960). The best introductions to the subject are Godfrey H. Thompson, *The Factorial Analysis of Human Ability* (New York: Houghton Mifflin and Co., 1951) and Benjamin Fruchter, *In-*

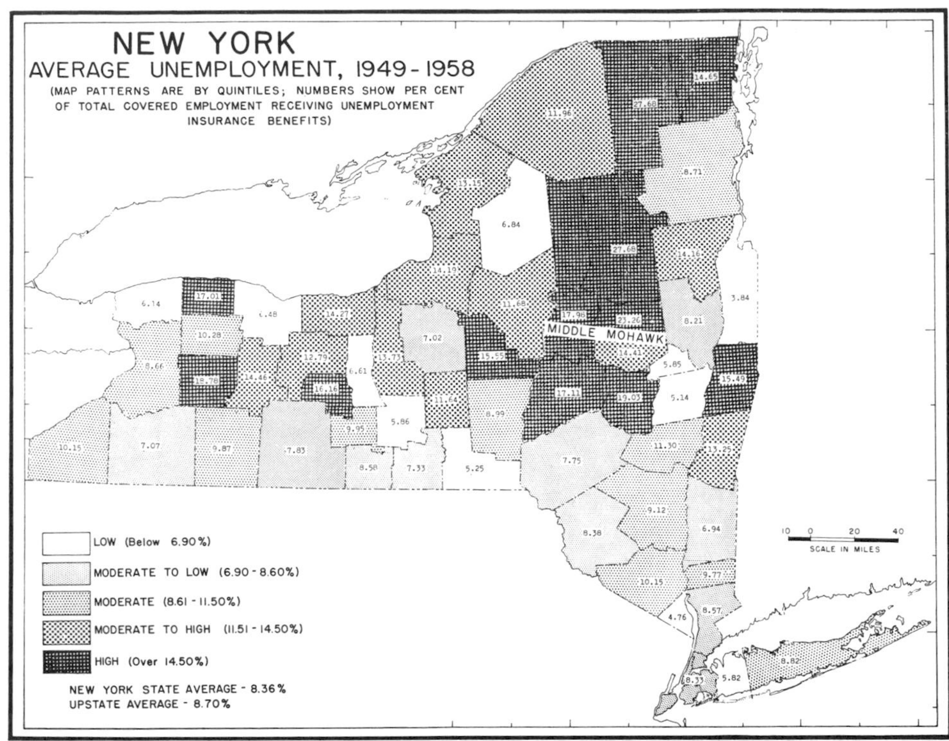

Fig. 4. Average unemployment, 1949–1958. Implication: the lower the unemployment levels the better the economic health. Unemployment is the indicator most widely used to identify economic distress, and this map points up some of the outstanding distressed areas, particularly the middle Mohawk region. It also reflects the seasonal character of job opportunities in some of the northern Adirondack and other rural counties. Where jobs are plentiful only in certain seasons, average unemployment figures always are high.

troduction to Factor Analysis (Princeton: Van Nostrand Co., 1954). A geographer might also note M. J. Hagood, "Statistical Methods for Delineation of Regions Applied to Data on Agriculture and Population," *Social Forces*, Vol. 21 (1943), pp. 287–97; Brian J. L. Berry, "An Inductive Approach to the Regionalization of Economic Development," in Norton S. Ginsburg, ed., *Essays on Geography and Economic Development*, University of Chicago, Department of Geography Research Paper No. 62 (1960), pp. 78–107; *idem*, "Basic Patterns of Economic Development," in Norton S. Ginsburg, *Atlas of Economic Development*, University of Chicago, Department of Geography Research Paper No. 68 (1961), pp. 110–119; *idem*, "A Method for Deriving Multi-Factor Uniform Regions," *Przeglad Geograficzny*, Vol. 23 (1961), pp. 263–282; and Christen T. Jonassen and Sherwood H. Peres, *Interrelationship of Dimensions of Community System: A Factor Analysis of Eighty-Two Variables* (Columbus: State University of Ohio Press, 1960).

tional complexities have hindered its use until the recent fairly widespread availability of electronic computers.[6] The factor analysis employed here is of the Principal Axes type and starts with a matrix (Table 2) of correlation coefficients measuring the degree of correlation between the indicators. Unities are placed in the diagonals, since each measure

[6] The program used was developed by Calvin E. Wright, *Principal Axis Factor Analysis Program for the IBM Type 650* (Seattle: University of Washington, 1957). This program calculated the factor loadings directly, rather than via the centroid method, the results of which have to be modified subsequently to achieve the unique principal axes solution from the original ellipsoid. The authors would like to thank Mr. James Geyert of the Computing Center at Syracuse University for the help he gave in running the program.

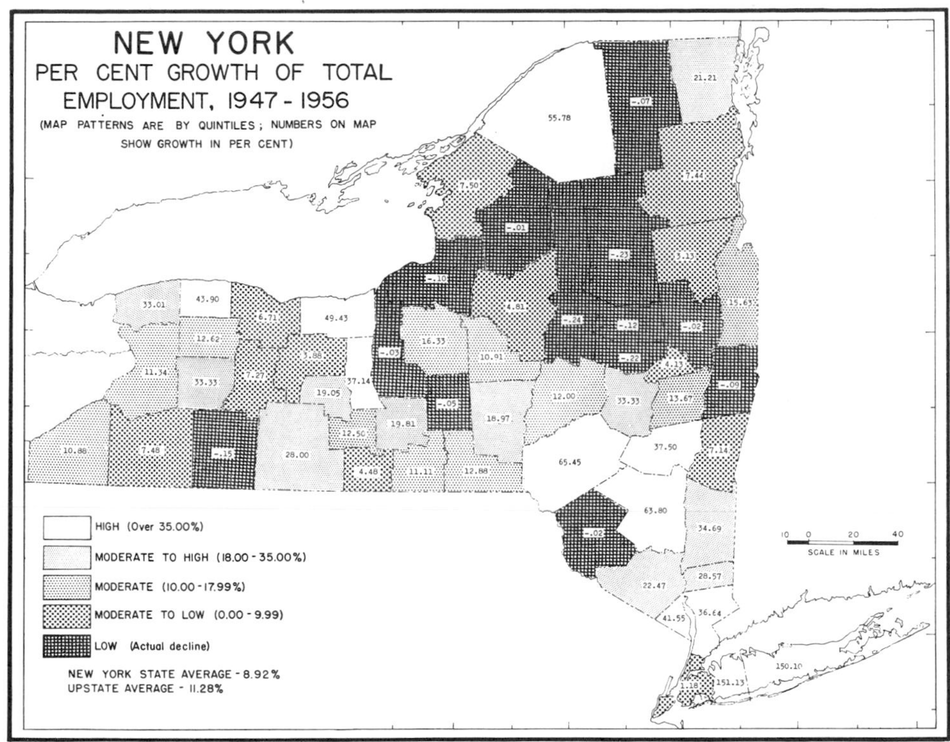

FIG. 5. Per cent growth of total employment, 1947–1956. Implication: the higher the growth rate, the better the economic health. Suburban areas, and counties which had relatively few working people in 1947 but which experienced subsequent sizable gains, rank high. St. Lawrence Seaway construction activities again raised the rank of St. Lawrence County. The major urban areas vary greatly but do not appear to be especially healthy. Their high levels of employment in 1947 would tend to preclude possibilities of spectacular percentage gains. Those sections of the state which show actual losses are in many instances the real trouble spots. The growth in counties surrounding New York City illustrates that these areas are more than dormitory communities. Some similarities exist between this map and Figure 4, especially in the middle Mohawk region and the Adirondacks. Elsewhere extreme dissimilarities support the validity of using multiple indicators. ("Total employment" refers to total employment covered by unemployment insurance.)

obviously correlates perfectly with itself. Operations upon the basic data matrix then extract the first factor which accounts for the greatest proportion of the intercorrelations, leaving those portions not accounted for in a residual matrix. These operations are repeated upon successive residual matrices and further independent factors are extracted, not all of which need be significant.[7] It is conceivable that only one significant factor accounts for the intercorrelations of the variables, in which case the notion of

[7] Identification of the significance of the successive factors is difficult. Only one test (M. S. Bartlett, "Tests of Significance in Factor Analysis," *British Journal of Psychological Statistics* Vol. 3 [1950], pp. 77–85) appears to be wholly reliable, but this demands extreme accuracy of the latent roots of all the matrices, original and residual. These values, sometimes referred to as the eigen values, are, in turn, calculated from the sum of the squared factor loadings and then multiplied together for the significance test. Any small error in the factor loadings would thus be magnified enormously rendering Bartlett's test useless. The iterative program used in this analysis set the smallest error term (0.00005) that could be used practically, but even so, factor loadings for the seventh, eighth, and ninth factors could hardly be relied upon.

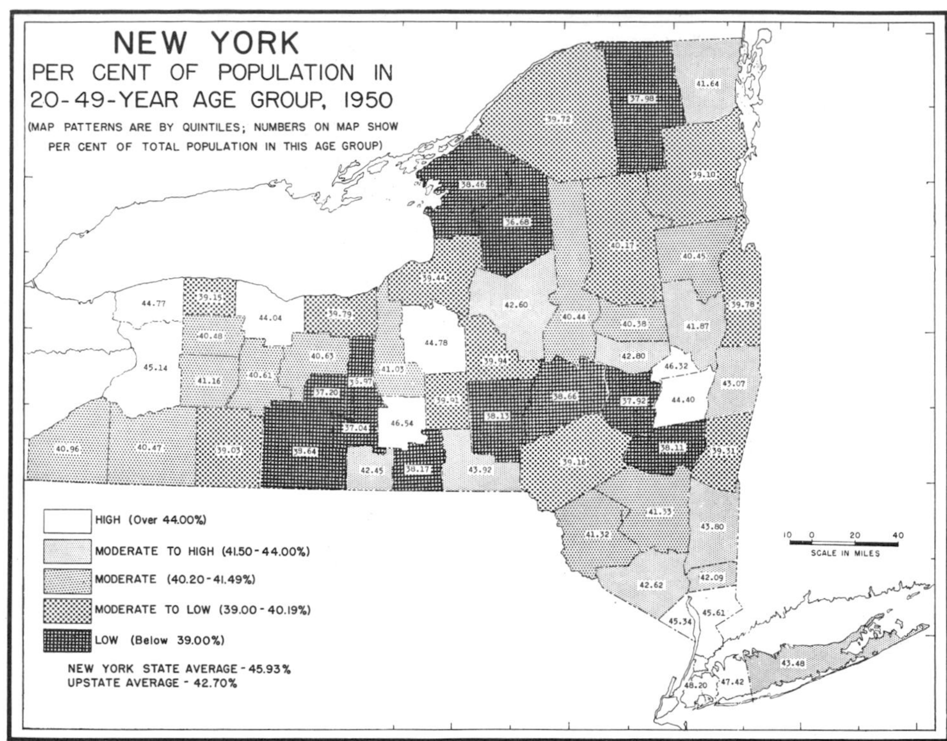

FIG. 6. Per cent of population in 20–49 age group, 1950. Implication: the higher the per cent of population in this age group, the better the economic health. Areas with the best work opportunities attract this most vigorous segment of the population. Counties with large urban centers, or adjacent ones profiting from proximity to these large centers, rank high. Primarily farming counties are especially low, indicating a lack of opportunities or attractiveness of farming to the "present generation."

economic health may be shown logically in one dimension or, cartographically, upon one map. If, however, more than one factor is significant, then there is a strong argument that the concept of economic health is multidimensional, each of the dimensions by definition being independent of one another and therefore incapable of being combined or shown in total on a single map.

Each factor is made up of a linear combination of all the indicators, and, to paraphrase Thurstone, the problem is somewhat similar to writing a linear regression equation in which the factor loadings or "weights" are analogous to regression coefficients, which give the proportion each indicator contributes to the factor. Loading on Factor I are shown in Table 4. The value of each county on Factor I is determined through use of different proportions of the indicators. Thus the county value on Factor I = 0.8015 (rank of county in increase in per capita income) + 0.7068 (rank of county in per cent of population growth) + 0.6479 (rank of county in per cent of population in 20–49 age group), and so on. Ranks of the counties are used because rank correlation coefficients made up the original data matrix. Then the values on Factor I are themselves ranked. The result, with quintile patterns, added, is shown in Figure 13.

Factor I, accounting for 50.1 per cent of all the intercorrelation of the indicators, and more than three times the amount of any other factor, must be interpreted as a general eco-

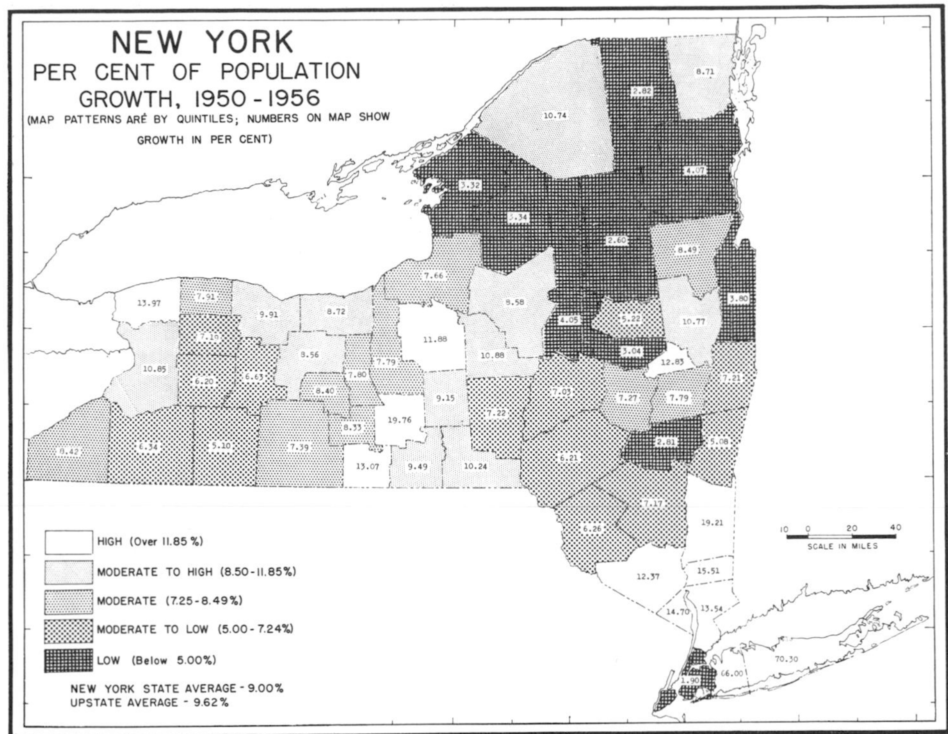

FIG. 7. Per cent of population growth, 1950–1956. Implication: the greater the population growth, the better the economic health. Except for the suburban phenomena, it is not likely that large population gains would show up in any area that is not providing substantial support for increasing numbers of people. Lack of population growth in the Adirondacks, Catskills (both limited because of physical handicaps and state ownership of land), and primarily farming counties is striking. Equally pronounced is the growth on New York City's periphery.

nomic health factor on which the counties are evenly spread.[8] The heaviest "weights," which tend to pull a county down the scale of economic health, are per capita income, increase in per capita income, and increase in average weekly earnings, whereas the lightest "weights," those which have the opposite affect, are per cent increase in value added by manufacture, per cent growth in retail sales, and per cent growth in total employment. The factor loadings do not differ widely, however, and it is interesting to note that the map of county ranks based on Factor I (Fig. 13), differs hardly at all from the map relying on equal weighting (Fig. 12).

County values on Factor II, which accounts for a further 15.7 per cent of the total intercorrelation of the measures, are normally distributed,[9] and the factor can be interpreted as a rural-urban scale, since there is a decided tendency for counties with high values to have large urban centers devoted to secondary and tertiary activities, whereas low values tend to be associated with rural counties. This interpretation is confirmed by a simple linear regression analysis of county values on Factor II and urban population, which indicated a

[8] A Kolmorogov-Smirnov test indicated no significant departure from even spacing along a linear continuum; $z = 0.57$ with $L(z) = 0.098$.

[9] On the Kolmorogov-Smirnov test $z = 0.23$ with $L(z) = 0.00$.

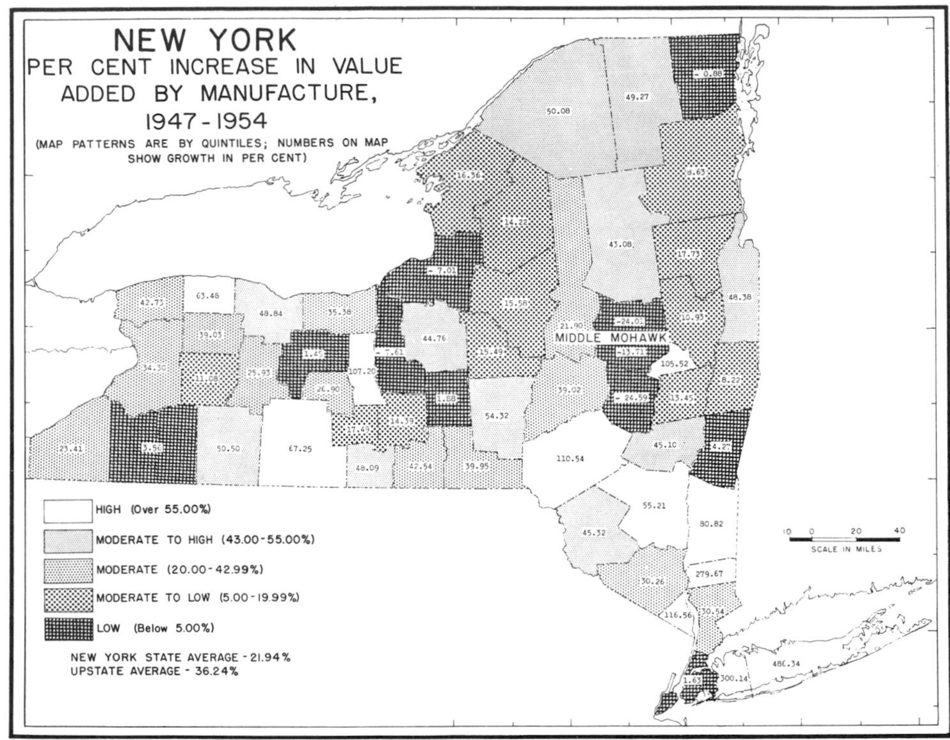

FIG. 8. Per cent increase in value added by manufacture, 1947–1954. Implication: the greater the increase, the better the economic health. It might be argued here that absolute gain in numbers of factory workers would be as good or even better an indicator, for the addition of one large factory would result in a substantial per cent increase in a county with little manufacturing, but only a tiny increase in one with a great deal of manufacturing. Both might be used to an advantage. On this map the great cities show only modest gains, but note the growth on Long Island. The middle Mohawk region again looks very weak. (1954 dollars are converted to 1947 dollars through use of the "All Commodities Other than Farm Products" index of the U. S. Dept. of Labor.)

weak, but significant, relationship (Fig. 14).[10]

It should be repeated that counties with high values on the factors have lower ranks in economic health. Thus, although the urban areas are generally supposed to be in relatively good economic health (a supposition supported by the values on Factor I), the spatial pattern of counties on Factor II, the regression analysis, and the highest factor loadings support the idea that, in some ways, the urban areas have a poor economic health of their own. This is undoubtedly true, for it is in urban areas that extreme problems of unemployment and very low living standards in slums occur even though relatively high overall economic vigor exists. The highest loadings for Factor II are on per cent growth of total employment, per cent of population in the 20–49 age group, per cent increase in the value added by manufacturing, and per cent growth of retail sales, all of which exhibit larger figures for urban than for rural areas.

County values on Factor III, which accounts for a further ten per cent of the total

[10] The linear regression analysis of county values on Factor II against the square root of the per cent of urban population indicated a weak $r = +0.33$, but a significant $P = 0.01$ relationship. Residuals were plotted in an attempt to identify further possible variables, but no rationale could be found for the spatial pattern.

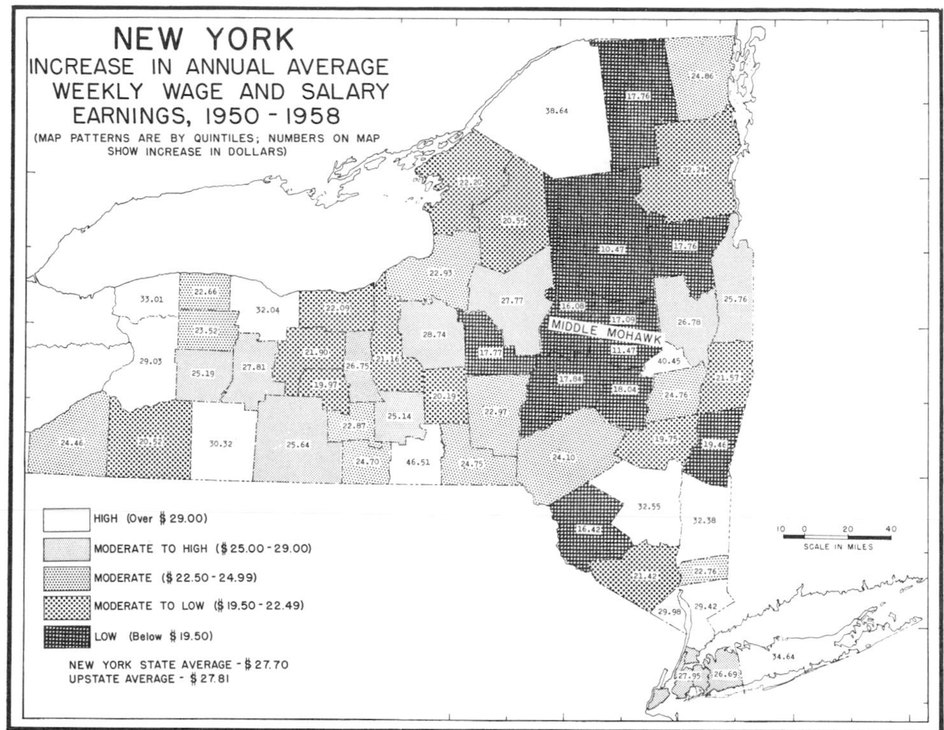

FIG. 9. Increase in annual weekly wage and salary earnings, 1950–1958. Implication: the greater the increase in earnings, the better the economic health. Once again the middle Mohawk region exhibits relative economic weakness while Seaway construction in St. Lawrence County has produced strength. Industrial growth in Tioga and Broome counties on the state's southern boundary had a major effect on the previously poor agricultural wage structure of the former. ("Earnings of employment" refers to earnings covered by unemployment insurance.)

intercorrelation of the measures, also are normally distributed,[11] but are more difficult to interpret. The significance of the factor rests upon interpretation, since, as mentioned previously, the tests of significance which have been devised up to this time are either unsatisfactory or impractical to apply. It is suggested here that Factor III reflects a dimension of economic-demographic growth upon which the factor loadings contrast growth (such things as population and retail sales) with unemployment (Table 4). The counties around New York City and near the Hudson-Mohawk corridor tend to fall into the economically healthier categories and demonstrate the still powerful pull of one of the oldest, magistral routes in the United States (Fig. 15). Apparently, this corridor still attracts the younger, economically vigorous people at the expense of some other parts of the state, but is unable to provide all the opportunities necessary to absorb the influx of job-seekers.

An examination of factor loadings and the spatial pattern of county values supports the conclusion that Factor IV and subsequent factors are unique or error terms.[12]

In summary, factor analysis has isolated three independent ways in which the counties of New York State vary according to their

[11] On the Kolmogorov-Smirnov test $z = 1.096$ with $L(z) = 0.822$.

[12] See Thurstone, *op. cit.*, pp. 73–75, and Fruchter, *op. cit.*, pp. 44–46.

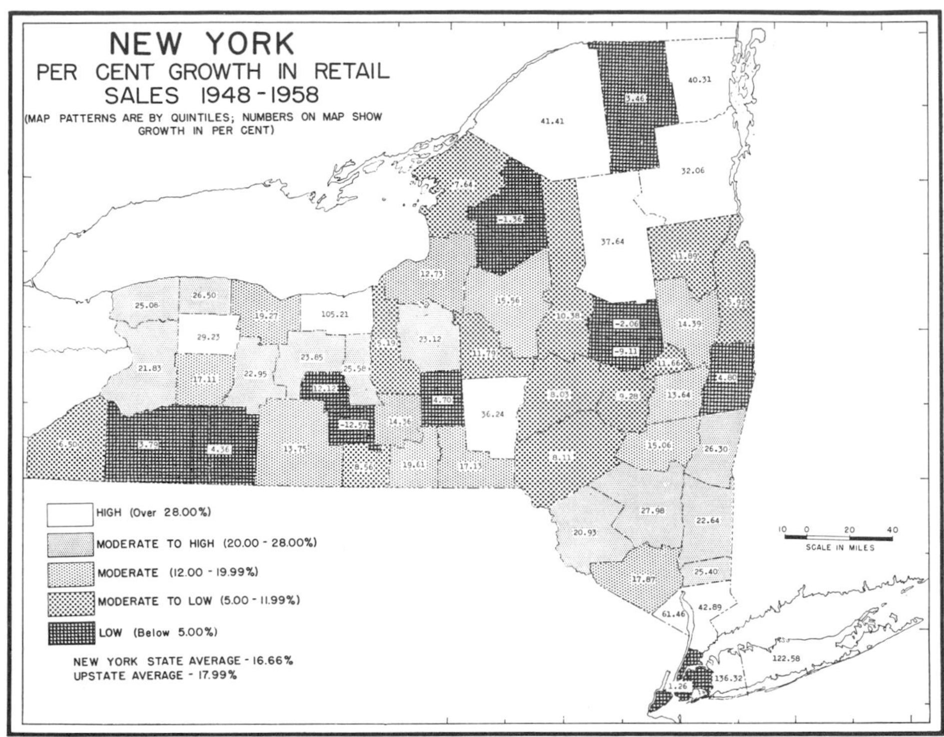

FIG. 10. Per cent growth in retail sales, 1948–1958. Implication: the greater the growth in retail sales, the better the economic health. The New York City periphery ranks high. Otherwise the urban counties do not show up particularly strongly. Rural counties which were very low at the base year but which prospered immensely by introducion of special new sales developments, tourist industries, or construction activities, nearly fill the top quintile. Of course, if retail sales per capita had been employed as an indicator, urban counties would have ranked higher. (1958 dollars are converted to 1948 dollars through use of the Consumer Price Index of the U. S. Dept. of Labor.)

degree of economic health: (1) a general economic health dimension to which all the indicators contribute roughly similar proportions, (2) an urban-rural dimension to which the indicators contribute widely different proportions, and (3) a dimension of economic-demographic growth which contrasts growth and unemployment.

MAKING GEOGRAPHIC REALITY OUT OF THE COUNTY CHOROGRAPHIC MAPS

Regardless of the procedure employed to arrive at a county ranking of economic health, the resultant chorographic map is far from realistic, and hence is not only objectionable to the geographically-trained mind, but perhaps even confusing to potential users of the map. The specific question considered in this case was how can the chorographic maps be converted to a single, relatively accurate, isopleth map. Figure 13 was used for basic control because Factor I accounts for 50 per cent of the intercorrelation of the indicators, and at the same time produces essentially identical results to the equal-weighting technique. Figures 14 and 15 aided in refinement of interpretations. In addition, the following demonstrably rational considerations were found to be pertinent to the isopleth drawing process: (1) Large metropolitan areas such as Rochester, Syracuse, and Binghamton generally have better economic health than smaller

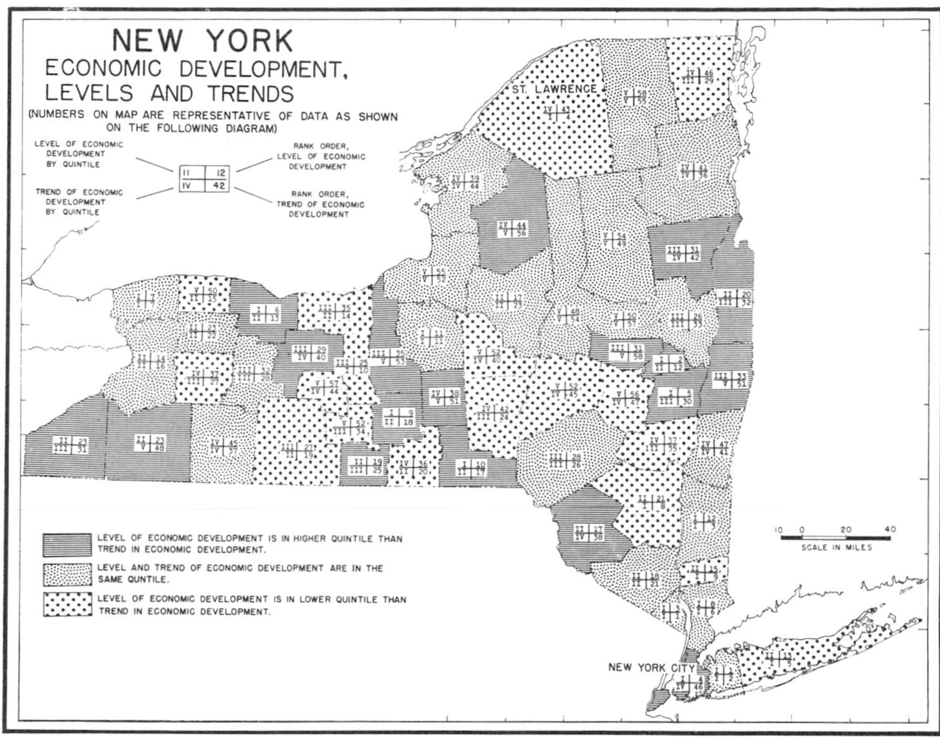

FIG. 11. Economic development, levels and trends. Some counties, such as Onondaga in which Syracuse is situated, or Oswego just to the north of Onondaga, show similar trend and level status. Others, however, including New York City and St. Lawrence County, exhibit great contrasts between level and trend. Explanation for these variations, and corrective measures for certain problem counties, need to be worked on by state and local agencies. The fact that rural areas exhibit low ranks in both level and trend supports the contention that their economic past and future is not bright. ("Levels" are based on equal weighting of per cent of population in 20–49 age group, 1950; per capita income, 1958; and per cent of average unemployment, 1949–58. "Trends" are based on equal weighting of increase in per capita income 1950–57; per cent of population growth, 1950–56; per cent growth of total employment, 1947–56; per cent growth in retail sales, 1948–58; increase in average weekly earnings, 1950–58; and per cent increase in value added by manufacturing, 1947–54.)

centers or rural sections. (2) Some urban areas, particularly medium-sized and small ones, are under considerable economic stress. Examples include places in the middle Mohawk region (between Utica and Schenectady), Auburn, and Oswego. Access to a variety of data on trends and levels for practically all cities of the state aided in placing them in their proper context in relation to the surrounding county or counties. (3) Within large metropolitan areas there is a "doughnut" effect, with poorer economic health in the old city than in its peripheral zones. (4) Areas dominated by farming are not experiencing a proportionate share of economic growth and in some instances are actually declining. (5) State-owned lands such as parts of the Adirondacks and Catskills, which by law have been set aside as "forever wild" areas, cannot be expected to show high levels of economic health when measured by the above indicators. (6) Areas of principally hilly or rough terrain are not advantageous to economic development and are generally becoming poorer and poorer. (7) Land largely in forests reflects a low intensity of land use. (8) The density

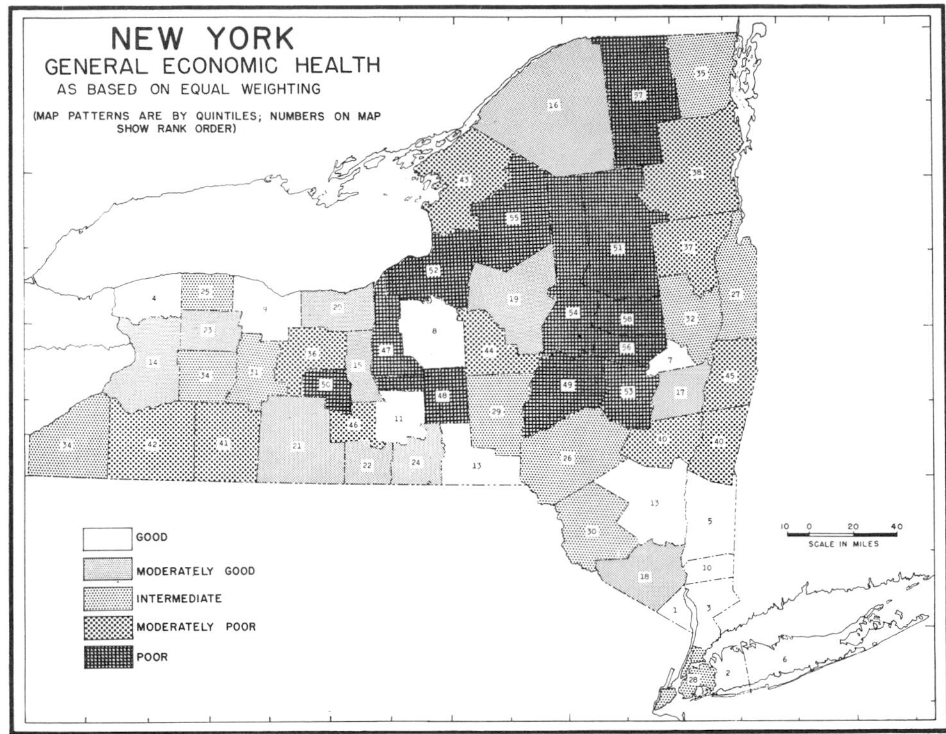

FIG. 12. General economic health (as based on equal weighting of indicators). This map reflects the relative economic health of the counties if all of the individual indicators shown on previous figures are arbitrarily weighted equally. Urban health is evident, although in some places it is not as good as might be expected. It is surprising to find New York City ranked 28th among the statistical units. Yet if one contemplates some of those aspects of New York City which reflect anything but robust economic health, he may accept a ranking of 28th as reasonable. Were levels of tertiary attainment given more prevalence among the indicators, New York City would rank higher.

of transportation networks of different kinds, although not always conclusive, gives some evidence concerning economic progress. (9) Population density and Klimm's empty areas map[13] are aids. Maps based on data related to the above considerations, when overlaid and compared with Figure 13, served as guides for drawing isopleths. Field checks further facilitated the isopleth drawing process. The result is Figure 16, a map of general economic health in New York State. It is interesting to note that some counties which were well up in the top quintile on Figure 13 actually have part of their areas in all quintiles from the highest to the lowest on the isopleth map (e.g., Albany County). Others, although in one quintile on Figure 13, may in reality have most of their areas in another quintile. In such cases, small but economically significant parts of a county dominate the whole county statistically.

[13] Lester E. Klimm, "The Empty Areas of the Northeastern United States," *Geographical Review*, Vol. 44 (1954), pp. 325–345.

BRIEF INTERPRETATION OF THE MAP OF GENERAL ECONOMIC HEALTH

Figure 16 portrays the patterns of economic health in New York State for approximately the 1950's. It reflects, in part, the economic evolution of the past and provides some insight into the future. Further, it mirrors some-

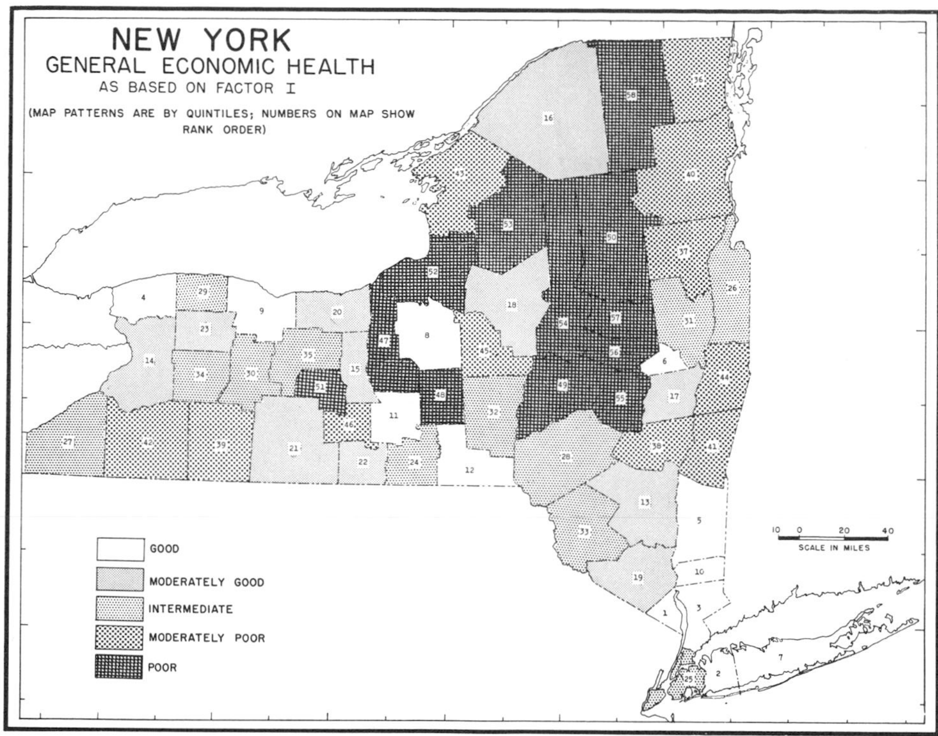

FIG. 13. General economic health (as based on Factor I). The application of the statistical procedure known as "factor analysis" lends underlying mathematical logic to the problem of combining the indicators. Factor I, accounting for 50.1 per cent of the intercorrelation of the indicators, and more than three times the amount of any other factor, serves as the statistical base for Figure 15. It is interesting to note that the rank of counties based on Factor I is essentially the same as that based on equal weighting of the indicators (cf. Figs. 12 and 13).

thing of what is happening in all of the northeastern United States. Whether or not Fig. 16 could ever function as a base for decision-making is problematical, but if decision-makers agree that the indicators of economic health employed here are valid, then it seems they might well give some serious attention to the patterns portrayed.

Clearly, the periphery of New York City, the Albany-Schenectady district, and the Syracuse, Buffalo, Rochester, and Binghamton areas stand out as being in relatively good economic health. They fall generally into the top two quintiles (cf. Figs. 1 and 16). These are the large urban areas, the places getting the largest share of new industrialization, expansion in tertiary activities, and residential construction. They have the size, the market, the services, and the general dynamism to attract economic activities of almost all types, and they compete favorably with growing urban areas elsewhere in the country. They will provide most of the additional jobs of the future and absorb most of the State's population growth. This phenomenon is not peculiar to New York State; it is part of the great wave of urbanism that characterizes the modern Western world.

Rural areas tend to be in the lower quintiles of economic health on Figure 16. They have been going downhill relatively for a long time and are likely to continue to do so. Little of the increasing population in the decades ahead can be expected to be supported in the

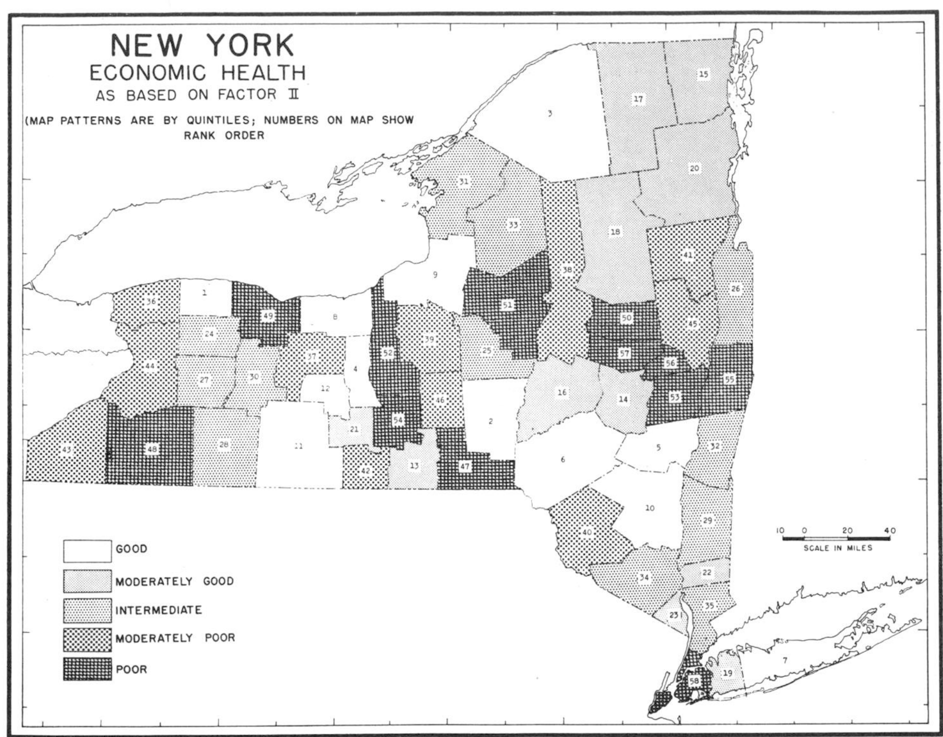

FIG. 14. Economic health (as based on Factor II). Factor II accounts for 15.7 per cent of total intercorrelation of the indicators. By ranking the urban counties relatively low, it points out the fact that urban areas have some economically unhealthy aspects.

areas shown in the lowest quintiles, except as the rapidly growing peripheries of the great cities may spread outward to encompass them.

Although there are some exceptions, urban areas with populations of about 50,000[14] or less are not doing so well. When places of this size show exceptional economic vigor, it usually is because of proximity to one of the larger metropolitan systems, which actually is inducing the economic growth, rather than the smaller place itself. Some of the smaller urban areas are in the lowest quintile. Standouts are those in the middle Mohawk region between Utica and Schenectady.

In spite of a vigorous early start and a position astride excellent transportation facilities, the middle Mohawk region may be described as the State's number one problem area. Although profiting a little because of proximity to metropolitan Utica on the west and Schenectady-Albany on the east, the middle Mohawk region lacks the really large metropolitan center which seems to be important to economic vitality. Instead it is composed of many small central places ranging in size from a few hundred to slightly over 30,000 population. Industry has been dominated by soft-goods production such as textiles, carpets, and gloves. At the national level, these types of industries have not expanded as rapidly as the American economy, and are less successful in the old industrial regions in the northeast than in newer regions like the American South. Unionism is strong, labor costs are

[14] It is quite possible that further study will show that this figure is too low. In any case it is undoubtedly a changing one reflecting the stage or conditions of economic progress.

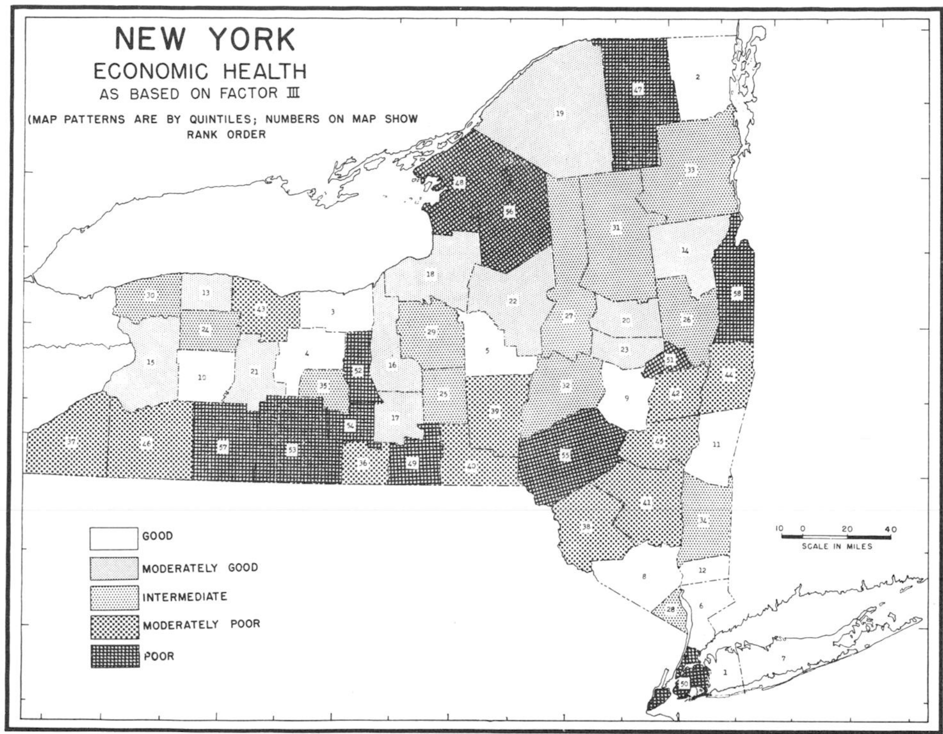

FIG. 15. Economic health (as based on Factor III). Factor III accounts for 9.7 per cent of the total intercorrelation of the indicators. The relative high ranks of many counties around New York City and along the Hudson–Mohawk Corridor suggest that these faster-growing areas attract ever-increasing numbers of people, but fail to provide sufficient employment opportunities for all.

high, and management lethargy is not entirely lacking. Locational advantages with respect to markets and materials have disappeared with the change of the national geography of markets and materials. Most new businesses considering moves into central New York State are likely to find the large metropolitan areas better suited to them than the small centers of the middle Mohawk region. Of course, efforts to attract new industry and business have been made, and with some success. On the other hand, there is always the likelihood that an area such as this, which over the years has had the qualities to produce economic distress, is not the best location for a new venture. If this reasoning is sound, then perhaps new enterprises should not in all cases be encouraged to move into distressed areas where they are likely to be subjected to the regional qualities which have already produced economic difficulties. Instead perhaps distressed areas should be helped to adjust to new lower economic equilibriums!

Interpretation of the geography of New York State's economic health could be extended into many pages, but such an interpretation is not a major purpose here. For this the reader is referred to the reference in footnote 2.

CONCLUSIONS

Four conclusions, largely of a methodological nature, can be stated: (1) Economic health is multi-dimensional. This conclusion has been supported by comparing individual indicators, differences between level and

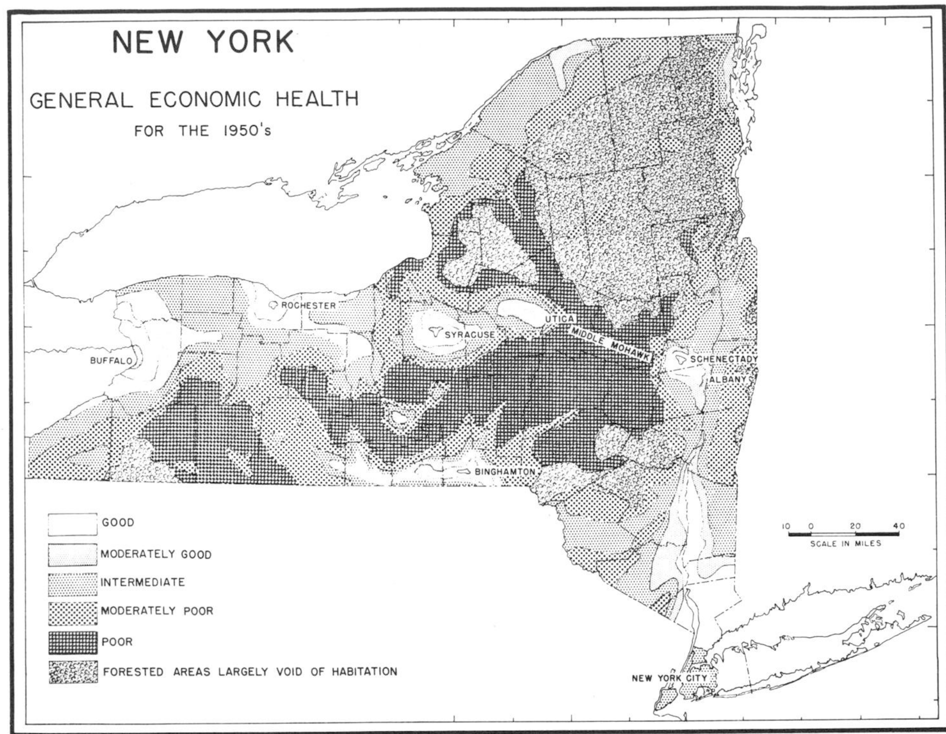

FIG. 16. General economic health for the 1950's. This isopleth map is the product of combining the statistical data on counties (Fig. 13) and knowledge concerning areal variation within counties. It was drawn by overlaying maps exhibiting relevant patterns. It is believed this combination of statistical and traditional geographic interpretations approaches the areal reality of economic health in New York State more rationally than either statistical or traditional geographic techniques alone. This map is derived in part from a county map based on Factor I. Community economic data, population, transportation, and terrain characteristics, and field observations facilitated the drawing of isopleths between health categories.

trend indicators, and contrasts between Factors I, II, and III. (2) The procedures employed in this analysis of New York State could be applied to any part of the United States and, theoretically at least, to any part of the world. (3) A map like Figure 16 represents a starting point for enquiry into causes and, as such, can become a basis for geographic and economic analyses as well as regional thinking and planning. (4) In a period when traditional methodology and newer statistical techniques are being compared and evaluated for use by the geographic profession, this paper demonstrates that these traditional and statistical methods can, and perhaps more often should, be blended.

PART III

Theory of Regional Development

Introductory Note

There is today no one theory of regional development that commands universal assent. The question might even be raised whether a single unified theory is possible. The processes are not only extremely complex, but our very manner of thinking forces us to choose between continuity and discontinuity in time and space, as discussed in the Introduction to Section II. Thus, we are afforded only partial theories which view that complex object, regional development, now from one angle, now from another.

Four of the principal approaches are represented by the selections in this section, each concentrating on a different aspect of the spatial differentiation of economic growth. The first concerns the role of natural resources; the second, the influence of labor mobility; the third, the function of cities; and the fourth, the response of the agricultural sector to urbanization.

The concept of resources is an economic, not a physical one. The value of a resource is not intrinsic in the material but depends on the structure of demand, the current state of technology, the cost of transportation, and the social and political organization for transforming the raw stuff of nature into marketable commodities. Thus, to make the resources in an area available in an economic sense, considerable investment may be required. But this investment will not be forthcoming unless its rate of return, private or social, is sufficiently attractive. Once the investment is made, however, the importance of the natural resource endowment shrinks in relation to the importance of other production inputs such as education, skill, research, technology, and organization. Consequently, some seemingly "poor" regions, such as the Arizona desert, may suddenly experience extraordinary economic progress, brought about by a shift in the structure of demand, while other regions, "rich" in natural wealth, such as Alaska, remain lodged in the category of problem areas.

Although physical resources have dwindled in importance as inputs of production, the start of development in a locality will frequently result from a unique resource advantage which attracts capital and the other factors of production. The irresistible magnet may be climate, as in Arizona, or raw materials such as petroleum, iron ore, diamonds, or forests. Typically, production will be at first primarily for export, and the income thus generated may be reinvested in the region, leading to further growth. Urban nuclei may form, local markets develop, early industries branch out into new lines, and the gradual expansion of the area's infrastructure of private and public capital, skills, and institutions enhance the general attractiveness of the area. As the local economy grows, it will cross one threshold after another, making possible larger and more diversified business operations. Eventually, a general threshold may be reached, which, if broken through, will lead to sustained and cumulative growth of the regional economy.

This, in brief, is the substance of the export-base theory of regional development discussed in this volume by Perloff and Wingo, North, Tiebout, Baldwin, and Pfister. It is stated here bluntly, without any of its refinements and sophistications such as the terms of trade, the effect of the business cycle, or the savings propensity of regional producers. Yet the theory makes economic growth contingent upon comparative locational advantage, initial resource endowment, regional exports, and the mutual reinforcement of linkage and multiplier effects. The theory is supported by considerable evidence, and is most successful in explaining the origins of regional growth. It is less successful, however, in explaining the mechanics of sustained and cumulative growth. After a heady start, an area's economy may slip or stagnate. Lack of industrial diversification, resource exhaustion, changes in demand, or technological change may adversely affect regional fortunes.

Much work has gone into the analysis of migration in relation to regional economic growth. A widely held theory, for which there is considerable empirical support, holds that migration occurs in response to differences in economic opportunities. Thus, it serves both to diminish regional differences in welfare and to stimulate growth. In areas of emigration, it allows economic reorganization to occur and tends to raise wage rates by contributing to the relative scarcity of labor. In areas of immigration, the inflow may depress local wages by making labor more abundant, but it also provides the work force necessary for an expanding economy and constitutes a hidden income transfer as a result of prior investment in the education of migrants.

Contrary to this theory, some authors, among them Gunnar Myrdal, have speculated that the massive rural-urban migration which has everywhere accompanied industrialization has tended to magnify existing differences between the urbanized center and the rural periphery. Although the evidence for this theory of the spreading welfare gap is far from certain, particularly for the long run, it has had a powerful influence on policy and, whenever asserted, has usually gone unchallenged. In their article, Bernard Okun and Richard Richardson dispute Myrdal's thesis on theoretical grounds, and conclude that migration may widen or narrow per capita income differences according to the circumstances.

The study of the role of cities is a third source of insight into the process of regional economic development. This focus on cities is justified by the fact that modern economic development has occurred chiefly in an urban-industrial matrix. Attention has been given to the effects of concentration in space upon the rate and the manner of economic growth and the corresponding social functions and organization. Concentrated growth gives rise to external economies which can have extreme importance for further growth and the location of new activity. Heterogeneity, combined with a high density of communications, favors creativity and innovation, so that cities are usually in the forefront of modernization. Thus growth tends to feed on growth; new needs are created and their satisfaction stimulates still greater wants. Political, social, and economic power are concentrated in the city and lead to further concentration.

The city's growth, however, cannot be contained. Urban influence will spread as an expanded and more varied food supply is needed, as factories call for larger quantities of raw materials, as local markets prove too confining. The city carries its way of doing things along as its imperium reaches outward: the network of communications is extended, banks, schools, and factories are built throughout the provinces, and urban values are widely adopted. New nuclei spring up, generally in accord with the rules for areal functional organization, in a hierarchy from local convenience centers to regional and national metropolises. While regionalism and particularism are worn down, national patterns of interaction are established among cities. At an advanced stage of development, city and nation may, in fact, appear to be coincident.

The final group of selections focuses on the problems of rural areas in an urbanizing society. Many of these areas are economically depressed; their "case" is discussed by the anonymous experts of the United Nations Economic Commission for Europe. The center-periphery theory is presented here with great force. More than a description of geographic position, center and periphery refer to a set of structural relations that hold the periphery in nearly permanent subordination to the urban-industrial heartland of Europe. Attempts to start new poles of growth within the periphery have met with only limited success.

The center-periphery relation is examined once more by William Nicholls, who concludes that the influence of urban institutions results in more efficient agricultural production in the vicinity of urban centers. The picture emerges of highly developed and well-integrated metropolitan-agricultural regions separated from each other by bands of essentially rural regions in economic decline. In a second and provocative article, Nicholls attributes the economic laggardness of the American South to dysfunctional social values and institutions which are a legacy of its historic regional ruralism. He places his hope in the transforming influences of the cities which, despite all obstacles, are beginning to replace the old order.

The final article returns to the topic of migration. Dale Hathaway reviews several recent empirical studies in the light of economic theory, and discusses the process of agricultural adjustment. In the main, he finds a positive value for the areas of emigration as well as for the receiving areas, but finds little evidence of a decreasing income gap between city and country in the United States.

Resources and Migration

11. Natural Resource Endowment and Regional Economic Growth*

HARVEY PERLOFF AND LOWDON WINGO, JR.

WE ARE CONCERNED in this paper with the relationship between the natural resources within the various parts, or regions, of a country and what might be called the geography of national economic expansion.

The development of the economy of the United States provides a case study of resources in space interacting with the other elements of economic growth that is especially illuminating: (1) It covers an extended spectrum of growth from early agricultural beginnings to status as an advanced, industrial-and-service-oriented economy, thus affording an opportunity to examine the role of resources in different stages of national economic growth. (2) It covers a wide variety of regional resources and growth situations, providing a rich set of variations on the interactions of the national economy with its geographic components. And (3) it can be examined with the help of a wealth of historical information and statistical data. Specifically, Resources for the Future has concluded a three-year study of the regional characteristics of the growth of the U. S. economy. The results of this effort have been made available in a book entitled *Regions, Resources, and Economic Growth.*[1]

[1] Harvey S. Perloff, Edgar S. Dunn, Jr., Eric E. Lampard, and Richard F. Muth: *Regions, Resources, and Economic Growth* (Baltimore: The Johns Hopkins Press, 1960). We owe a great deal to Messrs. Dunn, Lampard, and Muth; we wish to absolve them, however, of responsibility for any errors or inadequacies in this paper.

The discussion of growth here will be limited to changes in what we refer to as the *volume* of economic activities (e.g., increases in population, employment, value added, and the like), acknowledging that this is but one facet of economic growth. Growth as defined by changes in *welfare* (changes in per capita income, for example) is discussed in Part V of *Regions, Resources, and Economic Growth*; changes in state per capita are analyzed in some detail by Simon Kuznets in "Industrial Distribution of Income and Labor Force by States, 1919-21 to

* Reprinted from Joseph J. Spengler, ed., *Natural Resources and Economic Growth.*

This paper draws heavily on the research that went into this book and on the conclusions that emerge from it. Given this storehouse of materials, we have been tempted into speculation on the broad relationships involved in the resources-growth problem.

Resources and Growth in a Broad Historical Framework

One of the insights emerging from an examination of the history of American economic development is the difficulty of defining "resource endowment" in any long-run, substantive sense. In the short run, endowment is simply the inventory of those natural materials that are required in some degree by the national economy responding to internal consumption demands and to its position in international trade. As the requirements of the economy change, the composition of the inventory shifts, and in this sense "resource endowment" is a changing concept closely associated with the dynamics of economic growth. In short, the answer to what constitutes "resource endowment" is rooted in the determinants of final demand—consumer preferences and income distribution, as well as foreign trade—on the one hand, and in the current organization and technology of production on the other. As these variables change, so will the content of resource endowment. And, clearly then, as the composition of resource endowment changes, there will tend to be substantial changes in the relative advantage among regions supplying material inputs (and services) for the national economy.

The impact of these shifts can be sketched in with broad strokes by identifying stage by stage what have been the "natural resources that count" in the national economy. This requires us to tell again a familiar story, but with a special focus.

The Early Agricultural Period

From its colonial origins the American economy developed as a producer of resource inputs into the rapidly expanding European economy. To serve such a function the endowment which counted in early America was arable land with its environmental complements of climate and water, and this, with access to the growing European market for

---

1955," Part III of "Quantitative Aspects of the Economic Growth of Nations," *Economic Development and Cultural Change,* Vol. VI, July 1958.

We assume that the broad features of regional economic expansion in the United States are familiar to our readers, and so we have presented no figures to describe them here. Those interested in such detail are referred to Chapters 2 and 3 of *Regions, Resources, and Economic Growth.*

agricultural staples, set up the conditions for regional growth in early America. It was quite logical, hence, that the regional economies developed a certain archetype: a good deepwater port as the nucleus of an agricultural hinterland well adapted for the production of a staple commodity in demand on the world market.

The growth potential of these nucleated regions depended heavily on the extent and "richness" of the hinterland accessible to port. Since good agricultural land was almost a free resource while labor and capital were dear, the expansion of production was effected by bringing more land into production and so extending the limits of the hinterland. Much of early American history is dominated by the great rivalries for control of hinterland that emerged between New York and Boston, Philadelphia and Baltimore, Charleston and Savannah. This expansion of the hinterlands took place through social overhead investment in transportation facilities beginning with the Massachusetts road system in the seventeenth century,[2] later producing the Erie Canal, and finally motivating the half century of railroad construction stretching from the Baltimore and Ohio's first crude line reaching out to the rich wheatlands in Maryland and Pennsylvania to the driving of the golden spike at Promontory Point, Utah.[3] The force of the outward push for land is suggested by the fact that population west of the Alleghenies, which was estimated by the 1790 Census at 109,000, by 1840 had become almost six and a half million, with more than 87 per cent of the labor force involved in agriculture.

Even though the data on this period are not very satisfactory, we can draw these general conclusions: (1) the *regional* endowment that made for growth was "good" land advantageously situated with respect to the market centers; (2) the distribution of economic activity in the period before 1840 was essentially a function of the expanding, nucleated, agricultural regions reaching into the economic vacuum of an unsettled continent to bring ever greater areas of land under cultivation; and (3) this resource-dominated expansion of the economy set the stage for the next important development by establishing a geography of markets, transport, and labor force to condition the nature of succeeding growth.

[2] The importance of hinterland in the growth of the early centers is vividly described by Carl Bridenbaugh, *Cities in the Wilderness* (New York: Ronald Press, 1938).

[3] A detailed treatment can be found in Paul H. Cootner, "Transportation Innovation and Economic Development: The Case of the U. S. Steam Railroads." Unpublished Ph.D. thesis, MIT, 1953.

The Minerals-Dominant Economy

Somewhere around 1840-1850 the next important resource stage began—as a result of the emerging minerals-dominant economy. The rapid growth of the railroads and the expansion of processing industries resulted in new input requirements: a new set of resources became important and a new set of locational forces came into play. The first part of this period was dominated by the growing demand for iron and steel and by the rapid elaboration of their production technology.[4] At this point it was the geographical juxtaposition of coal, iron ore, and the market which afforded the great impetus for growth. The importance of minerals, unlike agricultural land, was not alone in their direct contribution to regional growth so much as it was in the nature of their linkages with succeeding stages of production. It was not so much the mining of coal and iron that was important for growth, as the making of iron and steel products, which could not be separated from the sources of its mineral inputs. The early concentration of steel making in western Pennsylvania was a result of these relationships, for this area was not only well endowed with deposits of iron ore and coal but was central to a concentrated market stretching from Boston and New York westward. As the center of gravity of the market shifted west and as Mesabi ores replaced depleted local ores, the iron and steel industry also shifted westward along the southern shores of the Great Lakes.

With the increase in the demand for nonferrous metals, the depletion of accessible ore deposits in the East and the penetration of the West by the railroad net, a new role in regional growth was played by mineral resources endowment. In the Mountain region stretching from the Canadian border to the Southwest states, the mining of metal ores was the lead factor in economic development: in 1870 when mineral extractions involved the employment of 1½ per cent of the labor force nationally, in the Mountain states it accounted for no less than 26.54 per cent, after which it declined until in 1950 the proportion was 3.44 per cent, still twice as much as the national average. Except for primary processing of ores, however, this resource base did not induce the location of any substantial amount of linked activity in the Mountain states. With most of the weight loss taking place during concentration and smelting, the distribution of the market governed the location of succeeding stages of metals fabrication, and the major markets were concentrated in the Northeast.

[4] In 1880, some 70 per cent of steel output went into rails. Cootner, *op. cit.*, Chapter V, pp. 13-14.

The extent to which changes in both demand and supply conditions influenced regional resources activities is suggested by the data in Table 1, showing figures for interregional production shifts for pig iron, copper and lead. Several points are worth noting: (1) the period of great growth in the output of these mineral products (1870-1910) corresponds with the most extensive interregional shifts in their production; (2) truly huge shifts in lead and copper production took place from the Great Lakes region to the Mountain states (and to a lesser extent to the Southwest and Far West) during this period; and (3) there has been a steady shift in pig iron production throughout the entire period 1870-1950 from the Middle Atlantic states to the Great Lakes and, to a lesser extent, the Southeast. These data underline the highly selective regional effects resulting from the growth of a mineral-based economy.

Some notion of the extent of changes in national requirements of material resources is provided by a measure of the changes in the composition of the value of purchases in constant dollars within the broad mineral categories over the period 1870-1950. (This measure is the same as that employed in Table 1; namely, the end of period total which would have to be redistributed among classes to recreate the beginning of period percentage distribution.) Thus, within the mineral fuels the total shift over the period was equivalent to 57 per cent away from bituminous and anthracite coals and toward petroleum and natural gas fuels, that is, towards materials which would hardly have been considered as resources ten years before this period. Among the metals during the same period the total shift was almost 34 per cent, away from iron, lead, and tin and in the direction of the light metals and ferroalloys—one-fourth of this shift has been in the direction of metals for which the economy of 1870 had little or no use, such as aluminum, manganese, nickel, and molybdenum. Finally, among the nonmetals (and here the availability of data limits us to the period 1910 to 1950) the internal composition in this shorter period shifted by 31 per cent, away from stone and toward other construction materials, as well as toward basic chemical materials. Something more than one-fourth of the shift was to materials which would not have been considered as resources in 1870.[5]

An especially important instance of the regional effects of changes in national requirements is provided by the case of petroleum and natural gas in the Southwest in recent decades. Here the effect resulted

[5] Calculated from data in a forthcoming RFF study by Neal Potter and Francis T. Christy, Jr., "U. S. Natural Resource Statistics, 1870 to 1955" (Preliminary Draft, with revisions to 11/1/59), Tables McT-22, 23, 24, 33, and 35.

TABLE 1.—PERCENTAGE CHANGE IN REGIONAL DISTRIBUTION OF U. S. PRODUCTION OF PIG IRON, COPPER AND LEAD, 1870-1910 AND 1910-1950

	Pig iron Percentage Shift[a]		Copper Percentage Shift[a]		Lead Percentage Shift[a]	
Region[b]	1870–1910	1910–1950	1870–1910[c]	1910–1950[d]	1870–1910[c]	1910–1950
New England..	− 1.62	− .06	− 6.90	0	− .41	0
Middle Atlantic	−15.98	−15.65	− 1.44	− .08	− 1.02	+ .34
Great Lakes...	+11.13	+ 7.37	−62.36	−17.72	−58.89	− .45
Southeast.....	+ 4.90	+ 5.80	− 6.39	− 1.57	− 3.89	+ .75
Plains........	0	0	0	+ .33	+ 7.09	− 7.89
Southwest.....	0	0	+27.73	+23.77	+ 1.63	+10.30
Mountain.....	0	0	+39.49	− 2.28	+54.61	−10.17
Far West......	+ 1.57	+ 2.54	+ 9.86	− 4.03	+ .88	+ 7.12
Total Shift....	17.60	15.71	77.08	24.10	64.21	18.51
Percentage growth of output......	1,538%	115%	2,727%	67.8%	1,983%	11.7%

[a] The end-of-period percentage of total national production *less* the beginning-of-period percentage. Thus, with respect to pig iron in the period 1870-1910, New England percentage share of national production was 1.62% less in 1910 than it was in 1870. The figure for Total Shift (sum of the absolute value of the shifts x ½), then, represents the percentage of total national production which would have to be redistributed in order to recreate the beginning-of-period percentage distribution by regions.

[b] The states composing the regions are as follows: *New England*—Maine, New Hampshire, Vermont, Massachusetts, Rhode Island, Connecticut. *Middle Atlantic*—New York, New Jersey, Pennsylvania, Delaware, Maryland, District of Columbia. *Great Lakes*—Ohio, Indiana, Illinois, Michigan, Wisconsin. *Southeast*—Virginia, West Virginia, Kentucky, Tennessee, North Carolina, South Carolina, Georgia, Florida, Alabama, Mississippi, Arkansas, Louisiana. *Plains*—Minnesota, Iowa, Missouri, North Dakota, South Dakota, Nebraska, Kansas. *Southwest*—Oklahoma, Texas, Arizona, New Mexico. *Mountain*—Montana, Idaho, Wyoming, Utah, Colorado. *Far West*—Washington, Oregon, California, Nevada.

[c] The 1870-1910 shift figures for lead and copper should be viewed with caution. The 1870 figures upon which the shifts are based represent the regional composition of the *current dollar value* of domestic mine production (the only data which were available), while all later figures used express domestic mine production in *short tons.* Since we are dealing with regional composition, the resulting shift figures would be seriously compromised if there were substantial price differentials at the mine head among the major producing regions in 1870. For the purposes of the discussion following, it is assumed that such price differentials would exert at worst a modest influence on the 1870-1910 shift figures.

[d] Excludes unallocated production in Pennsylvania, Tennessee, and Vermont of 1.59%.

(For sources see p. 7)

not only from a powerful, direct mining leverage (as was noted in the case of the Mountain region), but also from the availability of a cheap, convenient fuel which altered substantially the region's relative advantages for certain classes of industry. The happy coincidence of these mineral fuels with rich deposits of salt and sulfur provided a resource base for a rapidly expanding chemical industry. Thus, petroleum and gas extraction and refining, responding to a huge and growing national demand, served to change the economic conditions of production throughout the entire Southwest.

Summarizing the broad sweeps of the period of very rapid growth from about the middle of the nineteenth century, we note that during the first half of this period (to the end of the nineteenth century) there were two great overlapping resource effects conditioning the subnational distribution of economic activity: (1) geographically the more widespread effect was that of agriculture continuing to spread out over the arable lands—as in the early period of economic development, but pulling with it an increasing component of processing and servicing activities; and (2) the developmentally dominant effects emerged from the growth of the minerals economy, shifting rapidly among regions, triggering, intensifying, or transforming the nature of regional growth patterns.

The second part of this modern period—that is, the first half of the twentieth century—has been largely characterized by an elaboration and "deepening" of the subnational economy building upon the geographic pattern of activities brought about by the great interregional resource shifts of the nineteenth century. Resource activities declined in relative importance in the national economy throughout the period, but their real importance lay in the role they had played historically in defining the economic basis for the succeeding stages of regional growth—in the movements of population and industry among the regions. In a very real sense the classical resource effects were playing themselves out, as the service sector moved into a dominant position and as technological and other changes (such as price changes which made recapture of waste products economical) brought about a long-range

---

SOURCES for Table 1: Shift figures computed from Perloff, Dunn, Lampard, and Muth, *Regions, Resources, and Economic Growth* (Baltimore: The Johns Hopkins Press, 1960), T. 75, p. 205; T. 76, p. 208; T. 77, p. 210. Growth of output computed from the long-term series in a forthcoming RFF study by Neal Potter and Francis T. Christy, Jr., "U. S. Natural Resource Statistics, 1870 to 1955" (Preliminary Draft, with revisions to 11/1/59), Lead, Table MT-14; Copper, Table MT-12; Pig Iron, Table MT-28.

reduction in the proportion of raw materials to total output,[6] thus weakening the linkages of economic activities to their resource inputs. The power of the "market magnet" loomed as the dominant locational force operating in the economy.

The "Services" Era and "Amenity Resources"

By mid-century, moreover, an additional resource effect was beginning to influence the distribution of economic activity among the regions. To understand the importance of this effect requires us to move away from a definition of resource endowment which sees resources exclusively as tangible materials upon which technology works in the production of goods, and toward one which sees natural resources as including other features of the natural environment which have consequences for economic decisions. Natural resources, then, need not *enter* directly into the processes of production, but only *influence* directly the location of markets as well as of production. This broader definition embraces a group of physical environmental conditions which we will refer to as the "amenity resources"—that special juxtaposition of climate, land, coastline, and water offering conditions of living which exert a strong pull on migrants from less happily situated parts of the nation.

This amenity-resource effect derives from the interplay of a number of developments within the national economy and society, First, there is the growing importance of the nonjob-oriented, as well as the job-seeking, migrant. Some 8 per cent of the U.S. population is over 65 years of age, and the proportion of this age group in the total is growing. Approximately two-thirds of these persons are not working and many enjoy some form of paid retirement. Since most consumption items can be acquired with only minor interregional differences, many of these persons will seek out the more intangible resource services, such as climate and coast, that do have substantial interregional variations.

Another important development is the growth in the number and

[6] The Potter-Christy data indicate that between 1870 and 1955, when real GNP expanded 16 times, the output of the resources industries expanded only 5½ times. In terms of output (in 1954 prices), the extractive industries dropped over this period from ⅓ of GNP to 12 per cent. The greatest declines were in the products of forestry, fishing, and agriculture. Output in mining rose as a percentage of GNP until the 1920's and since has shown a moderate decline relative to GNP. Kindleberger finds a similar trend in the declining relative use of raw materials in Europe. Charles P. Kindleberger, *The Terms of Trade: A European Case Study* (Cambridge and New York: Technology Press and Wiley, 1956), Chap. 8, pp. 176-212.

significance of industries whose ties to resource inputs and national market centers are relatively weak. These are the so-called "foot-loose" industries which are distinguished from other industries in the fact that they have an unusually broad spectrum of locational alternatives available. Such an industry may be labor-oriented in terms of requiring unskilled or semi-skilled labor, such as the apparel industries, or in terms of a highly technical labor requirement, such as the research and development industries. It may be climate-oriented, as in the case of the aircraft industries. Or it may be an industry whose unit transportation costs are negligible in terms of the value of the product, such as instrument and optical goods producers. All of these have in common an array of locational possibilities which permits them to settle in amenity-rich areas without doing violence to the economics of their activities. The growth of the transportation equipment industry (mainly aircraft) in California is an excellent example. During the period 1939-54 California realized some 35 per cent of the national shift in employment in the industry, and this accounted for a very large share of California's total increase in manufacturing employment.

Finally, there is the effect of a rising per capita income throughout the nation. Given the high elasticity of demand for travel and recreation, rising incomes have meant an increasing export market for regional amenity resources in the form of tourist services to vacationers.

Even before mid-century the great shift in population was in the direction of states that had advantages in these amenity resources: Florida, the Southwest and the Pacific Coast states. During the 1940-50 Census period, this great arc of states stretching from Florida on the southeastern rim to Washington on the northwestern rim [7] (which contained 16 per cent of the national population in 1940) absorbed some 40 per cent of the total increment of national population growth.[8] The movement in the direction of the amenity resources is strong, and even though we are not certain how much of the movement to specific regions can be attributed directly to this resource influence and how much to

[7] Florida, Texas, New Mexico, Arizona, California, Oregon, Washington.

[8] In the case of Florida, between 1940 and 1950 the native white population of the state increased by 54 per cent, adding an increment of 707,300 to the 1940 population of 1,304,000. Of this increment the increase in Florida-born residents accounted for 210,000, while the increase of residents born in other states accounted for 497,300, some 251,600 of which were born in states north of the Ohio River. New York alone accounted for 30 per cent of these. Everett S. Lee, Ann R. Miller, Carol P. Brainard, and Richard A. Easterlin, *Population Redistribution and Economic Growth, United States, 1870-1950* (Philadelphia: The American Philosophical Society, 1957), Table P-3, p. 257.

other factors, given a highly mobile population with rising incomes and retirement payments, it seems fairly certain that the direct influence of the amenity resource will increase rather than diminish.

And so, in the broad perspective of history, the changing content of resource endowment has had a succession of effects in the interregional distribution of economic activity. As "new" resources moved to the forefront of the national economy, new advantages for economic growth were created for those regions well endowed. This much seems certain: in terms of the distribution of national economic activity over the landscape, resource endowment has mattered a great deal.

Resources and the Mechanics of Regional Growth

Regional growth typically has been promoted by the ability of a region to produce goods or services demanded by the national economy and to export them at a competitive advantage with respect to other regions. We have already referred to three such cases touching upon resources—the leverage of minerals in the growth of the Mountain states, of petroleum and natural gas in the growth of the Southwest, and of amenity resources in the growth of Florida. The role of timber in the development of the Pacific Northwest and the role of agricultural commodities in the development of the Plains states are equally instructive. This ability to export induces a flow of income into the region which, through the familiar multiplier effect, tends to expand the internal markets of the region for both national and region-serving goods and services. The extent of the multiplier effect is related to certain "internal" features that characterize the economic and social structure of the region. Regions tend to differ substantially in the degree of development that becomes associated with the growth of the export industries and in what happens to the income that flows in from the export sales.

Some of these internal features are related to the nature of the export industries and particularly to the localized industrial linkages, and services attaching to the export sector are also important here. Thus, for example, it has been noted by historians that the shipment of *heavy* export products from a region has influenced the development of substantial transportation facilities and services within the region. The quantity and type of labor required by the export industries and relative levels of wages paid has, of course, an obvious relationship to the "internal" development of a region. Another important feature is the income distribution that tends to be associated with a given type of regional export product. Douglass North has pointed to the differential effect on regional development in the nineteenth century of the plantation system in the Southeast for the production of cotton and tobacco—with its highly unequal distribution of income, as compared to the independent-farmer production system of the Midwest—with its broad income base and its growing markets for local goods and services.

"Internal" regional development takes the form both of internal structural changes (such as an increase in the proportion of the labor force employed in manufacturing and service industries) and an expansion of the local market for all sorts of goods and services. As the regional market expands and region-serving activities proliferate conditions may develop for self-reinforcing and self-sustaining regional growth, and new internal factors may become important in determining the rates of regional growth, such as external economies associated with social overhead capital and the agglomeration of industries, and internal economies of scale. At any rate, the occurrence of rapid self-sustaining growth involves a shift in the relative importance of growth factors—away from the dominance of the export sector and in the direction of the internal organization of production—which makes it possible for the region to play a more elaborate role in the national economy. This highly simplified exposition of the regional growth process needs to be hedged with many reservations, but it brings to the fore the context within which the effects of resource endowment play out their role.

The "export" and "internal" determinants of regional economic expansion can be brought together in the concept of *cumulative advantage*. But any advantage which a region may have *vis-à-vis* other regions is, of course, always relative. This is so whether the focus is in terms of input and market advantages in the production of a single product or the products of a single industry, or whether the focus is in terms of cumulative advantages for over-all economic growth.

The conditions making for relative advantage can be of many sorts. Given our focus on the role of natural resource in growth, it is suggestive to view relative advantage as resource-based and nonresource-based. As already noted, resource-based advantages have afforded the conventional route to regional economic growth in the United States. In terms of their consequences for regional economic expansion, resources can be described as "good" or "bad" depending on their capacity to provide a vigorous economic linkage with the national economy and to extend the internal markets of the region. A good resource for a region can be identified, first, by its ability to support an extensive stream of nationally-wanted production. Here attention is focused on the characteristics of the national demand curve for the resource and the relationship of the region's supply conditions to those of the other regions: these must afford a substantial promise that production of the resource in the region will expand. In short, the demand for the resource must be derived from final and intermediate demand sectors of the national economy exhibiting a high income-elasticity of demand. Secondly, production of the resource must be characterized by extensive locationally-associated forward and backward linkages. And, finally, the resource must be characterized by a high regional multiplier—that is, a substantial proportion of the returns from the export sector must find its way into active demand for regionally produced goods and services.

Thus, a region's resource endowment is "good" to the extent that it is composed of resource products which rate high by these criteria. A "poor" resource endowment is one whose potential for inducing growth is, accordingly, not very high. In general, the importance of resource endowment in regional growth derives from its ability to alter the region's over-all cumulative advantage position. This will vary among regions and among resource components, and especially will it vary over time as shifts in the composition of rapid and slow growth sectors of the national economy change the bill of inputs.

Most agricultural products rate low on this "growth" scale. The agricultural sector in recent decades has expanded at about the rate of population growth [9] and its products have had an income-elasticity of much less than one.[10]

Thus, taken in aggregate, agriculture will rarely make much of a contribution to the cumulative growth advantages of a region, except in the case of a region whose relative advantage for the production of agricultural products is improving relative to the rest of the nation, as in the Plains states for the period 1870-1910.[11] However, to focus our inquiry at the "1-digit" level is to conceal by aggregation the consider-

[9] The index of per capita agricultural production has changed as follows:

1870 . . .	86.33
1910 . . .	100.00
1950 . . .	100.05

Source: Agricultural production data from Potter and Christy, *op. cit.*, Series AT-28; Population data from *Historical Statistics of the United States,* 1789-1945, Series B-2, and 1950 Census of Population.

[10] Income-elasticity of demand for food has been estimated at 0.2 to 0.3; Harlow W. Halvorson, "Long Range Domestic Demand Prospects for Food and Fiber," *Journal of Farm Economics,* Vol. XXXVI, December 1953, p. 760.

[11] The index of the share of the Plains states in the value of the national agri-

able variation among agricultural products at the three- and four-digit level. Some agricultural products in some specific instances can make significant contributions to regional economic growth. Thus, where cotton and cattle would rate low across the board as growth-generating items, the ability of California to engage in capital-intensive cotton production, and of Florida to exploit new breeds of cattle on the basis of excellent feed conditions, make these comparatively "good" resource products for these states. In other cases, there are agricultural specialties whose patterns of consumption have suggested a relatively high income-elasticity of demand—such as fruits, nuts, and horticultural specialties—so that they tend to contribute to the economic growth of those areas which are suited to their production.

The minerals sector has expanded much more rapidly than agriculture as a whole and regional endowment in mineral resources has always been looked upon as a positive asset for regional growth. As in the case of agriculture, there are great variations among the various mineral categories as to their contribution to regional growth. In addition, there are two characteristics of minerals that deserve special attention: first, minerals are nonrenewable resources, so that the depletion phenomenon becomes important in assessing the relative advantage conveyed by them; second, there is a high degree of substitutability among mineral products, so that the advantage of an endowment involving bituminous coal, for example, may become ephemeral as petroleum products become utilized as a substitute fuel. The impact of substitution cannot always be easily identified; it would be difficult to say, for example, how much production of steel, copper, lead, and zinc have been displaced by the growing production of aluminum. In general, the big mineral-using manufacturing industries, and particularly, the metals-using industries, have been among the most rapidly growing sectors of the economy. Also, at the level of final demand, the products of these industries have a high income-elasticity of demand. Equally important, they are the terminal products of an intricately-linked production sequence.

---

cultural product is:

1870 . . .	41.48
1910 . . .	100.00
1950 . . .	91.07

Source: Perloff, Dunn, Lampard, Muth, *op. cit.*, T. 38 p. 138, and T. 100 p. 249: "Regional Distribution of Value of Resources Extracted, by Major Resource Industry, 1870, 1890, 1910, 1930 and 1950."

The role of petroleum and natural gas deserves a special comment. Throughout the first half of the twentieth century their production has continued to increase at a tremendous rate: over the period 1910 to 1950 the increase in output was almost elevenfold, and during this same period almost half of the total interregional shift in mining activities was accounted for by the oil-rich states of Texas, Oklahoma, and Louisiana. During the more recent period of 1939 to 1954, while employment in mining as a whole declined by 8.84 per cent, employment in this sector increased by 92.4 per cent. In terms of national levels of consumption, petroleum and natural gas have clearly been "good" resources. In terms of their multiplier effects and their linkages these resources do not rate so high. Production and refining of petroleum products is one of the most capital intensive activities in the economy so that a considerable proportion of the returns to these activities is in the form of returns to capital, which is largely imported. At the same time, while petroleum extraction and the manufacture of petroleum products are tightly linked together, the more general backward and forward linkages are relatively limited—for example, almost 80 per cent of petroleum products were destined for final demand in 1947, while absorbing only 13.1 per cent of the total inputs from other manufacturing activities. The answer to the question of how good an endowment is petroleum and natural gas is also affected by the nature of the regional supplies. These mineral fuels are strongly conditioned by the discovery-depletion cycle, so that areas narrowly specialized in the production of these mineral fuels may well find these products to have substantial disadvantages for growth if the depletion of reserves takes place at a greater rate than the augmentation of reserves by new discovery.

The fairly limited, direct, localized linkage with other economic activities is not only a characteristic of petroleum and natural gas, but of other minerals as well. For regional economic growth, the linkage between resources and other economic activities is not only a matter of *product-linkage* and value added (since the value may be added elsewhere geographically), but is even more a question of *locational linkage*—the extent to which other activities cluster in the same general area as the resources. There is some evidence to suggest that these types of "geographic" linkages are fairly limited, and that they are becoming even more so. In this category are data showing the rank correlation of employment in manufacturing with population and resources employment, by states, some of which are presented in Table 2, using data for 1954.

The proliferation of stages in the manufacturing processes has per-

TABLE 2.—RANK CORRELATIONS OF SELECTED RESOURCE-USING MANUFACTURING GROUPS WITH RESOURCE EMPLOYMENT AND POPULATION, BY STATES, 1954

Correlated Sectors	Coefficient
(1) Employment in 1st Stage Resource-Using Manufacturers with Resource Employment	.677
(2) Employment in 2nd Stage Resource-Using Manufacturers with Resource Employment	.583
(3) Population with Resource Employment	.666
(4) Employment in 1st Stage Resource-Using Manufacturers with Population	.915
(5) Employment in 2nd Stage Resource-Using Manufacturers with Population	.935

NOTE: These groups were based upon input-output relationships. The industries classified as 1st stage resource users were those sectors in the 200-industry BLS table that received more than 10 per cent of their inputs (by value) from the resource sectors. The 2nd stage resource users received little directly from the resource sectors but received more than 10 per cent of their inputs from the 1st stage resource users. These two groups combined accounted for slightly less than half of the total manufacturing employment. The 10 per cent dividing line was an arbitrary choice, but was based on what seemed to be in both cases a logical division in terms of the nature of the basic productive procesess involved.

SOURCE: Perloff, Dunn, Lampard, Muth, *op. cit.*, T. 148, p. 394.

mitted the increasing separation of resource processing stages from later stages. Since the processing stages are generally the primary weight-losing points in the production process, remaining stages become increasingly freed from their resource bases to seek more strategic market locations. This is reflected in the different correlations for the 1st stage and 2nd stage resource-using manufacturing groups with relation to resources employment and to population.

Employment even in the 1st stage, resource-using manufacturing industries has a high degree of geographic association with population, but a relatively limited association with resource employment (roughly equal to that between resource employment and population). The 2nd stage resource users show a higher degree of association with population and a lesser degree with resource employment. The major part of manufacturing (those not included in the two classes shown) is even further removed from resource association. For all stages of manufacturing, taken in broad categories, closeness to markets (intermediate and final) tends to be the dominant locational factor.

This underlines the point made earlier: while export of resource products provides the basis for regional economic development, extensive and continued growth can be expected to take place only in those regions which achieve sizeable regional (internal) markets. Here the notion of *cumulative* advantage is useful. Rapid advances are possible as a region reaches "threshold" size for the internal production of a wide variety of goods and services. This type of regional development is greatly enhanced where the building up of social overhead proceeds rapidly—especially in the development of an extensive internal transportation network—and where particular attention is paid to the human resources and to the conditions for living. The latter, as noted earlier, is in no small part helped by the natural conditions of the area. Where resource and nonresource advantages come together are to be found the best conditions for a high level of economic development.

Resources in the Relationship of the Regional and National Economies: Heartland and Hinterland

In the development of the U. S. economy the role of cumulative advantage is most clearly seen in the growth of the Middle Atlantic region and, later, of the Great Lakes region. Here are regions which have enjoyed unequaled access to national market. Each was endowed with unusually good agricultural resources from the beginning, and the emergence of the minerals-dominant economy found each with excellent access to vast deposits of iron ore and coal. With these resource and market advantages, they developed into the most significant feature of regional economic growth on the American scene—the emergence of an industrial heartland coincident with the center of the national market.[12]

The emergence of the industrial heartland set the basic conditions for regional growth throughout the nation—it was the lever for the successive development of the newer peripheral regions: as its input requirements expanded, it reached out into the outlying areas for its resources, stimulating their growth differentially in accordance with its resource demands and the endowment of the regions. The rapid growth of the U. S. economy was accompanied (and to some extent achieved) by this process of industrial nucleation.

A major consequence of the process of expansion and regional differentiation has been the *specialization* of regional roles in the national economy, and the nature of this specialization has influenced the content

[12] New England, which is also part of the Manufacturing Belt, can be considered a lesser-endowed, junior partner in the industrial heartland.

and direction of regional growth. In following this process of growth, we see the working out of the general principles touched upon in the previous two sections.

Using a three-sector classification of economic activity and eight multistate regions (as in Table 1) for the period 1870-1950, we can use a simple index of specialization [13] to describe the dynamics of regional specialization in the national economy during this period. This is plotted for two of the three major industrial sectors—resource activities and manufacturing—in Figure 1 (100 = national average). The data serve to highlight the nucleation process. In the three regions which have coalesced into the industrial heartland—New England, Middle Atlantic, and Great Lakes—strong manufacturing specialization has characterized the entire period; however, during this eighty-year period there has been a relative decline in manufacturing specialization (i.e., as compared to the nation as a whole) in the eastern end (New England and Middle Atlantic) and a continuing increase in the western (Great Lakes) end as (1) the center of gravity of the national market shifted toward the west, and (2) the superior resource endowment of the western end helped tip the scales in its favor.[14] The great outlying regions (with the exception of the Far West) have maintained or increased their relative specialization in resource activities over the whole period, while in the heartland resource activities in relative terms have continuously declined, suggesting the progressive reaching out of the heartland into the hinterland areas for its resource inputs.[15] These data highlight the significance of the heartland-hinterland construct in the development of the national economy, and its persistence and stability in the face of dramatic structural changes during this period. The nature of this process has a number of important implications for regional growth.

[13] $I = 100 \times \frac{\text{per cent of region's labor force in given sector}}{\text{per cent of nation's labor force in given sector}}$

[14] It is worth noting that the industrial "heartland" itself is not a static geographic area, but an area whose size and extent (and even role) shift with significant changes in the national economy.

[15] As in so many other indexes, the Far West (especially California) emerges as a unique case which, at least since the end of the 19th century, has followed neither heartland nor hinterland patterns, but which can be described in terms of a subnucleation in the national economy, or, if one prefers, as a second nucleation. The development of California thus suggests some interesting questions—for example, about the possibilities of "second-growth" (or new-conditions) nucleations, as well as the possibilities of a gradual spreading out of nucleation-type or high-level development in advanced stages of national economic growth. Even under the latter circumstance, the heartland-hinterland concept retains valuable explanatory power in analyzing regional development over time.

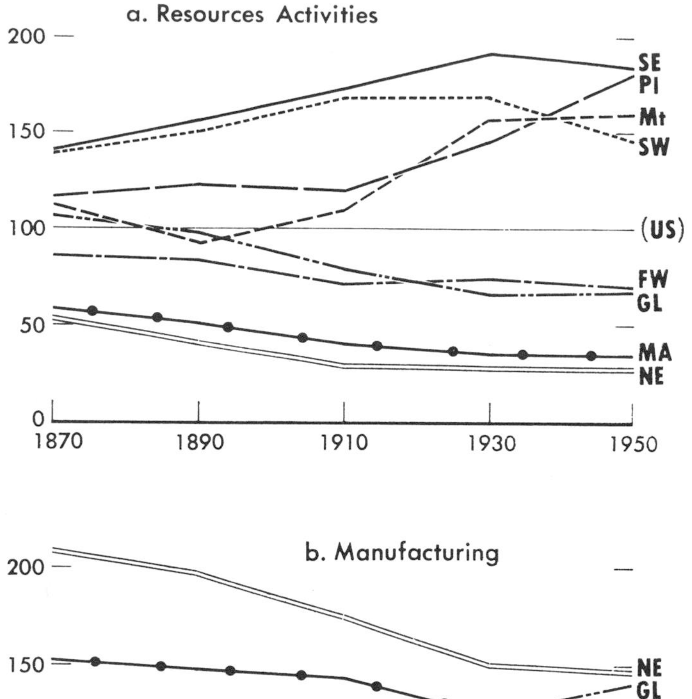

Figure 1. Indices of specialization in resources activities and manufacturing, multistate regions, 1870, 1890, 1910, 1930, and 1950 (U.S. = 100)

In the hinterland regions the working out of comparative advantage can result in a narrow and intensive specialization in a single resource subsector, in effect tying the future of the region to the vicissitudes of national demand for the products of that subsector. This will set at least ultimate limits to the region's growth rates: shifts in national demand patterns, the emergence of substitutes, depletion, technological advances, or the relative shifting of regional advantage may at any time choke off growth and leave behind enclaves of unemployed resources and economic stagnation. At its extreme, the western experience of "boom-town to ghost-town" is a dramatic illustration, but almost as severe has been the history of the tobacco and cotton producing areas in the South. These consequences are not confined to single-product specialization. Broader, sector-wide regional specializations may produce similar problems where the degree of specialization is great and where the products in the aggregate have a low income-elasticity of demand. Typical of this kind of problem is the experience of the Plains states which has been increasing specialization in agriculture since 1910, at the same time that their relative contribution to total national value of agricultural products has been declining.[16]

On the other hand a broad and diverse resource specialization involving products in growing demand may provide a continuing impetus to regional expansion, especially where there is some complementarity among the resource activities. The Southwest illustrates the advantage of such a condition. Here a flourishing chemical industry has emerged based on rich endowments of petroleum, natural gas, sulfur, and salt—this is doubly fortunate, considering the high rate of growth of chemicals industries in the national economy.[17]

In short, the economic expansion of the hinterlands is closely associated with their resource endowments and the manner in which their endowments contribute to the evolution of favorable patterns of specialization or substantial levels of cumulative advantage.

When we look at the manufacturing sector, some important regional facets also emerge. Thus, the economic expansion of the hinterlands is accompanied by a certain amount of induced manufacturing growth. This falls into two general classes: (1) Industries devoted to the processing of regional resource products loom large. If we classify all manufacturing into first-stage resource users, or "processing" industries, and later stage, or "fabricating" industries, and plot by State Economic Areas

[16] See n. 12, p. 16.

[17] Annual growth rates of the following chemical end-products groups are suggestive:

	Period	*Average Annual Growth*
1. Synthetic fibers (not including rayon and acetate)	1940-1954	36.1%
2. Synthetic organic plasticizers	1936-1954	16.8%
3. Synthetic plastics and resins	1940-1954	16.6%
4. Fixed nitrogen in fertilizers	1939-1955	13.4%

Source: Harold J. Barnett and Frederick T. Moore, "Long Range Growth of Chemical Industries," *Chemical and Engineering News,* April 7, 1958, p. 81.

which class of industry is dominant, we find that the processing industries dominate throughout the resource hinterlands, while the fabricating industries dominate in the industrial heartland, as shown in Figure 2. Thus, the process of industrialization not only defines the resource role of the hinterlands, but also sorts out the kinds of manufacturing activities between the heartland and the hinterland. (2) Less distinct is the role of region-serving industries in the regional growth process. These are generally market-oriented industries, producing products for regional final demand: As regions grow, their expanding markets offer increasing opportunities for economies of scale, so that one dimension of regional growth is a kind of "filling-in" generated by emerging regional market possibilities. This kind of growth frequently takes place at the expense of imports from other regions, so that one characteristic of regional growth may be a decline in the relative advantage of other regions from which imports have flowed in the past.

A general idea of this total effect is provided by a measure of the "differential shift" in manufacturing employment, as shown in Figure 3. This measures the extent to which the growth of employment in the major (two-digit) manufacturing industries within each of the states of continental United States has exceeded or fallen below "expected" growth; that is, the average national growth for each of the industry categories during a given period (here, over the period from 1939 to 1954). These "within-industry" shifts are netted out for each state, and each state total is shown as a percentage either of all the above-average growth states taken together (i.e., a percentage of the "upward shift") or of all the below-average growth states taken together (a percentage of the "downward shift"), depending on which category the state falls into. Thus, for example, Texas had 11.4 per cent of the total gain—or greater than expected increases—of all the states that experienced above-average growth in employment for all the two-digit manufacturing industries taken together.

At the same time, however, the rapid-growth (often the new) manufacturing industries have continued to find their most favorable location to be in the industrial heartland. This is shown by the "proportionality shift" in manufacturing employment—a measure of the relative change in manufacturing employment among the states due to their industrial *composition*.[18] (See Figure 4.) The significant role in regional economic

[18] Even if manufacturing employment in each industry had grown at the national average for the industry within each state, some states would have had a greater than average increase in total manufacturing employment because of a "favorable" industrial composition; that is, a high proportion of "rapid growth" industries. That is what is measured in the "proportionality" or composition effect,

(*Note* [18] *continued on page 23*)

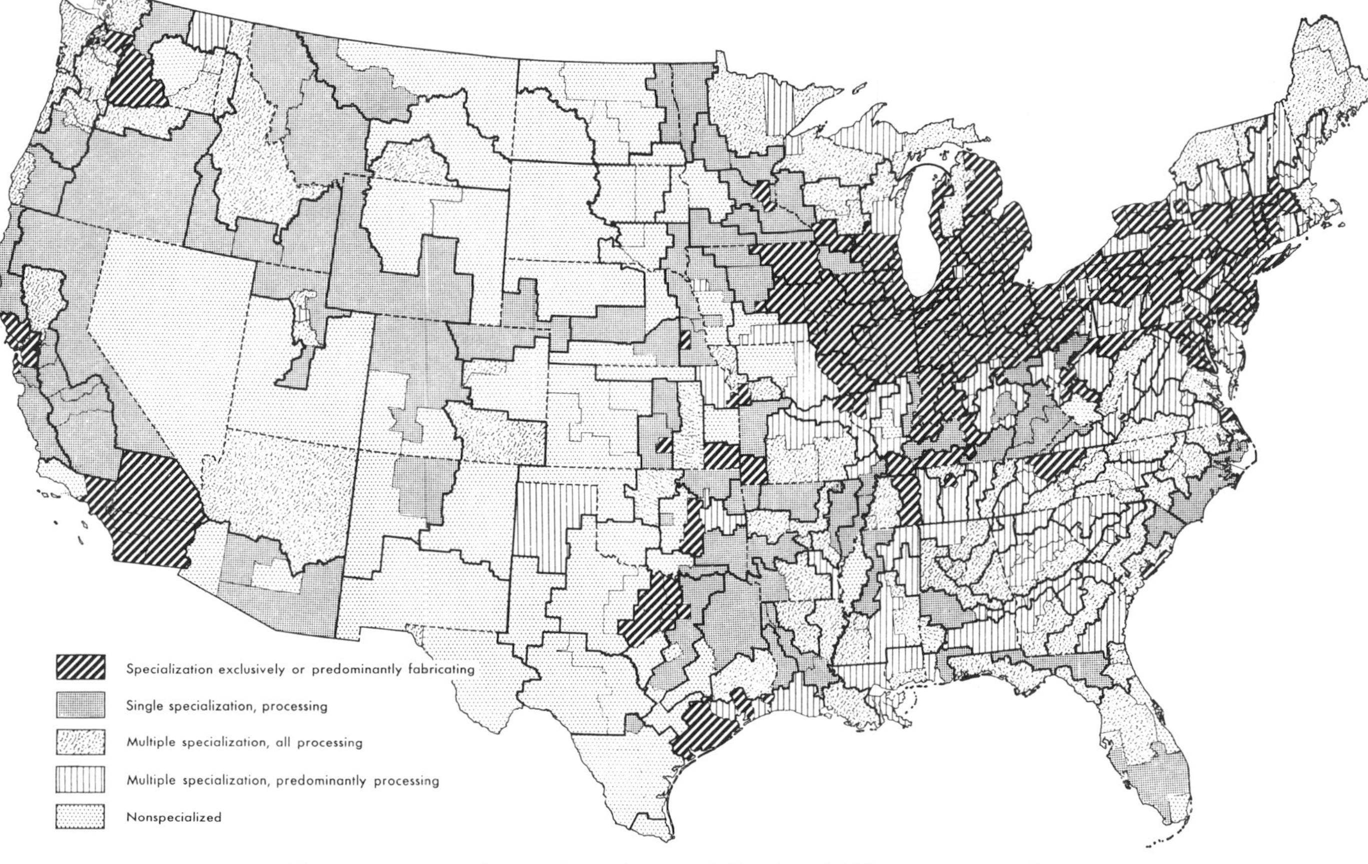

Figure 2. Type of manufacturing specialization, 1950, state economic areas.
(Source: An unpublished series of data for state economic areas prepared by Donald J. Bogue and Calvin L. Beale.)

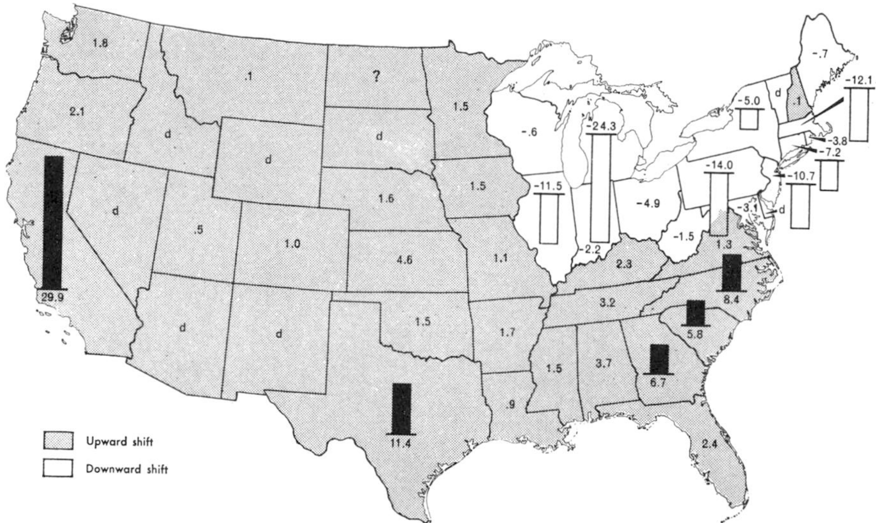

Figure 3. Total differential net shift in all manufacturing employment, 1939-54.

(Disclosure problems made it difficult to measure this dimension accurately for those states marked "d"; the direction of shift was ascertainable, however, in all states but North Dakota. The % figures are rough indications of dimension only.)

Figure 4. Total proportionality net shift in all manufacturing employment, 1939-54.

(Disclosure problems made it difficult to measure this dimension accurately for those states marked "d"; the direction of shift was ascertainable, however. The % figures should be taken as rough indications of dimension only.)

growth of industrial composition can be highlighted by noting the very wide range of industrial employment growth rates during the same period, 1939-54 (Table 3). The regions which have contained or attracted the machinery, metals, and chemical industries have, of course, gained volume-wise through the unusually rapid growth of these industries. It would seem that these industries find that the massive markets, economies of agglomeration, and the extensive social overhead investment of the Manufacturing Belt provide them with the economic environment most conducive to their growth and prosperity.

As highlighted by a comparison of Figures 3 and 4, the industrial heartland tends to grow in a different way than do the hinterland areas. The industrial heartland serves not only as the focal point of the national market taken as a whole, but also as the industrial seedbed of the economy. The newer products tend to be started here, nourished along, and as they find wide acceptance and volume grows, often the manufacturers find that they can supply the outlying markets more economically by producing on a decentralized basis. There are cases, of course, where the reverse is true and experimentation begins away from the center, but these have been relatively limited in number. In broad terms, the hinterland areas have grown mainly by the "filling-in" process referred to above, a threshold-by-threshold upward movement as resource exports expand and as the regional markets grow in size.

Focusing, then, on the specialized role of the regions in the national economy we get a picture in broad strokes of the spatial dimensions of the national economy. Central to it is the great heartland nucleation of industry and the national market, the focus of the large-scale, nation-serving industry, the seedbed of new industries responding to the dynamic structure of national final demand, and the center of high levels of per capita income.[19] Radiating out across the national landscape are the resource-dominant, regional hinterlands specializing in the production of resource and intermediate inputs for which the heartland reaches out to satisfy the input requirements of its great manufacturing

---

shown in Figure 4. For a more detailed description of these measures, see Perloff, Dunn, Lampard, and Muth, *op. cit.,* Chapter 5.

[19] While a discussion of the welfare aspects of regional growth is beyond the scope of this paper, it is worth noting at least briefly that among the more dramatic features of the evolving heartland-hinterland relationship has been its consequences for levels of per capita income. If we divide the nation into two parts—the heartland (including the Far West as a subnucleation) and the resource hinterland—and take the per capita personal income in the former as an index of 100, the comparable index for all the hinterland regions taken together is 58 for

TABLE 3.—PERCENTAGE CHANGE IN MANUFACTURING PRODUCTION WORKER EMPLOYMENT FOR 2-DIGIT MANUFACTURING SECTORS, 1939-1954

S.I.C. Code	Industry sector	% Change	Employment in the industry as: % of total 1939 employment	% of total 1954 employment
36	Electrical machinery	+191.39%	3.2%	5.8%
37	Transportation equipment	+143.70	7.0	10.7
38	Instruments & rel. prod.	+130.48	1.1	1.6
39	Miscellaneous mfg.	+129.91	3.1	4.5
35	Machinery (except elect.)	+118.50	6.9	9.5
34	Fabricated metal prod.	+ 82.04	5.8	6.6
28	Chemical & allied prod.	+ 81.84	3.5	4.1
30	Rubber prod.	+ 62.53	1.5	1.6
26	Paper and allied prod.	+ 61.24	3.5	3.5
	TOTAL MANUFACTURING EMPL.	+ 58.46	100.0	100.0
32	Stone, clay & glass prod.	+ 54.26	3.4	3.3
27	Printing & publishing	+ 54.04	4.2	4.0
29	Petroleum and coal prod.	+ 52.11	1.4	1.3
25	Furniture & fixt.	+ 51.36	2.4	2.3
23	Apparel and rel. prod.	+ 42.10	9.6	8.7
20	Food & kindred prod.	+ 41.90	10.3	9.2
33	Primary metal industries	+ 39.57	8.6	7.6
24	Lumber & prod.	+ 21.47	5.4	4.6
31	Leather & leather prod.	− 1.84	4.2	2.6
22	Textile mill prod.	− 12.41	13.8	7.7
21	Tobacco manufactures	− 19.78	1.1	0.6

SOURCE: Perloff, Dunn, Lampard, Muth, *op. cit.*, Table 147, p. 391.

1920 and 69 in 1950. Thus, although the per capita income differences have tended to narrow with the process of hinterland development, the advantage in welfare terms for the industrial heartland is still tremendous. As several studies have shown, the structural origin of the income differences is associated with the agricultural-nonagricultural dichotomy, so it is not surprising that we find such significant income dominance by the nuclear regions. This is, of course, not a hard and fast relationship. That a high degree of manufacturing specialization in industries with a relatively low income-elasticity of demand not only can dampen regional growth rates but depress a region's relative welfare levels has been indicated by the New England experience. At the same time, it is possible for resource regions to enjoy comparatively high per capita incomes, as the Mountain states have proven by turning up periodically with per capita incomes exceeding the national average. The important conclusion, however, is that so long as income differentials are associated with industrial structure, and structure is regionally determined by this ongoing process of nucleation, there are likely to continue to be interregional differences in welfare levels.

plant. Here in the hinterlands, resource endowment is a critical determinant of the particular cumulative advantage of the region, and hence of its growth potential. This heartland-hinterland relationship seems to be the basic morphology of the subnational economy; through it we can better understand the role of resource endowment in regional growth.

Summary

In summary, the U. S. experience suggests the following set of propositions. "Resource endowment" is continuously redefined by changes in national final and intermediate demand, production technology, and economic organization. The relative economic growth of a region is directly related to its relative advantages in the production of goods and services for the national market; these may result from resource endowment on the one hand, or from a favorable degree of access to the national markets on the other—more generally, from a combination of the two. These advantages are normally conditioned by other elements, such as the quality of the labor supply and relative labor costs. The working out of cumulative advantage is exhibited in the specialized role that a region plays in the national economy, and this specialized role can best be described in terms of the heartland-hinterland relationships.

12. Location Theory and Regional Economic Growth*[1]

DOUGLASS C. NORTH

I

DURING the past several decades there has been a growing interest in location theory in America. Building on the pioneering works of Thünen, Weber, Lösch, Palander, and others,[2] a number of economists and geographers have extended the analysis to apply to a wide range of problems and have attempted to synthesize location theory with other fields of economics.[3] However, very little work has been done in using the principles of location to analyze the historical growth of regions in America.[4] While economists concerned with location theory sometimes point out the implications of their analysis for the growth of regions, they have not followed up these discrete observations with any systematic analysis. A fundamental difficulty has been that the theory of regional economic growth[5] has little relevance for the development of regions in America. Not only does the sequence of stages outlined by the theory bear little resemblance to American development but its policy implications are also fundamentally misleading.

This paper will attempt to demonstrate the inadequacies of the existing theory of regional economic growth and will advance a number of propositions that may lead to a more useful theory, both for analyzing the historical development of the American economy and for understanding the contemporary problems associated with regional economic growth.

The analytical propositions advanced in this paper, though explicitly oriented to America's development, would apply equally well to other areas that meet the following conditions: (1) regions that have grown up within a framework of capitalist institutions and have therefore responded to profit maximizing opportunities, in which factors of production have been relatively mobile,[6] and (2) re-

[1] I am indebted for criticisms and suggestions to several of my colleagues at the University of Washington, particularly Philip Cartwright, J. R. Huber, Franklyn Holzman, and Robert Lampman. Dean H. W. Stoke and the Research Committee of the Graduate School at the University of Washington generously provided financial assistance for research, part of which is used in this article.

[2] A summary of earlier contributions to location theory may be found in E. M. Hoover, *Location Theory and the Shoe and Leather Industries* (Cambridge: Harvard University Press, 1937).

[3] In addition to Hoover's valuable study cited above, see his *The Location of Economic Activity* (New York: McGraw-Hill Book Co., 1948). See also Bertil Ohlin, *Interregional and International Trade* (Cambridge: Harvard University Press, 1935); National Resources Planning Board, *Industrial Location and National Resources* (Washington, D.C.: Government Printing Office, 1943); and the articles by Walter Isard cited below.

[4] A significant exception is Walter Isard's "Transportation Development and Building Cycles," *Quarterly Journal of Economics*, LVII (November, 1942), 90–112. See also William H. Dean, *The Theory of the Geographic Location of Economic Activities* (*Selections from the Doctoral Dissertation*) (Ann Arbor: Edward Bros., Inc., 1938).

[5] See Sec. II below.

[6] Obviously both profit maximization and factor mobility are relative notions and nowhere perfectly met. However, there is a vast difference between the response of an underdeveloped area where the social and economic structure is not fundamentally geared

* Reprinted from the *Journal of Political Economy,* Vol. 63 (June 1955).

gions that have grown up without the strictures imposed by population pressure.

II

Both location theory and the theory of regional economic growth have described a typical sequence of stages through which regions move in the course of their development.[7] E. M. Hoover and Joseph Fisher, in a recent essay entitled "Research in Regional Economic Growth,"[8] point out that "there is now a fairly well accepted body of theory regarding the normal sequence of development stages in a region."[9] This sequence may be outlined as follows:

1. The first stage in the economic history of most regions is one of a self-sufficient subsistence economy in which there is little investment or trade. The basic agricultural stratum of population is simply located according to the distribution of natural resources.

2. With improvements in transport, the region develops some trade and local specialization. "A second stratum of population comes into being, carrying on simple village industries for the farmers. Since the materials, the market, and the labor are all furnished originally by the agricultural populations, the new 'industrial superstructure' is located with reference to that 'basic stratum.' "[10]

3. With the increase of interregional trade, a region tends to move through a succession of agricultural crops from extensive grazing to cereal production to fruit-growing, dairy farming, and truck gardening.[11]

4. With increased population and diminishing returns in agriculture and other extractive industries, a region is *forced* to industrialize. "Industrialization means the introduction of so-called secondary industries (mining and manufacturing) on a considerable scale."[12] Typically the early stages of industrialization are based on the products of agriculture and forestry and include such activities as the processing of food, the manufacture of wood products, and the preparation of textile fibers. If industrialization is to continue, mineral and energy resources become critical.

As a second stage of industrialization, then, we see [in the regions possessing economically usable mineral resources] such industries as the smelting, refining, and processing of metals; oil refining; chemical industries based mainly

---

to capitalist stimuli and the kind of response one can expect in a basically capitalist society. The reluctance of the economic historian to make more extensive use of the tools of the theorist reflects in good part the fact that most of the world's economic history falls outside our first condition and that therefore economic theory is of little use in analyzing a large part of its development. On the other hand, the joint efforts of economic theorists and historians applied to the development of the United States and of some other areas hold out the promise of yielding valuable insights.

[7] See August Lösch, "The Nature of Economic Regions," *Southern Economic Journal*, V (July, 1938), 71–78; Hoover, *Location Theory and the Shoe and Leather Industries*, pp. 284–85, and *The Location of Economic Activity*, pp. 187–88.

[8] Universities–National Bureau Committee for Economic Research, *Problems in the Study of Economic Growth* (New York: National Bureau of Economic Research, 1949), chap. v.

[9] *Ibid.*, p. 180.

[10] Hoover, *Location Theory and the Shoe and Leather Industries*, p. 284. The second stage of regional growth has been elaborated by Hoover and Fisher to include some further specialization and interregional trade (*op. cit.*, p. 181).

[11] The theory of location diverges here from the theory of regional economic growth in stressing the historical pattern of the emergence from feudalism. Since this pattern has little meaning for American development, it is omitted here. However, it will be an important part of my argument that American location theorists have implicitly accepted a good deal of this stage sequence based on the European experience of emergence out of feudalism without recognizing the significant difference between this pattern and the pattern of American development.

[12] Hoover and Fisher, *op. cit.*, p. 182.

on coal, petroleum, potash, salt, and other minerals; and glass and ceramics industries. Where cheap hydroelectric power is available, industries requiring large amounts of cheap power (nonferrous metals refining, ferroalloys, and special steels, artificial abrasives, etc.) are possible, as in Norway, Switzerland, the Tennessee Valley, and the Columbia River Valley.[13]

5. A final stage of regional growth is reached when a region specializes in tertiary industries producing for export. Such a region exports to less advanced regions capital, skilled personnel, and special services.

The role of transport costs has been critical in the advancement through these successive stages of growth. Isard summarizes this effect as follows: "Historically we find that reduced transport rates have tended (1) to transform a scattered, ubiquitous pattern of production into an increasingly concentrated one, and (2) to effect progressive differentiation and selection between sites with superior and inferior resources and trade routes."[14]

III

When this sequence of stages is placed against the economic history of regions in America, two basic objections arise. (1) These stages bear little resemblance to the actual development of regions. Moreover, they fail to provide any insights into the causes of growth and change. A theory of regional economic growth should clearly focus on the critical factors that implement or impede development. (2) Furthermore, if we want a normative model of how regions should grow, in order to analyze the causes of arrested development or relative decay, then this sequence of stages is of little use and is actually misleading in the emphasis it places on the need for (and difficulties of) industrialization.[15]

The problems of industrialization will be explored later in this paper when the causes of regional growth are examined. Here we are concerned with the first objection: the lack of correspondence between the stages of the theory of regional economic growth and the economic history of regions in America. A major discrepancy is immediately evident; namely, that America was exploited in large part as a capitalist venture. Settlement in new regions and their subsequent growth were shaped by the search for and exploitation of goods in demand on world markets. The result was a kind of development very different from that implied by the theory of regional development in which regions gradually extended the market from a subsistence economy. From the early joint-stock companies on through the whole westward expansion, a basic objective was to exploit the land and its resources in order to produce goods that could be marketed "abroad" and would bring in a money income. This is in marked contrast to the experience of Europe (which appears to be the model for the early stages of the theory of regional economic growth), where a market-oriented economy emerged only gradually from the predominantly local economies of the manorial system. If a subsistence economy existed in a new region in America, it was solely because of a lack of means of transport, a condition that was swiftly remedied by the

[13] Hoover, *The Location of Economic Activity*, p. 193.

[14] Walter Isard, "Distance Inputs and the Space Economy. Part I. The Conceptional Framework," *Quarterly Journal of Economics*, LXV (May, 1951), 188–98.

[15] Hoover and Fisher stress the difficulties of achieving an industrial status and maintain that most of the bottlenecks and problems of arrested development occur in moving from an agricultural to an industrial economic base (*op. cit.*, pp. 182–84)

concerted efforts of the settlers.[16] This is not to deny that many homesteaders maintained a subsistence existance but only to affirm that such settlement was not significant in shaping the economic development of the region, any more than the modern subsistence farmer of the backcountry is shaping the development of contemporary agriculture.

This point may be illustrated briefly from the economic history of the Pacific Northwest.[17] Not only has this region never experienced a subsistence economy, but its markets from the very beginning have often been thousands of miles distant. Even before general settlement, the region was exploited for its furs by the Hudson Bay Company. With the decline of the fur trade and the coming of settlers, wheat, flour, and lumber were quickly developed as exportable commodities. They first found markets in California in the 1840's. With the gold rush the demand for both wheat and lumber expanded tremendously, and the region experienced rapid growth based on these two commodities. In 1868 the first wheat shipment went from Portland to Liverpool, and by the late 1870's Pacific Northwest soft wheat had become an important part of the world wheat trade; a fleet of ships sailed from the region around Cape Horn every year. In 1857 the first shipment of flour was made to Japan, and thereafter Pacific Northwest flour found markets in Australia, Hawaii, the Orient, Europe, British Columbia, and California.[18] In each decade after 1850 an increasing percentage of the crop was exported either as wheat or in the form of flour. Before the end of the nineteenth century over half the crop was being exported from the region.

The history of the lumber industry reflects a similar preoccupation with markets foreign to the region. The first lumber shipment went to California in 1847, and during the gold rush lumber exports from the Pacific Northwest expanded rapidly. The rate of growth of the lumber industry was directly related to the growth of the markets reached by water (primarily California, British Columbia, and some foreign markets). In 1894 James J. Hill established a 40 cent per hundredweight freight rate on lumber to Minneapolis on his railroads, and the industry began to compete with the southern pine region for markets in the Middle West. With this rapid growth of markets the industry expanded many fold. In the first five years of the twentieth century output more than doubled, and thereafter in each successive decade Pacific Northwest fir increased its share of the national market at the expense of southern pine. The rate of growth of the region has been directly related to these basic exports. Between 1860 and 1920 lumber and flour-milling accounted for between 40 and 60 per cent of the value of the region's manufacturing output. Almost all the rest of secondary industry (as well as tertiary industry) was passive in the sense that it served local consumer needs.

[16] More often than not, this concerted effort was directed toward getting the government to provide the necessary internal improvements.

[17] This brief summary of the development of the Pacific Northwest is condensed from a larger research project that I am currently undertaking. Support for the data presented here may be found in John B. Watkins, *Wheat Exporting from the Pacific Northwest* (State College of Washington Agricultural Experiment Station Bull. 201 [May, 1926]); the Silver Anniversary Number of the *Commercial Review* (Portland, Ore.), July 1, 1915; E. S. Meany, Jr., "History of Northwest Lumbering" (Ph.D. dissertation, Harvard University, 1935); and R. W. Vinnedge, *The Pacific Northwest Lumber Industry and Its Development* (New Haven: Yale University School of Forestry, 1923).

[18] A substantial amount of the wheat and flour sent to California was exported to Europe.

Its growth therefore reflected the changing fortunes of the region's exportable commodities.[19] Wheat played a similarly critical role in the development of the region, although by the end of the nineteenth century the agricultural export base had broadened to include a number of other commodities.

This brief account of the development of the Pacific Northwest bears no resemblance to the theory of regional economic growth. There was no gradual evolution out of a subsistence economy. Instead the whole development of the region from the beginning was dependent on its success in producing exportable commodities. Nor was the Pacific Northwest's history exceptional. Furs and the products of mining were typically the early exportable commodities of western America. Colonial America exported such products as tobacco, rice, indigo, naval stores, ships, and fish. Even the well-worn historical generalization of location theorists that reduced transport rates will transform a scattered, ubiquitous pattern of production into an increasingly concentrated one is not true of America. Many new regions in America developed from the beginning around one or two exportable commodities and only widened their export base *after* transport costs had been reduced.[20] In short, both this generalization of location theorists and the early stages in the theory of regional economic growth appear to be taken uncritically from European experience rather than derived from the economic history of this country.

A basic starting point for reshaping our views on regional economic growth might well be the insights of the late Harold Innis in his studies of the growth of the Canadian economy.[21] Innis' early research had convinced him of the crucial importance of the export staple in shaping new economies. His subsequent studies of the growth of these staple exports were always directed toward attempting to understand "how the Canadian economy had been generated and how it had been shaped as a working economy."[22] An analysis of the export staples of the Canadian economy became the basis for understanding the character of that country's economic development. Moreover, it provided real insights into the political and social institutions of the country.

The term "staple" refers to the chief commodity produced by a region. It is customarily thought of as describing products of extractive industry. Since my concept of the export commodities of a region may include products of secondary or tertiary industry as well, I shall use the term "exportable commodities" (or services) to denote the individual items and the export base[23] to denote col-

[19] This point will be elaborated and qualified in the following section.

[20] In the Pacific Northwest the export base (particularly of agricultural commodities) only broadened after the advent of the railroad.

[21] See *The Fur Trade in Canada* (New Haven: Yale University Press, 1920); *The Cod Fishery: The History of an International Economy* (New Haven: Yale University Press, 1940); *Problems of Staple Production in Canada* (Toronto: University of Toronto Press, 1933); and, in collaboration with A. R. M. Lower, *Settlement and the Forest and Mining Frontier* (Toronto: Macmillan Co., 1936).

[22] W. A. Mackintosh, "Innis on Canadian Economic Development," *Journal of Political Economy*, June, 1953, p. 188. This article provides an excellent summary of Innis' views.

[23] The use of the term "base" has become popular among urban land economists and city planners in the concept of the urban economic base, which refers to those activities of a metropolitan community that export goods and services to other areas. For a history of the development of the concept see Richard B. Andrews, "Mechanics of the Urban Economic Base: Historical Development of the Base Concept," *Land Economics*, XXIX (May, 1953), 161–67.

lectively the exportable commodities (or services) of a region. In young regions, typically dependent on extractive industry, my exportable commodities and Innis' export staples are synonymous.

Settlers in new regions typically experimented with a number of different crops before discovering one that was economically feasible.[24] The success of an industry in producing an exportable commodity can be understood in terms of the principles of location theory.[25] The development of an exportable commodity reflected a comparative advantage in relative costs of production, including transfer costs. Distributive transfer costs have served to limit the extent of the export market.

From the viewpoint of the region, the demand for the exportable commodity was an exogenous factor, but both processing and transfer costs were not. Historically new regions bent every effort to reduce these costs in their concerted drive to promote their economic well-being. The ceaseless efforts of new regions to get federally subsidized internal improvements, state aid for canal construction, federal and state aid for railroads, and river and harbor improvements were a part of the continuous effort of each region to reduce transfer costs to better the competitive position of its exports.[26]

As regions grew up around the export base, external economies developed which improved the competitive cost position of the exportable commodities. The development of specialized marketing organization, improved credit and transport facilities, a trained labor force, and complementary industries was oriented to the export base.

The concerted effort to improve the technology of production has been equally important. Agricultural experiment stations, state universities, and other local research groups become service adjuncts to export industries and conduct research in technological improvements in agriculture, mining, or whatever manufacturing comprises the region's export base.

The purpose of this concerted effort is better to enable the region to compete with other regions or foreign countries for markets. In new regions highly dependent on extractive industry, these external economies and technological developments tend to more than counteract diminishing returns in the staple product.[27] As a result, these efforts tend to reinforce a region's dependence on its existing staples rather than promote changes in the export base. This conservative bias is further reinforced by the

[24] The experiments with silkworm culture in the Southern Colonies are a famous case in point.

[25] For our purposes it is convenient to follow Hoover's breakdown of costs into procurement, processing, and distribution costs (see *The Location of Economic Activity*, pp. 7–9, 15–115). While processing costs reflect factor-input coefficients and factor prices, procurement and distribution costs depend fundamentally on transfer costs.

Isard has done a great deal of work attempting to introduce the problems of space into economic theory through the concept of distance inputs (the movement of a unit weight over a unit distance). The price of a distance input is the transport rate and, as in the case of capital inputs, a reduction in price has both a scale and a substitution effect. Distance inputs are conceived to be simply another factor of production whose price is the transport rate and whose optimum combination with other factors can be determined by the principles of substitution (see his "Distance Inputs and the Space Economy," *op. cit.*).

[26] Such efforts have not been confined to pressure-group activity but have erupted into political movements. The Grangers and the Populists were fundamentally concerned with a number of economic measures that would, for example, improve the position of American wheat on the world wheat market or provide the western miner with a better market for his silver.

[27] In the case of mining this statement probably would not hold.

role of capital. Capital is typically imported into new regions in the development of the export staple industries. Indeed, until a region develops sufficient income to provide a substantial share of its own investment capital, it must rely upon outside sources. External suppliers of capital tend to invest primarily in existing export industry rather than in new, untried enterprises.[28]

IV

The following section will deal with the way in which regions grow; first, however, we must explore the significance of the export base in shaping the whole character of a region's economy.

At the outset, export industries must be clearly distinguished from "residentiary industries."[29] The term "residentiary" is used to designate industry for the local market which develops where the consuming population resides. In order to determine the market area of each industry more precisely than can be done by a priori classification, the "location quotient" developed by Hildebrand and Mace[30] is employed. The location quotient measures the concentration of employment in a given industry in one area (the "subject economy," which for our purposes is the region) with another area (the "benchmark economy," which for our purposes is the nation).

Formally the location quotient is the numerical equivalent of a fraction whose numerator is employment in a given industry in the subject economy relative to total employment in the subject economy and whose denominator is employment in the given industry in the benchmark economy relative to total employment in the benchmark economy. *A priori* a location of 1.00 means no greater relative specialization in the subject economy than in the benchmark economy, for the particular industry. In each industry values significantly below 1.00 indicate much greater relative specialization in the benchmark economy; or if well over 1.00 much greater relative specialization in the subject economy.[31]

---

[28] This outside capital often comes in waves associated with (or in anticipation of) substantial reductions in costs or increases in demand. As a result the growth of regions tends to be uneven. This whole subject of the growth of regions is dealt with in more detail in Sec. V.

[29] The term "residentiary industry" was first used by P. Sargent Florence in National Resources Planning Board mimeographed releases. Rutledge Vining subsequently employed the concept in "Location of Industry and Regional Patterns of Business Cycle Behavior," *Econometrica*, XIV (January, 1946), 37–68.

[30] George Hildebrand and Arthur Mace, Jr., "The Employment Multiplier in an Expanding Industrial Market: Los Angeles County, 1940–47," *Review of Economics and Statistics*, XXXII (August, 1950), 341–49.

P. Sargent Florence developed the concept of a coefficient of localization. He first computed a "location factor" for each industry by computing the ratio of the percentage of employment in the given region found in the given industry to the corresponding percentage for the nation as a whole. If all industries were perfectly evenly distributed among regions, the location factor would be unity. "The coefficient of localization for a given industry is obtained by computing the weighted average deviation from unity of the location factors for all regions, the weight for a local region being the proportion of total national employment found in that region. This measure divided by two varies between zero and unity" (Vining, *op. cit.*, pp. 40–51). Completely even geographic distribution would give a coefficient of zero, while increasingly greater concentration of industry in a region would give a coefficient approaching unity. Although this method is somewhat different from that of Hildebrand and Mace, the result is the same.

[31] Hildebrand and Mace, *op. cit.*, p. 243. In their study of Los Angeles County these authors varied the subject and benchwork economies. Using the United States as the benchmark economy, they used successively the twelve western states, the eleven counties of southern California, and Los Angeles County as subject economies. Then using the eleven western states as the benchmark economy, they used southern California and Los Angeles County as subject economies and finally used Los Angeles County relative to southern California. As a result, they were able to delimit precisely the extent of the market for each export (while exports out of the country would increase the location quo-

Thus industries producing for export will show values significantly above 1.00.[32]

We are now in a better position to examine the role of the export base in shaping the economy of the region.

Clearly the export base plays a vital role in determining the level of absolute and per capita income of a region. While the return to factors of production[33] in the export industries indicates the direct importance of these industries for the well-being of the region, it is the indirect effect that is most important. Since residentiary industry depends entirely on demand within the region, it has historically been dependent on the fate of the export base.[34] Vining's analysis indicates that employment in residentiary industry tends to bear a direct relationship to employment in export industries. The median figure for employment in residentiary industry in individual states was approximately 55 per cent of the total employment.[35]

The export staple plays an equally vital role in the cyclical sensitivity of the region; it acts as the "carrier" in diffusing changes in the level of income from other regions to the subject region. Furthermore, the sensitivity of the region to fluctuations depends on the income elasticities of the export staples. Clearly regions that specialize in a few products with high income elasticities will have more violent fluctuations in income than more diversified regions.[36]

When we turn to the role of exports in shaping the pattern of urbanization and nodal centers,[37] we are on ground that has been more thoroughly explored by location theorists and geographers.[38] Again, however, the pioneering work has been done by German location theorists who have extended the implications of each stage of economic growth to embrace the logical pattern of urbanization that would ensue.[39] Since these

tient, they would not of course be isolated by this technique).

32 Hildebrand and Mace allowed for differences in demand functions, which might make some residentiary industry appear with a location quotient above 1.00. They came to the conclusion that 1.508 was the boundary line in their study (*ibid.*, p. 246).

This location quotient is not too well adapted to use in agriculture. There I have used a coefficient of specialization in which the numerator is the region's physical volume of production relative to the physical volume of production of the agricultural good for the nation. The denominator is the region's absolute popluation relative to the nation's absolute population. While such a coefficient has some obvious limitations and must be used with care, it is more adaptable to the available data than the one discussed above.

33 Obviously the disposition of nonwage income to residents of the region or outside the region is important here. It will be further considered in the next section.

34 This statement requires both substantiation and careful qualification. This article is primarily concerned with the historical development of the American economy, and here the statement needs little qualification. The fortunes of regions have been closely tied to their export base. However, it is conceivable that a region with a large influx of population and capital might simply "feed upon itself" and thereby account for a substantial share of its growth. Moreover, in older "mature" regions, economic activity may become so diversified as to make the export base less significant. This question will be dealt with in the next section.

35 Vining, *op. cit.*, p. 49.

36 For further discussion of this subject see Vining, *op. cit.*

37 The concept of nodes is one that has been extensively used by geographers. The term refers to *sites* that have strategic transfer advantages in reference to procurement and distribution costs and therefore become processing centers. Such advantageous points are limited in number and tend to develop into major metropolitan areas. For further discussion of nodes see Hoover, *The Location of Economic Activity*, pp. 119–30.

38 For a summary of recent developments in this area see Walter Isard, "Current Development in Regional Analysis," *Weltwirtschaftliches Archiv*, LXIX (September, 1952), 81–91.

39 An excellent summary of the German contributions is contained in Isard's "The General

stages do not fit the American development, the pattern of American urbanization likewise differs in many respects from the German models. However, it is beyond the scope of this article to explore the whole question of urbanization and the export base. We may note in passing the observations of August Lösch that in such areas as Iowa, with a rather even distribution of production of agricultural staples, the distances between towns increase with their size.[40] In contrast, cities in the English coal districts are the same distance from each other irrespective of size.[41]

While discussion of the spatial distribution of urban areas would take us too far afield, the role of the export base in shaping the growth of nodal centers deserves some attention. Nodes grow up because of special locational advantages that lower the transfer and processing costs of exportable commodities. Nodal centers become trading centers through which exports leave the region and imports enter for distribution throughout the area. Here special facilities develop to implement the production and distribution of the staples. Subsidiary industries to service the export industry, as well as specialized banking, brokerage, wholesaling, and other business services, concentrate in these centers and act to improve the cost position of the export.[42]

The character of the labor force will be fundamentally influenced by the export industries. The types of skills required, the seasonality and stability of employment, and the conditions of work will shape the social attitudes of the working force.

As already noted, the political attitudes of the region will be largely directed toward improving the position of its export base. The extent of such activity is too well known historically and too obvious in the contemporary American political scene to require extended discussion.

V

Previous sections of this paper have examined the significance of the export base for a region's economy. I have tried to indicate the primary role that such exports have played historically, but I have not yet touched on the critical question of the causes of the growth of a region. It is evident that this growth is closely tied to the success of its exports and may take place either as a result of the improved position of existing exports relative to competing areas or as a result of the development of new exports. However, a major question that must first be examined is whether a region must industrialize if it is to continue to grow. Such a necessity has been a major tenet of the theory of regional economic growth. Moreover, industrialization has been regarded as a difficult stage to achieve, so that it is the source of problems of arrested regional development. Hoover and Fisher stress three factors that make this transition difficult: (1) the need for greatly improved transportation facilities, which call for large-scale capital in-

Theory of Location and Space Economy," *Quarterly Journal of Economics*, LXIII (November, 1949), 476–506.

[40] Lösch, *op. cit.*, p. 75. In this article Lösch advances an interesting theoretical model of spatial location.

[41] *Ibid.*, p. 75. A summary of the development of concepts of spatial organization may be found in Isard's "Distance Inputs and the Space Economy," *op. cit.*

[42] These specialized facilities provide economies in addition to the general economies of urban concentration resulting from such things as fire and police protection, lower utility rates, and a specialized labor force. For further discussion of these aspects of urban concentration see Ohlin, *op. cit.*, pp. 203–4.

vestments; (2) the need for intensification of the geographic division of labor; and (3) the fact that industrial technology is novel to an agricultural region.[43] If these statements are correct, then the implications for our analysis are clear. At some point regions must shift from an extractive to an industrial export base, and this shift will be fraught with difficulties. However, the contention that regions must industrialize in order to continue to grow, as well as the contention that the development of secondary and tertiary industry is somehow difficult to achieve, are both based on some fundamental misconceptions.

The importance of industrializing is based upon the notion that, with increased population and diminishing returns in extractive industry, the shift to manufacturing is the only way to maintain sustained growth (measured in terms of increasing per capita income). This argument has been buttressed by evidence such as that gathered by Dr. Louis Bean correlating per capita income with percentage of the labor force engaged in primary, secondary, and tertiary occupations by states for 1939.[44] Bean's figures purport to demonstrate that increased industrialization leads to higher per capita income, and he goes so far as to say that "a 10-point [per cent] increase in industrial progress in the east and south . . . apparently tends to add $100 to $150 (1939 prices) per capita and in the western states substantially more."[45] In fact, Bean's statistics do not prove this, and the policy implications of such generalizations may be misleading and dangerous.

We may note first of all that his correlation is not very impressive. There were eleven states in which the percentage of the labor force in primary occupations was above the national average whose per capita income either exceeded the national average or was close enough to the average so that annual variations could well place it on one side or the other. Indeed, had the correlation been made for postwar years, it would have been substantially different.[46]

Furthermore, money-income data significantly understate the real income of the farmer,[47] because of the great variety of goods and services produced on the farm that require cash payment in the city.[48]

However, the real source of error has resulted from a basic misunderstanding of the nature of the economy. A state whose export base consists mostly of agricultural products may have a low percentage of its labor force in primary activity and a high percentage in tertiary occupations and *yet* be basically dependent upon agriculture for the high per capita income it enjoys. It is the agricultural export staples that provide the high income that enables the state to support a substantial level of services. In such a case both the secondary and the tertiary activities are "residentiary" and can sur-

[43] *Op. cit.*, p. 182. Hoover and Fisher go on to point out that "further difficulty arises from the fact that when a non-industrial region reaches a limit of growth it is likely to retrogress or decay" (*ibid.*, p. 184).

[44] *Studies in Income and Wealth*, VIII (New York: National Bureau of Economic Research, 1946), 128–29.

[45] *Ibid.*, p. 137.

[46] See "State Income Payments in 1950," *Survey of Current Business*, August, 1951, p. 18.

[47] There is also evidence to indicate that money incomes are disportionately understated.

[48] See Margaret Reid, "Distribution of Nonmoney Income," *Studies in Income and Wealth*, Vol. XIII (New York: National Bureau of Economic Research, 1951). See also Jacob Viner, *International Trade and Economic Development* (Glencoe, Ill.: Free Press, 1952), pp. 63–73. Professor Viner provides a number of trenchant criticisms of Bean's argument.

vive only because of the success of the basic agricultural export staples. In short, a percentage shift in such a state from primary to secondary and tertiary employment does not necessarily reflect a shift away from dependence on agriculture to dependence on manufacturing and services. Instead, it may reflect the simple fact that farmers are receiving high incomes for their staple crops and therefore buy more goods and services from residentiary industry.

This brings us to the related question of the difficulty of industrialization. The implication of the preceding paragraph is that a substantial amount of secondary industry of the residentiary variety will develop automatically as a result of high incomes received from the exportable commodities. Nor is this the only kind of manufacturing that can be expected to develop. We may distinguish four different kinds of manufacturing that will develop:[49]

1. Materials-oriented industries which, because of marked transfer advantages of the manufactured product over the raw material, locate at the source of the latter. Among the industries in this category are sugar-beet refining, flour-milling,[50] and lumbering.[51] Such industries may develop further stages of vertical integration until transfer cost advantages become equalized. Such industry is typically part of the export base.

2. Service industries to the export industry. Foundries and establishments that make machine tools, specialized agricultural implements, and logging and lumbering equipment are illustrations.

3. Residentiary industry producing for local consumption.

4. Footloose industries, where transfer costs are not of significant importance in location. A great many such industries develop purely by chance in some location.[52]

While footloose industries have typically developed by chance, the other three types of secondary activity develop naturally because of locational advantages in a society responsive to profit-maximizing stimuli. There is nothing difficult about the development of such industries. The difficulties arise when promoters seek to develop in a region industries which simply are unsuited for the area and which can therefore only be maintained under hothouse conditions.[53]

The argument may be advanced that the kinds of industry described above do not constitute industrialization. How much and what kind of secondary industry must a region possess to be termed "industrialized"? By 1950 census classification, the state of Oregon had almost

[49] This classification is similar to that of E. J. Cohn, Jr., in *Industry in the Pacific Northwest and the Location Theory* (New York: Columbia University Press, 1954), pp. 42–44.

[50] However, milling-in-transit privileges may modify this materials orientation.

[51] See National Resources Planning Board, *op. cit.*, chap. vi, for a further account of such industries.

[52] For further discussion of such industries see National Resources Committee, *The Structure of the American Economy*, Part I: *Basic Characteristics* (Washington, D.C.: Government Printing Office, 1939), p. 36.

[53] This does not mean that there is no room for appropriate public policy that may create the social overhead benefits that will make certain industries feasible. I can do no better here than to quote Viner: "There are no inherent advantages of manufacturing over agriculture, or, for that matter, of agriculture over manufacturing. It is only arbitrarily in fact that the line separating the two can be drawn. The choice between expansion of agriculture and expansion of manufactures can, for the most part, be left to the free decisions of capitalists, entrepreneurs and workers. To the extent that there is need for government decision, it should be made on rational grounds, in the light of considerations of costs and comparative returns from alternative allocation of scarce national resources, human and material" (*op. cit.*, p. 72).

24 per cent of its labor force in manufacturing, which was only slightly under the United States average (25.9 per cent) and exceeded the United States average in durable goods (16.7 per cent as compared with the national average of 13.8 per cent). It was well ahead of the neighboring states of Washington and California, despite the fact that these two states had a variety of manufacturing industries, in contrast to Oregon's specialized dependence on the Douglas fir lumber industry. Is such a state industrialized? Implicit in the concept appears to be the notion that industrialization is somehow tied up with steel and the capital goods industries. However, historically, the locational pull of coal and iron ore has shaped the development of the steel-producing centers, which in turn have attracted and concentrated heavy industry.[54] While locational influences in the steel industry have been changing significantly in the last half-century with the growing importance of scrap and the changing composition of inputs,[55] nevertheless, the possible areas for the development of efficient large-scale steel production[56] and, therefore, capital goods industry are severely circumscribed. A more useful concept of industrialization for our purposes is a region whose export base consists primarily of finished consumers' goods and/or finished manufactured producers' goods.

We may summarize the argument up to this point as follows: (1) There is no reason why all regions must industrialize in order to continue to grow. (2) A great deal of secondary (and tertiary) industry will develop automatically either because of locational advantages of materials-oriented industry or as a passive reflection of growing income in the region resulting from the success of its exportable commodities. (3) The concept of industrialization is an ambiguous one that needs further clarification if it is to be useful.

Since the growth of a region is tied to the success of its export base, we must examine in more detail the reasons for the growth, decline, and change in the export base. Clearly, the decline of one exportable commodity must be accompanied by the growth of others, or a region will be left "stranded."[57] Among the major reasons[58] for the decline of an existing exportable commodity have been changes in demand outside the region,[59] exhaustion of a natural resource,[60] increasing costs of land or labor relative to those of a competing region,[61] and technological changes that changed the relative composition of inputs.[62] A historically important reason for the growth of new exports has been major developments in transport (in contrast with mere cost-reducing improvements in transport, which may reinforce dependence on existing exports). Such developments

[54] National Resources Planning Board, *op. cit.*, p. 162.

[55] Walter Isard, "Some Locational Factors in the Iron and Steel Industry since the Early Nineteenth Century," *Journal of Political Economy*, LVI (1948), 213–17.

[56] The extensive utilization of scrap makes possible small-scale steel production as a residentiary industry wherever the local market achieves sufficient size.

[57] The cut-over region in the Great Lakes area is a case in point.

[58] For further discussion on shifting industry see National Resources Planning Board, *op. cit.*, pp. 92–104.

[59] Such as the decline in the demand for beaver hats, which affected the fur trade.

[60] Exemplified by the Great Lakes lumber industry.

[61] The most famous example is the decline in the New England cotton textile industry.

[62] Such as the case of steel cited above.

have often enabled a region to compete with other regions in the production of goods that were previously economically unfeasible because of the high transfer costs.[63] Growth in income and demand in other regions[64] and technological developments[65] have also been important. The role of the state and federal government in creating social overhead benefits has created new exports in many regions,[66] and the significance of war in promoting industries that may either continue or leave a residue of capital investment for peacetime use has also been important.

A region may expand as a result of increased demand for its existing exportable commodities, whether due to an increase in the income of the market area or to a change in taste. An improvement in the processing- or transfer-cost position of the region's staples vis-à-vis competing regions will likewise promote growth.

Historically, in a young region, the creation of a new export or the expansion of an existing export has resulted in the influx of capital investment both in the export industry and in all the kinds of passive and supporting economic activity described above. Meier has described this process for the Canadian economy in the first decade of the twentieth century, when increased world demand for wheat not only led to an expansion of warehousing, transport, public utilities, and construction in the Prairie Provinces, but also, by increasing income, augmented demand for secondary products and thereby induced investment in a host of other industries.[67] As a result the growth of a region will, in all likelihood, be uneven, coming in spurts of increased investment rather than proceeding at an even pace.

Increased capital investment in the export industry will go toward achieving optimum size of the enterprise, increased mechanization of the processes, and further development of the specialized services to the export. The source of capital will play an important part in the region's growth. Typically, the capital in young regions comes from outside. Profits (and some other nonwage income) flow out of the region. To the extent that the export base is profitable, a part of this income will be reinvested in the expansion of this base.

With the growth of population and income, indigenous savings will increase. Both indigenous savings and the reinvested capital can pour back into the export industries only up to a point, and then the accumulated capital will tend to overflow into other activity. As described above, some will go into residentiary industry and industries subsidiary to the export; but it is also very likely that some will go into locationally "footloose" industries, which may start out to serve only the region, but which can expand into export industries.

63 The whole history of canal and railroad development contains innumerable illustrations of such developments (see Isard, "Transportation Development and Building Cycles," *op. cit.*).

64 The growth in demand for wheat in England and on the European continent in the last half of the nineteenth century is a famous example.

65 The development of the petroleum industry is a typical illustration.

66 The development of hydroelectric power in the Pacific Northwest and the resultant development of the aluminum industry is an example.

67 G. M. Meier, "Economic Development and the Transfer Mechanism," *Canadian Journal of Economics and Political Science*, XIX (February, 1953), 1–19. M. C. Daly has attempted to work out a geographic multiplier between "localized" and "non-localized" industry, using data for Britain for the years 1921–31 ("An Approximation to a Geographic Multiplier," *Economic Journal*, L [June-September, 1940]), 248–58. See also Hildebrand and Mace, *op. cit.*

At this point a region is no longer young. The social overhead benefits that have been created through political pressure or as a part of the pattern of urban development and the development of a trained labor force and indigenous capital make it far easier to develop new exports. Whether such industries were originally residentiary and, by gradually overcoming transfer-cost disadvantages, became export industries, or were originally footloose industries not significantly affected by transfer costs, the result is to broaden the export base. As such a region matures, the staple base will become less distinguishable, since its production will be so varied.

We may expect, therefore, that the differences between regions will become less marked, that secondary industry will tend to be more equalized, and indeed in economic terms that regionalism will tend to disappear.

VI

The purpose of this paper has been to re-examine location theory and the theory of regional economic growth in the light of the historical development of regions in America and to advance some propositions that may lead to a new theory of regional economic growth.

It has been argued that the stages outlined in the theory of regional economic growth bear little relationship to the character of American development and more specifically do not focus on the crucial elements that will enable us to understand that growth. Furthermore, the traditional theory has policy implications that may be fundamentally in error.

The first stage of subsistence has been relatively unimportant, and, to the extent that it existed at all, it was because means of transport were lacking rather than because of a nonmarket orientation. In Europe a subsistence or a village economy with local markets was built into the social and economic structure for centuries. In America subsistence was only a frontier condition to be overcome as rapidly as means of transport could be built.

The second stage of the theory is based on a gradual widening of the market area with improved transport and the development of a second stratum to service the basic agricultural stratum. Far from moving through such a gradual progression American regions, as soon as any transport permitted, developed goods for export often to markets thousands of miles away. The early town centers were located not only so as to service the agricultural stratum but so as to implement the export of the region's staples. The prosperity of the region depended on its success in competing with other areas producing the same staple exports. Therefore, the region's economic and political efforts were oriented toward the reduction of processing and transfer costs. The struggle for internal improvements by the West, the agrarian pressure for inflation and cheaper credit, and the campaign for free coinage of silver were fundamentally economic movements. Their objectives included increasing the supply of capital, eliminating real or fancied transport discrimination, reducing interest rates, and improving the market for silver, however much they may also have been concerned with social justice.

The third stage of regional growth has been described as the gradual shift from extensive to intensive farming. While it is true that rising land values promoted such a shift, there were many other reasons for a shift in the staple base. New means of transport, changing demand, new technological developments, changing cost relationships vis-à-vis competing regions, government subsidization of social overhead benefits, and war have all been important.

The shift from an agricultural to an industrial base has been looked upon as the difficult, but indispensable, step for sustained economic growth. It is a major argument of this paper that such a step may be neither necessary nor desirable and that the evidence customarily advanced to support this argument proves nothing of the sort. There is nothing to prevent population and per capita income from growing in a region whose export base is agricultural. Moreover, there is nothing difficult about developing secondary and tertiary industry in such a region. Indeed, it will develop automatically, often to such an extent that analysis of the region in terms of distribution of employment will lead to the conclusion that it is an industrial region.

The final stage has typically been conceived to be the mature regional economy exporting capital, skills, and specialized services to less-well-developed regions. While this may be true for some regions, it is unlikely to be a final stage for all. Indeed, one would presume that some sort of balanced relationship would emerge among regions as transfer costs become less significant and income differentials tend to be ironed out by long-run factor mobility.

The major propositions that emerge from this paper are:

1. For economists' purposes the concept of a region should be redefined to point out that the unifying cohesion to a region, over and beyond geographic similarities, is its development around a common export base. It is this that makes it economically unified and ties the fortunes of the area together. This tends to result in the interdependent development within the region of external economies and unified political efforts for government assistance or political reform. The geographer has emphasized the distributive functions of the nodal centers of a region, but the role of the nodal center in providing external economies for the export industries has been equally important.

2. The success of the export base has been the determining factor in the rate of growth of regions. Therefore, in order to understand this growth, we must examine the locational factors that have enabled the staples to develop.

3. The importance of the export base is a result of its primary role in determining the level of absolute and per capita income in a region, and therefore in determining the amount of residentiary secondary and tertiary activity that will develop. The export base has also significantly influenced the character of subsidiary industry, the distribution of population and pattern of urbanization, the character of the labor force, the social and political attitudes of the region, and its sensitivity to fluctuations of income and employment.

4. In a young region dependence on staples is reinforced by the concerted efforts of the region's residents to reduce processing and transfer costs through technological research, and state and federal government subsidization of social overhead benefits, as well as the tendency for outside suppliers of capital to reinvest in the existing staple base.

5. Some regions, because of locational advantages, have developed an export base of manufactured products, but this is not a necessary stage for the sustained

growth of all regions. A great deal of secondary and tertiary industry will result from the success of the export base. This residentiary industry will, in all likelihood, provide for widening the export base as a region develops.

6. The growth of regions has tended to be uneven. A given increase in demand for the region's exports (or a significant reduction in processing or transfer costs) has resulted in a multiple effect on the region, inducing increased investment not only in the export industry but in all other kinds of economic activity as well.

7. As a region's income grows, indigenous savings will tend to spill over into new kinds of activities. At first, these activities satisfy local demand, but ultimately some of them will become export industries. This movement is reinforced by the tendency for transfer costs to become less significant. As a result, the export bases of regions tend to become more diversified, and they tend to lose their identity as regions. Ultimately, we may expect with long-run factor mobility more equalization of per capita income and a wider dispersion of production.

13. Exports and Regional Economic Growth*

CHARLES M. TIEBOUT

I

THE theory of the regional economic base has been bobbing around in the literature, implicitly and explicitly, for some time.[1] Its latest appearance comes as an explanatory factor in regional economic growth. In his recent article Douglass C. North has suggested that the theory of regional development which sees the region as passing through various stages—primary, secondary, and tertiary—is not adequate.[2] As a substitute, North maintains that a region's growth "is closely tied to the success of its exports and may take place either as a result of the improved position of existing exports relative to competing areas or as a result of the development of new exports."[3] He further points out that it is necessary to look into location theory to explain changes in the export base. The point involved is that the concept of the export base in regional analysis is called on as the major autonomous variable determining the level of regional income.

The concept of the economic base has been developed largely in the works of city planners and other researchers interested in urban problems.[4] As such—and this is neither slur nor praise—no attempt has been made to relate this concept to the general theory of income determination as used in national income analysis.[5] This failure and the continual identification of the exports of a region with the autonomous variable determining income have led to some erroneous conclusions about regional income and regional development. The purpose of this note is, first, to show how the export-base concept fits within the more general theory of income determination and, second, using this setting as a frame of reference, to point out some implications for the theory of regional growth.

II

It is useful to begin by presenting a simplified version of the concept of the export base. The economic activities of a region are divided into those which produce for the export market and those which produce for the local market. In defining exports allowance is made for such items as the earnings of commuters, capital flows, government transfers, and linked industries. Given these basic or export activities, the level of non-basic or residentiary activities follows. The ratio between export activities and residentiary activities, measured in income or employment, is then used as a multiplier. For example, a one-to-one ratio would mean that an increase in exports will cause an equal increase in residentiary activities. Whether or not this function is constant at all levels of in-

[1] See Richard B. Andrews, "The Mechanics of the Urban Economic Base," *Land Economics*, Vol. XXIX (1953), No. 3 (continuing series). For a more explicit statement see George Hildebrand and Arthur Mace, Jr., "The Employment Multiplier in an Expanding Industrial Market: Los Angeles County, 1940–47," *Review of Economics and Statistics*, XXXII, No. 3 (August, 1950), 241–49.

[2] "Location Theory and Regional Economic Growth," *Journal of Political Economy*, LXIII (June, 1955), 243–58.

[3] *Ibid.*, p. 251.

[4] See Richard Andrews, "The Mechanics of the Urban Economic Base: Historical Development of the Base Concept," *Land Economics*, XXIX (August, 1953), 161–67; and Homer Hoyt, "Homer Hoyt on the Concept of the Economic Base," *Land Economics*, XXX (May, 1954), 182–86.

[5] It is interesting to note that the work of Hildebrand and Mace (*op. cit.*), which deals with an employment multiplier, is rarely mentioned in discussions of the economic base. North's article is a notable exception.

* Reprinted from the *Journal of Political Economy*, Vol. 64 (April 1956).

come is not stated. There is no a priori reason to believe it is. From here, of course, it is a simple step to the statement that the income of the region is tied to the level of exports. For a small region this may be substantially correct, but for larger regions it is an oversimplification. A general theory of income determination at the national level rests on a knowledge of the level and stability of both the dependent and the autonomous variables. These are the necessary ingredients of an econometric model that forecasts income.[6]

There is no reason to assume that exports are the sole or even the most important autonomous variable determining regional income. Such other items as business investment, government expenditures, and the volume of residential construction may be just as autonomous with respect to regional income as are exports.[7] Under the assumption, which may have some validity, that the autonomous variables are the dynamic factors in determining the short-run level of regional income, these items may even be the chief source of instability. Only empirical studies will enable us to say something about their quantitative importance.

A further consideration will help to point up the error of identifying exports as the sole source of regional income change. In an exchange economy one person considered in a spatial context may be entirely dependent on his ability to export his services. Probably this is true of a neighborhood area, except for the corner grocer. For the community as a whole, the income originating in non-exports increases. In the United States economy, exports account for only a small part of national income. Obviously, for the world as a whole, there are no exports.

Thus the quantitative importance of exports as an explanatory factor in regional income determination depends, in part, on the size of the region under study. It is true that for a region considered at two different time periods, a change in the volume of exports may indicate a change in the level of income, but this is not enough. A region may grow with exports at a constant level, if internal autonomous activities are on the upswing. The larger the region, the more the dynamic forces causing income change will be found inside its borders.

The problem that arises because export volume is a function of regional size might be solved if it were possible to find some method of determining the boundaries of a region which not only made sense but allowed for interregional comparisons. North has suggested that the boundaries of a region should be determined by "its development around a common export base."[8] This basis of classification is useful, but it is by no means the only possibility.

Most researchers in the field of regional economics have come to the conclusion that there is no "ideal" region. Probably the closest approximation to the concept of an ideal region would arise in a Lösch production-oriented spatial system.[9] In this system an over-all area is mapped out according to sites of production determined by market networks. Other conditions which are also given for equilibrium need not concern us here. In the central city all goods are produced, with fewer produced in the other spatially arranged cities. If an over-all area, in this sort of orientation, could be divided into two or more identical parts, either one might be considered an ideal region.[10] Any statement concerning the nature of one region would be applicable to any other. Unfortunately, in the nature of market networks even in the conceptual construct, such regions do not exist. Given this Lösch mapping, it follows that regional boundaries are not clear-cut and any statement concerning

[6] See Lawrence Klein, *Econometrics* (Chicago: Row, Peterson & Co., 1953).

[7] North's consideration of the possible outlets of a region's indigenous savings suggests these considerations (*op. cit.*, p. 255).

[8] *Ibid.*, p. 257.

[9] August Lösch, *The Economics of Location* (New Haven: Yale University Press, 1954).

[10] In terms of set theory, this implies that the over-all area can be partitioned into disjoint subsets which map one-to-one into each other.

the importance of exports must keep this in mind.

In view of our inability to construct an "ideal" region, the selection of regional boundaries rests on other criteria. Usually, the regional boundaries are suggested by the variables one chooses to study. Non-economic considerations, such as the availability of data and the location of political divisions, may, of course, be the basis for the demarcation of a region. The important point is *not* which boundaries are chosen but the effects of this choice on the variables under study. If the researcher is aware at least of the direction of changes in the variables as a function of regional boundaries, the question of boundaries is of less importance. For example, increased regional size, with more internal trade, implies that the quantitative importance of exports decreases.

Perhaps the most surprising feature of the concept of the export base of a region is that no one, to my knowledge, has attempted to integrate this concept into the traditional foreign-trade multiplier analysis. The works of Metzler, Machlup, and Stolper are conspicuous by their omission from the discussions.[11] Usually the economic base of a region of any size from an urban area up to several states is merely assumed to be exports. Implicitly, no foreign-trade multiplier feedback is assumed. This is probably valid for smaller areas, but for larger areas the feedback can be an important factor. An example may illustrate this point.

Consider the exports of New England. Like those of any other region, its exports compete with products from elsewhere. Thus one expects and finds that export receipts fall off as a function of distance.[12] Few of the region's exports enjoy a worldwide market. The New York area would be expected to absorb a much higher percentage of New England's exports than would a market of equal size in the Far West. Conversely, the New England area would tend to absorb a greater percentage of New York's exports than would a more remote market.

Contrast this situation with that of a mill town. Here the exports may be considered as going off into some distant space. The income of the mill town will be affected by the income of its market, but the income of the market will not be affected by the income of the mill town. This merely places the mill town in the same position as the competitive wheat farmer who is too small to affect the market but is affected by it. In this case there is no foreign-trade multiplier feedback. This is not true in the regional case, and one is left in the uncomfortable position of having exports in part a function of domestic income. Thus in the short run it appears that the determination of regional income depends only in part on the region's exports. The larger the region under consideration, the smaller the role of exports. Other variables in the structural equations must be considered if income stability is to be more fully understood.

III

The concept of the export base, or even the fuller concept of regional income determination which includes other autonomous variables, is a short-run concept. As such it may be fairly accurate. Our knowledge of consumer behavior and the relative ease of entry into residentiary activities, such as baking and retailing, indicate that this may be a fairly safe assumption, at least for small regions. To extend this relationship to the question of regional development, however, can be dangerous.

Before we consider the question of the export base in regional development, one issue should be cleared up. It involves a dif-

[11] Lloyd A. Metzler, "Underemployment Equilibrium in International Trade," *Econometrica*, X (April, 1942), 97–112; Fritz Machlup, *International Trade and the National Income Multiplier* (Philadelphia: Blakiston Co., 1943); Wolfgang Stolper, "The Volume of Foreign Trade and the Level of Income," *Quarterly Journal of Economics*, LXI (February, 1947), 285–310.

[12] See Walter Isard and Merton Peck, "Location Theory and International and Interregional Trade Theory," *Quarterly Journal of Economics* LXVII (February, 1954), 97–114.

ference between regional growth and economic development in general. Suppose that we assume that general economic development means raising the per capita income of some area, say North America. Further, let us define regional growth as the rate of change of per capita income in some segment of this totality, say Canada. It is pertinent to ask whether these should be considered as presenting the same sort of problem. If we imagine that the continent had developed without Western influence, but assuming capitalism, some process of primary, secondary, and tertiary evolution might be expected to have taken place just as it did, in general, in the development of Europe. True, some areas might have specialized in agricultural activities; but if the concept of regional balance means anything, specialized areas of manufactures would be expected. If some island economy, unknown to the rest of the world, were studied as a case of economic development, the stage concept might be quite valid.

This sort of analysis should not be called on, however, to deal with questions of regional economic growth, which presents a different sort of problem. If a new peninsula were formed off the New Jersey coast, it would provide an ideal setting for studying regional economic growth. In this case there is no reason to expect the peninsula area to pass from the primary-subsistence to the secondary-tertiary stage as real incomes increase. If, as North points out, the region can develop an export base, it may develop in a variety of forms. It could become a center for truck gardens (primary); a cite for manufacturing (secondary); or a vacation area (tertiary). Note that this does not imply that it will develop even if it *seems* to have an export base, for reasons to be discussed later. The important point about the New Jersey example is that we are dealing with a region in the neighborhood of more advanced areas. The degree of specialization and of exporting will depend on the market. The higher the incomes in the neighboring areas, given the propensity to import, the higher the volume of their imports, that is, the exports of the peninsula. The volume of exports and, in turn, internal growth will depend not only on the factor endowment but also on the income of the surrounding area. It is useful to keep this distinction in mind when contrasting regional economic growth with economic development in general.[13]

The idea that essentially the export base is the necessary and sufficient condition for regional economic growth may be, by definition, a true statement. Given the transport network, the size and location of markets, and factor endowments, it appears that a region will develop if it can compete with other regions in the export market. This implies an ability to produce at lower cost. With factor mobility, growth will take place only if the return to the factors is equal to, or greater than, the return to the same factors in other regions. If this is what is meant by the ability to develop an export base, it is correct by definition, but it does not uncover enough to predict growth. Ability to find an export base depends not only on the value of the units of output but on the cost of the inputs. These costs cannot be assumed to be equal for all regions. Yet, if residentiary activities are assumed to be endogenous and are not considered as a factor in regional growth, the analysis will implicitly assume that all unit factor costs are equal among regions. Put another way, it is possible to define the necessary condition for regional economic growth as the creation of an export base. But location theory, which is called on to explain its creation, will work only if factor costs are known. The determination of factor costs depends in part on the nature of the region's residentiary activities.

[13] The development of the Pacific Northwest and the Canadian development cited by North (*op. cit.*, p. 246–47) may be analogous to the New Jersey example. Both occurred after the process of industrialization was under way. In contrast to this case, the position of the earliest colonies typifies the case of general economic development. Of course, this is a matter of degree and should not be taken as a statement that exports were unimportant to the early colonies.

An example may serve to illustrate this point. Going back to our hypothetical New Jersey peninsula, assume that a coal deposit is found some two hundred miles out on the peninsula. Will it be mined to compete in the New York market with Pennsylvania coal? Make one further assumption about the region. Assume that the rest of the area is all sand and marshland. If workers are to mine this newly found deposit, they must eat, and hence there must be imports. If the cost of these imports is high enough, no coal will be mined, and no export base will develop.

Contrast this with a situation in which the peninsula is rolling, fertile countryside. Truck gardening and dairy farming can develop. Some imports will still flow in, but some local needs—vegetables and milk—will be supplied locally, that is, supplied by residentiary activities. Under these conditions coal may be mined because of the lower cost of production, in this example lower dollar wages.[14]

Again, formally speaking, it is the ability to develop an export base which determines regional growth. Yet in terms of causation, the nature of the residentiary industries will be a key factor in any possible development. Without the ability to develop residentiary activities, the cost of development of export activities will be prohibitive.

The objection may be raised that this is a special case. No claim is made for general validity. However, if one seeks to explain the failure of certain parts of Alaska or Canada to develop, this consideration may uncover a more complete picture. Further, it is well known that cities usually develop in locations that are surrounded by good lands and not in the middle of less fertile areas.

[14] In both cases the real wages of the coal miners would be the same, but in the former case, because of the high cost of living, dollar wages would be higher. In location theory it is the dollar cost which determines location and development.

However, the idea of the export base is more useful when applied to certain areas, such as satellite cities in the suburban fringe. Here low transport costs and proximity to markets insure that, even if residentiary activities do not develop fully, their outputs can be imported from near-by areas. The larger the region under consideration, the less safe the assumption.

A final point is in order concerning regional growth and the ratio of export to residentiary activity. Given its population, boundaries, transport network and costs, markets, and factor endowment, a region must divide its energies between residentiary and export activities. If too little is devoted to one or the other, the economy will not be maximizing per capita income. Supposedly there is some optimum division. If export activities are relatively too large, it will pay to move resources into residentiary industries (witness the enviable position of the storekeeper during the gold rush), and the region's income will increase. Here we find an example in which regional growth is possible with a reduction of exports.

IV

This note has tried to show that the concept of the export base is merely one aspect of a general theory of short-run regional income determination. In the case of large regions, other variables may play as important a role as exports. Furthermore, the concept of the export base may be useful in describing regional income growth, but this need not be considered the same problem as general economic development. As an explanatory factor in regional growth, the idea of the export base should not subsume the key role of residentiary activities in determining factor costs of possible regional exports. Finally, since a region must optimize the use of factors as between exports and residentiary outputs, a decline in export activity may even be accompanied by rising regional income.

A REPLY

DOUGLASS C. NORTH[1]

PROFESSOR TIEBOUT's comment is a welcome addition to the literature on regional economic growth. The role of the export base in regional development requires further analysis, and Tiebout has raised some important questions that merit discussion.

The bulk of his criticism of the role of the export base in regional growth hinges on one critical point at issue between us. His is a *short-run* analysis, in which the export base is conceived to be only one of a number of important factors in income determination. I have no quarrel with this position, but it has little relevance for my article, which was explicitly concerned with *long-run* economic growth. Short-period income determination and long-run economic growth are not the same thing. In the former case the analysis is concerned with changes in the level of employment and the variables that will affect the rate of utilization of productive factors. In this case increased business investment will result in expanded employment and income in periods of less than full employment. Such analysis, however, has little relevance for long-run economic growth, where the objective is to determine the factors that will affect the decade-to-decade changes in the real aggregate and per capita income of an area under conditions of full employment. In the latter case secular expansion comes about because of increased output per unit of resources or an increase in the supply of productive factors, or both. Historically, this increase in labor and capital has come about as a result of long-run expansion of the demand for productive factors within the area. Not only has there been mobility of productive factors within the American economy, but also during a substantial period of our growth there has been international mobility of capital and labor for the entire Atlantic economy. Therefore, while the study of short-run income determination has been concerned with the rate of utilization of productive factors, the study of long-run growth has dealt with the determinants of changing efficiency and the immigration of labor and capital into an area. The variables used in income analysis are of limited use in the study of long-run growth. Indeed, the aggregates used tend to obscure rather than to illumine the factors generating secular expansion. An examination of Tiebout's major points will further clarify this distinction and highlight some important problems for further research.

[1] I am indebted to my colleagues Philip Cartwright and Donald Gordon for suggestions which have clarified some of the points at issue in this discussion.

I

Tiebout and I are in agreement that there is no "ideal" region. Since he concedes that the question of boundaries is of less importance if the researcher is aware of the significance of increased regional size, there is no apparent difference in our position. Yet one point requires emphasis. The usefulness of a region as an economic unit of analysis rests upon its specialization. It is this geographic division of labor, with different areas having special factor endowments and transfer costs, which makes the concept of the region valuable in economic analysis. The region's significance lies in its being a specialized part of the whole. If the size of the region is to be limited by its individual economic characteristics, then the concept of a geographically contiguous area held together by its development around a common export base is a useful (though certainly not the only) basis of classification.

It has the added advantage that, in terms of the long-run growth of different areas in America, the export base has been influential in shaping a good deal of the history of the region.[2] Such a classification necessarily limits the size of the region and minimizes the problems raised by Tiebout.

II

Given the region as defined, the role of the export base in regional growth may now be more precisely delineated. Tiebout and I are in agreement that it is not the sole source of regional growth,[3] but we are in disagreement when he states that it may not even be the most important factor in regional expansion. An examination of the differential rates of growth of regions throughout America's development inevitably focuses on the ability of areas to attract productive factors. Initially it was the rich land and resources capable of producing extractive goods in demand in existing markets which were the primary attractions. At a later date, with changing factor combinations and technological developments, it was frequently the opportunities in manufacturing for the United States market which led to immigration of labor and capital into a region. The important point is that the pull of economic opportunity as a result of a comparative advantage in producing goods and services in demand in existing markets was the principal factor in the differential rates of growth of regions.

Since residentiary industry depends on income within the region, the expansion of such activity must have been induced by the increased income of the region's inhabitants. Therefore, increased investment in residentiary activity is primarily induced investment as a result of expanded income received from outside the region, and, correspondingly, expanded employment in locally oriented industry, trade, and services primarily reflects long-run changes in income received from the export base.[4] The qualifications to this argument require examination in order that the significance of the export base in regional growth may be properly evaluated.

1. Disproportionate federal government expenditures in a region (as compared with tax withdrawals) can serve and have served as a cause of regional expansion. Not only may the character and amount of federal expenditure in a region be expansive, but also investment in social overhead facilities in a new area may alter its competitive position with other regions.

2. Migration for non-economic reasons may lead to expansion of residentiary activity without any expansion of the export base. In a high-income society such as ours the lure of pleasant living conditions—"amenities," to use Professor Ullman's term[5]—has been a force attracting immigrants (with capital) into California and other areas and leading to an expansion of residentiary activities.

3. The relationship between residentiary activity and imports changes in the course of regional development. With the opening-up of a new area, almost everything must initially be imported. Gradually, residentiary activity increases until locational factors

[2] A brief account of the role of the export base in shaping the character of a region's economy is given in my article, "Location Theory and Regional Economic Growth," *Journal of Political Economy*, LXIII (June, 1955), 249–51.

[3] See the qualifications in my article, *ibid.*, p. 250, n. 34.

[4] The employment multiplier has been conceived by Hildebrand and Mace ("The Employment Multiplier in an Expanding Industrial Market: Los Angeles County, 1940–47," *Review of Economics and Statistics*, Vol. XXXII, No. 3 [August, 1950]) to be primarily of use in short-run analysis. However, the study by the Federal Reserve Bank of Kansas City of "The Employment Multiplier in Wichita" (*Monthly Review, Tenth Federal Reserve District*, Vol. XXXVII, No. 9 [September 30, 1952]) strongly suggests that residentiary employment does not adjust to short-run changes in employment in export industries but does reflect long-run movements in export employment.

[5] Edward Ullman, "A New Force in Regional Growth," *Proceedings of the Western Area Development Conference, November 17, 1954* (Palo Alto, Calif.: Stanford Research Institute, 1955).

effect a balance between imports and locally oriented economic activity at a given level of technology and transfer costs. Since techniques and transportation have undergone radical changes over time, this relationship has been subject to important changes. Moreover, as a region's population and income grow, its regional market will become large enough to make it feasible to produce some goods and services locally which had previously been imported.[6]

Clearly, therefore, residentiary activity does not play a purely passive role in regional growth. Tiebout's point about factor costs is a good one. Both the nature of the supply curve of labor and the level of transfer costs are important determinants of the ability of a region to produce export commodities. Typically, new regions have been opened up and developed because they had such a tremendous advantage in natural-resource endowments that they could produce and market their export commodities at a cost competitive with other areas despite this disadvantage in labor and transfer costs (and in the case of the earlier development of American regions, when institutions for financial mediation were immature and capital was less mobile, higher capital costs as well). The subsequent inflow of capital and labor and the development of social overhead facilities typically reduced these cost disadvantages and made it possible to produce other export commodities whose comparative resource advantages were somewhat less pronounced. However, when the growth of residentiary industry is "stunted" and transfer costs remain high, then the export base will not expand in this manner. Alaska is an excellent case in point.

This examination of the major alternative sources of regional growth clearly indicates their secondary importance as compared with the export base in long-run regional growth. The first two qualifications are exceptional in character, while the third, though more important, is clearly not a primary determinant of growth but rather a factor that will exert some influence upon a region's rate of growth.[7] Any analysis of the secular growth of a region must be primarily focused on the success of its export base, and Tiebout's contribution here has been to point out some of the factors that must be considered.[8] However, his discussion of short-run factors in income determination, significant though these may be in determining the level of employment (or effecting a shift in resources in the case of full employment), is irrelevant to the analysis of long-run regional economic growth.

III

Tiebout's distinction between regional growth and economic development in general is surely a spurious one. It is hard to conceive of the economic growth of one region which would not favorably affect the per capita income of the nation as a whole (even though it might have adverse effects upon another region). In fact, America's entire development has illustrated this relationship. Growth has been generated in particular geographic areas which, as a result of favorable factor endowments and transfer costs, could produce goods in demand in existing markets. Whether it was the opening-up and development of a new region in the West capable of producing wheat for the world market or the development of an industrial region in the eastern and central states producing manufactured goods for the domestic market, the result in each case was to attract labor and capital (from Europe as well as internally) not only

[6] The changing character of residentiary activity with regional growth requires further research both in expanding regional markets and in the historical development of regions where changing technology and transfer costs have changed the character of residentiary goods and services.

[7] Tiebout's final point deals with the possibility of regional growth with a decline in exports. This is conceivable but flies in the face of the experience of growing nations, where international trade has typically increased with rising incomes rather than the reverse.

[8] In this regard the changing terms of trade of a region have been important. Regions whose export base consists primarily of agricultural commodities have been particularly affected.

into the expanding export industry but also into a wide variety of residentiary activities to meet the expanding needs of the region's population. The process of urbanization, which was an integral part of the growth of manufacturing regions, was as expansive in its effects as was the opening-up of new regions, their development, and their assimilation into the economy. In both cases the expansion of the region required a vast increase in imports from outside the area. The result was to induce investment throughout the rest of the economy. The multiplier-acceleration process that resulted was an essential part of America's economic growth.[9]

Tiebout's footnote about the difference between the later development of Canada and the Pacific Northwest, when there were well-developed markets, and the case of general economic development which typified the American colonies is, to the best of my knowledge, likewise incorrect. America was settled partly for the explicit purpose of producing goods in demand in the expanding European market. The prosperity of the colonies did not rest upon subsistence farms but resulted from the rich land and resources of the New World, which could produce tobacco, rice, indigo, ships, fish, cereals, and other products that were in growing demand in England, Europe, and the West Indies. The whole development of the New World has been within the context of the rapidly expanding Western world, and the prosperity of the colonists reflected the growth of income throughout the North Atlantic economy, which resulted in an expanding demand for their services (particularly important in the case of New England) and commodities.

[9] James S. Dusenberry has an excellent account of this entire process in his article, "Some Aspects of the Theory of Economic Development," *Explorations in Entreprenurial History*, Vol. III, No. 2 (December, 1950).

REJOINDER

CHARLES M. TIEBOUT[1]

PERHAPS the basic issues between Professor North and myself can be easily resolved. It is my contention that the concept of the "export base" is merely an oversimplified method of describing regions by structural equations of the national-income or general-equilibrium variety. The larger the region, the greater the oversimplification in designating exports as the exogenous variable. This is clearly true in the short run.

For long-run growth, merely to look at exports as the key factor in explaining regional growth is no more adequate than merely looking at investment at the national level. Yet if econometric models of national trends are useful in growth analysis, there is no a priori reason why the same type of more complete system cannot be applied to regional growth.[2] North is concerned about the factors determining the level of export activity. My concern, however, is not only with the factors affecting the level of export activity but with the level of other exogenous variables as well. Further, given their level, what does the nature of the structural relations between the exogenous and the endogenous or residentiary activities imply for total regional activity?[3]

Whether or not my classification of regional growth as opposed to general economic development is "spurious" is a matter of both judgment and degree. Unfortunately, no pure cases as such have ever occurred historically. Yet a fundamental difference does seem to appear. In describing the development of all the region known as western Europe, one is dealing with a substantially *closed economy*.[4] Development proceeded by stages, since there was no alternative. In the nature of the hierarchy of wants, it would have been impossible to pass directly to the tertiary stage.

The regional economy, which is an *open economy*, need not pass through the stage process. The region Florida, for example, may be considered as having started largely in the tertiary stage. The ability of a region to start at any stage, given factor endowment, depends on two conditions: (1) the regional economy must be open; (2) the region must deal with other regions which are able to supply it with products of other stages that it does not produce.

Thus one should not expect any particular region to pass through the three stages of development. However, the reason is not that the stage theory is necessarily wrong but simply that in some cases it may not apply.

[1] I am grateful to my colleague Bernard Kemp for sharpening some of the points involved.

[2] See Stefan Valavanis-Vail, "An Econometric Model of Growth: U.S., 1869–1953," *American Economic Review*, XLV (May, 1955), 208–21.

[3] North's contention that "the aggregates used tend to obscure rather than to illumine the factors generating secular expansion" (p. 165) seems to overlook this aspect of growth analysis.

[4] What is a closed or an open economy is also a matter of degree and may be considered in terms of the proportion of exports to total income.

14. Patterns of Development in Newly Settled Regions*

ROBERT E. BALDWIN

I.

To aid in the formulation of effective development programs, economists must seek to understand the reasons why certain parts of the "backward" world have become enmeshed in what appears to be a vicious circle of poverty. Why is it that these particular regions failed to become economically developed ? [1]

One economic relation which may be useful for answering some aspects of this question is the input-output variation among commodity production functions. Although everyone is aware that there are significant differences among commodities concerning the nature of the physical output possibilities from different quantities and combinations of the factors of production—as witness the frequent use of such terms as "labor intensive" and "capital intensive" commodities—these engineering differences among production functions only infrequently have been made an operational part of economic theorizing. By far, the most comprehensive use of these differences for economic analysis is the input-output studies initiated by Professor Leontief.[2] He has measured the average technical input coefficients employed in producing the outputs of various industries in the United States. These coefficients include both current or flow coefficients, *i.e.*, the quantities of various products (measured in dollars) and the number of workers (or man-years) which are used to produce a dollar's worth of a particular commodity per year, and capital or stock coefficients, *i.e.*, the quantity of capital (measured in dollars) used to produce a dollar's worth of a commodity per

[1]See Haavelmo, T., *A Study in the Theory of Economic Development*, No. III in the series *Contributions to Economic Analysis*, Amsterdam, 1954, pp. 1-6, for an excellent discussion of the objectives and possibilities of a theoretical approach to the problem of economic development.

[2]W. W. Leontief, *The Structure of the American Economy*, 1919–1939, New York, 1951. Also W. W. Leontief and others, *Studies in the Structure of the American Economy*, New York, 1953.

* Reprinted from the *Manchester School of Economics and Social Studies*, Vol. 24 (May 1956).

year. On the basis of these coefficients it is possible to estimate the derived demands which would arise from various changes in the final bill of goods.

Table I presents a few of the Leontief labor and capital coefficients. The figures in Table II are rough estimates of the labor coefficients for a few agricultural commodities that are produced to an important degree under a plantation system.

TABLE I

LABOR AND CAPITAL REQUIREMENTS FOR SELECTED UNITED STATES INDUSTRIES PER $1,000 OF OUTPUT, 1947 * †

	Capital (dollars)	Labor (man years)
Agriculture and fisheries	2524·4	·082
Textile mill products	493·6	·110
Chemicals	592·7	·049
Iron and steel	1026·3	·077
Agriculture, mining and construction machinery	838·6	·087
Motor Vehicles	565·8	·060
Coal, gas and electric power	2222·6	·099
Railway transportation	3343·3	·153
Trade	984·9	·165
Communications	4645·4	·163

* Leontief, Wassily, "Domestic Production and Foreign Trade; The American Capital Position Re-examined," *Proceedings of the American Philosophical Society*, Vol. 97, No. 4, September, 1953.

† Two other important studies dealing with inter-industries differences among capital-output ratios in the United States are: D. Creamer, *Capital and Output Trends in Manufacturing Industries*, 1880–1948, Occasional Paper 41, National Bureau of Economic Research, New York, 1954, and I. Borenstein, *Capital and Outlay Trends in Mining Industries*, 1870–1948, Occasional Paper 45, National Bureau of Economic Research, 1954.

TABLE II

SELECTED LABOR COEFFICIENTS IN TEA, RUBBER, AND SUGAR

Tea * (1940 Colombo price)	
Ceylon	6·0–6·3 men per $1,000 per year
Rubber † (1939 Singapore price)	
Malaya and F.M.S. estates ...	2·6–4·0 men per $1,000 per year
Ceylon (estate and total) ...	4·2–5·7 men per $1,000 per year
Sugar ‡ (cane)	
Cuba (1939 Cuban price) ...	2·1 men per $1,000 per year
Hawaii (1939 New York price) ...	·6 men per $1,000 per year
Or (1939 Cuban price) ...	1·1 men per $1,000 per year

* The sources for these figures are *The Census of Ceylon*, 1946, Vol. I, Part 1 (6·3 per $1,000) ; *The Annual General Report for* 1934 *on the Economic, Social, and General Conditions of the Island*, 1934–1936, (6·0 per $1,000) ; and V. D. Wickizer, *Coffee, Tea and Cocoa* (6·3 per $1,000 on the basis of information on p. 162 and his yield figures). It is interesting to note that using the real labor coefficient for India in 1915 (*Report of the Production of Tea in India*, 1915, Calcutta, 1916) together with the 1940 Colombo price gives a coefficient of 8·9 per $1,000.

† This information was obtained from P. T. Bauer, *The Rubber Industry*, pp. 266–267, (Malayan estates, July, 1940 to June, 1941—2·6 per $1,000 ; F.M.S. estates, 1933—2·6 per $1,000 ; F.M.S. estates, 1929—4·0 per $1,000) ; *Census of Ceylon*, 1946 (total exports 1946—5·7 per $1,000) ; and *The Annual General Report* (4·2 per $1,000).

‡ The sources are : U.S. Cuban Sugar Council, *Sugar—Facts and Figures*, 1952, (total production, 1950—2·7 per $1,000) ; *Printed Reports of the 68th Annual Meeting of the Hawaiian Sugar Planters' Association*, 1948, (total production of these companies, 1939—·6 or 1·1 per $1,000).

These coefficients are, of course, average figures. Even within the United States intra-industry differences are important because of variations in the techniques employed within an industry, differences among factor price ratios, dissimilarities in the quantity of the labor supply and natural resource conditions, differences in managerial skill, etc. For similar reasons, one would expect a wide degree of intra-industry variability among different countries.[1] However, if new firms, using the same technological and managerial

[1]Information on some of the international differences in capital-output ratios has been collected by Grosse, R. N., "The Structure of Capital," in Leontief, W. W., *Studies in the Structure of the American Economy*, New York, 1953 ; Bhatt, V. H., "Capital-output Ratios of Certain Industries : A Comparative Study of Certain Countries," *Review of Economics and Statistics*, Vol. XXXVI, No. 2, August, 1954 ; and Mandelbaum, K., *The Industrialization of Backward Areas*, Monograph No. 2, Institute of Statistics (Oxford University), Oxford, 1947.

knowledge, were established in the various industries and their means of production were secured from some common, perfectly competitive factor market, Professor Leontief's investigations do seem to indicate that there would be significant industry differences among the labor and capital coefficients employed in these firms.[1]

While the Leontief analysis assumes fixed production coefficients for each industry, this assumption will not be followed here, since the analysis will be conceptual rather than statistical. What will be assumed is merely that there are significant engineering differences among some commodity production functions over their input-output range. These variations concern the manner in which returns to scale behave for different factor ratios and also the manner in which the maginal rates of factor substitution vary for different output levels and factor ratios.

II.

This paper will utilize the concept of these production function differences in analyzing the problem of differential rates of growth between newly settled regions. While technological conditions of production influence the pattern of growth in an economy at all stages of development, it appears that they can be particularly important in conditioning the potential for growth in newly settled regions. Consequently, the procedure to be followed will be to contrast the *hypothetical* development of two regions—both of which, initially, are assumed to be sparsely populated. The two areas are assumed to develop simultaneously within a given and constant state of technology and to draw their immigrants and capital from some common, populated region where all the inputs and outputs are represented.[2] The socio-political environment of this more populated region is assumed to be conducive to the development of the two sparsely populated regions.

[1]The coefficient of variation of the capital-output ratios in 1929 prices in thirty-seven manufacturing industries analyzed by Creamer, D., *op. cit.*, for 1948 was 30·7%. However, the coefficient has declined steadily from 1900, when it was 66·9%.

[2]The effects of improvements in technological knowledge will be discussed later. In a general sense, the exploitation of these new regions may be considered a technological change.

Each region's economy is assumed to be small enough in its early stages of development to have no effect on the given hierarchy of factor and commodity prices prevailing in the more developed, third region.[1] Furthermore, the two regions are equi-distant from the older area and this distance is sufficiently great to make the costs of labor migration fairly substantial. It also is assumed that the economic development of each of the two sparsely populated regions begins in the export sector with the production of a primary commodity.

The differences between the two regions concern their natural resource conditions. One of the regions is assumed to possess a soil and climate highly suitable for the initial cultivation of a plantation crop in contrast to the other area which is assumed to enjoy conditions most conducive to the initial production of a non-plantation type commodity such as wheat. However, in both regions there is assumed to be an abundant supply of mineral resources such as coal, iron-ore, ferro-alloys, oil, etc. These are not exploited immediately since, initially, they are at a prohibitive distance from the export ports.

The purpose of most of these assumptions is to minimize differences among the many other factors which can cause dissimilarities between the two regions in their patterns of development. The development model to be analyzed can easily be compared with the differential growth patterns which might result by varying these initial assumptions. Some of the consequences of such other assumptions will be examined later. However, it seems that even with a wide range of possible initial conditions facing newly settled areas the effects of production function differences still emerge as an important (and neglected) determinant of development patterns.

Given the above conditions, the contention here will be that the extent to which the export sector induces the subsequent development of other sectors in the two economies depends to an important degree upon the technological nature of the production function of the export commodity (assuming there is only one major export item in each new region). For, given the price of the export commodity and the array of

[1]The labor supply is divided into a number of imperfectly competing groups.

factor prices in the third region, this function will greatly affect subsequent development by initially influencing the nature of the labor and capital supply which flows into each region and the distribution of each economy's national income. It is from this framework that some of the many other important factors which determine the pattern of development will be introduced into the analysis.

Assume that the following conditions exist in one of the two regions. Factor and commodity prices in the populated area and the climate and soil of the new region indicate that the most profitable opportunity for initial development is the production of a plantation type commodity. Assume the production function for this particular commodity is such that for a wide range of labor/capital price ratios the most efficient organization for any level of production is on a relatively labor intensive basis.[1,2] In other words, efficient production of a dollar's worth of the commodity technologically tends to require a relatively large number of laborers to perform comparatively simple tasks. Beyond a certain proportion of capital to labor, the amount of capital which must be substituted for a given decrease in labor in order to maintain a given level of output is relatively large. Furthermore, there are significant increasing returns to scale in the cultivation and processing of the commodity. Consequently, comparatively large amounts of both capital and labor are necessary for the most efficient size of the production unit. A high level of managerial and technical skill also is needed to direct large plantations effectively.

Small, family-size farms are attractive for the very low income groups in the older region, but the independent entrance of these groups is prevented by the cost of migration and the initial capital outlay on even this type of small productive unit. Nor are these people able to borrow the funds in the capital

[1]Since information concerning the variability of capital coefficients among agricultural commodities is meager, it will be assumed that optimal capital requirements per dollar of output are about the same for the two types of agricultural commodities discussed here.

[2]For a general survey of the methods of production for a few plantation type products, see V. D. Wickizer, *op. cit.*; A. Pim, *Colonial Agricultural Production*, London, 1946; P. T. Bauer, *op. cit.*; and C. R. Fay, "The Plantation Economy," *Economic Journal*, 1936.

market, since severe capital rationing tends to operate against these very low income groups.

Those establishing productive units migrate from middle and higher income groups of the developed region and either possess the necessary funds for migration or are able to borrow them in the capital market. In order to produce the commodity at the lowest possible costs, these entrepreneurs in turn create a demand in the older region for the labor of very low income groups (who are assumed to possess the requisite skill to perform the comparatively simple tasks involved in production or can be trained easily to perform them). Plantation owners or their agents seek out these low wage groups and finance their migration. And they protect this investment by attempting to tie the workers to the plantations for a certain number of years.

In the second sparsely populated region assume the following conditions hold. Prices in the older area and the environment of the new region favor the development of a non-plantation agricultural commodity. The production function for this commodity differs from the plantation commodity in two respects. First, a family-size farm gives an efficient scale of production. In particular, large scale production based on the intensive use of cheap, imported labor is not the best form of economic organization. Furthermore, the absolute amount of capital required is less for the optimum size of a production unit, and the level of managerial and technical skill need not be so high for a productive unit of the most efficient size. Secondly, the technological possibilities of capital intensification on the family-size farm are much greater. Varying the labor/capital price ratios over a wide range causes much more factor substitution in producing a given level of output than with the plantation crop.

As in the previous case, the very low income groups in the older region tend to be prevented from independent migration because of the costs of migration and the difficulty of borrowing funds. The level of knowledge and skill required for establishing a farm also rules out the migration of many from this labor group. Because of the assumed distance conditions, financing the movement of this type of labor is relatively costly. This fact and the wide range of alternative factor combinations prevent any extensive importation of cheap, unskilled labor by small-scale cultivators. Consequently, migrants flow from the income groups which can provide the necessary initial outlays on transportation and production. However, capital rationing also works against the latter group to some extent. The smaller scale of operations hampers the supervision of direct lending. Consequently, direct inter-regional lending is not as significant as in the plantation economy.

The agricultural development in both regions stimulates a simultaneous development of some supporting industries—such as transportation—which are directly linked with exporting the agricultural commodity.[1] The large amount of capital necessary for even a minimum amount of this type of social capital is supplied comparatively readily by foreign investors. Not only are these industries directly tied to the exchange-earning export industry and, consequently, are particularly attractive to foreign investors, but also they are organized on a large enough scale to take advantage of the established capital markets in the developed region.

III.

However, the obstacles to the vigorous expansion of the plantation economy into a developed, higher per capita income economy are much greater than with the non-plantation economy. The relevant factors for an analysis of the development potential of the two regions from the stage already discussed can be grouped into demand and supply forces. First, in order to introduce domestic production of commodities for which an export advantage does not exist, there must be the basis of an internal demand for such products. And, secondly, given the demand, the natural resource situation and the supply of capital and labor must be adequate enough to meet foreign competition.

[1]See Nurkse, R., "The Problem of International Investment Today in the Light of Nineteenth-Century Experience," *The Economic Journal*, December, 1954.

For both regions the composition of the family budget is assumed to depend upon the level of income.[1] At very low levels, the budget consists almost entirely of a few basic foodstuffs, clothing, household needs and shelter. As incomes rise, the food budget is diversified and, eventually, a smaller proportion of the budget consists of foodstuffs. Durable consumer good expenditures and savings increase in relative importance.

In the plantation economy at this initial stage a large part of the population is in the very low income brackets. Consequently, most of this group's effective demand consists of a few basic foods, simple clothing and other consumer durables, and minimum shelter needs. While production of the plantation crop requires large quantities of labor, this labor is not needed throughout the entire year. Consequently, workers lease small plots of land from the plantation owners (who also usually provide the capital) and supplement their income by growing part of their food requirements. During the idle period, the choice to a laborer of working more on the plantation and less for himself does not exist. The alternative essentially is between leisure and working for himself. And since his plantation income is very low, his marginal utility for commodities is relatively high. Therefore, he is willing to devote much of his free time to growing part of his own food in a very socially inefficient manner. He drives his marginal productivity in this line down to nearly zero. The same phenomenon tends to take place with respect to part of his clothing, shelter, and durable consumption goods needs. The family unit produces many of these items.[2]

[1]K. Mandelbaum in *The Industrialization of Backward Areas*, Oxford University, Institute of Statistics, Monograph No. 2, Oxford, 1947, utilizes a budget approach in estimating the flow of demand in his hypothetical model of development for south-eastern Europe. He also employs capital, labor, and commodity coefficients in computing the supply requirements for his program. Because of a lack of data, this procedure so far has been only used in a rough fashion for the formulation of actual development plans in the backward countries.

[2]For a general discussion of some of the production and labor conditions in such backward areas, see Greaves, I. C., *Modern Production among Backward Peoples*, London, 1935, and Moore, W. E., *Industrialization and Labor*, Ithaca, 1951.

Why do not the plantation workers break away from the plantation, produce the crop themselves, and raise their income level appreciably above the plantation wage? Some do break away. However, most of these unskilled, low income workers cannot save or borrow enough to start anything but a very small, low income yielding unit of production.

In attempting to expand from such small units, the cultivators are hampered by the technical constraints of the crop's production function. They must secure more labor, land, and capital, *i.e.* expand horizontally, for efficient production. But this is very difficult. First, the initial income level on these farms is so low that their saving is almost insignificant. Nor are they able to borrow sufficient funds for a large scale unit. Secondly, it is difficult for this group to enlarge gradually its holdings of good land. The fertile land is cultivated by the plantation method and its owners are reluctant to sell or lease parcels of it. Large tracts must be taken at one time. But the small farmers cannot overcome this discontinuity. The best they can do is obtain isolated parcels of good land or more contiguous but relatively poor land. However, expanded production on this type of land is not very efficient. Thirdly, the level of knowledge and skill of these people is so low that they are not capable of supervising and controlling the greater amounts of capital and labor necessary for increased production. The supervision of the labor is particularly important. It is probably more difficult to direct the greater amount of non-family labor than the increased quantity of capital. Finally, the plantation class tends to develop a social antipathy towards this very low income group. It does not want the group to move into the plantation class and erects social and economic barriers in the path of the group's expansion.

All of these factors tend to prevent this group from increasing the size of its farms and thus its income level. And, because production of the crop does not require the same amount of labor throughout the entire year, these small farm families (like the plantation workers) also grow part of the food they consume (or even a market supply) and produce many of the durable consumer goods they consume. Disguised unemployment tends to arise within this sector of the economy.

Small scale planters who employ some non-family labor are another important group in the economy. These individuals either break through the exclusively family-labor type of farming or initially possess sufficient funds to establish a small plantation. They resemble somewhat the middle income migrants in the other region. However, these planters face more difficulties in reaching the optimum productive unit. In the first place, they must accumulate much more capital to attain this level. And, as in the non-plantation area, the capital rationing barrier forces the planters to rely on current saving for most of their investment funds. Furthermore, given funds equivalent to the requirements for the smaller optimum size farm in the other region, a small scale planter will not earn as high an income as his counterpart in the other region. The production unit is too small. Even if organized as efficiently as possible, he cannot use his managerial skill to full advantage. Merely directing production does not require his full time nor yield a very high income. Yet the only alternative to leisure is to perform the low productivity tasks of the hired help. Consequently, because of their low income level, these planters cannot expand their productive units as rapidly as the farmers of the non-plantation region. In addition, most of these small planters do not possess the high degree of managerial ability and technical skill required to expand the scale of operations in an optimum manner. Consequently, they tend to keep the amount of labor and land employed about the same and reinvest their savings in capital improvements which do little in lifting their level of income, because of the nature of the crop's production function.

A reasonably stable hierarchy of export producers emerges within the economy. At one end stand the plantations employing large quantities of low wage labor. The other end of the scale is composed of many small, family cultivators who operate under a tenure system or perhaps own their land. The income level of these farmers is not much higher than the plantation wage, and the possibilities for expansion by these producers is not favourable. The small scale planter who combines family and hired labor lies between these two groups. While incomes among these planters are higher than the very small farmers, they are below the level achieved with a similar investment in the non-plantation economy.

Perhaps 70 per cent. of the economy's income is spent on foodstuffs.[1] The remainder is devoted to services, consumer durables (of which expenditures on items other than simple clothing and household articles are a small percentage), and saving. The effective market demand for the higher class of consumer goods and services stems largely from the middle and high income groups, who are composed of large plantation owners, those performing the marketing services associated with the export item, and to some extent the small planters. A large number of these commodities are imported from the more developed region.

Why do not efficient domestic industries quickly develop and capture both the import markets and the domestic markets which are supplied in a socially inefficient manner?

Consider the opportunities in the fields of simple, mass consumed durables and luxury durables—many of which are imported. A major obstacle confronting prospective domestic manufacturers is the problem of training the labor force to the factory system. The large, low income labor supply possess such a low level of education and skill that its costs of training represent a large, initial outlay. While there is always the alternative of recruiting skilled foreign labor, this too is expensive. At this early stage of development, the region cannot rely to any significant extent upon the voluntary migration of suitable labor. This labor migrates at its own expense only after the industrial sector has begun to expand vigorously and employment opportunities become well known. In addition, although the marginal productivity of the low income farm labor may be near zero, it is necessary to offer them a higher figure in order to induce them to move into urban factories. Both of these factors make it difficult to capture the import market.

They are particularly forceful with respect to luxury imports. Many of these items require a very high degree of labor skill. Conspicuous consumption also applies to some of

[1] T. W. Schultz, *The Economic Organization of Agriculture*, New York, 1953, Ch. 4.

these goods, and considerable outlays on advertising are necessary to overcome a preference for foreign commodities. Still another important factor with respect to some of these consumer durables is the internal and external economies involved in their production. The domestic market is too small to take advantage of these economies.

Most of these obstacles also apply to those consumption items produced on a household scale. However, another obstacle confronting more efficient domestic industry is one which prevents the importation of these items, namely, the high costs of internal transportation and the lack of other marketing facilities. In this region, the bulk of the population in the hinterland is so poor that the construction of transportation facilities (other than the minimum necessary for the export crop) proceeds very slowly. Governments cannot raise enough revenue from these people to build adequate facilities. The higher income groups are so spread out that they cannot support these facilities either. To obtain many of the commodities and services, which they desire, they travel to a few large cities where the marketing facilities for the export commodity are located. Outside of these central cities, few other trading cities spring up and, consequently, transportation facilities in the interior remain crude. Therefore, domestic manufacturers find it too expensive to tap the interior markets for mass consumption goods.

Two other factors on the supply side, which are relevant to this discussion, are the rate of saving and the supply of entrepreneurial labor. Because of the greater income inequality the proportion of saving to national income is likely to be higher in this region than in the non-plantation economy. However, a larger share of the saving flows back to the more developed area in the form of interest and dividend returns on foreign investments in the plantations and the auxiliary service industries. The foreign earnings which are retained tend to be employed for a further expansion of the export industry, since foreign investors prefer investments which are directly linked with the foreign exchange earning ability of the economy. Furthermore, foreign investments in industries producing for an internal demand are discouraged by the lack of an adequate market in addition to the other factors already enumerated. For the same reasons, large domestic savers also tend to employ their funds in the export and import trades or in such ventures as residential and business construction. But, because of the nature of the production function for the export crop, investment in this sector does little to improve the distribution of income ; it merely enlarges the existing productive structure as more cheap labor is imported.[1] Nor does the investment in elaborate homes, office buildings, shops, etc. do much in inducing a better pattern of growth. With respect to entrepreneurship, the most obvious source of leadership for manufacturing—the large plantation owners—provides a meager supply. This group, because of the unique non-pecuniary advantage of the plantation life, tends to develop a social antipathy towards occupations in the manufacturing field. And, the low income group possesses neither sufficient training nor the social and economic opportunities necessary to provide more than the occasionally successful entrepreneur.

All of these factors tend to restrain the economy from breaking out of its predominantly export-oriented nature.[2] As transportation facilities improve, the mineral resources are tapped, but this sector too becomes export-oriented. Domestic manufacturing industries based on these raw materials are blocked by the same obstacles previously mentioned. The only real possibility for exploiting the minerals is as raw material, export industries. And, because of the general lack of technological and entrepreneurial skill within the economy, many of the firms are owned and operated by foreigners. Although these industries may provide an important source of saving in the form of royalty payments and, depending on the

[1]W. A. Lewis employs the assumption of an elastic labor supply in his interesting article, "Economic Development with Unlimited Supplies of Labour," *The Manchester School of Economic and Social Studies*, May, 1954.

[2]See Mosk, S. A., "Latin America versus the United States," *The American Economic Review*, Papers and Proceedings, May, 1951, for a discussion of some of the development obstacles in this kind of economy ; H. W. Singer, "The Distribution of Gains between Investing and Borrowing Countries," *The American Economic Review*, Papers and Proceedings, May, 1950. Also on the general topic of the effect of foreign trade on newly settled areas see H. Myint, "The Gains from International Trade and the Backward Countries," *The Review of Economic Studies*, No. 58, 1954–1955.

quality of labor they require, may help to improve the distribution of income, these effects will not be as favourable for growth as those that would result if the internal market were large enough to induce related domestic manufacturing industries.

IV.

When the development potential in the other region is analyzed, a more optimistic outlook appears. The nature of the export crop's production function is an important reason for this view. As already mentioned, labor and capital requirements for an optimum size farm in this region are much smaller than for the plantation type commodity. The family unit gives an efficient scale of operations. As in the other region, the very low income families in the older regions are excluded from independent emigration by the relatively high costs of the movement. However, unlike the plantation region, the more wealthy individuals do not finance their passage, since very unskilled labor cannot be employed as effectively in this type of agriculture. Instead, most of the migrants come from the income groups which possess sufficient funds for migration. In this region there are relatively fewer individuals at both ends of the absolute income scale.

Unlike the plantation economy, as this region's export sector expands, the economy does not devote a large portion of its investment to securing and supporting a greater quantity of cheap, unskilled labor. Although many of the migrants to this region originally do not establish the most efficient size unit, the limitation is not so much labor, but rather the inability to secure sufficient capital. However, these migrants do not start, like those breaking away from the plantations, at such a low level of income that their saving is almost nothing.

In the early stages of development, these farmers also produce much of their food, clothing, shelter and simple durable consumer goods. But they are not blocked from optimum expansion as are most of the small planters and the family-size farmers in the other economy. Since the marginal productivity of labor and capital is higher in agriculture than in these activities, the farmers, by reinvesting their saving, increase the output of the cash commodity and curtail the family production of food and consumer durables. Moreover, as their income level increases, the family prefers to purchase more of its clothing, food, shelter, services, and other consumer durables in the open market.

The more equitable distribution of income, which arises as the economy develops its export production, is more favorable for the induced development of domestic industry. A smaller proportion of the national budget is devoted to food expenditure. And the production of this food is undertaken on efficient, family-size farms. Furthermore, there is a relatively larger market demand for services and durable consumer goods. Profit opportunities arise in these lines of commodities. Initially, some of these goods are imported, while others are not consumed at all because of the high costs of transportation. But gradually trading centers spring up to answer the demands for medical, legal and personal services as well as to provide the marketing facilities for the imported commodities. All of this means investments in homes, offices, warehouses, roads, schools, hospitals, etc., which have a multiplier effect on the volume of trade.[1] As this development occurs, the mineral resources begin to be exploited. However, instead of merely becoming exports, these resources are also used to supply domestic manufacturers. For, the more favorable distribution of income and thus the relatively large demand for durables stimulates domestic manufacturing. Because of the relatively larger market demand for such items and the higher level of skill of the agricultural population, the problem of recruiting foreign labor or training domestic workers for manufacturing activity also is not as difficult as in the plantation area.

All of these factors and their interaction tend to induce a faster and a more balanced type of development. This economy has a better chance of climbing from its initial export orientation. Domestic industries spring up which, in turn, stimulated the further expansion of other domestic or export industries through external economies and the familiar multiplier-accelerator interactions.

[1] J. S. Duesenberry, "Some Aspects of the Theory of Economic Development," *Explorations in Entrepreneurial History*, Dec., 1950, pp. 96–102.

V.

In order to emphasize the role which technological differences among production functions can play in the process of economic development, a number of restrictive assumptions were made in the preceding analysis. When these are lifted, the factors stressed in the traditional explanations of differential growth patterns re-emerge to a more prominent position.

First, there is the matter of the production functions themselves. In the above discussion, it was assumed that the production functions in the export industries of the two regions were such as to impose rigid constraints on the nature of the development process. While I believe this factor is and has been an important element in shaping actual development in several regions, this is not to say that it always plays an important role in the development process. For example, the production functions of some crops may be such that both plantation and small scale production are equally efficient. And, there may be wide possibilities of factor substitution with relatively slight changes in the factor price ratios. In these cases the engineering constraints of the production function will not be important in determining the character of development. It was also assumed that each region drew its productive means from a common equi-distant, purely competitive market. But obviously, if the array of factor and product prices differs in the older regions which initiate development in the two new regions and the distances to these new regions vary, the patterns of development will be affected accordingly. Differences among the factor supplying regions in the state of their technological knowledge, in their entrepreneurial spirit, in their tastes and in their social, economic and political ideas and institutions generally also will play an important role in determining the nature of development within the two regions. And, of course, the dissimilarities between the new regions with respect to their natural resource conditions are highly relevant. The effects on the preceding analysis which regional differences in the above factors can cause are fairly obvious.

Another condition which has been maintained in this discussion is the assumption of an unchanged state of technology. Probably, most of the technological knowledge actually introduced over the last 200 years has been of two types : (1) those changes which required more capital and less labor (or other resources) per unit of output than previously ; and (2) those changes which required less of all factors.[1] How do these types of technological progress affect economic development ?

Clearly, the development problem cannot be dismissed with the assertion that technological progress will guarantee successively higher levels of *per capita* income in an automatic fashion. Three major factors should be considered in analyzing the problem : demand, the supply of capital, and the nature and growth of the population. The first factor, demand, is extremely important for those agricultural exporting nations which are so large that changes in their output affect international prices. Price and income elasticities for many agricultural products are low in the higher *per capita*, agricultural importing regions. Consequently, part of the possible real income benefits of technological progress may be lost through an adverse movement in the terms of trade. Secondly, in order to achieve the maximum growth allowed by technological progress, the requisite capital must be forthcoming. But there is no reason to assume that the saving propensities of the public and business will adjust automatically to take advantage of the new technique. In low *per capita* countries this can be an especially serious problem. Rather similar barriers with respect to the nature of the labor supply also can prevent maximum growth. Shortages of particular kinds of labor and/or general lack of entrepreneurial ability are examples of this type of bottleneck. Finally, the growth of population in relation to the increase in income will determine what happens to *per capita* income.

But, of course, technological progress does operate in the direction of encouraging a more rapid rate of increase in national income. This is especially so if the progress in technological knowledge is such that less of all factors of production are

[1]See Grosse, R. and Duesenberry, J., "Technological Change and Dynamic Models," Prepared for the Input-Output Meeting of Conference on Research in Income and Wealth, Oct., 1952.

required per unit of output. However, to the extent that technological progress is such that the relative position of each commodity in the scale of labor and capital coefficients remains roughly the same, technological progress can be handled in the model by interpreting much of the development behaviour of the two regions in relative rather than absolute terms. But a radical shift in the relative position of a commodity in the labor and capital coefficient hierarchy must be treated as an autonomous change, and the analysis must be modified to take into account this new engineering relationship.

Even with the many special assumptions in this analysis, differences in the technological nature of production functions still, I think, emerge as an important factor determining actual patterns of economic development. Briefly, the argument is that the technological nature of the production function for the major commodities initially selected for commercial production influences the potentialities for further development in newly settled regions. In conjunction with market conditions in the more developed areas, these engineering constraints affect the nature of factor migration and the early distribution of income within a region. The latter factors, in turn, affect the stimuli for further economic development. While much more empirical and historical investigation is necessary to determine the extent of the technological restraints of various production functions, these differences can, I think, prove useful in contrasting actual historical development of some plantation-type economies in the world with those regions which at an early stage specialized on such commodities as livestock and grains. Furthermore, they must be carefully considered in the formulation of plans for future development.

15. External Trade and Regional Growth: A Case Study of the Pacific Northwest*

RICHARD L. PFISTER

Many of the hypotheses advanced in discussions of economic development and growth of nations should also be applicable to regions within a nation. This paper is concerned with testing three such hypotheses in the case of the growth of the Pacific Northwest, a region that is heavily dependent upon the export of crude and processed primary products. The first hypothesis is that foreign trade (external trade) tends to decline as a proportion of total product or output as economic growth takes place. The second is that specialization in primary products means that growth will necessarily be slow relative to more industrialized areas. The third hypothesis is that an economy is subject to relatively great instability if its exports are large compared to total output, and if its exports are concentrated in primary products.

The first hypothesis did not hold in this case. Data for the Northwest and for other states and regions showed that the second and third hypotheses were not valid in all cases. A primary conclusion of this paper is that the rate of growth and the stability of income depend not so much upon whether exports are concentrated in broad categories such as "primary products" or "industrial products," but upon the particular products being exported and upon the region's competitive position in supplying those products. The last two sections of the paper are devoted to a discussion of specialization versus diversity in exports and a brief digression on economic development.

The Pacific Northwest is defined to include the states of Idaho, Montana, Oregon, and Washington. Most of the data have been taken from a larger unpublished study.[1] The period included in the study is confined mainly to the years 1929 to 1955. In some cases, the data have been extended to more recent years.

The Northwest as an Exporter of Primary Products

In this paper, the Pacific Northwest is considered to be a region whose exports are heavily concentrated in crude or processed primary products. The basis for regarding the region in this manner is the export data presented in Table 1. The share of total exports accounted for by products of forests, animals and their products, and products of agriculture was 88.5 percent in 1929; it averaged 87.3 percent from 1934 to 1939 and 77.1 percent from 1948 to 1955. Although exports

1. Richard L. Pfister, "The Commodity Balance of Trade of the Pacific Northwest for Selected Years, 1929-1955," unpublished Ph.D. dissertation, Massachusetts Institute of Technology, 1959.

* Reprinted from *Economic Development and Cultural Change*, Vol. 11 (Jan. 1963).

TABLE 1

Percentage Distribution of Net Exports[a] by Commodity Group, Pacific Northwest, Selected Years, 1929-55

Product groups[b]	1929	Annual average 1934-39	Annual average 1948-55
Products of forests	44.1	35.8	44.6
Animals and their products	16.0	19.1	6.6
Products of agriculture	28.4	32.4	25.9
Petroleum and its products	3.0	-	-
Products of mines	8.5	11.3	8.2
Manufactures and miscellaneous	-	1.4	11.9
Other[c]	-	-	2.9
Total	100.0	100.0	100.0

a. Net exports means exports minus imports for each of the ICC commodity classes. Net exports for a product group, e.g., products of forests, consists of the sum of net exports for all commodity classes in that group that have an export balance.

b. For the most part these commodity groups are those of the classification scheme used by the ICC. A few exceptions were made, however. Petroleum products constitutes a new category that includes crude petroleum, taken from products of mines, and refined petroleum products, taken from manufactures and miscellaneous. Processed foods were transferred from manufactures and miscellaneous to either products of agriculture or animals and their products.

c. Includes defense-controlled water shipments and foreign trade by land transportation.

Source: Pfister, "The Commodity Balance of Trade...," op. cit., p. 74.

of manufactures grew sharply to account for 12 percent of the total in the 1948-55 period, over three-fourths of all exports were still in the broad category of crude and processed primary products.

The product groups in Table 1 do not follow the Standard Industrial Classification. For the most part, they follow the classification of the Interstate Commerce Commission. Lumber is included in products of forests, whereas it is included in manufacturing by the Standard Industrial Classification. The content of the product groups is explained in greater detail in a footnote to Table 1.

It should be pointed out that Table 1 is based on net exports. Gross exports would be better than net, but data limitations necessitated the use of the net figures (see footnote 4 below). The ICC publishes commodity flows for approximately 260 commodity classes. An export or import balance was obtained for each class. Net exports consist of the summation of the export balances for all commodity classes for which exports exceeded imports. Gross exports and gross imports are both understated by this procedure.

A calculation for rail shipments only showed that in 1955 gross rail exports exceeded net rail exports by 17 percent. A greater volume of exports and imports is "netted out" in manufacturing than in the other categories. There are large flows of both exports and imports for the broader commodity classes, such as the not-otherwise-specified categories, machinery and parts, electrical equipment, and a few others. As a result, the importance of manufacturing in the region's export base is understated in Table 1. The amount of understatement cannot be determined with the data available, although the "true" figures would certainly not materially affect the pattern shown in Table 1. There is no way of knowing what part of gross exports was just shipped through the region, or what part consisted of imported goods being re-exported in the form of other manufactured products.

It must be admitted that the Northwest is not an ideal case of an area dependent upon the export of primary products. The region's dependence upon exports of primary products declined significantly from the 1930's to the 1948-55 period, and it was less in 1955 than in 1948. This decline reflected a considerable change in the region's industrial structure. However, the decline in dependence upon primary products is not as great as is indicated by changes in the pattern of employment. The export data of Table 1 are in terms of current dollars. Over the period 1929-55 lumber prices rose much more than most other prices. Whereas the physical quantity of lumber exports did not increase greatly and employment in lumber production probably declined a little because of mechanization, the value of lumber exports rose sharply. This favorable movement in the region's terms of trade prevented products of forests from losing ground in value of exports despite a less rapid growth of employment and output.

There is still another reason why the Northwest is less than ideal as an example of a primary exporting region. Most of the area's exported manufactures are produced in Washington. Consequently, that state is much less dependent upon exports of primary products than the other three states. Also, the structural shift away from primary products has been much greater in Washington, with the growth of aircraft, primary metal, and chemical production, and Idaho, Montana, and Oregon are better examples of primary producing states. Aggregate data are strongly affected by Washington, which has approximately one-half of the region's personal income.

For these reasons, data will be presented for both the region and the four individual states in testing the second and third hypotheses. The Northwest will be compared, in terms of changes in population and income, with other areas— the Great Lakes (Michigan, Ohio, Indiana, Illinois, and Wisconsin); Mideast (New York, New Jersey, Pennsylvania, Delaware, Maryland, and the District of Columbia); New England (Maine, Vermont, New Hampshire, Connecticut, Massachusetts, and Rhode Island); and the Plains states (Minnesota, Iowa, Missouri, North Dakota, South Dakota, Nebraska, and Kansas). All of these regions except the Plains states can be classified as industrialized. The individual states of the Northwest will be compared with other selected states, including California, Michigan, Ohio, Illinois, Massachusetts, Pennsylvania, Oklahoma, Nebraska, Iowa, and South Dakota. The first six are predominantly industrial states, while the last four are predominantly agricultural.

The Relationship of Exports to Income

The hypothesis has frequently been advanced that foreign trade tends to decline as a proportion of income or product as an economy grows.[2] The primary

2. Charles P. Kindleberger, Economic Development (New York: McGraw-Hill, 1958), pp. 121-23.

reason advanced to explain this behavior is the following. Services are traded among nations much less than goods, while the income elasticity of demand for services generally is greater than for goods. Thus services grow and imports (or exports) decline as percentages of income as economic growth occurs.

Kindleberger suggested that this tendency is not always strong and that it is the net result of opposing forces of varying strengths.[3] Some events or situations tend to cause trade to increase relative to income. A country or region might be exporting goods with income-elastic demands, so that exports rise more than domestic output with growth of incomes in the buying regions. This situation is generally assumed to be exceptional and temporary. Technological changes leading to economies of scale and to relative decreases in transport costs tend to increase specialization and therefore the ratio of exports to income.

Exports as a percentage of personal income were positively correlated with personal income in the Pacific Northwest for the years 1929 to 1955 (Table 2).[4] If the hypothesis were to hold, the correlation would be negative. In 1929 exports amounted to 33 percent of personal income. For the period 1934-39, when personal income was somewhat lower than in 1929, exports averaged 27 percent of income. For the period 1948-55, when income was much higher than in the earlier periods, exports averaged 36 percent of personal income. These figures suggest that purely domestic and import competing industries did not grow as fast as regional income. In other words, the export industries contributed more to the region's growth during the 1929-55 period than domestic or local industries.

It has become customary to relate exports to income or exports plus imports to income in discussing this hypothesis. In view of the reasons advanced to explain it, a more appropriate comparison would seem to be between imports and income. In the case of the Pacific Northwest, the ratio of imports to personal income shows a trend nearly identical to that of exports. Exports were greater than imports, however, for most years included in Table 1.

Two other studies of regional trade revealed similar findings in the relation of imports or exports to income. In his study of Southern California for the years 1920-34, Terrill concluded that the income elasticity of demand for imports was substantially greater than for locally produced goods.[5] Simpson found that exports

---

3. *Ibid.*

4. The comparison in Table 2 is between net exports and personal income. Ideally, gross exports should be compared with geographic product. The necessary data for estimating geographic product were not available. The unavailability of data also dictated the estimation of net rather than gross exports for each commodity class. The net export figures are the summation of the export balances for those commodity classes with exports greater than imports. The Pacific Northwest has a considerable amount of through traffic in goods. Since there was no way of determining the imports that were destined for re-export, it seemed best to estimate net rather than gross exports and imports. On the basis of a rough calculation for 1955, gross exports would have exceeded net exports by nearly 17 percent. For the United States, gross national product exceeds personal income by about the same percentage. The ratio of personal income to geographic product in individual regions would undoubtedly vary around the national average.

5. Robert P. Terrill, "The Balance of Interregional Payments of Southern California, 1920-34," p. 166, unpublished Ph. D. dissertation, Stanford University, 1941.

TABLE 2

Regional Exports in Relation to Regional Income, Pacific Northwest, Selected Years, 1929-55

Year	Net exports[a] (millions)	Personal income (millions)	Exports as percent of personal income
1929	$ 769	$ 2,350	33
1934	415	1,515	27
1935	466	1,710	27
1936	541	1,999	27
1937	589	2,095	28
1938	481	2,075	23
1939	604	2,707	27
1948	2,580	7,441	35
1949	2,587	7,373	35
1950	2,839	8,151	35
1951	3,419	9,061	38
1952	3,264	9,590	34
1953	3,465	9,793	35
1954	3,530	9,801	36
1955	3,770	10,324	37

a. For each commodity class—the commodity classification of the ICC was used—imports were subtracted from exports to get net figures. The figures in this column are the totals of the net figures for those commodity classes with export balances.

Source: Personal income from U.S. Department of Commerce, Office of Domestic Commerce, Personal Income by States since 1929 (Washington: Government Printing Office, 1956), pp. 140-41; exports from Pfister, op. cit., p. 72.

---

tended to rise relative to personal income in the states of Washington and Oregon for selected years from 1939 to 1955.[6] Hartland's study of New England contained only the trade balance for that region, so there was no way of computing the ratio of exports or imports to income.[7]

The question now arises as to why the hypothesis did not hold in the case of the Pacific Northwest. Various conflicting forces are undoubtedly at work, as Kindleberger suggested. Since 1947 freight costs in the United States have risen sharply relative to all prices.[8] Other things being equal, this would cause a decline in the ratio of regional exports and imports to income and would lead to behavior in

---

6. Paul B. Simpson, "'Export' Requirements for Economic Growth of the Pacific Northwest," Oregon Business Review (September 1957), p. 1.

7. Penelope C. Hartland, Balance of Interregional Payments to New England (Providence: Brown University Press, 1950).

8. Benjamin Chinitz, Freight and the Metropolis (Cambridge: Harvard University Press, 1960), pp. 116-24.

support of the hypothesis. There are a number of reasons, however, why the relative rise in transport costs has not yet affected, or become the dominant force in determining, the ratio of exports to income. Some industries are so strongly tied to a low-valued raw material that transport costs may fluctuate within a wide range without affecting their locations. The same is true of industries producing high-valued, low-weight products for which transport costs are a small part of delivered prices. There could have been technological changes which enhanced the advantages of large-scale production, thus nullifying the effects of increased transport costs. Also, the size of the Northwest market for numerous products is not yet sufficiently large to induce plants to locate in the region, despite the forces tending to cause decentralization of production.

More fundamentally, the explanation of the failure of the hypothesis must concern the relationship between the demand for services and locally produced goods, as compared with the demand for exports and imports. Garnsey has pointed out that services tend to be traded more among regions than among nations.[9] This factor could not explain the trend noted in Table 1, as the export figures are for merchandise only—services are excluded.

The data of Table 2 indicate that the consumption of the region's exports has increased more than its consumption of internally produced goods and services. How is this possible if the income elasticity of demand for services is greater than that for goods? Much has been written recently about the rising share of service expenditures in total personal consumption expenditures. Some of these articles are not accurate in indicating trends, because they concentrate on only the last ten or twelve years. Whereas expenditures for services have risen as a share of total personal consumption expenditures since 1947, there is no rising trend if the data are extended back to 1929. The service share in 1929 was 40.6 percent (in current dollars); it rose to 46.5 percent in 1932 before declining to a low of 31.1 percent in 1947. By 1959 the figure had risen to 38.7 percent.[10]

Government expenditures are not included in services in the foregoing figures. The payment of taxes, or the purchase of services provided by government, is troublesome in a discussion of consumer demands. Should all government purchases of goods and services be considered as personal consumption in the same

---

9. Morris E. Garnsey, America's New Frontier, the Mountain West (New York: Alfred A. Knopf, 1950), p. 160.

10. Based on data from Economic Report of the President, January 20, 1960, p. 160. The Department of Commerce series on personal consumption expenditures goes back only to 1929. Various other individuals and agencies have developed estimates for selected years from 1909 to 1929. The most refined of these estimates are given in U.S. Bureau of the Census, Historical Statistics of the United States, Colonial Times to 1957, p. 179. Although the expenditure categories are not the same as those of the Department of Commerce, it is possible to collect nearly the same components as are now included in services. On the basis of these data, the service share of total personal consumption expenditures ranged from 44.1 percent to 45.9 percent, except for 1919, when it was 40.0 percent. Although these figures may not be exactly comparable to the more recent data, they lend support to the view that there has been no long-run rise in the service share of personal consumption expenditures.

manner as purchases of food, housing, clothing, etc.? In a broad sense all government spending is for the provision of services to the public; even defense spending provides the service of insuring our survival as a free and independent nation.

Non-defense expenditures support functions or activities that are closer to the usual concept of consumer services. Civilian expenditures of government include such items as education, highways, public health and sanitation, civilian safety, etc. The non-defense component of all government expenditures shows a much different trend than the total including defense spending. Civilian public spending for goods and services rose only from 7.5 percent of total non-defense output in 1929 to 10.3 percent in 1957; the percentage was lower in the postwar years than in 1939 and 1940.[11]

Total government purchases of goods and services, including defense, rose much more rapidly, of course. They increased from 8.2 percent of gross national product in 1929 to 20.4 percent in 1959. The rise for the federal government was from 1.3 percent to 11.2 percent, while for state and local governments it was from 6.9 percent to 9.2 percent.[12]

In studies of regional trade, the federal government is generally regarded as an external institution, so that goods sold to it are counted as exports. The federal government made major purchases of aircraft from the Pacific Northwest during the period 1948-55. If government purchases of goods are considered to provide services to the public, then the export data of Table 1 include a substantial amount of service exports.

The foregoing discussion leads to an interesting conclusion. Service expenditure has risen relative to income in the long run only if government purchases of goods and services are included in the service category. The other part of the basic explanation, i.e., that services are traded much less than goods, may not be valid if government expenditures are included in services, for the reason that much government spending, especially that for defense, gives rise to interregional trade in goods. Many of the services other than government—those that are considered as part of personal consumption—must be consumed on the spot and are therefore obtained primarily from local suppliers. There is thus relatively little interregional trade in such services. Therefore, if government spending is included in the service total, it may no longer be true that services are traded less among regions than goods. Or perhaps better, service expenditures give rise to interregional trade in goods so that regional commodity exports do not decline relative to income.

Primary Exports and Growth

Several economists have maintained that specialization in primary products dooms a country to a slow rate of growth and that resources must be shifted from

---

11. Francis M. Bator, The Question of Government Spending (New York: Harper, 1960), p. 21.

12. U.S. Department of Commerce, Office of Business Economics, U.S. Income and Output (1958), pp. 118-19; and Survey of Current Business (February 1960), p. 12.

primary production to manufacturing in order to speed up growth.[13] Advocates of this view stress that demand factors work against the country specializing in primary products. In the developed countries, demand for food grows slowly because of a low income elasticity, and demand for raw materials grows slowly because of increasing efficiency in the use of raw materials.

The measures of growth used in the following discussion are relative increases in population and per capita income. The increase of per capita income is undoubtedly the most widely used single measure of economic growth. Some countries, mainly those with great population pressure, regard population growth as a hindrance in their efforts to promote economic growth. Nearly all states, however, consider population growth to be desirable and a measure of their relative positions in the over-all picture of economic growth. For this reason, population growth was included in the discussion.

Table 3 shows the percentage gains in population and per capita income for the various states and regions from 1929 to 1955. Special circumstances such as crop failures or bumper crops may cause large irregular movements in the per capita incomes of individual states and regions. To reduce the distorting effects of such irregularities on the percentage increase of per capita income, three-year averages were used for the beginning and ending of the period. The base is thus a three-year average centered on 1930, since personal income by states is not available prior to 1929. The ending figure is a three-year average centered on 1955. No averaging was done for the population figures since they are much less volatile and do not show the irregularities that per capita income does.

From 1929 to 1955, the population of the Northwest increased by 60 percent, substantially greater than the U.S. average of 35 percent and the averages for the other four regions in the table. The population growth in the Northwest was not steady, of course; major increases took place during the 1930's and during and immediately following World War II. The Plains states, the only non-industrialized region among the other four, had the smallest population growth—just 12 percent.

The growth of population for the individual states shows more variation. Oregon with 79 percent led the Northwest states, although Washington was close behind with 68 percent. Only California had a higher percentage increase. Idaho's population growth of 36 percent was one point above the national average, and was greater than that for such industrialized states as Ohio, Illinois, Massachusetts, and Pennsylvania. Montana with only 20 percent growth exceeded the figures for the last six states on the list in Table 3. Two of the last four states, all of which are predominantly agricultural, actually lost population, while the other two had relatively little growth.

The increase in per capita income for the Northwest was 218 percent, which was greater than the U.S. average of 203 percent. The increase of 238 percent for the Plains states was the largest among the selected regions, while the lowest was 148 percent for the Mideast states. The rank of the five regions in percentage increase of per capita income is exactly the inverse of their rank in absolute level of

---

13. For a discussion of this view, see Norman S. Buchanan and Howard S. Ellis, Approaches to Economic Development (New York: Twentieth Century Fund, 1955), pp. 259-63. Most of the books on economic development mention and discuss this view.

TABLE 3

Percentage Gains in Population and Per Capita Income, Selected Regions and States, 1929-55

Regions	Population	Per capita income[a]
Pacific Northwest	60	218
Great Lakes	33	205
Mideast	29	148
New England	18	160
Plains	12	238
United States	35	203
States		
Washington	68	206
Oregon	79	208
Idaho	36	240
Montana	20	272
California	134	161
Michigan	53	222
Ohio	35	205
Illinois	22	181
Massachusetts	13	148
Pennsylvania	12	177
Oklahoma	- 7	309
Nebraska	1	227
Iowa	9	236
South Dakota	- 1	296

a. The base is a three-year average centered on 1930. The 1955 figure is a three-year average centered on 1955.

Source: Based on data from U.S. Department of Commerce, Personal Income by States..., op. cit.; and Survey of Current Business (August 1961).

---

per capita income in 1929. The regions with low per capita incomes were the relatively non-industrialized ones, but they experienced the more rapid growth of income. However, the industrialized regions still had somewhat higher per capita incomes in 1955 than did the Northwest or the Plains states. The per capita figure for the Northwest was actually above the national average from 1938 until 1955, but it has subsequently grown less rapidly and has fallen slightly below the U.S. figure.

All four states of the Northwest experienced a greater percentage rise in per capita income than the national average. Idaho and Montana had substantially greater relative growth than the other two in per capita income, although they trailed badly in population growth. In general, those states with low per capita incomes in 1929 showed the greatest growth. In terms of percentage increase, the industrialized states of Illinois, Massachusetts, and Pennsylvania were at the bottom, along with California.

Several conclusions can be drawn from these data. Specialization in primary production did not cause per capita incomes to grow slowly in the period 1929-55.

On the contrary, those states and regions that were least industrialized experienced the greatest relative growth in per capita incomes. In regard to population, it appears that primary production does not provide the basis for supporting a rapid growth of population. However, this statement has to be qualified, as the outcome depends upon what particular primary products are involved. Oregon, with heavy specialization in lumber and wood products, had the highest percentage growth of population in the Northwest and led all states in Table 3 except California.

On the other hand, a high degree of industrialization does not insure rapid population growth, as is illustrated by the relatively low percentage growth for Illinois, Massachusetts, and Pennsylvania. Demand for some manufactured products grows slowly because of a low income elasticity or because of competition from other products. Certain states may be producing goods for which demand is growing rapidly, but other states may have a competitive advantage which permits them to undersell the former. The over-all conclusion is this: growth depends not so much upon whether exports are concentrated in broad groups such as "primary products" or "industrial products," but upon the particular types of products from either or both groups, and upon the region's competitive position vis-a-vis other regions in supplying the particular products.

Primary Exports and Instability

The third hypothesis states that if exports are large relative to income and if they are concentrated in primary products, the economy will be quite unstable and especially vulnerable to external changes.[14] During recessions in the purchasing regions, the price and volume of exports both fall, causing a sharp decline in the value of exports of the producing region. Thus, an external recession is quickly transmitted to the producing region, where it has a sharply depressing effect on the economy. It is also assumed that the value of exports declines more than the value of imports for the primary producing areas, so their balance of payments is put under pressure.

This hypothesis was tested by comparing the average percentage changes in per capita income from year to year.[15] The data are presented in Table 4. The figures are simply the arithmetic means of the year-to-year percentage changes without regard to sign. The averages were computed for two periods, 1929-60 and 1945-60. The figures for the latter period should show the effects of changes in industrial structure over the period since 1929.

---

14. See Buchanan and Ellis, op. cit., p. 383, for a discussion of this point.

15. Gross regional or gross state product would be better for measuring instability, but such data are not available. Personal income probably fluctuates less than measures of product or output because it includes transfer payments which behave in a countercyclical fashion. Monthly or quarterly income data would be useful for indicating instability, but again they are not available. Covered employment by month can be obtained, but it omits a substantial volume of employment for states where agricultural production is important. If monthly employment data were used to show cyclical fluctuations, it would, of course, have to be corrected for seasonal variation. Despites its shortcomings, personal income should give a useful indication of instability in states and regions.

TABLE 4

Average Percentage Change from Year to Year in Per Capita Incomes, Selected Regions and States, 1929-60 and 1945-60

Region or State	1929-60	1945-60
Pacific Northwest	9.0	3.5
Great Lakes	9.8	5.3
Mideast	7.5	4.2
New England	7.2	4.5
Plains	9.8	5.5
United States	8.4	4.4
Washington	9.0	4.0
Oregon	8.9	4.2
Idaho	10.8	4.4
Montana	9.6	5.9
California	7.5	3.8
Michigan	10.9	5.6
Ohio	9.9	5.9
Illinois	9.4	5.3
Massachusetts	6.9	4.6
Pennsylvania	8.5	4.8
Oklahoma	10.1	5.0
Nebraska	11.6	7.0
Iowa	12.7	8.4
South Dakota	18.0	11.8

Source: Based on data from U.S. Department of Commerce, *Personal Income by States...*, *op. cit.*; and *Survey of Current Business* (August 1961).

For the period 1929-60, the average percentage change for the Northwest was 9.0 percent, which was greater than the U.S. average of 8.4 percent. The Great Lakes and Plains states both had 9.8 percent, the highest figure for the five regions. The Mideast and New England areas had the lowest averages; they also experienced relatively low percentage growth in per capita income and population (Table 3). In the 1945-60 period, the Northwest had an average variation of 3.5 percent, which was below the averages for the nation and for each of the other four regions. When the differences in averages is small, it may not be statistically significant.

Among the individual states of the Northwest, Idaho and Montana had the highest average changes in both periods. Washington and Oregon were close together in both cases. The industrial states of Michigan, Ohio, and Illinois had rather high percentage changes, substantially greater than those for Washington, Oregon, and Idaho for the 1945-60 interval. California had the most stable income from 1945 to 1960 and was second to Massachusetts for the longer period, 1929-60. Massachusetts and Pennsylvania were among the most stable for the longer period, but trailed Washington, Oregon, Idaho, and California, in the postwar years. Oklahoma, Nebraska, Iowa, and South Dakota showed unstable incomes in both periods.

The states most heavily dependent upon agriculture were thus the most unstable. South Dakota is not only heavily dependent upon agriculture, but upon a single crop—wheat. Oregon and Idaho, the states in which lumber and wood products were of great importance, fared well in the 1945-60 period. The instability for the predominantly agricultural states is primarily due to fluctuations in output. Weather conditions were undoubtedly the major determinant of output and incomes for these states in recent years. Changes in the incomes of lumber producers stem primarily from fluctuations in demand.

A high degree of industrialization does not insure stability of income, as the experience of Michigan, Ohio, and Illinois illustrates. The conclusion of the previous section also applies here: instability of income depends more upon the particular product mix rather than upon concentration of production in primary products or industrial products.

Triantis has shown that the vulnerability and instability of national economies that rely heavily upon exports of primary products vary a great deal, depending on the type of primary products.[16] He examined the trade balances of twenty-nine countries exporting chiefly primary products. From 1928-29 to 1931-32, the trade balance improved for fifteen countries and deteriorated for the remaining fourteen. Those countries with a wide variety of export products fared no better in general than those with highly concentrated export trade. The countries whose trade balances improved generally exported substantial amounts of goods with relatively high price elasticities of demand and only moderate income elasticities. Among such goods were non-staple and semi-luxury agricultural products and certain petroleum products. Those countries whose trade balances deteriorated exported large amounts of products with low price elasticities of demand and high income elasticities or with low price and income elasticities coupled with highly inelastic supply. The first type included numerous raw materials, while the second type consisted of staple foodstuffs plus a few other commodities.

The value of imported manufactured goods declined sharply in many of these countries, despite a rather high price elasticity of demand. For those countries whose trade balances improved, two factors overcame the effect of this elasticity: (a) a much sharper price decline for domestic than for imported goods; and (b) a fall in domestic incomes, in conjunction with rather high income elasticities of demand for the imported manufactures. Among the manufactures, the import values for consumer durables and luxuries and investment goods fell more than those for non-durable and essential manufactures. Triantis concluded that no general statement could be made concerning the effect of industrialization or diversification of exports on the trade balance of primary exporting countries during cyclical fluctuations.[17]

An examination of U.S. production indices for selected commodity groups shows that the output of certain primary products fluctuates less than the output of certain manufactured goods. Table 5 contains the indices for certain commodity groups which are important in the trade of the Pacific Northwest. The declines in the 1948-49 recession were roughly comparable for lumber, pulp and paper, all durables, fabricated metals, and machinery. The decline for primary metals was

---

16. S. G. Triantis, "Cyclical Changes in the Balance of Merchandise Trade of Countries Exporting Chiefly Primary Products," American Economic Review, XLII, 1 (March 1952), 69-86.

17. Ibid., p. 86.

TABLE 5

Indices of Production for Selected Commodity Groups, United States, 1947-55
(1947 = 100)

Year	Lumber and its products	Pulp and paper	Canned and frozen foods	All durables	Fabricated metal products	Machinery	Autos, trucks, and parts	Primary metals
1947	100	100	100	100	100	100	100	100
1948	105	105	103	103	101	101	106	104
1949	92	98	106	94	90	90	109	87
1950	112	117	113	115	112	111	139	112
1951	112	127	125	127	118	126	126	122
1952	110	121	121	135	117	143	107	113
1953	117	131	125	151	132	155	132	128
1954	114	133	115	136	119	138	114	105
1955	126	151	122	153	130	151	161	136
1956	122	158	137	157	131	166	132	134
1957	113	156	130	158	135	163	134	127
1958	109	156	138	140	121	136	118	96

Source: *Federal Reserve Bulletin*, December issues, 1953-59.

greater, while the indices for canned and frozen foods and autos actually rose. In the 1953-54 recession, the relative decline in lumber output was substantially less than that for all durables, fabricated metals, machinery, automobiles, and primary metals. A decline in lumber output began in 1956 and continued through 1958; the total decline was about 14 percent. The 1957-58 declines for automobiles, machinery, and primary metals were as great or greater, although these decline took place in one year rather than over three years. The 1957-58 decline for all durables and for fabricated metal products were roughly 10 percent, somewhat less than the 1956-58 decline for lumber. The index for pulp and paper rose during both the 1953-54 and 1957-58 recessions, while that for canned and frozen foods fell during the former and rose during the latter. These production indices support the view that regions specializing in primary products will not necessarily experience greater cycle fluctuation than those specializing in manufactured goods. The crucial questions are what particular primary and manufactured goods are being produced, and what is the area's competitive position in relation to other areas supplying the products.

The Northwest has also benefited by certain circumstances that have tended to reduce its cyclical declines in the postwar years. First, the countercyclical behavior of housing construction has reduced the cyclical decline in demand for lumber. Second, employment in aircraft production in the Seattle area has generally not been affected by cyclical downturns, and in some instances behaved in a countercyclical fashion. Third, the agricultural price support program may have reduced fluctuations of farm income.

Diversity Vs. Specialization

Closely related to the third hypothesis is the argument concerning the dangers to a region of a high degree of specialization. Hoover and Fisher wrote that "...specialization of a region in one main kind of activity, or a few closely allied lines, makes its growth precarious and vulnerable to economic changes originating either inside or outside the region."[18] The suggested disadvantages of specialization are that a region's market for its specialty might be undercut by discovery of new and cheaper sources, by improvements in production elsewhere, by improvement in transportation, or by shifts in demand. Also, it is suggested that the less the specialization, or the more the diversification, the greater the ability to cushion adverse cyclical effects.

Without doubt there is some validity to the case for diversification of exports, but it is not as strong as generally assumed and needs to be qualified in a number of ways. As the analysis in the previous section suggests, diversification cushions adverse cyclical effects only if it happens to consist of the "right" product mix. The usual argument for diversification as a cushion against cyclical downswings is based on the "law of large numbers."[19] This law validates the case only if the various

---

18. Edgar M. Hoover and Joseph L. Fisher, "Research in Regional Economic Growth," Problems in the Study of Economic Growth (New York, 1949), p. 190.

19. This point is discussed in Wolfgang F. Stolper and Charles M. Tiebout, "The Balance of Payments of a Small Area as an Analytic Tool," unpublished manuscript.

industries fluctuate independently. Industries frequently exhibit different cyclical patterns, but the patterns are not randomly distributed. Diversification is no help if all the diversified industries are linked and fluctuate together.

The Seventh Federal Reserve District (the Chicago district) has a highly diversified economy but encounters its share of difficulties during recessions. In commenting on the recession of 1957-58, the Federal Reserve Bank of Chicago stated:

> ...activity in the Midwest, Iowa excepted, had slumped somewhat further than the nation generally and has shown a lesser recovery to date...Despite substantial diversification, the well-being of the major industrial centers of this area is tied intimately to the demand for producers' and consumers' durable goods—machinery and equipment, autos, appliances, and furniture.[20]

The demand for durables, like the demand for some primary products, is subject to wide swings during the course of a business cycle.

Even if the fluctuations of diverse industries were offsetting, one could not conclude that the unemployed in the depressed lines would automatically be employed in the non-depressed industries. For this to occur, there must be an increase in demand in the latter industries, or wages must fall if demand does not change. Contrasting skills may be required by the different industries, and workers may be reluctant to shift occupations even if they could.[21]

Some arguments for diversification and self-sufficiency are less relevant for regions than for nations. The threat of warfare, economic or otherwise, with sudden loss of markets or sources of supply is not a problem of interregional trade relationships. Regions ordinarily do not have independent booms or recessions; neither do they have independent monetary and fiscal policies. Because of greater labor mobility among regions than among nations, a high rate of unemployment in a region does not have the same significance for policy as it would if it existed for the nation as a whole.

The question of diversification, or the lack of it, usually comes up when a region's employment pattern is compared with that for the nation, the latter being used as a norm or as the "ideal." A strict application of the national pattern of employment as a goal toward which the region should work would require that the region deny itself its own comparative advantage.

Hoover and Fisher stressed the possibility that a specialty might be undercut by the discovery of new and cheaper supply sources, by improvements in production elsewhere, by improvement in transportation, or by shifts in demand. Actually, each of these factors <u>could</u> work to the advantage of the specialized region instead of against it. Innovations, however, might have a tendency to work against the region specializing in the production of food and raw materials if, as capital grows relative to land, innovations cause the substitution of capital and ubiquitous resources for highly specialized resources.[22]

---

20. Federal Reserve Bank of Chicago, <u>Business Conditions</u> (October 1958), p. 2.

21. Stolper and Tiebout, <u>op. cit.</u>, pp. 10-11.

22. Charles P. Kindleberger, <u>The Dollar Shortage</u> (Cambridge: Technology Press, 1950), pp. 122-23.

When specialization is based upon an exhaustible resource, the region may be faced with a reduced rate of growth or an actual decline as the depletion progresses. The experience of the state of Washington provides an interesting case of adjustment to the depletion of an important resource. Lumber production in the Douglas fir region of that state declined by about 60 percent from 1929 to 1955. Despite the use of less accessible timber supplies, technological advances resulted in an increased output per worker in logging. From 1940 to 1950, log production in Washington dropped 11 percent, but employment in logging declined even more—17 percent.[23]

Even though lumber production decreased sharply, employment in all phases of wood-products manufacture in Washington remained remarkably steady. The available employment data for the period 1929-55 indicate that while employment in logging and in lumber mills declined, it increased in pulp and paper mills, planing mills, plywood mills, and in the production of various by-products such as Presto-logs, hardboard, and softboard. The relatively steady employment in wood-products manufacture was due to greater processing and utilization of a smaller quantity of logs. Since 1955, employment in wood products has declined somewhat due to cyclical factors and increased mechanization.[24]

It is interesting at this point to examine the data to see if the four-state region of the Pacific Northwest has experienced any diversification of its exports during the course of its growth since 1929. Table 1 gave the percentage distribution of the region's exports by major commodity groups. Those figures indicated some lessening of the specialization in forest products and agriculture, and a broadening of the export base by the rise in importance of manufacturing. The share of total exports accounted for by products of forests, animals and their products, and products of agriculture declined from 88.5 percent in 1929 to an average of 87.3 percent for the period 1934-39, and to 77.1 percent for the years 1948-55. Manufactures and miscellaneous contained 12 percent of total exports from 1948-55, whereas previously this group had virtually no exports on a net basis.

When the commodity groups of Table 1 are broken down to individual commodity classes, there appears to be no lessening in the concentration of exports in a few leading commodity classes. The top fifteen commodity classes among exports accounted for roughly 83 to 84 percent of total exports throughout the years 1929 to 1955.[25] The five largest export classes accounted for 52.5 percent of the total in 1929, for an average of 46.7 percent during 1934-39, and for an average of 55.4 percent during 1948-55. There has thus been no decrease in specialization of exports in the sense of their concentration in a few leading commodity classes. There were changes, however, in the commodity classes that appeared in the top fifteen and in the top five.

Two other comments are relevant in interpreting these data. First, "aircraft and parts" are overwhelmingly dominant among the manufactures that are

---

23. Walter J. Mead, "The Forest Products Economy of the Pacific Northwest," Land Economics (May 1956), p. 131; and U.S. Bureau of the Census, Sixteenth Census of the United States, 1940, Population, Vol. III, Part 5, p. 886; and Census of Population, 1950, Vol. II, Part 47, p. 202.

24. Miner A. Baker, "Economic Growth Patterns in Washington and Oregon," Monthly Labor Review (May 1959), pp. 502-08.

25. Pfister, op. cit., pp. 87-88.

exported. The rise in importance of manufactures among the region's exports thus does not represent diversification in the form of a variety of manufacturing activities. Second, even though products of forests have not diminished in relative importance among exports, within this category there has been a shift to more highly processed products. The greater the degree of processing of raw materials, the closer the activity comes to being footloose and thus outside the classification of primary activities. This shift in composition of the category products of forests represents more diversification and industrialization.

Some Comments on Economic Development and the Pacific Northwest

The Pacific Northwest has been described as an underdeveloped region of the United States, or one in the early stages of development, primarily because extractive and primary processing activities are so important in its economy. This view results from the popular idea of a natural line of economic development through various stages, full development being reached with the establishment of a diversified industrial economy that includes heavy industry. By the usual criteria, the Northwest is a developed economy, for its per capita income is high, production is primarily for the market, and modern technology is used.

A region may, of course, be rich in natural resources but still not become industrialized. It might not have the right resource mix and markets for industrialization. If it cannot import the needed resources at a sufficiently low cost so that its industrial products can compete in price with those of other regions, then its resources may lie unused, or worse in the view of some inhabitants of the region, be used "only as isolated, individual resources, the raw materials from which will be sent to regions more favorably circumstances for a diversified manufacturing development."[26]

Economic development should not be defined to consist solely of growth in manufacturing. A large part of the resources involved in primary activities is really engaged in filling the demand for secondary products through trade.[27] However, a region that lacks energy sources (oil and coal) or steel-making materials must be able to maintain large exports to pay for the imports needed for its continued economic growth.

The arguments here are not intended to suggest that the Northwest will always be primarily a producer of crude and processed primary products. Much of the region's growth can be attributed to increased production of aircraft, chemicals, non-ferrous metals, fabricated metals, and machinery. Growth in the latter two industries was in part related to the expansion of aircraft production. Among the primary processing activities, growth has been most rapid for those involving a high degree of fabrication. These changes have lessened the region's dependence upon primary products, although they have had the greatest impact upon Washington.

---

26. John H. Dales, "Fuel, Power, and Industrial Development in Central Canada," American Economic Review, Papers and Proceedings (May 1953), p. 198.

27. This point is made in Kindleberger, Economic Development, op. cit., p. 117.

Because so much of the Northwest's growth occurred during World War II and because its growth has slowed since 1953, some observers of the region's economy believe that its prospects for growth in the immediate future are not bright.[28] They point out that production of several of its major export commodities is not expected to increase much if at all. They expect the region to have difficulty keeping up with national trends in economic growth.

In the 1930's the National Resources Planning Board stated that the major problems of the Northwest's economy were heavy dependence upon agricultural and raw-materials production, a small regional market, and the great distance from major industrial markets.[29] Despite these problems, the region's growth since 1929 compares favorable with the national average and with several other states and areas.

It is true, of course, that its major export industries generally are not among the dynamic and fast-growing ones of the nation in the postwar period. However, the absolute growth in population, income, and production since 1929 means that the local markets for consumer and producer goods have grown. The size of a region's markets has an important bearing on the outcome of its economic development. The market in the Northwest for a number of commodities either has reached, or will soon reach, the "threshhold" in size, so that economic-sized plants can be built to serve this regional market. An example of this tendency is the recent establishment of petroleum refineries in the Seattle area. Other trends, particularly the increasing relative cost of transportation, point to the stronger pull of markets in location decisions. The region's future growth will probably be based more on the expansion of market-oriented industries than in the past. If this prediction comes about, then exports and imports will eventually decline relative to regional income.

---

28. See Simpson, *op. cit.*; James N. Tattersall, "River Basin Development Vital for Economic Growth of Northwest," *Oregon Business Review* (October 1957), pp. 1-7; and Philip W. Cartwright, "The Changing Pattern of Industry in the State of Washington," *Proceedings of the Thirty-Second Annual Conference of the Western Economic Association* (1957), p. 76.

29. U.S. National Resources Planning Board, *Pacific Northwest Region: Industrial Development* (Washington, 1942).

16. Regional Income Inequality and Internal Population Migration*†

BERNARD OKUN AND RICHARD W. RICHARDSON

Introduction

Recent literature on economic growth evidences increasing concern over what appears to be ever-widening economic inequality between the advanced and the backward countries of the world. While some countries have in a relatively short time effected enormous improvements in economic performance and generally commensurate gains in levels of living, other countries have failed to keep pace.[1] Less attention is paid to the fact that disparities in growth rates are equally typical among regions and areas within a country, whatever its overall state of economic development.

The factors governing the levels and trends of per capita income have been a major concern of the literature on economic growth. One traditional approach attempts to relate the size of a country's population to the objective of maximizing per capita income. A country, region or area is said to be "underpopulated" or "over-populated" if, respectively, an increase or a decrease of population would contribute to a rise of per capita income. Any "over" or "under" population must of course occur relative to one or more other economic variables, e.g., the supply of natural resources, the stock of capital, the state of technology, or the size of the labor force.

This paper is concerned with the effect of internal migration on regional inequality of per capita income. The use of population size as the reference variable is a very convenient analytic device for this purpose, for the immediate effect of net internal migration is obviously to change the population size of the region concerned. In order to assess the effect of migration on a region or area, we analyze the effect of the change in population on regional per capita income by examining the relation of the new population size to the other relevant economic variables noted above. In addition, an attempt is made to draw some inferences on the short and the long run effects on regional inequality of per capita income.

---

* This study was undertaken with financial assistance from the Ford Foundation.

1. Simon Kuznets, "Under-developed Countries and the Pre-industrial Phase in the Advanced Countries: An Attempt at Comparison," Proceedings of the World Population Conference (Rome, 1954), and G. Myrdal, Economic Theory and Under-developed Regions (London, 1957).

† Reprinted from *Economic Development and Cultural Change,* Vol. 9 (Jan. 1961).

Internal Migration and Economic Growth

As a preliminary to our central theme, let us briefly explore the general relationship between internal migration and economic growth, in order to stress the extreme importance of one phenomenon in the growth process--the mobility of human resources.

Assume, for the sake of simplicity, an economy with a closed population--that is, one in which no emigration or immigration takes place. A simple demand and supply model can be developed to explain the economic rationale for internal migration. Consider first the supply side. It is unlikely that rates of natural increase of population will be the same in all regions of the country. Though there are probably only small differences in mortality rates among regions in an advanced country, it is likely that regional differences in fertility rates are larger, causing regional differences in the natural rate of increase.[2] There is, similarly, no reason to believe that the natural rate of increase is the same in all regions of the typical underdeveloped country. Many factors account for regional differences in fertility and consequent differences in the natural rate of increase. Among these are regional differentials in the degree of urbanization, in the relative weight of agriculture vs. manufacturing activities, in the religious composition of the populations, in the level of education, etc. These and other factors help to account for the fact that some regions are, quantitatively speaking, more efficient producers" of people than other regions.

On the demand side, it is historically true that economic growth is typified by shifts in the relative importance of industries: from agriculture to manufacturing, from manufacturing to services. Equally characteristic are changes in the relative importance of activities within the broad industrial groupings, e.g., from textiles to automobiles, electronics and aircraft. The fact that natural resources are not homogeneously distributed geographically throughout an economy means that shifts in the importance of different activities, and consequent changes in relative resource demands, will generally be associated with shifts in the economic importance of different regions. Economic growth, with its concomitant and characteristically rapid changes in economic structure, will generally have an uneven impact on the different regions within an economy. Changing inter-regional differentials in the marginal productivity of labor, and in economic opportunities more generally, are a necessary by-product of the process of economic growth.

It is possible that those regions of an economy that demand relatively more labor are those which have relatively higher natural rates of population increase. If there were a close conformity between natural rates of increase and the growth of economic opportunity, then the need for internal migration would be diminished. But differential rates of natural increase cannot be counted upon to redistribute population in the optimal way. Crude death rates are not a function of economic opportunity. Also, the birth rate may fail to respond positively to economic growth. Even if it did, the time lag between new births and new entries into the labor force is longer than a region enjoying rapid economic growth is willing or able to wait for additional labor. It would, in fact, be necessary for the crude birth rate to lead movements in a region's demand for labor by twenty years.

---

2. For figures on state fertility rates in the United States, see Bernard Okun, Trends in Birth Rates in the United States Since 1870 (Baltimore, 1958), pp. 33-34.

Far from reducing the need for migration, regional patterns of natural population increase and growth of economic opportunity generally enhance the importance of mobility. For while the agricultural regions typically have the higher rate of natural increase, it is in the non-agricultural regions that the demand for labor grows more rapidly.

Internal Migration and Equilibrium Theory

From what has been said, it is clear that population migration must be the predominant force making for redistribution of human resources in response to changing relative opportunities among regions. Its role as a catalyst in the growth of the entire economy is apparent. The major part of this paper is addressed to an examination of the effect of such migrations on the economies of the individual regions.

Gunnar Myrdal has recently asserted that traditional economic theory suffers from what he terms an "equilibrium bias." According to him, traditional economic theory argues or implies that movements of capital and labor (as well as trade) all tend to reduce inequalities of per capita income among countries and among regions within a country. In the face of generally widening inequalities, Myrdal submits that theory is blind to reality, largely because of its use of unrealistic assumptions--particularly the notion of stable equilibrium.[3]

Myrdal seems to have misconstrued some of the propositions of traditional theory, and consequently much of his criticism is levelled against a non-existent body of doctrine. A fundamental proposition of general equilibrium theory and the theory of the competitive market is that discrepancies in factor payments, caused by shifts in supply and demand schedules, will lead to an appropriate reallocation of productive factors until equilibrium is restored. In the particular case in which we are here interested, theory asserts that inter-regional factor mobility is a force which tends to equalize prices for homogeneous factors in different regions.

Myrdal's critique appears to be based on a confusion between the concepts of equilibrium and equality. Equilibrium analysis addresses itself to the problem of equality, but only with respect to <u>factor payments</u>. Factor mobility is an instrument for the elimination of factor price differentials; nothing can logically be inferred from this, however, about the impact of spatial factor mobility upon the per capita income differentials between the geographical units which are the sources or recipients of the factors themselves. In other words, while spatial factor mobility tends to equalize the returns to homogeneous factors residing in different areas, it may or may not tend to reduce the differential in per capita income between these areas. Whether or not the effect is equalizing depends upon several variables: the income of the mobile factor relative to the average incomes in the regions of origin and destination; the direction of the migratory movement (from a lower to a higher per capita income region, or vice versa); and other variables which will be considered presently. Myrdal states that "according to the classical doctrine movements of labour and capital between countries would not be necessary to bring about a development towards and equalization of factor prices and, consequently, incomes."[4] The soundness of this observation, however, does not justify

3. Myrdal, <u>op. cit.</u>, pp. 12-13, 142-146.

4. <u>Ibid.</u>, p. 148.

the inference, which Myrdal first establishes and then criticizes, that the process of trade and growth reduces international and inter-regional inequalities of per capita income.

Internal Mobility and Regional Inequality

Though he fails to make the important distinction between equilibrium and equality, Myrdal nevertheless raises a question of considerable interest in his analysis of the process of growth: does internal mobility tend to widen or to narrow income inequality? Myrdal asserts that mobility widens inequality:

> The localities and regions where economic activity is expanding will attract net immigration from other parts of the country. As migration is always selective, at least with respect to the migrant's age, this movement by itself tends to favour the rapidly growing communities and disfavour the others.[5]

It is generally the case that the age distribution of migrants tends to favor the 20-40 age bracket relative to the population as a whole. Therefore, it probably would follow that migration tends to increase the proportion of the population in the labor force of the receiving region, and to decrease its proportion in the region of origin. From this, Myrdal infers that migration benefits the economy of the receiving region, and debilitates the economy of the originating region.

So strong an inference from the age-selectivity argument may prove seriously misleading. The beneficial effects upon the receiving region of age-selective migration may be exaggerated, while it may on the other hand be possible that emigration of any age distribution whatsoever may be helpful, rather than detrimental, to the region of origin. Consider first the region of origin. In the first place, there appear to be areas in the world where the marginal productivity of labor is zero, or very low.[6] Even if all the emigrants from such areas were members of the labor force, there would result no or little diminution of total income, and per capita income might well rise. A second possible consequence of such emigration--indeed, a likely consequence--is that the capital-labor ratio would rise, and this would also tend to increase per capita income.[7] Thus there is a strong presumption that when the marginal productivity of labor is zero or very low--and this is not, apparently, uncommon for backward agricultural regions in underdeveloped countries and perhaps even in some advanced countries--emigration from such regions, regardless of age distribution, is likely to increase the region's per capita income.

---

5. Ibid., p. 27.

6. Ragnar Nurkse, Problems of Capital Formation in Underdeveloped Countries (Oxford, 1957), pp. 32-36.

7. John D. Black, for example, shows that for the period 1925-30, the southern regions had, in agriculture, the lowest monthly wage rates and the lowest value of capital goods per worker of all regions in the United States. Cf. "Agricultural Wage Relationships: Geographical Differences," Review of dconomic Statistics XVIII, No. 7 (May, 1936), 74.

With respect to the receiving region, the age-distribution argument is similarly not so complete or straightforward as Myrdal suggests. Two obvious points come to mind. First, the in-migrants may be of such inferior quality as to lower the average output per worker in the region, perhaps to an extent which more than offsets the positive influence of the rise in the proportion of the population in the labor force. Second, the age distribution of the migrants is such that it tends to raise the proportion of the population in the child-bearing age groups. Most of the migrants are or will be married, and have or will bear children. This factor will, of course, tend to reduce the proportion of the population in the labor force, somewhat offsetting the positive effect on this proportion of the workers themselves.

Similarly, the proportion of the population of child-bearing age in the region of origin will be reduced, and this will tend to reduce the region's crude birth rate; consequently, the proportion of this population which is in the unproductive pre-labor force age will also fall. Such a consequence would, in the short run, have a salutary effect upon the per capita income of this region--the more so if it happens, as is not unlikely in backward agricultural regions, to be suffering from too high a birth rate.

These few counter-examples alone suffice to demonstrate that a simple interpretation of the age-distribution argument does not adequately deal with the complexities inherent in the relationship between migration and inequality of per capita income. To provide a fuller treatment of this problem, a model will be developed which, though it will not in all instances yield definitive conclusions, will point to the relevant variables that must be considered.

The Model

We assume a closed economy, not subject to international migratory movements, and composed of four paradigm types of region: (1) low per capita income and stagnant (LS); (2) high per capita income and stagnant (HS); (3) low per capita income and growing (LG); and (4) high per capita income and growing (HG).

Some elaboration of these concepts is in order. A "stagnant" region is here defined as one in which there occurs, over time, relatively little or no increase in per capita income; a growing region, correspondingly, is one in which there is sustained secular improvement in per capita income. Growing regions are generally characterized by advances in productive organization and techniques, and changes in industrial structure. Such characteristics are typically lacking in stagnant regions.

The "low" and "high" concepts are of course concerned, not with the rate of growth, but with the level of per capita income at a point in time. A low per capita income region is here defined as one in which per capita income is low by comparison with other regions in the same country, _and/or_ by comparison with some median per capita income level prevailing among advanced countries. It follows that a high per capita income region is defined so by comparison _both_ with income levels in other regions of the same country _and_ with some median level among the advanced countries. (The latter condition makes it possible that _all_ regions in an underdeveloped country may be classified as low.)

In the United States, to which we shall continually refer for illustrative purposes, the Pacific Coast would be described as "high growing" (HG); parts of

New England as "high stagnant" (HS); the East South Central region (particularly Mississippi) as "low stagnant" (LS); and Texas and North Carolina as "low growing" (LG).

Our model considers only migratory movements from one region to another of a different category, since nothing of economic interest can be discerned in the cause or nature of migration between similar regions. Since there are four categories, the direction of migration can theoretically vary in twelve ways:

I.	LS	to	LG, HS, HG
II.	LG	to	LS, HS, HG
III.	HS	to	LS, LG, HG
IV.	HG	to	LS, LG, HS

It is clear that the characteristics of the migratory group with respect to occupation, education, etc., and the consequences of the migration for regional inequality of per capita income, will depend on the direction taken by the migratory stream.

The Low Stagnant Region

For reasons which will presently be made apparent, the low stagnant region will tend to experience a net outflow of population. In 1950, for example, there were 442,500 native whites who were born in Mississippi but living elsewhere in the United States, while there were at the same time only 178,900 native whites living in Mississippi who were born in other states.[8] Assuming the quality of the in-migrants in such a case does not differ substantially from that of the out-migrants, we may treat Mississippi as an originating state, and need not be concerned with it as a recipient state. As a general proposition for present purposes, we shall regard the low stagnant region as a region of origin only.

In order to weigh the consequences of out-migration from a low stagnant region, it is necessary to specify certain characteristics typical of such a region. In both developed and underdeveloped countries, a stagnant and low per capita income region is generally agricultural. Labor-intensive methods of agricultural production are used, capital and modern equipment may be lacking, and per capita arable land tillage is low. These factors help to explain the low marginal productivity of labor which typically prevails in such a region. It is conceivable, in the extreme case, that marginal productivity of labor is zero--the case of disguised unemployment. Such a condition, however, is much more likely to be encountered in underdeveloped countries. This type of region also tends to have a relatively high fertility rate and natural rate of increase. This condition, combined with an excess labor supply, militates strongly in favor of out-migration, to the extent

---

8. Everett S. Lee *et al.*, *Population Redistribution and Economic Growth, United States, 1870-1950* (Philadelphia, 1957), I, 271.

that any migratory movement at all takes place. It seems reasonable, moreover, to assume that the out-migration will consist primarily of unskilled laborers and their families, because this is the segment of the labor force which is here relatively abundant. Now, if the marginal product of the out-migrants is lower than the average for the region as a whole, it is evident that per capita income will rise, provided that not too drastic a reduction in the proportion of the population in the labor force has resulted from their exit. Moreover, the out-migration of workers may cause the marginal productivity of the remaining workers to rise, because of the resulting increase in capital-labor and in arable land-labor ratios. For these reasons, a fair presumption may be said to exist that current out-migration will in general tend to help rather than hinder a low stagnant region, both in the immediate and the distant future.

The Low Growing Region

The case of the region with low, but nevertheless growing, per capita income is somewhat more complicated than the first. To begin with, the issue of whether there is likely to be net in-migration or out-migration is not clear-cut. Much depends on the economic status of the other regions of the country. If the low growing region is part of a country which is otherwise typically low stagnant, then it is likely to be a net recipient of population. This case is, of course, ruled out for an advanced country, which, by definition, must have at least one advanced region. For some underdeveloped countries, however, the greatest economic opportunities may well lie in the low growing region, thus tending to make it a recipient of population migration. On the other hand, in the advanced countries there may be regions--presumably high growing--which provide relatively greater economic inducements than the low growing region. In this case, the latter might be a net loser of population, though not to so great an extent as the low stagnant region in similar circumstances.[9]

Let us consider the case where the low growing region is a net loser of population. It is now necessary to distinguish two patterns of growth that may emerge in this region. The first involves progress chiefly in the agricultural sector; for example, more capitalistic techniques of production may be employed. In this situation, because capital serves within wide limits as a substitute for labor, the amount of labor employed per arable acre of land will decline; and because the available quantity of land is relatively fixed, a decline in the population and the labor force as a result of out-migration will probably not have deleterious effects, in either the short or the long run, upon the potential economic growth of the region. On the contrary, a reduction of population will probably facilitate the introduction of more capitalistic techniques, and accelerate the mechanization of agriculture.

A second possible growth pattern involves a shift from agriculture to manufacturing production. Assuming that this is an agricultural region with a high labor-to-land ratio, it is unlikely that investment of even a relatively labor-intensive variety will be sufficiently great in the early phases of the shift to absorb fully the excess population of the region. Furthermore, it is probable that population will

---

9. For example, North Carolina, with a population in 1940 of about 2.5 million native whites, had a net loss of 81,600 native whites between 1940 and 1950; Mississippi, with about 1.1 million in 1940, lost 94,300 in the same period. Data from ibid., I, 162, 185.

continue to grow in this region in the short run despite out-migration, because of the high natural rate of population increase that is historically characteristic of such situations. Hence, it is likely that a sufficiently large labor force will continue to exist in the face of out-migration, so that the demand for labor can be met at a wage which will not deter investment. For these reasons, it is unlikely that out-migration would in the short run prove harmful to the growth of the region.

For the long run, it is not possible to reach firm conclusions about the effect of migration on a low growing region with changing economic structure. Even the question of whether there would be net out-migration in the long run is in doubt. Such a situation could prevail, however, if there are other regions in the country which offer even greater economic opportunity, because their growth rate is higher and per capita incomes are higher, and/or they have a lower natural rate of population increase. If out-migration should indeed continue over a prolonged period, it would prove harmful to the region of origin if labor shortages developed which kept the long-run actual rate of growth of income per capita below the potential rate of growth. The possibility of labor shortages is increased if the out-migration is accompanied by the secular decline in the birth rate which so often attends a transformation from agricultural to manufacturing structure.

In the special case of a low growing region sparsely populated to begin with, any significant out-migration would impede the growth of manufacturing in the short as well as the long run. But this is an unlikely case. It is doubtful that such a region, with a limited labor supply, would attract manufacturing activity. Moreover, even if it did, the marginal productivity of labor would rise to such a degree that the region would probably become a net recipient of population.

In the low growing region which is not sparsely populated, it is also uncertain that out-migration will always prevail. We have remarked that in underdeveloped countries, which consist predominantly of either low stagnant or low growing regions, the low growing region can be expected to be a net recipient of migration. Even in an advanced country, if a region of low per capita income is growing sufficiently rapidly, a large demand for labor will often result in net in-migration. In the United States, for example, personal per capita income in Texas was 90 percent of the national average in the period 1949-1951, and had been growing rapidly to that time.[10] As a result of its rapid growth rate, Texas--which would here be characterized as low growing--had been (and still is) experiencing net in-migration. It is possible, therefore, that a low growing region may, as in the case of Texas, more than offset its population losses to other, higher per capita income regions by gains from low stagnant regions.

Whether or not such in-migration is helpful or harmful to the growth of such regions will depend on the actual rate of in-migration relative to the rate of regional investment and the availability of land. It is more likely to be harmful in the shorter run, when capital is probably not available in quantities adequate to absorb the suddenly enlarged population. With the passage of time, however, in-migration may prove fruitful for the regional economy, as it becomes better able to use the new arrivals efficiently.

Whereas the propositions concerning the low growing regions which are net migration recipients are relatively straightforward, those dealing with the net mi-

---

10. Data derived from ibid., I, 753.

gration losers are, as we have seen, less so, and therefore warrant a brief summary. It was noted that low growing regions are likely to experience out-migration only in advanced countries. In the short run, net out-migration is likely to prove beneficial, except in the special case of sparsely populated areas. In the long run, increasingly limited supplies of labor could well retard the rate of growth. But severe limitations of the labor supply would probably be a consequence, not merely of the out-migration itself, but of birth rate reductions accompanying a structural transformation of economic activity. If the economic changes that characterize the region are predominantly modernization and capitalization of agricultural production, the supply of labor is likely to remain adequate--indeed, more than adequate; out-migration might accelerate the rate of growth of regional per capita income. But if the changes are characterized predominantly by a shift from agricultural to manufacturing activity, then it is possible that out-migration will deter the rate of growth in the long run.

The High Stagnant Region

As in the previous case, two basic regional types are distinguishable in the high per capita income category. The first is the "old" region, in which the rate of growth of income has markedly declined. The second is the high per capita income region which continues to grow at a rapid rate.

Stagnation in a high per capita income region is usually associated with the presence of industries which enjoyed their secular peaks of activity at an earlier date, and the failure of a sufficient number of newer and rapidly growing industries to appear. An obvious empirical example of this type is provided by parts of New England. The decline and partial withdrawal of the textile industry from this region was a prominent factor in its economic retardation, and was not by any means offset by the appearance of some electronic and other firms. Large portions of the region have over a period of years experienced stagnation.[11]

A high stagnant region is likely to be a net exporter of people, particularly in countries which also have high growing regions, for the pull of economic opportunity from the high growing regions is likely to more than offset any in-migration which originates in the low stagnant or low growing regions. There are a number of forces operating in a high stagnant region which tend to push people in the direction of high growing regions, and which act simultaneously to thwart in-migration from the low per capita income regions. Why is this so?

A number of observations can be made concerning the characteristics of the inhabitants of a high per capita income region. First, if a high growing region elsewhere is offering improved economic opportunities--as is likely to be the case--many residents of the high stagnant region are likely to know about it. In this region, as contrasted with low per capita income regions, the communication of information--in this case concerning job possibilities elsewhere--is likely to be relatively efficient. The educational standard of the population of a high stagnant region is such that information media such as newspapers are relatively better utilized than they are in isolated rural areas in low income regions. Moreover, the sheer number of such sources of information is likely to be larger.

---

11. Cf. Seymour Harris, The Economics of New England: Case Study of an Older Area (Cambridge, Mass.).

Another factor of importance in contrasting the migratory potential of low and high per capita income regions is that the potential migrant from the latter is likely to possess the economic resources to move himself and his family to new areas of opportunity, whereas migrants from regions of the former type are more likely to find such resources unavailable. Finally, the general training of the high income potential migrant would tend to strengthen the demand for his services in high growing regions, as compared with the services of migrants from low per capita income regions.

While the high stagnant region is a likely origin of migration, particularly to high growing regions, it is not a likely candidate for migratory inflows from low per capita income regions. What inflow does occur is likely to originate predominantly in low income regions; however, the very fact of stagnancy implies that, despite high per capita income, the region does not offer sufficiently promising economic horizons to attract large numbers from elsewhere, particularly when compared to horizons in high growing regions. Even though per capita income may be high, its composition may not be such as to encourage significant in-migration. For example, property income per capita may be relatively high in high stagnant regions. Many families accumulated wealth in earlier periods when the region was economically dynamic. Although the rate of growth of the region has now declined, these families are still receiving returns for their past accumulations, in the forms of rent, interest, and dividends, all of which contribute to regional per capita income. But these income components provide no direct inducement to potential migrants who would be unable to share in it.

The recent Study of Population Redistribution and Economic Growth by the University of Pennsylvania provides some interesting figures bearing on this argument. The data in Tables 1, 2, and 3 are for the period 1949-1951 in the United States, and are taken as percentages of the national average.[12]

Table 1. Property Income Per Capita in the United States, 1949-1951

	(percent of United States average)
Maine	105.0
New Hampshire	111.9
Vermont	96.8
Massachusetts	131.4
Rhode Island	118.2
Connecticut	174.2

Table 2. Service Income Per Worker in the United States, 1949-1951

	(percent of United States average)
Maine	82.8
New Hampshire	82.9
Vermont	81.1
Massachusetts	102.0
Rhode Island	93.4
Connecticut	109.6

12. Data derived from Lee *et al.*, *op. cit.*, I, 253, 754, 757.

It is interesting to note, from Tables 1 and 2, that in New England property income per capita is greater than service income per worker, relative to the United States as a whole. This indicates that property income accounts for a larger proportion of total income in New England than in the United States at large. Moreover, the near-average figures for service income per worker in the three southern New England States suggest that these states really enjoy their high economic status almost solely because of the property component of its income, as is borne out by the figures on total per capita income in Table 3.

Table 3. Total Personal Per Capita Income, 1949-1951

	(percent of United States average)
Maine	82.4
New Hampshire	88.8
Vermont	81.0
Massachusetts	111.0
Rhode Island	106.1
Connecticut	125.1

Another factor that is probably significant in maintaining for a considerable period the high per capita income of relatively stagnant regions is the occupational distribution of the population. A lengthy previous history of growth and high income will probably have left the region with an endowment of superior educational facilities. In addition, high incomes will have permitted the inhabitants to postpone entrance into the labor force longer than would otherwise have been possible, meanwhile enabling them to acquire additional schooling and pre-job training. For these reasons, it is probable that, on the average, there are in high stagnant regions relatively more labor force members of professional and skilled status than in low stagnant or low growing regions. In such a region, there is also a greater demand for such workers than in regions of low per capita income. These factors, taken together, provide further explanation for a current higher per capita income in the high stagnant region. However, such sources of income would, as in the previous case of property income, fail to provide inducement to the potential out-migrant from low per capita income regions, who tends to fall in the unskilled, or at best semi-skilled, category. Neither high property nor high service incomes per capita provide powerful inducements for in-migration.

Some in-migration into high stagnant regions may occur, nevertheless, for different reasons. Potential out-migrants from low stagnant or low growing regions might find a high stagnant region attractive because the services offered by state and local government, particularly in the areas of education and welfare, may far surpass those available in the originating regions. There may, too, be a fairly substantial demand in the receiving region for certain types of service--for example, domestic help--which can be met by the untrained migrant. In general, however, limited opportunities for the relatively unskilled laborer in a stagnant region, for the reasons enumerated above, will usually reduce any population inflow to insignificant levels.

On balance, a high stagnant region is likely to be a net exporter of population. Aside from purely quantitative considerations, however, some extremely interesting consequences of a qualitative type may emerge from this case, which makes inadmissable the analytic netting of inflows against outflows. Consider, for example, the question of educational selectivity. As noted earlier, a region of historically high per capita income will probably have developed, over the years, a strong and ubiquitous educational tradition, which will have had the effect of creating a large amount of educational capital. The average educational level of the indigenous population will be higher than that of the economically more backward areas, and the out-migrants from such a region will tend to be of higher "quality" and potential productivity than the average for the country as a whole. At the same time, the existence of a population of this educational and productive quality, in a stagnant region where the demand for such a population is not growing very rapidly, will very likely mean that whatever in-migration does occur will not be of similar quality. The inflow will consist predominantly of the unskilled, who seek to improve their status in the high stagnant region.

What are the consequences for the high stagnant region of this "quality exchange?" The in-migration, in whatever numbers, of the unskilled and semi-skilled laborers and their families probably has a depressing effect on per capita income, for two reasons--one merely arithmetic and the other economic. In the first place, it is apparent that the average income of the in-migrant will be lower than the average for the region, given the presumption that he tends to be of lower "quality." This will necessarily reduce the average income of the recipient region. Secondly, because this is not a growing region, the capital-labor ratio will probably fall as a result of any increase in unskilled or semi-skilled labor, and this will tend to diminish the marginal productivity of these classes of labor. Thus, any net increase in the numbers of lower-quality workers through migration will probably have a detrimental effect on per capita income. One cannot, however, predict whether or not an increase of population of this category will result from inter-regional migration. While it is probable that the average quality of the out-migrant will be higher than that of the in-migrant, the <u>number</u> of low quality out-migrants may or may not exceed the number of low quality in-migrants.

The net out-migration of professional and highly skilled labor from the high stagnant region will operate upon per capita income of that region in the same downward direction as the inflow of the less skilled, as their exodus constitutes a reduction of the average productivity of the remaining population.[13] These considerations, taken together, point to the conclusions that inter-regional migration will prove detrimental to the per capita income of a high stagnant region. This conclusion is valid for both the short and the long run, assuming the persistence of stagnation in the region.

The migration figures for the New England states, in Table 4, illustrate some of the points mentioned above. Four of the six New England states had, in the decade 1940-1950, significant migratory losses. In Rhode Island there was no significant change. Connecticut, as a real exception, experienced significant net in-migration. This exception, however, strengthens the argument presented above. As Harris has noted, "Connecticut, with its close relations with the Middle Atlantic States and its concentration on thriving industries in the last generation, is a manufacturing state with a much better record than the rest of the region."[14] This state, therefore, should not be classed as a high stagnant area, and it is therefore not surprising that it experienced net in-migration.

---

13. Of course, the average income of the remaining higher-quality labor will presumably benefit from the depletion in the numbers of the highly trained, but the average income of the region as a whole will be reduced.

14. Harris, <u>op. cit.</u>, p. 73.

Table 4. Net Intercensal Migration by Nativity and Race, for the New England States, 1940-1950*

	Native Whites	Negroes	Foreign-Born Whites	Totals
Maine	-41,600	- 100	5,900	- 35,800
New Hampshire	- 12,600	300	3,300	- 9,100
Vermont	- 25,800	---	2,000	- 23,800
Massachusetts	- 73,800	10,600	33,600	- 29,500
Rhode Island	200	1,200	1,700	2,700
Connecticut	49,000	13,000	27,500	89,500
Totals	-105,000	25,000	74,000	- 6,000

* The data are derived from figures in Lee *et al.*, *op. cit.*, I, 119-21, 149-51, 154-56, 174-76, 199-201, 214-16. The totals do not all check because of rounding. The figures for the foreign-born include international as well as domestic migration.

The breakdown of Table 4 also supports our contention concerning the "quality exchange" that characterizes migration in high stagnant areas. While New England (except for Connecticut) experienced a large net loss of native whites, it gained considerable numbers of foreign-born whites and Negroes. Presumably, the occupational status and per capita income of the native white out-migrants was higher than that of the foreign-born and Negro in-migrants. This undoubtedly tended to depress the per capita income of the region.

It would, however, be incorrect to conclude that migration is an important prime cause of the plight of a high stagnant region. In the main, causality runs the other way. Because of the failure of old industries to grow rapidly, and of new ones to appear, growth rates have declined. It is this which causes the migration streams to behave as they do--contributing to, but not initially responsible for, the impairment of the region's economy.

High Growing Regions

Finally, we must consider the direction and effects of migration for a region characterized by relatively rapid growth of per capita income, starting from levels already high. It should be immediately evident, from what has already been said about the low per capita income regions and the high stagnant region, that the high growing region will be a net recipient of significant migratory inflows. All of the other regional types are likely to be contributors, in one or another degree, to the population of the high growing region. Because of its level and rate of growth of income, there is in this region a substantial and growing demand for labor, thus creating a wage structure which will prove attractive to labor in other regions. A further attraction is the educational and welfare facilities made possible by the already high per capita income.

The long-run effects of migration into such a region are fairly clear. This region is characteristically composed of relatively youthful industries, growing at a rapid pace, which have located there for some economic or other advantage. This is a region in which the birth rate (and hence the natural rate of increase) will be relatively low, particularly in comparison to the low-income rural areas of more backward regions. Typically, a substantial amount of population growth is required to facilitate the long-run expansion of the region's industries to their full potential. In the absence of a high rate of natural increase, in-migration at least partially fulfills this function and thus in the long run is conducive to higher levels of per capita income.

The situation is less clear in the short run. The entry of quantities of unskilled and semi-skilled labor mainly from the regions of low per capita income could in the shorter period have a depressing effect on per capita income; this is an arithmetic proposition to which we have already alluded. These migrants, whose average income is below the average income of the receiving region, tend in the short run to lower per capita income for the receiving region as a whole. For example, the influx of population into the state of Michigan in the 1920's very probably had a depressing effect on Michigan's per capita income during that decade. There were about 550,000 net in-migrants into the state between 1920 and 1930, representing about 15 percent of the average Michigan population in that decade, which was 3,769,900. Of the total migratory inflow, about 86,100 were Negro, and 224,000 were foreign-born.[15] Thus a large proportion were, we may infer, either unskilled or semi-skilled, and this probably had a depressing short run effect on per capita income.

Because of the enormous influx of population into Michigan, a heavy demand for housing and public facilities undoubtedly developed quickly. To the extent that this caused a diversion of resources into these sectors, where the capital-output ratio is relatively high, and away from other activities of lower capital-output ratios, the short run effect of the heavy in-migration may have been adverse. However, this may have been partially or wholly offset by a capital inflow from other regions which had been attracted by the economic prospects of the new automobile industry.

But despite any unfavorable initial impact of this migration of the twenties, it is evident that the subsequent phenomenal growth of the automobile industry, and the consequent growth of the state's per capita income, were directly contingent upon this influx of unskilled labor from other regions. The role of migration was highlighted by the fact that the natural rate of increase in Michigan during this period was relatively low.

The case of Michigan is particularly interesting in that it points to a close relation which sometimes exists between migration and technology. The assembly-line technique of automobile production could not have been successfully instituted without the presence of an adequate supply of unskilled and semi-skilled labor, and the economic opportunity generated by the introduction of this technique was probably responsible for encouraging and absorbing the large-scale unskilled in-migration.

California provides another illustration of a high growing region. The secular growth of the aircraft industry, as well as the growth of the rest of the state's economy, was made possible by the in-migration--the role of in-migration again

---

15. Lee _et al._, _op. cit._, I, 157-159. The foreign-born figure also includes persons coming to Michigan directly from foreign countries.

being highlighted by the fact that before 1940 the fertility rate in the state was among the lowest in the nation.

We may conclude from these observations that the significant in-migration probably experienced by high growing regions may have an unfavorable effect on per capita income in the short run. In the long run, however, it is bound to have a beneficial effect on the region's economy, for it provides the labor required for sustained growth.

Conclusions

On the basis of the foregoing analysis of regional migration, we may now attempt to assess the effects of such migrations on regional inequalities of per capita income.

It has been noted that low stagnant regions are quite likely, over time, to experience a net outflow of population. This outflow, it was argued, would in the short and probably in the long run prove beneficial to the region, whether it is in an advanced or in an underdeveloped country. When this outflow is in the direction of low growing regions, this will tend in the short run to retard the rate of growth of the latter regions, though in the long run the result may be either retardation or acceleration of the growth rate. We may therefore conclude that in the short run, migration from low stagnant to low growing tends to diminish the rate of widening inequality between the low stagnant and low growing regions. In the long run, out-migration is of benefit to the originating low stagnant region, but at the same time may prove to be either an aid or a detriment to the receiving low growing region. Thus, it is not certain whether in the long run migration will contribute to a widening or a narrowing of inequality in per capita incomes between the low stagnant and low growing regions.

A second important stream of migration flows from the low stagnant to the high growing regions. In the short run, the inflow of persons of probable "low quality" (in terms of educational and occupational status) to the high growing region tends to depress per capita income there, while the outflow from the low stagnant region reduces its excess labor supply, tending here to raise per capita income. It is evident, therefore, that in the short run migration from low stagnant to high growing regions will tend to narrow inequality between these regions. In the long run, however, because net in-migration probably is of benefit to the high growing region, nothing definite can be concluded regarding the effects upon inequality of per capita income.

A third important migratory stream flows from the high stagnant to the high growing regions. It was argued that the out-migrants may tend to be of relatively "high quality" in terms of occupation and education; hence, in this case, quality deterioration in the labor force of the high stagnant region is linked to quality improvement in the labor force of the high growing region. It follows that this migration will tend to accelerate the growing inequality in per capita income between the high stagnant and high growing regions.

It was also noted that there may be some migration of relatively "low quality" labor from the low stagnant to the high stagnant regions. Hence, migration may adversely affect the high stagnant region in two distinct ways--through a loss of relatively high-productivity labor to the high growing regions, and through a gain of relatively low-productivity labor from the low stagnant regions.

Finally, a migratory stream may flow from the low growing to the high growing regions. This case is the most difficult to assess in terms of its effects on per capita income inequality. In the short run, this movement probably contributes to lesser inequality. This is based on the assumption that the quality of the in-migrants is such as to depress the average level of labor productivity of the high growing region, thus tending to depress per capita income. On the other hand, the out-migration is not likely to prove detrimental to the low growing region, particularly since there may be a partially compensating inflow from the low stagnant region. Moreover, in the short run, with limited capital available, the low growing region is unlikely to experience a relative scarcity of labor.

What should now be abundantly clear is that no general proposition can be formulated concerning the effect of internal migration on regional inequality of per capita income. Any general statement, such as Myrdal's conclusion that migration widens regional inequality, based as it is only on an age-selectivity argument, is not valid. As we have shown, the effect on inequality depends on the direction of the migration, on whether one considers the short or the long run, and on whether the country involved is advanced or underdeveloped. And even when all of these factors are specified, there are important cases where the outcome is indeterminate.

The Role of the City

17. The History of Cities in the Economically Advanced Areas*

ERIC E. LAMPARD

1. Introduction

Though "cities" have existed in one form or another close on 7000 years, the past two centuries, 1750-1950, have witnessed an unprecedented urbanization of people and economic activity in areas affected by the industrial revolution. During this brief moment of history, many towns and villages in Europe and North America ceased to be mere regional markets for craftsmen and cultivators; they became vibrant centers for almost all the manufacturing, servicing, and distributive functions developed in an expanding economy. Only food raising and certain extractive processes remained tied to the countryside. The coincident growth of cities, population, and non-agricultural employments seems to have been a characteristic feature of all economically advancing societies.[1]

But the trend was not confined to western Europe and North America. During the first half of the present century, urban growth became more marked in some of the "underdeveloped" countries. Cities mushroomed in parts of the world which had previously felt little urban or industrial development; they expanded in areas of both high and low population density along the maritime fringes of Asia, Africa, and Latin America. The growth of urban population in Puerto Rico since 1898 is a dramatic illustration of this point. More recently there have been reports of urban-industrial concentration in some of the "sovietized" economies of eastern Europe and central Asia.[2]

These developments constitute a social transformation of which we know little beyond a bare statistical outline. It has been estimated that in 1800 less than 2 per cent of the world's population lived in cities of 100,000 or more inhabitants; by 1850 that proportion had perhaps reached 2.3 per cent;

---

(1) The forthcoming volume by K. Davis and H. Hertz, The Pattern of World Urbanization (Macmillan), will be the first comprehensive study of urban demography since A. F. Weber, The Growth of Cities in the Nineteenth Century (New York, 1899); meanwhile we must be content with disparate evidence culled from official sources. Thus in England and Wales the proportion of economically active men aged 20 plus engaged in agriculture fell from 31.4% in 1841 to 6.1% in 1951: rural population as a whole dropped from a little over 51% to less than 20% in the same period. In the U.S.A. about 89.2% of total population lived in rural areas in 1840, but by 1950 that proportion had fallen to about 36%; the proportion of all persons aged 14 plus employed on farms in 1950 had declined to about 11.7% of total employment.

(2) For a discussion of printed sources and literature, see E. E. Lampard, Urbanization and Economic Growth: A Report to the Committee on Research in Economic History (mimeo, May, 1954), notes to Section 1.

* Reprinted from *Economic Development and Cultural Change*, Vol. 3 (Jan. 1955).

in 1900 it stood about 5.5 per cent; but by 1950 it already exceeded 13 per cent. In view of the great increases in world population over this period, these changing proportions mark an enormous growth in the absolute numbers of contemporary (if not exactly "modern") city-folk.[3]

There are nearly 900 cities in the world today with populations over 100,000; in 1800 there were perhaps 20 of that size. By 1950 there were nearly 50 places with populations exceeding 1,000,000; in 1800 there were none. Nevertheless, of the great cities today "only about half . . . are located in countries whose level of socio-economic development is high enough to approximate that taken for granted by most writers on urbanism."[4] The mere presence of large cities in a region does not, therefore, ensure the existence of a developed economy. But it is no less clear that developed economies do not occur anywhere in the world without the presence of a large population, specialized away from subsistence agriculture, and residing in a "hierarchy" of different-sized cities ranging from one (or more) metropolitan centers at the peak to a broad base of medium and small-sized cities with less than 100,000 inhabitants.[5]

It is in the light of our own recent economic history, and that of the underdeveloped areas, therefore, that students of economic development have raised the question whether there can ever be widespread industrialization without concomitant growth of cities. We know, of course, from this same history that a few large centers may develop in a region without any marked industrialization. Many questions follow from these initial reflections. What has been the relation of urban development to economic growth in the past? Was the rise of the city merely a passive index or itself an active ingredient of industrial development? Did the economic advantages of urban-industrial concentration always outweigh possible disadvantages? Have cities in some way generated a dynamic force making for socio-economic change?

To some writers the connection between industry and the city was, perhaps, too obvious to require further elucidation. Others found a ready explanation at hand. The most common opinion was that cities were passive incidents in the growth and refinement of transportation systems. The great urban explosion of the second half of the 19th century was seen to stem directly from

---

(3) Population Division of the Bureau of Applied Social Research, Columbia Univ., World Urbanization Index; Progress Report (mimeo, March, 1952).

(4) N. Rogoff, "The Universe of Cities: Some Preliminary Considerations," Bureau of Applied Social Research, Columbia Univ. (mimeo, Jan., 1953), gives an account of "the modernization index," a composite of the distribution of cities according to four interconnected variables -- literacy, urbanization, industrialization (non-agriculturism), and *per capita* income.

(5) The term "urban hierarchy" suggests a functional interdependence among cities; A. E. Smailes, "The Urban Hierarchy in England and Wales," Geography, XXIX (1944), 41-51; J. E. Brush, "The Urban Hierarchy in Europe," Geog. Rev., XLIII (1953); also the paper by R. Vining in this number.

improvements in communications which served to concentrate economic opportunities in locations which offered the greatest cost advantages in the procurement, processing, the distribution of goods. According to this view, cities developed at convenient nodal points in an evolving network of more refined transportation services. The revolution in transport transformed a relatively scattered and uniform mode of rudimentary activities into a highly differentiated but closely integrated system of local specialization.[6]

The concept of urbanization as an incidental phase in the growth of communications proved fruitful in many areas of research; but in some respects its very completeness militated against the development of other, supplementary, perspectives. If much was learned about the city, much that was important economically tended to be overlooked. Even the city planners sometimes neglected the "economic base" on which their designs for better communities would ultimately stand or fall. As Gordon Logie put it in a recent study of industry in towns: industry was regarded "as the bad boy of the class to be stood in the corner well away from commerce and housing." In an age of comprehensive, graduated transport services, people even questioned the necessity for living in cities at all. A genuine disgust at urban conditions combined with an ingrained rural romanticism to spread the popular belief that cities were "abnormal" and costly deviants from some natural, more verdant, order of socio-economic growth.[7] Even those who did concern themselves in a more disinterested way often failed to appreciate the intimate and complex relation of urban nucleus to environing economy. To be sure, the great schools of urban geography and sociology at Paris and Chicago did much to elucidate this question, but cooperation from theoretically-minded economists in such endeavors was seldom forthcoming. The work had to be carried on by others -- political reformers, architects, city-planners, demographers, human ecologists, and geographers.

All of this work was valuable but it did not, of course, concern itself with the role or significance of cities in the economy. Location theorists and land economists eventually threw more light on this problem; but they rarely went on to link their discussion of spatial factors to the more complex phenomenon of economic growth. It is significant, perhaps, that, though there are established fields of research in urban sociology, urban geography, municipal government and finance, no branch of economics yet studies the city in a comprehensive way. There are valuable items on the economic growth of particular towns, the whole area of medieval cities has provided a constant challenge to historians, but, to our knowledge, no systematic study has ever been made of the role of

---

(6) F. Ratzel epitomized the process in the phrase: "Der Verkehr wirkt städtebildend," _Anthropogeographie_ (2 Vols., Berlin, 1891), II, 464. See also L. Mecking, _Die Entwicklung der Grossstädte in Hauptländern der Industrie_ (Hamburg, 1949), pp. 21-5. For a critique of this "transportation hypothesis" and its literature since J. G. Kohl, see E. E. Lampard, _op. cit._, Section 1, notes 9 and 10.

(7) G. Logie, _Industry in Towns_ (London, 1952), pp. 19-25; E. T. Peterson, ed., _Cities Are Abnormal_ (Norman, Okla., 1946).

cities in recent economic development.[8] We are still unable to counter the charge that cities are "abnormal" and "costly" with any considered account of the ways in which they have actually facilitated, let alone fostered, progressive economic change.

2. The Present Approach

Though this paper attempts some appraisal of the role of cities in the evolution of the economically advanced areas, it is not written in any confident departmental spirit. If I seemed churlish in commenting on the alleged shortcomings of others, it was not to imply that economic historians now bring some patent formula which enables them to fill existing *lacunae* or resolve every moot issue. On the contrary, any fruitful exploration of the city's relation to economic growth requires cooperation from every worker in the field -- from human ecologists and land economists to keepers of local archives.

I also recognize the special difficulty of generalization in the field of urban history. It has been said, for example, that cities developed in order to increase economic efficiency: to realize the optimal conditions of economy. But cities also provided a range of other social, civic, administrative, and psychological "services" -- each of which posed a different set of optimal conditions. Thus at various times and places cities were centers for religious and secular administration, communications, defense, recreation, and other community purposes in addition to economy. Each city, in fact, serves a variety of social purposes and meets an array of human needs. Yet no two are exactly alike in every respect of their functions; each is a more or less unique product of its individual history and circumstances. A city is a concrete manifestation of general social forces; but its identity stems from being a particular accommodation to them. Each city population attempts to reconcile its needs and purposes with the specific limitations of its culture and environment; limitations of size, resources, position, site, and technique. Our interest lies in formulating the generalities of urbanization in a way which may help in organizing and evaluating the diverse materials available in the history of particular cities.

Sir John Clapham has said that economic history treats the economic aspects of past social institutions and that its methodological distinctiveness among historical studies hinges on "its marked quantitative interests." Something more may be claimed on its behalf. Its materials may be selected and ordered in accordance with analytical schema drawn from economic theory. The economic historian may sometimes be in a position to emphasize potentially relevant factors in socio-economic growth which are not readily treated within the more rigorous confines of economic analysis. *In the present case we are seeking to differentiate urban and non-urban influences relevant to some conceptual framework of economic progress.*

---

(8) The only comprehensive survey of the vast urban literature is E. Pfeil, *Grossstadtforschung* (Bremen, 1950), but this work is weak in respect of non-German material. Also, E. E. Lampard, *op. cit.*, Section 1, Notes 12-16, for a discussion of urban bibliographies and historiography.

In such a reconnaissance as this a certain tactical license must be assumed in order to speed the assault on the final objective. Thus I did not linger long over the vexed question of definitions but proceeded to a survey of diverse materials from sociology, geography, and economics which might bear on our theme of cities and economic development. Two promising lines of approach were revealed. The first was to consider urban-industrial growth as a phase in the history of culture, as a cultural process. The second involved looking at urban-industrial growth as an economic contingency, i.e., as meeting fundamental conditions of economy or as realizing certain economic optima.

The second line of approach is familiar and more or less self-explanatory. The first may cause some difficulty. We will follow E. B. Tylor's celebrated definition of culture as "that complex whole which includes knowledge, belief, art, morals, law, custom, and any other capabilities and habits acquired by man as a member of society."[9] Such a broad formulation is not just another catch-all. It implies that modern urban-industrial society is an integral whole in which modes of life, values, and typical socio-economic relationships form a distinctive cultural pattern. A cultural approach has several advantages for the historian of the modern city. It enables him to treat the rise of an urban-industrial society as a whole, in all its interrelated aspects -- technical, administrative, social, economic, intellectual, etc. He can hope to avoid the worst errors of mechanistic determinism, since technology, ideology, and socio-economic institutions are alike integral parts of the cultural whole. Such an approach seems particularly appropriate in an evolutionary, historical study, for culture is a continuum of many interacting elements -- ideas and behavior, symbols and techniques. It is a process *sui generis*; a culturally ordered and transmitted whole.[10]

I shall first establish criteria of "economic progress" and develop a general hypothesis of the culture process linking modern urban and industrial growth. This argument is then checked against certain theoretical notions from economics and specific evidences from economic history. A final section

---

(9) E. B. Tylor, *Primitive Culture* (5th ed., London, 1928), p. 5. C. F. Ware, ed., *The Cultural Approach to History* (N.Y., 1940), pp. 3-16, speaks of a cultural pattern which "conditions individuals, providing their basic assumptions and their tools of observation and thought, and setting a frame of reference for their living. It determines the forms of institutions, the types of conduct which will be sanctioned . . . Every culture acts selectively . . . stressing some characteristics, discarding others, and molding a culturally acceptable personality."

(10) A. A. Goldenweiser, *History, Psychology, and Culture* (N.Y., 1933), p. 59; L. A. White, *The Science of Culture* (N.Y., 1949), pp. 363-94; C. E. Ayres, *The Industrial Economy: Its Technological Basis and Institutional Destiny* (Boston, 1952), pp. 84-9; idem, *The Theory of Economic Progress* (Chapel Hill, 1944), pp. 187-88; C. Wright Mills and H. Gerth, *Character and Social Structure* (N.Y., 1954), pp. 375-404. But see also J. J. Spengler, "Theories of Socio-Economic Growth," *Problems in the Study of Economic Growth*, Universities Nat. Bur. Com. on Econ. Res. (mimeo, 1949).

suggests some "lessons" from our own experience for the so-called underdeveloped areas.

3. Cities and Economic Growth: The Role of Specialization in Cultural Change

(a) Assumptions regarding economy and economic progress: The word "economy" is commonly used to describe the social system which is concerned with the management and use of a community's resources. It also denotes the more efficient utilization of such resources in producing an output of goods and services. Economy, as Sargant Florence has suggested, takes output for granted and directs attention to costs.[11] Efficiency is the obverse of economy: it takes costs as given and focuses attention on return or output. Improvements in productive efficiency, whereby the physical output from a given input is increased, are held to enhance the community's potential for economic welfare.

Thus we find that real national output in the U.S.A. increased five-fold between 1900 and 1950, while population doubled in the same period. Output per head increased two and one-half times but the actual human effort expended -- as measured by total man-hours of labor input -- increased by only 80 per cent. Hence we conclude that the immense gains of the period reflect a fast-growing productive efficiency, or "unit efficiency of effort," in the American economy.[12]

Rising productive efficiency has, in fact, been the mainstay of material advances achieved in all the industrial areas of western Europe and North America. Increases in output per man-hour of work (the productivity increment) are generally recognized as the principal source of higher living standards. But it is not enough that goods and services be produced in greater magnitude and with greater efficiency; they must also be consumed and give greater satisfaction to their consumers. Any proper definition of "economic progress" requires that enhanced productivity be realized and sustained in higher average levels of consumption, after allowing for the maintenance of existing capital and adequate new formation.[13]

Some part of the amelioration of conditions in economically advancing areas is, of course, attributable to increases in the size of the labor force and the stock of capital. The major portion, however, has probably stemmed from increases in productive efficiency which, other things being equal, govern the rate of change in stocks of labor and capital. Moreover, of all the influences affecting productivity in advanced areas, the principal consists in improvements

---

(11) P. S. Florence, The Logic of British and American Industry (London, 1953), pp. 48-55.

(12) F. C. Mills, Productivity and Economic Progress (New York, 1952), pp. 2-5.

(13) H. S. Davis, Economic Progress (Philadelphia, 1947), pp. 146-49; E. E. Lampard, op. cit., Section 2, notes 6 and 7.

in productive technique and organization which have the progressive effect of reducing the real costs of enlarged outputs.[14] Given the distribution of resources, the quantity and quality of capital equipment appear to determine the real cost of any output and, therefore, the possibility of progress.

These few considerations regarding means and sources of economic progress furnish an essential framework for the study of urbanization and economic growth. They provide a rough yardstick against which to measure the effect of changes in technique and organization. But how are such changes when identified as "improvements" related to the cultural phenomenon of city growth? The theory of economic progress as such throws little light on that subject. It mostly ignores social-institutional factors and is generally oblivious to considerations of "space" or area. Nevertheless, it does call attention to the dynamic influence of techno-organization itself.[15] We must therefore examine how such factors and considerations contribute to improvements in the level of techno-organization. We must enquire, for example, whether there are features of urban socio-economic structure and function which may affect such improvements. Are there features common to both technical and locational change which may link industrialization to the growth of cities? If so, in what ways do urban situations differ from non-urban situations in these respects? If particular urban sites and situations facilitate change, do all cities equally generate such a force, and, if not, why do they differ? Such questions bring us to the heart of our problem, but before they can be answered, it is necessary to look more closely at the cultural process of techno-organizational change.

(b) Specialization and improvements in technique: Technological developments are events in the evolution of cultures. They are an outcome of changes which, in greater or lesser degree, pervade every area of cultural experience, namely, innovation and emulation. The mechanical inventions of the last two centuries, for example, are a class of innovations representing new syntheses of technical and intellectual elements made available in the cultural stream of western Europe. As one recent writer put it: inventions are "those imaginative combinations which men make of previously existing elements in the cultural heritage and which have emergent novelty as combinations."[16] But for novelties to acquire any great socio-economic significance, they must, in effect, cease to be novelties. They must become generalized in, and characteristic of, their particular techno-organizational system.

The history of industrialism in Europe and North America vividly illustrates these processes at work. It shows the importance of antecedent elements

---

(14) On the special importance of organizational as opposed to technological changes, e.g., new lay-outs, types of line production, multiple work-shifts, etc., see W. Baldamus, "Mechanization, Utilization and Size of Plant," Econ. Jnl., LXIII (1953), pp. 66-9.

(15) This is not to imply that the technological sphere of culture is autonomous or self-determining.

(16) B. Barber, Science and the Social Order (Glencoe, Ill., 1952), p. 194; also the opening chapters of A. P. Usher, A History of Mechanical Inventions (2nd ed., Cambridge, Mass., 1954).

in every "novel" technique: it emphasizes social-institutional factors which make an effective demand for their exploitation, e.g., the ideological and institutional concomitants of widespread capital accumulation. It helps explain the growing interaction of science, the useful arts, and economic institutions during the last three centuries. Finally, it throws light on the intense division and subdivision of labor which occurred in all areas affected by the industrial revolution. In short, industrialization was a phase of cultural history in which certain communities (and not others) became marked by an increasing differentiation of economic functions, skills, instruments, institutions, and regions.[17] It was this ongoing specialization among men and machines which gradually transformed the techno-organizational base of society and, with it, the spatial order of economic activities. Specialization provides an essential link between the technical and spatial conditions of economic progress. It holds an important clue to the nature and creative significance of urban-industrial growth.

(c) Specialization and the economy of resources and effort: I have implied that the division of labor is culturally determined but, from Adam Smith to the present day, most economic writers have explained it as having a purely mechanical relation to "the extent of the market." They have held that the degree of specialization at any time is a function of the size of the market; it depends on the volume of goods which the market can absorb, since the possibility of exchange is a necessary preliminary to any specialization.[18] There is much to be said for this formulation. Markets have certainly exerted a powerful influence on the potential division of labor. Constriction of trade or the prohibition of exchange have slowed the rate at which novel techniques could be adopted: changes in taste or shifts in demand have likewise created dissatisfaction with existing modes of supply and prompted innovation. All this is true; but to argue that A conditions B is not to establish A as the adequate cause of B.

The old dictum regarding the division of labor and the extent of the market was, to say the least, misleading in its simple finality. It repeatedly led economists to ignore or underestimate the "inner dynamisms" of specialization as a cultural process. For example, on one level of culture -- that of technique -- research may come to have a greater influence than markets on the course of specialization. On another level -- that of socio-economic institutions -- there may be strong inducements to specialization which themselves create wider markets.[19]

---

(17) J. A. Hobson, The Evolution of Modern Capitalism (London, 1926 ed.), pp. 77-80; G. N. Clark, "Early Capitalism and Inventions," Econ. Hist. Rev., VI (1936), 149-53; J. D. Bernal, Science and Industry in the Nineteenth Century (London, 1954); B. Barber, op. cit., pp. 52-9, 191-206.

(18) A. Smith, Wealth of Nations (Cannan ed., London, 1904), pp. 6-14; G. Schmoller, "Die Thatsachen der Arbeitstheilung," Jahrbuch für Gesetzgebung, Verwaltung, und Volkswirtschaft, XIII (1889), 95-128; K. Bücher, Industrial Evolution (N.Y., 1901), pp. 282-314; L. Deschesne, "La spécialization et ses conséquences," Revue d'économie politique XV (1901), 155-62; F. von Wieser, Social Economics (tr. N.Y., 1927), pp. 310-14.

(19) C. E. Ayres, The Industrial Economy, pp. 88-91. Speaking of communities

Yet such heresies concerning process are not incompatible with much that is sound in orthodox accounts of specialization. The division of labor, for example, was always regarded as progressive when it contributed to productive efficiency. By concentrating a limited stock of energy or talent on one operation, each worker acquired greater skill and dexterity. Specialization along these lines fostered a more intensive use of tools and broke down all but the most complex muscular tasks to levels of simplicity where they could be mechanized. As a consequence, resources are saved for other employments and, to that extent, the productive potential of a community is raised. In theory, at least, each factor tends to find work for which it is best suited; for which it earns the highest return. The object of specialization, therefore, is a greater economy of time, effort, and resources -- the sources of higher productivity and material advance.

This emphasis on the "object" of specialization throws important light on the inherent dynamisms of the cultural process of division of labor. The very circumstances and incentives which make for specialization in the first place will, other things being equal, tend to foster its cumulative development. Specialization will thrive best where it is most developed. Specialization tends to breed specialization. It develops furthest where it is most prized; where socio-economic institutions are best adapted to its forms.

There is, as was suggested above, another sense in which "inner dynamisms" of specialization generate new specialization. For example, the growth of science in the last century had a potent "specializing" effect. A. N. Whitehead gave it the deceptively simple title -- the invention of "the method of invention." As a consequence of scientific advances, technical improvement has become, in part, the function of a self-motivating, self-controlling, technique called "research" which may be carried on without regard for the market.

In an urban-industrial society there is likely to be both wider opportunity and greater necessity for specialization than in earlier, more relaxed, modes of existence. In the city, for example, to specialize is to enjoy scarcity value, whereas in the country it is usually acquiescence rather than initiative which pays. An increasing rivalry for place and preferment under urban conditions puts higher premiums on more specialized roles, functions, and instruments.[20] Some may even make a specialty of "anti-specialism." Nevertheless, the specialist, the expert, the man with know-how and know-who, becomes a commanding figure in communities which have the income to buy his services. Professional achievement no less than private ambition impels the specialist to seek higher returns and greater security (scarcity value) in deeper, albeit narrower, ranges of specialism. It is no longer a matter of taste or inclination, but a condition of survival and fulfillment; a rule in the urban success game, a cultural norm. We might generalize and say that, in the

---

with an industrial background, S. G. Checkland writes, "change seems to stem from technology almost as an independent variable," "English Provincial Cities," Econ. Hist. Rev., VI (New Series) (1953), 200.

(20) G. Simmel, "Die Grossstadt und das Geistesleben," in Th. Petermann, ed., Die Grossstadt (Dresden, 1903), pp. 187-206.

socio-psychological atmosphere of metropolitan existence, there is an inherent inducement, a "built-in" tendency, to specialize. The effort of entrenched groups and individuals to limit entrance in their particular fields is some measure of the drive to, and expectation from, specialization.

Thus the process is cumulative and dynamic, working at many interactive levels of particular cultures. Vast technical, economic, and emotional resources are invested in its behalf in every advancing economy. The outcome is always a more complex, potentially richer, more efficient order of life. Given the tendency to seek material advance through the unlimited application of science and technology to available resources and there is no end to this process of economic specialization. The ultimate outcome need not concern us here except to note that differentiation of functions and roles in a community "committed" to specialization raises a demand for more comprehensive and systematic coordination, if the object of greater economy is to be reached. Much of the saving realized in specialization, however, may later be used in developing new modes of socio-economic behavior and institutional structure to preserve the whole as a going concern, e.g., bureaucratization.

(d) Ecological consequences of economic specialization: If specialization makes for higher productivity over time, it also tends to concentrate productive activities over space. It is a dynamic process which transforms the spatial order of production and distribution. In pre-industrial societies, where factors are relatively unspecialized, economic functions and organizations tend to be uniform, simple, and scattered -- very much according to circumstances of geography.[21] The small urban nuclei which often develop in such societies are essentially service centers of an agrarian way of life. The services they provide have to do with religious and political administration, defence, the facilitation of mercantile exchange. To be sure, towns are sometimes centers for craftsmen, but the bulk of so-called primary and secondary activities remain undifferentiated in space and are tied to the "self-sufficient" hinterland where the mass of population perforce resides. Specialization revolutionizes the spatial pattern of economic activity and increasingly undermines the older social structure in so far as it is inseparable from a relaxed rural-agrarian base (the village and small market town).

The increasing specialization of functions, which marks an industrializing economy, imposes a greater measure of interdependence among the differentiated parts. Sometimes the interdependence is indirect (social) in the sense that everyone in the community now sinks or swims together. Individuals, firms, industries, whole areas rely on the general prosperity for their particular welfare and are more closely tied by some "common bond of stable

---

(21) S. Kuznets, "National Income and Industrial Structure," Econometrica, XVII (1949), Supplement, describes a pre-industrial economy as one "in which a large part of production is within the family and rural community, a minor share of resources is devoted to advanced industrial production, and a minor part of its population lives in cities." An industrial economy is one "dominated by business enterprises, using advanced industrial techniques and ordinarily with a large proportion of its population in large cities."

interest." Direct interdependence, on the other hand, is ecological: it arises from the necessity of overcoming structural and environmental frictions which may impede the smooth, efficient, operation of differentiated parts. As a rule, the more specialized a function, the greater its dependence on other functions to keep it regularly and fully employed. Operational interdependence of this type requires more comprehensive cooperation and coordination of functions and areas, giving rise to more complex, "round-about" patterns of production.[22]

This ecological interdependence is essentially a centripetal force. To reduce operational imperfections and space frictions (which, from an economic standpoint, represent costs), interdependent specialisms tend to draw together and "link" in more integrated local sequences. Differential and complementary production requirements modify the geographical distribution of economic activity as greater advantages attach to local specialization. Production is increasingly concentrated in areas adjacent to workable deposits of coal, iron, and non-ferrous ores, and at more accessible sites along the primary routes of trade; larger volumes of food, fuels, and other budgetary materials swell the burgeoning channels of commerce. The older balance between agricultural and industrial, rural and urban, populations is disturbed and regions of specialized activity emerge. From the strictly economic standpoint, local concentration is only limited by the physical distribution of resources and the costs of surmounting intermediate space (a composite of transfer charges and site rentals). It is this marked operational-structural attachment -- what J. A. Hobson called the "integrative tendency" -- which is at the root of urban-industrial concentration. The growth of the modern city and the march of the industrial revolution are joint products of a single cultural strand -- specialization.

The relation of functional specialization to the integrative tendency is seldom stated in this bald fashion: it doubtless needs some qualification as simplifying assumptions are removed. Nevertheless, its recognition is essential in a cultural-historical approach to the industrial city. There is, to be sure, a real sense in which specialization and integration can be represented as opposing forces, since differentiation often involves the disintegration of tasks formerly performed by one person, machine, or plant. But, by our definition, the specialist is one who provides a narrow range of goods or services; his specialty only achieves its profound economic significance as it is incorporated with, or absorbed in, the work of other specialists. We use the word "integrated" here to denote the fact that specialized operations must be fitted together, juxtaposed and joined, if the objectives of specialization -- greater economy of resources and effort -- are to be realized. It is precisely the task of an

---

(22) Cooperation and coordination not only transform spatial relations between economic functions but also foster "vertical," bureaucratic, structures of control. A. W. Hawley, *Human Ecology: A Theory of Community Structure* (N.Y., 1950), pp. 182-203, 371-404. L. Deschesne, *op. cit.*, p. 162: "It (specialization) increases the interdependence of the diverse factors co-operating in a common production." F. von Wieser, *op. cit.*, pp. 314-15, characterizes the division of town and country as "the historical result of the articulation of labor." See also G. Schmoller, *op. cit.*, pp. 95-6; R. D. McKenzie, *The Metropolitan Community* (N.Y., 1933), pp. 50-65.

"economic system" to achieve this felicitous orchestration of diverse themes with whatever instruments a culture makes available.

Specialization of functions makes inevitably for specialization of areas: it prompts a territorial division of labor between town and country and differentiates town from town. Areal differentiation is, in fact, the spatial corollary of functional specialization and logically serves the same end -- economy. The closer integration of interdependent functions means that less of a community's limited stock of energy and material need to be devoted to overcoming the various disutilities of distance. Local concentration of specialized activities is thus an ecological response to certain technical and cost considerations which impel a more selective use of space, a more efficient pattern of land-use. In varying time and degree, technical limitations on power transmission, the state of the arts, the linking of processes, more effective communications, better procurement of materials and skills, closer control over business functions, readier access to markets, etc., have all transformed the spatial pattern of economic activity. From a socio-ecological standpoint, city growth is simply the concentration of differentiated but functionally-integrated specialisms in rational locales. The modern city is a mode of social organization which furthers efficiency in economic activity.

4. The Economics of Urban Growth

(a) The logic of space economy: location analysis and land economics: The cultural approach to urban-industrial growth sketched in the preceding pages is not inconsistent with certain approaches of economic theory. Thus the effort involved in surmounting spatial frictions in the economy can be visualized as a sum of physical inputs which represent a charge on scarce resources. Resources utilized in overcoming such imperfections are, by definition, no longer available for alternative uses: the "mobility" of factors and products always involves some cost contingency. In the interests of economy, therefore, "distance inputs" should be minimized, except where their substitution for other inputs brings a higher return. These spatial problems of economy are most readily treated with the techniques of location analysis and land economics and, as Walter Isard has shown, such an approach adds an important dimension to conventional production theory: it focuses attention squarely on the spatial aspects of economic activity.[23]

The optimum location for any enterprise is determined by striking a balance of all possible sites in terms of differences to be achieved in operating cost (including site rent) plus differences in transfer cost. A rational choice of site should represent the most advantageous locus for the given type of activity in the light of all existing business conditions and prospects. Similarly, consumers should locate themselves so as to minimize the proportion of their income spent in the "consumption" of transport services and

---

(23) W. Isard, "The General Theory of Location and Space Economy," Quart. Jnl. Econ., LXIII (1949), pp. 476-506. For a brief review of location literature and a caution regarding the role of transport in locational change, see E. E. Lampard, op. cit., Section 1, Notes 9 and 10, Section 3, Note 2.

other "distance inputs." The indiscriminate siting of production and consumption may result in charges on the economy no less serious than the employment of wasteful production-functions. Thus, if all producers and all consumers were located in one place, maximum efficiency of location would be achieved; no resources or effort need be devoted to surmounting disutilities of space.

But the actual location of activities at any time, like the level of technical efficiency itself, is deeply rooted in past history and present circumstances. The pattern never approaches the high order of rationality sketched in the previous paragraph. Nevertheless, the geographical distribution of activity is rational to the extent that, given the natural disposition of materials and the level of the arts, all output is secured at a minimum cost to the community's limited stock of resources and energy. The rationality of an economy, as Professor Hoover has shown, "can only be understood in terms of the interrelations among units of production."[24]

In a culture which emphasizes the virtue of economic competition, there will be a continuing tendency for producers to scatter or concentrate according to the principle of minimum cost. Conventional production theory has led many to suppose that economies of scale and mobility of factors would eventually bring all activities into great centers, but the persistence of small-scale plants and widely dispersed towns is not necessarily a token of irrationality. It may merely indicate, for example, that transfer costs to scattered markets cannot immediately be offset by economies of large plant operations. Similarly, as we shall argue later, the clustering of smaller plants in particular localities yielding "external" economies may provide a viable alternative in some lines to the highly centralized large-scale operation yielding mostly "internal" economies.

From time to time the economic historian notices substantial changes or shifts in the location of activities, changes which often defy simple explanation in terms of comparative cost. Many short, medium, and long-run influences determine these historical movements: the growth of population, the depletion or discovery of resources, the force of technical improvement, alterations in the level and distribution of income, the course of the trade cycle, etc. But few of these currents work in the same direction simultaneously or with equal force. The most that can be said is that countervailing tendencies in an advancing economy should evidence a more rational distribution of activities over time. There is a presumption that the more salient shifts in the history of economically advanced areas will mark responses to the "pulls" of progress. Notwithstanding difficulties in the measurement of locational change over long periods, studies from at least two advanced areas, Great Britain and the United States, broadly confirm this expectation. The long-run trend has been towards local concentration.[25]

---

(24) E. M. Hoover, "The Location of Economic Activity," in H. F. Williamson, ed., The Growth of the American Economy (N. Y., 1944), pp. 580-85; C. Woodbury, ed., The Future of Cities and Urban Redevelopment (Chicago, 1953), pp. 118-43.

(25) E. M. Hoover, The Location of Economic Activity (N.Y., 1948), pp. 145-85; A. J. Wensley and P. S. Florence, "Recent Industrial Concentration,"

Robert Murray Haig was perhaps the first economist to adapt location analysis to a general theory of urbanization. In two articles published during the mid-twenties he offered an explanation of urban growth and a rationale of the internal economic arrangement of cities. He argued that improvements in communication services had reduced the time and cost involved in factor movements and had increased the over-all capacity of the system. These considerations led him to develop the model of a "frictionless" distribution of economic activities.[26]

As Haig saw it, "(t)he most favored spots are those from which the richest resources can be tapped with the lowest transportation costs." In an industrializing economy, moreover, a diminishing proportion of the labor force is required for primary production and a correspondingly larger proportion "is under no compulsion to live 'on the land.'" But if this "economically footfree" population is to earn a living, it must reside in places where it can obtain work; in places where opportunities exist in manufacturing, distribution, and related business functions and where consumption goods can be supplied in quantity at lowest cost. "Instead of explaining why so large a portion of the population is found in urban areas," declared Haig, "one must give reasons why the portion is not even greater. The question is changed from 'Why live in the city?' to 'Why not live in the city?'" All activities apart from basic food-raising, extraction, and long-distance transport should remove to the nearest metropolis: there could be no economic reason for anyone to live or work far from the great city.

Haig knew this to be an extreme position, yet he meant it to exhibit the rational possibilities of a territorial division of labor based on the tested principles of location analysis. Despite all qualifications required by the facts of life, his argument showed that cities were, from a standpoint of transfer efficiency, optimum points for production and consumption. While conceding certain diseconomies and "consumption advantages of non-urban locations" in particular cases, Haig made urban-industrial concentration the first premise of his spatial logic.[27]

The internal structure of urban land-use was likewise conditioned by the controlling circumstance of spatial frictions: the physical task of surmounting imperfections at minimum cost. Within the city, however, transfer charges were only one of two principal friction costs: the other was site rental. All urban enterprisers must therefore take account of the costs of assembling their materials and merchandise and the costs of their employees' journey to work. The retailer must reckon with an additional factor, namely, the travel costs of his customers who come from all around to shop. It was the convenience of customers which, according to Haig, looms largest among

---

Rev. Econ. Studies, VII (1940), 139-58; A. C. Hobson, "The Great Industrial Belt," Econ. Jnl., LXI (1951), 562-76.

(26) R. M. Haig's articles from the Quart. Jnl. Econ. (1926) were reprinted in Major Factors in Metropolitan Growth and Arrangement (N.Y., 1927)

(27) R. M. Haig, op. cit., pp. 21-2, 37-9.

considerations affecting retail locations and which explains why high rents are paid for the most accessible sites. It also helps explain why modern department stores sometimes seek locations in suburban sections along the perimeters of great cities.

Haig concluded that every businessman should seek the site for which the sum of his friction costs was lowest. In the absence of "artificial" restrictions, he thought that competition would ensure that the activity which capitalizes most on the locational advantages of a site would occupy it; that which exploits the locational character of the site most efficiently. In last analysis, the residents of the community, the customers, determine the pattern of land-use, the "grain" of the city, through the evaluation of site-attributes expressed in their purchases. Thus the most efficient lay-out for a city would be one in which the total of land-values was lowest; efficiency being inversely proportional to the sum of all costs of friction.[28]

Haig's contribution to the logic of space-economy was immense. He developed a theory which showed urban growth to be part of a great rationalizing process in the industrial society and he indicated some of the obstacles and frictions which frustrate the realization of more rational patterns of land-use. The economic historian of cities must be eternally grateful to Haig since much of his time is spent in tracing divergences between economic logic and historical fact. Sometimes the situations which offend theoretical logic, however, have what Sargant Florence called "a practical logic" of their own.[29] For example, the theory of maximizing returns at minimum cost indicates an economy of large-scale operations in large plants, but in practice the logic must often be modified "by reason of technical, distribution, and risk factors. The facts often diverge even from this practical logic, a divergence attributable either to a logical producer having to cope with an illogical situation, or to his own illogic, or both."

Yet when all qualifications on rationality are admitted, the evidence of economic history affirms the continuing vitality of localized concentrations of industry within an expanding economy. What then are these potent economies of urbanization which tend to overcome all but the most stubborn of geographic and social circumstances? Why hasn't some principle of diminishing returns to concentration compelled a drastic decentralization and a decline in the size of our leading industrial centers? Why, on the other hand, isn't everything by now completely centralized according to the Haig model?

It is precisely because urban sites offer an array of "scale"-type economies almost regardless of actual plant-size that concentration endures. For example, better transfer facilities, broader and more flexible labor markets, numerous auxiliary business services like banking, insurance, brokerage, utilities, or fire and police protection. To these may be added

---

(28) *Ibid.*, pp. 43-4, especially "Economic Basis of Zoning."

(29) See R. U. Ratcliff, "The Dynamics of Efficiency in the Locational Distribution of Urban Activities," Columbia Univ. Bicentennial Conference I (Jan., 1954, mimeo), pp. 5-14. P. S. Florence, *op. cit.*, pp. 92-7, 339.

increasing returns to larger operations, various economies of integration (used here in the sense of control), bulk purchase and handling, complementary factor requirements, greater density and frequency of customers: in short, most of the advantages of scale-economy and greater specialization.[30]

The fact that many activities, especially those of a service nature, have low "coefficients of localization" does not mean that urban incentives have lessened, as such a low coefficient does not indicate that the function is better situated in a non-urban locale. We find that bakeries, building supplies, road trucking, and banking have a characteristically wide geographical distribution in many of the advanced economies. Yet none of them could properly be classed as a "rural" activity, nor does the smallness of their particular operation preclude membership in a large-scale organization, e.g., the joint-stock banks in Britain. Similarly, iron, steel, and shoe industries tend to integrate in certain localities, while others, such as the branches of electrical engineering, scatter and differentiate with population itself. Wherever income is created on a sufficient scale locally, such activities will thrive, despite the fact that more specialized forms of the same activities may favor a central or metropolitan location. It can be said, therefore, that either through the nature of their product or the character of their materials, some activities remain tied to relatively scattered sources or dispersed markets.[31]

Broadly speaking, we can say that "economies of urbanization rest on the same basic principles as those of the individual producing unit: multiples, massing of reserves, and bulk transactions."[32] Diminishing returns to concentration merely set some limit to any particular agglomeration, to the economies derived from some individual site. In most areas diminishing returns do not seem to have affected the long-run trend to urbanization.[33] Large cities, in fact, grow larger (on the perimeter).

(b) External economies: the economies of urban atmosphere: The study of locational changes makes an important contribution to our knowledge of the city's role in economic development. It establishes the broad rationalizing effect of concentration and, to that extent, supports the hypothesis that urbanization of economic activities tends to facilitate progress. Yet it does not develop the full implications contained in some of the axioms of location theory; implications which, we believe, bear on the "creative force" of cities. Using

---

(30) E. M. Hoover, *op. cit.*, pp. 116-41; P. S. Florence, *op. cit.*, pp. 85-8.

(31) The coefficient of localization is based on the deviation of the distribution of workers in industries or areas from the distribution over the whole industry or country; A. J. Wensley and P. S. Florence, *op. cit.*, pp. 139-55. Also P. S. Florence, *Investment, Location, and Size of Plant* (Cambridge, 1948), Tables IVB, IVN.

(32) E. M. Hoover, *op. cit.*, pp. 120-21.

(33) P. S. Florence, "Economic Advantages and Disadvantages of Metropolitan Concentration," Columbia Univ. Bicentennial Conference I (Jan. 1954, mimeo).

ideas which have since become common ground among location analysts, Alfred Marshall was able to provide a somewhat broader perspective on the role of cities.

In Book IV of the Principles, and again in Industry and Trade, Marshall emphasized that not all gains from concentration were attributable to large-scale operations. Some additional savings, he thought, were derived from "the aggregate volume of production of the kind in the neighborhood." To the "internal" economies of scale (ultimately derived from managerial capacity and the volume of business), he added certain "external" economies which stem from the "industrial atmosphere" of individual towns (he had Sheffield and Solingen in mind) and "yield gratis to the manufacturers . . . great advantages that are not easily to be had elsewhere."[34]

Thus far his views do not differ markedly from those of the location analysts. If less rigorously formulated, however, his statement is the more evocative; he goes on to suggest that the "atmosphere" or socio-economic structure of towns generates a powerful force for innovation and change.

Two things had especially impressed Marshall as he considered the changing location of industry and commerce in the Britain of his day. (1) He noted that once an industry develops in an area, it is prone to stay there a long time -- "so great are the advantages which people following the same trade get from near neighborhood to one another." (2) The existence of strong local roots seemed a powerful stimulus to innovation and change:

> "Good work is rightly appreciated, inventions, and improvements in machinery, in processes and the general organization of business have their merits promptly discussed; if one man starts a new idea, it is taken up by others and combined with suggestions of their own; and thus become the source of further new ideas. And presently subsidiary trades grow up in the neighborhood, supplying it with implements and materials, organizing its traffic, and in many ways conducing to the economy of its materials."[35]

Each new synthesis, so to speak, becomes a potential matrix of a new development.

Marshall was likewise one of the first to hint at a theory of local transformation. As the old center continued to beget or attract other manufactures and related trading activities, there was increased competition for central sites, since "contacts" were essential to the conduct of modern commerce. The newer factories tended to drift to the outskirts or even move to adjoining towns where land was cheaper and producers might enjoy higher returns to

---

(34) A. Marshall, Principles of Economics (2nd ed., London, 1891), pp. 325-32; idem, Industry and Trade (London, 1919), pp. 284-87.

(35) Ibid.

scale. The whole urban district thus offered a continuing opportunity for further adaptation and specialization; "the mysteries of the trade . . . are as it were in the air, and children may learn them unconsciously." Meanwhile, the predominance of artisans in the town center gradually gives way before the swarming of clerks, salesmen, and wholesalers. Despite the onset of maturity, the dynamism and creativeness of old centers remained impressive. In face of vast technical changes, the old industrial towns maintained vitality and adaptability, quickly turned to account new departures in technique, and often attracted "new shrewd energy" to their midst.[36]

Marshall did not, of course, formulate a theory of urban-industrial growth. The gleanings of his wisdom gathered here are scattered through two major books and three decades or more of careful observation and reflection. Yet his remains the boldest, most imaginative, account of urban influences to appear in the literature. Unfortunately little has been done to test his generalities with empirical studies. For example, the putative relation between "external" economies of atmosphere and the emergence of novel technique has never been adequately explored. Indeed, the whole subject of "external" economies remains a rather large "empty box."

Some have argued that "external" economies are a will-o'-the-wisp affecting "a very small proportion of the total costs of an industry," and therefore have no significant influence on the rate of return (diminution of cost). This may be true in part but it does not permit our writing off the strategic importance of such a proportion, however minute it may be in comparison with total costs. Conceivably, the "external" economies might just provide the competitive difference between two or more locations with otherwise identical procurement and transfer costs.

E. A. G. Robinson made a useful distinction between mobile and immobile "external" economies: between those accruing to whole industries and those confined to localized plants or firms.[37] From the history of Lancashire's cotton industry he inferred that the proportion of "external" economies "of the international mobile type" is steadily increasing at the expense of the immobile variety. In other words, the economies of local concentration were to this extent lessened and the optimum size of local industry correspondingly reduced. Yet, he implied that the newer, more remote, subconcentrations of cotton manufacture, such as those in Central India, were likely to remain dependent on the older Lancashire concentration "for developments of machinery, of techniques, and of fundamental research . . ." If these three contingencies alone exhausted the influence of centers with immobile "external" economies, they would still be of great significance for progress. A backward area developing certain segments of its manufactures for the first time may well find the absence of such economies a serious handicap, and almost certainly a drain on limited capital resources.[38]

---

(36) Ibid.

(37) E. A. G. Robinson, The Structure of Competitive Industry (Cambridge, 1931), pp. 140-44.

(38) W. J. Baumol, Welfare Economics and the Theory of the State (Cambridge,

The case for immobile economies receives further force from the study of their influence on plant-size. Some local economies even outweigh advantages derived from lower transfer costs in procurement and distribution. Small and medium-sized undertakings prove viable in certain local situations and are not impelled towards larger, more centralized, operations. Such economies are occasionally decisive influences in location. For example, Sargant Florence has spoken of their significance in regard to

> "the possibilities of division of labor between plants in 'linked' processes, products and service industries. The advantage of full use of specialist plants can be combined with proximity. Several specialized plants, if close enough together, may have much the same economies as the separate departments of a large plant . . . a given scale of production by several small firms will undoubtedly offer more points where the powerful profit incentive is applied than a large plant with a salaried servant of a joint stock company in charge."

Thus "external" economies arising from special features of localized concentrations of industry may have a critical importance for the general profitability and development of business enterprise.[39]

Allyn Young once postulated a significant connection between higher returns from specialization (internal and external economies thereof) and general economic progress. He noticed that, with every increase in industrial differentiation, new opportunities for specialization occurred and new advantages attached to it. Though elasticities of demand and supply varied for each line, there was a real sense in which new divisions of labor in one sector might stimulate developments in related sectors. Little was ever done to put these bold ideas to the test, but, in so far as such theorists as Marshall, Young, and Jones attributed an "external" character to so many of the economies of expansion,[40] there seems justification for insisting on some investigation of the urban hypothesis. There is ample evidence in the study of locational trends in Britain, Germany, and the United States to suggest that the economic advantages of urban-industrial concentration still outweigh the sum of the known disadvantages.

(c) Economic progress and the growth of tertiary activities: In earlier sections I suggested that the progressive differentiation of work which underlay urban-industrial growth had proven a powerful stimulus to tertiary activities. As technical advances augmented productivity in agriculture and manufacturing,

---

Mass., 1952), pp. 165-66.

(39) P. S. Florence, The Logic of British and American Industry, pp. 85-8; West Midland Group, Conurbation, Ch. 8; E. E. Lampard, op. cit., Section 3, Note 20.

(40) A. A. Young, "Increasing Returns and Economic Progress," Econ. Jnl., XXXVIII (1928), 529-39; G. T. Jones, Increasing Return (Cambridge, 1933), pp. 5-27, 245-48; A. G. B. Fisher, "Capital and the Growth of Knowledge," Econ. Jnl., XLIII (1933), 379-81.

a growing proportion of the labor force was freed to engage in other so-called "tertiary" occupations -- defined by difference as "all other activities producing a non-material output." More recently, the development of self-service merchandising, automatic elevators, adding machines and computators, and the craze of "do it yourself" gadgets, marks a tendency for technical change to invade labor's preserve in the "service" industries.

But if some such transfer of workers into the tertiary area had not occurred in the past, the worst prophecies of the early machine-breakers might have been fulfilled. The numbers of technologically-displaced persons would soon have hobbled labor-saving innovation and lessened the desirability of "progress." That our society has never been wholly disenchanted with "progress" is due, in large part, to the proliferation of tertiary employments. The shift from agriculture and manufacturing has no doubt been painful for those caught in times of rapid techno-organizational change, but the great increases in wealth accruing to communities from their enhanced productive capacity has provided both a cushion and a rationale for the change. It is precisely this prospect of greater productivity which draws people of underdeveloped areas towards the industrial revolution. One hopes that the social costs of industrialization will not prove a rude awakening.

A. G. B. Fisher has described the process in this way: as wealth increases after an indeterminate point, new demands are made effective in the direction of products requiring relatively _less capital_ and relatively _more labor_ as compared with other products. In short, the higher a community's income, the greater the demand for tertiary products. In its (over)simplest form, the argument may be stated: _economic progress is accompanied by a rise in the percentage of the labor force occupied in tertiary production._[41]

Despite the many difficulties in definition which complicate the statistical task of measuring tertiary employment, there is a volume of general evidence from the history of advanced economies to support this hypothesis. For example, it appears that the larger an individual's income above subsistence, the higher will be his marginal propensity to consume such tertiary items as travel, education, amusement, domestic service, and even research. Similarly, the marginal propensity to consume tertiary products at all levels of income exceeds the average propensity. Progress produces large, albeit unequal additions to income at most levels of society, and it is broadly true that all levels, except the very lowest, tend to increase their consumption of tertiary items correspondingly. Tertiary production, moreover, appears to have furnished an increasing share of the total value of national output in the more advanced economies; while labor productivity has risen more sharply in primary and secondary occupations than in tertiary. Hence, despite the difficulties of measurement, we conclude that most tertiary items have a higher income-elasticity of demand than most non-tertiary items; and that technical development has proceeded, at least until very recently, at a slower rate in tertiary than in other sectors. The expansion of specialized tertiary employments thus seems a useful index of a progressive economy, though it is by no

---

(41) A. G. B. Fisher, _loc. cit._, pp. 379-85; idem, _Economic Progress and Social Security_ (London, 1946), p. 57.

means certain that the experience of underdeveloped societies must necessarily follow this exact pattern.[42]

If the growth of tertiary employment may be regarded as symptomatic of progress, it is significant that it also points in the direction of the city. Primary activities are best located where resources abound; near fertile farm land, in great forests, or on rich ocean banks. Secondary production is most advantageous in or about industrial centers, or at points variously distant -- depending on frictions of bulk or perishability -- from suppliers of materials and consumers of products. The area of tertiary activities, however, is even more confined in that its product is closely tied to a consuming population which is overwhelmingly urban or suburban. As Colin Clark has suggested, the city is the only feasible locus for the mass of specialized servicing.

The proportion which tertiary bears to total employment and income in a locality provides a useful tool for the study of city growth and size. At a given average level of income, a population might wish to consume a variety of tertiary services, but if no urban center exists in the vicinity, it is unlikely that people will be able to meet their expectations. They must do without them or make a periodic pilgrimage at personal cost to the nearest regional center. Clark argued that "(a) city cannot be said to be of optimum size unless it can provide its own inhabitants and the inhabitants of the surrounding region with at any rate all but the most specialized . . . services."[43] His argument shows that the "proper" amount of service employment in a locality should vary with the income of that locality. Though accurate figures on urban income were not available, he took some localareas given in the United States, British, Canadian, and Queensland census tables in order to compare numbers employed in service industries per million dollars of "regional income" with the national average in each case. When the volume of tertiary employment per million dollars of local income fell below the national average, the size of the central city in the locality was adjudged below the economic optimum. It could not attain sufficient specialization to give the area the range of services which, on the basis of income, the population would wish to purchase.

Where city population ranged between 100,000 and 200,000, inhabitants of the immediate vicinity might expect an adequate array of commercial services. For most other activities -- education, domestic help, government, "body and clothing" services, etc. -- a somewhat smaller central population would suffice. We need not be concerned with these details, but the broad implications of the argument are important. The principal function of the city today in terms of the employment it creates is the provision of services rather than manufactures. This is not to say that manufacturing no longer

---

(42) See literature cited by S. G. Triantis, "Economic Progress, Occupational Distribution, and International Terms of Trade," Econ. Jnl., LXIII (1953), 627-37; E. E. Lampard, op. cit., Section 3, Notes 22, 23, and 24. But see P. T. Bauer and B. S. Yamey, Econ. Jnl., LXI (1951), 741-55; ibid., LXIV (1954).

(43) C. Clark, "The Economic Functions of a City in Relation to Its Size," Econometrica, XIII (1945), 97-8; P. S. Florence, op. cit., p. 86.

imposes its essential location requirements. Despite some relaxation of these requirements in the present century, Clark found manufacturing concentrated in the established centers of industry much as they were in Marshall's day. Only the proportions of the labor force had changed somewhat with the trend set towards servicing.[44]

---

(44) Ibid., pp. 112-13; K. S. Lomax, "A Criterion of Efficiency in Local Administration," Jnl. of Royal Stat. Soc., Series A, CXV (1952). W. W. Rostow, The Process of Economic Growth (N.Y., 1952), pp. 22-54, identifies six propensities affecting growth -- to develop fundamental science, to apply science to economic ends, to accept innovations, to seek material advance, to consume, to have children. All except the last are characteristic propensities of the industrial city.

18. Cities in Social Transformation[1*]

John Friedmann

I. THE CITY AS A CROSS-CULTURAL TYPE

The clustering of populations into communities is one of the basic forms of human settlement. It arises from man's need for cooperation in order to survive, from his gregarious instinct, from certain external economies that may be obtained when his activities are centralized, and from the fact that distance is a physical obstacle that can be overcome most rationally by centralizing certain functions within geographic space. But not all population clusters grow into cities, and different clusters have been called by different names: hamlet, village, burg, town, city, and even megalopolis. The fundamental distinction, however, remains between the village and the city. "The relations between city people and country people form a major separation, a principal frontier of human relations."[2] Although this distinction is common in every-day speech—and therefore has something to recommend it—its rigorous application is by no means easy, and for various purposes of analysis different distinguishing criteria may be used.

Despite their being conceived as contrasting types, village and city do not represent the extremities of a continuum of modalities. There are, to be sure, some arguments in favor of a continuum theory. Villages often expand into full fledged cities, passing through what seem to be intermediate stages. Together with cities, they come to form a hierarchy of central places through which society, at least in its spatial dimensions, will be organized. And finally, one may observe the lingering of selected rural characteristics in many,

[1] For general bibliography see *Economic Development and Cultural Change*, October 1954, and January and April 1955; Bert F. Hoselitz, *Sociological Aspects of Economic Growth* (Glencoe, Ill., 1960), pp. 159-250; Philip Hauser, ed., *Urbanization in Asia and the Far East* (Unesco, 1957); Oswald Spengler, *Decline of the West*, vol. 2; Ralph Turner, *The Great Cultural Tradition*, 2 vols. (New York, 1941); Gordon V. Childe, *Man Makes Himself* (New York, 1959); Max Weber, *The City* (Glencoe, Ill., 1958); *Cities and Society*, ed. Paul K. Hatt and Albert J. Reiss, Jr. (Glencoe, Ill., 1957); Harold Mayer and Clyde Kohn, *Readings in Urban Geography* (Chicago, 1959); and my own article, "L'influence de l'intégration du système social sur le développement économique", *Diogène,* 33 (Jan.-Mars 1961), pp. 80-104.

[2] Robert Redfield, *The Primitive World and Its Transformations* (Ithaca, N.Y., 1957), p. 57.

* Reprinted from *Comparative Studies in Society and History,* Vol. 4 (July 1961).

if not in most, cities, while villages will occasionally exhibit social and cultural traits characteristic of urban areas. In rebuttal it may be said: a village is not simply a tiny urban cosmos, nor are cities outsized villages. The two are fundamentally distinct in kind, exhibiting peculiar socio-cultural, as well as physical configurations. Instead of a continuum joining the extremes, there is a radical break between them: by simply projecting the growth patterns of a village, one will never obtain a characteristically urban structure. It is consequently best to think of the city as a type that must be studied and understood on its own terms.

In contradistinction to Gideon Sjoberg's position,[3] my approach is through Julian Steward's "cross-cultural type", that is, through the concept of a characteristic social system that may be found in several historically unrelated areas or traditions. According to Steward, similarities which recur cross-culturally may be referred to as "regularities", whereas "uniformities" designate the similarities of form and content which characterize a single area or co-tradition.[4] Thus Kyoto and Kalamazoo, Basra and Bruges, Hangchow and Helsinki, Manaos and Mandalay, are seen primarily as cities, as exhibiting the important "regularities" that form the subject of this study.

Though social and economic structures may differ markedly among cities throughout history, a common trend may be observed to run through all of them. No one who wanders through the neat grid of Pompeian streets, visiting its shops and workmen's quarters (with virile *graffiti* on the walls), its baths and theatre and forum, and the residences of its rich merchants and retired politicans, can fail to be impressed with the sense of modernity that the city conveys. What strikes one most about Pompeii is how small the differences are that distinguish it from any provincial Italian city of corresponding size today: it is the regularities and not the contrasts that surprise us.[5] Preindustrial cities that have survived essentially undisturbed by modern innovations, such as Rothenburg, Venice, or Siena, give the same impression. To the sensitive observer, the very stones and mortar of the city still reflect the vibrant life of the past.[6]

[3] See Gideon Sjoberg, "The Preindustrial City", *American Journal of Sociology*, March 1955, pp. 438-45. (Editorial note: This article was accepted prior to the publication of Gideon Sjoberg's book of the same title, reviewed above, pp. 60-63).

[4] Julian H. Steward, *Theory of Culture Change* (Urbana, Ill., 1955), p. 88.

[5] It is not greatly different with cities which culturally are more remote. Marco Polo's description of ancient Hangchow is that of a genuine metropolis. It had, of course, a character appropriate to its time and place. Yet Marco Polo describes it as "far ahead of any European city in the excellence of its buildings and bridges, the number of its public hospitals, the elegances of its villas, the profusion of facilities for pleasure and vice, the charm and beauty of its courtesans, the effective maintenance of public order, and the manner and refinement of its people" (Will Durant, *Our Oriental Heritage*, New York, 1942, pp. 761 ff.).

[6] This has been excellently demonstrated in Georg Simmel's "The Metropolis and Mental Life", in Paul K. Hatt and Albert J. Reiss, Jr., *op. cit.*, pp. 365-646. His

II. WHAT IS A CITY?

One must, to start with, see the city as a whole.[7] There are many different kinds of city, classifiable according to size or density of population, economic base, principal functions, legal institutions, provision for defense, or place in a hierarchy of cities; indeed there is no end to the number of viewpoints that may be adopted. The names given to different types—garden city, coketown, *civitas,* metropolis, linear city, temple city, market city, capital, satellite, railroad city—evoke concrete images of their essential character. Yet all are cities. The common denominator among them is principally a way of life, a frame of mind, and a manner of thinking, speaking, and behaving. It is its spirit that makes a city. What is this spirit? What is the urban prototype?

The spirit of the city arises from its social heterogeneity. The city may also be culturally, even racially, heterogeneous, a place where different languages are spoken, different customs practised, different gods worshipped. Always it is a brilliantly exciting contrast to the monotony of a village in which life is bound to the cycle of the seasons. The city has the heady excitement of politics with its periodic crises and occasional pomp, its whispering campaigns, conspiracies and rumors, its public press and factionalist parties, with its essential mystery of power. The city has color and variety in its markets, bazaars and workshops. It has the glittering bubble of entertainment: circuses, games, dancing-girls, music, theatres, restaurants, taverns. Was a wineshop in Alexandria so different from a *Weinstube* in medieval Schwaebisch Hall or a modern tea room in Tokyo? It is to visits in these and to stimulating talk with friends and colleagues that many a peasant boy looks forward on moving to the city.

The city thus becomes a place of immense cultural vitality, where the consciousness of self is brought to an acute sensibility. Ideas are formed, change in fads and fashions is the order of the day. News and the discussion of news are essential to it. Here the present and the future intersect. The true urbanite is always *en courant.* There is a place also for scholars who peer into the past and into cosmic space. Every major creative effort either originates or comes to full bloom in the city. Here the important decisions are made.

The city has also a rationality that acts as a sobering influence upon the hurly-burly of its life. It is thrown down, indeed, as a rational act in defiance

portrayal of the urban psyche is unthinkable apart from an environment that, if it does not exclude nature, allows her to intrude in only a controlled and highly selected fashion.

[7] Failure to do so will lead to such unconvincing statements as Max Weber's, that "cities are peculiar to the Occident" (*The City*, p. 80), or that Peking was merely an assembly of "five large villages", *General Economic History* (Glencoe, Ill., 1958), p. 380. The only similar approach to the definition of what constitutes a city is Louis Wirth's famous article, "Urbanism as a Way of Life", *American Journal of Sociology*, July 1938.

of nature. If on a grid plan, its lines are carefully drawn in a Euclidean pattern that is in contrast with the curving and organic forms of nature. Parks and gardens are carefully delimited, if they are permitted at all, and are parcelled out according to what are believed to be the special requirements of the urban population. The life of the city is *zwecksrational*: means are fitted to ends agreed upon, and efficiency is introduced as a unit of measure relating input to output. With the city comes administration and the law, compiled into a rational code and a legal-administrative apparatus. Money and accountancy govern its trade, and most things become eventually reduced to their value in cash—whether it be labor, a work of art or a parcel of land. Universities pursue science, mathematics and philosophy (all three distinctively urban forms of mental activity) to the limits of reason and into the realm of ultimate doubt. "What can I know?" is a question the urban immigrant from a traditional rural environment learns to ask.

Civic political consciousness has declined since the days of the city-states, but there is still a consciousness of belonging to a unique cultural habitat. Bert Hoselitz has questioned whether such an urban consciousness exists in the modern cities of Asia, Africa and Latin America,[8] but in doing so he was apparently referring to that segment of the population in underdeveloped regions that lives in cities temporarily and continues to be emotionally tied to kinship groups that have remained back in the village. This segment may be large, perhaps excessively large,[9] and it may lead to the co-existence of a modern and a folk sector within the administrative confines of the city. But in fact it is the modern sector of the city that represents whatever is uniquely urban about the local environment. And in this sector, it is the "down-town" district that plays the decisive role. For it is the urban elite that frequents it—the business people, literati, intellectuals, politicians, and bankers—that most represents the spirit of the city. It is the members of this elite who make the critical decisions that will shape the future of their city's history within the usual constraints by which decisions such as these are bound. The folk sector is in the city but not a part of it.

It must be recognized that there has been a tendency for the city to disappear as a distinctive way of life in recent decades, as urban culture has successfully invaded the countryside in what is surely the most comprehensive imperialism known to history, and urban populations have vastly increased

[8] Bert F. Hoselitz, "The City, the Factory, and Economic Growth," *American Economic Review*, May 1955, pp. 166-84.

[9] Kingsley Davis and Hilda Hertz Golden have introduced the suggestive concept of "over-urbanization" to describe a situation, reported to exist in countries like Egypt and Korea, where the size of urban populations is far in excess of the existing requirements for full-time productive employment. It is especially those cities which suffer from over-population that may appear to possess a distinctly rural atmosphere. See their article "Urbanization and the Development of Pre-Industrial Areas", *Economic Development and Cultural Change*, October 1954, pp. 6-26.

in number and proportion, overflowing the old boundaries and sprawling in more or less unruly patterns over vast portions of the earth.[10] In a sense, the mass communications industry has placed the city in everybody's living room, from the shores of Alaska to the Belgian Congo. And yet, something of the city remains and probably will always remain, if only as a sense of the city as we approach it: the hum and vibrations of life become louder, the intersection of intelligences becomes more frequent and intense, vitality and movement are raised to a high pitch. *This is the center:* it may be physically distinguishable or not; but it is here.

III. FUNCTIONAL HIERARCHIES OF CITIES

Within a given area, cities may be systematically arranged in hierarchies according to the functions they perform.[11] One such hierarchy, for instance, might consist of primate, regional, provincial, and local-service cities.[12] Relative position in the hierarchy will tend to be associated with a certain size-group of urban population—given as parameters the total population of the area over which the hierarchy extends its influence, the level of economic development achieved in the area, and the state of existing transportation technology—as well as the specific functions that establish the characteristic relations of cities to each other. Thus, the *primate* city may be a great center of manufacturing and of specialized services (finance, publishing, science, arts, communications, fashions, and government), as well as the area which has the greatest relative market potential; the *regional city,* comprehended within the radius of influence of the primate city, may be a regional service and trade center, especially for wholesale trade, but may also serve as a regional administrative center; *provincial* cities are generally sub-regional trade centers and occasionally important centers of manufacturing, but they may serve as the capital of a major political sub-division as well; and finally, the *local service* city will provide a limited number of essential services to the rural areas immediately surrounding it and may have some manufacturing activity which will be usually related to the processing of local agricultural raw materials. Irregularly interspersed within this basic structure may be *satellite* cities in the vicinity of the larger urban centers, and *special function* cities, devoted predominantly to single economic or other activities such as manufacturing,

[10] For instance, along the Northeastern Seaboard in the United States, a continuous area, 600 miles long and containing some 30 million people in 1950, has been classified as essentially urban. See Jean Gottlieb, "Megalopolis, or the Urbanization of the Northeastern Seaboard", *Economic Geography*, July 1957, pp. 189-200.

[11] Brian J. L. Berry and William L. Garrison, "The Functional Bases of the Central Place Hierarchy", *Economic Geography*, April 1958, pp. 145-154.

[12] John Friedmann, "Locational Aspects of Economic Development", *Land Economics,* August 1956, pp. 214-227; also Walter Isard, *Location and Space Economy* (New York, 1956) and the literature cited in both works.

education, entertainment, mining, administration, religious devotion, and so forth.

The hierarchy sketched above is only one of several such hierarchies that may be delineated, and the nature of each hierarchy will have to be studied specifically for each area.[13] The one presented here reveals a pattern typical for a "mature" or "maturing" modern economy. Surrounding each urban center will be two related types of regions, defined by prevailing modes of social and economic interaction with the central city: the city region and the region of interdependency. The *city* or *urban region* is marked by a relatively dense interaction of production, buying and selling, and other activities within its area: the city itself lies at the hub, and culturally as well as economically, the urban region blends into an organic extension of the city proper. In the United States, it is most closely approximated by the census definition of a Standard Metropolitan Area. The physical extent of this region will vary with the size of the urban center, as well as with topography, urban functions, and transport means. Somewhat less intensive relationships with the central city mark the *region of interdependency* which will often, though not necessarily, coincide with the wholesale area of the central city. It is the area for which specialized central services are provided by the city, such as administration or higher education. The region of interdependency is, by definition, always larger than the city region, and in the case of a primate city, it may extend over the entire country. In general, however, its size will vary with the available forms of transportation, and with competition from other cities in providing similar services for their own areas. Particularly in ancient times, the region of interdependency was often discontinuous with the central city, so that the major trade and supply areas might be located overseas in provinces that could be reached only by ship, today by telephone and airplane, and had no common boundaries with the city proper. The bulk of trade and other exchange activities, however, generally takes place between contiguous regions. These two types of regions, then, and the central city common to them both, tend to rise and decline together, economically as well as politically.

This description of an urban structure refers to what would be the outcome of a long period of economic growth under modern conditions. But there are also relatively underdeveloped urban-regional structures, with the degree of their "development" roughly corresponding to the level of economic growth achieved. What criteria may be employed to measure the level of "maturity" attained? Lampard has shown how the growth of cities and gains in productive efficiency were usually accompanied by specialization of economic activ-

[13] See, for example, Rupert B. Vance and Sara Smith, "Metropolitan Dominance and Integration", in Rupert B. Vance and Nicholas J. Demerath, eds., *The Urban South* (Durham, N. C., 1954).

ities in space.[14] According to this view, *area specialization, functional differentiation, and the degree of interaction among activities distributed in space may be accepted as one of the more important criteria for measuring the relative degree of maturity of regional urban structure.*

Less developed urban structures may consequently be characterized by a low order of functional specialization, with many small communities existing more or less independently side by side. Each little community (village or small city) will be the economic center of an agricultural production region. To be sure, a larger city may spring up here and there, such as an important religious or administrative center or a port for transacting commerce with the outside world. Yet, during the early stages of a region's development, significant "gaps" in the hierarchical structure of its communities will be observed, with a few cities growing disproportionately to the rest of the economy, and with vast areas remaining largely outside the sphere of any urban influence. At the other extreme, having attained to a degree of maturity, the pattern of cities and their relationships might well resemble the one already described, with linear cities, conurbations, and belts of continuous urbanization emerging in due course within the more densely settled areas.

What has been sketched in the foregoing is only a generalized scheme for the analysis of cities and in no way pretends to give a perfectly accurate picture of the actual conditions in any region. But it also suggests the conclusion that *the hierarchy of urban places represents the ultimate means for organizing a geographic area into its component social, political-administrative and economic spaces.*

By this is meant: a mere area becomes "effective space", in any of the three senses referred to, solely through the agency of urban institutions which extend their influences outward, binding the surrounding regions to the central city and introducing to them urban ways of thought and action.[15] The nature and spatial extent of urban influence will correspond to the position of each city in the hierarchy. And as the hierarchy evolves from its rudimentary stages of structural development to greater maturity, it will help organize the entire area over which its influence extends into an interdependent system of "nested" city-orientated regions. These regions will themselves partake increasingly of the urban way of life. The resulting changes in the social order, the disruption of accustomed patterns of behavior and their reintegration around new value principles, are identical with the processes of social transformation that include, but are not limited to, the processes of economic growth.

[14] Eric E. Lampard, "The History of Cities in the Economically Advanced Areas", *Economic Development and Cultural Change,* January 1955, pp. 86 ff.

[15] For a more detailed explanation of this concept of "space", see John Friedmann, "L'influence de l'intégration du système social sur le développement économique", *Diogène,* 33 (Jan.-Mars 1961), pp. 80-104.

IV. THE GROWTH OF CITIES

The rise and growth of cities has been tied in fundamental ways to innovations in agriculture and transportation that have had the effect of increasing the efficency of both. The first cities of which we know, were located in the naturally most fertile areas, in the delta regions of the principal world rivers.[16] Rural and urban economies interpenetrated each other from the very beginning. This relationship grew more intense: cities required food, raw materials, and labor from the country, and the country became a major market for the urban producer. But the country also required the city: farmers had to sell their surplus to private urban consumers and to industries, and the bigger these markets were, the greater also were the possibilities for expanding the economic potentialities of rural areas.[17] It is evident, however, at least for the preindustrial era, that the city was more dependent upon the farm than the other way around: instead of a symbiotic (mutual), there tended to be only a parasitic, one-sided relationship, with the city exploiting the countryside, an exploitation that could ultimately be justfied only in terms of the city's ability to draw all areas into its own cultural horizon.[18]

Be that as it may, primitive agricultural and transport technics effectively prevented the emergence of large urban concentrations until relatively recent times. Exceptions to this rule are few. The world was not yet settled densely, so that in any case large cities could not be expected in great numbers, but the lack of an agricultural surplus and difficulties of transport were the chief reasons inhibiting the development of large cities. Coastal cities were in a somewhat preferred position but even they would find it difficult at times to assure themselves of a sufficient supply of food for a large population.

Since the beginnings of urban history, the world has undergone a series of cycles of urbanization, growth and decline succeeding each other either within the same geographic region or in different parts of the world, decline in one area being "compensated" for by the emergence of new cities in another. Changes in political stability, food-growing capacity, health, and transportation technology all contributed to these fluctuations. But until the onset of the 19th century, cycles of urbanization took the form chiefly of an increase in the number of cities instead of an expansion in their size. The great majority of cities prior to 1800 AD did not exceed 50,000 inhabitants. The

[16] The impetus to the growth of cities, however, arose out of the commerce that developed to supply these regions with essential raw materials, especially timber and minerals from far-distant regions. See Gordon Childe, *op. cit.*, chapter VII.

[17] The interrelations between farm and city are of course far more complex than these few phrases would suggest. Important additional "linkages" may be found in connection with farm mechanization, agricultural research and extension, rural development, capital formation in rural areas, living standards, employment opportunities, and so forth.

[18] The consequences of such an unbalanced, one-sided relationship are discussed in John Friedmann, "Regional Planning: A Problem of Spatial Integration", *Papers and Proceedings of the Regional Science Association*, V (1959), pp. 167-179.

giants in the preindustrial western world were Rome and Byzantium, each with close to one million inhabitants during the peaks of their ancient power, and it is probable that certain Asiatic cities such as Peking, Hangchow, and Edo during the Tokugawa Era, rivalled the larger contemporary European cities in size.[19]

The introduction of technical innovations in agriculture, manufacturing and transportation released a decisive urban "revolution" in Europe. By the middle of the 18th century these were already leading to a hyper-centralization of economic activities within a few concentrated areas. With the vast expansion of the world's cultivated area made possible by railroad and steamship in the 19th century large-scale urbanization spread. But it has been only during the last 25 or 30 years, as a result of further innovations in communications, transport and industrial technology, and in scientific agriculture, that a break-through into cumulative self-sustaining economic growth could be achieved and that the thorough organization of social, political and economic space, as a tripartite entity, has become a real possibility.

V. SOURCES OF URBAN INFLUENCE AND POWER

What are the sources of this spell that cities cast over the regions that surround them? In what manner does the city participate as an active force in the ongoing processes of social transformation? In what sense is the social, political and economic integration of an area achieved as it moves towards the threshold of cumulative economic growth? Some answers will be proffered below. There will be no pretension to completeness, but simply a suggestion of some ways in which the city acts to draw surrounding areas into the net of urban influence through the pervasive actions of her intellectual, administrative, and enterprising classes.

The Intellectuals

Every city is to some degree a center of high culture and intellectual life, and it is principally the intellectuals who are involved in keeping active and if necessary in transforming, the cultural traditions they inherit. High culture, in this context, refers to that tradition of fundamental values by which men live. It is the one insistent theme which underlies all social conduct; it is the

19 Kingsley Davis, "The Origin and Growth of Urbanization in the World", *American Journal of Sociology*, March, 1955, pp. 429-37; Robert E. Dickinson, *The West European City* (London, 1951), chapter 15; Irene B. Taeuber cites the following populations for Japanese cities for the period between 1725–29): Edo (= modern Tokyo) 472,000, Osaka 369,000, and Kyoto 374,000, in "Urbanization and Population Change in the Development of Modern Japan", *Economic Development and Cultural Change*, IX, no. I, Part II, p. 4.

social norm against which both conforming and deviating actions may be judged.

The geographic limits of a population whose basic values are derived from a single high cultural tradition define the boundaries of an effective social space. A stable political equilibrium cannot be maintained unless the fundamental assumptions regarding political institutions, also, are shared by a preponderant part of the population. The extension of an effective social space is thus a precondition to an area's political and economic integration.

The United States provides a good example of this thesis. Perhaps the single most important problem in its development has been to urge upon the millions of new immigrants the basic features of a uniquely American tradition. What to some contemporary observers appears to be an almost obsessive concern with "un-American activities", the worship of the flag, and similar patriotic manifestations, is simply a consequence of the tremendous effort to weld a multiplicity of peoples into a single, integrated social space of national dimension. The fabulously rapid growth of the United States from a dependent colony to a supreme world power can be ascribed, in part, to her successes in this undertaking.

A low level of social integration, on the other hand, is normally associated with conditions of political and economic backwardness. In so-called dualistic societies, cities will represent the economically and socially most integrated areas, high cultural traditions being there most widely shared, while rural populations will participate in only a restricted way in these traditions. For the expression of high culture will frequently be one of literary sophistication and lie beyond the normal range of intellect of the illiterate. Nor are tradition-minded intellectuals so eager to popularize their closely guarded heritage. Not without cause are they dubbed Mandarins or Brahmins where their preeminence depends, in part, on the exclusive, occultistic nature of their knowledge.

Any vital cultural tradition is capable, of course, of being understood at different "levels" of meaning, from the excessively abstract to more mundane, concrete manifestations. The American democratic tradition, for instance, is enunciated in the lofty principles of the Declaration of Independence, the Constitution, and in the philosophical lucidities of the *Federalist Papers*. But it is also strongly in evidence in the popular tradition of the "cracker barrel" where every man enjoys the right to speak his mind.

But differing interpretations as to the meaning of a high tradition may result in the serious disruption of a potentially effective social space, especially in areas where cities remain largely isolated from peasant communities and urban influence is consequently weak. Among the peasantry, a high tradition may be little more than hear-say and being overshadowed by popular traditions, folkways, local customs, and beliefs, have little practical significance. The peasant, after all, is a *paganus*, a heathen fellow, who in the face of higher truth clings stubbornly to pagan idols. Social space in the less developed countries is therefore often fragmented into isolated "island" regions. Brazil, for instance, no less than India, Indonesia, or China, has been called a cultural archipelago, and the United States was compelled to assure its political and social integration through a civil war in which a genteel southern tradition was locked in fatal conflict with the urban-industrial tradition of the North.

It is the cities however that are responsible for ultimately breaking down the barriers of dualism and for effecting a widespread social revolution whose aim is the integration of culturally diverse areas into a social whole. It is the disaffected urban intellectual, now uncommitted to his cultural inheritance, who mediates the values that will challenge the prevailing ways. He is the progenitor of a new cultural tradition and of a renovated social order. And it is he who formulates the ideologies required to provide for and sustain the socially disruptive changes taking place.

The values of the budding new tradition are dynamic. Change is posited as the natural and fundamental condition of mankind. Only those who live in history or even better who are a jump or two ahead, will be successful. Success becomes synonymous with the successful mastery of change. The origin of these values is in the cities of the West from whence they spread to other cities in new continents, arriving in successive waves that are about to engulf all parts of mankind. They include the belief that:

1. Constant striving is the *summum bonum* of existence and that the result of such striving is progress infinitely extended into the future;
2. Environment can be successfully mastered and turned to man's advantage through the practice of science and scientific technology;
3. Significant truth is established only empirically and that achievement in performance is a major standard of practical as well as moral excellence;
4. Social and political equality is either a natural right or an historical inevitability;
5. Suffrage should be extended to all adult persons possessing minimum qualifications, and that participation in at least some of the processes of governing a nation is a right no less than an obligation of each citizen.[20]

In short, they are the broadly democratic and scientific-experimental values of our time. They are not everywhere interpreted in the same way; but with some modifications, they form the core of our modern faith. They form the creed of socialists and liberals alike.

As these values become widely accepted throughout city-centered regions and as disaffected intellectuals in each take up the common banner and carry it triumphant through the streets, effective social space will be extended to always larger areas. Initial impulses are strengthened through application of

[20] For a discussion of these values and their role in social transformation see my forthcoming paper on "Intellectuals in Developing Societies", *Kyklos,* XIII (1960), pp. 513-44.

modern technology to communication, through schools and universities, through more frequent contact with Westerners, and through migrations to the city. In time, new cities will be founded to fill the gaps left in the urban hierarchy.

To consolidate these gains, and to preserve a sense of national identity under the impact of an international urban culture, it will be necessary to distinguish this newly-created social space from every other, to differentiate it sufficiently to give the population a heightened self-consciousness and a faith in their collective powers. Hope in the future is largely related to the creation of a national self-image. It is again the urban intellectual who will eventually provide an image of this kind.

The Administrators. As social space is being extended with increasing effectiveness to encompass larger areas, the city comes to oppose the traditional order of communal life with the administrative order of a rationally organized society.[21] As the seat of the administration of public affairs, presided over by bureaucrats and politicians, the city is able to exert substantial pressures upon the life of rural populations.[22] For smaller centers, these influences may not extend beyond a few square miles of countryside, but for the largest cities, they will reach out over whole provinces, the nation, and even overseas possessions. Hand in hand with the integration of a dual, or rather, multiple society into an effective social space, an urban administrative hierarchy will gradually become entrenched, specific areas of authority and competence being delineated for each city. Through this authority, the claims of the State or, more generally, of Society organized into a State, are laid upon the individual, his family, and his community. With the organization of

[21] For a penetrating discussion of these issues, see Robert K. Lamb, "Political Elites and the Process of Economic Development", in B. F. Hoselitz, ed., *The Progress of Underdeveloped Areas* (Chicago, 1952), pp. 30-53, and S. N. Eisenstadt, "Internal Contradictions in Bureaucratic Polities", *Comparatives Studies in Society and History*, I, 1 (October 1958), pp. 58-75.

[22] Cities do not assure this while the aristocracy, as in medieval Europe and in colonial Latin America, live on their estates and shun urban life. Effective political power was thus dispersed, and economic expansion thereby drastically curtailed, for economic space must be combined with political and social space to become totally effective. Thus, Brazil did not begin her rapid rise as a modern industrial nation until the aristocracy, which had been a law unto itself, moved permanently into the cities following the repeal of slavery towards the end of the last century. This move led to the complete breakdown of the traditional plantation economy and made possible, through the accumulation and contralisation of wealth in the cities, the present development based on urban industrialism and agricultural diversification. Economic development was most retarded in precisely those regions, such as Bahia and Pernambuco, where this dissolution of the old aristocratic order was not carried to its logical completion. On the other hand, where a strong central power was lacking and where one city was neatly belanced off against another, the tendency was for cities to form States within the State, leading to political atomization. Modern industrialism could not spread until this atomized system of government was consolidated into a strong and unified nation-State. It is therefore not surprising that the period of great nationalism coincided with the rise of industrial civilization during the past 150 years.

Society through adoption of a common value system and the extension of an effective social space beyond the limits of daily face to face contact through institutions which embody these new values, and the growing interdependency of economic activities, it is inevitable that a person's life should be increasingly held accountable to Society. For the State demands that a certain portion of a person's labor should be for the common good, and that his conduct should conform not only to the unwritten code of his immediate community, but also to the written law.

The evolution of political-administrative space is closely geared to the functional hierarchy of central places. Through a process of cumulative causation,[23] the establishment of political-administrative authority will first affect those populations that live within the ambience of larger cities. In countries where the urban hierarchy is present only in its rudiments, the capital city will have only a tenuous hold upon more distant regions, each region living by a law unto itself. This is the well-known phenomenon of the frontier. Only with maturing urban hierarchy will political-administrative space be organized so as to facilitate significantly the processes of economic growth.

Administrative order extending with compelling force over subordinated towns and villages will form a rational and stabilizing element in what would otherwise be a fragmented social order. It will create the basic rules of social conduct and establish the common points of reference wherever public interests are involved. The law, its institutions, and its processes will then supplant the customary ways of doing business and of arriving at just and equitable solutions of potential social conflict. It is the law that will enunciate objective principles above and beyond the subjective desires of private parties and thereby give expression to the "will" of a collectivity defined by the limits within which the written law can be enforced. This collectivity may encompass less than the total population of a nation.

Within any given political-administrative space, conditions will favor rapid economic expansion. Standardized systems of measurement, weight, and coinage are adopted. Local rules concerning the rights and administration of property are superseded by universally valid standards. Taxes and services are imposed for common purposes of public projects. From these and other measures results an awareness of the existence of a larger political unity beyond the city walls which leads to the recognition of that unity as the logical area for public policy and planning.[24]

Perhaps the first sign which betrays administrative order emanating from

[23] See Gunnar Myrdal, *Rich Lands and Poor. The Road to World Prosperity* (New York, 1957), for an exposition of the concept of "cumulative causation".

[24] John Friedman, "The Concept of a Planning Region: The Evolution of an Idea in the United States", *United Nations Social and Economic Council, Working Paper* no. 12, E/CN.11/RP/L.14, June, 1958.

the city, breathing that rational and calculating spirit of the city, is the taking of a census.[25] In census work, heads, hogs, and houses are reduced to numbers by the objectively rational mind of those whose business is the management of national territory. Censuses are required for the basic decisions of how to allocate society's resources. They are the ledgers of national weaknesses and strengths, the basic documents for planful, goal-directed action. The taking of a census is a first indication that a political-administrative space is in the making.

The second crucial instrument for spatial integration of which administration will avail itself is planning.[26] In planning, collective purposes are set forth as guidelines for policy and are detailed in course of a laborious, time-consuming administrative process into proposals for public action, contained in budgets, maps, and accompanying charts and documents. Again, it is the whole of the political-administrative space with its varying needs, its differing and often clashing interests, and its regional subdivisions, that will be taken into account. Planning will assist in the integration of the space economy. An ideological force in its own right, it will provide for the orderly, sequential development of all parts of the effective political-administrative space and of the activities of populations residing in it.

Eventually, a plan will issue into public action, setting into motion the entire machinery of government administration. A legal framework for the conduct of private affairs will be established; taxes will be levied and collected; helping to break down the dualism in society by furthering the expansion of urban institutions and a maturing of the urban hierarchy. Public projects will be started for roads, railroads, communications, electric power, housing, irrigation, schools, health, and various forms of resources development. Initially, the tendency will be for projects to be centered upon cities and the areas immediately surrounding them. But as progress continues to be made, as successes are beginning to be scored, as the voices of disaffected intellectuals become louder and more urgent, as surpluses of capital accumulate, public projets will also penetrate into remoter and less developed regions.

Behind these efforts will be discovered the spirit and the social patterns of an administrative class, resident in cities, and acting as surveyors of the creative, organizing powers of the city. In the conduct of their work, administrators as a class are largely rational, impersonal, and socially responsible. Their outlook is materialistic, and their thinking geared to the scientific-technological world-view. Of course, there will be waste and graft and self-seeking associated with any administrative system, but the standard by which administration will be judged emerges as self-evident from this description of the type.

[25] John Chadwick, "A Prehistoric Bureaucracy", *Diogenes*, summer 1959, pp. 7-8, cites evidence to this effect for Mycenaean Greece around 1500 B.C.
[26] John Friedmann, "Introduction to the Study and Practice of Planning", *International Social Science Journal*, IX, no. 3 (1959), pp. 327-339.

The Entrepreneurs. If intellectuals are responsible for the formation of a social space, and administrators for political-administrative space, it is the enterprising spirit in economic affairs that is responsible for organizing economic space. Enterprise, despite significant exceptions, is to a large extent an urban phenomenon. It is the city as a center of economic affairs that breeds that restless type, the entrepreneur, venturesome, ambitious, and always ready to strike out in new directions.

What is meant by an effective economic space becomes evident as we attempt to visualize a geographic area whose limits are defined by a higher relative frequency of economic transactions within it than between itself and any other area. Internally, an economic space will have a structure defined by (1) the location of its centers of economic activity, (2) their functional characteristics, (3) the physical extent of local market areas, and (4) the flows of goods and services between cities and regions. Preconditions to its establishment are a common money economy, a common market area, and a common set of economic rules necessary for obtaining economies of scale. The boundaries of the area over which these principles extend draw the rough outlines of a rudimentary economic space possessing as yet little internal structure and organization. A common or freely convertible medium of exchange—the first condition of a space economy—is basic to realizing external economies of buying, selling, and investing and to functional specialization according to the principle of comparative advantage. The continued division of the economy into a monetized and subsistence sector where barter is predominant, precludes the creation of a unified economic space. Similarly, the existence of artificial obstacles to trade and to the flows of capital and labor—whether through customs tariffs or other institutional devices—will tend to divide an area into as many regional economies, each striving to attain to a degree of self-sufficiency and seeking to protect itself against the actions of competing regions. Finally, as a third precondition to the forming of an economic space, the rules of economic conduct must be the same throughout an area, preparing institutional foundations for centralizing certain activities and effecting essential economies of scale. Banks, stock exchanges, corporations, cooperatives, and labor unions are all means for carrying out economic activities more efficiently. They represent a significant step towards a maturing space economy, they are the focal points of economic power from which will flow the multipliticy of urban influences for organizing economic life.

These preconditions to the further development of space economy are usually brought about in concert with the creation of a political-administrative space, throwing into relief the intimate connection which exists between economy and government. For the issuance of money and the control of its value as a medium of exchange, the elimination of barriers to trade and to the flows of capital and labor, and the enactment and enforcement of basic economic legislation, are normal functions of the State. These preconditions will exist in areas where the effective powers of administrative hierarchy extend. Therefore, a primitive political-administrative space precedes the further elaboration of an economic space into its structural components. But once the general outlines of economic space have been defined, the evolution of social and political-administrative institutions runs parallel to the progressive differentiation of economic space. Eventually, the three types of space will become so intertwined that they become indistinguishable from one another. This movement towards the spatial integration of the social system as a whole is accompanied by and at one with the processes of economic growth.

The internal structure of the space economy, as suggested above, is the result of investment-location decisions and of the rational economic calculus which underlies them. Within the framework of a rudimentary space economy, these decisions lead to increasing areal specialization as determined by natural resource advantages, distance to existing markets and to sources of raw material, available labor supply, climate, topography, etc. Such specialization will come to a head in the city, each city acting for its own immediate region as a supplier of credit and capital, as a buyer and seller of products, as a processor of locally produced materials, standing in line of communication with other cities in the emerging hierarchy of city regions and regions of interdependency. For specialization is, of course, feasible only because of trade and the exchange of goods.

It is the cities that have accumulated the largest economic surpluses for investment, and it is urban interests that make investments and thus give shape to the maturing space economy. It is completely natural that urban enterprises should seek out other cities and regions as the most logical localities for these investments. For cities:

1. Occupy the most stategic points of access within an area, being situated at the nodal points of a transport and communication network at some one place within the hierarchy;
2. Offer the possibility for realizing substantial external economies through certain public services they provide in common to all citizens: water, sanitation, police protection, and electric energy;
3. Possess a variety of services, including those of communication, and certain institutional arrangements for facilitating the smooth flow of economic transactions;
4. Have the largest relative market potential, wealth and population being concentrated in cities, with industries forming inter-related complexes of mutually supporting production activities; and
5. Provide for agreeable and comfortable living according to the almost universally desired urban standard.

Attrition of dual economy through the location decisions of urban investors is one of the principal effects of investment activities. It is the entrepreneur who first introduces money economy on a large scale into subsistence-barter areas. It will be his decisions that result in the differential centralization of economic activities, bringing about the rise of cities in the wilderness, and drawing these cities into an ever tighter network of trade and economic relations of all kinds, thereby enlarging the effective economic space and adding to the total resources of society. At first, his purpose will tend to be narrowly self-seeking, as he will consider non-urban areas primarily fit for the colonial exploitation of their natural resources. But gradually, this unenlightened policy will yield to a dawning recognition that between city and rural areas exists indeed a mutuality of interests. For in the end, the urban product markets will be limited by the purchasing power of the population of both the city and its hinterland. The State, however, may be sooner aware of this complementarity than private individuals and will therefore frequently assume the role of entrepreneur in the development of the city's former "colonial" domain.

VI. SUMMARY

This essay has sought to bring out salient points that can throw light both upon the vexing problems of cultural transformation and on the related phenomena of economic growth. It has employed concepts that are relatively recent in the social sciences and that when synthesized provide the elements of a theory of social change. The five main concepts are: the city as a cross-cultural type; the functional urban hierarchy; the nodular regional structure; effective social, political-administrative and economic space; economic growth as being part of a more comprehensive process leading to successively higher levels of integration of the social system.

From the concept of the city as a cross-cultural type it follows that there are no fundamental distinctions between industrial and preindustrial cities, but both are sharply distinguished from communal village life. All cities have in common a way of life that is characterized by varying degrees of social heterogeneity and cultural vitality, and by inventiveness, creativity, rationality, and civic consciousness. From the fact that cities and the regions related to them may be seen as functionally differentiated and arranged in hieratic fashion it follows that the extent of urban influence will vary with (a) the stage of evolution reached by the hierarchy as a whole, and (b) the relative position of any given city within the hierarchy.

Economic growth has to be seen as part of a comprehensive process of cultural transformation. From the ruthless destruction of old social forms no aspect of society will be spared. It is the influences spreading outward from cities that accomplish both the disruption of the traditional social patterns and the reintegration of society around new fundamental values. The city acts as a coordinating, space-creating force, thus achieving the integration of the social order in its spatial dimensions. Intellectuals, administrators and entrepreneurs are the city's agents in this task. With their success in organizing the life of a society, both as a pattern of activities and as a pattern in space, the traditional notion of a city as a place having definite geographic limits will tend gradually to disappear. Just as Karl Mannheim speaks of fundamental democratization as one of the tendencies of our age, so one may speak of fundamental urbanization as the end-result of modern economic growth. With this, the former distinction between town and country will be blurred and will leave a thoroughly organized, impersonal, and functionally rational society to carry on.

19. Latin American Cities: Aspects of Function and Structure*†

Richard M. Morse

This essay will advance two interrelated hypotheses about the Latin American city. The first of them has to do with the role of the city in the settlement of the New World. The second suggests certain characteristics of the modern Latin American metropolis.

The analysis of the colonial Latin American city is frequently prefaced by a review of its medieval Iberian origins. These origins are clearly reflected in the internal workings and institutions of the New World city: in the municipal control of common lands; in the function and structure of craft and trade guilds; in the procedures for election of town officers by property owners; in municipal supervision of prices and trade practices; and in the role of the church and of religious brotherhoods. Significantly, however, these quasi-medieval organizations and procedures were assembled — in the Spanish if not in the Portuguese lands — within a Renaissance city plan whose geometric lines of force radiated out to the vast and often loosely settled surrounding space.[1]

This leads us to perceive the New World city not solely as a projection of municipal and cultural traditions from the Middle Ages but as a protagonist in a large scheme of imperial colonization. The Spanish and Portuguese monarchs claimed a territory the size of thirty or forty Iberian peninsulas. The conquerors and colonizers were largely urban types from two urban-minded countries. Yet, ironically, their task was to make contact with the soil and subsoil from which all wealth would flow, given the labor of millions of Africans and American Indians.

In Spanish America ultimate title to all land was vested in the crown, which delegated the right to grant lands to the conquistadors, and later to viceroys and governors by agreement with town councils. In practice, the town councils tended at first to allot lands directly, operating at the margin of the law. By the seventeenth century the crown, desperately needing income, was asserting its right to sell vacant lands or to question the rights

* This paper was read in abbreviated form at the December, 1960, meeting of the American Historical Association. Some of the research upon which it rests was done on a grant from Columbia University in the summer of 1958.

1 Erwin Walter Palm, "Los orígenes del urbanismo imperial en América", *Contribuciones a la historia municipal de América* (Mexico City, 1951), p. 258.

† Reprinted from *Comparative Studies in Society and History,* Vol. 4 (July 1962).

of those who already claimed land titles. When royal inspectors came to examine questionable titles, however, it was common for a town council to request a "composition" that allowed it to pay a lump sum for the properties in question, thus legitimizing the *de facto* distribution. Until well into the eighteenth century the juridical doctrines applying to crown lands were still in formulation.[2] One historian goes so far as to say that the municipality was essentially "the juridical agent authorized by the crown to effect concessions and allotments of land, whether rural or urban, according to the needs and interests of each particular locality".[3]

The city, then, is the point of departure for the settlement of the soil. And we can say that, whereas the Western European city represented a movement of economic energies away from extractive pursuits toward those of processing and distribution, the Latin American city was the source of energy and organization for the exploitation of natural resources.

This relation of city to land helps to explain several characteristics of colonial Latin American cities.

First, the abandonment or transfer of cities was frequent because of errors of judgment by the founders, who had incomplete knowledge of local geography and who could not accurately predict the patterns of future trade routes which might have been expected to guarantee stability and commercial prosperity to the administrative, military and religious nuclei.[4]

Second, crown officials were in many regions thwarted in their attempts to nucleate the sprawling settlement patterns into towns or villages. Smaller municipalities lived under threat of dissolution as their leading citizens were drawn off to regions of greater economic promise or else devoted themselves to rural pursuits to the detriment of municipal administration.

Third, many towns became encircled and their common lands absorbed by the individual holdings preempted by firstcomers. Status was defined by ownership of the land rather than, as in older societies, the relation to the land being a function of status. This caused the early growth of municipal oligarchies which controlled without putting into full production circum-adjacent town lands.[5]

[2] José María Ots Capdequí, *Manual de historia del derecho español en las Indias* (Buenos Aires, 1945), pp. 273-292.

[3] Francisco Domínguez y Compañy, "Funciones económicas del cabildo colonial hispanoamericano" in *Contribuciones . . ., op. cit.*, p. 166.

[4] José María Ots Capdequí, *Nuevos aspectos del siglo XVIII en América* (Bogotá, 1946), p. 283; R. MacLean y Estenós, "Sociología de la ciudad en el Nuevo Mundo", *Proceedings of the 14th International Congress of Sociology (30th August-3rd September 1951)*, II, 277; Pierre Deffontaines, "The Origin and Growth of the Brazilian Network of Towns", *The Geographical Review*, XXVIII, 3 (July 1938), 399; Raimundo Lopes, *Antropogeografia* (Rio de Janeiro, 1956), pp. 162-163.

[5] José María Ots Capdequí, *El régimen de la tierra en la América Española durante el período colonial* (Ciudad Trujillo, 1946), p. 45; Juan Agustín García, *La ciudad indiana* (Buenos Aires, 1937), *passim.*

Fourth, the urban network was weakly developed. The lack of commercial reciprocity among the cities, which was accentuated by Iberian mercantilist policies, insulated them and tied them individually to Lisbon and Seville.[5a]

If we assume such characteristics, we may permit ourselves the analogy between the Iberian colonization of America and the Roman colonization of Western Europe, fifteen hundred years earlier. In both cases the location of the colony-town is decided more by political, strategic and agricultural considerations than by industrial or commercial ones. (The Latin word for "colony", *colonia,* is in fact related to *colere,* meaning "to cultivate".) The administrative unit is a *civitas* or municipality, centering on a nuclear grid plan that is surrounded by arable fields, to be allotted to the colonists or to be held aside as an *ager publicus* or *ejido*. The Roman *civitas* was an old tribal unit, comprising a tribe and its territory. Its chief town served as its administrative center, having a government organized on the standard Roman model. "Gaul was . . . too large, its tribes too backward and scattered, to be welded into the Italian type of a network of municipalities. A tribal territory was like a French department, or often larger."[6] In Spanish America, similarly, municipal jurisdictions might extend scores or even hundreds of miles. The early Roman colonists were soldier-farmers, and their towns had a camp-like appearance. In Spanish America certain land grants were called *peonías* and *caballerías,* because they were allotted to foot soldiers or horse soldiers.

If both situations yield the example of the geometrically planned town functioning as a metropolitan outpost and as a colonizing agent, so do they exhibit functionally comparable agrarian institutions. The latifundium, controlled by a single proprietor, originally from an urban background, becomes the agency by which rural workers are organized for production. In both cases a large number of these workers is culturally alien to the colonizers, and, whatever the dictates of the metropolis may be, it is largely the latifundium which determines the workers' relation to the soil and the nature of the justice which they may expect to receive. Potentially, the *latifundista* has mixed rural-urban allegiances. When the social or economic promise of the hinterland is great, or when life in the town is penurious and oppressive, he will be drawn to reside in the country. This deprives the town of administrative leadership and of chances for economic growth to the extent that the latifundium becomes self-sufficient in agriculture and manufactures.[7]

In Roman Europe by the third century A.D. the wealthiest landowners were spending little time in the chief towns, which were being exploited by

[5a] These historical aspects are further developed in Richard M. Morse, "Some Characteristics of Latin American Urban History", *The American Historical Review,* LXVII, 2 (Jan. 1962), 317-338.

[6] Olwen Brogan, *Roman Gaul* (London, 1953), pp. 66-67.

[7] Ferdinand Lot, *The End of the Ancient World and the Beginning of the Middle Ages* (New York, 1931), pp. 115-130, and *La Gaule* (Paris, 1947), pp. 201-203, 406-407.

the metropolis, diminishing in size, and becoming gloomy fortified outposts. Rural workers, reduced to servile dependency upon the landholders, came to live in clusters of huts, and to form a kind of agricultural proletariat. A great villa not only had hand-mills, bakeries and such workshops as forges and carpentry shops needed for farm maintenance but might also support embroiderers, chasers, goldsmiths, sculptors and hairdressers. In short, the villa replaced the town as the vehicle of Romanization. "The towns", wrote Collingwood with respect to Roman Britain, "represent romanization as the central government wished to have it; the villas represent it in the shape in which it commended itself to the individual British landowner."[8] Of Gaul Brogan observes that with the decay of imperial authority over municipal life by the fifth century, the "great estates in the country and the bishoprics in the towns were the chief institutions which eased the transition to the Middle Ages".[9]

The Spanish American encomienda was not strictly a latifundium, for it was not a grant of territory but a stipulation of reciprocal duties and privileges obtaining between Spaniards and Indian laborers. Within the limits indicated earlier, land grants (*mercedes*) were generally made by town governments, while encomiendas were awarded by governors, audiencias and viceroys. As a definition of social organization the encomienda showed a medieval imprint. It scarcely corresponded, however, to the medieval manor, for *encomenderos* and their tributary Indians did not share the common traditions which underly a manorial regime of community and mutuality. The prominence of dispositions affecting the encomienda in Spanish laws revealed the crown's constant fear of the *encomenderos'* separatism and their exploitative use of Indian labor. In Brazil, moreover, the latifundiary fazenda rather than the encomienda was introduced from the start, while in Spanish America the encomienda gave way in the eighteenth century to the hacienda, which appears to have had its origin in municipal land grants.[10]

Reverting to the Roman analogy, we will recall the insistence of Fustel de Coulanges that the structure of rural social organization in Western Europe as determined by the villa persisted as late as the ninth century. Village communities tended to lead a somewhat marginal existence and were usually scattered among and upon, and subordinated to, the villas. It was the villa, controlled by a single proprietor, and not the village which originally divided the land and organized rural life and agricultural production.[11] Neither the

[8] *The Cambridge Ancient History*, 12 vols. (Cambridge, 1923-1939), XII, 288.

[9] Brogan, *op. cit.*, pp. 210-211.

[10] Silvio Zavala, *Estudios indianos* (Mexico City, 1948), pp. 207-353; Louis C. Faron, *The Acculturation of the Araucanian Picunche during the First Century of Spanish Colonization in Chile: 1536-1635* (Ph. D. dissertation, Columbia University, 1954), pp. 62-67, 157-172.

[11] Fustel de Coulanges, *L'Alleu et le domaine rural pendant l'époque mérovingienne* (Paris, 1889), pp. 38-42, 198, 229-231, 436-437.

Latin language nor Burgundian and Salic law contained a term that unequivocally denoted "village".[12] In general, a "village" was a grouping of coloni and serfs on a villa, or else a small commercial or parochial center without agricultural functions. From roughly the fourth till the ninth century this situation prevailed. In Carolingian Gaul the "village, as a personality, did not yet exist, seeing that the 'parish' was scarcely beginning to be formed in the country districts".[13] Only in the late Middle Ages did independent village communities come into being, growing in most cases out of the old villas.[14]

In the settling of Latin America the village community was of secondary importance alongside the town or "municipality" and the encomienda or later hacienda. The colonization of central Chile has been described as a concentration of land in the hands of a few, "an extensive domination over large territories rather than small village economies".[15] In modern Venezuela the most frequent form of rural social organization is not the village but the dispersed and nomadic farm families. Eighty-five percent of the centers of population have 25 houses or less, and 92.4% of them have fewer than 200 inhabitants. The resulting conditions of "solitude and isolation are contrary to the development of a spirit of communal cooperation".[16]

The colonial Brazilian village came often as an "afterthought", a spontaneous grouping to care for whatever needs of the settlers were not being served by the fundamental rural unit, the farm or fazenda. The nucleus of today's rural community is the neighborhood, rather than the village center to which a cluster of such neighborhoods may or may not be tributary.[17] An eighteenth-century captain-general despaired of implanting the Portuguese village system in Brazil because of the centrifugal tendencies of the settlers.[18] His letters are similar to those of Spanish administrators in the viceroyalty of New Granada who, during this same period, were unable either to maintain the agricultural Indians in nucleated settlements or to gather the white settlers into systems of villages, or "parishes of Spaniards". Even the larger towns were partly

[12] *Ibid.*, pp. 200 ff. Fustel's theory needs the qualifications that are set forth in Robert Latouche, *The Birth of the Western Economy: Economic Aspects of the Dark Ages* (New York, 1961), pp. 59-72.

[13] Lot, *Ancient World . . .*, *op. cit.*, p. 369.

[14] Roger Grand and R. Delatouche, "Les Communautés paysannes dans la France du Moyen-Age", in François Perroux (ed.), *Agriculture et communauté* (Paris, 1943), pp. 40-62.

[15] Jean Borde and Mario Góngora, *Evolución de la propiedad rural en el Valle del Puangue*, 2 vols. (Santiago de Chile, 1956), I, 57.

[16] J. A. Silva Michelena, "Factores que dificultan y han impedido la reforma agraria en Venezuela", in *Resistências à mudança*, ed. by Centro Latino-Americano de Pesquisas em Ciências Sociais (Rio de Janeiro, 1960), pp. 138-139.

[17] T. Lynn Smith, *Brazil: People and Institutions*, rev. ed. (Baton Rouge, 1954), pp. 495-502.

[18] Carlos Borges Schmidt, "Rural Life in Brazil", in T. Lynn Smith and Alexander Marchant (eds.), *Brazil: Portrait of Half a Continent* (New York, 1951), pp. 169-171.

abandoned because of an exodus of inhabitants to rural haciendas.[19] Today the nuclear rural group in this area — that is, highland Colombia — is still the neighborhood or extended family (*vecindario, vereda*) rather than the village, although there are signs that functional differentiation of the groups is finally causing complementariness among them and therefore the gradual integration of larger communities.[20]

In describing the autonomous and self-sufficient hacienda of northern Mexico in the seventeenth century, formed outside the pale of the encomienda "already drained by the Crown", Chevalier explicitly advances the analogy with post-Roman Europe. Settlements of free workers were absorbed into the hacienda, and the Indian communities became hired labor upon it. Military power and judicial authority in effect devolved upon the *hacendados,* who attracted large retinues of relatives and hangers-on. Mexico City alone broke the monotony of this disintegrated society, "as the *point d'appui* of a State whose authority threatened to dissolve in the vast country".[21]

The regions of the most advanced Indian civilizations, where systems of permanent nucleated settlement had grown up before the Spanish conquest, did not necessarily offer exceptions to the generalizations being developed. Such Indians were often regrouped into small areas for use as a labor force. In the case of Guatemala this "led to cultural integration on a 'township' basis", with the *municipios* becoming "the fundamental cultural units". Divisions tended to reflect preexisting ethnic groupings, "though it is probable that many of these lines were entirely arbitrary".[22] In short, the uprooting and regrouping of highland Indian populations under Spanish administrative arrangements, and the disruption of pre-Columbian economies, might produce unknit or disarticulated hinterlands, as did the settling of empty lands.

To complete the analogy between post-Columbian America and post-Roman Europe, of course, one would have to imagine a gradual cessation of all contact between the Old World and the New once the colonization was effected. Under such circumstances one might further imagine the universal decadence of town life and the decentralization of New World society around the landed estate, as Chevalier has described the process for northern Mexico. Finally, allowing the Americas many centuries of isolated history, one might envision the growth of village communities on or near these estates, as well as a network of exchange among them.

In some regions, especially the more outlying ones, parts of such a process did certainly occur. In counterpoint to it, however, the more important cities

[19] Orlando Fals Borda, *El hombre y la tierra en Boyacá* (Bogotá, 1957), pp. 47-50.
[20] *Ibid.*, pp. 188-198.
[21] François Chevalier, *La formation des grands domaines au Mexique. Terre et société aux XVIe-XVIIe siècles* (Paris, 1952), pp. 390, 404-406.
[22] Felix Webster McBryde, *Cultural and Historical Geography of Southwest Guatemala* (Washington, 1945), pp. 88-89, 100-101.

of Latin America continued to serve as bureaucratic, commercial and cultural outposts of metropolitan Europe and, after Latin America independence, as the centers of national political life. Furthermore, the economy of Latin America as a whole, far from becoming autarkic, came to hinge more and more upon the export of a few raw materials and tropical or semitropical food crops in return for manufactures and other necessaries. This commercial relation with the increasingly industrialized temperate countries brought about erratic, externally induced shifts in the centers of production. It tended to create exploitative patterns of agriculture and an easily uprooted rural proletariat. And it militated against the emergence of a stable network of towns and villages, producing a variety of economic surpluses and linked in commercial exchange.

The history of the settlement of what is today the department of Norte de Santander in Colombia exhibits many features characteristic of the urban history of Latin America as a whole.[23] Six settlement phases have been identified for this north Andean region. (1) The conquest. Towns were founded along strategic routes between the coast and inland administrative centers, or between such centers. Some towns, like Salazar and Ocaña, had multiple foundings before certain military or commercial criteria were empirically satisfied. (2) Rural dispersion. During the seventeenth century no new towns were founded, but some existing Indian centers were "Spaniardized" and brought into encomiendas as the rural taproots of economic life were struck. Also the earthquakes of 1610 and 1644 produced some changes of town sites. (3) Cacao phase. The intensification of agriculture, and in particular the new commercial possibilities of cacao, attracted population from the highlands to the hot, humid river valleys. Cúcuta and other lowland towns were founded, some at the cost of depopulating previous nuclei. The careful regulations for founding cities contained in the Spanish Laws of the Indies were now no longer followed.

(4) Rehabilitation of Indian centers. Overlapping the cacao boom came a period when old encomiendas or Indian settlements took on more importance owing to the wealth of the whites who resided in them. Some towns were formed by the grouping together of scattered Indian nuclei. (5) Improved communication. Intensified agriculture and a denser population caused an increase in transportation among population centers and the appearance of new way-station settlements along the routes. Before the nineteenth century, however, it can be said that the three main towns of the region — Pamplona, Salazar and Ocaña — were still tributary to their surrounding encomiendas and haciendas, and that among them "there was no settlement net by which they might be unified".

[23] Miguel Marciales (ed.), *Geografía histórica y económica del Norte de Santander* (Bogotá, 1948), I, 230-239.

(6) Coffee phase. The early nineteenth century saw the ruin of the cacao industry and a consequent dislocation of people from the valleys to the uplands that was accentuated by the impact of the independence wars. The coffee boom after 1840 caused an indiscriminate founding of towns at centers of coffee production and at temperate altitudes, with little attention paid to topography and other factors of site selection. The thrust from this most recent colonizing phase continues into the twentieth century, and is finally giving a more cohesive set to the human geography of the region.

Returning to the urban history of Latin America as a whole, we may now identify it as having two broad stages. The first was the centrifugal phase, when the towns distributed status- and fortune-seekers out to the land. The social organization of the town was often unstable, and its very life sometimes ephemeral. Social power tended to flow to the rural estate, especially in Brazil and outlying Spanish America. Such towns offer contrast to those of medieval Europe which, through the centripetal process represented in Henri Pirenne's *faubourg* theory, acquired larger populations and new economic processes.

Latin American rural settlement, however, was exploitative, badly articulated and, we might say, of a provisional nature. It is easy to suppose that the loosening of latifundiary ties and a tip in the balance of social and economic expectancy might have caused heavy migration to the cities, giving urban development a sharply centripetal character. This is precisely what happened in the nineteenth and above all in the present century.

Preliminary signs of the new cosmopolitanism and appeal of the larger cities were the urban reforms of such eighteenth-century administrators as Governor Gomes Freire de Andrade in Rio de Janeiro and Viceroy Revillagigedo in Mexico City.[24] Under Gomes Freire and his successors Rio received new public buildings, hospitals, streets and streetlights, parks and defense installations. The city's famous aqueduct was built; pestilential areas were cleaned up or paved; reforms in municipal administration were introduced.[25] Mexico City benefitted from very similar improvements, which included better policing, paving and lighting of streets, a new aqueduct, and such buildings as the mint, the custom house and the school of mines. Lima was almost completely rebuilt and modernized after the earthquake of 1746. "And what was true of Mexico and Lima was true only in lesser degree of the principal provincial cities."[26]

With the coming of Latin American independence in the early nineteenth century, cities — and especially the new national capitals — assumed a

[24] Ladislao Gil Munilla, "La ciudad de Hispanoamérica", *Estudios Americanos*, X, 48 (Sept. 1955), 307.

[25] Vivaldo Coaracy, *Memórias da cidade do Rio de Janeiro* (Rio de Janeiro, 1955), pp. 563-574.

[26] C. H. Haring, *The Spanish Empire in America* (New York, 1947), p. 345.

pivotal role as the cockpits of national politics, as centers for trade now free of mercantilist restraint, and often as refuges from the disruption and banditry of rural life. For Gilberto Freyre the key trend of the social and institutional history of nineteenth-century Brazil is the shift of power from the rural "big house", or *casa grande,* of the planter class to the town house, or *sobrado,* of the urban bourgeoisie.[27] The ascendancy of economic liberalism in the new nations helped to commercialize and build up capital in the urban economy, and to make available the multiplying products of the industrialized societies. Even before banks were established, the Brazilian city of the early nineteenth century "began to extend its dominion over the country in the form of loans".[28] In 1844 a Venezuelan observed that, in his country, newly passed Benthamite legislation authorized high, even usurious interest rates that were giving the urban moneylender a stranglehold on the nation's agricultural development.[29]

Statistics for the province of Buenos Aires show that the rural population continued to grow at a faster rate than that of the city until the 1830's, when the failure of the government's colonization policy and the city's greater economic attractions swung the balance the other way.[30] From then until the First World War Buenos Aires, like other cities of Uruguay and southern Brazil, depended for its growth largely upon foreign immigration. This, however, was unusual in Latin America; and even in Argentina the total number of permanent immigrants was only one half of the 6.5 million arrivals, owing to the country's relatively limited agricultural and industrial possibilities.[31]

By and large, Latin American city growth since independence has been fed by internal migrations. The nature and extent of these migrations are related to the patterns of settlement already described, and particularly to the lack of a seigneurial or village-community basis for rural social organization. Certain social and technological changes of the nineteenth century cast adrift large numbers of rural workers. These changes included the abolition of Negro slavery; the disruption of Indian communities or *resguardos* by ostensibly "liberal" legislation; the commercializing and industrializing of agriculture; and the intensifying of single-crop production that offered only seasonal employment.

Reinforcing the push from the country was the pull of the city, especially the capital cities, now modernized with gas lights, trolley lines, broad prome-

[27] Gilberto Freyre, *Sobrados e mucambos,* 2nd. ed., 3 vols. (Rio de Janeiro, 1951).

[28] Smith and Marchant, *op. cit.*, p. 201.

[29] Fermín Toro, *Reflexiones sobre la Ley de 10 de abril de 1.834 y otras obras* (Caracas, 1941), pp. 162-163.

[30] Miron Burgin, *The Economic Aspects of Argentine Federalism 1820-1852* (Cambridge, 1946), p. 27.

[31] Richard Robbins, "Myth and Realities of International Migration into Latin America", *The Annals of the American Academy of Political and Social Science*, 316 (March 1958), 106.

nades, theaters, opera houses and monumental public buildings. By urban improvements the national strong man catered to the increasingly absentee and city-based landholders of an oligarchical, almost clan-like society. The same improvements, however, attracted rural masses to the cities, where eventually they were to exert their own pressures in national politics.

Since the rural-urban migration was common to the whole Western world after the Industrial Revolution, one must bear in mind special characteristics of the process as it occurred in Latin America.

First, the Latin American migration to cities, taken globally, represents a pressing against a social and technological system rather than against the soil itself. Latin America contains 16% of the world's habitable area but only 6.8% of its population.[32]

Second, the migration has been out of proportion to the opportunities for employment in manufacture. The ratio between employment in manufacturing and employment in "services" in Latin America is 1.4 to 1, as against a 1 to 1 ratio in Western Europe. In the United States the "services" ratio is high (1.5), but growth in this sector was preceded by tremendous expansion of industrial productivity. The increase in the "services" category in Latin America partly precedes industrial development, and it reflects activity in what are often called the least productive services, such as petty commerce and certain personal services. Moreover, half of the Latin Americans said to be employed in manufacturing are really in handicrafts.[33]

Third, migration has favored the large so-called "primate" city, usually one in each country, thus creating a topheavy pyramid or hierarchy of cities, and leaving the networks of secondary towns underdeveloped. Transportation nets radiate out from the primate cities, and give frequently poor direct connections among hinterland towns.

Finally, migration tends to assume an unselective, diluvial character, and rural migrants often bypass the intermediate forms of non-agricultural, semi-rural employment.[34] In Mexico and Ecuador there are even localities where the Indian becomes a factory worker or becomes urbanized without passing through the rural mestizo cultural stage.[35]

[32] Kingsley Davis, "Recent Population Trends in the New World: An Over-all View", *The Annals of the American Academy of Political and Social Science,* 316 (March 1958), 7.

[33] Harley L. Browning, "Recent Trends in Latin America Urbanization", *The Annals of the American Academy of Political and Social Science*, 316 (March 1958), 117; Davis, *loc. cit.*, p. 9.

[34] Browning, *loc. cit.*, p. 118. The more gradual process by which rural migrants were absorbed into the European urban proletariat is described in Georges Friedmann (ed.), *Villes et campagnes, civilisation urbaine et civilisation rurale en France* (Paris, 1953), pp. 159-161.

[35] Ralph L. Beals, "Urbanism, Urbanization and Acculturation", in Olen E. Leonard and Charles P. Loomis (eds.), *Readings in Latin American Social Organization & Institutions* (East Lansing, Mich., 1953), p. 172.

A sociological study of Lima, Peru, published at the turn of this century gives a trenchant if somewhat impressionistic account of the life and institutions of that city.[36] Many of its observations might be generalized for the other urban societies of modern Latin America. Lima, we are told, lacked the "superorganic unity" of European cities. The regime of association was exceedingly weak. Neither professional groups nor workers' unions had passed beyond a rudimentary stage. Political parties were organized not around principles but around personalistic leaders and their cliques who were seeking wealth and power. Class demarcations and identifications were loose, which impelled people to simulate higher class positions than they in fact enjoyed and to substitute appearance for reality.

The citizen's sense of civic responsibility and of loyalty to the larger community, or municipality, was faint; and his opportunities for enterprise were smothered by the triple evils of monopoly, usury and heavy taxes. A large proportion of the population was therefore non-functional. Some 30,000 persons, or 30% of the inhabitants, were idlers who drifted among the cafés or, if youths, formed platoons on street corners to block the way and insult passing women. Only one child in three in Lima attended school.

The nuclear social unit of Lima's society, the author continues, was the extended family, which might range across all the class strata and afford a permanent means for its indolent members to prey upon the industrious. "Every family has its links scattered from the beggars' asylum to the wealthiest class." The main cause of Lima's poverty and political corruption is that "the chief of this tribe, however much he may work, can never, by the honest path, acquire sufficient resources to provide sustenance for so many people".[37]

At the time this study of Lima appeared, the modern growth of Latin American cities was still gathering momentum. Only four countries had over 10% of their population in cities of 20,000 or more. By 1950, however, 25% of the total Latin American population was in cities of 20,000 or more, and 17% was in cities of 100,000 or more.[38] This last percentage was 9% above the average for Asia, 4% above the world average, and only 4% below the average for Europe. But while Latin America had nearly as many people in large cities, proportionately, as Europe, about two-thirds of its labor force was still in agriculture, as against slightly over one-third for Europe.[39]

Enough has been said of the causes and nature of growth of the Latin American city to suggest that its structure fails to conform to other city types of the Western world. A contrast that has been drawn between the sociogeographic structure of São Paulo, Brazil, and that of Paris makes the point

36 J. Capelo, *Sociología de Lima,* 4 vols. (Lima, 1895-1902), III, *passim.*

37 *Ibid.*, III, 258-264.

38 Browning, *loc. cit.*, p. 111.

39 Kingsley Davis and Hilda Hertz Golden, "Urbanization and the Development of Pre-industrial areas", *Economic Development and Cultural Change,* III, 1 (Oct. 1954), 8.

that whereas Paris is divided into scores of autonomous administrative units, São Paulo is an urban agglomeration that lacks any "organic subcenters of collective life".[40] This does not mean that São Paulo is a disorganized mass of individuals. It means that there is archaic, paternalistic centralization of control at the top and a multitude of quasi-familial, potentially vital social cells at the bottom, with weak structures and organizations mediating between them. The attempt to develop such intermediate structures need not and probably should not follow closely the model of the classic cities of the Western commercial and industrial world.

A baseline frequently used in studying the Western city is a unilinear scale which ranges from the close-knit folk village to the metropolis and which is foreshadowed in the writings of Maine, Tönnies and Durkheim. An ultimate model for the urban end of the continuum — for the competitive, depersonalized, anomic metropolis — was identified by American sociology as the Chicago of the 1920's. One version of this bipolar scale was formulated for a Latin American setting by Robert Redfield in his study of rural and urban communities in Yucatan. In comparison with the town, the village and the tribal settlement, he described the Yucatecan city of Mérida as culturally heterogeneous, disorganized, secularized and individualized.[41] It may be inferred, however, that Redfield was more interested in constructing an ideal, universal typology than in identifying the specifically Mexican or Latin American characteristics of Mérida.

A leading trait of the Western metropolis is its highly developed regime of impersonal associations. This trait implies the condition of anomie, which pertains not to a man who lives in an unorganized world, but to one whose world offers a bewildering excess of possibilities for impersonal group affiliation. The Latin American city, however, is not richly endowed with associations. A study of Guadalajara, Mexico, (1950 population, 378,000) revealed that over 60% of 415 respondents belonged to no voluntary association at all; only 11 respondents (or 2.7%) belonged to three or more associations. Of the memberships, 49.8% were in church groups and 26.3% in athletic or "social" clubs. The fact that many of the city's associations paralleled those of American cities and were therefore explainable by cultural diffusion, raised a question as to the extent to which they even answer "the functional necessities of an urban social structure *per se*". Moreover the diffusion has been selective. The sample contained no memberships at all in secular women's clubs, fraternal lodges, local political or "ward" clubs, or veterans' associations. There was little evidence of organization into pressure groups.[42]

[40] A. Delorenzo Neto, "O aglomerado urbano de São Paulo", *Revista Brasileira de Estudos Políticos,* III, 6 (July 1959), 121-127.

[41] Robert Redfield, *The Folk Culture of Yucatan* (Chicago, 1941).

[42] Floyd Dotson, "A Note on Participation in Voluntary Associations in a Mexican City", *American Sociological Review*, XVIII, 4 (Aug. 1953), 380-386.

In Latin America, rationalistic, depersonalized forms of organization are making uneven headway against primary and personalistic forms. This is borne out when we examine the structure of labor unions, political parties or business enterprise;[43] or when we are told that a resident of São Paulo, a city of some four million, can be expected to be in touch with anywhere from 30 to 500 relatives;[44] or when we observe that only 3% of the 47,000 manufacturing plants in Colombia have more than twenty employees.[45]

Rural migrants to the big cities, however bewildered and disoriented they may be, are not, strictly speaking, "massified".[46] They carry with them or, as circumstances permit, re-create quasi-familial or neighborhood arrangements. It has been pointed out that whereas rural migrants to European cities in the eighteenth and nineteenth centuries soon found new homes and loyalties in the city, their modern counterparts in underdeveloped countries continue "belonging" to their places of origin. The city remains strange to them and forces them to seek out as associates persons from their own kinship group or region. Patterns of co-operation, authority and responsibility are fashioned upon rural models rather than upon those of the Western city.[47]

In a Latin American city rural migrants and, in general, the proletariat are not customarily crowded into a blighted area at the urban core, as in the schema devised for the North American city by the sociologist E. W. Burgess; but they are scattered, often in makeshift dwellings, in peripheral or interstitial zones. The Latin American city center with its spacious plaza was traditionally the residence area for the wealthy and was the point of concentration for urban services and utilities. The quickening of commercial activity in this center may displace well-to-do residents without necessarily creating "contaminated" and overcrowded belts of social disorganization. The poor are often not attracted into transitional zones by cheap rents; they tend to move out to unused land as the city expands, erecting their own shacks. The downtown area becomes converted for commercial uses or for compact and modern middle- and upper-income residences.[48]

In Guatemala City in the 1940's the four worst slums were all peripherally

43 For São Paulo see Richard M. Morse, *From Community to Metropolis: A Biography of São Paulo, Brazil* (Gainesville, 1958), pp. 209-212, 228-230.

44 Emílio Willems, "The Structure of the Brazilian Family", *Social Forces*, XXXI, 4 (May 1953), 343.

45 Ford Foundation Mission to Colombia, "Political and Economic Profile of Colombia", June 1960 (offset).

46 Yolanda Ortiz, "Algunas dificultades de adaptación de las poblaciones rurales al pasar al medio urbano en los países latinoamericanos y especialmente en Colombia", *Revista Mexicana de Sociologia*, XIX, 1 (Jan.-April 1957), 25-38.

47 Bert F. Hoselitz, "The City, the Factory, and Economic Growth", *The American Economic Review*, XLV, 2 (May 1955), 176.

48 Floyd and Lillian Ota Dotson, "Ecological Trends in the City of Guadalajara, Mexico", *Social Forces*, XXXII, 4 (May 1954), 367-374, and "La estructura ecológica de las ciudades mexicanas", *Revista Mexicana de Sociología*, XIX, 1 (Jan.-April 1957), 39-66.

located and all brand new. Within two kilometers of the city center there was only one area of distinctly poor housing. The "lower class half-urbanized" groups in great misery but without being overcrowded on the American scale; "the tendency to interior breakdown of the urban configuration which so concerns contemporary North American planners is not a problem in Guatemala". And while it is clear that the city's acculturation of the rural migrant is a disorganizing experience which entails a period of cultural marginality, we are led to question "the assumption that individual and institutional disorganization are progressive functions of urbanism per se".[49]

Recent studies shed light upon the formation, structure and social processes of the urban areas settled by rural migrants. In the case of Rio de Janeiro the first *favelas*[50] appeared in the late nineteenth century. However, most of the city's poor continued to live in collective dwellings, usually converted from houses of the wealthy, until about 1930, when there came a surge of rural migration. Construction of "rustic" dwellings in the city rose to an average of 1,000 per year in the 1930's and to 2,700 a year in the 1940's. By 1957 650,000 people, or a fifth of Rio's population, lived in *favelas*.[51] Of the population of Lima, Peru, about 10% live in *barriadas,* or communities of dwellings on unimproved land generally peripheral to the city. On a single night in December, 1954, it is reported that 5,000 persons "invaded" Lima to establish a colony on a tract along the Rimac valley.[52]

The majority of the urban proletariat tends to be of rural origin. Of the family heads in the Lima *barriadas* studied, 89% were born in the provinces, only 11% in Lima. Of the former, more than three-fifths came from the Indian cultures of the mountain area.[53] A sample of semi- and unskilled factory workers in São Paulo showed that no less than two-thirds of them had either worked in agriculture or lived in rural settings.[54] Some of the migrants to cities — those from the Andean or Middle American Indian areas, for example — may carry with them developed traditions of collective action. In Brazil, on the other hand, the rapid disappearance of the *mutirão,* a rural

[49] Theodore Caplow, "The Social Ecology of Guatemala City", *Social Forces,* XXVIII, 2 (Dec. 1949), 114-115, 124-125, 127, 133.

[50] A *favela* is defined as a grouping of at least fifty rustic huts or barracks, unlicensed and uninspected, built by squatters on lands that lack any urban improvements.

[51] Andrew Pearse, "Some Characteristics of Urbanization in the City of Rio de Janeiro", United Nations document E/CN.12/URB/17 - UNESCO/SS/URB/LA/17 (30 Sept. 1958), pp. 1-4. This study and those below by Matos Mar and Brandão Lopes are now published in Philip M. Hauser (ed.), *Urbanization in Latin America* (New York, 1961).

[52] José Matos Mar, "Migration and Urbanization, the 'Barriadas' of Lima: An Example of Integration into Urban Life", United Nations document E/CN.12/URB/11 - UNESCO/SS/URB/LA/11 (30 Sept. 1958), p. 12.

[53] *Ibid.*, p. 14.

[54] Juarez Rubens Brandão Lopes, "Aspects of the Adjustment of Rural Migrants to Urban-industrial Conditions in São Paulo, Brazil", United Nations document E/CN. 12/URB.3 - UNESCO/SS/URB/LA/3 (30 Sept. 1958), pp. 5-6.

institution for mutual aid, has left few such traditions "beyond the orbit of kinship and neighborhood relationship".[55] Even, however, in the *barriadas* of Lima with their migrants from Indian highlands, the insecurities and mixed origins of the inhabitants work against cooperation, so that "the family remains the sole effective compensating unit". In rural areas the family, the community and tradition are all cohesive forces, "whereas in the city there is nothing left but the family".[56]

The fact that large extended families do not move from country to city intact and in a moment of time does not necessarily mean — as much urbanization theory would assume — that the migrant family is stripped down to the nuclear or conjugal unit. In the *favelas* of Rio de Janeiro, to be sure, Pearse found only 17 "nuclear families with accretions" in a total of 279 families studied. He also found, however, that migrants to the city came as links in a chain of kin groups "both preceded and followed by kin in persistent movement citywards". City dwellers give every assistance to in-migrants belonging to their kin group. New kin groups are created within the city by marriages, and the appointment of godparents may either reinforce existing groups or extend them by incorporation of non-kin. Visiting tends to occur among kin-group families of the same or different *favelas* rather than among neighbors. Little sentiment attaches to the geographic neighborhood, and attendance at general gatherings for the public is not well looked upon. The kin group serves as "the dominant and almost exclusive sanction group" for the behavior, protection and collective action of its members.[57]

Some version of the extended family seems to be a basic social unit common to all the urban working-class zones. Moreover, the family size of the average dwelling unit is not always so small as in the Rio *favelas* observed by Pearse, nor always limited to the conjugal family. A comparison between rural Venezuelan communities and migrant communities in Caracas reveals that the number of extended-family households drops by only 1% in the city, and that the average family size actually increases.[58] Oscar Lewis followed his study of the Mexican village of Tepoztlán with studies of districts, or *vecindades*, of Mexico City peopled by migrant Tepoztecans. Not only was the average household size in the city larger than in the village (5.8 against 5), but the city households contained a slightly larger percentage of extended families. Lewis found "very little evidence of family disorganization in the city". There seemed to occur no weakening of parental authority over children and no decline in church attendance and religious practices. It even appeared that the trials of urban life gave continuity to a family solidarity which was

[55] *Ibid.*, p. 14.
[56] Matos Mar, *op. cit.*, pp. 17-18.
[57] Pearse, *op. cit.*, pp. 7, 10-12.
[58] Inter American Economic and Social Council, Pan American Union, *Causas y efectos del éxodo rural en Venezuela* (Washington, n.d.), p. 188.

evoked in the village only during crisis or emergency.[59] Lewis reports one *vecindad* in Mexico City in which most of the families, originally migrants, have lived for fifteen to twenty years. Over a third of the households have blood relatives within the *vecindad,* and a fourth are related by marriage or kinship.[60] In Lima, the associations of residents based on provinces of origin, the associations of residents of the *barriadas* and the trade unions are all secondary to the family, "which provides the greatest source of security for the inhabitants of these areas".[61]

The point is not that rural or familial institutions are indefinitely preserved, or precisely duplicated, in the Latin American city. It is, rather, that the utilization and *adaptation* of such forms are a necessary alternative in the near-absence of mechanisms for the rapid assimilation of migrants into the urban milieu. Thus we find that lower-class residents of the fast-growing city of Cali, Colombia, maintain not only the traditional *compadrazgo* (extended family or coparenthood relation) but also an improvised urban variety of it. The conventional one, carried from the country, acknowledged the *compadre* as "the trusted person who may eventually replace the father of the family", while the city-born version is designed to obtain "economic aid, even though sporadic, from a person of higher income". "Thus the traditional *compadrazgo* binds neighbors among each other, while the economic one binds them to the city."[62]

A study of political behavior in Rio de Janeiro concludes that the city worker, "failing to find in the urban structure the powerful organizations of professional and social solidarity which constitute the bulwark of urban life in the highly industrialized countries, seeks to rebuild his political behavior following the guidelines of agrarian patriarchalism". The local ward boss is utilized by his higher-ups in the same way that the agrarian "clan" leader once utilized the *compadre,* the authority figure of the extended-family relation.[63]

Of the *compadrazgo* in Mexico City Lewis finds that it has made urban adaptations without becoming weakened. In the city many types of godparent fall into disuse; by and large it is only the godparents of baptism and marriage that continue to be named, and these are generally blood relatives because the family has not the friends it knew in the village. Thus the urban *com-*

[59] Oscar Lewis, "Urbanization without Breakdown: A Case Study", *The Scientific Monthly*, LXXV, 1 (July 1952), 36-37. Lewis recognizes that Tepoztecans, coming from a traditional and stable community, are not typical migrants; he calls for similar studies of poor and landless migrants from plantation areas. *Ibid.*, p. 41.

[60] Oscar Lewis, *Five Families: Mexican Case Studies in the Culture of Poverty* (New York, 1959), pp. 13-14, 63.

[61] Matos Mar, *op. cit.*, p. 10.

[62] Centro Interamericano de Vivienda y Planeamiento, *Siloé, el proceso de desarrollo comunal aplicado a un proyecto de rehabilitación urbana* (Bogotá, 1958), p. 9.

[63] José Arthur Rios, "El pueblo y el político", *Política*, 6 (Feb. 1960), 34-35.

padrazgo is reinforced by blood ties and becomes more personal, less ceremonial. It comes in fact to resemble more nearly the version originally introduced in Mexico City by the Spaniards.[64]

Hand in hand with the quasi-rural forms of social organization found in the city goes the conventionally agrarian attitude of dependency of the poor or weak upon the rich or strong. The urban or "economic" *compadrazgo* of Cali described above is a product of such an attitude. The migrant in Rio de Janeiro is not content with a mere wage nexus, and he looks for the patron, the *bom patrão,* who will advance him money or medicine, or help him cope with the bureaucracy. He may even appeal for tutelage to a strong saint through prayers or communication via a medium. Pearse uses the term "populism" to describe the system of patronage or "clientage" which preserves for the urban scene the spirit of rural face-to-face dependency relations. The common man receives his benefits — jobs, welfare services, recreation facilities, and so forth — through the intervention of "populist" and well publicized leaders who utilize informal patronage structures that usually lie outside the formal structures of administration. "Populism does not favour the organization of common interest groups or cooperative groups, and power is usually delegated downwards rather than upwards." The common man fits easily into this situation, for "he does not know either how to obtain his legal rights or how to operate successfully even in the lower echelons of the power and influence structures".[65]

Of course, the obverse to dependency is "independence". That the latter sentiment is no less intimately a part of the migrant's outlook is attested by his stubborn preference for the one-family dwelling, however crude and makeshift, even in the largest metropolises. Nearly every migrant to São Paulo looks for the chance to work on his own. "Any job where I'd give the orders", said one; "it could be anything, a liquor shop, a food store. Anything that could be mine. Nobody would give me orders there, see?"[66] A factory worker employed some years may frequently be expected to lower his production rate so that he will be dismissed and may then set up his business with the dismissal compensation. Each worker's performance tends to be guided by an internalized norm, deriving from rural traditions but reworked under city influences and in answer to his particular needs as he sees them. That is, his job behavior is guided more by personal, *independent* criteria than by the requirements of the *system.*

Given the urban worker's lack of experience with secondary groups and lack of identification with the industrial structure, it is no surprise that his most effective group participation is on an *ad hoc,* cooperative basis. It is through mutual-aid residents' associations that the inhabitants of the Lima

[64] Lewis, "Urbanization . . .", *loc. cit.*, p. 38.

[65] Pearse, *op. cit.*, pp. 13-15.

[66] Brandão Lopes, *op. cit.*, p. 12.

barriadas exert pressure on the bureaucracy, the church and other entities to acquire the essential services of urban life. Organized communities are thus constituted which have "as their specific objective home ownership".[67] An example of such an association in Cali is the Central Pro-Vivienda de Colombia, a virtually spontaneous organization of 3,850 lower-class family heads who each pay about twenty cents a week to a common fund for acquiring residential land and urban services. The Central is governed by its own general assembly, board of directors and governing committee. Its objectives include: legal acquisition of land for individual home ownership; assistance in home construction; studies to determine the greatest needs of the poor classes and the ability of each family to pay for its land; solidarity of homeless persons without attention to political, religious or racial considerations; exertion of pressure to bring down land prices near the city; encouragement of cooperation and self-help among the poor, especially for the construction of dwellings; moral and cultural improvement of the poor and defense of the nuclear family; resistance to the creation of new slums and the "invasion" of private lands.[68]

In all, some 4.5 million Latin American families live in urban slums and shanty towns. Often it is they themselves who take the initiative and organize to improve their living conditions and administer their own affairs, to become on occasion effective political groups.[69] There exists an economic argument against high governmental expenditures to improve the material condition of these urban poor. It is that a fixed capital investment in Latin America of $100 generates $40 to $50 of production per year. The same money invested in residential building generates only $10 to $12.[70] This is an important consideration for an underdeveloped country. As a cold dollars-and-cents argument, it becomes more palatable when taken in combination with a sociological one — namely, that the hiatus between urban bureaucratic structures and the agrarian background of the migrant is so great that accommodation of one to the other can be expected only after the migrants have grouped themselves, if possible with understanding guidance, in *ad hoc,* transitional associations. In short, the alternative to the urban worker's personalistic "dependency complex" is not necessarily impersonal, bureaucratic regimentation but might be an appeal to his "independence complex".

Wherever we pick our way in the study of the modern Latin American city we must be careful not to trip over concealed premises that derive from

[67] Matos Mar, *op. cit.*, pp. 11-12.
[68] " 'Central Pro-Vivienda de Colombia:' Síntesis sobe origen, organización y finalidades", ms. by Eduardo Burbano R., secretary general of the Central, June 1960.
[69] "Report of the Seminar on Urbanization Problems in Latin America", United Nations document E/CN.12/URB/26/Rev. 1 - UNESCO/SS/URB/LA/26/Rev. 1 (29 Feb. 1960), pp. 57, 61-62.
[70] *Ibid.*, p. 31.

familiarity with West European or North American cities. At least three such premises have come to the surface in this paper:

(1) *The primate city.* It is customary to deplore overwhelming concentration of persons and services in a single primate city which is said to be parasitic and to be a "cause" for the underdevelopment of the hinterland. One observer asks, however, whether urban concentration does not offer advantages in countries which cannot afford to dissipate their meager resources. If Montevideo, which contains 40% of the population of Uruguay, were divided into two or three cities, would these still offer the existing services and amenities? Also, the beef-and-wool economy needs relatively few rural workers to run it. The question is raised, is not Latin America perhaps "over-ruralized" rather than "over-urbanized"? Is not the present afflux to the cities healthy, as helping to provide both a solution for agricultural underemployment and a better opportunity for rationalizing rural production? [71]

(2) *The "services" sector.* Another observer asks us to be wary of a facile distinction between the high proportion of tertiary employment, or employment in "services", found in rich countries (seen as an index of progress) and the high proportion found in the poor countries (seen as an index of poverty). "Services" in Latin America are often loosely referred to as "petty" ones in which "excessive" numbers are employed, though with no definition of terms. The question occurs, do not people generally seek out the most advantageous employment, and would not those who are in "petty services" tend to be less productive in the other occupations open to them? May not Latin American city growth be reallocating the working force into more effective occupational patterns? [72]

(3) *The city as "Gesellschaft".* The assumption is frequently made that the urbanization of modern Latin America implies the depersonalization of social ties, the ascendancy of the secondary over the primary social group, and the bureaucratization of the occupational structure. While it is clear that such processes are at work, it is less certain that they are as unequivocal or as overmastering as in the classic model of the Western metropolis. Certainly there is nothing prescriptive about them, and the attempt to build an independent theoretical model for the Latin American city would be of solid practical value for the reconstruction of its society.

There is already much evidence that similar analyses need to be done for cities throughout the underdeveloped world. William Kolb suggests that these cities cannot "afford" the diversity and anarchic conflict of Chicago in its heyday. They will industrialize and achieve fitting levels of welfare largely under governmental control. Diffuse bonds of neighborliness and kinship in

[71] Browning, *loc. cit.*, pp. 116-118.

[72] Simon Rottenberg, "Note on the Economics of Urbanization in Latin America", United Nations document E/CN.12/URB 6 - UNESCO/SS/URB/LA/6 (30 Sept. 1958), pp. 8-11.

cities can be further developed and may long endure. What Talcott Parsons calls the universalistic-achievement values of the Western city may never receive full stress in other settings. "Primary controls of a community oriented variety can be much more prominent both in the control of individual action and of corporate action." [73]

Marriot speculates that in India extended primary group organization may even have grown stronger with the growth of cities.[74] Banton gives us a study of the city of Freetown, Sierra Leone, which has a population that is about three-quarters tribal. Here the fusion points of African and Western culture often produce new cultural forms which are outwardly European but retain a latent content of tribal significance.[75] It should in fact be noted that an attack has even been launched upon the assumption that extended family relationships are incompatible with the democratic industrial society of the West. It is now asserted that the isolated nuclear family was the most functional type only during earlier stages of industrialization. A modified version of the extended family, no longer characterized by geographic propinquity, occupational nepotism or strict authority relations, appears to be coming into a more important role in the Western industrial city.[76] If this is the case, it would almost seem that the Latin American city is, in certain respects of social organization, more "developed" than that of the developed nations.

At this point we may restate the two interrelated hypotheses which have been set forth in this paper regarding the process of Latin American colonization and the structure of the modern Latin American city. The early settlement patterns had, by and large, a municipal point of origin. During the colonial period, however, rural institutions developed to an important extent outside the radius of municipal control. Under such conditions, rural social organization was thrown back upon extended-family, *compadrazgo* or neighborhood units.[77] These were reminiscent of the *hermandad* or *adfratatio* of early medieval Europe, a social unit which at the time of the discovery of America had given way to a more complex type of community organization.[78]

[73] William L. Kolb, "The Social Structure and Functions of Cities", *Economic Development and Cultural Change*, III, 1 (Oct. 1954), 43-46.

[74] McKimm Marriott, "Comments" on Kolb's article, *loc. cit.*, pp. 50-52.

[75] Michael Banton, *West African City: A Study of Tribal Life in Freetown* (London, 1957).

[76] Eugene Litwak, "Occupational Mobility and Extended Family Cohesion" and "Geographic Mobility and Extended Family Cohesion", *American Sociological Review*, XXV, 1 and 2 (Feb. and April 1960), 9-21, 385-394.

[77] Fals Borda, *op. cit.*, p. 188.

[78] Alfons Dopsch, *The Economic and Social Foundations of European Civilization* (London, 1937), p. 158; Eduardo Hinojosa, "La comunidad doméstica en España durante la Edad Media", *La Lectura*, V, 2 (1905), 233-241, and "La fraternidad artificial en España", *Revista de Archivos, Bibliotecas y Museos*, IX, 7 (July 1905), 1-18; Sidney W. Mintz and Eric R. Wolf, "An Analysis of Ritual Co-parenthood (Compadrazgo)", *Southwestern Journal of Anthropology*, VI, 4 (Winter 1950), 341-368.

As the Latin American city entered its centripetal phase in the nineteenth century, it began to reap as it had sown. It drew massively from the rural areas, and the migrants depended heavily upon traditional or impromptu primary group organizations for their accommodation to urban life. Thus the city, which imparted an individualistic, exploitative spirit to the settling of the land, exhibits internally the traces of agrarian, familialistic social structure. Any attempted reconstruction of the Latin American city which relies upon secondary associations to the neglect of primary groups would seem, therefore, to have only tenuous chances of success.

20. Urbanization, Political Stability, and Economic Growth*

SHANTI TANGRI

Sociologists and economists have in general tended to agree about the mutually beneficent influence of urbanization and economic development. The argument runs in terms of economies of population aggregation and value transformations conducive to economizing, enterprising, and innovative behavior. Generalizations in this field are based largely on the historical experience of Western developed economies.[1]

I have argued elsewhere that urbanization is neither a necessary nor a sufficient condition for economic growth.[2] Under certain conditions, however, and up to a point, it can be a desirable condition for growth, while under other conditions, or beyond a certain point, it can be a factor in slowing down growth. In contemporary India the process of urbanization, in both magnitude and nature, seems to be a factor retarding rather than accelerating growth.

Here I do not propose to review the highly important but well-

[1] For a brief (and unsympathetic) review of non-Weberian theories of the city see Don Martindale and Gertrude Neuwirth's Prefatory Remarks (pp. 9–62) in their translation of *The City*, by Max Weber (Glencoe, Ill.: Free Press, 1958). For a more limited and relevant discussion see William L. Kolb, "The Social Structure and Functions of Cities," *Economic Development and Cultural Change*, III, No. 1 (October, 1954), 30–46.

[2] "Patterns of Investment and Rates of Growth, with Special Reference to India" (Doctoral dissertation, University of California, Berkeley, 1960). For a historical criticism of the "industrialization through urbanization" thesis see Carl Bridenbaugh, *Cities in the Wilderness* (New York: Ronald Press, 1938), and *Cities in Revolt* (New York: Knopf, 1955).

* Reprinted from Roy Turner, ed., *India's Urban Future.*

discussed issues of social overhead capital, economies of scale for industrial plants and cities as a whole, external economies, consumer densities, pools of labor, skills and knowledge, centers of communication and innovation, etc.[3] My contention is rather that we cannot determine the role of urbanization without estimating the economic costs or benefits of such urban phenomena as *anomie*, political and ideological ferment, and transformation of cultural and social values. For drawing policy conclusions we need also to know comparable costs and benefits associated with social change among rural populations. I have been unable to find comparative studies of this nature. Reviewing the literature on social and economic change leads me to believe, however, that the socio-economic costs of tradition-oriented rural attitudes, though never measured, are usually assumed to be prohibitive enough to make growth extremely slow, if not impossible, while similar costs of urbanization are seldom considered to be high enough to prevent or retard change. Indeed, this is what the historical experience of Western societies seems to indicate.[4] That perhaps is not and will not be the case in India and some other underdeveloped countries. As the benefits of urbanization have been discussed extensively in the literature, I will discuss primarily the other side of the case. In this context a few words about the relative rural-urban potential for economic development are in order.

The Rural-Urban Potential for Asset Formation

In the cities, the savings of entrepreneurial and managerial classes tend to be high, and those of middle and lower classes to be low or negative, because of low incomes and/or higher consumption standards and lower earner-dependent ratios in families. Thus, while the proportion invested out of industrial incomes tends to be relatively high, compared to investments out of agricultural income,[5] it is not clear how the total urban savings-income ratio compares on a per capita basis with the rural savings-income ratio.

[3] See, for example, Eric Lampard, "The History of Cities in Economically Advanced Areas," *Economic Development and Cultural Change*, III, No. 1 (October, 1954), 81–136.

[4] *Ibid.*, p. 132.

[5] P. N. Rosenstein-Rodan thinks the former ratio is often as high as 35 per cent and the latter between 10 and 15 per cent. (This and other references to him are based on personal conversations and a seminar he gave at the Massachusetts Institute of Technology in the spring of 1959.) Wilfred Malenbaum derives the figure 10 per cent for the latter ratio from sample data on India; cf. *The Non-Monetized Sector of Rural India* (Cambridge, Mass.: Center for International Studies, M.I.T., 1956), p. 11. He thinks the figure may be a slight overestimate. Some economists think the figure is much lower. For an argument that most estimates of rural capital formation are downward biased see Basil S. Yamey, and Peter T. Bauer, *Economics of Underdeveloped Countries* (Chicago: University of Chicago Press, 1957), pp. 16–31.

Lack of empirical information precludes judgment on the relative rural-urban potential for asset formation out of internal savings.

However, the possibilities of asset creation without prior or concomitant savings are quite extensive and impressive in rural areas[6] and insignificant in urban areas. In the villages people often cooperate to help each other in building houses or fences, or in other acts requiring group effort; not so in the cities, where exchange of labor is monetized and thus involves problems of financing. Again, in the villages there are unused resources—such as common village lands, forests, tanks, wells, ponds, labor, and skills which can be used for asset creation given an appropriate program of mobilization. A villager repairs his own home more readily than a city dweller. Also there is a lesser expectation, on the part of an idle villager, as compared to an urbanite, of finding alternative sources of income, whether the relative expectations of the urbanite and villager are justified or not by the realities of job markets.[7] Thus, lower opportunity costs of the villager make it easier for him to donate his labor to his neighbor or to his community. Finally, many materials and assets which the villager has use for are not desired by the urbanite. The villager can dig up clay and lime and bring palm leaves from the outskirts of the village and husks from his fields, to thatch his roof or plaster his walls or add a room to his house. The urbanite will live in a crowded brick hovel rather than in a thatched mud house. He may not be able to afford a new brick house, but a mud house is not an asset in his eyes—and if it were, the municipal authorities would probably not tolerate, much less encourage, its construction.

The deepening, cleaning, and lining of village tanks and wells as sources of water supply for humans and animals and for irrigation and the construction of warehouses for storing agricultural produce—a vital step for stabilizing agricultural prices and increasing output, for preventing significant losses in food supplies, and for freeing the cultivator from the usurious controls of money-

---

[6] Yamey and Bauer, *op. cit.* A detailed analysis of the rural-urban potential for capital formation in the underdeveloped countries is given in my "Patterns of Investment and Rates of Growth . . ."

[7] Whether people are pushed or pulled to towns, one can argue that economic opportunities in towns must be better than in villages, that potential migrants must believe them to be so, and that in the long run their perception must be validated by experience, otherwise the flow of population would cease or reverse itself. If this reasoning is correct, differentials in reality and perceptions of reality by villagers about relative opportunities become irrelevant for long-run population flows. This reasoning assumes that migration can be based on "irrational" considerations only in the short run. In fact, only a small minority of the migrants need realize their expectations in order for the myth to survive that opportunities in the city are greater than in the country—in other words, people's irrational behavior in regard to spatial mobility can persist even in the long run.

lenders—involve the use of local labor, materials, skills, and organization. Constructing schools, clinics, and community centers, digging ditches and canals and building roads, terracing, bunding, and hedging fields, planting suitable trees on fallow land, controling soil and wind erosion, and developing village ponds as sources of fish supplies: these also are dependent on similar uses of labor and skills.

In addition, the potentialities of increased agricultural output resulting from better practices and marketing, and the consolidation of holdings, net of expenses of innovation, seem impressive.[8] Addition of new facilities, such as brickkilns, multiplies this potential several times, brickmaking being one of the simplest and least expensive operations, ideally suited for local production, distribution, and use in most communities.[9]

In ten years of planned development India has not come anywhere near to exploiting this potential fully, and this in spite of the demonstration by Communist China of its powerful role in the initial phases of development.[10]

The Cost of Theologies and Ideologies

Around the theory of indivisibilities, ably propounded by Professors Rosenstein-Rodan, Nurkse, and others, has grown an almost mystical complex of belief with many variations.[11] Crudely put, it amounts to this: in underdeveloped countries you have got to have a "big push" if you want to generate self-sustaining growth (enough to outstrip population growth). The big push is then related to big projects and the most up-to-date technology.

All of these ideas have some validity. But political beliefs and historical associations have taken this discussion partly from the realm of theory and reality into that of dogma. Many Marxists are for this way of thinking because it fits the Russian model. Some ardent nationalists are for it because other theories seem to stress rural and agricultural development, a thing which the British rulers used to stress.

---

[8] See, for example, Albert Mayer, McKim Marriott, and Richard L. Park, *Pilot Project, India: The Story of Rural Development at Etawah, Uttar Pradesh* (Berkeley and Los Angeles: University of California Press, 1958), pp. 233–287.

[9] *Kurukshretra: A Symposium on Community Development in India, 1952–1955* (New Delhi: Community Projects Administration, 1955), pp. 298–308. The facts reported here are also cited in Mayer *et al., Pilot Project, India*, pp. 272–278.

[10] Wilfred Malenbaum, "India and China: Contrasts in Development Performance," *American Economic Review*, XLXI, No. 3 (June, 1959), esp. pp. 305–307. See also Durdin Tillman, "Red China Plans Vast Irrigation," New York *Times*, November 3, 1958, and other similar reports in the *Times*.

[11] For a brief review of these theories see Benjamin H. Higgins, *Economic Development, Principles, Problems and Policies* (New York: Norton, 1959), pp. 384–408.

Rightly or wrongly, to many this British attitude was an indication of Britain's desire to keep India a nonindustrial, raw-material-supplying colony. To some, like Pandit Nehru, the big dams are "temples of a new faith" in India.[12] To others, steel mills are the crux of economic development. To yet others, steel mills and shipyards are the symbols of national power and autonomy. Psychological symbols and national power may legitimately compete with economic goals. Steel mills, unlike shipyards, are perhaps economically justified in India. The point, however, is this: if economic criteria indicate that a network of rural feeder roads is more productive for the economy than an airline, or fertilizer factories are more remunerative than steel mills, it needs to be explicitly stated that the choosing of steel mills and airlines involves the adoption of other criteria. Indeed, the commitment of the bulk of the nation's resources to construction of dams and irrigation systems with long gestation periods is not easy to justify on economic grounds, when the urgent problems of food, shelter, and clothing can be solved much more quickly with simple technologies, less capital, and more labor.[13]

The example of big dams illustrates that gigantomania is not always biased toward urbanization. However, due to the correlations between economic development, industrialization, and urbanization which most people carry in their minds, it tends to favor urbanization and industrialization, particularly capital-using industrialization at the cost of labor-using, agricultural, and industrial development. It results in inefficient use of resources for the "short run" (which may extend to fifteen or twenty or more years) in exchange for added but more uncertainly anticipated benefits in the "long run." In an economy like that of India, when high interest rates of 40 or 50 per cent per annum,[14] reflecting the scarcity of

[12] Takashi Oka, "Dam in India Looms as 'Temple of Faith,'" *Christian Science Monitor*, January 28, 1958.

[13] If it is assumed that both the production of more consumers' goods and the labor-intensive mode of production for consumers' as well as capital goods will only stimulate population expansion and not raise per capita incomes, and that population growth cannot be checked otherwise, then a "capital-intensive" investment program may be the only economically feasible program for development. Cf. Walter Galenson and Harvey Liebenstein, "Investment Criteria, Productivity and Economic Development," *Quarterly Journal of Economics*, LXIX, No. 3 (August, 1955), 343–370. As I have argued elsewhere (see note 2), such a program is not politically feasible in a democracy. It amounts to controlling population growth by starving a section of the people (the unemployed) or spreading consumption goods more thinly over an expanding population, thus keeping general mortality rates high. Even in Communist Poland such a program was overthrown by the people, and only terror and purges enabled Stalin to carry it through in the Soviet Union.

[14] Rates of interest as high as 5 or 6 per cent per month have been reported to the author by several people in villages and traditional sections of old cities.

capital (and not the artificially controlled low rates of interest, such as 3 or 4 per cent in the imperfect capital market), are used to discount the flow of future outputs, it is not at all clear that such long-run investments are always more productive, even in the long run, than a series of short-run, quick-maturing, and quickly depreciating investments.

I am not aware of any published information which attempts to justify long-run projects in India on such economic grounds. When people are so wedded to their theories that they apply them without even trying to test them, wasteful allocation of resources is likely to occur—and the theories take on the character of theologies. Thus, very often the zeal for setting up the most modern factories and transportation systems increases the real costs of industrialization and urbanization.

Another important reason for the increased expensiveness of urbanization in India is the modern and egalitarian ideology of public welfare. England in the 18th and 19th centuries could ignore the social costs of slums, unsanitary conditions, and fire hazards to a greater extent than can India in the 20th century.

Because of bad sanitation, Josiah Strong believed, there were 156,600 "unnecessary" deaths in U.S. cities in 1890.[15] Today, public health measures are introduced first in the cities. The resulting population growth, with overcrowding of housing, schools, hospitals, and transport systems, and shortages of food and other necessities, is a well-known story. Thus are being built the pressures, the strains, and the tensions which may lead to political turmoil or to an authoritarian regime. And hence, as Rostow has stated, the responsibility of the "non-Communist literate elites in . . . transitional societies [to] ensure that the humane decision to save lives does not lead to an inhumane society." [16]

This welfare philosophy is affecting villages also. Describing wastages of cement and steel in one Indian village, René Dumont wrote, "Even European villages do not yet possess all these amenities. India has tried to become a welfare state before creating the basic economy required to sustain it. Comfort has been given priority over production."[17] But this priority of comfort over production becomes operative first in the cities and then radiates out.

Most experts expect housing conditions to get worse in the urban

---

[15] *The Twentieth Century City* (New York: Baker and Taylor, 1898), p. 58.

[16] W. W. Rostow, *The Stages of Economic Growth: A Non-Communist Manifesto* (Cambridge: Cambridge University Press, 1960), p. 144.

[17] "Agricultural Defeat in India," *New Statesman and Nation*, LVIII, No. 1501 (December 19, 1959), 871.

areas of the underdeveloped areas in the coming decade or two.[18] This certainly appears to be the prospect in India.[19] As congestion and slums grow, the need to spend more on urban areas to provide for public health services and social amenities will also increase. The amenities are more expensive because of higher standards expected by urbanites. And if, in addition, a city has already exceeded the population mark of 400,000–500,000, which Rosenstein-Rodan considers optimal from the point of view of social overhead capital, per unit costs of social services may rise rapidly. The number of cities in excess of this size is likely to increase very rapidly in the coming decades in India, thus making urbanization an increasingly expensive process.

If many of the economic, social, and political troubles of the developed economies flow from the fact that ideology lags behind technology, the troubles of the underdeveloped areas become more acute because ideology outruns technology.

Economic Frustrations: Unemployment, Underemployment, and Misemployment

In spite of all the deficiencies in the available employment statistics,[20] it is evident that the trend of growing unemployment in India is not likely to reverse itself in the near future. Urban unemployment accounts for perhaps half of the total. In the larger cities, Malenbaum points out, of all the employed 51.8 per cent were literate and only 3 per cent had any college education, while of the unemployed 78.4 per cent were literate and 5.1 per cent had college education. Some 46 per cent of all the educated unemployed are concentrated in the four major cities of India.[21]

The interval between completion of education and first employment is often quite long. "Thus, while some 50 per cent of the illiterate unemployed have been out of work for at least a year, 75 per cent of the matriculates and intermediates are in this category." [22] Majumdar's study of a large sample of alumni of Lucknow University holding Master's degrees indicates that the more highly educated are unemployed longer. Of the unemployed

[18] See, for example, Burnham Kelley (ed.), *Housing and Economic Development* (Cambridge, Mass.: Massachusetts Institute of Technology, 1955).

[19] Pitambar Pant's confident optimism about the housing situation is based on minimal average-cost estimates for the Third and Fourth Plans, far below those actually achieved in the first two Plans.

[20] For a review of these see K. N. Raj, "Employment and Unemployment in the Indian Economy: Problems of Classification, Measurement and Policy," *Economic Development and Cultural Change*, VII, No. 3, Part I (April, 1959), 258–278.

[21] Wilfred Malenbaum, "Urban Unemployment in India," *Pacific Affairs,* XXX, No. 2 (June, 1957), 138–150.

[22] *Ibid.*, p. 146.

in this sample, 44 per cent had been unemployed for over two years, 18 per cent for a year and a half, and 27 per cent for a year. A somewhat similar pattern emerges from a sample survey conducted by the Delhi Employment Exchange.[23]

Corresponding to underemployment and seasonal or disguised unemployment in the villages, there is considerable disguised unemployment and/or misemployment in the cities, as reflected in the rapid growth of the low-productivity service sector in which unskilled, uneducated workers, and especially the transients, seek means to subsist. Among the educated in the Majumdar sample, "about three-quarters of those who sought service in a firm and a substantial majority of those who sought service in government or sought a profession of their own failed to achieve it." Economic frustration can only be high in such situations. None of the 237 who answered Majumdar's question as to the factors responsible for difficulty in getting a job blamed it on their own shortcomings. While only about 12 per cent blamed it on bad luck, the rest blamed society in one way or another, to wit: "government," 48 per cent; "society," 13 per cent; "lack of proper and systematic training," 26 per cent—which usually meant lack of opportunities for these.

If the educated unemployed provide leadership, these transients, whom Hoselitz calls the *lumpen proletariat,* provide the raw material for mobs. Political parties, trade unions, business and religious groups, displaced landlords, and princes willing to provide ideological, financial, and organizational resources for making effective use of these two groups are not scarce in the cities.

Rapidly increasing enrollments in colleges and schools, and demographic and economic trends, are likely to swell the ranks of both of these groups in the coming decade. This *lumpen intelligentsia,* as Lewis Feuer calls it, with little skill, opportunity, or capital for entrepreneurship in economic activity, turns to political entrepreneurship where, with less capital, training, and skills, a man can manage to exist, if not get ahead. Moreover, opportunity costs in economic enterprise are higher than in political enterprise. Social values, historical associations, and ideological fashions make economic enterprise a less and political a more desired activity as a means to status and power.

Physical densities, communication, and other facilities make political organization relatively easier in cities. Groups with re-

[23] For the Lucknow sample see D. N. Majumdar, *Unemployment Among the University Educated: A Pilot Inquiry in India* (Cambridge, Mass.: Center for International Studies, Massachusetts Institute of Technology, 1957). For the Delhi survey see Motilal Gupta, "Problems of Unemployment in India" (Doctoral dissertation, Netherlands School of Economics, Rotterdam, privately published, 1955), p. 43.

sources and tightly knit organizations, like the Communists or the Rashtriya Swayam-Sewak Sangh (R.S.S.) are at a relative advantage in such situations. Part of the success of Communists in Kerala and Bengal, two of the most densely populated areas in India, may be due to this reason.[24] The R.S.S. similarly is, by and large, an urban lower-middle-class movement. Psychological densities—intense interchange of ideas, rumors, and stimulations in crowded situations—are conducive to demagoguery and crowd formations. Speakers and audiences tend to stimulate each other into states of irresponsibility and frenzy in situations of crowding and anonymity which are more easily obtained in cities than in villages. Extremist groups with less scruples and more resources stand to gain from situations in which crowds can be turned into mobs.

Noneconomic Frustrations: Sex, Sports, Recreation, and the Arts

Education, urban environment, increasing interregional and international contacts, and foreign and native motion-pictures are either widening the gap between the old and new generations, or promoting a double standard of morality among many. Students and some illiterates watch Hollywood movies—the former partly and the latter mainly—for their sex appeal. And these very people often turn around to criticize American society, as depicted in these movies, as lewd, materialistic, and corrupt, while describing their frustrating cultural framework as spiritualistic and pure. There is less segregation of the sexes in big cities, particularly among students. But economic insecurity and intellectual fashion, by preventing early marriages, are choking off the traditionally accepted avenues for sex gratification, while extramarital sex gratification is severely limited because of strong social mores, joint family living, overcrowded housing and the consequent lack of privacy, and relative immobility of most people (due to the lack of money, motorcars, "metros," and motels). Strong cultural sanctions also operate against prostitution among the educated middle classes. Sexual frustration in this group is, thus, quite high. In addition, there are neither sufficient opportunities to participate in sports nor to attend sports spectacles where, on weekends, like their American counterparts, they may work off their steam by yelling some team to victory. There are few opportunities for youth to develop and display its talents in the theater, literature, or other forms of creative life—the market for art being limited. Rowdy politics be-

[24] Benjamin Higgins explains the success of the Communist party in the crowded sections of Indonesia partly on the same grounds.

comes a channel for youth's repressed exuberance. For many it is an inexpensive substitute activity, and for some an attractive avenue to social climbing and psychic satisfaction. The dictatorships of Russia, Nazi Germany and Latin America have well demonstrated their understanding of the role of sports and stadia in politics. Even in an affluent democracy like America, one wonders to what extent the political apathy of college students may be attributable to the existence of vast opportunities for economic, artistic, romantic, and extracurricular satisfactions. In the contemporary Indian urban context, political apathy is conducive and activism is detrimental to political stability. Unless there is a change in the nature of this activism, or in economic trends, the politics of irresponsibility are likely to increase in the cities.

Sources and Patterns of Extremism

Cities either give birth to political and other leaders or draw them there. A major consequence of Western education has been the growth of nationalist and culturally revivalist, as well as socialist and Communist, ideologies.[25] A conservative-liberal coalition is in power in India, but liberalism has as yet not taken deep roots there. It is from the villages that the ruling Congress party derives its support. In the cities it has been losing steadily. Calcutta, though not quite typical of other cities, may yet turn out to be the model of political sickness likely to spread in other cities.

Revolutions, Brinton has remarked, leave behind both a uniting tradition and a memory of successful revolt.[26] The process of winning independence developed self-confidence in the common man and it trained cadres of politically active workers. Students participated more heavily than perhaps any other group in the revolutionary struggles. Theirs were the highest aspirations—theirs also the deepest disappointments—and theirs the strongest and most emotive reactions. Education, youth, and unemployment produce explosive mixtures.

A political party in India, Weiner has pointed out, is often an alternative social structure vis-à-vis the traditional family.[27] Some bolt from the discipline, frustration, and pettiness of the joint family wedded to the past to take sanctuary in the discipline, dedi-

---

[25] For the Indian case see Bruce T. McCully, *English Education and the Origins of Indian Nationalism* (New York: Columbia University Press, 1940).

[26] Crane Brinton, *The Anatomy of Revolution* (New York: Vintage Books, 1957), pp. 262–264.

[27] Myron Weiner, *Party Politics in India: The Development of a Multi-Party System* (Princeton, N.J.: Princeton University Press, 1957), p. 8. He treats this theme at length in "Politics of Westernization in India," (Institute of East Asiatic Studies, University of California, Berkeley, April, 1957). [Mimeographed.]

cation, and intrigues of the political party devoted to the future. Purposelessness of life is transformed into a cause and an overriding loyalty that makes many young persons sacrifice health, money, and other careers. The more demanding the discipline of a party, the greater the dedication of its members. Again, in India, dedication and self-sacrifice, per se, as Singer has noted, are time-honored traditions.[28] Thus, the same person will often respect and admire a liberal humanist like Nehru, a conservative reformer like Gandhi, a fascist like Subhash Bose, and a rightist revolutionist like Savarkar. This ethos of dedication, though quite useful for maintaining political unity around charismatic symbols like Nehru and Gandhi, is dangerous for democracy. Fanaticism can grow more easily and nondemocratic charismatic symbols can replace the present ones, in this psychological climate. The tradition has not lost ground in the cities. If anything, it has been intensified by two puritanic movements—Gandhism and Marxism. The saving grace of the villager is his belief in many gods—often warring gods. Through the centuries he has learned to pray to them and yet live without them. Divergences of professed and practiced faith do not generate serious anxieties. But the urbanite is a monotheist, and a true believer. His rationalism leads him to a passion for consistency, and in the context of limited knowledge, poor education, poverty and insecurity, and an atmosphere of superstition, this often leads to intolerance. Educated, urban middle classes provide most of the political leadership, including that of the Communist party.[29] The strongholds of Muslim fanaticism before the creation of Pakistan were in educational centers like Aligarh, Dacca, Lahore, Calcutta, Karachi, Peshawar, and Rawalpindi. Hindu conservatives and reactionaries have derived large numbers of their leaders and workers from Delhi, Nagpur, Poona, Lahore, and Benares. The chances are that in India, if dictatorship comes, it will be of the Left. Left radicalism appeals more to the science-worshiping mind of youth. It also offers a more complete and intellectually satisfying credo. It has international support as well as internationalist ideology. The first yields tremendous organizational advantages, while the second appeals to urban cosmopolitanism.

The ruling party has a reservoir of material resources in its business supporters, but it lacks youthful manpower. The socialists have manpower, but lack material resources. The rightists get their financial backing from feudal social classes which are on the way

---

[28] Milton, Singer, "Cultural Values in India's Economic Development," *The Annals of the American Academy of Political and Social Science*, CCCV (May, 1956), 81–91.

[29] Gene D. Overstreet, and Marshall Windmiller, *Communism in India* (Berkeley and Los Angeles: University of California Press, 1959), pp. 357–364.

out. Only the Communists have access to both youthful manpower and finances in ample and increasing quantities. The budget of the Communist party in one state alone is reported to be larger than that of the Praja Socialist party for the entire country. Moreover, the Communist credo has "worked" elsewhere. Communist countries are developing rapidly. To the man in a hurry to change the world, communism seems the wave to ride.

Few young men seek political activity in the ranks of the party in power. To defend the *status quo* is not heroic, especially when there are unemployment, poverty, crime, waste, inequalities, and corruption all around. Besides, the party in power has a fairly well-established hierarchy with large numbers of older people, wherein social climbing is more difficult, while opposition groups have use for any man—trained or untrained. There is more room for expansion of the party machinery—hence more opportunities for status or power within the party structure, and, if one has faith enough in the rightness of one's cause, in society at a later date. Communists, in general, are in a better position to absorb newcomers. Well integrated, well financed, with a ready-made ideology tailored to all levels of comprehension, they have a well-designed program for action, so that each new entrant finds plenty to be busy with. The newcomers work like missionaries for a cause and a judgment day. Their internal and external supporters give finances in a big and religious way. Living in a democracy, they are free to organize and operate. When their irresponsible actions are repressed, they acquire a halo of martyrdom. This adds another dimension of romance and adventure to oppositional politics, which thrives in an atmosphere where jailgoing has acquired social prestige.

Whether urban educated youth goes Right or Left,[30] it is not likely to be the standard-bearer of liberal democracy if social and economic conditions continue to worsen. It is perhaps the lower middle class in the cities, unskilled and semieducated, culturally conservative or confused, and politically adrift, whose politics are the most volatile. This floating population in the political arena makes it easier for opportunistic (as well as idealistic) politicians to resign from and reënter political parties, and to reshuffle political alliances with a staggering and confusing frequency. A kind of unrestrained laissez-faire politics prevails. Individuals as well as parties seek to maximize their political gain with little regard to rules and

[30] For the view that the collapse of democracy would lead, initially, to the emergence of a Rightist or military rather than a Communist dictatorship in India see M. F. Millikan and W. W. Rostow, "Foreign Aid: Next Phase," *Foreign Affairs*, April, 1958, pp. 418–436. For the opposite view see Taya Zinkin, "India and Military Dictatorship," *Pacific Affairs*, XXX, No. 1 (March, 1959), 89–91.

principles essential for the maintenance and growth of a responsible representative political system.[31]

Cities also reveal patterns of mutative extremism. After the death of S. P. Mukerji, the leader of the rightist Jana Sangha, his parliamentary seat was captured by a Communist. Aligarh University, which was a hotbed of rightist Muslim politics, became a center of Communist activity after the creation of Pakistan.[32] Egalitarian, populist, and welfare-state ideas are shared by most, it not all, political parties. Emotive issues, like language or corruption, unite radicals of the Right and the Left against all moderates. All kinds of opportunistic alliances between all kinds of political groups take place all the time, but the spiritual and psychological affinity of what Hoffer calls the "True Believers" [33]—the fanatics of all faiths, political and otherwise—makes the actual or potential union of Right and Left radicals more dangerous. As the power of the ruling party declines and as youth becomes increasingly disillusioned with the *status quo,* the liberals and moderates are likely to lose. It may be that the old administrative, religious, and cultural cities like Delhi, Banaras, and Ajmer will move to the Right and industrial-commercial cities like Calcutta, Madras, and Bombay to the Left. Where responsible and strong trade-unions take root, as in Bombay, socialists rather than Communists may gain by this shift. But if unemployment and living conditions continue to worsen, the greatest gains will ultimately be for the extremists.

In such conditions even the villages are likely to go over to extremist politics—but perhaps with a time lag. The swastika may appeal to the peasant and the hammer and sickle to the intellectual,

---

[31] For a description of such politics see S. L. Polai (ed.), *National Politics and 1957 Elections in India* (New Delhi: Metropolitan Book Company, 1957), esp. pp. 12–15; also, Margaret W. Fisher and Joan V. Bondurant, *The Indian Experience with Democratic Elections* (Indian Press Digest, No. 3 [Berkeley: University of California, December, 1956]), pp. 69 ff. For Pakistan see K. S. Newman, "Pakistan's Preventive Autocracy and Its Causes," *Pacific Affairs,* XXXII, No. 1 (March, 1959), 18–33.

[32] For the Calcutta by-election see Polai (ed.), *op. cit.,* p. 157. The social, historical, and political causes for this political mutation of Leftist into Rightist extremism, and vice versa, differ from situation to situation. For the Italian case see, for example, "Party-Ocracy versus Democracy: An Exchange Between Ignazio Silone and J. K. Galbraith," *Radical Humanist*, XXII, No. 45 (November 9, 1958), 527–528 and 531.

The psychological factors that make this mutation possible are, however, fairly constant. See Eric Hoffer, *The True Believer: Thoughts on the Nature of Mass Movements* (New York: Harper, 1951) and *The Passionate State of Mind* (New York: Harper, 1955), and Brinton, *op. cit.;* also, T. W. Adorno *et al., The Authoritarian Personality* (New York: Harper, 1950), and A. H. Maslow, "The Authoritarian Character Structure," *Journal of Social Psychology*, XVIII, 2nd half (November, 1943), 401–411.

[33] In his book of that title, previously cited.

but their transmutation or alliance is not inconceivable—and if it comes it will, like plague and cholera, come from the cities.

Intellectuals and Slums

Growing slums, worsening sanitary conditions, lowering living standards, and unemployment concentrate misery visibly, not in inaccessible villages, but in areas which are the habitat of writers, social reformers, artists, poets, teachers, religious preachers, humane societies, dreamers, city planners, sociologists, journalists, and economists. They arouse the concern and the ire of these and other socially sensitive and articulate individuals and groups. Some of their protest—especially when it comes from professional groups—helps rectify some evils, such as graft, inefficiency, and waste. But, by and large, it merely adds to feelings of dissatisfaction with the *status quo*. Believing that they are bystanders, not participants, in processes of social change, many intellectuals become angry men—young and old. Their anger, in turn, leads only to callousness on the part of authorities, who dismiss their criticism as "destructive." A vicious circle of irresponsible and angry criticisms on both sides is thus initiated.

A society in a perpetual state of anger is not a stable society.

Transients and *Anomie*

Because of housing shortages, low incomes, transportation costs, and other factors, immigrants from rural areas are primarily males. In the four biggest cities, 60 per cent of the population is male as compared to 51.4 per cent for India as a whole.[34]

This ratio is even higher among working classes and migrants. Gambling, racing, dope peddling, prostitution, and cult religiosity tend to spread in rapidly growing cities. The result is a demoralized, unhealthy, pitiful mass which, unlike an industrial reserve army, Hoselitz asserts, is not easy to convert into a disciplined factory work-force.[35] It is true, as Knowles points out, that these people can be converted into an effective labor force if fed and trained properly.[36] But it is easier to turn them into a riotous mob; it needs less training and discipline, and the demand for this alternative is fairly high and frequent in the cities.

[34] Malenbaum, "Urban Unemployment in India." The number of women per thousand men is as follows: Calcutta, 602; Bombay, 569; Ahmedabad, 764; Kanpur, 699. See also Bert F. Hoselitz, "The City, the Factory, and Economic Growth," *American Economic Review*, XLV, No. 2 (May, 1955), 178–179.

[35] *Ibid.*

[36] William H. Knowles, "Discussion on 'Urbanization and Industrialization of the Labor Force in a Developing Economy,'" *American Economic Review*, XLV, No. 2 (May, 1955), 188–190.

Opportunity costs of political rioting are very low for these marginal people. Crowded housing or, more commonly, lack of any housing whatsoever (one quarter of Bombay's population sleeps on the streets) makes physical access to them very easy. They are eager to talk about their troubles. Political workers find the uprooted urban "rice-roots" receptive to their ideas and leadership. The Communists often have the most convincing explanations for all the troubles of these unfortunates, even though at times, as among the refugees from Pakistan, the rightists manage to get a foothold.

There are no estimates of the total economic costs of social disorganization that arise in such contexts. Juvenile delinquency, drunkenness, murder, theft, and robbery involve increased costs, including those for police and justice administrations and for institutions for the detention, reform, and rehabilitation of convicts. Some sketchy information available for three rural-urban districts in Bombay State indicates that over-all crime rates and their economic costs are much higher in the cities.[37]

Besides, political demonstrations and rioting dislocate traffic, trade, and production and result in loss of property and sometimes even of life. No cost estimates for these are available. The greater frequency and magnitude of these in the cities suggests that these costs are higher there.

Workers and Entrepreneurs

Per capita output and income are generally higher in cities than in villages. This is, however, largely a result of the higher per capita investment and the associated modern technology in cities. Effects of urban environment, per se, as distinct from those of more investment or superior technology, on labor morale, productivity per man-hour, hours of work, quality of work, and mobility of the labor force need to be ascertained. It is not inconceivable that the proportion of time lost due to strikes (many for noneconomic reasons) increases while the pace of work slows down—at least in the very big cities where relatively more workers are unionized. Unions in India, being largely controlled by political workers from outside their ranks, can and often do use labor for organizing

[37] See, for example, *Annual Police Administration Report of the State of Bombay, Including Railways for the Year 1957* (Bombay: Government of Bombay, Police Department, 1959), pp. 96–101, 160–171.

Several limitations of the data, as published, do not permit a more definite conclusion, or an exact statement of comparative costs. Available data for 1925 indicate that drunkenness is increasing and social maladjustment is more rife in industrial cities. See B. S. Haikerwal, *Economic and Social Aspects of Crime in India* (London: Allen & Unwin, 1934), p. 46. Haikerwal, however, is inconsistent about his feelings regarding the relative incidence of crime in cities and villages; see, e.g., pp. 12, 48.

strikes, protest marches, and demonstrations for furthering their political ends. Language riots in Bombay are a case in point.[38] Husain's study of industrial location in East Pakistan indicates that social disorganization is minimal and workers' morale is maximal where workers are not torn away from their rural habitat.[39] In this respect trade unions can play an important role in reducing rather than aggravating costs of urbanization. By providing a new sense of community and a web of social relationships and activities, they can integrate immigrants into new meaningful and satisfying life-patterns and help build their morale. The responsibility of the unions is high, because in Indian cities there are few secondary social organizations or religious institutions which can create a sense of belongingness corresponding to that provided by the growth of sects like Methodism and Presbyterianism during the Industrial Revolution in England.[40] There are no such significant movements for creating a new social milieu for immigrants in place of the one they left behind. The operation of caste panchayats in cities to some extent prevents the alienation of the worker from his traditional society. In the years to come, however, the strength of this institution is likely to diminish.[41] And to the extent it does not diminish, city society will merely duplicate village society on a large scale. Cities then become collections of villages. The argument for urbanization as a vehicle for value transformations conducive to industrialization then disappears.

Cities, by concentrating the labor force in relatively small areas, and by making possible the organization of labor, are creating conditions in which the clash of labor and entrepreneurial interests becomes more well-defined. Unions are already exercising an influence on governmental policies much greater than is warranted by the size of their membership.

The consequent upward pressure on wages and consumption may

---

[38] For the crucial role of unions in precipitating such disturbances in the autumn of 1956 see Marshall Windmiller, "The Politics of States Reorganization in India: The Case of Bombay," *Far Eastern Survey,* XXV, No. 9 (September, 1956), 129–144.

[39] A. F. A. Husain, *Human and Social Impact of Technological Change in Pakistan* (Dacca: Oxford University Press, 1956). This study contradicts the contrary view expressed by Hoselitz, *op. cit.,* pp. 181–184.

[40] On the role of religion in both resisting and aiding social change, and that of Protestant sects in reintegrating communities disrupted by rapid industrialization and urbanization see W. Arthur Lewis, *The Theory of Economic Growth* (Homewood, Ill.; Richard D. Irwin, Inc., 1955), pp. 101–107.

[41] The role of caste in economic development is the subject matter of much writing which is excellently reviewed by Morris Davis Morris in "Caste and the Evolution of the Industrial Workforce in India," *Proceedings of the American Philosophical Society,* CIV, No. 2 (April, 1960), 124–133; also, see his "The Recruitment of an Industrial Labor Force in India, with British and American Comparisons," *Comparative Studies in Society and History,* II, No. 3 (April, 1960), 305–328.

not be a bar to increased investment, if such wage increases result in equal or larger productivity increases. The relation of wages to productivity in India, however, has not been empirically explored. Again, if entrepreneurial consumption can be kept in check, it will be somewhat easier to restrain workers' consumption. In practice, it has not been easy to restrain the consumption of either group.

Successful measures to keep both wages and profits—or, strictly, the share of wages and profits that goes into consumption—from rising would necessitate greater regulation of both groups by government, entailing more political, economic, and social controls, more administrative personnel, and increased costs. It would also necessitate a greater capacity for public agencies to fulfill roles of entrepreneurship if private enterprise should become discouraged as a result of such measures. How far the new educated groups, pouring out of colleges and universities with largely a nontechnical and half-baked education and with a tradition of averseness to economic enterprise and initiative, will make better managers, directors, and planners of enterprises under public rather than private control is yet an open question.

Exposure Effects: Sociological, Economic, and Political

Cities are being integrated into a growing network in and outside the country more rapidly than villages. With rapidly increasing contacts between different groups, tensions are mounting. Patterns of in-migration tend to heighten the tensions associated with regionalism in India.

Increased intergroup contacts are raising the levels of aspiration, without increasing levels of achievement. Consequently, the sense of *absolute deprivation* is increasing among urbanites. Closer contact with upper classes and their modes of living increases the sense of *relative deprivation.* At the same time, urban political and social ideologies are sensitizing the norms whereby people evaluate "social injustice," thus increasing the intensity of resentment and hostility. English commoners may derive satisfactions from the luxuries that their Queen enjoys—as Samuelson suggests[42]—but commoners in India are becoming averse to such "vicarious consumption" in proportion to the degree of their urbanization. Indian motion-pictures and literature, platforms of political parties and political speeches, and the sermons of preachers and social reformers often reflect as well as stimulate this emergent social ethos. The

[42] Paul A. Samuelson, "The Dilemmas of Housing," in Kelley (ed.), *Housing and Economic Development*, p. 35.

darshana-seeking villager loses his sense of awe and respect for political and other heroes and elites as he observes them from closer quarters and imbibes urban egalitarian ideas. As the erstwhile demigods look more human to him, their actions appear more inhuman. Both the numbers of malcontents and the intensity of discontent increase.

Patterns and levels of consumption also change as a result of exposure or demonstration effects. Lower expenditures on food within some income groups, and a substitution of refined-processed foods and sugar for more nutritious foods, have implications for the health and productivity of urbanites. But the changed pattern, particularly among middle- and upper-income groups, also involves more use of luxuries and foreign goods. Thus, there is the flow of scarce resources away from socially useful expenditure into the manufacturing of luxuries, and also a drain on foreign exchange. Levels of consumption also tend to rise, affecting the volume of internal savings available for capital formation.

Successful revolts in some countries raise the morale of revolutionists in others. The revolution of communications transmits knowledge as well as social unrest across oceans.

Slowing Down the Dynamo

W. Arthur Lewis has said,

> Towns tend to be prominent in organizing most political movements, whether their aim is greater freedom or less, if only because government is usually done from cities to which the politically ambitious are attracted. . . . Town is the home of the mob, and mobs are as prone to sweep tyrants into power, who reduce the opportunities for economic freedom, as they are to take part in liberating movements. The town is also the home of monopolists—the traders' associations, the guilds, the workers' combinations—whose aim is to restrict opportunities and to keep out new men. The town takes the lead in movements for reducing the amount of work done, and for working sullenly or resentfully. . . . If therefore a case can be made for saying that towns lead out of stagnation into growth, as good a case can be made for saying they lead out of growth into stagnation.[43]

In India, towns are not likely to lead into stagnation, but they can lead into slower economic growth and political instability, because of the diversion of resources from more to less productive investments. Urban populations have more access to, and influence on, political processes. As conditions worsen, towns are likely to demand and get progressively larger proportions of the national pie at the cost of the countryside.

[43] *Op. cit.*, pp. 150–151.

As the international economy developed, disparities of income grew between the rich and the poor nations, in the past century or so. Now, as the Indian economy develops, disparities are likely to grow between the village and the city. But what worked politically in the 19th-century world of colonial powers is hardly likely to work in the egalitarian 20th century. This trend can be reversed by appropriate allocations and actions for development of the countryside. There is little reason to believe that the rural exodus would continue if economic and social opportunities for advancement were expanding rapidly enough in the villages. In the Majumdar study, out of 327 respondents, 35 per cent were rural in origin. Of these, 35 per cent were willing to return to their villages after the completion of their studies. The other 65 per cent, who were unwilling to do so, were largely motivated by economic considerations. When the entire group of former students from rural areas was asked whether they were willing to return to villages if given a job similar to the one they held, 61 per cent said yes. Of the rest, 63 per cent again gave an economic reason for their answer—they expected chances for their economic advancement to be better in the cities.[44] If a majority of these highly educated (they all had Master's degrees), "westernized," urbanized Indians of rural origin were willing to return to the villages, given proper opportunities there, it is not unreasonable to assume that unskilled and tradition-oriented migrants can be persuaded to return with as much, if not greater, ease under similar conditions. And it should certainly be easier for those who are still in the villages to keep on living there.

Economic measures for correcting the pace and nature of urbanization can be supplemented by an ideological campaign, especially, because the village still has a romantic, emotional, political, or philosophical attraction for many, even among the intelligentsia and other groups of urban origins. There is no reason to believe that many idealistic and educated men will not choose to work in villages if they are assured that it is not the end of the road for their careers.

Conclusion

There are more opportunities for making a person a participant in economic planning and development in rural than in urban areas. This, by itself, reduces political disaffection. Also, in villages there is a greater level of tolerance for the old and familiar problems of unemployment and poverty. By exporting these problems to cities, political instability is increased. There are many avenues for sig-

[44] Majumdar, *op. cit.*, pp. 33–34.

nificant increases in agricultural and rural industrial output. There are greater opportunities for capital formation with the use of idle labor and other resources in villages. The levels and patterns of consumption unfavorable to economic growth can be prevented from emerging with less difficulty in rural than in urban areas.

Higher direct and indirect costs of social disorganization, welfare ideologies, and overhead capital in cities are reducing the flow of output obtainable from investment of available resources—some of which, like labor, are going to waste partly because of a pattern of development which is urban-oriented. If these trends continue, political discontent will grow in the cities, and if public discontent fails to change governmental policies peacefully, streets may become the arbiters of political destiny. But the problem cannot be solved by expanding employment only or largely in urban areas. The employment elasticity of urbanization may be greater than one—every new job in the city is likely to attract more than one person from the country, thus worsening the problems and tensions in cities.

Increased sports, circuses, sex, spectacles, festivals, cultural shows, and demonstrations of military prowess can provide some substitute satisfactions and distractions to discontented youth. But the real effective solvent of tensions is rapidly expanding social and economic opportunity for advancement through orderly processes, in rural as well as in urban areas. The former have progressively lost their human and material capital to the latter. This flow can and needs to be reversed for the benefit of both. Communist China is doing it by coercive measures.[45] India has to do it by economic inducement and persuasion.

Meanwhile the great march of men from the backwoods to the metropolises continues at an ever accelerating pace. The new frontier—albeit a dangerous one—is not the wilderness with its promise of freedom, gold, or virgin lands, but the skyscraper with its promise of food and shelter.

Unlike the promise of the wilderness, the promise of this frontier may turn out to be an illusion. Like the countless who fell by the wayside or collapsed after reaching the streets of Calcutta in the Bengal famine of 1942, many more are likely to discover that escaping from the stagnation of the village does not necessarily mean salvation in the city slum.

Development patterns which cannot slow down this explosive and skewed growth of cities (big ones growing faster than the

[45] Gordon Walker, "Old Chinese Socialism Tested," *Christian Science Monitor*, February 8, 1958.

others) will involve a great wastage of human resources. "A social order is stable," Hoffer has said, "so long as it can give scope to talent and youth. Youth itself is a talent—a perishable talent." [46] This is one resource which if not utilized for development is likely to become political lava in a country where the social fabric of democracy is still very inflammable.

[46] *The Passionate State of Mind,* p. 20.

Problems of the Rural Periphery

21. Problems of Regional Development and Industrial Location in Europe*

United Nations, Department of Economic and Social Affairs

The growing interest in the problems of economic development which is an outstanding feature of post-war economic thinking has, quite naturally, been focussed mainly on the wide differences existing between countries and on the problem of stimulating economic progress in those which have been left behind. Both in public debate and in government policy increasing attention has, however, been paid in recent years to the related problems of regional disparities in levels of economic development within one and the same country. In the United Kingdom overall policies to reduce regional disparities in economic activity and standards of living were initiated already in the thirties. In the Soviet Union considerable resources were devoted to the industrial opening-up of the vast eastern parts of its territory.[1] In Germany a conscious policy of industrial decentralization was carried out, but this was motivated mainly by strategic considerations and the effects it may have had in reducing regional disparities in income and economic activity were incidental. In the post-war period regional policies have become still more important in the United Kingdom and in the Soviet Union, and a number of other European countries both in the west and in the east have embarked upon regional development plans and other schemes of regional economic policy.[2]

The purpose of this chapter is to describe the nature and importance of regional economic problems within European countries and to discuss different methods of regional economic policy on the basis of the experiences of the various parts of Europe. In the first section, an attempt is made to identify the problem regions in Europe and to determine whether the gap between poor and rich regions within countries

* Reprinted from United Nations, Department of Economic and Social Affairs, *Economic Survey of Europe, 1954*. Tables 70–76 have been eliminated from this edition.

has, on the whole, been widening. In the second section, the common features of the structural weakness of under-developed regions and the existing location of manufacturing activity are examined, with the purpose of ascertaining whether the present pattern is due to actual differences in factor endowment between regions or to legacies of the past, reinforced by certain institutional factors, which might tend to perpetuate the existing concentration of industry. In the third section, certain conclusions are drawn as to the type of industry best suited for establishment in poor regions both from the point of view of checking the cumulative process of concentration in the highly developed areas and from that of promoting the balanced growth of the under-developed regions. Sections 4 and 5, after describing the various methods applied in regional policies in western and eastern European countries respectively, deal with the most effective way of using the various policy instruments at the disposal of Governments. The chapter ends by referring briefly to the possibilities for cooperation between countries in regional policy and to the implication of international integration policies for regional differences within countries.

1. DISPARITIES IN REGIONAL DEVELOPMENT IN EUROPEAN COUNTRIES

The Broad Geographic Pattern

Figure 1 is intended to give a first impression of the variations in the degree of economic development between different regions within each individual country. The degree of shading of each region is determined by the relationship between incomes in that region and the average for the country of which the region forms part. No comparisons can therefore be made directly across political boundaries. The criterion by which the regional differences are measured is relative levels of *per capita* income and it is subject to certain limitations which are discussed below. It may perhaps be accepted as adequate for a first broad identification of the location and size of the problems. A glance at the map shows that the poor regions in individual countries are generally those situated at the periphery of Europe: the western and northern regions of the British Isles and the Scandinavian countries, the western regions of France and the southern parts of nearly all southern European countries. A similar pattern is found in virtually all central and eastern* European countries up to the borders of the Soviet

* Sufficient information is not available to permit the inclusion of eastern European countries in the map.

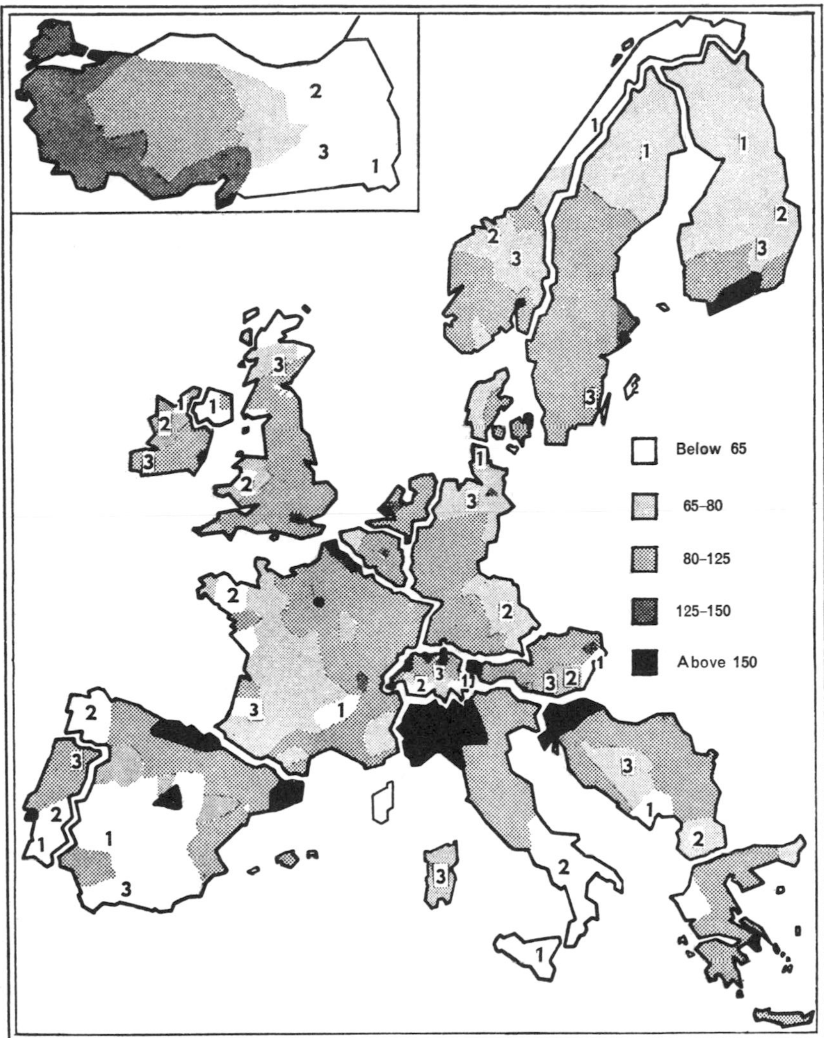

FIG. 1. Regional income disparities within Western European countries. Estimated *per capita* income in each region expressed as percentage of income in each country.

Union. Thus, in all countries of Europe the levels of economic development tend to be lowest in the regions furthest removed from the relatively small area which developed as the main European center of industrial activity, embracing England and the valley and outlet of the Rhine.

The lower level of activity and income at the periphery of Europe can, to a certain extent, be accounted for by natural factors. The climate is more unfavourable in most regions of the European periphery than nearer the center, and some of the outlying regions, for instance northern Scandinavia and eastern Turkey, are handicapped by the mere fact of geographic distance from their own national centers of population and production. However, the smaller or larger distance from the industrial center of Europe has no doubt been in itself a powerful location factor which has contributed to mould the pattern of settlement inside most European countries, making the regions nearer the center more, and those furthest away from it less, attractive from the point of view of industrial location. Location of economic activity in Europe is still predominantly determined by historical patterns which emerged in times of economic liberalism, and—what is still more important—in times when proximity to coalfields and navigable rivers was virtually indispensable to a more developed pattern of activity. Although development of other sources of power and transport have brought decisive changes in relative location advantages of various regions, the existing concentrations of population and the distribution of capital stock, particularly that invested in transport facilities, have so far prevented any major shifts away from the old centers of activity.

It is a well-known fact that the countries situated near the economic center of Europe are, in general, richer and more developed than those at the periphery. This, combined with the geographical pattern of regional disparities within countries described above, the most prosperous and developed regions of each country tending to be those closest to the economic center, produces the result that, as a general rule, national frontiers separate the relatively poorer regions of the richer of two neighbouring countries from the relatively richer regions in the poorer country.* The opposite constellation—rich regions of rich countries neighbouring on poor regions of poor countries—does not exist, and examples of two underdeveloped regions of different countries con-

* Examples of this abound: the relatively poor southwestern regions of France are neighbours to the richest regions of Spain, some very poor regions of Spain to the northern richer part of Portugal. The depressed Belgian regions of northwest Flanders are neighbours to the rich northeastern France and some very poor districts of France and Switzerland to the richest regions in Italy. Other examples can be found on the German frontiers with Poland, Czechoslovakia and Austria, on the Austrian frontiers with Yugoslavia and Hungary, on the Czechoslovak frontiers with Hungary, and on the British "frontiers" with Scotland and Ireland.

tiguous to each other are very rare, the northern regions of Norway, Sweden and Finland being the most notable examples. Rich regions on each side of a common frontier are, of course, found in the valley of the Rhine at the frontiers between France and Germany, and on the two shores of the eastern part of the Channel. The implications of this international pattern of developed and underdeveloped national regions will be dealt with later in this chapter after the regional problems of individual countries have been discussed.

While the map gives a reasonably correct picture of where the low-income regions are to be found in each country, the impression it conveys of the amplitudes of the regional deviations from the average income of the country is very imperfect. This is partly because the underlying figures are based on taxable income—without adjustment for differences in the cost of living—or on even less reliable indicators of real income. It is also because the delimitation of regions is to some extent arbitrary since the available statistics refer to administrative units of very different sizes, sometimes cutting across what would appropriately be defined as regions in the economic sense. Nevertheless, it can safely be inferred from the map that regional income disparities are much wider in the poor countries of Europe than in the richer ones. Large regions in southern European countries show *per capita* incomes less than two thirds of their respective national average levels, while no such wide regional disparities are found in western Germany, Sweden, or the Benelux countries. The differences in this respect between rich and poor countries are even more pronounced than would appear from the map, because most of the poorest regions in the rich countries are very sparsely populated, while large parts of the poor regions in southern and eastern Europe are, on the contrary, very densely populated. While the population in regions with average incomes below two thirds of the national average account for only a few per cent in the United Kingdom, Switzerland, and Austria and for some 10 per cent in Norway and France, it accounts for about one third of the population in Italy, Turkey, and Spain.[3]

Differences in regional incomes as shown by the map may, of course, arise in some cases simply from the inability of an already developed region to use its resources fully. Thus, areas which suffer from the loss of markets may more accurately be described as depressed rather than underdeveloped, but they remain a problem nevertheless. Otherwise, however, low incomes in particular regions of a country may be taken as indicative of underdevelopment in the sense that productivity per head in these regions is low in comparison with the country as a whole.

In principle, low productivity in a particular region can be explained in two different ways. It may either be the case that all, or nearly all, the industries in the region have a lower productivity per head than in other parts of the country, or it may be that the region contains a disproportionate share of activities which are generally of low productivity throughout the country. The first case is clearly one of regional under-development. The second case may be typified by agriculture or fishing, which in most European countries yield a lower output per head than other industries, and here it may well be argued that the problem is really one of improving productivity in these particular branches of activity throughout the country as a whole rather than one of increasing productivity in general within a particular region.

In practice, however, neither the first nor the second situation exists in isolation. In nearly all low-income regions in Europe a particularly large share of the population is engaged in agriculture, while at the same time the level of productivity within these regions, both in agriculture and in industry, is lower than in the same branches of activity elsewhere. It may be in some cases that poor natural conditions for agriculture, uncompensated by any other location advantages, are the main reason for under-development of a region, but much more often it is the general backwardness of the region which perpetuates low productivity *per capita* in agriculture along with that in other branches.

The tendency for low income to be associated with a high degree of dependence on agriculture can be observed in Table 70, which includes information for selected low and high income regions inside a number of European countries.* In virtually all cases the share of population in agriculture is considerably higher in the poor than in the rich regions. Moreover, yields or other indicators of agricultural productivity are lower in the poor than in the rich regions.[4] Unfortunately, hardly any information is available on agricultural output per man in particular regions.

There is little statistical evidence of regional differences in productivity in non-agricultural occupations,[5] but there is no doubt that they are much smaller inside developed countries than inside the relatively under-developed countries of southern and eastern Europe, where

* Table 70 of the original text details the economic and population characteristics of rich and poor regions in Turkey, Yugoslavia, Spain, Portugal, Italy, France, Switzerland, Austria, Western Germany, Norway, Sweden, Finland, Ireland, and United Kingdom.

capitalist methods of production have pervaded some regions only, while others are still dominated by pre-capitalist methods.

Growing Regional Disparities in the Poorest Countries of Europe

The regional disparities in the poor countries of Europe are partly due to the fact that these countries include islands of progress—usually the capital city or other large cities—in the midst of a sea of relative backwardness, partly to differences of natural resources, climate and topography, and partly to systems of land ownership and other institutional factors. In Yugoslavia the wide regional disparities are largely legacies of the past, when the present-day regions were either independent States or peripheral provinces of the Ottoman Empire and Austria.

Favourable location from the point of view of international trade gave the major cities of Greece, Turkey and the Iberian countries the first impetus to development. Industry there, as almost everywhere else, has drawn its leadership and finance from the commercial classes whose initiative has traditionally been oriented outwards, and this, as well as the heavy demands on imports during the initial stages of industrialization, meant that either the ports or their immediate vicinity took the lead in development. The attraction of proximity to administration is also an important factor in the concentration of industry in the neighborhood of Lisbon and Athens-Piraeus. Istanbul derived part of its economic power in the past from its role as the hub of the Ottoman Empire, while Ankara, the capital of modern Turkey, is rapidly becoming a dynamic centre of industry.

In the poorest regions of the southern European countries, three-quarters of the population draws its income from exceedingly primitive agriculture. Farming in these regions is in many cases extensive as in the latifundia of Portugal south of the Tejo, the Spanish Meseta and eastern Turkey; but in Galicia, southeastern Spain, the Turkish Black Sea coast, Thrace, and the Yugoslav southern provinces, the land is divided into very small peasant holdings. In general, the fertile areas are most heavily populated, so that differences of income per head are reduced. In Spain the difference in population density in agriculture between the infertile and fertile regions is nearly sufficient to redress the balance of agricultural *per capita* income. In Thrace and in the Black Sea region of Turkey, the pattern of settlement is distinctly perverse: population density is greatest on low-quality soil and, in spite of specialization in such intensive occupations as tobacco cultivation and fruit growing, *per capita* income is very low even in relation to generally prevailing low standards; moreover, the market for the products in which these regions specialize is mainly external and subject to wide fluctuations.

In under-developed countries poverty is generally less closely dependent on purely natural conditions than in richer countries. The natural resources of the more advanced parts of poor countries are by far the best known, and, except where national needs put a premium on particularly favourable features of the backward regions (as is the case for the expansion of wheat production in southern Portugal and the improvement of livestock breeding in eastern Anatolia) the tendency is for these countries to concentrate the bulk of their limited investments on those areas which are most favoured in terms of known resources and social capital, and which are therefore likely to pay quicker dividends. It is not surprising therefore that not only has industrial development continued to be most rapid in the old centres, but progress in agriculture and education (measured by the degree of literacy) has also generally been least rapid in the poorest regions. In recent years, however, comprehensive efforts of regional planning in some of these countries are beginning to bear fruit.

Regional Changes in the More Advanced Countries

There is a general tendency for economic development to concentrate where it has already reached the highest levels. Both in Poland and Czechoslovakia most of the development in the inter-war period[6] took place in the most industrialized regions and eastern Poland and Slovakia remained in a state of extreme poverty and backwardness.

In Italy and France, too, the gap in economic development between regions has been steadily growing. In both of these countries, the differences in the degree of industrialization as between regions[7] are considerably larger than in the other industrialized countries, and employment in industry is expanding fastest in the most industrialized regions. Moreover, in both Italy and France, agricultural productivity is very low in the poor regions and is also making less progress there than in the rich regions. The population factor, however, acts differently in the two countries. In Italy the situation of the poor southern regions is made still more difficult because natural population increase has been faster there than in the rich, and internal migration is kept at low levels because of unemployment in the rich districts. In France, on the contrary, the much more favourable employment situation in the rich regions has resulted in migration on such a scale that some of the poor regions have become depopulated to a considerable extent. This is true of the mountain districts in the centre and south-east of France and of many parts of the west and south-west, but not of Brittany, which has a considerable agricultural surplus population even at the existing low standards of mechanization in agriculture.

Depopulation of the countryside in France has been of far greater dimensions than in other European countries. In other countries too, for instance in Sweden and Norway, unfavourably situated valleys and many villages have lost a large share of their population during the process of industrialization and urbanization; but in those countries many of the migrants have moved only to the regional centres and the population of the region as a whole has, in most cases, continued to grow, although much more slowly than in the richer regions of the country. In France, on the contrary, stagnation in total population and strong centralization, both administratively and economically, have combined to make population decline a normal phenomenon throughout the country, while only the richest regions and a few large towns continued to expand. Of the 90 departments of France, two-thirds reached their maximum population in the nineteenth century and no more than 20 continue to grow. While population in all the poor regions listed in Table 71* is no higher, or even lower, than a hundred years ago, it has increased by some 75 per cent in the rich north-eastern region.

Although natural conditions for agriculture are poor in some of the under-developed provinces of France and Italy, as well as in Poland and Czechoslovakia, these facts of geography are only a minor element in explaining the wide regional gaps in economic levels which have developed in these countries. The unification of Italy, under the political hegemony of the northern part of the country, was followed by a long period of decay in the south and expansion in the north.[8] Political factors were of major importance also in shaping the industrial pattern of Poland and Czechoslovakia. Before the creation of the national States at the end of the first World War the ruling classes in those territories were often more influenced in their investment decisions by political considerations and national group interest than by purely eco-

* Table 71 (not shown) lists long-term trends in population in the regions of Spain, Italy, France, Germany, Norway, Sweden, and United Kingdom. The poorer regions of France referred to here are Corse, Massif Central, Bretagne, and South West.

nomic factors. The case of France is somewhat different, because easy access to coal and iron in the north-east was a powerful element in causing the large regional differences, but strong political centralization and the consequent radiation of the whole transport network from Paris was of major importance too. The result was that the growing utilization of energy in the form of oil and electricity, particularly hydro-electricity, although causing some industrialization in the northern part of the Alps, was unable to reverse the trend towards concentration in the north-east, and depopulation continued in many regions.

In the sparsely populated countries of Norway, Sweden and Finland, as in Switzerland and Austria, hydro-power or discoveries of mineral resources have tended to shift the balance between the regions. Industrialization has been very rapid in all these countries during the last two decades and the shift of population from agriculture to industry has been large even in the poor areas, although part of the population surplus has continued to migrate from the poor to the rich areas. The improvements that have taken place in the poorest areas were, however, by no means sufficient to eliminate the regional inequalities in development and income; in particular, the northern regions of the Scandinavian countries have lagged behind, a fact which is accentuated by the far more rapid population growth in these districts than elsewhere.

In the major highly industrialized countries—the United Kingdom and Germany—differences in the degree of industrialization as well as in incomes within broad regions are relatively small. It would be tempting to argue therefore that regional disparities are only a temporary phenomenon in the process of industrialization and can be expected to disappear with rising economic levels even in the absence of particular regional policies. It should be remembered, however, that industrialization in the United Kingdom was accompanied by population decline and economic stagnation in the region which is now the Irish Republic and that regional differences in Germany were much larger before the predominantly agricultural regions east of the Oder and Neisse were incorporated in Poland and the Soviet Union.[9]

In such densely populated countries as the United Kingdom and Belgium, the problem of congestion or of structural unemployment in some of the highly industrialized districts is causing more concern than problems of under-developed or depopulated regions, although the United Kingdom has such problem areas in the north of Scotland and in parts of Wales. Congestion becomes still more serious in western Germany and the Netherlands, where density of population is combined with rapid population increase.

The Impact of Refugees on the Regional Problems of Western Germany

In western Germany, the pressing need of finding immediate shelter and food for over 8 million refugees who suddenly poured into the Western Zones at the end of the war—and later for the 2 million further refugees from the Eastern Zone—swept aside all consideration of the development of problem regions of old standing. The emergency situation required hurried day-to-day decisions, since the concentration of a vast number of people devoid of any occupation and means of livelihood produced great hardship and constituted a grave political problem. Refugees were therefore directed to those regions which, owing to their predominantly agricultural structure, had suffered least war damage and where emergency accommodation, as well as food, could most readily be found.

There were two possible lines of approach for remedying the over-population and the extremely high unemployment ratio in the main refugee regions. One was resettlement in other parts of western Germany, and the other the creation of employment opportunities on the spot. Since the size of the problem was overwhelming and time was pressing, resettlement was the first solution to be tackled. The Government worked out three consecutive resettlement programmes whereby some 600,000 refugees were to be moved from the most burdened provinces—Schleswig-Holstein, Lower Saxony and Bavaria. The re-settlement was carried out according to quotas established for each programme. After some experimentation with the distribution of quotas among the receiving provinces on the basis of what turned out to be inadequate criteria, government-directed migration was adapted to the main flow of free migration which had moved to the old concentration regions of Nordrhein–Westfalen, the Rhein–Main and Rhein–Neckar regions and industrial parts of Baden-Württemberg. Thus, both government-sponsored and free migration followed the pull of the great industrial centres.

Although, as will be shown in a subsequent section, some measures were taken to assist the development of the new problem regions, these remained on a relatively modest scale. Thus, under the pressure of circumstances, an opportunity of decentralization through the employment of the refugees on the spot was lost and the task of developing the problem regions was rendered more difficult in the long run by the exodus of skilled workers to the highly developed regions, whereas those who remained were often of a type difficult to integrate. The situation is most problematic in the poorest region, Schleswig-Holstein, which has had the largest increase in population and the lowest increase in industrial production. In that region, in contrast to other regions of western Germany, industrial production has increased less than population, and unemployment in June 1954 was 12 per cent against 3 per cent in the Ruhr.

Austria and Finland also had to face a serious problem of integrating refugees into their economies; but, unlike western Germany, the influx was not concentrated on the poor regions and the refugees could be absorbed without increasing the regional disparities in those countries.

The Effects of Migration

The short review of regional differences in European countries given above can be summarized as follows: the gravest problems of regional under-development are found in countries where the rate of growth of industry has been insufficient to absorb the population surplus even in the most industrialized regions, so that the way to emigration from the poor regions has been barred (except for possibilities of emigration to other countries). Where industrial expansion in the rich regions has been more rapid, the difficulties of the poor regions have been alleviated by migration of part or most of the population surplus. However, in some poor regions, in particular in France and Ireland, either the natural increase has been negligible or much smaller than net migration from the region, so that total population has declined.

While emigration of part of the population surplus is often desirable from the point of view of the poor area, the effect has been quite different where migration has caused a decline in total population in whole regions. The exodus of a large share of the younger generation, the decline in investment needs following from depopulation, the increased burden when there are fewer to pay for the upkeep of public and private services all combine to produce an atmosphere which paralyses technical and economic progress. In such circumstances the ensuing shortage of agricultural manpower is likely to result in part of the land being taken out of cultivation rather than in mechanization and other labour-saving improvements. Thus, in a region whose population is declining, the labour shortage, instead of being the highroad to a rational and modern agriculture, leads only to a decline in total agricultural output. Even if, in this process, production is concentrated on the better lands, productively, either per man or per hectare, is unlikely to increase significantly.

Owing to the rapid growth of population, which until recently was normal for European countries other than France, the continued expansion of industry in the old centres has only rarely led to an absolute decline of population in the less industrialized regions. The migration towards the traditional centres of industry has caused much concern in some countries because it added to the congestion in the receiving regions, but at least when the absolute numbers engaged in agriculture did not decline, it was considered an advantage from the point of view of the region of departure. With the modest increase in population which can be expected in the next decade, this situation is bound to change. If industrial expansion continues to be more rapid in the old centres of industry than in the less industrialized regions, the resulting migration will cause an absolute population decline and changes in the age structure which, in turn, will lead to stagnation and decay in many regions.

In these countries demographic developments increasingly give rise to a serious dilemma: on the one hand, it is essential that agriculture should be modernized in the backward regions, and this normally involves a decline in the agricultural population. On the other hand, it is desirable, for the reasons just mentioned, to avoid a decline of total population in those regions. The only escape from this dilemma is in a policy of industrial decentralization, the conditions and methods of which will be discussed below.

Short of policies aiming at a genuine equalization of levels of productivity, there remains the possibility, at least for the richer countries, of alleviating the social effects of regional discrepancies through income transfers from the rich to the poor areas. In fact many countries pursue such policies, partly in the form of financial transfers, and partly in the form of tariff protection or price support to products which are of basic importance to the economy of poor regions. But for the consideration given to the interests of poor regions, prices for certain agricultural products would probably be lower than they are in many countries. This form of regional policy has, however, certain inconveniences: first, it gives help to producers other than those it was intended to help, and therefore lays more burdens than necessary on consumers or on the public budget; secondly, it does not provide a true solution because it raises income instead of productivity, and may thereby even reduce the incentive to improve productivity, for instance by migration to other regions or to other occupations within the same region.[10] When the increasing social cost of incorporating new inhabitants and new industries in the already congested areas is added to the cost of supporting poor and perhaps depopulated regions, the total sum may well become very much larger than the costs of industrial decentralization.

2. THE ECONOMIC STRUCTURE OF UNDER-DEVELOPED REGIONS

The preceding section has shown the great variety of regional problems in Europe. Nevertheless, it was found that certain characteristics are common to nearly all the poor regions. Thus, the share of population occupied in agriculture is higher and the share in industry lower in poor than in rich regions inside the same country, the main exceptions being certain areas in the United Kingdom and Belgium, where a very large proportion of the population is engaged in industries which have been or are still depressed, such as coal and shipbuilding in the case of the United Kingdom and textiles in both countries. There is a less clear rule as to the variations in employment in services between rich and poor districts (as can be seen from Table 70). A large share of the population engaged in services may be a genuine sign of high living standards, but it may also be an indication that the region is congested and many people have to be employed in local transport; for both reasons, there tend to be more people employed in services in rich districts. In regions with too scattered a population, however, a large share of the population may likewise be absorbed in services such as distribution, administration and transport, and lack of other employment possibilities may swell the numbers in services although the amount of services provided is small. The last two cases explain why some poor regions have a very great number of people employed in services.

Since differences in the degree of dependence upon agriculture are the main structural differences between poorer and richer regions inside the same country as well as between poorer and richer countries, it is not surprising that the pattern of commodity trade as between regions likewise corresponds to that between countries: the poorer regions do as a rule export food, forest products and raw materials derived from agriculture to the richer regions and import manufactures and services.[11] The analogy does not, however, hold for mineral raw materials. These are often exported by under-developed countries, but under-developed regions export them only rarely to rich regions inside the same country because processing of such raw materials, if it takes place at all in the country, will normally be carried out near their extraction.

The Development of Agriculture and of the Extractive Industries

A large part of the discussion about the possibilities of development of under-developed countries has centred round the problem of the relative merits of developing either agriculture or industry or both at the same time, and the last solution is generally favoured. When this problem is posed for under-developed regions inside countries in Europe, the choice will never be "either or" since very few regions can be developed by means of improvements in agriculture alone, and at least some improvements in local agriculture will always be a necessary element in any co-ordinated effort to develop a backward region. In exceptional cases, extensive schemes for irrigation or other land improvement may make it possible to absorb all labour that has hitherto been unemployed or employed in occupations of low productivity, but such a solution requires not only rather exceptional conditions in the region itself, but also that a market for a large share of the increase in agricultural production can be found inside or outside the country. It is this last condition which does not seem to be fulfilled for some of the ambitious proposals for developing large regions of France exclusively by means or irrigation and other improvements of agricultural land.[12] In cases where the demand for food in the richer regions is relatively inelastic and the expansion of export markets cannot be counted upon, or in cases where the natural conditions for agriculture in the region that should be developed are so poor that more intensive production could not compete with production in other regions, the means to develop the region must consist solely in the implantation of non-agricultural activities. On the other hand, once such activities are started, local demand may increase for certain foodstuffs with particularly high transport costs and this may then make it possible to intensify agriculture somewhat. For instance, the measures to increase agricultural production contained in the development scheme for northern Norway are meant to meet these secondary demands only, while the basic development is to be provided by industrialization.

Even where it is possible, as it may be in limited districts in southern Europe, to base development of a poor district mainly on improvements in agriculture, this will nearly always necessitate certain investments in transport facilities and in manufacturing industry, particularly food processing. Where a development programme for a region is based mainly on utilization of mineral or forest resources, it will also inevitably involve considerable investments in transport and processing industries. It has already been noted that in less developed countries some poor regions are rich in unexploited mineral resources and this would probably prove to be true for many more if geological prospecting were made more systematic than at present.[13] Even in much more developed countries like France and the Netherlands, modern prospecting has in recent years brought evidence of hitherto unknown mineral resources in some of the poorer regions.[14] Utilization of these resources will in nearly all cases require assistance from Governments in the form of improvements in transport and other social capital, and in some cases also in the extraction and processing, because these activities may involve the investment of risk-taking capital in larger amounts than are likely to come forth from private sources. The State-financed steel industries utilizing local ore in northern Norway and northern Sweden and the State-owned copper mines in eastern Finland provide examples of this.

It is well known that lack of public services, in particular power and means of transport, is a very important hindrance to the development of backward regions in the poor countries of Europe, but even in countries which have reached a fairly high stage of industrialization, their inadequacy may be the decisive bottleneck which prevents profitable economic activities in the poor regions. Thus, for instance, although the continued shortage of timber in the post-war period has made forestry extremely profitable, there still exist enormous forest districts in the poor regions in the north and east of Finland where the trees are going to waste because of lack of roads or railways to bring them out.[15] If, on the other hand, means of transport were provided, processing industries would have to be built in the region in order to make possible the utilization of waste and inferior qualities of timber. Similar cases where simultaneous development of social capital and of extractive industries and the expansion of processing are able to produce substantial results exist in parts of eastern Europe. For instance, the development plan for Slovakia consists of such co-ordinated measures to promote extractive industries (forestry and mining) as well as agriculture and at the same time to set up manufacturing industries processing the expanding output of raw materials. By such consolidated schemes a region avoids too narrow specialization and a varied range of employment possibilities is opened up to local labour. Moreover, the region is protected against the risk of becoming a depressed area at a later stage owing to excessive specialization in one or a few products, a risk which is all the greater when the products are raw materials.

In southern Europe the forestry problem is of a quite different nature. In these countries, as well as in southern France, deforestation, often continuing up to recent times, has transformed large areas into barren mountain pastures, which have been further deteriorated by overgrazing, while hillsides and adjacent lowlands suffer from erosion and a disturbed water economy. This destruction of natural wealth has been an important cause of the impoverishment of some of the most destitute regions in southern Europe.[16] The problem of recovering the lost forestry resources is exacerbated by the fact that reafforestation is a long-term investment. Hence, this investment, although tremendously productive in the longer run, tends to be given a relatively low priority in countries which are struggling with short-term problems and where the investment decisions are coloured by the shortness of the perspective of private investors.

The Location of Manufacturing Industry

Among the poor regions of Europe, under-developed as well as depressed, there are many which have very few or no natural resources which it would be economically advantageous to develop. In such regions the choice is between depopulation or establishment of such manufacturing industries as need not be located near their raw materials.

A statistical method of determining the extent to which various industrial branches are concentrated in particular regions or dispersed over the country has been devised by Professor Sargant Florence, whose coefficients of localization[17] measure the degree of geographical concentration of a particular industry. Inter-country comparisons based on such coefficients are naturally subject to considerable qualifications, mainly due to differences in the size of regions and the density of their population, but they can nevertheless be usefully employed as illustrations of the general framework of location.

It is seen from the comparison of coefficients of localization for Sweden, the United Kingdom and the United States* that the coefficients show both considerable agreement as to the overall localization and divergences where special factors operate in one of the countries. The processing industries mentioned above, which tend to be located near their raw material sources (that is, food processing industries, pulp mills and the first stages of processing of textile fibres and ores), show high coefficients, indicating a large degree of concentration in certain regions, except in cases where they are based on raw materials produced all over the country or on raw materials which are mainly imported from other countries. Apart from these raw-material-oriented industries, high coefficients are found in some industries where the optimum size of the plant is very large. In these cases, the high coefficients are explained by the fact that employment is concentrated in a few large plants the number of which is smaller than the number of regions chosen. (There are, of course, many more such industries in Sweden than in the two other countries in the table, which have a much

* Coefficients are given in Table 72 of original text.

larger population.) The high coefficients for these large-scale industries do not necessarily indicate that one particular location is more favourable than another. The group of industries with very low coefficients includes, apart from some of the raw-material-oriented ones mentioned above, some for which the final product is much more expensive to transport than the raw material (concrete products, beverages), and some which have to be freshly made each day (bread, newspapers).

In between these extremes there is the bulk of manufacturing industries with location coefficients somewhere between 30 and 50. This group includes some of the industries with very large numbers of employed: the metal-using industries, chemicals, more advanced stages of textile production, clothing and many other industries manufacturing a large variety of goods. These, together with the large-scale industries mentioned above, provide the field for policies attempting to influence the regional dispersal of manufacturing, and it is therefore of importance to investigate in which regions they are actually located in European countries.

There is a very characteristic difference between the industrial structure of rich and poor areas, which is accounted for by wide divergencies in a few important branches of industry: in under-developed regions, textile, metal, metal-using, and chemical industries hardly exist, while they are the predominant branches in all the rich regions. Differences in employment between rich and poor regions are much less pronounced in such branches as the clothing, food-processing, wood and building-materials industries, as well as in building activity partly because in the poor regions larger numbers in handicrafts tend to counterbalance the smaller numbers in industry proper. This difference in industrial structure between rich and poor regions is much more pronounced in Spain, Italy and France than in western Germany and the United Kingdom, but it is clearly discernible also in the latter countries. In Spain, the richest regions employ ten times as many in the first group of industries as the poor regions, while in the rich industrialized regions of the United Kingdom only 25 per cent more are employed in this group than in the poor regions.*

It is natural to ask the question if it is poverty itself—i.e., the narrowness of the local market—which has kept industries like engineering and textiles away from the poor regions, or whether it is the absence of these industries which is the main explanation of their poverty. There is no simple and uniform answer to this question. First of all, it should be noted that none of these industries would seem to be particularly

* The differences are detailed in Table 73 of the original text.

dependent on nearness to their customers, a statement that needs no further proof than the fact that they account for a very large share of European exports. The pronounced tendency to locate these industries in already highly industrialized regions or, in the case of engineering, in the biggest towns, is no doubt much more due to the attraction of a big labour market than to the advantages of a big market for sales of the products. This is in particular the case for large-scale industries which will normally have sales agencies in other localities than the place of production.

The attraction of a large market for labour already possessing some skill or at least some adaptation to work in factories is no doubt a very important location factor for particular industries in the least developed countries of Europe, and it was equally so in the early stages of industrialization in the countries that are now highly industrialized. This is probably the main explanation why some branches of industry that are more scattered over the territory in the United States and Sweden show a very high regional concentration in the United Kingdom. Cotton[18] and wool processing, cutlery and hand tools—some of the oldest British industries—started their existence in isolated spots of capitalist development, as industries still do today in some southern European countries. Once they were started, they were maintained by tradition, including the traditional skill of the labour force in the original locations. So the original centre continued to grow and prosper until the day came, for some of them, when structural decline revealed the dangers of too high a degree of regional specialization. Other industrialized countries, too, show examples of such early specialization, although to a lesser extent than in the United Kingdom. Thus, the French silk industries are centred in Lyons and production of cutlery in Thiers and Nogent. Another example of regional specialization is provided by the watch industries in western Switzerland, eastern France and southwestern Germany. Some of these industries developed originally in regions which had no particular location advantage other than that their agriculture was so poor that the need for secondary employment made labour extremely cheap. It would be interesting to know how far these industries still obtain real advantages from their geographical concentration and how far they are now kept there by pure tradition. The much lower and, as it seems, "normal size" localization coefficients shown for some of these industries in more newly industrialized countries suggest that tradition may be the main explanation. It could be added that a British Government report of 1940[19] analyzed the behaviour of some of the industries traditionally located in London and found that those plants which had been located outside London had proved just as able to resist the depression of the 'thirties as those located in London.[20]

It is commonly assumed that room for manœuvre in policies of industrial location is seriously restricted by the fact that skills for a certain industry or group of industries have accumulated during generations in traditional centres. It may well be, however, that the importance of this is often exaggerated. For a wide range of industries, the skills required of the bulk of the labour force can be easily developed once training facilities are available. But the present distribution of technical schools is very uneven.* The figures suggest that the insufficiency or complete lack of facilities for industrial training in the less industrialized or under-developed regions is an important factor tending to project the existing distribution of industry into the future.

Institutional Factors which prevent the Decentralization of Industry

A number of institutional factors have the effect of perpetuating and even accentuating the existing location pattern of industry. One of these factors, the insufficient availability of social capital in the poorer regions, has already been mentioned. Another factor has been the reduction in regional wage differences brought about by the growing strength of trade unions and the introduction of social considerations into national wage policies. In some countries in Europe, the range in wages still shows considerable differences between regions, but in others regional wage differences have almost ceased to exist except for somewhat higher wages in the largest towns as a compensation for the higher cost of living. In economic theory, it is normally assumed that there are two mechanisms, both related to income differentials, through which the population in backward areas within a country should be able to overcome their disadvantages, one of these being migration, the other the tendency to attract through lower wages those industries for which the location disadvantages are smallest. While, as shown above, migration has actually been very important in relieving population pressure in the poor regions in most countries, it is clear that the small regional wage differences now prevailing in a number of countries are wholly unable to compensate industries for the many other drawbacks confronting them in the under-developed regions. In Sweden and Finland, the situation in this respect is rather paradoxical because nominal wages

*Table 74 of original text gives figures for students in industrial schools by regions, in Spain, Portugal, Italy, Austria, Western Germany, Norway, and United Kingdom.

have been fixed at a level about one-third higher in the poor northern regions than in the rest of the country to compensate for the higher living costs and other disadvantages there. This has been possible because export prices for the main products of these regions (iron ore and forest products) are very favourable, but it does, of course, act as a brake on the expansion of other industrial production in these regions.

In a number of European countries, such as the United Kingdom, Germany and Sweden, differences in local taxation have had perverse effects on the location of industry, either because a chronically low level of income necessitated higher tax rates to meet local expenses and this made the place unattractive as a location for new industries; or because depression in one major industrial branch led to higher taxation to meet increased expenditure for unemployment relief. Although many countries operate a system of financial transfers between rich and poor local authorities, these do not normally fully compensate for differences in taxable incomes and consequently do not offset the adverse effects on industrial location of differences in tax rates.

Imperfections in the credit market are another distorting element in regional balance, since centralized banking systems with branch banks in the provinces will usually supply credit only to large and well-established firms, and small and medium-sized businesses in poor regions often find it difficult to secure funds at reasonable terms. Moreover, not only are investment funds from the centres prevented from flowing into the provinces, but branch banks in the under-developed regions often serve as a collecting instrument of local funds for investment in the centres, thus depriving the poor regions of the productive use of their own savings. This was the case in Germany until the 'thirties[21] and has also been one of the difficulties from which southern Italy has been suffering.

In railway freight policy, the traditional and still dominant principle is tapering rates for long distances* and lower charges per ton/km. for raw materials than for manufactures. Part of the difference in rates does, of course, correspond to cost differences for the railways, but in many countries it goes far beyond this and amounts to subsidies for raw materials and for long hauls paid for by charging above cost for the transport of manufactures. This freight-rate policy tends to free location of manufacturing industry from being tied to raw material sources. It may, of course, have decentralizing effects for mining, and manufacturing from imported raw materials or from materials

* Rates for Italy, France, Western Germany, Netherlands, and Belgium are given in Table 75 of original text.

produced in concentration areas. More frequently, however, it will work as a centralizing factor because it reduces the advantage of processing agricultural raw materials or the products of decentralized mines on the spot rather than in the industrialized areas. An example of a measure deliberately intended to favour decentralized mines, which had a centralizing effect on manufacturing, was the choice of a fictitious base for freight rate calculations adopted by the German steel cartel in the inter-war period. Oberhausen in the Ruhr was selected as the freight base for the transportation of steel within the cartel, whereby favourably situated steel plants subsidized those in less favoured locations. This had the effect of discriminating against metal-using industries outside the base region and of attracting them to Oberhausen. On the side of the steel-processing industries this system favoured concentration, while on the side of steel production it fostered dispersal. But since the number employed in metal-using industries is much larger than that occupied in the steel industry itself, the centralizing effect of these measures was much greater than the decentralizing effect.[22]

While the subsidies given by the railways to the transport of raw materials tend to encourage location of the raw-material-oriented industries in the big towns, the high transport charges for manufactures provide a protection for decentralized manufacturing industries producing for local markets. The rising competition of road transport in recent years has forced railways to reduce their high rates for finished goods and, to compensate for this, to raise their highly degressive rates for raw materials. While the second measure may improve the competitiveness of some decentralized processing industries, the first reduces the competitiveness of industries producing for local markets in the poor districts. It would seem, however, that the rapid development of road transport has much more dangerous effects for local industries outside the congested areas than merely reducing the protective effect of transport costs. In fact, this protection is beginning to disappear altogether for an increasing number of commodities. This is because it becomes more and more usual for large-scale industries to sell their products at a single price throughout the whole country, a tendency that is reinforced by the growing importance of road transport. Road vehicles are often owned by manufacturing firms themselves and transport costs enter into total cost calculations. The consequence of charging the same prices everywhere is that local consumers have to subsidize the more distant ones. Decentralized industries, which do not depend on local raw materials, are thereby put in an exceedingly difficult position; they have to pay transport on their raw materials, but their competitors cover their transport costs for the finished products partially in other markets. The lack of progress made in the efforts to implant new industries in Northern Ireland, in spite of special facilities granted to local manufacturers, is supposed to be partly explained by the practice of British manufacturers of charging the same prices throughout the whole of the United Kingdom.[23]

The reduced power of competition of local industries in the poor districts is not the only unfavourable effect of the practice of charging a uniform price for the whole country. Equalized prices increase the incentive for large-scale industry to settle near the large consuming centres, since the cost of transport to more distant regions can thus be borne by a larger number of local customers.[24]

As previously mentioned, the growing use of electricity in place of coal facilitated industrial decentralization. The system of power rates decided in most cases by Governments or with Government agreement does, however, often discourage decentralization. This is particularly the case in some of the countries of southern Europe. Thus, the cost of electricity in the Greek provinces is about three times higher than in Athens. In Portugal, the difference is not quite so large, rates in the south amounting to one and a-half times the rate in Lisbon. The unification of electricity rates throughout the whole territory in some of the more developed countries, for instance Sweden and Finland, is an improvement over a system whereby prices are higher in the poor regions. However, this still deprives the industries in the poor mountain regions of their main location advantage. In these regions, it would be more rational for electricity to be sold at prices below the uniform national rate, because important transport losses are avoided when consumption takes place near hydro plants and it moreover seems unjustified that local consumers should share in the investment cost for long-distance transfers. Thus, it has been proposed in Finland[25] that, in order to assist industry in the north, electricity should be sold here at prices 10 to 15 per cent below the uniform rate of the rest of the country. In France, public tariff policy since the war has hit industries in the Alps in a double way: freights for raw materials from the north have been increased and electricity prices have been raised and have come closer to those prevailing in the industrial centres.

More examples could be added of the various artificial impediments to the development of poor regions. The fact that all these factors interact reinforces the cumulative process of growth in the concentration areas and makes these barriers extremely powerful in preventing the spreading of industry to the poor regions. Probably these obstacles are of much greater weight in explaining the backwardness of many poor regions than any natural handicaps from which they might suffer.

3. THE PROBLEM OF ECONOMIC BALANCE BETWEEN AND WITHIN REGIONS

Development of Manufacturing in Poor Regions

It is, of course, of crucial importance for any policy of regional development to determine what types of manufacturing industry can most advantageously be promoted in poor regions. As was mentioned in the preceding section, one important factor to take into account is the endowment of the region in question with natural resources and, in particular, the possibility of creating industries for the processing of local raw materials. Although possibilities of this kind are never wholly absent, they are often rather limited and, hence, the availability of local raw materials cannot be the only criterion for the choice of industries to be promoted in poor regions. The question needs to be considered in the broader context of the industrial structure of the country as a whole.

It might seem, at first sight, that when—as will occur in most cases—the industrial development of a backward region cannot be based on local raw materials alone, the best alternative would be to promote industries processing imported[26] raw materials for local consumption. It could be argued that the region would thereby reduce its dependence on imports of manufactures from the richer regions, and even in the absence of any protection for the new local industries in the poor regions, it might be thought that they would be in a better competitive position vis-à-vis the industries in the more developed regions than large-scale industries which would have to depend on exports beyond the region and, therefore, be at a disadvantage in transport costs both on their raw materials and on their finished goods.[27]

This reasoning is clearly one of analogy with the process by which the development of poor countries has most often been seen to take place; policies of industrialization have regularly been directed towards the substitution of imported manufactures, and the most important policy tool has been tariff protection for the new import-saving industries. It is, however, pertinent to ask whether this analogy between the development problems of poor countries and of poor regions is at all valid. As a matter of fact, the much closer economic ties between regions within a country than between countries set narrow limits to the possibilities of developing "import-saving" industries in backward regions.[28] The textile industries provide an illustration of the problems involved.

As already seen in Table 73, the textile industry hardly exists in any of the under-developed regions in the countries listed. Yet the low transport costs for both raw materials and finished goods, the high labour intensity and the modest demand for skilled labour would seem to make manufacturing of textiles for local consumption a particularly promising field for expansion in the poor regions, and in certain countries, for instance in Yugoslavia, the setting up of textile industries is being used as one of the means to develop the poor regions. Most European countries have, however, excess capacity in the textile industry and employment in this branch is on the decline in a number of them. This does not hinder the continuous development of textile industries in the under-developed overseas countries, but, in the poor regions in European countries, establishment of textile industries meets with considerable opposition from the traditional textile regions, whereas the setting up in poor regions of the more dynamic branches of industry, like engineering and chemicals, is likely to encounter much less resistance.

A lot depends, however, on the overall employment situation in the country: if the country is short of capital and the richer areas suffer from unemployment and have idle capacity in the industries which it is proposed to set up in the under-developed regions, the decision to transfer some of the unemployment burden from the very depressed to the less depressed areas naturally meets with criticism from the vested interests in the richer areas, irrespective of the beneficial effects which are assumed to follow from the change in the longer run. Such a situation exists for instance in Italy, where the choice of industries to be implanted in the south is limited by the existence of mass unemployment and considerable unutilized capacity in most industrial branches in the north. In a country like Norway, on the other hand, where full employment prevails, and certain lines of industry in the rich regions which it is felt should be fostered in the national interest are hampered by labour shortage, the Government may find it easier to encourage a change in the occupational structure of the richer areas for the sake of developing their backward regions. Even where such shifts are deemed desirable, it may, however, be considered whether it is in the true interest of the poorer areas to be saddled with industries which, although suitable from an employment point of view because they are labour-intensive, are in structural decline. It would therefore seem more in the interest not only of the rich but also of the poor areas to concentrate development on those lines of industry which show the greatest tendency to expansion, even if they may be of the large-scale type for which the local market alone is not sufficient.

There are, however, further reasons for basing the development of backward regions not on relatively small-scale local industry of the more simple type but on the most modern and expansive type of industry. One of these reasons is to be found in the structural problems in the rich regions, the other in the long-term interests of the poor regions; these two aspects are now to be considered in turn.

The Structural Problems of the Highly Industrialized Regions

In nearly all European countries, increasing attention is being paid to the economic and social consequences of the rapid growth of population in some key towns or highly industrialized regions. The urgency of the problem does, of course, vary widely from country to country, not only because of differences in overall population density and geographical factors, but also because the degree of concentration of the town population[29] is very different, influenced as it is by historical differences in political and administrative systems. Federal States, such as Switzerland or States which have fairly recently been constituted such as Germany, Italy and Yugoslavia, have, of course, smaller capitals than old centralized States such as the United Kingdom or France, or those which have lost territory, such as Austria and Denmark.* On the other hand, some countries, like the Netherlands and Germany, which have no particularly large towns (measured in relation to total population) contain big regions where a large number of middle-sized towns have grown so close to one another that the whole region has become one large urban agglomeration.

It is obvious that the optimum size of towns or the optimum population density of industrialized regions cannot be decided on economic grounds alone; economic considerations are even far from being the most important in the solution of this question. A considerable number of studies have been made, mostly in the United States, but also some in European countries, to determine the optimum size of towns according to a large number of different criteria varying from industrial needs, *per capita* cost of municipal administration, and time wasted on daily transport, to fertility, mortality, cultural needs and access to the open country.[30] These studies are far from giving any precise

* The population distribution in these countries is given in Table 76 of original text.

answer even for individual criteria, but they seem to agree in finding no significant advantages on any grounds and many very important disadvantages of towns above the size of some 300,000 inhabitants. Even without putting the maximum quite as low as that[31] it could be concluded that it would be desirable to stop the further growth of a very large number of European cities, and some European countries actually do try, by various means, which will be discussed in following sections, to prevent one or more big cities or congested areas from growing further. The aspect of the question which is most relevant for the present discussion relates to the occupational distribution of the population in those cities and agglomerations.

It is well known that growth in *per capita* national income is accompanied by a much more than proportionate growth in the demand for services and that demand for certain services such as local transport increases more than proportionately with the growth of population when the size of a town exceeds a certain limit. In large cities, or in regions which have become so industrialized that the share of population in agriculture is insignificant, the increasing demand for services arising from growth in *per capita* income can only be met either by transfer of people hitherto employed in industry or by population increase through immigration.[32] Immigration, however, increases the demand for services still more and the process goes on cumulatively, unless measures are taken to bring about an absolute reduction in industrial employment.[33] In the richest countries of Europe, it seems that not only the biggest towns but also other highly industrialized regions have arrived at the point where the share of population in industry is declining, because the share in services increases more than the already very low share in agriculture decreases. That this is the case in Sweden can be seen from the figures below, showing the number of workers in industry proper (excluding handicrafts) per 1,000 inhabitants:

	1930	*1945*	*1951*
Average for regions including 3 largest towns	91	102	96
Average for 5 highly industrialized regions	50	133	132
Average for 12 less industrialized regions	65	88	91
Average for 4 non-industrialized regions	34	40	43

Sources: Figures for 1930 and 1945 from S.O.U., 1951:6, *Näringslivets Lokalisering* (Swedish Government Reports), page 22. Figures for 1951 from S.O.U., 1951, *Industri,* and *Statistisk Arsbok,* 1953.

If one accepts the assumption made above that in a large number of European congested cities and districts further immigration is contrary to the interests of the people already living there, it follows that it is also in the interest of the local population to avoid the introduction of new industries of the type which can be expected to expand rapidly in the coming decades, because the growth of these industries would inevitably attract new immigrants and increase the congestion. It would therefore be in the interest of the congested districts if new industries, like nylon, plastics, television, electronics, etc., could be induced to install themselves in the less developed regions.

Table 73 gives an impression of the dominant position of engineering industries in such towns as London and Paris, where this single branch of industry occupies approximately 33 per cent of the active population in industry. The particularly fast expansion of this branch of industry in recent decades has been one of the main reasons for the rapid growth of these cities. The case would therefore seem very strong for trying to get this expanding as well as labour-intensive industry to settle in the regions where expansion of industrial employment is desirable and not in those where it should, if possible, be avoided. And this holds true not only for the most highly industrialized countries, but also for those where most of the growth of engineering is still to come.

Difficulties of Long-term Balance in the Poor Regions

The desirability of introducing the most modern and expansive industries in the poor regions is due not only to the need to avoid them in the congested districts, but also to long-term considerations for the poor regions themselves. In order to make this clear, it is necessary to discuss in further detail the process by which poor regions develop or fall behind in development in relation to more prosperous areas of the country.

First, it should be noted that it is easier to provide activity and higher incomes for a short period than in the longer run. The poor regions are virtually all in dire need of basic improvements in transport systems, public utilities and dwellings and, especially in the backward regions in southern Europe, there are immense possibilities for land improvement. Hence, there is no dearth of investment opportunities. As regards supply, there is in most cases an abundance of unemployed or under-employed labour and since the basic investments—notably road-building, power, irrigation and afforestation—are highly labour-intensive, the problem is not one of availability of physical factors directly needed for the investments but of financing them.

Even if finance is provided for these basic investments through public grants and credits, or through inducements to private capital, there remains the problem of securing long-term balance for the region after these investments in social capital and in the improvement of natural resources are completed. As long as these investments go on, further activity will of course be generated in local services, handicrafts and small-scale industry, and if the region is among the promising ones where the exploration of considerable unutilized natural resources has only been kept back for lack of the social capital now invested, the stimulus given by the investments and the resulting increase in local incomes may be sufficient to start a genuine productive development of the region. But in regions which are poor not only in social capital but also in unutilized natural resources, activity and income may, once the investments are completed, fall back to a level not very much higher than the original one. The population would live more comfortably, but employment and current incomes may not have improved much. In such a case some of the local industries and services which had been set up in the days of greater activity may even have to close down. The importance of this problem has been recognized by the Italian Government, which—as will be shown later—has tried to overcome it by taking more positive measures for the establishment of industries in southern Italy than had been contemplated in the original development plan.

If, however, no recession in activity takes place, but the workers released from employment in the original investments are transferred to local industries which have expanded partly because of the increase in income and partly by replacement of imports from other regions,[34] the balance may then be preserved also after the completion of the investments. But difficulties may nevertheless be expected to arise at a later stage. The reason is that the region in question will not be the only one in the country that develops and, simultaneously with the development process in the poor region, technical progress takes place in the richer regions. However, technical progress in one region tends to disturb the balance in others, because part of the consumption in the technically lagging regions will shift from home-produced to "imported" goods. If the persons who previously produced the local goods remain in the region as under-employed or unemployed, and if the increased demand in the other region where the technical progress takes places does not direct itself towards export products of the poor region, the position of the latter will have deteriorated permanently.

It is this mechanism which makes it vital to spread the most dynamic industries[35] over the country, and in particular to make sure that some of them are located in under-developed areas. If the most modern

—and especially the most dynamic—industries are not established in the poor regions they will be set up in other parts of the country and the competition from their output will directly, or via their increasing share in total consumers' expenditure, make inroads into the markets for the products produced in the poor regions. Since the poor regions will be mainly exporters of food and producers of manufactures for local consumption, it is highly improbable that they will be able to compensate for the loss of internal markets by increased exports to the expanding regions. The most rapidly expanding element in the consumption of rich regions is services, which are produced primarily within these regions. It is therefore necessary, in order to preserve inter-regional balance, to give the poor regions more than their proportionate share of the most dynamic industries.

In other words, industries which produce mainly for the local market in a backward region cater only for limited needs and can be expected to advance only so fast as the region as a whole. "New" industries, on the other hand, are designed to meet needs which arise primarily in the more developed parts of the country, and in this manner the development of the poor region becomes geared to the development in more fortunate regions. An equally important result is the introduction through these industries of standards of technology far in advance of those prevailing in the region, thereby giving it a chance to take the lead in technical development if only in a limited field. Some leadership in technology is needed if a new gap in development is not to appear at a later stage.

Given that the value of the "new" industries would lic in their exceptional possibilities for further expansion, it is obvious that little importance attaches to the amount of employment they provide per unit of capital invested, particularly since it is the same capital market which will have to supply the capital wherever the industries are placed. Here again, the analogy with under-developed countries does not hold. From considerations of this nature it appears to have been a wise policy on the part of the Dutch Government to set up their continuous-strip mills in one of their development areas and to induce the company producing nylon to establish itself in another. Similarly, the Italian plans to make Naples, the depressed "capital" of southern Italy, a centre of the electronic industry would seem well motivated.[36]

Limits to Decentralization

The discussion has so far been concerned with the desirability of shifting the pattern of industry so that the poor regions receive a larger share and the congested districts a smaller. The problem to be dealt with briefly here is that of the location of industry inside the poor regions—namely, the problem of how far decentralization ought to go.

Some of the enthusiasts for industrial decentralization—mainly those who have closer ties with agriculture than with industry—argue in favour of bringing manufacturing industry into the villages. The object of this would be to prevent the spread of rural depopulation which is already resulting from the rapid mechanization and rationalization of agriculture.

Though there may be exceptional cases where industrial plants could without great disadvantage be situated in not too isolated villages, the general rule is that the disadvantages of industrial decentralization grow considerably when industry moves from middle-sized towns down to the village level. While the studies concerning optimum size of towns mentioned above seem to agree still less on the desirable minimum than on the desirable maximum, it is quite clear that below a certain level economic disadvantages tend to grow and non-economic advantages to diminish or become clearly negative.

The argument in favour of industrial decentralization and against gradual depopulation of whole regions is not directed against the concentration of population *inside* each region. On the contrary, concentration of settlement within a region is precisely the method by which the two objectives of securing economic progress and of avoiding gradual depopulation of the region can be reconciled. Rural romanticism and petty local interests often combine in the claim, vociferated through political channels, that both the population and the means of subsistence should be preserved, even at very high cost,[37] in small isolated islands, secondary valleys and remote mountain villages. Often such places had better be evacuated entirely, although sometimes there may be an escape in turning old farmhouses and fishermen's cottages into summer habitations for town dwellers. This has happened for instance in some poor agricultural districts in Sweden and, in America, in the New England states.

Even where agricultural land is too valuable to be taken out of cultivation, the justified desire that agriculture should not be left as the only activity in a depopulated district without access to services or cultural life would be satisfied if the effect of industrial decentralization were to strengthen economic activity and thereby commercial and cultural life in middle-sized towns. With the development of modern means of transport and especially of the motor scooter, these towns are now within much easier reach of the rural population. Experience has shown that it is no easy task to halt the growth of industry in the heavily industrialized areas and to stop the flow of migrants towards them. This goal may, perhaps, become attainable if industry can be attracted to, and the flow of migrants from agriculture halted in, a large number of expanding middle-sized towns which revive economic activity and cultural life in their regions. Attempts to go still further and spread individual plants over the countryside would run grave risks of failure, partly because of the higher costs and partly because workers may be inclined to use such rural industries as only a temporary halt on their way to town.[38] While it would be desirable from the point of view of agriculture if such rural industries were set up in districts where agriculture is overcrowded with manpower, it would be much less satisfactory for the industries themselves, which would be faced by a very fluctuating labour force and may run into difficulties of recruitment once the agricultural surplus had been eliminated.

This whole problem is, of course, of much more urgency in countries with scattered populations like Sweden, Norway or France than in the densely populated countries. In Sweden, a Parliamentary Committee dealing with industrial localization[39] has suggested that, parallel with industrial decentralization, there should be developed relatively small service towns in the countryside. The function of these towns would be to serve as commercial and cultural centres for the agricultural population.

NOTES

[1] Regional problems and policies of the Soviet Union are not dealt with in this chapter.

[2] An outstanding example is the Italian plan for development of the *Mezzogiorno,* which was discussed in the SURVEY for 1953, which also contained a more summary description of regional problems in other southern European countries. See *Economic Survey of Europe in 1953,* Part III, in particular pages 92–94 (Turkey), 103–104 (Greece), 121 (Yugoslavia), 123–140 (Southern Italy), 142 (Spain), 154 (Portugal) and 184–186 (General).

[3] These figures must, of course, be taken only as broad indications because of the arbitrariness necessarily involved in the definition of regions.

[4] There is, of course, no such correlation to be expected in the case of industrially depressed areas. For instance, western Flanders, the depressed area of Belgium, shows agricultural incomes about 20 per cent above the Belgian average. See Guido Declercq and Olivier Vanneste: *Structurele Werkloosheid in West-Vlaanderen,* Roeselare, 1954, page 306.

[5] However, it was shown in a study of productivity in England and Scotland made by H. W. Singer and C. E. V. Leser (*Journal of the Royal Statistical Society,* Vol. CXI, Part IV, 1948) that the 5 per cent lower value of output per

person employed in industry in Scotland compared with England and Wales (according to the 1935 census of production) was not caused by differences in industrial structure, but could safely be interpreted as a difference in productivity.

[6] Post-war regional problems and policies in these countries are dealt with in Section 5.

[7] As measured by the share of active population in industry (see Table 70).

[8] For a further description, see *Economic Survey of Europe in 1953,* pages 131 *et seq.*

[9] In the 'thirties, income per head in both East Prussia and Pomerania was around half of that of Schleswig-Holstein and also quite considerably below that of Lower Saxony and Bavaria, the other two poorest regions of western Germany at present.

[10] For a more detailed discussion of these problems, see *European Agriculture —A Statement of Problems,* ECE/FAO, Geneva, 1954, Chapter 3, pages 33 *et seq.*

[11] There are exceptions, of course, one of the most important being tourism in poor regions.

[12] For a discussion of this problem, see Chapter 7.

[13] See *Economic Survey of Europe in 1953,* Chapter 13.

[14] For instance, mineral oil has recently been found both in one of the poor regions in the Netherlands and in the southwest of France. Moreover, uranium has been discovered in the Massif Central and in Brittany, and coal in the Jura.

[15] In the district of Maanselkä in north-east Finland alone about 260,000 ha. of forests could be brought within the border line of economic utilization by building a forest railway which would have to transport 13,000 wagons of timber a year. On shorter distances also there may be great advantages in improving transport; in one case, for instance, a road—4 km. long—which had cost 3.75 million Finnish marks to build was already after six years' use able to save transport costs of 8.6 million Finnish marks by shifting from horse to truck transport. See Henrik Gripenberg, "Aktuella spörsmål inom vårt skogsbruk," *Ekonomiska Samfundets Tidskrift,* Helsinki, 1954.

[16] According to an estimate made in the ECE/FAO study *European Timber Trends and Prospects,* Geneva, 1953, barren areas in the whole of Europe, which could again become productive through afforestation, extend over 7 to 8 million hectares, a large part of which is to be found in southern Europe.

[17] For an explanation of the method used, see note in Table 72.

[18] A high coefficient of localization for the cotton textile industry is also apparent in the United States but the reasons are different: two-thirds of the employment in the cotton industry is in the three southern states of North Carolina, South Carolina and Georgia, which together accounted for only 7 per cent of total employment in manufacturing (the figures relate to 1939). The attraction of these states is due not only to the nearness to raw material supplies but also to lower wage rates and lower taxes.

[19] *Report of the Royal Commission on the Distribution of the Industrial Population* (Barlow Report), Cmd. 6153, January 1940, page 272.

[20] The advantages for small firms in the same branch of industry being located together, thereby benefiting from common services (auxiliaries, repairs, etc.), have often been stressed. The recent tendencies for large firms to break up their production into several fairly independent departments, often located very far

from the main operating unit, seems to point to the limited importance of this in countries benefiting from modern transport facilities. Such tendencies of geographical spreading of large firms are visible not only in the United States but in Europe as well, for instance in the Netherlands and Switzerland.

[21] The Deutsche Industriebank was set up before the war with the purpose of putting financial means at the disposal mainly of provincial banks which granted long-term credits to small enterprises.

[22] See H. Doerpmund, *Die Mittel der Industriestandortlenkung und die Grenzen ihrer Anwendbarkeit,* Bremen-Horn, 1950.

[23] See C. F. Carter, "Northern Ireland—An Economic Survey: The Last Depressed Area," *The Banker,* August 1954.

[24] Moreover, small industries producing the same commodities may also be induced to locate themselves in the big concentration areas near the large firms, since the gap between costs and prices of the large firms will be wider than in the remainder of the country.

[25] *Report of the Industrialization Committee,* Helsinki, 1951.

[26] From other regions or from abroad.

[27] This is, of course, based on the assumption—nearly always valid—that the poor regions are, at least at the initial stage of development, less favourably located from the point of view of transport either for geographical reasons or owing to previous capital investment in transport in the rich regions.

[28] Economic ties between poor and rich regions may in certain respects resemble more those between a country and its colonies than those between sovereign countries.

[29] The share of total population living in towns does correlate somewhat more closely with the degree of industrialization of the country, as can be seen from Table 76.

[30] Robert M. Lillibridge ("Urban Size: An Assessment," *Land Economics,* November 1952, page 341) reviews a number of such studies.

[31] However, the Dutch Government has decided on an optimum size of 100,000 inhabitants, except where particular circumstances (for instance, the existence of very large industrial plants) require a somewhat higher number.

[32] The natural increase of population is most often negative in big cities.

[33] There may, of course, be cases where industry is so badly in need of rationalization or certain services so overcrowded that the demand caused by raising *per capita* income could, for a time, be met by rationalization alone.

[34] The relative size of payments for these imports will vary from region to region and country to country according to the degree of development and of adjustment in consumption standards. Estimates made by *Svimez* (the Association for the Development of Industry in Southern Italy) of the repercussions of a two-year programme of basic works for southern Italy show that for every unit of employment in this project in the south, only 0.3 unit can be taken to be employed subsequently in the south itself for the provision of the additional goods and services which the initial expansion will require, the remaining extra consumption provided by the expansion in employment serving to increase employment in northern Italy and abroad. (See *Economic Effects of an Investment Programme in Southern Italy,* published by *Svimez,* Rome 1951, Tables 27 and 28, pages 50 and 52.)

[35] These dynamic industries being, of course, not the same, for example, in Turkey and in the United Kingdom.

[36] Naples, although a town of one million inhabitants, has only 18 per cent employed in industry proper against 27 per cent in Milan.

[37] For instance, to keep schools, postal services and communication lines may become very expensive in isolated villages. See examples given in *Dépeuplement rural et Peuplement rationnel,* Cahier No. 8 de Travaux et Documents (INED), Paris, 1949.

[38] A Swedish study of population movements in a forest district in central Sweden, which had as its purpose to find out how the exodus of workers from the forest could be halted, warned against all plans of setting up more local industries in the villages because it was found that the existing ones attracted the forest workers, who once they were accustomed to industrial work moved further away to other regions or to towns. (See Jan Wallander: *Flykten från Skogsbygden,* Stockholm, 1948.)

[39] S.O.U., 1951:6, *Näringslivets Lokalisering* (Swedish Government Reports), pages 78–81.

22. Industrialization, Factor Markets, and Agricultural Development[1]*

WILLIAM H. NICHOLLS[2]

Reverse cannot befall that fine Prosperity
Whose sources are interior.

EMILY DICKINSON

I. INTRODUCTION

For nearly a decade, we have had under way at Vanderbilt University a large-scale research project on Southern Economic Development and Agriculture. This project has been concerned with testing for selected southern areas the locational hypothesis first advanced by T. W. Schultz in 1950 to explain wide international and interregional divergences in per capita incomes.[3] As Schultz himself recognized, it would be virtually impossible to test his hypothesis on an international basis because of the vast number of uncontrollable variables.[4] Instead, Tang and I have dealt with relatively small and homogeneous areas for which one might hope to isolate more successfully the effects of industrial-urban development (via factor

[1] A revision of a paper prepared for the Conference on the Role of Agriculture in Economic Growth, sponsored by the Social Science Research Council's Committee on Economic Growth, at Stanford University, November 11–12, 1960.

[2] I am greatly indebted to my colleague, Anthony M. Tang, on whose own contributions to the present subject I have drawn so freely in what follows as to give him the status of virtually a joint author. I am also grateful to the Rockefeller and Ford Foundations for the financial support which made our various studies possible.

[3] T. W. Schultz, "Reflections on Poverty within Agriculture," *Journal of Political Economy*, LVIII (1950), 1 ff.; "A Framework for Land Economics—the Long View," *Journal of Farm Economics*, XXXIII (1951), 204–15; and *Economic Organization of Agriculture* (New York: McGraw-Hill Book Co., 1953), chaps. ix and x. According to Schultz's hypothesis, economic development occurs in a specific locational matrix which is primarily industrial-urban in composition and near the center of which the existing economic organization (factor and product markets) works best. He further hypothesized, with particular reference to agriculture, that those parts of agriculture situated favorably relative to the industrial-urban center enjoy more efficient factor and product markets than those situated at the periphery.

[4] However, as Meier and Baldwin (*Economic Development: Theory, History, Policy* [New York: John Wiley & Sons, 1957], p. 147 and Part II) have shown, the mid-nineteenth-century world economy can be rather successfully analyzed in the general terms of center (Britain) and periphery.

* Reprinted from the *Journal of Political Economy*, Vol. 69 (Aug. 1961).

markets) on agricultural productivity and income. Tang has presented most of his findings in his path-breaking book on industrial-urban development and agriculture in the South Carolina-Georgia Piedmont.[5] The findings of my parallel study of the Upper East Tennessee Valley have been reported in a long series of journal articles.[6] Since our investigations are now virtually complete, the purpose of the present paper is to bring together within the compass of a single article the principal generalizations which have emerged from our joint efforts.

Objectives and methodology.—While our approaches have differed in detail, Tang and I have each sought to test a series of subhypotheses which may be grouped into three major hypotheses: (1) that the labor, capital, and product markets facing agriculture are relatively more efficient in local areas which have enjoyed considerable industrial-urban development than in similar nearby areas which have not; (2) that the effects of differences in rates of industrial-urban development have accordingly been increasingly wide inter-area differences in per worker agricultural capital and farm output (income); and (3) that there are fundamental impediments to equilibrating factor movements which tend to perpetuate differences in market efficiency and agricultural productivity between the more and less industrial areas. To this end, each of us selected a group of twenty to twenty-one contiguous counties (each with a combined area equivalent to that of Massachusetts or Connecticut) which have had a common historical and cultural background; which some fifty to seventy-five years ago had a similar dependence on agriculture and similar farm output per worker; but some of which have since experienced substantial rates of industrialization while others (the control group) have remained largely rural-agricultural.

Each of us has made a very thorough analysis of the economic development of his area during the entire century 1850–1950, but we have put greater emphasis upon the period since 1900 and have analyzed with special intensity the dynamic years since 1940. For sources of data, we have relied primarily upon the United States Census, supplemented insofar as possible from other important statistical compendiums which contained relevant socioeconomic data on a county-unit basis. Our statistical methodology has been relatively simple, consisting largely of correlation techniques applied to the ranks of our data rather than to the original data themselves. Tang successfully employed Wilcoxon's rapid sum-of-ranks technique which often enabled him to eliminate calculations of various socioeconomic indexes for all but his five top-ranking (most industrial) and five bot-

[5] Anthony M. Tang, *Economic Development in the Southern Piedmont, 1860–1950: Its Impact on Agriculture* (Chapel Hill: University of North Carolina Press, 1958).

[6] In order of their publication, my own journal articles were: "A Research Project on Southern Economic Development, with Particular Reference to Agriculture," *Economic Development and Cultural Change*, II (1952), 190–95 (which set forth in detail the various hypotheses of the entire project): "Some Foundations of Economic Development in the Upper East Tennessee Valley, 1850–1900," *Journal of Political Economy*, LXIV (1956), 277–302, 400–415; "The Effects of Industrial Development on Tennessee Valley Agriculture, 1900–1950," *Journal of Farm Economics*, XXXVIII (1956), 1636–49; "Human Resources and Industrial Development in the Upper East Tennessee Valley, 1900–1950," *Quarterly Journal of Economics*, LXXI (1957), 289–316; "Relative Economic Development of the Upper East Tennessee Valley, 1850–1950," *Economic Development and Cultural Change*, V (1957), 308–24; "Industrial-Urban Development and Agricultural Adjustments, Tennessee Valley and Piedmont, 1939–54," *Journal of Political Economy*, LXVIII (1960), 135–49; and "Factors Affecting Gross Farm Income Per Worker in the Upper East Tennessee Valley, 1899–1954," *Journal of Farm Economics*, XLII (1960), 356–62.

tom-ranking (least industrial) counties. Because of the more erratic nature of several of the counties in my study area, I found the Wilcoxon method less satisfactory. Instead, I applied Spearman rank-correlation techniques to my entire sample of twenty counties, in each case correlating their ranks in industrial development[7] with their ranks in numerous other socioeconomic indexes. While our choice of these simpler statistical methods was primarily based on their economies in computing time, their use also appeared to be appropriate in view of the crudeness of our data, the small numbers of our observations, and the failure of our data to fulfil the assumptions implicit in parametric techniques.

In the remainder of this paper, I shall present a summary of the generalizations which emerge from these two case studies. However, because Tang's statistical methods differed substantially from mine, I shall normally not present the statistical findings of the two studies comparatively. Instead, I shall state various generalizations in strictly verbal terms, using only my own statistical results for support or illustration. In each case, I shall also indicate in general terms whether Tang's findings are in agreement or in conflict with my findings. I shall begin with a section on the pre-industrial period, when any differences in agricultural productivity and incomes might be expected to have reflected differences in "original" physical resources. I shall then turn to the more recent period since 1900, during which both study areas were subject to the dynamic effects of substantial industrial-urban development. For the latter period, I shall center attention on the responses to industrialization of capital and labor markets serving the nearby agriculture. First, however, let us gain some perspective by looking briefly at the major patterns which emerged during the ninety years 1860–1950.

II. SOME COMMON PATTERNS IN INDUSTRIAL-URBAN DEVELOPMENT, 1860–1950

The pre-industrial period.—Despite many significant differences in their natural and socioeconomic attributes, the agricultures of the Tennessee Valley and Piedmont study areas shared one important characteristic—the tendency for intra-area geographical differences in per worker farm income and farm capital to be substantially reduced during 1860–1900 and to be markedly increased during the half-century beginning in 1900. This common agricultural pattern of initial convergence and subsequent divergence corresponded roughly with an initial, essentially pre-industrial period, followed by a period of rapid and notable industrial-urban development within each area. These long-run tendencies may be illustrated by some summary indexes taken from my Tennessee Valley study and presented in Table 1.

During 1860–1900, per capita value added by manufacture in the Tennessee Valley never exceeded its peak of 17 per cent of the national average attained in 1860. In fact, relative to the nation as a whole, the Tennessee Valley underwent significant industrial retrogression during 1860–90 (reaching a low of 8 per cent in 1890) and had not quite recovered its

[7] In our earlier work, Tang and I used "per capita value added by manufacture" as our measure of industrial development since the necessary basic data were reported by the Census from 1860 on. However, beginning in 1930, the Census reported data permitting the computation of a moderately comprehensive index of "per capita non-agricultural payrolls" (manufacturing, retail and wholesale trade, and selected service industries), which was almost invariably more highly correlated with other socioeconomic indexes than was per capita value added. Hence, here as in our other more recent work, I have adopted per capita payrolls as my measure of industrial-urban development.

1860 level by 1900. The Piedmont area did not show the same relative industrial retrogression and, during 1880–1900, gained sharply on the rest of the nation's manufacturing with the expansion of its new textile industry. Nonetheless, even the Piedmont's per capita value added stood at only 30 per cent of the national average in 1900.[8] To be sure, there were in 1900 already considerable *relative* differences in the levels of industrialization of the several counties within each area, as illustrated by the fact that there was a very strong tendency (.878**)[9] for today's more industrial-urban counties to have greater per capita values added than did today's less developed counties. (In fact, the corresponding coefficient of rank correlation, .432*, for 1860 indicates that even forty years earlier this particular index had some predictive value for the relative development of the several counties a century later.)[10] Despite these significant relative differ-

TABLE 1

SOME SUMMARY INDEXES OF INDUSTRIAL-URBAN AND AGRICULTURAL DEVELOPMENT, UPPER EAST TENNESSEE VALLEY STUDY AREA, SELECTED YEARS, 1860–1954[a]

	1860	1880	1900	1920	1940	1950	1954
Per capita value added by manufacturing:							
Index for area (U.S. average = 100)	17%	11%	15%	21%	55%	62%	68%
Coefficient of variation	0.87	0.97	0.95	0.94	1.63	1.43	N.a.
Coefficient of rank correlation	.432*	.650*	.878**	.868**	.869**	.911**	.979**
Population per square mile:							
Index for area (U.S. average = 100)	242%	213%	187%	157%	162%	155%	N.a.
Coefficient of variation	0.24	0.26	0.22	0.29	0.47	0.62	N.a.
Coefficient of rank correlation	.236	.114	.280	.644**	.774**	.792**	N.a.
Per worker gross farm income:							
Index for area (U.S. average = 100)	N.a.	58%	58%	52%	53%	45%	39%
Coefficient of rank correlation	N.a.	.268	.185	.186	.678**	.624**	.744**
Per worker farm capital:							
Index for area (U.S. average = 100)	95%	66%	49%	43%	56%	59%	50%
Coefficient of rank correlation	.488*	.568**	.344	.484*	.808**	.798**	.841**

[a] Coefficient of correlation between county ranks in the particular index in each selected year and the county ranks in my index of economic development, per capita non-agricultural payrolls in 1954.

* Significant to 5 per cent level.

** Significant to 1 per cent level.

[8] While both areas had per capita values added which were 11 per cent of the national average in 1880, the Piedmont's industrial progress during 1880–1900 was obviously much greater—standing at 30 per cent as compared with the Tennessee Valley's 15 per cent in the latter year.

[9] Here and in subsequent analysis, the figures in parentheses will (unless otherwise specified) represent the coefficients of rank correlation between my index of industrial-urban development (per capita non-agricultural payrolls) for 1954 and the particular socioeconomic index and year indicated in the text, for the twenty counties of the Tennessee Valley study area. (One asterisk indicates statistical significance at the 5 per cent level; two asterisks, significance at the 1 per cent level.)

[10] That the same was true for the Piedmont area is emphasized by the indexes of Table 8 in Tang, *op. cit.*, p. 88; see also pp. 60–63.

ences, it seems clear that as late as 1900 (*a*) all of the counties within each area were primarily agricultural (the estimated proportions of the male work force engaged in agriculture in the twenty Tennessee Valley counties ranged from 69 to 92 per cent) and (*b*) the absolute differences in the degree of their industrialization were as yet not sufficiently great to cause substantial differences in local agricultural productivity and incomes.

Furthermore, insofar as industrial development had taken place during 1860–1900, its unevenness among the several counties of each area was not yet marked (the coefficient of variation in per capita values added during 1860–1900 increased only from .87 to .94). In addition, intercounty differences in population density had, if anything, slightly declined (the corresponding coefficients of variation were .24 and .22), and as late as 1900, for the Tennessee Valley at least,[11] today's more advanced counties did not have significantly greater population densities (the coefficient of rank correlation was only .280) than did today's less developed counties. Hence, our choice of 1900 as the approximate date ending the preindustrial period of each area would appear to be reasonable enough.

The period of industrial development.—In any case, during the half-century following 1900, both the Tennessee Valley and the Piedmont experienced rates of industrial development far in excess of the nation as a whole. Between 1899 and 1947, the per capita value added by manufacture in the Tennessee Valley area increased from 15 to 62 per cent of the national average (Table 1); in the Piedmont area it increased from 30 to 120 per cent.[12] Within each area, however, the various counties shared far from equally in this industrial growth. For example, for the Tennessee Valley area, the coefficient of variation in county per capita values added increased from 0.95 to 1.63 during 1899–1939, although it then declined to 1.43 in 1947. The corresponding coefficient of variation in county population densities increased steadily from 0.22 to 0.62 during 1900–1950. Furthermore, although today's more industrial counties did not have significantly greater population densities (.280) in 1900, by 1950 they showed a very strong tendency to do so (.792**). Whereas, in 1900 only one of the Tennessee Valley's twenty counties (and five of the Piedmont area's twenty-one) had per capita values added by manufacture exceeding the modest level of 40 per cent of the national average, by 1947 seven (and fifteen) counties did so. In fact, by the latter year, two (and nine) counties actually exceeded the national average. Thus, industrialization (and concomitant urbanization) proceeded at a rapid but highly uneven pace within each study area.

Trends in agricultural income differentials.—Finally, as Table 1 makes clear for the Tennessee Valley, within each study area there was a convergence in county indexes of per worker farm capital and income during 1860–1900, fol-

[11] In the Piedmont area, today's more industrial counties already had significantly greater population densities (although absolute differences were still small) in both 1850 and 1900 (Tang, *op. cit.*, p. 97).

[12] While the Piedmont's industrialization far outstripped that of the Tennessee Valley, the latter had the advantage of greater diversification of industries and greater relative male employment in manufacturing. As late as 1950, textiles accounted for 76 per cent of the Piedmont's manufacturing employment; the Tennessee Valley's leading industry, chemicals, accounted for only 29 per cent, followed by textiles and apparel (22 per cent) and furniture, lumber, and wood products (19 per cent). In the same year, females were responsible for 40 and 24 per cent, respectively, of total manufacturing employment in the two areas.

lowed by an increasingly divergent movement during 1900–1950. (Here we are concerned primarily with intercounty differences, although the generally unfavorable trend in farm capital per worker relative to the national average may be noted.) Thus, prior to 1900, today's more industrial counties showed a tendency to have higher per worker farm capital and income than their less industrial neighboring counties, but this tendency was weakest in 1900. During the subsequent period of substantial industrial-urban development, however, this tendency had become much stronger than at any other time during the entire century.[13] To what extent can we attribute the increasingly favorable position of the more industrial counties after 1900 to their more rapid rates of industrialization? Before seeking to answer this question, let us consider the pre-industrial period 1860–1900 and particularly the extent to which today's more advanced counties owe their superior achievements both agricultural and industrial to superior "original" resource endowments.

III. FACTOR ADJUSTMENTS IN THE PRE-INDUSTRIAL YEARS, 1850–1900

Differences in "original" resource endowments. Within both the Tennessee Valley and the Piedmont today's more industrial counties had in 1860 an agriculture with certain significant advantages over the agriculture of today's less industrial counties. Among these advantages were superior "original" agricultural land, certain differential windfall gains from new cash crops, and higher rates of capital formation in agriculture. While in 1860 today's more industrial counties did not have any more total acreage of land per farm (−.141), they showed in both areas some tendency to have more improved acreage per farm (.393) and a highly significant tendency to have a higher value per acre of farm land (.639**). In each area, there was some tendency for today's more industrial counties to have in 1860 greater production per thousand acres of improved farm land of some major cash crop—cotton in the Piedmont, wheat (.816**) in the Tennessee Valley. This combination of superior "original" agricultural resources and greater suitability for a profitable new cash crop was capable of giving rise to important intercounty differences in capital formation within agriculture. Thus, in both areas in 1860 today's more industrial counties had significantly more farm capital per worker (.488*).[14]

The fact that in each area today's more and less industrial areas showed certain significant differences in 1860 may at first seem surprising. It should be remembered, however, that both areas were approaching the end of their first century of settlement, so that enough time had already passed for differences attributable to differential "original" resource endowments to have become apparent. Initially, all counties had had a self-sufficing agriculture in a still largely unsettled and uncleared wilderness so that "original" differences in land productivity were of less importance. As time went on, however, those people who had settled in counties with less productive land found themselves increasingly disadvantaged. Their continuing self-sufficiency perpetuated their economic and cultural isolation and made it difficult for them to finance out of agricultural sur-

[13] For a discussion of the parallel pattern of convergence and divergence in the Piedmont, see Tang, *op. cit.*, pp. 85–90, 69–76.

[14] For the supporting data for the Piedmont, see Tang, *op. cit.*, pp. 29–30, 87–88. Cf. my article, "Some Foundations of Economic Development . . . ," *op. cit.*, esp. Table 8 and pp. 293–302.

pluses the beginnings of local industrial development. Today's more advanced counties, on the other hand, tended to have superior "original" agricultural resources and mineral resources (particularly iron ore). Their agriculture was capable of accommodating the use of large quantities of capital and was productive enough after such capital became available to finance some industrial development by 1860. As a consequence, there was already a significant tendency in both areas for today's more developed counties to have a higher per capita value of commercial manufactures (.550*) than today's less developed counties.[15]

Had the advantage of today's more developed counties in terms of such indexes as per worker farm capital and gross farm income persisted during subsequent decades, we might settle the matter by simply attributing today's wide farm-income differentials to differences in "original" resource endowments. Instead, however, as we have already observed, there was in both areas a convergent movement in county indexes of per worker farm capital and gross farm income during 1860–1900.

Equilibrating factor adjustments, 1860–1900.—During the immediate post bellum decades, in which industrial development in both areas fell far short of keeping pace with national industrial development, important equilibrating forces seem to have been at work, making today's more and less developed counties more alike than before. Thus, in both areas, today's more advanced counties had significantly higher farm capital per worker in 1860 (.488*) but not in 1900 (.344).[16] The convergence of gross farm income per worker is less clear cut, especially in the Tennessee Valley area,[17] but in 1900 today's more advanced counties did not have per worker farm incomes significantly different (.185) from today's less advanced counties in either area. Such convergent movements might have been brought about (*a*) under conditions of complete immobility of factors of production, if today's more developed counties had had sufficiently more rapid natural population increase to have leveled down differences in per worker farm capital or income; or (*b*) under conditions of sufficiently great mobility of the factors of production (particularly labor) to eliminate initial differences.

Can the tendency toward convergence be explained by differentially higher rates of natural increase in the counties with superior "original" resources? The evidence supports a negative answer. In the Tennessee Valley at least, today's more industrial counties already showed in 1850 some tendency to have *lower* fertility rates (−.374) and by 1880 the negative relationship had become statistically significant (−.426*). In both areas, there was also a slight tendency for today's more industrial counties to have in 1850 *smaller* mean family size (−.229),

[15] Nicholls, "Some Foundations of Economic Development . . . ," *op. cit.*, pp. 414, 281–86, and Tang, *op. cit.*, pp. 57–60, 88.

[16] For the Tennessee Valley area, after reaching a peak of .591** in 1870, this relationship steadily declined to .344 in 1900, when it was at its lowest level for the entire period 1850–1954.

[17] For the Tennessee Valley area, this relationship rose from .098 to .417* during 1870–90, then fell to .185 in 1900, its lowest level during 1880–1954. During 1880–1900, the relative dispersion of this index (quartile difference divided by quartile sum) declined from .094 to .088 while, for the Piedmont, the coefficient of variation declined much more sharply from .207 to .094. For the latter area, the coefficient of variation of per worker farm capital dropped from .265 in 1860 to .160 in 1900, but, for the Tennessee Valley, the corresponding coefficient increased from .206 to .297 (see Tang, *op. cit.*, pp. 64, 71, 86, 88; and Nicholls, "Some Foundations of Economic Development . . . ," *op. cit.*, Table 9, p. 301).

although this tendency had by 1900 become stronger in the Tennessee Valley (−.394*) while being virtually eliminated in the Piedmont. In any case, it is clear that the tendency toward convergence in per worker farm capital and income during 1850–1900 cannot be attributed to today's more developed counties having had *greater* rates of natural increase than their less industrial neighbors. Hence, we must turn to the evidence on degree of factor mobility for an explanation. Throughout 1850–1900 in the Piedmont, today's more industrial counties showed some tendency to have lower net outmigration rates than today's less industrial counties. While the same was not true initially in the Tennessee Valley, by 1890–1900 this tendency had become statistically significant (−.453*). As a consequence of the joint effects of differential rates of human fertility and migration, in both areas today's more industrial counties tended in 1900 to have larger percentages of their male population in the productive age group 18–44 (.457*), although, in the Tennessee Valley at least, this tendency had become much weaker since 1860 (.626**).[18]

We may therefore conclude that, in the absence of substantial industrial development during 1850–1900, the initial advantages today's more industrial counties enjoyed in terms of superior "original" natural resources and differential windfall gains derived from profitable new cash crops did not suffice to prevent a significant reduction in, or even the elimination of, their initially favorable differentials in per worker farm capital and income. Instead, the indications are that during 1850–1900 there were in both areas long-run equilibrating factor adjustments (particularly in labor) of sufficient magnitude to reduce very substantially any intercounty income differences which, had they persisted, might still have been plausibly attributed to differences in "original" resource endowments alone.[19] It is against such a background that the subsequent *divergence* in per worker farm capital and income within each area must be viewed.

IV. DIFFERENTIAL INDUSTRIALIZATION AND DIVERGENT AGRICULTURAL INCOMES, 1900–1950

I have already noted that after 1900 both the Tennessee Valley and Piedmont study areas experienced a substantial,

[18] Nicholls, "Some Foundations of Economic Development . . . ," *op. cit.*, pp. 415, 405–6, and Tang, *op. cit.*, pp. 88, 171.

[19] In my analysis of the pre-1900 economic development of the Tennessee Valley, however, I did note certain cultural differences between today's more and less industrial counties which may have persisted throughout the century 1850–1950 and which may have had their roots at least partly in differences in "original" resources. Thus today's more industrial counties had initially enjoyed during 1850–70 an ephemeral industrial development based on local mineral resources that played out, but perhaps not without leaving favorable local attitudes and entrepreneurial talents that encouraged and supported new industries as new opportunities arose after 1900. Similarly, even in their less prosperous days around 1900, today's more advanced counties had lower fertility rates and higher educational investments per school child (.564* in 1850, .244 in 1880, but .590** in 1900), which probably reflected somewhat superior total community resources and, probably more important, a continued belief in the importance of maintaining the "quality" of their population. As a consequence, they probably laid the groundwork for their subsequent industrial rebirth, which was based largely on outside rather than local capital and managerial resources ("Foundations of Economic Development . . . ," *op. cit.*, pp. 413–15, 410–11) .

It should also be noted that, in the Tennessee Valley area, the windfall gains which wheat brought to today's more advanced counties during 1850–70 were ephemeral: interregional competition eventually took its toll. In the Piedmont area, on the other hand, the initial windfall gains which the introduction of cotton brought to today's more advanced counties were gradually spread (as happened during 1920–40 with burley tobacco in the Tennessee Valley) to even the less advanced counties (*ibid.*, pp. 293–94, 415, and Tang, *op. cit.*, pp. 35–36).

but highly uneven, degree of industrial-urban development and that during the same period intercounty differentials in per worker farm capital and income sharply increased. As Table 1 shows, while today's more industrial counties did not in 1900 have significantly higher farm income per worker (.185) than their less industrial neighboring counties, by 1940 they clearly did so (.678**), and in 1954 this relationship stood at its highest level (.744**) in history. For either study area, the agriculture of today's more advanced counties—after starting on a nearly equal footing in farm income per worker in 1900—had forged increasingly far ahead of the agriculture of those neighboring counties which had not enjoyed comparable industrial-urban development during the subsequent fifty-year period.[20]

Can we attribute these persistent and increasing intercounty differentials in per worker farm income after 1900 to differences in county rates of industrial-urban development? Tang and I have both concluded that we can. Despite the fact that the period 1900–1950 saw a quickening of factor mobility, such resource adjustments no longer appear to have been as effective in dampening existing agricultural income differentials between counties as they had been in the pre-industrial period. Apparently, the dynamic nature of industrial-urban development had a disequilibrating effect on farm incomes per worker which far more than offset the equilibrating effect of continued factor transfers during the more recent period of industrialization. Presumably, the reason was that local industrial-urban development transmits its effects on local agricultural productivity and incomes through its impact on local factor and product markets, which function more efficiently the greater the level of nearby industrial-urban development. Let us examine this basic hypothesis further, first with reference to the capital market and then with reference to the labor market.

[20] Tang, *op. cit.*, pp. 66–72.

The impact of industrialization on the local capital market.—One would expect that those counties which have since 1900 enjoyed differentially greater industrial-urban development would, because of an initial influx of outside capital (most new industry was so financed) and subsequent growth of local employment and income, have shown increasingly greater bank deposits per capita as compared with those of the less developed counties. In both the Tennessee Valley and the Piedmont, today's more advanced counties had as early as 1900–1905 significantly larger per capita (primary) bank deposits. For the Tennessee Valley, this relationship was highly significant throughout 1900–1954 but slightly weakened during the half-century (.809** in 1900, .714** in 1950) as the number and dispersal of banks in the study area grew (Table 2). However, as in the Piedmont area, the absolute differences in per capita bank deposits (in constant prices) increased enormously as between more and less industrial counties of the Tennessee Valley (for example, in 1926 prices, the interquartile range of per capita bank deposits for the twenty Tennessee Valley counties increased from \$15 to \$135 during 1900–1950). As a consequence, the increasing advantage of the more rapidly industrializing counties in terms of volume of bank deposits was presumably reflected, through the greater availability of agricultural credit, in a higher rate of capital formation in the nearby agriculture.[21]

[21] *Ibid.*, pp. 113–17. Tang went on to demonstrate (pp. 118–22 and 124–25) that, per farm worker, both short- and long-term bank loans to agriculture were significantly greater in the more industrial counties than in the less industrial counties of the Piedmont.

Of course, insofar as today's more industrial counties had higher rates of capital formation in their agricultural sector, these higher rates might be in part attributable to inherently superior land resources. For example, the Tennessee Valley's more developed counties already had in 1900 significantly higher per acre farm-land values (.627**). Furthermore, throughout 1900–1954, they maintained a strong relative advantage over the less developed counties in per acre yields of wheat, although the relative advantage in corn and oat yields which they enjoyed during most of 1900–1940 had been eliminated or substantially weakened by 1954 (Table 2). These latter data suggest that, unlike in the Piedmont area,[22] those counties enjoying higher rates of industrial-urban development after 1900 at best maintained, rather than strengthened, their favorable position in terms of crop yields. On the other hand, the Tennessee Valley's more industrial counties did strengthen their already strong tendency to have higher per acre farm-land

[22] *Ibid.*, pp. 142–44. In the Piedmont, Tang found that during 1900–1940 the industrial counties gained sharply on their less industrial neighbors in per acre yields of cotton, wheat, corn, and oats.

TABLE 2

COEFFICIENTS OF RANK CORRELATION BETWEEN PER CAPITA NON-AGRICULTURAL PAYROLLS, 1954, AND SELECTED INDEXES RELATED TO LOCAL CAPITAL MARKET, UPPER EAST TENNESSEE VALLEY STUDY AREA, SELECTED YEARS, 1900–1954[a]

Item	1900	1910	1920	1930	1940	1950	1954
Per capita bank deposits	.809**	.805**	.826**	.779**	.746**	.729**	.714**
Per acre value of all farmland	.627**	.561**	.722**	.805**	.773**	.773**	.792**
Per cent of all farmland improved	.233	.255	.272	.242	.549**	.516*	N.a.
Per acre yield:							
Corn	−.071	.492*	.395*	.441*	.426*	.226	.063
Wheat	.701**	.486*	.593**	.577**	.763**	.529*	.787**
Oats	.542**	.550**	.460*	.456*	.543**	.503*	.320
Tobacco	−.030	.161	.256	−.308	.247	−.051	−.236
Per cent of gross cash farm sales:							
Tobacco	N.a.	N.a.	N.a.	−.072	−.418*	−.603**	−.632**
Livestock	N.a.	N.a.	N.a.	−.004	.312	.580**	.621**
Per farm acreage of all farmland	.282	.089	−.161	−.233	−.242	−.234	−.198
Per farm total value of capital	.553**	.441*	.504*	.633**	.448*	.559**[b]	.651**
Per farm man-years of labor input	.582**	.501*	.414*	−.158	−.609**	−.316[b]	−.386*
Index of total inputs per farm	.673**	.546**	.541**	.359	−.028	.198[b]	.191
Per farm gross farm income	.283	.463*	.388*	.418*	.298	.382*[b]	.304
Per farm net farm income	N.a.	N.a.	N.a.	N.a.	.147	.182[b]	.039
Per worker total value of farm capital	.344	.387*	.484*	.663**	.808**	.798**[b]	.841**
Instructional expenditures per school child	.590**	.559**	.719**	.719**	.740**	.699**	.714**
Per cent of children 16–17 years old attending school	N.a.	−.204	−.406*	−.134	.585**	.689**	N.a.
Median years of school completed by persons 25 years old and over	N.a.	N.a.	N.a.	N.a.	.790**	.820**	N.a.

[a] Coefficients of correlation between county ranks in the particular index in each selected year and county ranks in 1954 per capita non-agricultural payrolls.

[b] The coefficients for commercial farms and part-time farms separately were:

	Commercial	Part-Time
Per farm capital	.627**	.812**
Per farm labor	.281	−.674**
Index of total inputs per farm	.540**	.100
Per farm gross income	.479*	.206
Per farm net income	.392*	−.064
Per worker farm capital	.671**	.800**

* Significant to 5 per cent level.

** Significant to 1 per cent level.

values between 1900 (.627**) and 1954 (.792**); and their initially weak tendency (.233 in 1900) to have larger percentages of "improved" farm land had become significant by 1940–50 (.549** and .516*). Therefore, to a limited extent at least, the more industrial counties were apparently able to increase their rate of investment in their farm land more than the less industrial counties found possible. While this fact was probably in part due to the greater ability of their farmers to finance their own improvements because of a superior resource base, we have already seen that such superiority was not sufficient in 1900 to give them a significant advantage in per worker farm income—the crucial variable so far as internal savings and capital formation are concerned. Hence, as in the Piedmont, their increasing rate of investment in their farm land was primarily attributable to the greater availability of farm credit which accompanied nearby industrial-urban development and to the consequent more perfect functioning of local capital markets.

It is also worth noting that industrial-urban development was in both areas associated with new enterprise combinations in agriculture in which livestock products played an increasingly important part. In the Tennessee Valley, today's more advanced counties did not derive larger proportions of their gross cash farm income from livestock in 1930 (−.004) but showed a very strong tendency to do so by 1954 (.621**). During the same period, the more advanced counties—which in 1930 had not differed significantly in terms of the proportion of their gross cash farm income derived from the major staple cash crop, tobacco (−.072)—had by 1954 become relatively far less dependent upon tobacco than the less industrial counties (−.632**). These sharp shifts in the relative importance of different farm products in the more and less industrial counties undoubtedly reflect not only (*a*) an increasing relative farm-labor scarcity (via improved labor markets) unfavorable to a labor-intensive crop and (*b*) the improved local markets for livestock products created by nearby industrial-urban development, but also (*c*) concomitant improvement in the functioning of local capital markets by which expansion of livestock enterprises might be financed.[23]

What was the influence of industrial-urban development on the resources (inputs) and income (output) of the average farm (Table 2)? In the Tennessee Valley, at no time during 1900–1954 did the average farms of the more developed counties have significantly different acreages of all farm land than those of the less developed counties. Indeed, over the fifty-year period, there was some tendency (primarily due to their more rapid increase in part-time farms) for the more developed counties to have average farms with *less* acreage than the average farms of the less developed counties (the coefficient was .282 in 1900 and −.234 in 1950). Furthermore, largely because of the persistently higher land values in the more advanced counties, their average farms had throughout 1900–1954 significantly greater total farm capital than those of the less advanced counties. While this tendency weakened somewhat between 1900 (.553**) and 1940 (.448*), by 1954 it had reached its highest level (.651**). On the other hand, throughout 1900–1954, the average farms of the more developed counties had significantly different man-years of labor inputs from

[23] *Ibid.*, pp. 104–9. Unlike in the Tennessee Valley, however, in the Piedmont the major cash crop (cotton rather than tobacco) as late as 1940 was not of significantly less relative importance in the more than in the less industrial counties.

those of the less developed counties. In the earlier years they showed a strong tendency to have *more* labor inputs (.582** in 1900), but from 1940 (−.609**) on, the tendency was reversed due to the increasing relative importance of part-time farms in the averages. (For commercial farms only, the relationship in 1950 was still positive at .281.)

To what extent are these contrary trends indicative of mere factor substitution without scale adjustments? In other words, did the average farms of the more industrial counties simply use greater capital inputs to offset fewer labor inputs, without increasing their total inputs or value of output? To answer this question on the input side, I devised an index of total inputs (which may be viewed as a crude index of scale), based on the ranking of the sum of ranks of each county's per farm capital and labor inputs. According to this index, the average farms of today's more industrial counties enjoyed a strong relative scale advantage in 1900 (.673**) which, as industrialization proceeded with a concomitant increase in numbers of part-time farms, had disappeared by 1940 (−.028). Thereafter, there was a tendency for the relationship to be restored, with the average *commercial* farms of the more industrial counties in 1950 employing significantly larger total inputs than their counterparts in the less industrial counties (.540**).[24]

Alternatively, we may measure farm size by total value of output instead of total inputs. If we do, we find that, relative to the average farms of today's less industrial counties, the average farms of the more industrial counties showed a moderate tendency during 1900–1954 to have larger gross farm incomes. However, this tendency did not become markedly stronger as industrialization proceeded. Again, however, the reason would appear to be primarily the result of the depressing effects of the growing number of part-time farms in the industrial counties upon per farm averages. Thus, in 1950 (the only year in which commercial and part-time farms can be separately treated), the average *commercial* farms of the more industrial counties had significantly larger gross farm incomes than those of the less industrial counties (.479*), whereas the average part-time farms did not (.206). These coefficients may be compared with .283 for *all* farms in 1900.

Nonetheless, it is evident that, whether measured in terms of total inputs or total output, our indexes of average farm size (scale) are rather imperfect and are relatively insensitive to the effects of differential industrial development. The value of farm capital per farm worker, on the other hand, reflects very fully these effects. Thus, as we saw in Table 1, in 1900 today's more industrial counties did not have a significant larger amount of farm capital per farm worker than did today's less industrial counties (.344). By 1940, however, they showed a very strong tendency to do so (.808**) and maintained their advantage through 1954 (.841**). These indexes strongly support the view that industrial-urban development was highly associated with relatively high capital-labor ratios in the agriculture of the Tennessee Valley as in Piedmont agriculture.[25] However, for both areas the weight of the evidence suggests that the strengthening of this association was much more the result of

[24] For a more detailed treatment of this matter of total inputs, see my most recent articles, "Industrial-Urban Development and Agricultural Adjustments . . . ," *op. cit.*, pp. 139 and 141–42, and "Factors Affecting Gross Farm Income . . . ," *op. cit.*, pp. 358–62.

[25] Tang, *op. cit.*, pp. 126–28.

differentially greater reductions in the more industrial counties' farm-labor inputs (the denominator of the capital-labor ratio) than to differentially greater increases in their farm capital (the numerator).[26] Hence, the relative impact of industrial-urban development on the efficiency of local factor markets appears to have been greater in the labor market than in the capital market.

Under such circumstances, a comparison of the responses of commercial and part-time agriculture (possible only in 1950) is instructive. In his Piedmont study, Tang concluded that the part-time sector was far more responsive to the positive income effect of local industrial development. This difference he attributed (*a*) to the greater ease in the more industrial counties of transferring underemployed farm labor to other employment without appreciably changing total capital or output, part-time farms by definition being the principal beneficiaries; and (*b*) to the slowness and difficulty with which the commercial farms, even in the more developed counties, were able to acquire additional land and other capital that might have justified the retention in agriculture of larger labor forces per farm. In the Tennessee Valley area, however, I found that the commercial farms responded favorably to local industrial development at least as well as neighboring part-time farms in terms of farm capital per worker, and considerably better in terms of total inputs and income and per worker net farm income. The stronger response of commercial farms in the Tennessee Valley, as compared with commercial farms in the Piedmont, was, I concluded, due to a larger proportion of its commercial-farm capital being agriculturally productive, to its less imperfect capital markets, and to its greater availability of superior managerial talent.[27]

Finally, on the capital side, today's more industrial counties in both areas have shown higher rates of investment in human beings than have their less industrial neighbors. In the Tennessee Valley area, educational outlays per school child were relatively greater in today's more industrial counties throughout the century 1850–1950. However, between 1900 (.590**) and 1920 (.719**), this tendency was strengthened somewhat and has been maintained to date. School attendance of children aged 16–17 in the more and less advanced counties was not significantly different in 1910 (−.204) but by 1920 was significantly *less* (−.406*) in today's more advanced counties. However, these initially adverse effects of industrial development had been fully reversed by 1950, when the more industrial counties had a very strong relative advantage over their less industrial neighbors in both high-school attendance (.689**) and median years of school completed by persons of 25 years of age or older (.820**). Thus, as in the Piedmont[28] we find that industrial-urban development has been associated with relatively greater capital investment in the human agent—a factor clearly favorable to further economic development through its positive influence on both labor productivity and awareness of economic opportunities.

Our findings on the capital market may be summarized as follows. Local industrial-urban development, typically made possible by an influx of outside

[26] *Ibid.*, pp. 197–98; Nicholls, "Effects of Industrial Development . . . ," *op. cit.*, p. 1648. See below, p. 334.

[27] Nicholls, "Industrial-Urban Development and Agricultural Adjustments . . . ," *op. cit.*, pp. 144–49. See below, pp. 334–36.

[28] Tang, *op. cit.*. pp. 138–41.

non-agricultural capital, increases local personal incomes and savings, and by increasing the total resources of local banking and credit institutions redounds to the benefit of the nearby agriculture. Agriculture benefits directly from the consequent greater availability of capital which facilitates investments in land improvement, the development of more profitable capital-intensive enterprises (particularly livestock), the raising of capital-labor ratios, and often an increased scale of farming operations as well —all of which increase farm incomes per worker relative to those in the less industrial-urban neighboring counties. Agriculture also benefits indirectly from the effects of more adequate credit on the development of local firms serving agriculture as suppliers of farm-production goods and as purchasers of farm products; and from the effects of an expanding tax base on the supply and quality of public services (education, roads, health, etc.) available to nearby rural people.

The impact of industrialization on the local labor market.—In 1900, today's more developed counties in the Tennessee Valley did not have a significantly smaller percentage of rural population than today's less developed counties (—.162), but from 1920 on they showed a very strong tendency (−.884** in 1950) to do so (Table 3). Even in 1900, today's more developed counties strongly tended to have larger percentages of their total work force engaged in manufacturing (.635**) and smaller percentages in agriculture (−.808**). Thus these particular indexes in 1900 had excellent predictive value with reference to the relative economic development of the several counties in the study area during the next half-century. Nonetheless, intercounty differences in these indexes were too small in 1900 to have much differential effect on the nearby agriculture. During 1900–1950, however, the interquartile range in percentage of manufacturing employment increased from 3.7 to 13.4 and the corresponding range in percentage of agricultural employment increased from 10.6 to 29.1. With these rapidly growing intercounty differences in relative non-agricultural employment, the counties enjoying the most industrial-urban development have also in recent decades greatly increased their per worker gross farm income relative to the counties which lagged behind. For the latter index, the interquartile range (in constant 1926 dollars) increased from $54 to $259 during 1900–1950 and, by 1954, the tendency for today's more industrial counties to have higher per worker gross farm incomes was very strong (.744**). The same was true for rural levels of living (.780**).

By 1940, annual average earnings per worker in manufacturing and retail trade in the Tennessee Valley were $899 and $759, respectively, as compared with $440 gross farm income per worker in agriculture. Since the latter figure includes net returns to all factors of production in agriculture rather than labor returns only, an attempt was also made to estimate for 1940 the *residual* returns to the labor factor in agriculture.[29] For the twenty Tennessee Valley counties, the average net labor return per worker in agriculture was $270—less than one-third of the annual earnings per non-agricultural worker. Within the Tennessee Valley (as in the Piedmont), today's more advanced counties in 1940 enjoyed relatively favorable labor returns in the non-agricultural industries and agriculture alike. For per worker annual earnings in manufacturing and retail trade,

[29] The method used was the same as Tang's (*ibid.*, pp. 129-36).

the coefficients in 1940 were .629** (as compared with only −.056 in 1900) and .652**, respectively. For per worker gross farm income, the relationship was even stronger (.678**) but for per worker residual labor returns in agriculture the coefficient was considerably smaller although still significant (.414*).

It is worth noting that this relationship between net labor returns per farm worker and industrial-urban development was substantially weaker in the Tennessee Valley than in the Piedmont. Furthermore, for 1940 my estimates of net returns on all capital (land, service buildings, and non-real estate inventories) per $100 of capital indicated that in the Tennessee Valley the more industrial counties did not earn significantly different returns on their productive farm capital (.069) than did the less industrial counties. In the Piedmont, on

TABLE 3

COEFFICIENTS OF RANK CORRELATION BETWEEN PER CAPITA NON-AGRICULTURAL PAYROLLS, 1954, AND SELECTED INDEXES RELATED TO LOCAL LABOR MARKET, UPPER EAST TENNESSEE VALLEY STUDY AREA, SELECTED YEARS, 1900–1954[a]

Item	1900	1910	1920	1930	1940	1950	1954
Per cent of population:							
Rural	−.162	−.352	−.627**	−.678**	−.553**	−.884**	N.a.
Rural-farm	N.a.	N.a.	N.a.	−.773**	−.816**	−.808**	−.828**
Per cent of work force employed:							
Agriculture	−.808**	−.816**	−.792**	−.785**	−.806**	−.816**	N.a.
Manufacturing	.635**	N.a.	.852**	.869**	.836**	.878**	N.a.
Per worker average earnings:							
Manufacturing	−.056	N.a.	.344	.423*	.629**	.802**	.802**
Retail trade	N.a.	N.a.	N.a.	.356	.602**	.622**	.531*
Per worker gross farm income	.185	.313	.186	.438*	.678**	.624**[b]	.744**
Per worker net farm income	N.a.	N.a.	N.a.	N.a.	.586**[b]	.633**[b]	.375
Rural level-of-living index	N.a.	N.a.	N.a.	.564**	.705**	.729**	.780**
Crude rate of natural increase	−.456*[c]	N.a.	−.267	−.669**	−.578**	.007	N.a.
Fertility rate	−.426*[c]	N.a.	N.a.	−.663**	−.761**	−.606**	N.a.
Average size of family	−.484*	−.292	−.382*	−.562**	−.468*	−.744**	N.a.
Net out migration rate, previous decade	−.453*	−.511*	−.608	−.783**	−.528*	−.902**	N.a.
Per cent of male population aged 18–44	.457*	N.a.	.418*	.879**	.828**	.851**	N.a.
No. males per 100 females, aged 18–44	N.a.	N.a.	−.120	.054	−.575**	−.708**	N.a.
Per cent of total farm-operator man-years worked off farm	N.a.	N.a.	N.a.	N.a.	.402*	.599**	.662**
Per cent of farms on all-weather roads	N.a.	N.a.	N.a.	.784**	.325	.391*	N.a.
Per cent of gross farm income from dairy, poultry, vegetables, and horticultural specialties	N.a.	N.a.	N.a.	N.a.	.390*	.481*	.558**

[a] Coefficients of correlation between county ranks in the particular index in each selected year and county ranks in 1954 per capita non-agricultural payrolls.

[b] The coefficients for commercial farms and part-time farms separately were:

	Commercial	Part-Time
Per worker gross farm income	.525*	.738**
Per worker net farm income	.444*	.531*

Other important indexes produced the following coefficients for *all* farms: residual (net) labor returns per worker in agriculture 1940, .414*; and median net cash incomes (all sources), rural-farm families 1950, .847**.

[c] Data for 1880 rather than 1900.

* Significant to 5 per cent level.

** Significant to 1 per cent level.

the other hand, the more industrial counties strongly tended to have *lower* returns on their farm capital than did their capital-poor, less industrial neighbors. While our estimates of net factor returns are very crude, these inter-area differences support the view that the Tennessee Valley had much less imperfect capital markets and somewhat less imperfect labor markets than did the Piedmont.[30]

In the previous section, we nonetheless saw that the agriculture of the more industrial counties in both areas enjoyed a higher rate of capital formation and an increasingly favorable ratio of farm capital to farm labor as compared with the agriculture of the less industrial counties. In the present section, we have just seen that the agriculture of the more industrial counties also enjoyed higher net returns to labor. If local labor markets had functioned perfectly, however, the direction and magnitude of movements of agricultural labor would have been such as to offset these differential rates of capital formation while narrowing, if not eliminating, the gap in net labor returns in agriculture. To what extent, and why, did local labor markets in the two study areas function less than perfectly?

In any given county, the farm-labor force is a joint function of demographic characteristics (particularly fertility rates) and changes of residence and/or occupation. Let us look at the matter of demographic characteristics first (Table 3). In recent decades, as one would expect, the Tennessee Valley's more industrial-urban counties had significantly lower crude rates of natural increase, lower fertility rates (−.606** in 1950), and smaller average family sizes (−.744**) than did its less developed counties. Such relationships might be expected to be the consequence of industrial-urban development. It is important to emphasize, however, that these intercounty differences clearly antedated the area's modern period of industrial-urban development, hence may have been in considerable part cause rather than effect of later differences in rates of economic progress.[31]

Because through higher fertility rates they historically kept the inflow of new persons into their population reservoirs at higher levels, today's less industrial counties would have had to have higher outmigration rates than today's more advanced counties, even if the latter had not experienced any significant industrial-urban growth. Indeed, this appears to have happened during 1850–1900, with today's more industrial counties having had sufficiently smaller outmigration rates (the coefficient for 1890–1900 was −.453*) so that in 1900 they did not have significantly greater per worker farm capital (.344) or per worker farm income (.185). Thus, in the pre-industrial period, local labor markets, though imperfect, apparently sufficed to eliminate substantial intercounty differences in agricultural productivity and income. As today's more advanced counties pulled ahead industrially during 1900–1950, however, increasingly great intercounty differences in outmigration rates were not enough to prevent their agriculture from also pulling ahead in per-worker capital and income. For example, throughout 1900–1950, today's more industrial counties had significantly lower outmigration rates per decade—a relationship that never fell below −.51* (1900–1910) and reached −.902** during 1940–50. Since it was not unusual for the least industrial third of the twenty

[30] *Ibid.*, p. 133, and above, p. 331.

[31] See n. 18. For a more detailed analysis of population characteristics, see my article, "Human Resources and Industrial Development . . . ," *op. cit.*, pp. 300 ff.

counties to lose over 20 per cent of their total populations per decade by net outmigration, it should be clear that outmigration alone can hardly be expected to bring about a general equilibrium in the area's agricultural productivity and income.

Since we have here been dealing with *county* rates of outmigration, however, the question still remains as to how much of the migration was internal to the study area and how much was from the area as a whole to other regions. That much was internal is shown by the fact that today's more industrial counties showed an increasingly strong tendency to have larger proportions of their male populations in the most productive age group 18 through 44. This tendency, unlike in the Piedmont,[32] was already significant in 1900 (.457*). By 1940, however, it was highly significant in both study areas (.828** in the Tennessee Valley). That the more industrial counties have had larger proportions of their male populations in the more productive years is, of course, a very favorable situation, reflecting not only their lower fertility rates but the age-selectivity of their inmigration.

However, many outmigrants from individual counties clearly moved beyond the study area to other regions in which economic opportunities were better. For example, in every decade during 1900–1950, the Tennessee Valley study area as a whole lost from 5 to 14 per cent of its population by migration to other areas. That increasingly these outmigrants from the study area were disproportionately male is shown by the fact that since 1940 today's more industrial counties in both the Tennessee Valley and the Piedmont[33] had *fewer* males per hundred females in the age group 18–44 (−.708** in 1950)—a difference which can be explained only by sex selection in migration patterns, with females more frequently migrating shorter distances from less to more industrial counties within the study area and males more frequently migrating out of the area as a whole.

In this connection, it is interesting to note that during 1940–50 both the Tennessee Valley and the Piedmont had increases in total real farm capital (in constant 1939 dollars) of 10 per cent but that the decline in farm-labor input was substantially less in the Tennessee Valley (16 per cent) than in the Piedmont (35 per cent). Since during 1940–50 the Tennessee Valley area had a net outmigration rate (12 per cent) almost twice that of the Piedmont (7 per cent), it would appear that the reduction in the farm-labor force in the Tennessee Valley was to a much less extent the result of shifts to local non-farm employment within the area than of outmigration from the study area. While in both areas the counties less developed *at the beginning of the decade 1940–50* subsequently had significantly higher net outmigration rates (−.813** and −.641**, respectively), in the Tennessee Valley they also made relatively larger downward adjustments in their farm-labor force than did the more developed counties (−.483*), whereas in the Piedmont the initially less developed counties at best matched those of the more developed counties (.034) in reducing the farm-labor force.[34]

Despite such differences between the two study areas, it is clear that in both

[32] Tang, *op. cit.*, p. 171. Unlike in the Tennessee Valley, net outmigration rates in the Piedmont were not significantly different in today's more and less industrial counties during 1900–1920 although they were thereafter (*ibid.*, p. 166).

[33] *Ibid.*, p. 173.

[34] See my article, "Industrial-Urban Development and Agricultural Adjustments . . . ," *op. cit.*, pp. 144, 141, 138.

areas the magnitudes of migration rates and reductions in the farm-labor force were very large. Nonetheless, in neither area was the outmigration of farm people (and the influx of farm capital) sufficient to raise returns to the human agent in the agriculture of the less industrial counties to a level comparable with that earned in the agriculture of the more industrial counties. Since both areas continued to be deficit areas in terms of non-agricultural employment, nearby job opportunities have been "rationed," in the sense that more farm people would shift to local non-farm jobs at prevailing wages if these jobs were available. In this rationing process, industrial employers can find numerous rational reasons (apart from emotional ties) for giving local residents some preference over long-distance commuters. Furthermore, the time and cost of commuting is in part a function of physical distance, a factor which is compounded by the typically poorer rural roads in the less developed counties. As late as 1950, today's more industrial counties in the Tennessee Valley had significantly larger percentages of all farms on all-weather roads (.391*), although their relative advantage had sharply declined since 1930 (.784**).[35]

Of course, as an alternative to commuting long distances, farmers in the less developed counties can move to the more developed counties. But changes of occupation are much more difficult to effect if they also require changes of residence. Farm operators of the more industrial counties have found it possible to work relatively more of their time in off-farm work than those in the less developed counties (.402* in 1940, .662** in 1954). For such nearby farm operators, not only are the opportunities for off-farm work greater but the choice of off-farm employment (since it involves no change of residence) is a much easier one to make, particularly in an area (such as the Tennessee Valley) where most farms are owner-operated. Despite his stronger attachment to the land, the owner-operator of a small farm in a more industrial county can rather readily solve his problem of underemployment (as can the members of his family) by shifting part of his labor to non-farm work—which may also supply an excellent source for self-financing of farm capital improvements—thereby raising his labor productivity and income. Thus, unlike his counterpart in a less developed county, he can keep his small acreage and raise his combined income too. On the other hand, the farm tenant is not always as mobile as his more tenuous attachment to the land might suggest. This is especially true where (as in the Piedmont) not only are tenancy rates high but most tenants are Negro sharecroppers, because landlords commonly strongly discourage sharecropper families from engaging in off-farm work. In addition, if they are Negroes, they may have to resort to long-distance migration beyond the area if they are to overcome their agricultural underemployment.[36]

In spite of such impediments to farm-labor mobility as high non-economic valuations placed on land ownership and the rigidities imposed by landlord-tenant relationships and race, it is clear that superior non-farm employment opportunities in the more developed counties make for significantly more efficient labor mar-

[35] Tang, *op. cit.*, pp. 100, 156–58.

[36] *Ibid.*, pp. 162, 158, 136–38, 177–90. Because of the much greater importance of tenancy and Negroes in his study area, Tang has given much more attention to the effects of both than I needed to. See also his recent article, "Economic Development and Changing Consequences of Race Discrimination in Southern Agriculture," *Journal of Farm Economics*, LI (December, 1959), 1113–26.

kets. As a consequence, local industrialization increases the actual or imputed cost of the human agent in agriculture toward (or, in the absence of job rationing, to) the prevailing level of non-farm wages, in turn forcing those who remain in agriculture to reorganize their farms to raise labor productivity enough to cover the higher labor cost. Such a reorganization may take one of two forms.

First, as we have just seen, nearby uneconomically small, full-time farms can become part-time farms without any increase in the amount of farm land or other capital (although self-financing of farm capital is also facilitated) if one or more members of the farm family takes off-farm employment. This adjustment, which is obviously easiest to effect, will tend to raise the productivity of the residual farm labor to the level in alternative non-farm employment. Small full-time farmers in the less industrial counties, on the other hand, lack both equal opportunities and comparable economic pressures to raise their productivity and incomes by part-time farming. Thus in both the Tennessee Valley and the Piedmont the part-time farms of the more industrial counties had in 1950 larger per worker farm capital (.800**), per worker gross farm income (.738**), and per worker net farm income (.531*) than did the part-time farms of the less developed counties (Table 2, nn. *a* and *b*; Table 3, nn. *a*, *b*, and *c*). In the Tennessee Valley the part-time farms of the more industrial counties strongly tended to have relatively larger capital inputs (.800**) per farm and, in both areas, relatively smaller labor inputs (−.674**) per farm than did those of the less developed counties, but these differences were almost completely offsetting as far as average farm scale was concerned (Table 2, nn. *a* and *b*). For example, the part-time farms of the more and less industrial counties did not have significantly different *total* inputs (.100), gross farm income (.206), or net farm income (−.064) per farm. These findings indicate that, as far as the part-time sector was concerned, the more industrial counties of each study area enjoyed a strong advantage not only in farm-labor productivity but in the ratio of farm capital to farm labor—with the Tennessee Valley experiencing larger capital adjustments and smaller labor adjustments than the Piedmont—but neither area made significant scale adjustments in its part-time farms.[37]

The second type of economic reorganization of farm firms resulting from local industrialization and its effects on farm-labor costs (and the availability of farm capital) is the enlargement of full-time farms, by which farm-labor productivity might again be raised enough to cover the increased opportunity cost of labor. In many instances, it may be possible to reorganize such full-time farms without enlargement of acreage or reduction of the farm-labor force. Since farm-land values may tend to be relatively high (although for quite different reasons) in both the more and less developed counties, a solution involving more intensive land use will presumably be favored insofar as feasible in either setting.

However, in the less developed counties, the possibilities of intensive land use in any case will probably have been exhausted. Lacking both alternative local non-farm employment opportunities and adequate rates of intercounty labor and capital mobility, these less developed counties have large numbers of farm workers the alternative use value of

[37] Tang, *op. cit.*, pp. 160–61, 204–7; and my article "Industrial-Urban Development and Agricultural Adjustments . . . ," *op. cit.*, pp. 146–47.

whose labor locally approaches zero. As a consequence, they have probably bid up the local price of farm land to levels which produce no more than a very low residual contribution of labor to agricultural output. At the same time, they have probably concentrated on labor-intensive products (for example, tobacco or cotton) which, while using land intensively, require little non-real estate capital, hence are associated with low farm-labor productivity. As we have already observed (Table 2), the less developed counties have shown an increasingly strong tendency to derive relatively larger shares of their gross cash farm income from tobacco (−.632** in 1950).

In the more developed counties, farm-land values may also be high because of the greater competition for land for non-agricultural uses, again favoring farm enterprises which demand intensive land use. However, full-time farms in such counties will probably have access to more non-real estate capital and more favorable local product markets, permitting concentration on other intensive farm products which will enable given farm labor to be more fully utilized while raising the productivity of labor to cover its locally higher opportunity cost. For example, it is significant in this connection (Table 3) that in both study areas the more industrial counties derived significantly larger percentages of their gross farm incomes (cash and kind) from dairy and poultry products, vegetables, and horticultural specialties between 1940 (.390*) and 1954 (.558**).[38] Being perishable, these products are probably more sensitive to local industrial-urban development than most other products.

Finally, full-time farms may be reorganized by an increasing emphasis on farm enterprises (for example, hay and beef cattle) which make less intensive use of labor and more extensive use of land. In this case, a reduced farm-labor force and increased acreage (through consolidation of small farms) are required. Such adjustments are very difficult to make in the less developed counties unless (as rarely happens) the rate of out-migration is sufficiently high to reduce substantially the pressure of the population on the local farm-land supply, farm-land values falling to levels which make economic the consolidation of the land by remaining farmers. Even then, lacking adequate access to capital, such community-wide economic reorganization of agriculture may not be possible in the less industrial counties. Even in the more industrial counties—despite more favorable capital, labor, and product markets—economic reorganization involving land consolidation faces considerable difficulties in view of increasing non-agricultural site values of farm land and the peculiar institutional barriers to the purchase of contiguous parcels of land. Nonetheless, one would expect a tendency toward this type of reorganization of full-time farms, particularly in the more outlying agricultural areas of the more industrial counties.

In any case, with or without land consolidation, the full-time (commercial) farms of the Tennessee Valley's more industrial counties had in 1950 larger per worker farm capital (.671**), per worker gross farm income (.525*), and per worker net farm income (.444*) than did those of its less developed counties (Table 2, nn. *a* and *b*; Table 3, nn. *a*, *b*, and *c*). While the Tennessee Valley's more industrial counties did not have significantly larger labor inputs per commercial farm (.281), they enjoyed substantially larger capital inputs per commercial farm (.627**). As compared with

[38] Tang, *op. cit.*, p. 105.

the commercial farms of the less developed counties, those of the more advanced counties showed larger "scale," whether measured by total inputs (.540**), gross farm income (.479*), or net farm income (.444*) per farm. The commercial-farm sector of the Piedmont showed similar but somewhat weaker relationships. Hence, the commercial (full-time) farms of both areas responded significantly to local industrial-urban developments. However, their response was somewhat greater in the Tennessee Valley, not only in terms of somewhat greater "scale" adjustments but through far greater increases in the ratio of capital to labor, with much more substantial gains in farm-labor productivity as a result. While the more industrial counties of each study area enjoyed more efficient capital and labor markets, those of the Tennessee Valley showed the greater advantage, perhaps because they had relatively fewer farm tenants, Negroes, and female manufacturing employees than the Piedmont.[39]

Elsewhere, I have shown that there was a much weaker tendency in the Tennessee Valley (.378*) than in the Piedmont (.540**) for per worker net farm income on part-time farms to be a larger percentage of per worker income on commercial farms, the more industrialized the county. Despite this evidence of the greater relative inefficiency of part-time farming in the Tennessee Valley, the inclusion of non-farm income presents a much more favorable picture. Unlike in the Piedmont, per capita non-agricultural payrolls (Table 3) were much more highly correlated with median net cash income, from *all* sources, of rural farm families (.847**), than with per worker net farm income on all farms (.633**).[40] Apparently the effect of the lesser response of farm-labor productivity on the Tennessee Valley's part-time farms was more than offset by greater non-farm income and by a greater response in the labor productivity of its commercial farms.[41]

V. SUMMARY AND CONCLUSIONS

The findings of our research at Vanderbilt on southern economic development and agriculture may be summarized as follows:

1. Within each area, today's more industrial counties had in 1850–60 an agriculture with certain significant advantages over the agriculture of today's less industrialized counties. Among these advantages were superior "original" agricultural land, certain differential windfall gains from new cash crops, and higher rates of capital formation in agriculture. Under conditions of perfect factor immobility, such "original" differences might have sufficed to account for today's wide income differentials within each study area. During the pre-industrial years 1860–1900, however, these earlier intercounty differences—for example, in agriculture's capital-labor ratio—virtually disappeared. Our analyses thus indicate that, despite imperfections in the factor markets, there were sufficient factor transfers (particularly labor) to eliminate these income differences attributable to differences in "original" physical endowment.

2. In 1900, today's more industrial counties did not have significantly different levels of farm capital per worker or farm output per worker from today's less industrial counties. By 1940, however,

[39] Nicholls, "Industrial-Urban Development and Agricultural Adjustments . . . ," *op. cit.*, pp. 145–46; and Tang, *op. cit.*, pp. 201–4.

[40] The corresponding coefficients for the Piedmont were .57** and .58**, respectively.

[41] Nicholls, "Industrial-Urban Development and Agricultural Adjustments . . . ," *op. cit.*, pp. 147–48.

today's more industrial counties had not only experienced differentially high rates of industrial-urban development but their agriculture also clearly enjoyed superior capital-labor ratios and higher farm-labor productivity. Although equilibrating factor transfers (as measured by relative rates of human migration) had meanwhile continued at substantial levels, these were obviously insufficient to prevent an increasing divergence in farm incomes and productivity between counties within each area. Instead, our analyses strongly support the view that local industrial-urban development made an important positive contribution to the efficiency of the local factor and product markets, thereby greatly facilitating the transfer of excess labor out of agriculture and of needed capital into agriculture within the immediate environs of the growing industrial center. Counties lacking such dynamic conditions of industrial-urban development were unable to hold their own through outmigration alone, even though such labor transfers had once sufficed to overcome income differences attributable only to "original" resource endowments.

3. The period 1940–54 permits the acid test for our conclusion that local areas cannot, in the absence of the industrial-urban development enjoyed by neighboring areas, overcome their differential disadvantage in farm incomes and productivity through outmigration alone. This most recent period provided not only sustained prosperity and full employment but conditions of war-induced resource mobility as well. The consequence was exceptionally high migration rates, particularly for our less industrial counties. Yet, within each area, the more industrial counties have since 1940 been able to maintain most if not all of their relative advantage over the less advanced counties in per worker farm capital and farm output. Thus the ability of the more industrial counties to offer redundant farm workers a change of occupation without necessitating a change of residence was of paramount importance.

While our research at Vanderbilt has been applied to relatively small, homogeneous areas, I believe that its policy implications[42] have considerable relevance to the problems of much larger underdeveloped regions or countries (Brazil is a paramount example). First, industrial-urban development offers the major hope for solving the problem of low agricultural productivity, once prior problems of an inadequate food supply have been met. Second, insofar as it is not inconsistent with fundamental economies of location and scale, the more widely dispersed such industrial-urban development, the more generally can agricultural productivity be increased. Finally, particularly for these areas which lack the attributes required for sound industrialization, public policy must provide for facilitating farm-labor and farm-capital mobility at rates far in excess of those which can be expected under complete laissez faire.

[42] For a broader and more detailed translation of our research findings into policy recommendations for solving the low-income problems of the whole southern region of the United States, see my recent book, *Southern Tradition and Regional Progress* (Chapel Hill: University of North Carolina Press, 1960), pp. 164–76.

23. Southern Tradition and Regional Economic Progress*†

WILLIAM H. NICHOLLS

Apothecary. My poverty, but not my will, consents.
Romeo. I pay thy poverty, and not thy will.
—Shakespeare, *Romeo and Juliet*

The South has been poor for a century. Relative to the rest of the nation, it is still poor today. To be sure, the South has made considerable economic progress, but in doing so it has held with surprising tenacity to traditional values. In some degree, the South has been traditional because it was poor. At the same time, it has also remained poor in part because it was traditional. It is these interrelationships between Southern tradition and Southern poverty which will concern me here.

Defenders of Southern tradition have sometimes argued that, unlike Romeo's apothecary, the South could and should remain "poor but honest." They have also warned that, if the South accepts offers of greater material well-being (Romeo's forty ducats), it will not only corrupt itself but will be condemned, along with the giver, to pointless self-destruction. On the other hand, critics of Southern tradition have denied that Southern poverty has necessarily precluded a measure of dishonesty. If Romeo's gold was "worse poison to men's souls" than the apothecary's potion, he nonetheless saw that "famine is in thy cheeks, need and oppression starveth in thine eyes" and knew that the apothecary would never say nay. From this point of view, as a defense of poverty, Southern tradition has constituted a rationalization and a mythology. Thus, it has (in Lewis Munford's colorful phrase) encouraged the South "continually [to] gaze with enamored eyes upon its own face, praising its warts and pimples as beauty marks."[1]

As an economist, I am not here interested in Southern tradition as such. However, as one who has devoted the last decade to scholarly investigations of the problems of Southern economic development, I have become very much aware of the extent to which certain peculiar non-economic factors in the Southern tradition have offered formidable barriers to the material progress of the region and which, if ignored or unrevised, will continue to do so.[2] Hence, in this address, I shall try to identify those elements of Southern tradition which may be appropriately associated with Southern poverty and whose abandonment may be a prerequisite if the South is finally to put an end to its poverty. Before turning to this major objective, I must set the stage for my investigation and, since clashes between systems of values are inevitable in such an endeavor, make my own personal values explicit.

I. OLD SOUTH V. NEW SOUTH: THE PERENNIAL BATTLE

Gonzalo. Here is everything advantageous to life.
Antonio. True; save means to live.
—Shakespeare, *The Tempest*

Some seventy years ago, Henry W. Grady made his famous lament that, in burying one of its native sons, Georgia could provide only a minister and a hole in the ground. Today Georgia

* Presidential Address, delivered at the twenty-ninth annual conference of the Southern Economic Association, Jacksonville, Florida, November 20, 1959. While I initially intended to encompass my treatment of this subject within an hour's lecture time, it quickly grew to the proportions of a book which, under the same title, is being published by the University of North Carolina Press. This address is based only upon half of Chapter One and most of Chapter Seven of that book.

[1] Quoted in Howard W. Odum, *Southern Regions of the United States* (Chapel Hill, N. C.: Univ. of North Carolina Press, 1936), p. 531.

[2] Economists interested in economic development cannot avoid concerning themselves with non-economic factors. Even in underdeveloped *countries*, economists have frequently made analyses and policy recommendations which have suffered because they have failed to take the non-economic factors sufficiently into account. (Cf. my recent article, "Accommodating Economic Change in Underdeveloped Countries," *Amer. Econ. Rev.*, Vol. 49 [Proceedings], May 1959, pp. 156–68.) Therefore, it is not surprising that in the underdeveloped South—where these barriers to economic progress are less extreme, hence less perceptible—economists and business leaders have too easily overlooked their importance.

† Reprinted from the *Southern Economic Journal*, Vol. 26 (Jan. 1960).

could undoubtedly dispatch her native son much more impressively in material terms. In the realm of the spirit, however, the native son might take a whirl or two in his grave at the lurking suspicion that his minister, secretly harboring integrationist sentiments, ought to have a "hole in the *head.*" If the material accoutrements of a decent burial today bear the label, "Made in the South," so does the tradition which still keeps our departed Georgian a Rebel beyond the grave. Thus, do times change yet remain the same.

The struggle between Old South and New South is nothing new; it dates at least from early Reconstruction days. In fact, it is ironic that two great Southerners who shared the common family name of Page should have personified so well the opposing forces of this struggle. Edwin Mims compared the two as follows:

> [Thomas Nelson Page] was distinctly a romantic, looking back upon a vanished age which for him had many of the characteristics of a golden age; [Walter Hines Page] was a critic, seeing with clear eyes the shortcomings of his people, and attacking with brave heart the barriers that hampered them in their struggle toward a more progressive life. One was a [Virginia] aristocrat, fully conscious of the charm and prestige of the aristocracy whose traditions he had inherited; the other was a [North Carolina] democrat, believing in the possibilities that lay in the training of the backward people of the South, for to him democracy was not simply a theory of government but a state of society in which all men might find the opportunity for the development of their distinctive talents.[3]

To be sure, Mims was not an unbiased observer. He not only favored Southern industrial development but hailed (Preface, p. vii) the "veritable war of liberation. . . . against the conservatism, the sensitiveness to criticism, the lack of freedom that have too long impeded Southern progress." Thus, he firmly aligned himself with the critics of the Old South and the proponents of the New South—from Henry Grady, Gen. Daniel Harvey Hill, and Walter Hines Page through Ellen Glasgow, Howard W. Odum, and Rupert B. Vance to W. J. Cash, Harry S. Ashmore, and James McBride Dabbs.

However, the essential accuracy of Mims' characterization of the traditionalist position can be clearly demonstrated from the writings of those most faithful to the Old South—from Thomas Nelson Page to and beyond the Vanderbilt Agrarians[4]—who left no doubt whatsoever as to where they stood. Thus, they were satisfied with developing nothing less than a positive defense (as their forebears had once done for slavery) of the Southern agrarian-aristocratic tradition in all of its aspects. To them the fundamental cause of the Civil War was the fact (Frank L. Owsley) that "the North was commercial and industrial, and the South was agrarian. The fundamental and passionate ideal for which the South stood and fell was the ideal of an agrarian society." The Agrarians deplored this triumph of industralism over agrarianism and added (in Donald Davidson's words): "What was worse for the nation [the South] lost the peace—first in the Reconstruction, second by temporarily conforming, under the leadership of men like Walter H. Page and Henry W. Grady, to 'new South' doctrines subversive of its native genius." Unlike the North, wrote John Crowe Ransom, "The South never conceded that the whole duty of man was to increase material production, or that the index to the degree of his culture was the volume of his material production." Thus, they rejected the values of industrialism, which "is an insidious spirit, full of false promises and generally fatal to [tradition]."[5]

Given the shallowness of Southern thinking of their times, the advocates of both New and Old South frequently showed great courage in the vigor and forthrightness with which they expressed their views. However, since it took more courage to be a rebel than a Rebel in the South, it was not uncommon for the proponents of the New South to seek escape from a hostile environment by self-exile or even suicide.[6] Fortunately,

[3] Reprinted from Edwin Mims, *The Advancing South* (Garden City, N. Y.: Doubleday and Company, 1926), p. 24. By permission of Doubleday & Co., Inc.

[4] Since the hard core of Vanderbilt's Agrarians was in the University's Department of English, of which Professor Mims was long Chairman, his progressive views were probably the prime if unnamed target of his agrarian colleagues.

[5] Quoted from Twelve Southerners, *I'll Take My Stand* (New York: Harper and Brothers, 1930), pp. 69, 52, 12, and 15. By permission of Harper and Brothers.

[6] As V. O. Key, Jr. (*Southern Politics* [New York: Alfred A. Knopf, 1949], p. 664) has observed: "A depressingly high rate of self-destruction prevails among those who ponder about the South and put down their reflections in books. A fatal frustration seems to come from the struggle to find a way through the unfathomable maze formed by

in recent decades the *fact* of Southern industrial-urban development has gradually reinforced the voices of the New South and has at least reduced the region's intolerance of dissenters from Old South traditions. Nonetheless, I shall seek to demonstrate that, insofar as the New South has made material progress, it has done so *in spite of* strongly inhibiting social, political, psychological, and philosophical elements in the Old South's cultural heritage. I shall also argue that, if the transition from the Old South to the New South is to be completed, many of those still-strong qualities of mind and spirit which have made the South distinctive must largely disappear.

With such an immodest objective in mind, I shall find myself compelled not only to invade the normal preserve of the other social sciences but must even project myself further into the uncertain realm of philosophy and ethics. Hence, my findings may too often appear to be impressionistic and subjective rather than solid and scientific. If so, given the paramount importance of the problem at hand, I shall not apologize. Rather, I shall hope that my analysis, with all its faults, will make Southern economists and business leaders more aware of the non-economic barriers to Southern economic progress; that it will stimulate other social scientists (not to mention humanists and philosophers) to bring to bear more fully and effectively the insights of their particular disciplines upon these vital matters; and that it will help the intelligent Southern layman to perceive and to resolve in his own mind any inconsistencies between traditional values and the will to progress.

II. THE ECONOMIST AND THE PROBLEM OF VALUES

Go put your creed into your deed,
Nor speak with double tongue.
—Ralph Waldo Emerson, *Ode, Concord*

Having no professional obligations to separate values from analysis, the Southern Agrarians usually minced no words in arguing that the South could not industrialize and urbanize without destroying distinctly Southern traditions which they valued above all else. Hence, they did not hesitate to demand that Southerners *ought to* reject material progress and hold fast to the old traditions. As a social *scientist,* I must exercise more self-discipline. To be sure, I shall not be able to avoid making important value judgments. But, for this very reason, I am obligated to make explicit my own value premises, the most important of which may be stated as follows: (1) I *favor* the achievement of sufficient additional Southern economic progress to eliminate interregional differences in per-capita real incomes; (2) I *believe* that further industrial-urban development of the South is not only essential but that it inevitably means the destruction of many of the Southern traditions which your ancestors and mine held dear; and (3) forced thereby to make a choice, I *prefer* that the South seek further material progress even at the cost of abandoning these traditional values. Even so, as economist, I cannot appropriately say that Southerners *ought to* want higher per-capita real incomes or that they *ought not* give the non-economic elements of the Southern tradition a higher priority than material progress. Nor can I, as economist, say that those who would put the preservation of certain Southern traditions first are "wrong" and that I am "right," since here we are in the extra-scientific realm of philosophy and ethics. Instead, as economist, I must state my problem in the following terms: *if* a majority of Southerners (here an unrepressed bias in favor of democracy remains) want as their foremost objective to achieve higher per-capita real incomes, what are the barriers to and means of attaining this social end?

But why, some may ask, be such a purist? Didn't the Agrarians demand that means be found to help "the little agrarian community resist the Chamber of Commerce of its county seat" and "to stop the advances of industrialism, or even undo some of them"?[7] Would more than a tiny minority of Southerners still accept such romantic, nostalgic, and even utopian views today? Isn't it clear that the South's rapid economic progress of recent decades has not only further weakened the hold of tradition but has become the primary social goal of most Southerners?

In reply I must admit that until recently any re-examination of Southern Agrarianism would have looked like flogging a dead horse. However,

tradition, caste, race, poverty." Cf. W. J. Cash's strangely prophetic eulogy of Clarence Cason, whose suicide Cash attributed to fear of the fiercely hostile attitude which he knew would result from his forthcoming book critical of the South. (W. J. Cash, *The Mind of the South* [Garden City, N. Y.: Doubleday & Co., 1956], p. 327. Copyright 1941 by Alfred A. Knopf, Inc.)

[7] By permission from Twelve Southerners, *op. cit.*, pp. xix, xx.

the current crisis surrounding school desegregation has revealed that, even though the old gray mare of Southern tradition "ain't what she used to be," she is still "alive and kicking." These more recent equine convulsions may represent either the death throes preparatory to Ashmore's "Epitaph for Dixie" or the renaissance of the traditional Southern values which some latter-day sectionalists still demand. Lest we underestimate the strength of tradition, however, let us recall Edwin Mims' words of 1926. After hailing the South's "remarkable industrial development, [and] an even more important and significant intellectual renascence," Mims tempered his optimism with a comment that has a familiar ring today:

> The stage seems all set for wonderful progress; the obstacles seem to be removed; and then something happens; there is a resurgence of the old reactionary spirit, policies, and ideas. And in some respects the South looks worse . . . than it has looked at any time within the last decade or more.[8]

In any case, whether one views the South's current convulsions with hope or alarm, a diagnosis of the causes is vital to understanding why the South has lagged behind in economic development and why its further progress is fraught with extra-economic impediments.

For this purpose, I find the Vanderbilt Agrarians more useful than their more moderate successors.[9] To be sure, it is easy to give the Agrarians a place of prominence greater than they deserve, since they were always a small voice, little heeded even in their own environs. However, because their views were both extreme and explicit, the Vanderbilt group did place in bold relief important elements of the Southern tradition. Being more literate and articulate than most Southerners of conservative persuasion, yet giving their emotions free rein, this group's views offer relatively faithful (if highly intellectualized) reflections of some of the more broadly held traditional values which interest us here. Being innocent of social science, though hating the "sociologist" with a purple passion, they also offer an excellent example of (in Ashmore's words) "the Southerner's remarkable capacity for unreality, which still enables him to hold out against the logic of argument and of events."[10] Particularly were they unrealistic in choosing traditional values over material progress without considering the relative costs of the alternatives. While the social scientist cannot properly say which alternative Southerners should choose, it is within his special competence to indicate the nature and extent of the costs which Southerners must weigh if their choice is to be rational and well-informed.

Less frequently, apparently seeking to broaden their appeal, the Vanderbilt Agrarians became even more unrealistic in implying that the preservation of Southern tradition was not inconsistent with achieving at least a modicum of material well being, although they carefully avoided saying for whom and for how many. Thus, in this more persuasive mood, John Crowe Ransom wrote: "The South must be industrialized—but to a certain extent only, in moderation . . . it will be fatal if the South should conceive it as her duty to be regenerated and get her spirit reborn with a totally different orientation toward life."[11] Here, however, the Vanderbilt Agrarians offended less than some of their own successors or even their more recent antagonists. Repeatedly, one finds both of the latter groups saying in effect what Rubin recently wrote: "The South must find a way to control industrialism, to admit it only on the South's own terms."[12] To be sure, the very

[8] By permission from Mims, *op. cit.*, pp. vii and 9. Cf. Howard W. Odum, *op. cit.*, pp. 211–13.

[9] For example, the Fourteen Southerners who contributed essays to Louis D. Rubin, Jr., and James Jackson Kilpatrick, Editors, *The Lasting South* (Chicago: Henry Regnery Co., 1957). Copyright 1957 by Henry Regnery Company.

[10] Quoted by permission from Harry S. Ashmore, *An Epitaph for Dixie* (New York: Norton & Co., 1957), p. 19.

[11] By permission from Twelve Southerners, *op. cit.*, p. 22. In what was in many ways a sequel to *I'll Take My Stand* (Herbert Agar and Allen Tate, Editors, *Who Owns America?* [New York: Houghton Mifflin, 1936]), Ransom added with a touch of good humor (p. 190): "The Agrarians have been rather belabored . . . as denying bathtubs to the Southern rural population. But I believe that they are fully prepared to concede the bathtubs." In the later book, however, the Agrarians appear to have conceded much more. Whereas the earlier book had been full of uncritical praise of essentially aristocratic values, strongly smacking of the big planter class, the later book presented a political program whose hero was explicitly the small yeoman farmer, their views having meanwhile taken on strong overtones more congenial with the agrarian radicalism of the old Southern Populist movement.

[12] Quoted by permission from Rubin and Kilpatrick, *op. cit.*, p. 15; cf. Walter Sullivan (*ibid.*, pp. 118–19), Ronald F. Howell (*ibid.*, pp. 161–62) and James Jackson Kilpatrick (*ibid.*, pp. 192–93). On the other side, cf. the similar views of Odum

lateness of the South's economic development offers a real opportunity to avoid some of the excesses of Northern industrial-urban growth and, with proper foresight and planning, the South can still do so. But it is unrealistic to argue, as most lay writers (both conservative and progressive) have tended to do, that the South can somehow eat its cake and at least have bread too. Rather, the social scientist can appropriately insist that the South cannot have it both ways—that is, that fundamentally a choice between the values of agrarianism and industrialism (however painful and unpleasant it may be) must be made.

So much said, I now turn to the heart of my analysis. What are the key elements in the distinctively Southern tradition, way of life, and state of mind which have hampered economic progress?

III. TRADITION AS A BARRIER TO PROGRESS

. . . the South once took a great tradition and made it a hitching-post instead of a steppingstone.
—Dykeman and Stokely, *Neither Black Nor White*

In its recent advertisements, the Southern Company has declared: "The march has just begun! The last half of the twentieth century belongs to the South!" Whether or not such extravagant claims are possible of fulfilment is still unsettled. To the extent that the South still belongs to the *nineteenth* century, it must fail to make its full and wholly realizable claim to the twentieth. Hence, let me attempt to summarize briefly here my analysis of those elements in the Southern tradition which have seriously impeded its economic progress. The list is long but can be classified for convenience into five principal categories: (1) the dominance of agrarian values, (2) the rigidity of the social structure, (3) the undemocratic political structure, (4) the weakness of social responsibility, and (5) conformity of thought and behavior.[13]

First, what were the effects of the *dominant agrarian values* in the Southern heritage? Early American tradition combined the philosophy of agrarianism with a strong spirit of progress. The South embraced agrarianism but, given its burgeoning system of slavery and plantation, lost interest in progress even with reference to agriculture. Increasingly, in ante-bellum days, the South's dominant agrarianism took the form of a positive antagonism toward industrial-urban development as an inferior way of life. With defeat and Reconstruction, the South's agrarian philosophy first came into serious question but the region's frenzied efforts to industralize produced only modest results, so that the traditional agrarian values were ultimately reinforced and largely restored to a position of dominance. As a consequence, agrarianism impeded balanced and broadly-based regional economic progress in the following ways: (1) *It created an agrarian-oriented scale of social prestige*, which has directed a disproportionate share of the South's indigenous capital into agricultural rather than business assets and too much of its superior human talent into non-business fields. (2) *It insulated the large planter from competing economic forces*, which otherwise might have weakened his excessive social, political, and economic hold upon his local community. (3) *It perpetuated a strong love of the land and outdoor life*, which has discouraged human mobility and created a belief that Southerners are unsuited for the discipline of the factory system. (4) *It made a tradition of leisure*, which has discouraged economic enterprise on the part of the wealthy class and has produced, and even given sanction to, laziness and lassitude on the part of poor whites and Negroes.

Second, what were the effects of the South's *rigid social structure*? The Revolution largely ended the tendency in America to take over the British system of large landholdings and a socio-politically dominant landed aristocracy. However, the British pattern, already firmly established in the Southern Tidewater in colonial days, became the model for a new planter aristocracy which waxed fat on the rich new combination of cotton, slavery, and plantation after 1800. The consequence was an environment unusually favorable to the perpetuation of a carefully stratified rural society in which first the Negro, and later the typical white, had his place. Whereas the rest of the United States largely rejected the "aristocratic ideal" derived from England, the South took it over as a major element in its value system. As in England, the new Southern aris-

(*op. cit.*, pp. 22, 55–57, 225–29), Cash (*op. cit.*, pp. 197–99, 243–45, 383), and James McBride Dabbs (*The Southern Heritage*, New York: Alfred A. Knopf, 1958, p. 169 *et seq.*).

[13] Each of these categories is treated in detail as a separate chapter of my book, *Southern Tradition and Regional Economic Progress* (Chapel Hill, N. C.: Univ. of North Carolina Press, 1960), Chs. 2–6

tocracy at its best accepted *noblesse oblige*, which made the social system sufficiently attractive to win rather general acceptance by the masses of yeoman farmers and poor whites.

However, the net effects of this rural social structure on regional economic progress were distinctly unfavorable for the following reasons: (1) *The "aristocratic ideal" was seriously corrupted* through its association with the positive defense of slavery before the War and with "white supremacy" after the War. (2) *The spirit of extreme individualism became increasingly dominant over noblesse oblige*, so that the aristocrat increasingly held that his less fortunate neighbors were wholly responsible for themselves rather than being either his responsibility or a product of the social system. (3) *There was an abnormal subordination of the Southern rural middle class*, which was unable to contribute nearly as much to the democratization and economic development of its region as did its counterpart in the other American regions. (4) *The South took on a backward-looking, pessimistic, and static outlook* which was the natural product of its status society as the region emerged from the ordeal of military defeat. (5) *The South's upper classes came to accept as normal and inevitable socio-economic arrangements based on a disproportionate number of low-income people*, arrangements made tolerable to lower-income rural whites by a social structure which at least clearly supported their claims to superiority over the Negro race. (6) *The relatively rigid, rural social substructure gave little ground before the development of Southern cities* which, despite their more fluid social substructures and their growing urban middle classes, were handicapped by inadequate growth rates and a discriminatory political structure.

Third, what of the effects of the South's *undemocratic political structure*? Early interregional conflicts of economic interests over the tariff and slavery formed the political basis for the South's sectionalism and ultimately civil war. During this period, a relatively small minority of large slaveholders were not only able to persuade most of their white neighbors to take up arms in defense of slavery but also succeeded in defeating the threat of post-bellum agrarian radicalism by raising the battle-cry of white supremacy. The consequence was a monolithic political structure, based on the overriding end of maintaining white supremacy whatever the cost, which has seriously impeded regional economic progress in the following ways: (1) *It embodied a blind sectionalism which has encouraged the trend toward coercive federalism*, instead of a healthy federalism under which the nation's resources might be used to promote greater regional balance in economic development. (2) *It embraced a negative and defensive states'-rights doctrine* which, being too narrowly based on considerations of race, has offered a serious political impediment to much-needed Federal grants-in-aid to the low-income South. (3) *It was based upon a narrow electorate*, reflecting not only restrictions on the suffrage of most Negroes and many whites but also low voter-participation rates attributable to a one-party system and the generally low educational and income status of much of the citizenry. (4) *Consequently, it gave a disproportionate political influence to black-belt whites* relative to Negroes and low-income rural whites. (5) *It insulated rural political leaders from the political counterforces of Southern industrial-urban development*, because of the general failure of legislatures to reapportion legislative districts in response to radical rural-urban population shifts. (6) *It perpetuated political control by a coalition of economic conservatives and racial extremists*, who continue to use racial antagonism as a means of maintaining the status quo against the liberalizing influences of the new social forces abroad in the South.

Fourth, what were the effects of the *weakness of social responsibility* in the Southern tradition, particularly as reflected in inadequate support for public-school education? Even before the Civil War, the development of public-school systems in the South was severely handicapped by the preference of the dominant planter class for private schools and the general view that public schools were "schools for paupers." While Reconstruction brought a partial social revolution which for the first time established a sound basis for the public financing of common school systems in the South, the indifference or even antagonism of the dominant socio-economic class seriously inhibited the general advancement of public education. At the same time, this same dominant class has allowed its self-interest in perpetuating a cheap labor supply to override any feeling of general social responsibility for the economic development of the local community.

This weakness of social responsibility on the part of the South's traditional socio-political leadership has been a formidable barrier to regional economic progress in several ways: (1) *It has kept the masses of Southern people, white and Negro, in relative ignorance* in a world in which knowledge and skills are increasingly the key to both personal and social betterment. (2) *It has led responsible political leaders to propose abolition of public schools* as a solution to the school-integration controversy, without regard for the educational needs of the vast majority of their people or for the effects on concurrent industrialization campaigns. (3) *It has caused large planters and the managers of local low-wage industries to oppose measures to facilitate out-migration and local industrialization,* despite the general community interest in such developments. (4) *It has encouraged a continued belief that the South's low-income people are poor because they are innately inferior,* rationalizing a policy of inaction toward the improvement of schools and other public services and the attainment of a more efficient and equitable social and economic organization. (5) *It has resulted in too easy an approval of the recent high out-migration rates by Southern Negroes,* which, while undoubtedly contributing to an easing of racial tensions, must increasingly represent a substantial social loss—in terms of potential industrial labor force and prior public educational investments—to the states from which they migrate.

Finally, what were the effects of the Southern tradition of *conformity of thought and behavior*? The South's extreme cultural and ethnic homogeneity was transformed into strait-jacket conformity and intolerance of dissent, first by intersectional rivalry before the Civil War, and later by solidification against the vindictive forces of the Reconstruction period. Thus, in rejecting Yankee thought and the Yankee mind, Southerners closed their minds on every other important social doctrine as well. The results were a general intolerance of intellectualism, an acceptance of violence as an ultimate weapon against nonconformity and dissent, and a corruption of higher education as it too increasingly repudiated innovation and novelty in thought and behavior. In all these respects, the Southern tradition of conformity has been a serious handicap to regional economic progress: (1) *It created an environment hostile to the use of intellectual processes as a means to technological and social innovation and advancement,* with consequent intellectual stagnation and the draining off of the South's best intellectual and industrial talent into other regions. (2) *It gave public acceptance of, and often official sanction to, the use of violence as a means of enforcing conformity,* even though an atmosphere of law and order is a fundamental condition for attracting industrial plants from other regions. (3) *It seriously threatened both the academic freedom and the public-school base which are so vital to the development of great Southern universities,* and without which the South cannot attract and hold superior faculties, develop its own indigenous industrial and intellectual leaders, or provide the research and training facilities which are a prerequisite for sound and broadly-based industrialization of the South.

Earlier in this address, I asserted that the South must choose between Tradition and Progress. It must choose because, as the above summation makes abundantly clear, Southern tradition has essential elements—its value system, its social and political structure, its weakness of social responsibility, its intolerance of nonconformity and the intellectual process—which are irreconcilably at war with regional economic progress.

IV. THE INEVITABLE CHOICE: TRADITION OR PROGRESS

Superfluous branches
We lop away that bearing branches may live.
—Shakespeare, *King Richard II*

At the very outset of my essay, I stated that the major problem which would concern me here was the following: *If* a majority of Southerners want *as their foremost objective* to achieve higher per-capita incomes, what are the barriers to and means of attaining this social end?

But is this in fact what a Southern majority wants? I don't know; but Southern politicians, whose job it is to assess majority opinions, ought to know. Like their constituents, however, most politicians are confused. Certainly there is considerable evidence that Southerners do want more industrialization, which most economists agree is the factor essential to further progress. But few Southerners have yet faced up to the question as to whether they want industrialization badly enough to give up firmly held Southern traditions which are inconsistent with it. And fewer politicians have yet had the foresight or the courage to make clear to their constituents that a fundamental choice between Southern economic development and cherished traditions must be made.

Senator Fulbright of Arkansas recently extolled the goal of regional economic development in the following words:

> The South is no longer the nation's No. 1 economic problem; it is now the nation's new economic frontier. The level of economic development in the South is still considerably below that of the rest of the nation. However, we no longer view our difficulties as a national problem, but as a challenge to ourselves; a challenge to develop our potentials to reach the national level of economic development so that the people of the South may share fully in the American standard of living.[14]

Yet Senator Fulbright has had to tread very lightly on the matters of tradition raised by the school integration issue in his state, where he faces the fact of Rep. Brooks Hays' defeat and the threat of Gov. Faubus as a potential rival for his Senate seat. On the other hand, the full costs to Arkansas of the Faubus fiasco are gradually coming to light.

Therefore, if most Southern states today stand at the crossroads between Tradition and Progress, their choice may be the wiser because of the increasingly strong evidence that Arkansas took the wrong turn. While the atmosphere is still murky, it appears that in Tennessee and North Carolina, and probably in Florida and Virginia as well, moderate political leadership has now recognized the necessity of choosing between Tradition and Progress and has firmly chosen Progress. On the other hand, most political leaders in the Deep South appear to have chosen Tradition—a choice epitomized by the vow of Gov. Vandiver of Georgia that "There will be no mixing in the class rooms come hell or high water"—although they may still be under the false illusion that Tradition and Progress are not irreconcilable. That the two goals are in fact irreconcilable has been well expressed by Ralph McGill when he wrote that Souther leaders "seeking new enterprises never saw themselves as carriers of the virus which was to destroy the *status quo* in their towns . . .—and also, therefore, the old 'way of life in the South'. . . . They sought with a kind of desperation to maintain the *status quo*—all the while laboring to bring new industries and payrolls which could only accelerate the change."[15]

Thus, the South has been choosing Progress over Tradition almost in spite of itself and has done it so gradually as to be largely unaware of what was happening. However, Progress by drift is at best bound to be slow enough and, unless the South faces the conflicts between Tradition and Progress squarely and realistically, its stubborn and recently intensified adherence to Tradition may well slow Progress to a snail's pace at the very time when its rapid acceleration might normally have been expected.

If any single generalization emerges from our analysis of Southern tradition, viewed from whatever angle, it is that the race issue dominates all other elements of the picture. While the Negro was physically emancipated from the Southern white in 1862, the psychological emancipation of the Southern white from the Negro is yet to be achieved a century later. As Jonathan Daniels recently put it, "The whites have sometimes seemed to carry segregation to the point of insisting upon carrying the Negro as a load."[16] Yet, as a low-income region, the South is peculiarly ill-equipped to carry this self-imposed load, which has so heavily drained off the region's energies from the constructive channels leading to economic progress. Thus, I do not believe that Key has exaggerated in concluding his *Southern Politics* with the following final words: ". . . until greater emancipation of the white from the Negro is achieved, the southern political and economic system will labor under formidable handicaps. The race issue broadly defined must thus be considered as the number one problem on the southern agenda. Lacking a solution for it, all else fails."[17]

While one might easily despair about finding such a solution in the present disturbed Southern scene, I believe that it can and will be done. As solid as the race-oriented traditions of the South appear to be, they are being steadily weakened by the much more solid economic progress that the South has already made and, with patient and wise leadership, will continue to make. Since so much of the South's traditional race antagonism has had its roots in community-wide rural poverty, the key to its solution clearly lies in the

[14] Quoted in Wilma Dykeman and James Stokely, *Neither Black Nor White* (New York: Rinehart, 1957), p. 322.

[15] Quoted in *ibid.*, pp. 332–33.

[16] *Virginia Quarterly Review*, Spring 1955, Vol. XXI, p. 222.

[17] Key, *op. cit.*, p. 675.

additional industrial-urban development by which such poverty can be largely eliminated.

With Southern urbanization, more and more Negroes (and poor whites) are able to escape to an environment which, despite all of its limitations, offers far less formidable obstacles to political participation and economic advancement. As the late President of Fisk University, Charles S. Johnson, put it: "We cannot escape the fact that the Negro minority market alone, even when held down by unequal opportunity and limited education to one half its potential, is equal to the total (national income) of Canada or to our total foreign exports."[18]

Furthermore, as Dabbs has so wisely observed:

> As [the Negro] gains economic power, he moves toward equality in economic relations. He is already equal in a detail of our financial life: at the bank counter he is plain Joe Doe. He is rapidly becoming an equal in the world of merchandising: all folding money is green. As he gains the ballot, he will become a political equal. As he gains legal support, he moves toward equality in civil relations. . . . And now, as the Negro gains equality, he will tend to accept himself as an equal, and this will put added pressure on the white man to accept him. For to some degree we accept every man's evaluation of himself.[19]

Similarly, Key has pointed to important factors altering the central place of the Negro in Southern politics, including the heavy outmigration of Negroes from the plantation areas, the increasing organization of urban labor in the South, and the increasing fellow-feeling of Southern industrial and financial interests with northern Republicanism. He particularly emphasizes the effects of Negro migration to Southern cities, arguing that the movement of Southern Negroes to Houston, Atlanta, and Birmingham "has somewhat the same political effect as [their] movement to points outside the South." To be sure, the moderating and liberalizing influences of Southern urbanization on race relations have been held in check by widespread gerrymandering against urban centers and by the dominance of the plantation counties in the conservative wing of the Southern Democratic Party.[20] Furthermore, the thousands of low-income rural whites moving into Southern cities do not leave their race prejudices and hatreds behind. Even so, as ways are found for the Southern cities to throw off the tyrannical rule of rural minorities, and as these cities accelerate their industrial development sufficiently to remove the feeling of economic insecurity among their vast new white wage-earning classes, a gradual improvement in urban race relations appears highly probable.

Thus, if they are left to their own resources and given that local autonomy without which the states'-rights doctrine is hypocritical and empty, the South's cities can ameliorate the race problem as its semi-feudalistic rural areas as yet cannot. The difference between the South's primitive rural folk society and its modern industrial-urban society are profound. In the South's traditional folk society, laws do follow customs, whereas, in the South's rapidly growing industrial society, "custom is becoming less important and law more important." Increasingly, in Dabbs' words, "Daily, abstract justice is of more concern, concrete habits of less. The demand that the South change, perhaps rather sharply, its customs is simply the demand that it act in the fashion of the industrial society to which it aspires and which it is rapidly becoming." Thus, in the process of its industrial-urban development, the South is at last learning "how men may live generously and easily without oppressing the laboring class; . . . indeed, [how] the entire society can advance only as all its members, its [white and Negro] laborers included, advance also." In doing so, the South is finally "substituting an etiquette of equality for one of inequality."[21]

V. THE NEED FOR WISE LEADERSHIP

> There is a tide in the affairs of men,
> Which, taken at the flood, leads on to fortune;
> Omitted, all the voyage of their life
> Is bound in shallows and in miseries.
> —Shakespeare, *Julius Caesar*

While the industrial-urban development of the South has already contributed much to removing the heavy load of history from its tired old back, the danger remains that another round of demagogues may yet have their day. If Southern political leadership allows the closing of its hard-won and priceless public-school systems, the break-

[18] Quoted in Dykeman and Stokely, *op. cit.*, p. 325.

[19] Reprinted by permission from Dabbs, *op. cit.*, pp. 163–64. Copyright 1958 by Alfred A. Knopf, Inc.

[20] Key, *op. cit.*, pp. 669–70, 672–74.

[21] By permission from Dabbs, *op. cit.*, pp. 162–63, 179.

down of law and order and freedom of discussion, the continued virtual disenfranchisement of its more moderate and liberal urban sector, and the destruction of its rising state universities, Southern economic development for whites and Negroes alike can easily be set back by half a century. As the contrasting experiences of North Carolina and Arkansas make painfully clear, the directions set by state leadership are of paramount importance. How much better for the South if its social, economic, and political leaders would heed the voices of its great native sons of the past!

Thus, Thomas Jefferson wrote a friend in 1786: "Preach, my dear Sir, a crusade against ignorance; establish and improve the law for educating the common people. Let our countrymen know that . . . the tax which will be paid for this purpose, is not more than the thousandth part of what will be paid . . . if we leave the people in ignorance." A century later, unembittered by defeat, Robert E. Lee not only demanded "the thorough education of all classes of [Southern] people," but stated that the great aim of every Southerner should be to unite in "the allayment of passion, the dissipation of prejudice, and the restoration of reason." "Abandon all these local animosities," he exhorted, "and make your sons Americans." Woodrow Wilson wrote in a similar spirit: "Any man who revives the issue of sectionalism in this country, is unworthy of the government of the nation; he shows himself a provincial; he shows that he himself does not know the various sections of his own country; he shows that he has shut his heart up in a little province and that those who do not see the special interests of that province are to him sectional, while he alone is national. That is the depth of unpatriotic feeling.[22] Jefferson, Lee, Wilson—these are the great and immortal voices of that South which is eternally worth preserving! Judged against such giants among men, the South's Tillmans, Bilbos, Faubuses, and Griffins are seen for the pygmies they really are.

Unless the South is again willing to secede from the Union—and no one really believes that it is—it is high time that the region faced up to its obligations as an integral part of the Union. Gov. Leroy Collins of Florida clearly did so in a recent statement: "Talking . . . in terms of realities, we should recognize the United States Supreme Court decision can only be changed by the court, itself, or by a constitutional amendment declaring racial segregation in public schools permissible. And no one seriously expects that either of these things will happen."[23] While Southerners have always had a remarkable capacity for unreality, this reality they must somehow bring themselves to face and face squarely. This is admittedly asking a lot for, as Louis D. Rubin, Jr., recently wrote in a somewhat different context:

> Working against a successful outcome is that characteristic ingrained in Southern life . . .—the willingness to ignore practical problems requiring common effort, planning and foresight, in favor of a concentration on personal inner satisfactions alone. The Southerner is . . . temperamentally opposed to the kind of necessarily abstract analysis that would permit him to work out a long range solution . . . . [Nonetheless, the South] must do what it has never done before—sit down and think out its course, prepare for the future without waiting until the next crises is upon it . . . . [Such behavior] is also most un-Southern . . . [but the South] must rise to the occasion.[24]

If the South could at last take such a fresh, honest, and hardheaded look at the race problem, the gains which would accrue to the region would extend far beyond matters of race. For race has so shackled the Southern mind that it has been incapable of accepting social responsibility for the general welfare or of organizing common efforts for common benefit in other important directions as well. To be sure, there is indeed a danger that the South, "in accepting the new, the urban, the industrial, [will] wantonly . . . discard the old [which] would quickly make the South a second-rate North at best, with all moorings gone."[25] However, with proper foresight and constructive planning, the South's industrial-urban development need not take such an unhappy turn. As Polk recently wrote, ". . . the South is being industralized at a time when industry has at-

[22] Jefferson's letter of August 13, 1786, to George Wythe; Lee as quoted in Mims, *op. cit.*, pp. 4–5; Wilson as quoted in Odum, *op. cit.*, p. 257. Wilson's criticism of provincialism, it should be noted, need not be limited to Southerners.

[23] Quoted in *New South*, December 1958, p. 15.

[24] By permission from Rubin and Kilpatrick, *op. cit.*, p. 15.

[25] By permission from Ellington White in *ibid.*, p. 162. Cf. Dabbs' similar good-humored warning (p. 179) that "Industrialism is the one abstraction we're buying now, lock, stock, and barrel. We'll have to be on our toes to keep it from making Yankees of us all."

tained not only a new efficiency but a new sense of social responsibility, and when city planning is a technique by which cities, instead of degenerating into blighted areas and slums, can grow in convenience, comfort, and beauty as well as size."[26]

Thus, with effective and constructive leadership, it is wholly possible that "the last half of the twentieth century belongs to the South!" Unfortunately, however, an adequate supply of such leadership has not been forthcoming. The plain fact is that the Southern social and political structure has maintained the form, while losing the ameliorative socially-responsible substance, of an aristocratic system. Thus, the South's privileged classes have largely abdicated their positions of leadership, while leaving the masses inadequately prepared educationally and economically to provide effective leadership of their own through more democratic channels.

While there is a great need for democratizing the Southern political structure, it is too slow a process to fill immediately the vacuum of leadership in these current troubled times. Hence, it is the South's citizens who presently occupy high social, economic, and political positions that must fill the gap in the meantime. If they are to do so, they must relearn some of the long-forgotten aristocratic principles of the Old South at its best—"sacrifice and obligation and a concern for the welfare of others."[27] Or, in Dabbs' challenging words: "As leaders of society, they should be able to see that at long last their society is changing and that it's their job to lead it. The leaders of the Old South were not afraid to stand upon their own feet. The leaders of the New might do well to be more truly traditional than they are."[28]

Thus far, I have directed my criticisms of a failure of constructive leadership against such broad and admittedly ill-defined groups as the South's "upper class," "privileged class," and so on. Even if they agree with me, most Southern economists probably do not identify themselves with such groups enough to have personal twinges of conscience about their own inadequate role in these important matters. Yet, as part of the South's small but growing intellectual *elite*, we Southern economists are members of the region's "privileged class" and opinion leadership—by training if not by wealth or family position. As such, have we not also shirked our own obligations as social scientists and citizens? Cash has observed that, in Southern universities during the early part of the present century, the field of economics advanced even more slowly than did the field of history. "Adam Smith still was generally presented as having the same absolute validity as Isaac Newton. And the teaching of [economics] was mainly in the hands of dull men who carefully avoided examining the current scene in the South itself."[29] Certainly, our profession in the South can no longer be so charged with being outside of the mainstream of American (and Western) economic thought. But haven't we found it too easy to leave it to our more courageous colleagues in sociology the analysis of the most important and controversial social issues of today, most of which have enormous economic implications?

I believe that we have. In his recent review of Becker's book, *The Economics of Discrimination*, Donald Dewey of Duke University was undoubtedly right in his melancholy observation that "apparently, economists in the South must still look to Chicago for pioneer work on the region's important problem."[30] While our principal professional obligation is sound and objective economic analysis of (among other things) problems of regional economic development, such analyses can hardly be adequate or realistic if they ignore the direct economic effects of race and other non-economic factors. Nor can we afford to hide such broader analyses, once made, under a bushel simply because life will be more comfortable if we do. While, as economists, we cannot say that the South should choose Tradition over Progress, I believe that we have a firm obligation to use our analytical tools to make clear to the Southern public the inconsistencies in trying to achieve both objectives at once.[31]

[26] William T. Polk, *Southern Accent: From Uncle Remus to Oak Ridge* (New York: Wm. Morrow & Co., 1953), p. 253.

[27] By permission from Robert Hazel in Rubin and Kilpatrick, *op. cit.*, p. 170.

[28] By permission from Dabbs, *op. cit.*, pp. 119–20.

[29] Cash, *op. cit.*, p. 323.

[30] *Southern Economic Journal*, Vol. 24, 1958, p. 496. Professor Dewey has been virtually the only white economist in any Southern university to devote a substantial amount of research to the economic aspects of race.

[31] Professor Lorin A. Thompson of the University of Virginia deserves a favorable citation here. His recent economic analysis of Virginia's public-school crisis was not only comprehensive and sound but was courageous and influential as well. ("Some Economic Aspects of Virginia's Current Educational Crises," Charlottesville, undated, processed.)

What I have said of the obligations of the Southern economist apply with almost equal force to other Southern social scientists and university professors, not to mention the important business and professional leaders who are the products of Southern university education. Collectively, we are the South's "intellectual aristocracy" or the South has none. Furthermore, quite apart from our professional or leadership obligations, we of this "intellectual aristocracy" have vital duties to perform as enlightened citizens and as men of flesh-and-blood and moral convictions.[32] Whether native sons or ex-Yankees, we are now Southerners by choice rather than necessity. There is something pleasant and precious about the Southern "way of life" which we like or we wouldn't be here. But like all ways of life, the Southern way is not perfect. If, against one of the South's least fortunate traditions, we are permitted to express even unpopular ideas freely and can feel hope for the South's economic future, most of us want to stay. But if we do, it will be because, in Walter Hines Page's striking phrase, "We look forward to a golden age that we may surely help to bring, not back to one that never was."

[32] In closing this paper, I should perhaps make explicit the extent to which, quite apart from the lessons of social science, my own maturing interpretation and application of Christian teachings have influenced my attitudes toward race relations. I have been forced to conclude that, quite apart from their economic and social aspects, traditional Southern racial attitudes inescapably have a *moral* aspect as well. That so few of my co-religionists in the South seem to see this moral issue never ceases to discourage and amaze me. It is a paradox that the South, which by every objective standard is the most religious region in America, could be so blind to the practical implications of Christianity. Somehow, the Southern religious tradition has never progressed from the Old Testament's God of Wrath to the New Testament's God of Love and Brotherhood, nor from an ethereal concern for the other world to a concrete moral concern for social injustice in the here-and-now. Thus, in my view, Southern religious views have been hopelessly schizophrenic and outrageously self-righteous.

On the race issue, it is the South's *moral* leadership which has been found most wanting, particularly in terms of what might be most reasonable to expect. For every Brooks Hays, there have been a hundred lay leaders of the Southern church who have remained silent or worse. For every minister of the Gospel who has, individually or collectively, spoken out, there have been scores who have followed rather than led their flocks. To me, the importance of religion has been one of the finest elements in the Southern tradition. But, if we are not to make a mockery of this grand religious heritage, can we Southerners any longer refuse to carry it to its logical and spiritual conclusion?

24. Migration from Agriculture: The Historical Record and Its Meaning*

DALE E. HATHAWAY

The low returns to human effort throughout most of United States agriculture and the very low incomes of most persons in some regions of U.S. agriculture have long been recognized. The most common prescription offered by economists for these ills has been a large-scale transfer of labor from agriculture. It usually is argued that such a transfer would: result in a recombination of resources in agriculture that would provide a solution to the major problems of United States agriculture; increase incomes in agriculture relative to incomes in the nonfarm economy; and reduce the disparity in agricultural income between regions.

For the last four decades there has been a large out-migration from agriculture to the nonfarm economy. This is sometimes cited as having significantly contributed to the improvement of agriculture's ills, and more of the same is prescribed as the method of complete cure. Therefore, it seems pertinent to examine in some detail the impact of the recent out-migration from agriculture to help us judge whether this simple prescription is enough or whether we must, perhaps, treat some serious secondary symptoms at the same time.

The Size of the Out-migration

Because it has become so commonplace in our society we sometimes fail to grasp the magnitude of the migration from agriculture. Yet, for a nation lacking a positive policy to induce migration and which has fortunately largely avoided widespread natural or man-made disaster, the record is truly amazing. Since 1920 more than 25 million people have migrated from farms to urban areas and nonfarm occupations. Migration from farms has persisted through depressions and wars. Although the farm population in 1950 was only about two-thirds that of 1920, the absolute number of migrants during the past decade has been above earlier periods.

However, economic conditions have had a strong influence on the rate of out-migration from agriculture. In the 1920-30 decade more than 6 million people left agriculture—a rate of 19 per cent of the begin-

* Reprinted from the *American Economic Review,* Vol. 49 (May 1960).

ning population.[1] During the thirties only slightly over 3.5 million migrated, a rate of about 13 per cent. In the ten years from 1940 to 1950 the net migration exceeded 9 million persons, giving a rate of 31 per cent. It appears that the number of out-migrants during the 1950-60 decade has been about the same as in the forties, so that the rate probably has exceeded one-third.

All regions of the country have experienced an out-migration from agriculture. However, the rates have varied between regions in different ways at different times (Table 1). The variation between regions in rate of out-migration was relatively low during the twenties. During the thirties, however, there was a wide variation between regions, with

TABLE 1

NET CHANGE IN RURAL-FARM POPULATION BY MIGRATION, UNITED STATES AND REGIONS, 1920–30, 1930–40, 1940–50

AREA	RATE OF CHANGE IN FARM POPULATION DUE TO MIGRATION		
	1920–30	1930–40	1940–50
United States	−19.3	−12.7	−30.9
New England	−13.0	+ 2.6	−21.8
Middle Atlantic	−18.7	− 1.3	−20.7
East North Central	−19.7	− 5.3	−22.6
West North Central	−17.5	−17.7	−29.2
South Atlantic	−25.0	−13.8	−31.9
East South Central	−19.8	−13.2	−33.4
West South Central	−17.3	−19.9	−44.0
Mountain	−19.4	−16.3	−32.6
Pacific	− .3	+ 4.9	−15.1

SOURCE: *Net Migration from the Rural Farm Population, 1940–50,* Statistical Bulletin No. 176, June, 1956, Table 1, p. 16.

the west North Central and west South Central having the highest rates. During the 1940-50 period the relative variation between geographical regions was again reduced, although the entire south and the west North Central regions experienced rates of out-migration above those for other regions.

One should not conclude immediately that this has been entirely a movement of people from what we generally classify as "the low-income areas" in agriculture (Table 2). For the decade 1940-50 the net migration from serious low-income farming areas was only one-third above that of the higher income areas. Among the generalized low-income farming areas classified by the Department of Agriculture there were many geographical regions from which the rate of out-

[1] The method used to compute the rate leaves out the migration of persons born and those dying during the decade. See Gladys K. Bowles, *Farm Population—Net Migration From the Rural-Farm Population, 1940-50,* Statistical Bulletin No. 176, U.S. Dept. of Agric., June, 1956, p. 167, for the methodology used in estimating rates.

migration was below that from medium- and high-income areas. Thus the rate of out-migration from a specific area depends upon a complex of socioeconomic factors of which relative income level is but one.

A majority of the migrants from agriculture have gone to the large urban metropolitan areas of the North and West. The popular concept of large-scale movements from the South to Detroit and Chicago are

TABLE 2

NET MIGRATION RATES FROM DIFFERENT FARMING AREAS CLASSIFIED BY INCOME LEVELS, UNITED STATES

AREA	RATE OF NET MIGRATION*	
	1930–40	1940–50
Rural-farm	−12.7	−30.9
Medium and high-income farming areas	−13.2	−28.0
Low-income farming areas†	−12.5	−33.8
Moderate low-income farming areas	− 8.3	−27.8
Substantial low-income farming areas	−13.9	−34.9
Serious low-income farming areas	−14.2	−36.9
Generalized low-income farming areas‡		
Appalachian Mountains and border areas		−27.8
Southern Piedmont and Coastal Plains		−34.8
Southeastern Hilly		−34.5
Mississippi Delta		−39.9
Sandy Coastal Plains of Arkansas, Louisiana, and Texas		−49.1
Ozark-Ouachita Mountains and Border		−33.4
Northern Lake States		−29.2
Northwestern New Mexico		−39.6
Cascade and Rocky Mountain areas		−16.0

* Change due to migration expressed as a percentage of farm population alive at both beginning and end of decade.

† Areas delineated in "Development of Agriculture's Human Resources—A report on Problems of Low-Income Farmers." Low-income farms were classified on the basis of three criteria for State Economic Areas: (1) Farms in State Economic Areas average less than $1,000 residual farm income to operator and had farm-operator family level-of-living index below the regional average and 25 per cent or more of commercial farms classified as "low production." (2) Average farm-operator level-of-living index for the State Economic Areas was in the lowest fifth for the nation. (3) Fifty per cent or more of commercial farms in State Economic Areas were classified as "low production." Areas denoted as *Serious* in Table 2 met all three criteria; areas denoted as *Substantial* met any two of the criteria; areas denoted as *Moderate* met any one of the criteria.

‡ The generalized areas represent geographic groupings of the low-income farming areas.

SOURCE: *Net Migration from the Rural Farm Population, 1940–50*, Statistical Bulletin No. 176, June, 1956, Table A, p. 13.

based on fact. The 1950-57 net imigration to Michigan is estimated at about 520,000 persons.[2] The high concentration of the in-migrants is illustrated by the estimate that two-thirds of the in-migrants went to the three counties including and adjacent to Detroit. Other northern and western metropolitan areas have had approximately similar experiences.

[2] J. F. Thaden, "Population Growth Components and Potential in Michigan" (Inst. for Community Devel. and Serv., Contin. Educa., Michigan State Univ., mimeographed, Jan. 16, 1959), Table 11.

What has been true generally for migration from agriculture has been particularly true of nonwhites. They have concentrated very heavily in large urban areas.[3] Thus the migration from farm areas has contributed very significantly to the growth of the labor force of the large urban areas. Some of the impacts of these movements upon the receiving areas will be discussed in a subsequent section.

Who Has Migrated from Agriculture?

Much economic theory has as an underlying assumption that units of resources are homogeneous and that, therefore, resource transfers are neutral as to the resulting character of that portion of the resource not transferred. We know, however, that human resources in agriculture are not homogeneous, so that who migrates from agriculture has an effect beyond the mere numbers involved upon both agriculture and the receiving sector of the economy.

Sociologists have attempted to isolate the differential characteristics of migrants. However, no clear-cut generalizations appear possible as to whether migration selects the least able or the most able, those with the most initiative or those with less.[4]

There is little question that migration from agriculture is closely related to age.[5] More than one-half of the farm population age 10-19 in 1940 had left the farm by 1950. About 40 per cent of the age group 20-24 in 1940 migrated prior to 1950. However, less than 20 per cent of those 30-49 years old in 1940 migrated from the farm during the subsequent decade.[6]

There is some relationship between the age at which out-migration has generally occurred, race, and educational attainment of the out-migrant. One study shows that migration rates from the rural farm areas for the 1940-50 decade were highest from the lower levels of education and roughly similar among those completing more than five years of schooling.[7] The migration rate from the nonwhite rural farm population aged 20-34 in 1940 was roughly similar for all educational levels up to high school. The migration rate for nonwhites with a high school education or beyond was much higher.

These conclusions for the 1940-50 period are approximately the reverse of those of Bogue and Hagood for the 1935-40 period. They

[3] Conrad Taeuber, "Economic and Social Implications of Internal Migration in the United States" (a paper presented for the joint meeting of the American Farm Econ. Asso. and the Rural Sociological Soc. at Ithaca, N.Y., Aug., 1959), p. 11.

[4] Conrad Taeuber, *ibid.*, p. 10.

[5] This apparently has been true for as far back as 1920. See Carter Goodrich *et al.*, *Migration and Economic Opportunity* (Univ. of Pennsylvania Press, 1936), p. 690.

[6] Gladys Bowles, *op. cit.*, p. 17.

[7] C. Horace Hamilton, "Educational Selectivity of Rural-Urban Migration: Preliminary Results of a North Carolina Study," *Selected Studies of Migration Since World War II* (Milbank Mem. Fund), Table 3.

found that migration during that period selected the better educated of the rural farm population, except that migration from the cotton belt contained disproportionately large numbers of the least well educated as well as the better educated.[8]

These two studies of rural-urban migration suggest that the pattern of educational selectivity has changed. This hypothesis is supported by two studies of migration over time from specific rural areas. They suggest that during the thirties there was a positive selectivity related to education among rural-urban migrants. However, during and since World War II there has been much less selectivity.[9] This probably can be attributed to the improved economic opportunities in the nonfarm economy and to a general increase in educational levels in rural areas, at least up through the eighth grade.

One final point should be made regarding who has migrated. The statistics discussed relate only to net migration, which is the result of movement in both directions. Thus some of the present agricultural population are persons who left agriculture and for some reason returned. Unpublished data from the Bureau of Old Age and Survivor's Insurance (Social Security) show that about one-third of the covered farm operators in 1955 worked off the farm in covered employment in previous years but were not doing so in 1955. Many of these farmers had higher incomes in their nonfarm employment than from farming in 1955. Apparently these individuals either found values in farming that overrode income considerations, or they were unsuccessful in making a transfer to the nonfarm economy and had to return to farming. Thus it is probable that even the high migration rates of the past twenty years do not reflect all of the persons who would be willing to leave agriculture if permanent employment opportunities were available.

The Impact of the Out-migration on the Agricultural Economy

One of the effects of the out-migration has been to reduce the number in the farm population, since the out-migration has exceeded the rate of natural increase. Thus an out-migration of about 25 million has reduced the farm population from 32 million in 1920 to about 21 million at the present time. Between 1929 and 1958 agricultural employment declined more than 40 per cent. The number of places classified as farms by the Census also has declined rapidly, and as a result we have had encouraging rises in statistical averages relating to per

[8] Donald J. Bogue and Margaret J. Hagood, *Subregional Migration in the United States, Differential Migration in the Corn and Cotton Belts,* Vol. II (Scripps Found., 1953), p. 57.

[9] See B. H. Luebke and J. F. Hart, "Migration From a Southern Appalachian Community," *Land Econ.,* Feb., 1958, p. 50, and Joe A. Martin, *Off-Farm Migration: Some of Its Characteristics and Effects Upon Agriculture in Weakley County, Tennessee,* Bul. 290 (Univ. of Tennessee Agric. Exp. Sta., Aug., 1958), p. 21.

farm and per capita incomes. However, these aggregate statistics can often be misleading, and it is necessary to raise other questions as to the effects of the out-migration. The pertinent questions would seem to be: (1) Has the out-migration reduced the gap in income between farm and nonfarm people? (2) Has out-migration brought an improvement in the relative income position of areas of chronic poverty in agriculture?

If the average per capita income of the farm population from farming is compared with that of the nonfarm population for the five years prior to World War I, five years in the late twenties, and for the most recent five years, there is no evidence that the gap is closing. From 1910 to 1914 the farm population's per capita income from farming averaged 38 per cent of the nonfarm average per capita.[10] From 1925 to 1929 the income from farming of the farm population averaged 33 per cent of the nonfarm level, and for 1954-58 the comparable figure was 35 per cent. Of course, in recent years the income from farming accounts for only two-thirds of the per capita income of the farm population. However, earnings from outside agriculture do not enter into the question of whether the agricultural industry is producing a relatively higher level of income after a period of heavy out-migration. Actually, inclusion of the nonfarm sources of income for earlier periods would probably make little difference.[11]

Since the average family size in agriculture has been larger than in the nonfarm population, comparisons of income per worker might be considered more valid. Income per worker in agriculture from farming amounted to 61 per cent of the average annual wage per employed factory worker for the years 1910-14.[12] The average for 1925-29 was 44 per cent and in 1954-58 was 45 per cent. There is no evidence of significant relative gains on either a per capita or per worker basis. Therefore, while there have been significant gains in real income in agriculture in the past four decades the rate of gain has probably little more than kept pace with that in the nonfarm economy.

Neither does the evidence support the contention that rapid out-migration has greatly improved the relative position of the low-income areas in agriculture.

It has been generally known that the poverty problems of agriculture are largely concentrated in the South so that it might be assumed that the heavy out-migration from this area would result in a sharply lower proportion of the total farm population now in that region. Surprisingly, however, the change has been only moderate. In 1920 the South had 53 per cent of the farm population and in 1958 it had 49 per cent of the

[10] Computed from Table 7, *Farm Income Situation* (July, 1959).
[11] See *Possible Methods of Improving the Parity Formula* (U.S. Dept. of Agric., mimeograph, Jan. 31, 1957) for some estimates of the effects.
[12] Computed from Table 8, *Farm Income Situation* (July, 1959).

total farm population. One-half of this percentage decline has occurred since 1950. Thus high birth rates in the South have partially offset the higher rates of out-migration over much of the last four decades.

Cheng found in his Michigan study that the disparities in farm income and wages between the higher income and lower income regions of the state have widened in spite of the fact that out-migration has been much higher from the low-income regions.[13]

Bishop found that despite the out-migration and increased resource productivity, net income per farm family in the southeast declined relative to the net income per farm family in other regions from 1939 to 1949.[14]

Figures are not presently available which give us regional and state comparisons of per capita incomes in agriculture for earlier periods. Therefore, it is not possible to determine accurately whether the heavy out-migration from southern agriculture has improved its relative income position. There are, however, some trends in the aggregate figures for regions which support the conclusions that the South has made little relative gain during the past fifteen years despite the large out-migration from its low-income agriculture.

An analysis of regional trends in per capita incomes of the total population by the Department of Commerce shows for the period 1927-29 to 1944 there was a marked reduction in the disparity in per capita incomes between regions.[15] Most of the reduction occurred between 1940 and 1944.[16] Since 1944, when the greatest out-migration from agriculture has occurred, there has been little change in the relative position of the regions. Even when the relative incomes were converging, the absolute gains in income were much larger in the higher income regions.

There are several reasons why out-migration has not resulted in significant and dramatic reductions in income differentials within agriculture and between agriculture and the nonagricultural economy. They are: the migration to date has affected commercial agriculture less than we realize; where migration has occurred its selectivity has created conditions tending to retard the recombination of remaining resources; and much more than a simple recombination of existing resources is necessary to bring an improvement in the income levels of most of the poverty plagued areas in agriculture.

Turning to the contention that out-migration has affected commercial

[13] Kenneth C. I. Cheng, "Economic Development and Geographical Wage Rates in Michigan 1940-57" (unpublished Ph.D. thesis, Michigan State Univ., 1959).

[14] See Charles E. Bishop, "Economic Development and Adjustments in Southeastern Low Income Agriculture," *J. of Farm Econ.*, Dec., 1954, p. 1151.

[15] U.S. Dept. of Com., *Personal Income by States Since 1929, A supplement to the Survey of Current Business* (1956), pp. 24-26.

[16] U.S. Dept. of Com., *U.S. Income and Output, a Supplement to the Survey of Current Business* (Nov., 1958), p. 37.

agriculture less than might be assumed, some evidence is seen in the statistics relating to changes in numbers of farms. For our purposes it might be useful to classify farms as falling into one of three types: commercial farms (roughly Class I through IV of Economic Class of Farm defined in the last Census of Agriculture); low-production farms (Class V and VI); and rural places to live (part-time, residential, and subsistence farms). If past censuses are adjusted for changes in farm prices, the trends in agriculture are these:[17] the number of commercial farms has been remarkably stable since 1929; the number of rural places to live has trended slightly upward; and the number of low-production farms has declined very sharply.

About 1.1 million of the 1.8 million low-production farms that disappeared between the 1930 and 1954 Census of Agriculture were in the South. However, this does not imply quite the degree of resource mobility for nonlabor resources that it might seem to, because about half of the reductions were of cropper farms which were not actually independent management units. Whereas the decline in the number of low-production farms has been greater in the South, the largest decline in the number of management units has been in the North and West.

There are further indications that the farms that have disappeared as people left agriculture were the smaller, less-productive farms. The decline in number of farms has been greatest among farms of ten to ninety-nine acres in size. In 1920 farms in this size group made up 54 per cent of the total number of farms, but they controlled only 17 per cent of the land in farms.[18] Between 1920 and 1954 there was a decline of 1.4 million in the number of farms between ten and ninety-nine acres. However, the amount of land which these farms contained and which, under ideal circumstances, might have been consolidated into larger units amounted to less than 6 per cent of the total land in farms in 1954. Thus the 63 per cent increase in the average size of farm in the United States from 1920 to 1954 is largely a statistical freak. Actually, there have been few increases in the numbers of farms in the various larger size groups and in the average size within the various groups.

The high degree of age selectivity in migration appears to be an important factor inhibiting the adjustment of resources remaining in agriculture. As a result of the disproportionately heavy out-movement in the younger age groups the average age of farm operators has risen. Whereas 21 per cent of the operators in 1920 were in the twenty-five to thirty-four age group and 26 per cent were over fifty-five years old,

[17] Jackson V. McElveen, *Family Farms in a Changing Economy* (USDA Inf. Bul. No. 171, Mar., 1957), p. 20.

[18] U.S. Dept. of Com., *1954 Census of Agriculture*, Vol. II, Chap. V, pp. 353 and 355.

in 1954 only 13 per cent were in the younger bracket and 37 per cent were over fifty-five.[19]

Older farmers are less likely to undertake drastic reorganizations of existing resources themselves because of limits of their physical capabilities and the limited span over which they might realize returns on large investments. Studies of low-income farming areas in South Carolina, Tennessee, and Arkansas all mention that the advanced age of many farm operators inhibits the adjustment of agricultural resources.[20] Apparently many older owners are unwilling to enter into contractual arrangements which will make it possible for the remaining younger farmers to organize existing agricultural resources in a satisfactory fashion. Thus institutional arrangements relating to tenure and credit, which were developed in a period of greater stability in technology and in the agricultural labor force, do not seem to be adjusting adequately to the rapid changes of recent years.

Adjustment problems in agriculture following a decline in the labor force are much more complex than a mere change in the capital-man ratio. Generally, the type of farming operation needs to be changed. New technology, new investment, and new management skills are required in order for the recombined resources to be productive. Old investments in buildings and equipment are often obsolete, requiring large additions of capital in new forms. The mere out-movement of labor from agriculture is a necessary, but not sufficient, condition to achieve these adjustments. Unfortunately, most of the people capable of making such adjustments may be among the out-migrants.

Even where heavy out-migration has occurred resource adjustments in agriculture may not tend to correct income inequalities. Bachmura found that population movements as a whole within a group of Mississippi Valley counties were not corrective in an income equilibrating sense.[21] In addition, he concluded that movements in capital investment per worker were noncorrective over the decade.[22]

Long-distance migration may be of much less help to agricultural adjustment than nearby nonfarm growth. There are indications that the adjustments are made more rapidly where the growth in nonfarm

[19] U.S. Dept. of Com., *1954 Census of Agriculture,* Vol. II, Chap. II, p. 83. The relative rise in noncommercial farms and the Census definition of an operator contributed to this rise.

[20] See Thomas A. Burch and Charles P. Butler, *Physical and Economic Characteristics that Limit Adjustments on Full-Time Medium Sized Farms in the Piedmont Area of South Carolina* (South Carolina Agric. Exp. Sta. Bul. 453, Mar., 1958, p. 47; Martin, *op. cit.,* p. 34, and William H. Metzler and J. L. Charlton, *Employment and Underemployment of Rural People in the Ozark Area* (Univ. of Arkansas Agric. Exp. Sta. Bul., 604, Nov., 1958), p. 55.

[21] Frank T. Bachmura, "Migration and Factor Adjustment in Lower Mississippi Valley Agriculture: 1940-50," *J. of Farm Econ.,* Nov., 1956, p. 1033.

[22] *Ibid.,* p. 1041.

employment is local. Ruttan found that rural farm areas in the southeast which "caught up" with the national average between 1930 and 1950 were close to developing urban centers.[23] Cheng found the same tendencies in Michigan.

The Impact of the Out-migration on the Nonfarm Economy

In the nonfarm economy as well as in the farm economy the heavy out-migration from agriculture has had both positive and negative aspects. During the periods of extreme labor scarcity the migration was appreciated and encouraged, but more recently some of its negative aspects have received more attention.

The nonfarm economy has attracted over 25 million people from the farm population since 1920. A high proportion of the migrants have been in age groups enabling them to be in the productive labor force. The migration, coming as it did at a time when new entrants to the labor force were low because of low urban birth rates in the twenties and thirties, was about the only way in which a large expansion of the nonfarm labor force could occur without immigration. Ducoff estimated that one-half of the expansion in the nonagricultural labor force from 1930 to 1954 came from migration from the farm population.[24] It would have been impossible to have increased nonfarm output to wartime and postwar levels without this increase in the labor force. Without the migration from farms, the price of nonfarm labor relative to other inputs probably would have risen more sharply than has been the case.

The nonfarm economy has received through the process of migration a large transfer of capital from the farm economy in the form of investment in the rearing and educating of farm youth to the age at which they migrated.[25] As a result, the nonfarm economy has received a large and significant quantity of productive resources in the form of productive labor without having to incur most of the initial expense of its rearing and education. This should contribute to a rapid rate of capital accumulation and growth in the nonfarm economy.

Not all of the effects of rural-urban migration have been positive for either the migrants or the receiving areas. First, the assimilation of large groups of people from different cultural backgrounds has presented some of the same problems as did the earlier mass influx of immigrants. Existing educational systems, social groupings, and eco-

[23] Vernon W. Ruttan, "Discussion of Development and Adjustment," *J. of Farm Econ.*, Dec., 1954, p. 1159.

[24] Louis J. Ducoff, "Trends and Characteristics of Farm Population in Low Income Farming Areas," *J. of Farm Econ.*, Dec., 1955, p. 1407.

[25] James D. Tarver estimated that an investment of $15,000 in 1954 prices was required to rear and educate a farm child to age eighteen. See his "Costs of Rearing and Educating Farm Children," *J. of Farm Econ.*, Feb., 1956, pp. 144-56.

nomic structures have been disrupted by the rapid influx of migrants into some urban areas. There has been a problem in some areas of the rapid replacement of the old population of central cities by migrant nonwhites whose economic status is low, adding considerably to the difficult adjustment problems already mounting in urban areas.

The receiving areas have become increasingly aware of the cost of assimilating the migrants. A recent Michigan study reported that although persons born in the South make up only 9.5 per cent of the state's population, they accounted for 31 per cent of the prison commitments.[26] When a commitment rate is computed for different population groups, the rate for whites born in the South is more than twice the rate for whites born in Michigan. Approximately the reverse was true for Negroes. The heavy burden of welfare costs to migrant groups has prompted recent suggestions of sending migrants out of one city and of increasing the residence requirements for welfare in several others.

The public problems that have arisen as a result of the migration to urban areas are partially because the migrants themselves sometimes have found the adjustment to the new economic and social environment difficult. They have found themselves unskilled labor in an industrial society which is increasingly replacing unskilled labor with skilled labor and machines. They have found that the impact of the nonfarm business cycle falls heaviest on the younger, the less skilled, and the nonwhite worker. They have found racial and other forms of discrimination among labor unions.

A recent paper summarized several sociological studies of the position of rural migrants in urban society.[27] It made the following points: (1) Many of the rural migrants lack the educational training or social background necessary to make them other than marginal members of the nonfarm society. (2) Rural migrants tend to move to lower standard housing areas and upgrade their housing less through moving than do urban migrants. (3) The rural migrant tends to participate less in formal and informal social and political organizations than other groups of the urban population. (4) Despite many of these less favorable aspects, the migrant generally would make the move if he had to make the decision again.

Summary and Conclusions

Migration from agriculture over the past four decades has touched virtually every community in the United States, both farm and non-

[26] "Non-natives Cause Most Crime in State," *The State J.* (Lansing, Mich.), Nov. 3, 1959, p. 16.

[27] George M. Beal and Wallace E. Ogg, "Secondary Adjustments from Adaptations of Agriculture," in *Problems and Policies of American Agriculture* (Iowa State Univ. Press, 1959), pp. 226 ff.

farm. Without out-migration the present problems of United States agriculture would have been magnified manyfold, and the gap between per capita incomes in the farm and nonfarm economy certainly would have widened. As yet, however, there is no evidence that the rapid rate of out-migration has appreciably closed the gap that existed in per capita incomes of farm and nonfarm people. Neither has the migration from agriculture apparently significantly changed the per capita income distribution between regions in agriculture.

Despite its magnitude, the out-migration from agriculture probably has affected that portion of agriculture producing the bulk of our food and fiber relatively little. Most of the out-movement has been from farms with few resources. There are widespread indications that the out-migration has severely strained the social and economic structure of many rural communities, causing serious problems for churches, schools, and rural businesses dependent on numbers of population.

Most of the policy proposals to facilitate the migration from agriculture have been to improve rural education, job information, and human mobility. These would be of primary benefit to the migrants themselves and to the receiving communities. Few, if any, policies have been proposed that are aimed at alleviating the serious social and economic problems of communities which have been or will be rapidly losing population. Also, little attention has been given to policies to promote the new institutions that will be necessary to facilitate rapid adjustment of the resources remaining in the agricultural economy.

The farm-nonfarm migration has had desirable effects and yet has created problems for the nonfarm economy. Migration made possible an expansion of the nonfarm labor force when the pressure for increased nonfarm output was great. It has also created social and economic problems for which solutions are not yet apparent. It seems probable that the problems will become greater and the benefits of farm-nonfarm migration somewhat less evident to the nonfarm areas in the decade ahead. Unlike the past twenty years, during the next decade there will be a rising number of persons annually available to enter the labor force from within the nonfarm economy. This will be due to the marked rise in birth rates during and since 1940. Thus the need for attracting new labor from the farm population will diminish and the problems of assimilating migrants will probably weigh more heavily upon the consciousness of prospective employers.

All this is to say that even with the favorable economic and social conditions of the past two decades a simple policy of rapid out-migration from agriculture has not, by itself, been sufficient to bring significant improvement in the relative position of the farm economy.

Migration has left unsolved many pressing problems it has helped create.

The total effect of the migration from farms has apparently been of value to both the farm and nonfarm economies. Therefore, it would appear that the nation could well afford some public policies to cope with the social and economic problems attendant to migration. Without such supplemental forces it is unlikely that migration will, by itself, bring about a significant improvement in the position of agriculture.

PART IV

National Policy and Regional Development

Introductory Note

Countries throughout the world, such as England, France, the East European nations, Venezuela, Brazil, and India, are trying to formulate national policies for regional development. Their economic planning tries to take explicit account of the geographic incidence of economic growth and its concomitant social effects. Yet, despite growing experience and the clear political importance of the problem, systematic knowledge has evolved only slowly, and there are few uncontested guidelines for policy.

Regional planning may be described as concerned in the first place with the informational bases for decisions of geographic relevance, ranging from regional survey and analysis to forecasting, project development, and programming. It is also concerned with the statement of appropriate goals for the economy in its spatial dimension, and with the institutional means for the effective coordination of action programs on an areal basis. The readings in this section have accordingly been grouped into three main parts.

The first part has to do with the organizational aspects of regional planning. The articles by John Friedmann and Paul Ylvisaker explore possible criteria for the establishment of regions for administration and programs of development. This is a crucial question, but it often receives excessive attention from policymakers, who sometimes excuse their failure to formulate an adequate regional policy by pointing despairingly to the difficulty of defining an *objective* set of workable planning regions. Since every regional definition is, of necessity, bound to a purpose derived from a national delineation of problems and goals, the definition is generally more mindful of what is socially valuable and politically significant than of scientific accuracy. Planning regions are best defined to be congruent in space with the socioeconomic functions to be carried out. A malaria-control region will consequently be different from one for forestry development or agricultural resettlement. Yet often the search is for a composite region to serve as a framework for developmental planning of a general sort. This effort may lead to contradictions between the requirements of functional planning and those of administration, and even to contradictions among various functional requirements.

Difficult as this problem may be, it is worth recalling that one seldom starts with a clean slate in defining regions. The planning region must be one in which effective action can be taken, and will therefore tend to coincide with existing spatial definitions of authority, such as provinces, states, or counties. It must also be one for which information is available and, since data are normally tabulated according to the traditional governmental divisions of space, the planning region is seldom drawn freely over a map, but is rather composed of predefined building blocks. Except in cases where the function is very narrowly defined, experience has shown the wisdom of emphasizing effectiveness over scholarly nicety in the defining of a region.

The two selections approach this issue in different ways. Friedmann reviews the concept of regional planning as it has evolved in United States planning history and concludes that, in economically advanced countries, the city-region is the most appropriate focus for planning efforts. Paul Ylvisaker, on the other hand, develops a set of general criteria for the decentralization of governmental powers. In essence, he asks who should carry out what functions at what level of government. Such a question involves the making of many value judgments, and Ylvisaker takes pains to make his premises explicit. Debate will continue to rage over the issues he has posed, but they are crucial ones, well deserving of the attention they are receiving. In the United States, the seesaw struggle continues to engage the energies of local, state, and federal interests. In many transitional countries, the mounting pressures of social change are forcing governments to face this question for the first time and to adapt to the changed requirements of modern administration.

The remaining two articles in the first section deal principally with the problems of administrative organization. Too often it is thought that regional planning, which inevitably involves a great deal of coordination, is best carried out by a single authority, and this may explain the proliferation of regional development authorities all over the world. These selections, however, dispute this approach. Ostrom, Tiebout, and Warren construct a model of regional administration based on decentralized decision-making and control, which, they argue, is more effective than the Leviathan based on the popular principle of "one region, one authority." Charles McKinley's article anticipates many of his ideas in *Uncle Sam in the Pacific Northwest,* an outstanding critical study of governmental relations in a large region. It constitutes a valuable assessment of the Tennessee Valley Authority experiment, which for thirty years has exercised a fascination both in the United States and abroad as a prototype of planned regional development. McKinley questions the validity of defining all-purpose regions on the basis of the functional area of a single resource (water), particularly in regions such as urban-industrial ones, in which the particular resource is not of great relevance for their development. He also argues the impracticability of subdividing a national territory into a mosaic of river basin authorities. The general question of the proper balance between functionally defined agencies, such as a Ministry of Agriculture, and geographically defined agencies, such as the TVA, is still very much alive; witness, for example, the frequent reorganizations of Soviet planning and governmental structure in recent years.

The second group of papers deals with the question of the "proper" aims for regional development, and the closely related question of how to measure regional progress. For instance, the meaning of a set of regional goals changes according to the definition of regional boundaries. Consider the issue of regional income equalization. The larger the number of regions in a country, the smaller their average area, and the likelier they are to differ from the national average. Achieving income equalization between two large regions might leave untouched income differences internal to each region. Thus, regional definition and goal formulation are parts of the same intellectual operation.

The practical aims of a polity, however, are inevitably in dispute, and not always substantially rational in Karl Mannheim's sense. In his stimulating discussion of regional objectives, Charles Leven recognizes this fact explicitly. He shows how possible regional goals may be in logical conflict with one another and, in particular, how the goals for all regions taken separately may be at odds with development goals for the nation as a whole. Thus, maximizing growth for every region, however defined, will not necessarily maximize growth for the entire nation. Leven makes use of a linear programing model to illustrate this point. While technical clarification will not remove all sources of conflict, it helps to define with greater precision the policy issues upon which the political process and political authority must ultimately be exercised.

John Krutilla doubts the possibility of aggregate regional welfare measures with which to evaluate accurately development programs. Consequently, he holds that a careful analysis of the costs and benefits of each component project is the best way to evaluate the effectiveness of a program. This often remains good practical counsel, but the decade since Krutilla's article has seen significant progress in the methods of regional social accounting, and the future may yet refute him. Edgar

Hoover and Benjamin Chinitz, two pioneers in this type of analysis, point to how the questions asked by policymakers determine the suitability of alternative analytic approaches. They emphasize the need to put regional social accounting on a long-term, systematic basis to derive the full benefit from such techniques.

The final group of papers deals with questions of development strategy and the criteria of investment allocation. These criteria are rules for making decisions toward ends which are already defined. Since we never can know in advance the direct costs and benefits and the full economic impact of all possible projects in all regions, we must proceed by a close accounting of the direct profitabilities of a relatively few specific projects at particular locations, within the context of some more general rules that deal with more elusive factors such as external economies or the indirect payoffs of social overhead investment. The need to make decisions about specific projects argues for the advisability of having at all times a repertory of possible projects, analyzed to a degree sufficient to permit choice among them within the context of the over-all strategy of a path of development and its timing.

A certain consensus has been building up concerning the strategy of regional development. There is now widespread agreement with Albert Hirschman's view that, in transitional societies, resources should be concentrated in the more promising and dynamic metropolitan centers, permitting development to spill to the other regions from these foci. Louis Lefeber supplements this principle by pointing to the importance of efficiency in the allocation of resources and the key role played in this by a pricing policy that reflects the long-term marginal social costs of the services provided. He further argues that investment should be diverted to the less developed regions only when the more developed have reached a point of self-sustaining, cumulative growth.

M. A. Rahman extends the discussion by calling attention to the significance of the differences in the rate of savings among regions. Thus, by considering the creation as well as the productivity of capital, he shows that an optimal strategy may involve a number of switches in investment priorities between the more and the less productive regions.

In the final paper, Hollis Chenery discusses planning for Italy's Maezzogiorno, which has become the classic case of a backward region within an otherwise developed nation. The original intent was a "welfare" one, trying to reduce the income gap between the North and the South of Italy. However, when a decade's effort had failed to reduce the gap appreciably, a new and more attainable "efficiency" goal was adopted. This was to achieve the structural changes within the southern region necessary to effect self-sustaining growth. The concern with the income gap remained, but in the background.

Four general objectives for regional development in transitional societies emerge from the literature: (1) the spatial integration of the national economy by the encouragement of regional specialization, interregional trade, and factor mobility; (2) efficiency in the pricing and location of investment projects; (3) the maintenance of a politically acceptable balance among regional levels of living; and (4) the promotion of a national growth rate consistent with the other objectives. The balance among these objectives, the tools for achieving them, and even the measures of progress toward them are still being worked out; however their logic is becoming clearer.

Organization for Regional Planning

25. The Concept of a Planning Region—The Evolution of an Idea in the United States*

JOHN FRIEDMANN

Part II of this paper was written in 1955. It does not purport to describe the *practice* of planning in the United States; it attempts, rather, to sketch the *evolution* of an idea: the concept of what is a suitable area for the administration of planning programs. Reference is to the United States, of course, and the focus is on planning activities that in scope exceed municipal boundaries. For urban and regional planning in this country have developed as two different specializations as, indeed, they have in most parts of the world. City planners have been concerned mainly with creating a more efficient physical environment; regional planners have been principally engaged in solving problems of resources and economic development. The reason for this divergence is shown to lie chiefly in the controls available to urban, state, and federal governments for the implementation of policy objectives. The article concludes with a plea for the integration of the regional and urban approaches to planning within areas that have the city as their center of dominant influence.

PART I

American planning practice, and not only the practice but the idea of planning itself, has always been in sharp contrast to the approach popular in Central Europe and elsewhere. Characteristically, it is almost completely devoid of ideological overtones; it is, for the most part, loose and informal; and it is closely linked to operations.[1] As such, it is congenial to the American pragmatic temperament and well adapted to the federal system of decentralized government and ad-

* Reprinted from United Nations, Department of Economic and Social Affairs, Working Paper No. 12, June 25, 1958, and *Land Economics,* Vol. 32 (Feb. 1956).

ministration. The Grand Conception, the Five-Year Plan, is a phenomenon unknown in the United States. Planning tends rather to be piecemeal and experimental.

This is well illustrated by the history of American economic development, a development which might almost be called spontaneous. It was certainly not and still is far from being a centrally directed or planned development. This should not be taken to mean, however, that government has not taken a very active part in economic affairs, be it through fiscal policy, grants-in-aid, subsidies, regulations, research, or resources management. But programs such as these were never, except superficially, related one to the other in a total planning operation. And consequently, there has been no attempt to achieve a regional integration of national policies. Just as no priorities are assigned according to function, so also are there no priorities according to area. Spatial integration has been left to take care of itself. That this approach has, on the whole, been successful is a tribute to the American system. There is no assurance, however, that it would work equally well in other parts of the world.

Regional planning in the United States has at various times had reference to different types of activity as well as to different types of area. There was a time, roughly from 1933 until the end of World War II, when regional planning meant primarily the development of water resources and adjacent land resources within a given river basin. The basic planning unit was the watershed and the objective, the fullest possible use of all physical resources for the improvement of living levels within the area. The Tennessee Valley Authority has been the outstanding example of this type of planning, but a number of other river basins have followed suit: the Columbia, the Central Valley of California, the Missouri, the Arkansas and Red Rivers. Several administrative schemes were tried. The TVA, however, remains the only "authority" in full charge of a comprehensive development program.

The postwar era brought to the fore a different set of problems, and the undogmatic character of planning in the United States made possible a quick adjustment to the new conditions, as attention shifted from the watershed to the metropolitan region as the major planning area. As more and more people streamed into the sprawling urban communities, problems of urban settlement leaped suddenly into the limelight of public concern. City limits had lost their practical significance as population spilled beyond it and as large parts of the United States came within the immediate influence of urban centers. In consequence, so-called regional metropolitan planning agencies sprang up in many parts of the country.

At the same time, there was also a sharp and growing awareness that many states and groups of states had been left behind in the race for industrialization or, at least, were growing less rapidly than the more advanced centers. There were, for instance, the older industrial areas that had failed to create favorable conditions for the expansion of dynamic industries: chemicals, synthetics, electronic machinery. And there were the "new" regions whose spectacular economic growth had, within a few years, created pressing social and physical problems of adjustment. The phenomenal expansion of industrial and commercial investments following the war had thus created a highly competitive mood in all of the 48 states. Each state wanted to get its share of the new wealth. And so there came into being a new type of "regional planning"—area development. Nearly all of the states established planning or development agencies whose principal job was research into the resource possibilities of their respective areas, information about industrial opportunities, and promotion. In very few instances, however, were these agencies also given control over the planning of state capital budgets.

All told, there are in the United States today a vast number of organizations and institutions concerned with various aspects of regional development. Dr. Perloff lists 19 types of groups, comprising hundreds of individual organizations, from City Planning Commissions in the multimillion cities such as Los Angeles and New York, to official Metropolitan Planning Organizations, Metropolitan and Rural Special Districts, State Planning and Development Agencies, Interstate Organizations, private Area Development Agencies, Regional Authorities, consulting firms, and so forth.[2] This multiplicity of "planning" is truly amazing; and yet there is no plan! A plan is largely an instrument for the integration and coordination of policies. But there exist other means for integration, and Americans have generally preferred more informal methods for bringing together various programs to the rigid "blueprint" of a master or development plan.[3]

What is the relevance of this approach to regional planning for other countries, especially for those which are only now beginning their march towards economic independence and higher levels (and standards) of living? In some respects, the approach is difficult to copy, if only because it assumes certain habits of mind and of administration that are peculiarly American. On the other hand, U.S. experience suggests some guidelines that it may be useful to explore, regardless of what the national style may be.

Experimental Character of Planning

As has been mentioned before, American planning has been particularly undogmatic. As new problems have arisen, the approach to planning—concepts, methods, administration—has changed to meet new challenges in the best possible way. Intellectually, this may not be as satisfying as a more theoretical approach; on the other hand, it is appropriate to a view that considers planning not as an end in itself but as a means toward the solution of specific problems. Much, of course, will depend on the definition of the problem itself, the scope that is given to it, and on the objectives to be reached. But in each case, it is the problem that suggests the means for solution, and not the other way around. In situations that are rapidly changing—as with all of the transitional economies throughout the world—the experimental attitude is much to be preferred to the dogmatic.

Flexible Planning Regions

Flexibility in the application of regional concepts is a corollary to the experimental character of planning. Economic development proceeds through different geographic or spatial arrangements: from rural to urban areas—a shift from agriculture to industry; from one or a few small urban-industrial centers and their surrounding regions to progressive regional decentralization of industrial activities; from "dual" economies to a single national market area. At each stage of development, different regional delimitations will be the most convenient and efficient for purposes of planning. Thus, large multistate regions may be the answer in the beginning, and upon these may be superimposed river basin development schemes; later, the metropolitan region may be the answer, with special programs designed for subregions that need particular attention. No one set of regions is ever completely satisfactory. Each problem must be analyzed in its own terms.

Integration of City and Regional Planning

Cities may be considered as centers of economic development: they affect economic patterns in the areas over which their influence extends, and, at the same time, they are affected by the growth which surrounds them. No effective regional planning can be done—in the sense of resource and economic development—without considering the role of cities, without considering the *core* of economic progress. Similarly, a good city planner cannot afford to ignore the character of the "city region" and the whole vast hinterland that surrounds the urban nucleus: the characteristics of growth and the requirements of planning are determined by it. The recent trend in the United States toward metropolitan planning recognizes this interrelationship and is taking measures to cope adequately with it. But even less urbanized countries must face up to this problem, and the delimitation of planning regions and the organization of planning administration should take the unity of city and region into account.

Program Planning

Planning is not really planning unless it is effectively related to action programs and administration. That is partly the reason why planning in the United States has been relatively unobtrusive, so that many visitors to this country have, in fact, gone away convinced that planning here does not exist. But it does exist—as an approach to problem solving. Planning activities are very much a part of the way in which existing organizations carry on their daily business. There may not be any specific group indicated to do the planning because everybody is in a sense engaged in planning. A plan that lacks operational significance is a museum piece, and planning does not necessarily begin with a plan but with introducing greater rationality into public decision-making, through better information (research and analysis) and through foresight (projection). Many alternatives for organizing the administration of planning present themselves. But one of the cardinal rules should be that every planning endeavor must be intimately related to the operations of the institution for which the planning is to be done.

It is reasonable to expect that at least these characteristics of American planning are transferable to other parts of the world. There are other aspects which probably are not, and in certain respects, U.S. experience may not be applicable at all to less developed countries. For example, in the question of evolving a national policy of regional development; or in adjusting national policies according to the unique problems and characteristics of the different regions in a country; or, again, in the integration of national programs within individual regions. These are essentially new problems for much of the world and each country will have to feel its own way, perhaps committing mistakes, but learning from them also, and so, by a method of trial and error, evolving an approach to regional and national planning which will be adequate to meet present and foreseeable problems and will be designed to fit within an existing structure of values and institutions.[4]

NOTE

Part I of this essay is reprinted from United Nations Economic and Social Council, Working Paper No. 12, June 25, 1958, pp. 1–6, by permission of the United Nations Publications Office. The remainder is reprinted from *Land Economics,* Vol. 32 (February 1956), pp. 1–13, by permission of *Land Economics.* (Copyright, 1956 by the University of Wisconsin.)

NOTES

[1] Harvey S. Perloff, *Education for Planning: City, State, and Regional,* Baltimore, The Johns Hopkins Press, 1957, pp. 89–103.

[2] *Ibid.,* pp. 101–103.

[3] Master plans, however, have been used very successfully in city planning, and "blueprint" planning is, of course, customary in private industry. Only in relation to public economic life has formal, over-all planning been rejected.

[4] Interest in problems of regional development has in recent years received great stimulus from the activities of the Regional Science Association with headquarters at the University of Pennsylvania and Resources for the Future, Inc., a Ford Foundation subsidiary located in Washington, D. C. These organizations have contributed greatly to the general revival of academic concern with regional questions, and much interesting work is now going on at a number of universities throughout the country.

PART II
THE CONCEPT OF A PLANNING REGION*

With few exceptions, public planning activities are delimited and organized in space. The region, the county, the metropolitan area, and the city are usually considered to be the basic units for planning.

In the present essay we shall be primarily concerned with the functional relation between the two main forms of areal planning, between city and regional planning. Theoretically, there should be little to distinguish one from the other. In both cases the major problem is the same: how to bring the physical environment in which men live under the controlling influence of the public interest. In practice, however, city and regional planning in the United States have proceeded along diverging paths.

* The writer is indebted to Drs. Harvey S. Perloff and Harold M. Mayer, both of the University of Chicago, for many helpful comments and suggestions during an earlier formulation of this essay.

To explain this lack of unity we would have to go far into the historical origins of planning in this country—a task too ambitious for the present essay.[1] But the basic distinction between city and regional planning appears when we consider it as primarily a difference in *controls* available to local and federal government for guarding the public interest.

In the cities, planning has evolved largely as an effort to maintain existing rental values and to improve the circulation of people and the flow of goods.[2] Zoning, subdivision control, and the powers of eminent domain are among its principal and most effective tools. Occasionally, too, city planners are charged with the preparation of capital improvement budgets, and the planning function has been extended to problems of internal growth and development. In most cities, however, the predominant concern is still with the present. Only peripheral attention seems to be given to a comprehensive approach which would determine the "needs" of the community ten, twenty, or even fifty years ahead and would proceed to show how these "needs" might best be met in the present. Rarely is the community offered a choice to consider what kind of a future it would have. The element of *design* in planning is almost totally lacking, and the evolution of life in the community is left by default to the haphazard interaction of private interests.

Regional planning, on the other hand, has grown up under quite different circumstances.[3] "Regional planning," wrote the National Resources Committee in 1935, "should, in the main, confine itself to dealing with the physical resources and equipment out of which socio-economic progress arises."[4] By this definition, regional planning has one major focus of interest: the development of physical resources. But the control powers of the federal government were so restricted that its point of entry into regional planning was the field of water resources where it had primary jurisdiction. Through the development of water resources for a multiplicity of uses it was hoped that social and economic advance in the watershed would be furthered.[5] The watershed, therefore, became rapidly identified as the "proper" region for planning, and the recognition that land resources are intimately re-related to the use of water only strengthened this view. Whether it was called the Tennessee Valley, the Columbia Basin, the Missouri Valley, the Central Valley, or the Arkansas-Red River Valleys, the physical setting was always a major drainage basin organized for comprehensive resource development. Flood control; the development of facilities for navigation, electric power, irrigation, and recreation; stream sanitation; erosion control and reforestration; even mineral development came to be included under development schemes in major river basins.[6]

The best known and certainly the most advanced regional planning agency in the United States is the Tennessee Valley Authority. Elsewhere in the United States a more complex scheme for regional planning has been worked out which involves a multiplicity of federal agencies such as the Bureau of Reclamation, the Corps of Engineers, the Soil Conservation Service, and the Forest Service; and, to an increasing extent state and local organizations. In every instance, however, administration is found to be organized along regional (watershed) lines.

The contrast between city and regional planning which we have attempted to sketch may be summarized by saying that city planning has been primarily concerned with community conservation through land use planning and control while the purpose of planning for regions has been economic progress through the development of natural reresources. What Catherine Bauer calls an "iron curtain" has descended between city and resources planners.[7] Two different professions, two different vocabularies have grown up. Communication between them has become exceedingly difficult, and on the level of practical action there appears to be little coordination between schemes of regional and urban development.

Now, coordination is no absolute value. It becomes valuable only where it furthers a particular objective. Thus, we may well ask whether regional planning as currently organized can achieve the end of sustained economic progress without taking explicitly into account the existence of urban centers and whether city planning in its present form can effectively achieve *its* purposes while ignoring the larger regional framework within which the city has to function. These questions have not as yet received adequate attention.

The concept of the region as a tool for planning had its origin in the Great Depression. There had been forerunners, of course, such as the Regional Planning Number of the *Survey Graphic* in 1925,[8] and the writings of Benton MacKaye[9] but, as late as 1934, Hedwig Hintze could write in the *Encyclopedia of the Social Sciences* that "in the United States regionalism has never really appeared."[10] To be sure, there existed many examples of metropolitan planning in New York, Boston, Washington, Chicago, Los Angeles and several of the other large American cities but, as we shall see, the "new regionalism" explicitly rejected the metropolitan area as a logical unit for planning.

The new philosophy took hold especially in the South where planning came to be looked upon as the truly dynamic aspect of regionalism.[11] It was an essential particle of the regionalist's fate that planning would provide the means toward the "rehabilitation of the people, toward the reconstruction of regional economy, toward increasing the region's revenue to the nation as well as its own wealth, and toward general regional, cultural adjustment."[12] The South saw in regional planning an opportunity to halt the decline of its resources and its people and to achieve what came to be vaguely referred to as "regional balance," while yet maintaining its unique agrarian culture and tradition. Whether there was not, indeed, a conflict among these objectives is a question that was not apparently considered.

The writers primarily responsible for elaborating on this concept of the planning region were teaching at Southern universities.[13] And the South, in their view, was indeed the archetype of a "true" region. It was identified with a distinctive "folk culture," the region being "an expression of the folk who occupy it and who give it a distinctive character through their 'natural' extra-organized, extra-technological, and unrationalized ways of life."[14] Folk culture, no doubt, was the cohesive bond that held a region together. But it was not sufficient for a definition. The region was also a distinctive area because it possessed "the largest possible degree of homogeneity measured by the largest possible number of economic, cultural, administrative, and functional indices, for the largest possible number of objectives."[15] Clearly, only a rural economy could, by any stretch of the imagination, be considered sufficiently "homogeneous" to qualify as a region. Though urbanization had made progress in the South, it had not yet drawn the focus of regional interest upon itself.[16]

An imagery of rural values still prevailed in the 1930's.[17] Perhaps the most amazing document of the times is a collection of essays written by twelve Southern writers in which the issue was unambiguously posed: agrarian versus industrial society.[18] These essays turned into a vigorous defense of the "Southern way of life," of traditionalism against what the authors called the "American or prevailing way," against progressivism. Industry must never come to the South in large numbers; the South was to remain a separate cultural enclave, a sanctuary of leisurely culture in the "European" sense.[19] And when a few years later TVA set about to develop the great hydro-electric potential of the Tennessee River, even *Fortune* magazine in an otherwise sympathetic article expressed grave doubts that all of the energy produced by federal dams could ever be sold to industrial consumers.[20]

Economic betterment in the South could be accomplished only by over-all planning—that, at least, was the current belief. *Laissez-faire* as a solution to the difficulties confronting the South was rejected as "futile and cruel."[21] The New Deal provided the impetus for planning. And the homogeneous, natural region seemed to be ideally suited to the comprehensive planning approach. No one, it might be added, seemed to be especially surprised by this strange wedding between Southern rural conservatism (region) and Northern progressivism (planning).[22]

The National Resources Committee which sponsored an extensive study of the region for planning tried to avoid some of the pitfalls of the ideological approach taken by its Southern proponents. "Regional planning," the Committee stated, "is not an end in itself; rather it is an instrument for arranging certain things more successfully. It is a basis for action. It is a means for deriving sensible policies and programs, and it should be an aid in determining what kinds of devices are most suited to carrying out these policies and programs."[23] But the ideology was in the air; it was pervasive, and it entered as an unconscious bias into the thinking of the Committee when it rejected the concept of the region based upon metropolitan influence:

> "To construct regions which would adhere to cities rather than to the broader aspects of resources, economic patterns and regional interests is to place the emphasis upon one factor rather than the total region. Upon such a basis, regional planning tends to become an expanded form of city planning. On the other hand, it is by no means certain that planning has not arisen at least in part out of necessity of preserving local rural culture and resources against chaotic economic and social forces emanating from the city. Even were cities themselves carefully planned, this would still be true, for the city is an organism whose very nature places its nutritive processes above larger regional considerations."[24]

This was in 1935. In 1938, Lewis Mumford published his brilliant study on *The Culture of Cities*.[25] While generally sympathetic to the Southern exponents of regional planning, he could not—and would not —escape the basic fact that it was the city which gave a region its cultural vitality. Like his Southern brothers-in-arms, he thought he recognized the region as a "natural area." But, he added, "to define human areas, one must seek, not the periphery alone but the center."[26] The city was thus a fact of the utmost geographic importance "for the urban center tends to focus the flow of energies, men, and goods that passes through a region, concentrating them, dispersing them, diverting them, rerouting them, in short, exerting a close and controlling influence over the development of region as a dynamic reality."[27] The city was viewed as analogous to the heart of the body: a controlling mechanism which pumps the life blood of energy, people, and commerce to all parts of the regional organism.

Shortly after the appearance of Mumford's book came the war, and with it began the sudden and startling rejuvenation of the American economy. Already by 1942 there were signs that the wind had shifted: the city was beginning to make an impression on the consciousness of the nation. In a challenging article, Louis Wirth proposed the metropolitan region as a planning unit.[28] That a restatement of the principles of metropolitan planning was necessary at this time only emphasizes the pervasive influence which the Southern School of regionalists had had on the spatial organization of planning. Wirth proposed that the immediate area constituting the region should be the area of daily intimate and vital interrelation between the city, its suburbs, and periphery and, further, that the region should be a unit "which takes account of the city's and its surrounding area's place in the national and world economy."[29]

Toward the end of the war there appeared a sharply critical article which attacked what it recognized as the rural traditionalist bias of regionalism on the grounds that it had failed to do justice to the facts of the technological revolution that was remaking America. "Regionalism," wrote Kollmorgen, "runs counter to the technological aspects of society which are universal and dominant and will eventually prevail over discordant folkways which regionalists may try to perpetuate."[30] Urbanism, to Kollmorgen, was the "wave of the future" that would sweep everything before its onrushing advance.

But the rural values propounded by the regionalists derived from a hardy stock and would not die so easily. Two years after Kollmorgen's incisive critique, and already well into the postwar era, a group of Yale University social scientists and planners resurrected the imagery of a natural region with its foundation in folk culture.[31] This time, however, the regionalists went beyond the traditional requirements of "geographic unities" and "homogeneous desires, attitudes, and wants," and suggested a forceful analogy of the region with individual living organisms.[32] Living in one of the most urbanized, industrial "regions" in the United States, the authors of the Yale Report searched for a regional philosophy that would somehow conform to their urban experience. In "biologism" they found an adequate basis for their beliefs by which they could challenge the mechanistic aspects of an urban society which they at once accepted and opposed. In this, they came very close to Lewis Mumford's own interpretation a decade earlier.

The Yale Report was perhaps the last outburst of the regional planning ideology in this country. But it did not mean the end of regional research as such. Since 1947 a number of regional studies have been published which continue the long line of such studies first begun by the National Resources Planning Board in the 1930's. The *Economy of the South,* sponsored by the United States Council of Economic Advisers, was one of these and a typical example of the difficulties that the older regionalists encountered.[33] The study included 13 Southern states, chosen on the basis of a "certain homogeneity in geography, population, climate, income, and history," but especially because each of these states was felt to be vitally concerned "in the production of one or both of the two great cash crops which dominate the agriculture of the region, cotton and tobacco."[34] But no sooner had they stated it, than the authors of the Report retracted this inclusive definition. "In fact," they continue, "the problem of homogeneity arises almost as soon as more than one State is included if, indeed it does not arise within the borders of a single State."[35] From a rigorous, scientific viewpoint a definition of the region according to homogeneous factors seemed rather a shaky one in 1949.

A second important regional study dealt with the New England economy.[36] But here the problem of definition appeared in even a more striking form. While purporting to deal with the whole of the "region," the report is actually preoccupied with southern New England, to the relative neglect of rural Maine, Vermont, and northern New Hampshire. Although in their statistics the authors were compelled to admit the basic north-south distinction inherent in the human geography of the region, they described New England elsewhere as an "old industrial community." But surely this is no more than half of the story. The "region" turns out, in fact, to be two, divided among an even greater number of metropolitan spheres of influence.

The very ambiguity of both these reports regarding the nature of their "regions" suggests that the old conceptions had become of doubtful value. A new regional order and a new kind of planning appeared in the making, an order based on "interdependence" instead of a spurious homogeneity. And again it was Louis Wirth who spoke out for the new concept.[37] In such a region, he wrote, "the component parts are not necessarily similar or identical but stand in a relationship of significant interdependence or integration of life in one or more respects. Such a region finds difficulty in delineating its boundaries, but is more likely to have a salient or dominant center . . . ."[38] His article helped to clear the way to a view of regional planning that would be in greater accordance with the facts of economic development. To an elaboration of this view we shall now proceed.

It was primarily through the efforts of the Chicago school of sociologists during the 1930's—building on the pathbreaking work of McKenzie—that the concept of the metropolitan region as the logical unit for planning was developed and refined.[39] Concurrently with these studies at Chicago, the German geographer, Walter Christaller, suggested that any inhabited area would exhibit a certain structure of settlement which may be read as a hierarchy of central places standing in a mutually dependent relationship to each other.[40] The validity of Christaller's rigid geometrical pattern of central places has been variously questioned.[41] Its main influence, however, was to provide a new perspective on regionalism and regional structure. To the attentive reader it suggested an approach which by-passed the old problem of delineating homogeneous "folk-regions."

The first major advance beyond these pre-war researches was achieved in this country by Donald Bogue, who provided large-scale empirical evidence for the theory of metropolitan dominance advanced by McKenzie and offered aggregate measurements of metropolitan regional structure.[42] The next step in the development of metropolitan theory soon followed with an attempt to bring together the theories of regional structure as a system of central places (Christaller) and of metropolitan structure (Bogue). Rutledge Vining of the University of Virginia, in a highly stimulating paper, proposed to view the human landscape as an "inter-connected system of central places."[43] Vining appeared to be strongly influenced in his theory by certain traffic flow maps he had seen for the United States. Indeed, his maps seemed clearly to indicate an hierarchical pattern of cities that transcended any "regional" boundaries and presented instead a picture of economic "flows" of different densities, joining one city to another.

This novel view of the "region," in effect, dispensed with the traditional regional concept altogether. Rather, it pictured a *system of cities* having certain properties of stability, though individual units within the system might always be shifting.[44] Considerable support for this view can be found in the long-run trends of the American economy.

An ever-increasing proportion of the total population lives today in cities or on the periphery of cities. According to Bogue, 57 percent of the population in 1950 lived in the 162 metropolitan areas defined by the Census, and the proportion continues to rise with each year.[45] Shift of population from rural to urban-metropolitan areas implicit in these figures is well portrayed in recent Census maps: population appears to move into clusters around a relatively small number of central places, and most of the rural countryside is becoming rapidly depopulated. Much of this growth during the past two decades occurred within the "rings" of metropolitan areas, however, rather than in central cities.[46] A rough picture of this important trend may be got by comparing the growth rates of urban and rural non-farm populations during recent decades. Between 1930 and 1950 urban population in the United States increased by 30 percent, contrasted with a 64 percent gain in the rural non-farm sector.[47] Most of this gain was in the suburbs.

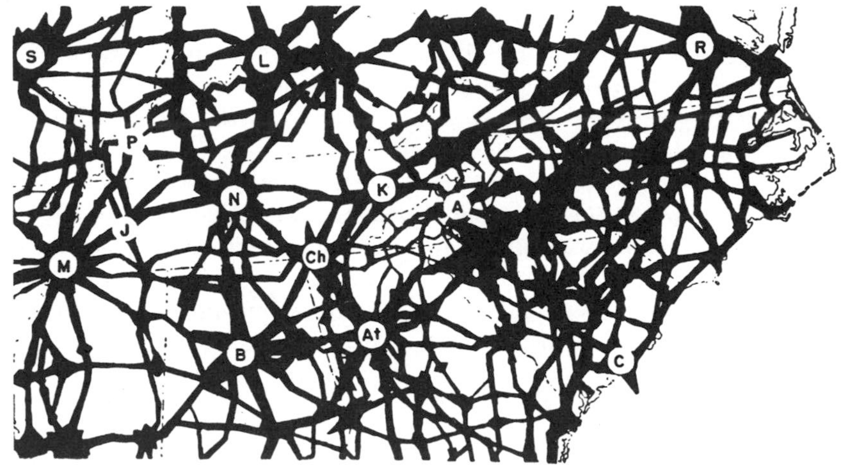

FIG. 1. Traffic flow map, southeast United States, 1952: average daily volume of traffic on main routes with lines proportional to density of traffic. *Source:* United States Department of Commence. Bureau of Public Roads.
Legend: **A** Asheville **At** Atlanta **B** Birmingham **C** Charleston **Ch** Chattanooga **J** Jackson **K** Knoxville **L** Louisville **M** Memphis **N** Nashville **P** Paducah **R** Richmond **S** St. Louis

With a high concentration of population in cities and in the areas peripheral to them, central places also gained relatively in economic power. Transport and communications systems came increasingly to focus on the dominant cities. The traffic flow map reveals the striking instance of "nodality" in the flow of the economy.

Population growth centering around cities must be viewed in the context of the upheaving changes in the American economy which have led to a progressive reduction of employment in farming and to a corresponding increase of opportunities in manufacturing and other sources of employment. The full development of a system of cities is related to economic changes and the particular pattern to which it conforms is dependent on the stage of economic maturity which the economy has reached. With rapid industrialization, new non-farm jobs tend to become available at a faster rate in the larger cities of an area than elsewhere.[48] And income changes, on the whole, parallel this movement of jobs to the large cities.[49] Economic development seems, indeed, to act in such a way as to enhance the possibilities of further growth at central places.[50] Not only does industrialization tend to improve the accessibility of an area by encouraging the provision of a wider variety of transportation services in the center, but it creates its own markets, tends to tip the balance of available capital for investment in favor of the city, and contribute to the progressive specialization of the labor force.[51] And once a pattern of urban settlement is established, its basic structure tends to perpetuate itself.

As the larger cities become more heterogeneous, the smaller cities and communities within their sphere of influence become functionally more specialized. Some grow into "satellites" of the center, others into specialized service, industrial or market cities. While the center of economic power in this pattern is the metropolis, all the communities within its economic reach are mutually dependent upon one another and upon the metropolitan center in its turn.[52]

The emerging pattern of the economy—what Lampard calls its metropolitan phase[53]—is thus built up increasingly around the *city region* with its dense urban core, its less densely populated outer "ring" (population declining outward toward the periphery of this "ring" along the major routes of access), and its satellite communities.[54] With increasing industrialization the conditions for further rapid growth in city regions tend to improve, and the "links" between and among city regions—in terms of population flows and the flows of goods and communications—tend to be strengthened. There is increasing interdependency throughout, and the structure of the whole economy tends to become more precisely defined along functional lines.

If this description of the spatial structure of a developing economy is substantially correct, we conclude that the city region has, in fact, become the basic areal unit for carrying out comprehensive developmental planning below the national level. It is a region defined by an intricate pattern of economic and social interdependencies; it is, therefore, a "community" informed of certain common interests; and above all, the locus of socio-economic power for a broader geographic area.

The basic requirement for the existence of a city region is transportation. Modern transportation facilities permit the outer "ring" to extend outward from the city core for about one hour's driving distance along major highways and connecting tributary roads.[55] Rapid transportation makes possible the ingathering of materials (e.g., lumber) from within this "ring" as well as the distribution of goods to outlying points of consumption. And it enables individuals to commute freely to most places of employment within the city region which, in turn, permits a more rational ordering of residential, industrial, commercial, and recreational areas. Accessible and rapid transportation is the means by which the various sections of the city region are welded together into a unified whole; it is modern transportation which has made the city region at all possible.

In the past, regional planning in the United States has dealt primarily with the problem of resource development as a means for improving the economic welfare of people, while city planning has been mainly concerned with problems of land use control and circulation. Now we may argue that both of these functions—development and control—should be brought together in a common framework and that the logical framework for this purpose is the city region.

The focus of economic development is thus shifted from a broader territorial basis and an emphasis on *natural* resources to the city region and an emphasis on *metropolitan* resources, such as transportation, space, and community organization. Given this focus, planning for the city region should proceed along two parallel courses of action: (1) in the direction of developing metropolitan resources with a view to encouraging general economic prosperity; and (2) in the direction of controlling land use so as to create a pleasing, no less than an efficient, environment for living. Thus conceived, the planning function should extend across the entire area dominated by the central city.

The resources of most city regions in the United States are far from being fully developed. Yet the socio-economic reality of city regions will not be wholly attained until its resources have been brought to optimum productive levels.

Transportation is perhaps the most strategic of these sources where it unfolds the locational advantages of the city region. It allows for accessibility to the center and for rapid circulation among the various parts of the city region. Speaking in metaphor, we may say that transportation is the "nervous system" of a regional organism and is absolutely vital to its survival. It will influence both the structure and the efficient functioning of the city region as a center of economic development. Robert B. Mitchell, in the foreword to a study of accessibility in southeastern Pennsylvania, writes much in the same vein:

> "Our 20th century technology makes possible a close and rapid contact among all parts of a great metropolitan area. Distance need be measured no longer by miles, but by minutes and convenience. This is the one most powerful fact in shaping the nature and arrangement of the various metropolitan localities. The potential of each locality is largely determined by its accessibility to other parts of the region. In turn the prosperity of the region as a whole will be very much affected by the quality of its internal circulation system."[56]

In improved internal transportation, Mitchell sees a way to "maximize opportunities for the good life and for prosperity in the Region."[57]

Second in importance only to transportation, are the space resources of the region. It is true that both transportation and space have traditionally been recognized as areas central to the concerns of city planners, but they have seldom been looked upon as *resources* which may be *developed* to assist in the economic growth of a "region."

Space is always in limited supply, modified as it is by its location, physical attributes, and the extent of man-made improvements on the land. It would be a radical mistake to believe that useful or "economic" space in the area surrounding a central city is co-extensive with the total number of square miles of this area, simply because this area does not as yet appear to be densely settled. The techniques of land use planning, subdivision control, and zoning are becoming quite as necessary in the less inhabited areas of a region as within the crowded urban core itself.[58]

A third important resource of the city region is found in the organization of its community life. As the city proper is itself often composed of different "neighborhoods," and as these join with one another in the polity of city life, so does the city region form a "community" which is composed of a number of interrelated parts: the urban core, industrial "satellites," "suburban" residential areas, village communities, and areas reserved for recreation and agricultural use. The economic integration of the city region will be expressed through the proper planning of its transportation and space resources, but it must be reflected in the social integration of the city region as well. Social integration sets limits to the possible economic integration of regional life. No part of the city region can fully develop its potentialities except within this larger regional framework. Functional differentiation compels the component parts of the region to strive for closer mutual ties and always greater interaction. It is the development of the city region as a truly urban *community* which assures to each component part its special advantages and resources.

The basic spatial relations in an economy are found (1) between a central city and its surrounding region and (2) between one city region and another. The first type of relationship and its significance for planning has been described in the foregoing section. The second type of relationship has greater relevancy for national planning. Differences in the level of economic development among larger socio-economic "regions," such as those defined by the Census, are gradually disappearing in the United States.[59] A truly *national* economy is emerging, with individual "regions," in the old sense, gradually losing their claims to special federal attention. Regional criteria of "need" are no longer as determining to policy as criteria derived from purely national "needs."

Not only are the old regional differences in the United States disappearing, but most of the more densely settled parts of the country may eventually come within the influence of city regions. The landscape will be overlaid with a network of such regions, one region joined to the other. Donald Bogue came to a similar conclusion when he wrote:

> "In the not too distant future . . . . the number of metropolitan centers may increase to such an extent that 65 miles will be the maximum distance which most areas lie from a central city, and technological improvements in transportation may permit all communities within this radius to participate directly with the metropolis."[60]

If this hypothesis is correct, and already it seems to hold true for large sections of the country, attention in national planning will have to shift increasingly to the relations *among* city regions. Transportation assumes a major role in defining these relations, and the current high pitch of interest in express highways is indicative of this trend.

In addition to planning for the city region and inter-regional relations, special resource problems may arise from time to time which call for a different areal organization than the one we have emphasized in this essay. In the case of power, water, or recreation resources, to cite some prominent examples, development may be organized on the basis of "functional" regions. Such a region may consist of an integral number of city regions grouped together for the purpose of planning a single function. In view of the interlinked pattern of city regions emerging in the more densely populated parts of the country, this particular form of regional organization is one likely to be followed. There are other possibilities, of course, where a functional region such as a watershed would cut across city regional boundaries or where several states would join in the solution of a mutual problem. But even here, the fact that city regions exist will loom large in planning considerations.

Although as much as 90 percent of the total population of the country may eventually reside within city regions, there will be large areas of sparsely settled land that fall outside the immediate influence of central cities. Such areas as the Cumberland Plateau, the Blue Ridge Mountains, the Ozarks, the Great Lakes cut-over regions, parts of northern New England, and large sections of the Southwest and West fall in this category. They pose special planning problems due to the poverty of their populations and their limited resources. An extensive type of development through recreation, forestry, or grazing will ofen form the basic approach to these areas. They are regions characterized by special physical disadvantage for a more intensive development. They may be called "functional regions" when public policy addresses itself specifically to problems related to the development of their resources. However, the name is unimportant. What is important is the recognition that special problems beset these areas; that they fall outside the existing pattern of city regions and thus outside the main stream of economic progress; and that only a small proportion of the country's population will reside in them.

Apart from these special areas, the United States economy maintains a definite spatial structure expressed in the pattern formed by city regions, and functional planning will usually be carried out successfully where it is closely related to this pattern, point for point. City regions are the nerve centers of economic life in an area. They are the seats of economic power where most of the population is concentrated, where most of the vital decisions affecting larger areas are made, and where the financial means are present for carrying these decisions into action. Any planning which ignores this primary fact about the spatial structure of an economy must be judged unrealistic.

NOTES

[1] For an excellent and comprehensive summary, cf. R. G. Tugwell and E. C. Banfield, "Governmental Planning at Mid-Century," *The Journal of Politics,* XIII (1951), p. 133–163.

[2] Robert B. Mitchell and Chester Rapkin, *Urban Traffic: A Function of Land Use* (New York: Columbia University Press, 1954).

[3] In the present context, metropolitan planning will be treated as a form of city planning. This coincides with the view expressed by Benton MacKaye and Lewis Mumford in their article on "Regional Planning" which first appeared in the 14th edition of the *Encyclopedia Britannica* in 1929.

[4] National Resources Committee, *Regional Factors in National Planning* (Washington: U. S. Government Printing Office, 1935), p. 156.

[5] For example, Gordon Clapp, shortly before his resignation as Chairman of the Board of TVA wrote: "Those who urged the enactment of the TVA Act apparently believed that, if the Tennessee River were conquered and its water power harnessed, the river would help transform the economic life of the region and increase the productive capacity of the nation. Nothing less than the resources of the United States Government could cope with this task." *TVA: An Approach to Regional Development* (Chicago: The University of Chicago Press, 1955), p. 14.

[6] President's Water Resources Policy Commission, *A Water Policy for the American People,* Vol. I (Washington: U. S. Government Printing Office, 1950).

[7] Catherine Bauer, "Economic Progress and Living Conditions," *The Town Planning Review,* January 1954, p. 303.

[8] *Survey Graphic,* May 1925.

[9] Benton MacKaye, *The New Exploration: A Philosophy of Regional Planning* (New York: Harcourt, Brace and Co., 1928).

[10] In the article on "Regionalism."

[11] Howard W. Odum and Harry Estill Moore, *American Regionalism* (New York: Henry Holt and Co., 1938), p. 253.

[12] *Ibid.,* p. 254.

[13] Howard W. Odum, "The Case for Regional National Social Planning," *Social Forces,* October 1934, pp. 6–23; Rupert B. Vance, "Implications of the Concept 'Region and Regional Planning'," *Publication of the American Sociological Society,* August 1935, pp. 85–93; T. J. Woofter, Jr., "Southern Population and Social Planning," *Social Forces,* October 1935, pp. 16–22; Harry E. Moore, *What Is Regionalism* (Chapel Hill: The University of North Carolina Press, 1937); John V. Van Sickle, *Planning for the South* (Nashville, Tenn.: Vanderbilt University Press, 1943).

[14] Moore, *op cit.,* p. 13.

[15] Odum and Moore, *op. cit.,* p. 272.

[16] Walter J. Matherly, "The Urban Development of the South," *The Southern Economic Journal,* February 1935, pp. 3–26. For more recent evidence, cf. Rupert B. Vance and Nicholas J. Demerath (eds.), *Urban South* (Chapel Hill, N. C.: Univ. Press, 1955).

[17] A dawning recognition that the rural way of life in the South might be in the process of being swallowed by progressive urbanization is found in Van

Sickle, *op. cit.,* pp. 76 ff. Van Sickle wrote his book at the crest of the war-time wave of expansion of industry in 1943.

[18] Twelve Southerners, *I'll Take My Stand* (New York: Harper and Brothers, 1930).

[19] *Ibid.,* p. 3.

[20] "TVA: Federal Power," *Fortune,* May 1935, pp. 156–160.

[21] Van Sickle, *op. cit.,* p. ix.

[22] That planning had struck its roots in the urban reformist movement during the early part of this century and that its methods and techniques were carried over into the national scene during the New Deal has been strikingly demonstrated by Rexford G. Tugwell in "The Sources of New Deal Reformism," *Ethics,* July 1954, pp. 249–276.

[23] National Resources Committee, *op. cit.,* p. 167.

[24] *Ibid.,* p. 159.

[25] Lewis Mumford, *The Culture of Cities* (New York: Harcourt, Brace and Co., 1938).

[26] *Ibid.,* p. 315.

[27] *Ibid.*

[28] Louis Wirth, "The Metropolitan Region as a Planning Unit," *National Conference on Planning,* Proceedings of the Conference held at Indianapolis, Indiana, May 25–27, 1942 (Chicago: American Society of Planning Officials, 1942), pp. 141–151.

[29] *Ibid.,* p. 150.

[30] Walter M. Kollmorgen, "Crucial Deficiencies of Regionalism," *American Economic Review,* Papers and Proceedings, May 1945, p. 377.

[31] Yale University, *The Case for Regional Planning,* with Special Reference to New England (New Haven: Yale University Press, 1947).

[32] *Ibid.,* p. 36.

[33] Joint Committee on the Economic Report, (Washington: U. S. Government Printing Office, 1949).

[34] *Op. cit.,* p. 1.

[35] *Ibid.*

[36] U. S. Council of Economic Advisers, *The New England Economy* (Washington, U. S. Government Printing Office, 1951).

[37] Louis Wirth, "The Limitations of Regionalism," *Regionalism in America,* edited by Merrill Jensen, (Madison, Wisconsin: The University of Wisconsin Press, 1951), pp. 381–393.

[38] *Ibid.,* p. 383.

[39] Roderick D. McKenzie, *The Metrooplitan Community* (New York: McGraw-Hill Book Co., Inc. 1935). Indeed, metropolitan regionalism in 1951 was not a new phenomenon; but it was now new in its more or less self-conscious opposition to the Southern regional school.

[40] Walter Christaller, *Die Zentralen Orte in Sueddeutschland* (Jena: Gustav Fischer Verlag, 1933). See also the discussion of Christaller's theory in Robert E. Dickinson's *City Region and Regionalism* (London: Kegan Paul, Trench, Trubner and Co., 1947); for a more recent critical review, Rutledge Vining, "A Description of Certain Spatial Aspects of an Economic System," *Economic Development and Cultural Change,* January 1955, pp. 160–165.

[41] The most recent example is Vining, *op. cit.*, pp. 164–5. Also August Lösch. *The Economics of Location* (New Haven: Yale University Press, 1954), p. 433.

[42] Don J. Bogue, *The Structure of the Metropolitan Community* (Ann Arbor, Michigan: Horace H. Rackham School of Graduate Studies, University of Michigan, 1950).

[43] Rutledge Vining, "Delimitation of Economic Areas: Statistical Conceptions of the Spatial Structure of an Economic System," *Journal of the American Statistical Association,* March 1953, pp. 44–64.

[44] Vining, "A Description of Certain Spatial Aspects . . . ," *op. cit.,* p. 185.

[45] Donald J. Bogue, *Population Growth in Standard Metropolitan Areas, 1900–1950,* (Washington: Housing and Home Finance Agency, 1953), p. vii.

[46] *Ibid.,* p. 18.

[47] *U. S. Census of Population,* 1930, 1940, and 1950. To insure comparability of data, the old Census definitions of "urban" and "rural non-farm" were used for 1950.

[48] John R. P. Friedmann, *The Spatial Structure of Economic Development in the Tennessee Valley,* Research Paper No. 1, Program of Education and Research in Planning (The University of Chicago, March 1955), chaps. II and III.

[49] *Ibid.,* chap. V.

[50] *Ibid.,* chap. VI.

[51] *Ibid.,* pp. 31–36.

[52] The metropolitan center is itself related to other centers and, according to Vining, occupies a place in the hierarchy of cities within the national system as a whole. What we have attempted to describe in the preceding pages is only the growth of one of the sub-systems within the larger system for the nation.

[53] Eric E. Lampard, "The History of Cities in the Economically Advanced Areas," *Economic Development and Cultural Change,* January 1955, p. 102.

[54] The term "city region" is preferred to "metropolitan region" because the concept is meant to apply also to cities which are smaller than those defined by the Census as "metropolitan." According to the Census, the population minimum for the central city of a standard metropolitan area is 50,000. "City region," as here defined, may be areas with a central urban core of about 30,000 population. The parallel British term would be "town region."

[55] Friedmann, *op. cit.,* p. 67. Cf. also Frank G. Coolsen *et al., Paducah and Western Kentucky:* Income, Labor, and Retail Trade Patterns (Frankfort, Ky.: The Agricultural and Industrial Development Board of Kentucky, 1952); and Robert N. Gold, *Manufacturing Structure and Pattern of the South Bend-Mishawaka Area* (Research Paper No. 36, Department of Geography, The University of Chicago, June 1954).

[56] The Southeastern Pennsylvania Regional Planning Commission, *Time-Distance* (Bridgeport, Pa., 1954).

[57] *Ibid.*

[58] The consequences of ignoring these problems are vividly stated by Karl Belsen in his "Misuse of Land in Fringe Areas and Inadequate Subdivision Standards," *Problems of Decentralization in Metropolitan Areas,* Department of City and Regional Planning, University of California, 1954. (Mimeographed.)

[59] Charles A. R. Wardwell, *Regional Trends in the United States Economy* (Washington: U. S. Government Printing Office, 1951), especially Chap. I.

[60] Bogue, *The Structure of the Metropolitan Community, op. cit.,* p. 55.

26. Some Criteria for a "Proper" Areal Division of Governmental Powers*

PAUL YLVISAKER

I

THE PURPOSES OF THIS SYMPOSIUM, as I understand them, are two: a) to tackle the substantive problem of developing a theory of the areal division of governmental powers; b) to do so in a way which will hopefully facilitate further and more systematic inquiry, not least in that tradition of empirical research and model-building which is so representative of American social science. These are some formidable assignments, and we can obviously do no more than nibble at them. My own efforts here will be, *first:* to identify the instrumental values which the areal division of power is presumed to realize, and the ultimate values in terms of which it must find its reason for being; *second:* to suggest a few criteria (or maxims) for dividing governmental power on an areal basis so that in fact this division realizes, or helps realize, both sets of values.

II

At this very early point it is the better part of wisdom and honor to make a few qualifying remarks, and to state a number of conditions which will be assumed; in short, to show how and why the argument will be biased and hedged.

1. The argument deals with the areal division of powers as a working device of an already united state, not as an instrument of courtship to attract independent areas into a govern-

*Reprinted from Arthur Maass, ed., *Area and Power: A Theory of Local Government.*

mental alliance. The results of the distinction are significant. To illustrate, a premium is likely to be placed—during what Professor Macmahon has called the "emergent" stage—on the assignment and legal guarantees of exclusive powers, whereas in the "mature" or "working" stage which we will be concerned with, the trend and proper emphasis is toward a sharing of power, worked out largely on a pragmatic and informal basis.[1]

2. By instruction of the editor, the argument assumes "a country much like the United States" (i.e., a democratic and industrialized state), though with a clean slate of areal institutions. It follows that the argument is, to that considerable extent, culture-bound; and there would seem to be good reason for making it so. The ultimate test of governmental institutions is whether they express and help realize the basic values of the society they are intended to serve. World-wide, we are forced to recognize differentiated value systems; in the case of the fictional state in point, the argument assumes what are held to be the three basic values of the modern democratic state: liberty, equality, and welfare.

To admit this much is not very painful, since it does no serious damage to the analysis being developed: assume either a fixed set of eternal values, or any different set, and the mode of argument remains the same.

But there is more to confess, which introduces a note of provincialism and bias into the argument that ought to be recognized and allowed for. Try as I have to abstract myself from the limiting circumstance of intergovernmental relations in the United States, what follows is influenced by that experience, and may be nothing more than a selection and rationalization of what I believe to be its proper lessons and principles. In which case all we can do is hope that my reading of that experience is not too far wrong, and that the lessons and principles are of some general validity.

That much confessed, the remaining assumptions can be listed with but one further caution. The factors which appear in these assumptions are fuzzy and overlapping. For that reason, and because supporting research is so sadly lacking, it is impossible in most cases to identify these factors as either dependent or independent variables. All of which makes systematic inquiry in this field inordinately difficult—and as I can now testify, frustrating in the extreme.

3. A relatively mobile and undifferentiated society, experimental and pragmatic in its approach to governmental problems, disposed to debate and compromise rather than to the use of force.

4. Social and economic pluralism; or as John Fischer has put it, a society in which the elements of real power are in reasonable balance.

5. A tradition of the rule of law, and a dedication to peaceful change.

6. Political tolerance or maturity to abide whatever attenuation of the governmental process there may be as a result of the areal division of powers.

7. Economic capacity to afford whatever waste there may be in the fact of several governments rather than one.

8. No unusual barriers to communication among the component areas, such as might be introduced by the language and race factor in South Africa, the physical isolation of Pakistan from East Pakistan, or the nationality question in some of the pre-War states of Central Europe. ("Usual" barriers—such as the current differences between North and South, suburb and central city, business and labor, rural and urban—are admitted as proper obstacles to the argument.)

9. No such emotional, historical or mystical attachment to the areal division of powers as would create or preserve that division for its own sake. This is the one possible departure from our own cultural circumstance which the argument must necessarily make. It may be that the areal division of powers as we practice it in the United States is an obsolescent institution, kept because we are fond of it, used to it, and have the illusion it protects us from tyranny, poverty, and abuse. On an understanding of man and the irrationality of his political process, we may want to return to these as reasons enough to justify the institution; for now, however, our working hypothesis is that

the areal division of powers is an effective part of a more rational process.

10. The existence of alternatives to the areal division of powers. A forceful argument can be made that there is no choice, that some form of an areal division of powers is inevitable in any culture, and under any governmental system. The premise here, however, is that there are alternatives, ranging from systems (of estates, guilds, syndicates etc.) by which power is deconcentrated, to the slightest form of decentralization, under a unitary state with but tightly controlled administrative outposts.

11. An area of free will in establishing and perfecting governmental institutions. This is to deny, but not disprove, the contention that the areal division of power is wholly a function of economic or other environmental conditions.

All of which, I cheerfully admit, leaves the argument seemingly very little to contend with. But given the scarcity and lack of direction of dispassionate inquiry in this field, we may still have accomplished something merely by identifying the variables that have to be dealt with, and by giving some sense of proportion and direction, if only by the simplest of analytical guides. And, to borrow a convenient "out" from our colleagues in science, the complicating factors can always be introduced later.

III

Values Associated with the Areal Division of Governmental Powers. By one or the other protagonist—only occasionally by some dispassionate theorist—a variety of claims have been made on behalf of the areal division of governmental power. So far as I know, no one has ventured to present them all at once as part of a systematic brief or general theory; this, for two reasons, both worth noting. In the first place, most of what has been said on the subject has been provoked in the heat of battle over whether or not to adopt or keep some variety of the system. As a result, we have inherited a congeries of expedient claims, supported only by casual examples and fragmentary arguments chosen on the run, bearing very much the stamp of what has been referred to as the "courtship" phase in the areal division of powers.

Further, these claims have accumulated over time in three distinguishable layers, deposited by passing generations of advocates and critics who have successively been concerned with the great values of liberty (the 18th Century), equality (the 19th Century) and welfare (the 20th Century). Few efforts have been made to relate these categories of claims; I suspect most of us assume that if anything there is a strain of incompatibility among them, addressed as they are to vastly different times, needs, and ends.

By a snip or two of the Procrustean shears, and the methodical tactic of Linnaeus, one can assemble these claims in a diagrammatic way which—without glossing over the inadequacies of this haphazardly accumulated rationale of an areal division of powers—makes the most of what plausibility and coherence there may be in it. But more important for our purpose, the diagram takes us an analytical step forward, by focussing on the ultimate criteria—the basic values of a given society—by which the areal division must be judged. And as well, the relevance and adequacy of any instrumental criteria or analytical models we may hope to develop.

To repeat, the diagram advances us one analytical step along our way by outlining the framework of values within which the areal division of powers is to be structured and judged. (Even so obvious a step as to admit again that there are other and more values to be served than "efficiency" should have the significant effect of flagging down some of us who under the immediate pressures of the administrative state are trying to build models and theoretical systems within the confines of that instrumental value alone.)

But the diagram does nothing to establish the validity of the several claims. They are and remain only claims; all that can be said of them is that they are plausible enough to have convinced many passing generations of their validity (interestingly enough, with the single exception of "efficiency," as witness the democrat's ever-ready apology for the Rube Goldberg character of his local institutions). How fragile the support

The Rationale for an Areal Division of Governmental Powers within the Modern Democratic State

BASIC VALUES	*INSTRUMENTAL VALUES OF THE AREAL DIVISION OF POWERS* —i.e., The means by which *adp* is presumed to realize the given basic values; expressed in terms of the: *Individual*	*Governmental Process*
	Gives further assurance of protection against arbitrary or hasty governmental action	
LIBERTY (Constitutionalism, with a goodly admixture of laissez-faire)	—by providing additional and more readily available points of *access, pressure,* and *control;* —by making it possible for minorities to avail themselves of governmental position and power; —by serving to keep governmental power close to its origins, and governmental officials within reach of their masters.	—by providing a system of *countervailing* power among governmental levels, assuring *friction* and *debate;* —by creating a network of compartments, to localize ills which may beset the body politic.
EQUALITY (Especially as embodied in its corollary of democracy and the axiom of wide-scale participation)	On the negative side, provides a further barrier to the concentration of social, economic, and political power. On the positive side, provides additional and more readily available opportunities for *participation* as a means of contributing to the development both of the individual (in the Aristotelian tradition of citizenship) and of public policy.	Gives further assurance of: —*responsiveness* and *flexibility;* —*energy* and *"collective wisdom";* —*consent* and *loyalty*
WELFARE (service)	Additional assurance that demands will be heard and that needs will be served.	Gives further assurance that governmental action will be effective (granted the claims listed immediately above), and that performance will be more efficient, in accord with the administrative principles of: —scale; —delegation; —decentralization; —specialization; —the availability and yardstick effect of comparative costs.

for these claims actually is can be demonstrated by the ease with which arguments and evidence can be mustered against them. One could cite H. G. Wells and his devastating account of "democracy" in the English hamlet, or the well-documented charges against state government in this country which are so readily at hand. Any reader could without difficulty trace through the diagram and insert rebuttals to each of the contentions listed.

This game of point and counterpoint is familiar, but not in all parts relevant; when over, and the smoke clears away, a number of conclusions regularly emerge which are material to the line of analysis being developed here.

One, there is no quarrel over any of the listed values, either basic or instrumental. There would be over any attempt to weight them or otherwise establish priorities among them. That has not been tried here. Frankly, I don't relish the task, don't see how it can be done, and am inclined to dodge the problem for the moment by assuming the values in their different categories to be of equal importance. Sooner or later, if a more precise theory or set of criteria is to be developed, someone may have to face the problem more squarely than I have here.

Two, all the listed values are compatible, but only if tempered, not maximized. A "maximum" of control can throw a monkey wrench into the machinery of government; a "maximum" of participation can re-create the confusion of Babel. This tempering of values involves a process of balance, which suggests the applicability of some type of equilibrium analysis. But the problem of devising a workable model seems formidable, to say the least; to begin with, there is lacking a unit of measurement or common denominator which can do for political science what the dollar has done for economic theory.

Three, we may assert that the areal division of powers helps realize the basic and instrumental values of our society, but we have no conclusive proof. We are fairly certain on the record that it does no serious damage to these values; we also know, if its effect is in fact positive, that this effect is only an incremental one, reinforcing the influence of such other factors as the capital division of powers, economic competition, and group rivalry.[2] But we have no clue, even speculative, to the measure of this increment.

IV

Those Promised "Criteria." Having shown that we do not know—and for a variety of methodological reasons, may have no way of knowing—precisely and for certain whether an areal division of power plays an effective role in helping realize the basic values of a given society, we may have reached something of a logical impasse in the attempt to make good the promise of a set of criteria for a "proper" areal division of governmental power. The only course open, I think, is to act on faith and venture some long intuitive leaps, observing as faithfully as possible the ground rules laid down in the sections above and moving in the general direction they indicate.

The quest, to repeat, is for criteria which can fill the blank in the following sentence: "To the degree to which (this condition, proposition, etc.) is satisfied, the areal division of governmental power will be a more effective means of realizing the basic values of liberty, equality, and welfare."

The following criteria are actually stated as maxims. They seemed to come naturally in that form, and being so flagrantly subjective serve nicely as reminders of the shrouded process by which they came into being. Appended to each of these maxims is a supporting set of assertions and explanations, which serve as connecting links with the line of argument developed in the preceding sections. There are many gaps: some of them I can see, and have neither the wit nor the data to do anything about. Some I have no doubt overlooked.

MAXIM ONE: *The areal division of powers should be concerned basically with what is meant by the phrase "the power to govern." The assignment of powers to component areas should in each case be a general one, covering the whole range of governmental functions, rather than a partial one related only to particular functions.*

I would admit only two possible exceptions, both justifying an exclusive grant to the central government: formal conduct of international relations, including the power to declare war; and control of the monetary standard.

This maxim, if nothing else, reflects a trend which is a matter of record and which we might as well recognize: away from the tradition of exclusive powers, toward a sharing (and hopefully a harmonious exercise) of common powers.

And there is logic in the trend. The semantics and legal fictions of exclusive allocations of powers do not accord with the "seamless web" of governmental operations in our times. They suggest boundaries where there are no boundaries, absolute distinctions where there are only relative ones; they invite spurious controversy and discord beyond the measure of "friction," which among the given values of our system would be their only possible justification. To coin an aphorism which implies a century of proof: "The Civil War began an era which, through the Kestnbaum Commission, we have finally recognized and sanctioned."

And more, if governmental action at each level is to be well conceived and effective; if the citizen is to be drawn as a whole person into participation (rather, I am tempted to add, than being drawn and quartered by the divisive effects of partial grants); and if the system of countervailing power is to have any meaning or vitality, then the concerns and the decisions which the component area can legitimately undertake ought to embrace the whole range of matters assigned to the governmental process by that society in its time.

And if, as I suspect, the process of balancing and weighting the different values is so subjective and complex that it can be done only in the actual moment and act of choice by the individual himself, then the agenda ought to be set so that the full range of choice is before him.

This maxim is not meant to exclude the whole variety of ingenious devices for getting specific things done in specific ways (e.g., TVA, Port of New York Authority, etc.). It assumes them, depends upon them, and by broadening the base of power from which they stem may even make them more effective. But it may also help curb what we have seen is a pathological aspect of these special devices—to the extent, that is, that a broader grant of power to the component areas may make it unnecessary to have so many of them, and to the extent that we stop trying to make of these devices what they are not, which is a vehicle for the whole process of government and a central claim on citizen participation.

Finally, the grant of general power helps ensure the capacity of the areal components to survive and remain effective. As we know from the experience of the township, and perhaps of TVA, the specialized instrument tends to disappear over time, because of obsolescence and/or the lack of adequate resources of power and support.

MAXIM TWO: *The optimum number of levels among which to share the power to govern would seem to be three.*

Two is an invitation to abiding conflict and stymie, or at the other extreme to subordination and quiescence.

At least in the American experience, the "third force" has been a dynamic factor in the interplay of governmental levels: the states in the early development of regulatory and administrative service; the federal government during the Thirties; and I would nominate local (especially urban) government as the gadfly of the moment.[3]

If I have any doubt, it is about the "middle tier" which chronically seem to suffer in comparison with local and central governments, having neither the attachment of the one nor the prepossessing qualities of the other. Interest in it tends to be languid;[4] vitality and efficiency correspondingly drop off.

Still, two further considerations reinforce the conclusion that a third force is nonetheless desirable: one, that two-level systems seem naturally to progress toward the establishment of a middle level; two, that the factors which tend to minimize interest in the American states are the very ones which prevent the states from operating as general instruments of government: restricted powers, inflexible constitutions, etc.

I have an intuition against more than three levels, but no real argument or proof. Certainly there is an upper limit which would accommodate very few more than three.

MAXIM THREE: *The component areas should be constituted of a sufficient diversity of interests to ensure effective debate within each component and transcending communities of interest among the several components.* This criterion marks the point beyond which one should not press the search for "natural" (i.e., homogeneous) communities to serve as jurisdictions for the component areas.

This maxim represents at least an apparent break from the earlier assumptions of equal importance among the instrumental values; it implies that *debate* has a higher priority than either *efficiency* (as conventionally talked about in the literature of administration) or *participation, loyalty,* and *interest* (as thought to be more assured if governmental and especially social boundaries coincide).

Actually the maximum may not stir up much of an incompatibility between debate and the other values. No one has ever demonstrated, except by reference to exceptional cases, that participation, loyalty, and interest increase as political boundaries more nearly coincide with "natural" social groupings or economic areas (the proposition might be tested in a very rough way, sometime, by simply checking the voting turn-out and other indices of participation in more homogeneous, as against more heterogeneous, constituencies). The fact may well be otherwise, as conflict arouses interest. And as we sometimes too painfully have experienced, loyalty is as much *generated* by the very creation and symbolism of boundary lines, as it is by whatever elements of alikeness these lines may happen to include.

The matter of efficiency is a much tougher proposition to contest. The administrative logic of conformance between area and rational grouping is authoritative and compelling. But three things might be said in favor of the hint of heresy being suggested here. First, a search for a scheme of general administrative areas has proved more disappointing than that for the Holy Grail; the perplexing map of special administrative areas in the United States is full testimony in itself. Second, to the extent that the administrative process is linked with the process of policy, and subordinate to it, it contains its own caution that debate and a diversity of interest are among the conditions of its operating success. And if these arguments fall, the third stands on its own as an assertion: that to the degree there is an incompatibility, the value of debate is to be preferred.[5]

This emphasis on the central importance of diversity of interests and debate as instruments of liberty and welfare does not have to be argued elaborately. If authority is wanted, we need only turn to Madison in the tenth Federalist and to John Stuart Mill; if pungency, we can return to H. G. Wells's trenchant piece on the vicious parochialism of "small" units.

What may need support is the proposition that a diversity of interests within the component areas helps ensure a consensus which transcends these areas. The defense is simple enough, and is suggested in part by one of the physical laws of equilibrium: *If pressures within are equal to those without. . . .* This condition of equilibrium, true, can be one of stymie as well as one of a facilitating consensus. But it provides at least the conditions necessary for competing groups in the society to form and reform the shifting alliances upon which we depend for the "ties that bind," and for our system of impermanent and safe majorities.

And one might as well offer as further evidence that part of the democratic myth—not unsupported by what we have come to know of the nature of man—which runs: ". . . argue it out, and you'll end up friends."

The maxim says nothing about ensuring a diversity of interests among the three "levels" and among component units. These are essential conditions which I doubt we shall have to struggle to create; they will exist as soon as the areal division of powers is made, and two or more parties begin worrying about different customers and/or are made partners to one decision.

The requirement of a diversity of interests will mean in practice larger (and therefore fewer) jurisdictions than we have become accustomed to. The change would be a happy one, if one accepts the many and persuasive arguments addressed to enhanced efficiency, responsibility, and citizen interest. Larger jurisdictions would also be more likely to have the expanded financial and leadership resources which, if they are not necessary now, would certainly be necessary under the conditions we are positing.

The resulting jurisdictions may still not be able to pay their own way. As long as their financial deficiencies are not so great as to cost them self-reliance and make them ineffective countervailing influences, I think we need not worry. The grant-in-aid has proved an effective remedy, with few harmful side-effects.

MAXIM FOUR: *The components should not as such be represented in the legislatures of the higher levels.* And it is an open question whether the areas of the components ought even to coincide with the legislative constituencies of the next higher level.

The underlying purpose of this maxim is to provide further insurance against stymie and parochialism (history being replete with examples), and to maximize the fluidity and generality of the process of government at the higher levels.

The degree to which this maxim applies, varies inversely with the degree to which the component areas satisfy the criterion of a diversity of interests (Maxim Three).[6]

I would offer as a sub-maxim that the executive, if chosen independently of the legislature, should in every case be elected at large. And to retain the integrity of the executive process and to avoid unproductive competition with the peculiar role of leadership it represents, it might even follow that *no* legislative members should be chosen at large.

MAXIM FIVE: *Four processes affecting intergovernmental relations should be provided for: one, a process of last resort to settle intergovernmental disputes and questions of jurisdiction; two, a process (or processes) of intergovernmental cooperation; three, a process by which the several governments may act separately and independently, as well as in cooperation; and four, a process of organic change which can neither be dictated nor stopped by a minority of components.*

The first process is a logical necessity, which when admitted seems to bring back through the rear door what Maxim One throws out the front—viz., grants of exclusive powers. Not entirely, though here we're certainly hip-deep in semantics. To summarize the argument: each component is to be free to tackle the whole range of governmental problems as they affect its area (exceptions having been noted above). This is admittedly a vacuous phrase, and will give rise to continuous dispute among the different governments. Ultimately, the disputes must be settled—and hence the need for a process of last resort. This need not be a legal process exclusively or even principally, although as Chief Justice Holmes once pointed out, the United States Supreme Court has demonstrated its real value in defining the jurisdictions of the states. Add to that the ingenuity of the interstate commerce and elastic clauses of the American constitution, which operate as convenient fictions and workable expressions of the ambivalence which is being deliberately sought after here. But the process may be even more informal; in the mature stage of the areal division of powers it will likely depend upon the practical dictates of governmental operations, the development of standards, and a common sense ingrained of long experience. In any case, it should be emphasized, this process should be one of *last* resort; before being entered upon, a good deal of policy debate and administrative competition should be tolerated.

The second process is meant to exploit the whole variety of devices (grants-in-aid, cooperative programs, intergovernmental planning and consultation) which have been developed within the multiple-government context of the modern democratic state. The value of cooperation seems so obvious and fundamental as to need no defense in depth. But two things are worth special note: (a) as the Anderson-Weidner studies in Minnesota show,[7] perhaps the most significant factor in assuring intergovernmental cooperation in the United States is the link which has been, and almost inexorably will be, forged among officials and administrators of the different levels who are engaged in the same functions. The extent of this cooperation is obviously enlarged by the degree to which the components each operate over the whole range of governmental functions. And (b) while much more of the democratic tradition enters into the pragmatism and responsibility which over time yield cooperation rather than conflict, the very participation of any one unit, rather than its exclusion, helps develop locally a sense of responsibility, and puts a premium on performance rather than inaction.[8]

The third proposition is the obverse of the second, and the necessary concomitant of several instrumental values: on the negative side, friction and countervailing power, which restrain the higher levels and give each component a fighting chance of doing things in its own way. On the positive side, flexibility and the incentive of competition, to do things differently and better, or to do things which any given unit may think important though the others do not.

The fourth process is inserted to recognize the need for change and accommodation (a recognition to which the democratic tradition owes much of its vitality and survival), and to give an instrument for change which will not make a mockery of the whole concept of the areal division of powers or violate beyond reason the integrity of the individual components.

I need not add that the minority referred to should most likely be the residual of that "extraordinary" majority upon which we have come to rely for organic change.

V

Some Emerging Trends. As admitted earlier, this whole analytical scheme builds heavily upon observations of American experience. Yet it does more than describe, for the maxims point well beyond the current development of American institutions and practice.

To illustrate and to impress the dimension of time unmistakably upon the theoretical model, consider two current trends on the American scene: one, the emergence of metropolitan government; the other the dispersion of governmental and social power. In these two trends, one can find at least the hint of further maxims for the proper areal division of powers.

A. The Emergence of Metropolitan Government: The explosive growth of our population, its fall-out into a pattern of massive urban areas, and the congealing of these metropolises into roughly distinguishable economic and social systems, are calling dramatic attention to one clear gap between maxim and practice. The lack of a *general* process of government at the metropolitan level, as Mr. Wood's study shows, is a crucial missing link in the American system of areal division of powers. That such a general process *should* be developed can be deduced from the theoretical framework outlined above. That sooner or later it *will* be developed seems clear from the growing ferment in almost every American metropolis. Precisely how it will be brought into being is a practical question that tears us from the philosophical comforts of the long run, into the hard realities of institution-building in the here and now.

The immediate question our 20th Century framers must face is a strategic one: whether to try heroically to create these general instruments of metropolitan government full-blown, or to move gradually toward them through intermediate devices of limited scope and partial jurisdiction. My own hunch, very likely a reformist's bias, is that public opinion is more favorable to a general and immediate solution than is commonly thought; and I can't help wondering what 1787 might have led to, had the Founding Fathers played it cautiously, merely tinkering with the system in a "practical, functional" way.

Be that as it may, much of the current agenda of action seems committed to a gradualist philosophy and the functional approach. Query, is this functional approach incompatible with the development of a general process of government, and therefore inconsistent with the criteria so far established for an effective system of divided power?

Even though it may represent the long and precarious way around, I think not—*if the transitional phase is deliberately planned as such, and if the function selected as a first step toward metropolitan government is chosen as the cornerstone of a more general system.* Mr. Wood suggests that transportation may be the most likely of these functions; another candidate might be the combination of zoning and planning, which strikes at an earlier phase of the community's development, evokes equal interest, and permits more general debate and control.

Whatever function or set of functions is chosen, their ultimate purpose will be defeated if they are fashioned and survive entirely unto themselves. The least protection one can ask is that the law which creates these functional authorities be of limited term, that after, say, ten years the question be raised again and automatically whether they should be absorbed into a more general process of government.

But to deal with the question of metrogovernment merely as one of timing and tactics is to oversimplify the problem and the process of institutional change in a given system (or model) of areally divided powers. For here, as in the physical world, we are dealing with forces in flow, with continuous adjustments and counter-adjustments, with successive imbalances, the resolution of one precipitating the next—all told, a *process* of equilibrium, but never a *state* of equilibrium.

So it is with the development of metropolitan government. Metrogovernment in the long view appears to represent an inexorable gathering of forces to overcome one imbalance in the system of areally divided powers; just as inevitably, one or more new imbalances will be created when the first is resolved.

Almost certainly, the principal expression of this new imbalance will be adverse to the middle (state) level of government. (The national level will also be affected, but its equivalent time of trouble and major readjustment will not come until an analogous gathering of forces begins to produce a genuine international level of government.)

Some states will escape the threat of demise by an exercise in definition, simply absorbing their metropolitan areas or otherwise becoming indistinguishable from them (as possibly Rhode Island, Connecticut and Hawaii). Others will contain the threat by adroit and positive gubernatorial leadership, and by liberalizing constitutions and revenue systems well in advance of metropolitan reorganization, so as to keep metrogovernment within a more or less familiar pattern of hierarchical state-local relations. Still others may delay the day of reckoning by a strategy of divide and conquer, exploiting local differences of race and boundary in such a way as to forestall the rise of a politically self-conscious metropolitan community. In all cases, of course, local eccentricities of history, geography, power structure, and leadership will greatly influence the outcome.

But in no instance will the states emerge entirely unscathed. In this coming era of the powerful metropolis, becoming politically self-conscious and economically more self-sufficient, state governments will come under heavy competitive pressures. Unless states become fewer and larger, unless they overcome the inflexibilities and social lag which are now characteristic, *unless, in short, they themselves develop as effective general instruments of government,* governors will be taking back seats to the new metromayors, legislatures will dance to the pipes of metropolitan political blocs, and the states may well suffer in full the lurking fate of all "middle levels."

This is obviously drawing the case in the extreme. Given the penchant of Americans for making marginal adjustments rather than major ones, and given the dispersion of political power and advantage, which for all practical purposes allows Americans no alternative but to express their penchant, we can expect something of a half-way house to be constructed between the transcendent metropolis and the defunct state.

To the extent this reconciliation of extremes is accomplished, and to the extent that general instruments with the capacity to govern are developed and perfected at all three levels, Americans will have satisfied the "dynamic" criteria of a proper areal division of powers. As a corollary to the maxims, this might read:

The criteria which govern the mature system of an areal division of powers are the standards by which to judge measures of transition and reform. And the test of such measures should be in terms of their total—and not just their immediate or partial—effects upon all elements of the system.

B. The Dispersion of Governmental and Social Power, and the Emergence of New Values: This corollary suggests a closed and immutable system predicated on the existing value structure. Obviously, the value structure will change over time; certainly so, if the past is any guide.

Obviously, too, it hardly is given to any person in the present to talk confidently about emerging trends in value structure; that job is one for the far historians.

Still, some stab ought to be made in this direction to give a sense of the dynamics which govern—and which plague—systematic political analysis of the sort being attempted here.

One can start with the centrifugal effect on governmental and social power which our dedication to *Liberty* as a principal value has produced. This outward pull has not abated over time. I suspect that if some quantitative measure of it were possible, we would find a secular trend line almost as constant as that showing the increase in economic productivity. Even the emergence of the later "great values" has not appreciably slowed the dispersive tendency: equality and welfare, each in its turn, have taken on the coloration of the first value, and if anything, have over time reinforced its effect. There has been a certain rhythm to the cycle by which this has taken place: as a new value appears, government is seized upon as an instrument to achieve it, and for a time power for that purpose is reassembled and concentrated; then, as the new value is recognized and the law adapted to its defense, power is again and further dispersed.

This is perhaps but a variation on de Tocqueville's vision of an "equalizing American democracy." It differs in that it (a) ascribes the basic thrust to liberty as a value rather than equality; and (b) is not so quick to conclude that the ultimate effect may be to approximate a tyrannic Babel of mass mediocrity.

True, there are some disturbing evidences of what the dispersion of power can bring. One of these, Reisman and Whyte have been pointing to in their recent jeremiads on organization society: a self-defeating attempt by an atomizing society to reproduce order via conformity, when suddenly that society becomes aware that its "separatenesses" are proliferating at a geometric rate.

The other is reflected in the fragmentation of American politics and governing institutions. In response, political science, too, has produced its Jeremiahs ranging from the "strong two-party" phalanx who decry the localism of American politics to those who, with Lippmann, are anguished by the growing difficulty of assembling enough power to make firm decisions and long-range commitments in matters of public policy, domestic no less than international.

If there is this long-range tendency to dispersion of power, what relevance does it have to the areal system and model we have been developing here? I see three points of relevance.

One, we shall have to be aware of this dispersive trend as the moving and changing base upon which the system is constantly struggling to achieve equilibrium. As with a constant shift in geological formations, those living on the surface must accept and anticipate change. One of our maxims already does that: *The growing measure of decentralization implicit in the broad grants of power to sub-national levels is itself a recognition of the need for dispersion of power throughout our society and policy.*

"Will this dispersion continue?" is a question which shows a second order of relevance. It may not. Already, a fourth major value is appearing on the American scene which may counter the centrifugal effect on power which liberty has exercised so long and so relentlessly. That value is *Security*. Its origins lie too obviously in the fact that we live now, as de Tocqueville a century ago predicted we would, hard against the boundaries of hostile nations, not simply those of a challenging Nature. If we should make security an operative ideal of our society, it will almost certainly exert a centripetal effect on power; and though I personally would abhor the shift, it would (if we could achieve the same scientific dispassion which led Aristotle to prescribe for varying value systems, each to its own perfection) argue for a restatement of the maxims, to provide less generous allocations of power, and a more hierarchical arrangement among areal institutions.

There is a third point of relevance, which returns us again to the "shorter long-run." Does the dispersion of power require more of an institutional adaptation than our present maxims provide? I think so; but I advance only an hypothesis which, had I more experience to go on, might develop into a maxim:

To the extent that power is dispersed throughout a given social and political system, the institutional arrangements through which the areal division of powers is effected should within certain fixed limits, be simplified and executive leadership strengthened: i.e., fewer levels (to a minimum of three); streamlined and more integrated executive agencies; smaller legislative bodies; fewer independent authorities, etc.

If I have real uncertainty about this hypothesis, it is because I am vaguely aware of falling prey to a psychological quirk which I have criticized in others: viz., attempting to impose order on a complexity which, if I properly understood it, I would the more appreciate. In short, the very reverse may actually be true: as power is dispersed, let institutions proliferate, and their character and function become more diffuse.

What swings me to the other side are two arguments: 1) The struggle for civilization—all the way from building sidewalks to containing the Russians—places a premium on action, performance and decision. Not all of these can or should await the infinitely elongated process of "multiple consensus" to which we have been forced in our rabbit-hutch tradition of breeding governmental agencies. 2) We can afford a good deal of governmental simplification. Not only do we have a surplus, the dispersion of power itself is a counterbalancing device and an assurance not present in the days when we adopted the set we did against institutional simplicity.

NOTES

1. Arthur Macmahon (ed.), *Federalism: Mature and Emergent* (New York, 1955).

2. One of the things one might ask of David Truman is that he push farther than he has into the relationship between his theory of groups and the areal division of governmental powers. His *Governmental Process*

(New York, 1951) almost wholly ignores the relationship, concentrating instead (and characteristically, as Mr. Maass would note) on the more topical questions relating to the capital division of powers. Thus his chapters on "Interest Groups and the Judiciary"; "The Ordeal of the Executive"; ". . . The Legislative Process"; ". . . The Administrative Process"; etc.

3. I suspect there may be a rhythm in the process by which—over time—the several levels of government, singly or in pairs, wax and wane in their relative dynamism and importance. And I have a hunch, too, that the determining or symptomatic element is the relative strength of executive leadership which obtains at any given moment as among the several levels. Whatever the cause, or whatever the pattern, the ebb and flow of relative strength is a vital part of any system of areally-divided powers, and worth some good research.

4. This impression, a seemingly general one, is confirmed in an intriguing little poll reported recently by Belknap and Smuckler in the Spring, 1956 issue of *Public Opinion Quarterly*. No more than 4% of either category of persons interviewed (Active, and Not Active in the Community) thought state problems more serious, interesting, and absorbing of attention than local and national problems. Fair to say, however, that the results might not have been so clear-cut had the questions been phrased differently. "State problems," etc., were left undefined, but were implied to be distinct—whereas very few governmental problems indeed can be distinguished as being local, state, *or* national. But the very fact that so few are aware of the state's partnership in so many governmental activities, may be proof enough of the underlying contention.

5. Despite this argument, and reserving comment about any governmental conclusions they may reach, I am intrigued by the effort of Douglas Carroll and others to develop formulae for defining areas of community and influence (*Traffic Quarterly*, April 1955). This being a theoretical inquiry, I have claimed immunity from questions which would force me to apply the analysis in other than a descriptive way. But if pressed to name areas which would most happily express a balance between diversity and community of interest, I would nominate river basins as areas of the middle level, urban transportation or trade areas for the local. And wonder whether the rural areas might not be left to tag along with the cities, or to work directly through the middle level.

6. If pressed again to describe a practicable balance, I would vote for a bicameral legislature, the lower house chosen from constituencies which singly or in groups coincide *in area* with the component units, the upper house selected from larger constituencies which do not coincide.

7. Professors William Anderson and Edward Weidner have directed a survey of *Intergovernmental Relations in the United States as Observed in Minnesota,* which includes 10 monographs.

8. Proof can be found, I think, in the study of intergovernmental relations in Blue Earth County, Minnesota (Ylvisaker, "Intergovernmental Relations at the Grass Roots," No. 7 in the Minnesota Intergovernmental Relations Series). The essential moral is retold as a short story in "The Battle of Blue Earth County" in Harold Stein (ed.), *Public Administration and Policy Development* (New York, 1952).

27. The Organization of Government in Metropolitan Areas: A Theoretical Inquiry†

VINCENT OSTROM, CHARLES M. TIEBOUT AND ROBERT WARREN*

Allusions to the "problem of metropolitan government" are often made in characterizing the difficulties supposed to arise because a metropolitan region is a legal non-entity. From this point of view, the people of a metropolitan region have no general instrumentality of government available to deal directly with the range of problems which they share in common. Rather there is a multiplicity of federal and state governmental agencies, counties, cities, and special districts that govern within a metropolitan region.

This view assumes that the multiplicity of political units in a metropolitan area is essentially a pathological phenomenon. The diagnosis asserts that there are too many governments and not enough government. The symptoms are described as "duplication of functions" and "overlapping jurisdictions." Autonomous units of government, acting in their own behalf, are considered incapable of resolving the diverse problems of the wider metropolitan community. The political topography of the metropolis is called a "crazy-quilt pattern" and its organization is said to be an "organized chaos." The prescription is reorganization into larger units—to provide "a general metropolitan framework" for gathering up the various functions of government. A political system with a single dominant center for making decisions is viewed as the ideal model for the organization of metropolitan government. "Gargantua" is one name for it.[1]

The assumption that each unit of local government acts independently without regard for other public interests in the metropolitan community has only a limited validity. The traditional pattern of government in a metropolitan area with its multiplicity of political jurisdictions may more appropriately be conceived as a "polycentric political system."[2] "Polycentric" connotes many centers of decision-making which are formally independent of each other. Whether they actually function independently, or instead constitute an interdependent system of relations, is an empirical question in particular cases. To the extent that they take each other into account in competitive relationships, enter into various contractual and cooperative undertakings or have recourse to central mechanisms to resolve conflicts, the various political jurisdictions in a metropolitan area may function in a coherent manner with consistent and predictable patterns of interacting behavior. To the extent that this is so, they may be said to function as a "system."

The study of government in metropolitan areas conceived as a polycentric political system should precede any judgment that it is pathological. Both the structure and the behavior of the system need analysis before any reasonable estimate can be made of its performance in dealing with the various public problems arising in a metropolitan community. Better analysis of how a metropolitan area is

* Ostrom is Associate Professor of Political Science, U.C.L.A.; Tiebout is Associate Professor of Economics, U.C.L.A.; and Warren is Assistant Professor of Political Science, University of Washington.

Ostrom and Warren wish to acknowledge the early support of their work by the Bureau of Governmental Research at U.C.L.A. Background for discussion of the final section on "conflict and conflict resolution" was derived from research supported by the Water Resources Center of the University of California, help which Ostrom wishes to acknowledge.

[1] The term is taken from Robert C. Wood, "The New Metropolis: Green Belts, Grass Roots or Gargantua," this REVIEW, Vol. 52 (March, 1958), pp. 108–122. Wood defines gargantua as "the invention of a single metropolitan government or at least the establishment of a regional superstructure which points in that direction." We do not argue the case for big units *vs.* small units as Wood does in his discussion of gargantua *vs.* grass roots. Rather, we argue that various scales of organization may be appropriate for different public services in a metropolitan area.

[2] We use this term for want of a better one. An alternative term might be "multinucleated political system." We do not use "pluralism" because it has been preempted as a broader term referring to society generally and not to a political system in particular.

Polycentric political systems are not limited to the field of metropolitan government. The concept is equally applicable to regional administration of water resources, regional administration of international affairs, and to a variety of other situations.

† Reprinted from the *American Political Science Review,* Vol. 55 (Dec. 1961).

governed can lead in turn to more appropriate measures of reorganization and reform.[3]

This paper is an initial effort to explore some of the potentialities of a polycentric political system in providing for the government of metropolitan areas. We view the "business" of governments in metropolitan areas as providing "public goods and services." The first section of the paper will examine the special character of these public goods and services.

We shall then turn to an analysis of the problems of scale in constituting the public organizations which provide them. This discussion seems relevant to an analysis of any political structure in a metropolitan area, and equally applicable to gargantua or to a polycentric political system. A brief reference will then be made to the problems of public organization in gargantua. Finally, patterns of organization in a polycentric political system will be analyzed with particular regard to the experience of the Los Angeles metropolitan area.

I. THE NATURE OF PUBLIC GOODS AND SERVICES

The conditions which give rise to public rather than private provision of certain goods and services are examined in this section. Three views of these conditions can usefully be distinguished: (1) public goods arising from efforts to control indirect consequences, externalities or spillover effects; (2) public goods provided because some goods and services cannot be packaged; and (3) public goods consisting of the maintenance of preferred states of community affairs.

The Control of Indirect Consequences as Public Goods. The basic criterion traditionally offered for distinguishing between public and private affairs was formulated some years ago by John Dewey: " . . . the line between private and public is to be drawn on the basis of the extent and scope of the consequences of acts which are so important as to need control whether by inhibition or by promotion."[4] The indirect consequences of a transaction, which affect others than those directly concerned, can also be described as "externalities" or "spillover effects." Those indirectly affected are viewed as being external to the immediate transaction. Some externalities are of a favorable or beneficial nature; others are adverse or detrimental.

Favorable externalities can frequently be recaptured by the economic unit that creates them. The builder of a large supermarket, for example, may create externalities for the location of a nearby drugstore. If the builder of the supermarket also controls the adjacent land, he can capture the externalities accruing to the drugstore through higher rents or by common ownership of the two enterprises. From the builder's point of view he has "internalized"[5] the externalities.[6]

Where favorable externalities cannot be internalized by private parties, a sufficient mechanism to proceed may be lacking, and public agencies may be called upon to provide a good or service. A privately owned park, even with an admission charge, may not be able to cover costs. If the externalities in the form of the dollar value of a better neighborhood could be captured, such a park might be profitable.

Unfavorable spillovers or externalities are another matter. The management of a refinery which belches out smoke has little incentive to install costly equipment to eliminate the smoke. Control or internalization of diseconomies usually falls upon public agencies. A function of government, then, is to internalize the externalities—positive and negative—for

[3] By analogy, the formal units of government in a metropolitan area might be viewed as organizations similar to individual firms in an industry. Individual firms may constitute the basic legal entities in an industry, but their conduct in relation to one another may be conceived as having a particular structure and behavior as an industry. Collaboration among the separate units of local government may be such that their activities supplement or complement each other, as in the automobile industry's patent pool. Competition among them may produce desirable self-regulating tendencies similar in effect to the "invisible hand" of the market. Collaboration and competition among governmental units may also, of course, have detrimental effects, and require some form of central decision-making to consider the interests of the area as a whole. For a comprehensive review of the theory of industrial organization see Joe S. Bain, *Industrial Organization* (New York, 1959).

[4] John Dewey, *The Public and Its Problems* (New York, 1927), p. 15.

[5] John V. Krutilla and Otto Eckstein, *Multiple Purpose River Development: Studies in Applied Economic Analysis* (Baltimore: The Johns Hopkins Press, 1958), p. 69 ff. Krutilla and Eckstein develop the concept of "internalizing" external economies as a criterion for determining scale of a management unit in the administration of water resources.

[6] In practice, shopping centers may also give favorable rents to large supermarkets as "traffic generators." This recognizes the externalities they create.

those goods which the producers and consumers are unable or unwilling to internalize for themselves, and this process of internalization is identified with the "public goods."

Not all public goods are of the same scale. Scale implies both the geographic domain and the intensity or weight of the externality. A playground creates externalities which are neighborhoodwide in scope, while national defense activities benefit a whole nation—and affect many outside it. Thus, for each public good there corresponds some "public." As John Dewey has formulated the definition, "the public consists of all those who are affected by the indirect consequences of transactions to such an extent that it is deemed necessary to have those consequences systematically provided for."[7] The concept of the public is important to later considerations in determining the criteria of scale appropriate to public organizations.

Packageability. Public goods and services and, in turn, the functions of governments in metropolitan areas can be distinguished from private goods by a criterion commonly used by economists. A private good must be "packageable", *i.e.*, susceptible of being differentiated as a commodity or service before it can be readily purchased and sold in the private market. Those who do not pay for a private good can then be excluded from enjoying its benefits. This notion is formulated by economists as the "exclusion principle."[8] In contrast with Dewey's formulation of the nature of public goods, the exclusion principle focuses attention on the practicability of denying benefits. National defense, for example, will not be provided by private firms because, among other reasons, the citizen who did not pay would still enjoy the benefits. Furthermore, if citizens understate their preferences for defense—as by failing to build bomb shelters—on the assumption that it will be paid for by others, the result will be an inadequate provision for defense.

Most municipal public goods such as fire and police protection, or the abatement of air pollution, are not easily packageable, either; they cannot be sold only to those individuals who are willing to pay.[9] This suggests two problems for public organizations.

First, private goods, because they are easily packageable, are readily subject to measurement and quantification. Public goods, by contrast, are generally not so measurable. If more police are added to the force, output will presumably increase. But how much, is a question without an exact answer. Moreover, when factors of production can be quantified in measurable units of output, the production process can be subject to more rigorous controls. A more rational pricing policy is also possible. With quantifiable data about both input and output, any production process can be analyzed and the performance of different modes of production can be compared for their efficiency. Rational control over the production and provision of public goods and services therefore depends, among other things, upon the development of effective standards of measurement; this gets into the allocation of joint costs as well as of joint benefits.

A second, closely related, problem arises in the assessment of costs upon persons who can benefit without paying directly for the good. Only public agencies with their taxing powers can seek to apportion the costs of public goods among the various beneficiaries. The scale criterion of political representation, discussed below, takes account of how this difference between private and public goods affects the organization of public agencies.

Public Goods as the Maintenance of Preferred States of Community Affairs. The exclusion principle provides a criterion for distinguishing most public goods from private, but it does not, as commonly stated, clarify or specify the conditions which determine the patterns of organization in the public service economy. However, by viewing public goods as "the maintenance of preferred states of community affairs," we may introduce a modified concept of packageability, one that is amenable to some measurement and quantification, and that therefore may be more helpful in clarifying criteria for the organization of public services in metropolitan areas. The modification consists in extending the exclusion principle from an individual consumer to all the inhabitants of an area within designated boundaries.

The concept can be illustrated on a small scale in the operation of a household heating system which uses conveniently measurable units of inputs. However, the household temperature it maintains is a joint benefit to the family and a marginal change in family size will have no material effect upon the costs of maintaining this public good for the family. Yet since the family good derived from it is effectively confined to the household, outsiders are excluded and there are no substantial spillover effects or externalities for them. The

[7] John Dewey, *op. cit.*, pp. 15–16.

[8] Richard Musgrave, *The Theory of Public Finance* (New York, 1959), esp. ch. 1.

[9] Charles M. Tiebout, "A Pure Theory of Local Expenditures," *Journal of Political Economy*, Vol. 64 (October, 1956), pp. 416–24.

family good is not a public good in the larger community. So household heating is treated as a private good in most communities. Similarly, a public good on a neighborhood or community scale can be viewed as "packaged" within appropriate boundaries so that others outside the boundaries may be excluded from its use. In this way, in some communities adjacent to New York City, for example, the use of parks and beaches is restricted to local residents whose taxes presumably support these recreation facilities.

Wherever this is practicable, the analogy of a household as a "package" for an atmosphere with a controlled temperature may be generalized and applied to the maintenance of a desired state of affairs within particular local government boundaries. Just as the temperature and the cost of heating can be measured, so it may be possible to develop direct or closely approximate measures both of a given state of community affairs resulting from the production of many public goods and services and also of the costs of furnishing them. An air pollution abatement program, for example, may be measured by an index of quantities of various pollutants found in air samples. Given costs of abatement, some preferred tolerance levels may then be specified.

Similarly, any community has a "fire loss potential," defined as the losses to be expected if no provision for fire protection is made. The difference between this potential and the actual fire losses is then the output or "production" of the fire protection service, and the net fire loss can be termed the "state of affairs" in that community with respect to fire losses. Fire protection, of course, does not eliminate but only reduces fire losses. Any effort at complete elimination would probably be so expensive that the costs would greatly exceed the benefits. The "preferred" state of affairs is some optimal level of performance where benefits exceed costs. The provision of a community fire department as a public good can thus be viewed as the maintenance of a preferred state of affairs in fire protection for that community, and the benefits can ordinarily be confined to its residents.

Police protection can be regarded in the same way. The traffic patrol, for example, operates to optimize the flow of traffic while reducing the losses to property and injury to persons. Even if perfect control were possible, the costs would be so great that the preferred state of affairs in police protection would be something less.

It must be acknowledged, however, that in the case of police protection and many other public services, in contrast, say, with garbage collection or air pollution abatement, the performance level or net payoff is much more difficult to measure and to quantify. Proximate measures such as the gross number of arrests for different types of offenses per month or per 10,000 population annually have little meaning unless considered in relation to various conditions existing in the community. Decision-makers consequently may be forced, for want of better measurements, to assume that the preferred state of affairs is defined as a balance between the demands for public services and the complaints from taxpayers.

While the output of a public good may not be packaged this does not of course mean that its material inputs cannot be. The preferred state of affairs produced by mosquito spraying is enjoyed by the whole community, while spraying supplies and equipment are readily packageable. Mosquito spraying, that is to say, can be produced by a private vendor under contract to a public agency.

This illustrates an important point, that the *production* of goods and services needs to be distinguished from their *provision* at public expense. Government provision need not involve public production—indeed, at some stage in the sequence from raw materials to finished products virtually every public good, not already a natural resource, is of private origin. So, a public agency by contractual arrangements with private firms—or with other public agencies—can provide the local community with public services without going into the business of producing them itself.

When the desired performance level or the net payoff can be specified by a measurable index, an element of rigor can be introduced to assure substantial production controls in providing a public good, even where the production itself is the function of a separate agency or entrepreneur. The producer can be held accountable for maintaining affairs within certain tolerances, and the agency responsible for providing the service can ascertain the adequacy of performance. Advances in the measurement and quantification of performance levels in the public service economy will consequently permit much greater flexibility in the patterns of organization for the production and provision of public goods and services.

If Dewey's definition is extended to include "events" generally rather than being limited to "acts" or to "transactions" among actors, his formulation is consistent with the conception of public goods as the maintenance of preferred states of affairs.[10] Public control seeks to internalize those events, viewed as consequences which impinge directly and indirectly upon diverse elements in a community, in such a way that adverse consequences will be inhibited and favorable consequences will be promoted.

In the final analysis, distinctions between private and public goods cannot be as sharply made in the world of human experience as this analysis might imply. In part, the technical character of specific goods influences the degree of differentiation or isolability that characterizes their distribution and utilization. Vegetables and landscapes cannot be handled in the same way. Many private goods have spillover effects such that other members of the community bear some portion of the benefits and losses, whatever the degree of public regulation. In every large community most people philosophically accept some of the costs of bigness—air pollution, traffic congestion, noise, and a variety of inconveniences—on the assumption that these are inevitable concomitants of the benefits that derive from living in a metropolis.

II. SCALE PROBLEMS IN PUBLIC ORGANIZATION

Viewing the boundaries of a local unit of government as the "package" in which its public goods are provided,[11] so that those outside the boundaries are excluded from their use, we may say that where a public good is adequately packaged within appropriate boundaries, it has been successfully internalized. Where externalities spill over upon neighboring communities, the public good has not been fully internalized.

In designing the appropriate "package" for the production and provision of public goods several criteria should be considered. Among these are control, efficiency, political representation and self-determination. Needless to say, they are sometimes in conflict.

The Criterion of Control. The first standard applicable to the scale of public organization for the production of public services requires that the boundary conditions[12] of a political jurisdiction include the relevant set of events to be controlled. Events are not uniformly distributed in space; rather, they occur as sets under conditions such that boundaries can be defined with more or less precision. Rivers flow in watershed basins, for example. Patterns of social interaction are also differentially distributed in space and boundaries can generally be defined for them too. In other words, all phenomena can be described in relation to specifiable boundary conditions and the criterion of control requires that these be taken into account in determining the scale of a public organization. Otherwise the public agency is disabled in regulating a set of events in order to realize some preferred state of affairs. If the boundaries cannot be suitably adjusted, the likely result is a transfer of the governmental function to a unit scaled to meet the criterion of control more adequately.

Pasadena, for example, is subject to severe smog attacks, but the city's boundary conditions do not cover an area sufficient to assure effective control of the appropriate meteorological and social space that would include the essential variables constituting the "smogisphere" of Southern California. None of the separate cities of southern California, in fact, can encompass the problem. Instead, county air pollution control districts were organized for the Los Angeles metropolitan community. The failure even of these counties to meet adequately the criterion of effective control has led the California state government to assume an increasingly important role in smog control.

The Criterion of Efficiency. The most efficient solution would require the modification of boundary conditions so as to assure a producer of public goods and services the most favorable economy of scale, as well as effective control. Two streams with different hydrologic characteristics, for example, might be effectively controlled separately; but, by being managed together, the potentialities of one may complement the other. This has certainly been the case in Los Angeles' joint management of the Owens River and the Los Angeles River by making one the tributary of the other through the 300-mile Los Angeles Aqueduct, skirting the Sierras. Joint management permits a greater

[10] *Op. cit.*, pp. 4–5. Dewey's use of the terms "acts" and "transactions" implies that only social behavior is contemplated in public action. But physical events, *e.g.*, floods, may also become objects of public control.

[11] See the discussion of "district boundaries and the incidence of benefits" in Stephen C. Smith, "Problems in the Use of the Public District for Ground Water Management," *Land Economics*, Vol. 32 (August, 1956), pp. 259–269.

[12] The boundary conditions of a local unit of government are not limited to the legally determined physical boundaries but should include reference to extra-territorial powers, joint powers, etc.

joint payoff in recreational facilities and water and power production.

Other factors such as technological developments and the skill or proficiency of a labor force can bear upon efficiency as a criterion of the scale of organization needed. If machinery for painting center stripes on city streets can only be efficiently used on a large scale, special arrangements may be required to enable several small cities to act jointly in providing such a service. The same may be true in the utilization of uncommon and expensive professional skills; and it accounts for the fact that mental institutions and prisons are apt to be state rather than municipal undertakings.

The Criterion of Political Representation. Another criterion for the scale of public organization requires the inclusion of the appropriate political interests within its decision-making arrangements. The direct participants in a transaction are apt to negotiate only their own interests, leaving the indirect consequences or spillover effects to impinge upon others. Third-party interests may be ignored. Public organizations seek to take account of third-party effects by internalizing the various interests in rendering public decisions and in controlling public affairs. Specification of the boundary or scale conditions of any political jurisdiction is important in determining the set of interests which are to be internalized within the organization.

In considering the political design of a public organization three elements of scale require consideration. The *scale of formal organization* indicates the size of the governmental unit which provides a public good. The *public,* as noted above, consists of those who are affected by its provision. The *political community* can be defined as those who are actually taken into account in deciding whether and how to provide it. Those who are affected by such a decision may be different from those who influence its making. An ideal solution, assuming criteria of responsibility and accountability consonant with democratic theory, would require that these three boundaries be coterminous. Where in fact the boundary conditions differ, scale problems arise.

If both the direct and indirect beneficiaries of a public transaction are included within the domain of a public organization, the means are in principle available for assessment of the cost of public control upon the beneficiaries. Except where a re-distribution of income is sought as a matter of public policy, an efficient allocation of economic resources is assured by the capacity to charge the costs of providing public goods and services to the beneficiaries.[13]

The public implicated in different sets of transactions varies with each set: the relevant public for one set is confined to a neighborhood, while for another the relevant public may be most of the population of the globe. Between these two extremes are a vast number of potential scales of public organizations. Given certain levels of information, technology, communication, and certain patterns of identification, a scheme might be imagined which had an appropriate scale of public organization for each different public good. As these conditions and circumstances change, the scale of the public for any set of transactions should be altered correspondingly. If it is not, what then?

Where the political community does not contain the whole public, some interests may be disregarded. A city, for instance, may decide to discharge its sewage below its boundaries, and the affected public there may have no voice in the decision. On the other hand, where the political community contains the whole public and, in addition, people unaffected by a transaction, the unaffected are given a voice when none may be desired. Capricious actions can result. The total political community in a city of three million population may not be an appropriate decision-making mechanism in planning a local playground.

Nevertheless, the statement that a government is "too large (or too small) to deal with a problem" often overlooks the possibility that the scale of the public and the political community need not coincide with that of the formal boundaries of a public organization. Informal arrangements between public organizations may create a political community large enough to deal with any particular public's problem. Similarly, a public organization may also be able to constitute political communities within its boundaries to deal with problems which affect only a subset of the population. It would be a mistake to conclude that public organizations are of an inappropriate size until the informal mechanisms, which might permit larger or smaller political communities, are investigated.

Seen in relation to the political community, the scale of formal public organizations merely specifies the formal boundaries. Since the feasible number of governmental units is

[13] This factor might be separately characterized as a criterion of equitable distribution of costs and benefits, but we have chosen to consider it here in the context of political representation.

limited when compared to the number of public goods to be provided, a one-to-one mapping of the public, the political community and the formal public organization is impracticable. Moreover, the relevant public changes. Even if, at one time, formal public organizations, political communities and the publics were coterminous, over time they would become dislocated. As a result, public organizations may (1) reconstitute themselves, (2) voluntarily cooperate, or, failing cooperation, (3) turn to other levels of government in a quest for an appropriate fit among the interests affecting and affected by public transactions.

The Criterion of Local Self-Determination. The criteria of effective control, of efficiency and of the inclusion of appropriate political interests, can be formulated on general theoretical grounds, but their application in any political system depends upon the particular institutions empowered to decide questions of scale. The conditions attending the organization of local governments in the United States usually require that these criteria be controlled by the decisions of the citizenry in the local community, *i.e.*, subordinated to considerations of self-determination.

The patterns of local self-determination manifest in incorporation proceedings usually require a petition of local citizens to institute incorporation proceedings and an affirmative vote of the local electorate to approve. Commitments to local consent and local control may also involve substantial home rule in determining which interests of the community its local officials will attend to and how these officials will be organized and held responsible for their discharge of public functions.

Local self-government of municipal affairs assumes that public goods can be successfully internalized. The purely "municipal" affairs of a local jurisdiction, presumably, do not create problems for other political communities. Where internalization is not possible and where control consequently, cannot be maintained, the local unit of government becomes another "interest" group in quest of public goods or potential public goods that spill over upon others beyond its borders.

The choice of local public services implicit in any system of self-government presumes that substantial variety will exist in patterns of public organization and in the public goods provided among the different local communities in a metropolis. Patterns of local autonomy and home rule constitute substantial commitments to a polycentric system.

III. PUBLIC ORGANIZATION IN GARGANTUA

Since all patterns of organization are less than perfectly efficient, responsive or representative, some consideration should be given to the problem of organizing for different types of public services in gargantua, in contrast to the problems in a polycentric political system. This brief discussion will only touch on theoretical considerations involved in organizing diverse public services in the big system.

Gargantua unquestionably provides an appropriate scale of organization for many huge public services. The provision of harbor and airport facilities, mass transit, sanitary facilities and imported water supplies may be most appropriately organized in gargantua. By definition, gargantua should be best able to deal with metropolitan-wide problems at the metropolitan level.

However, gargantua with its single dominant center of decision-making, is apt to become a victim of the complexity of its own hierarchical or bureaucratic structure. Its complex channels of communication may make its administration unresponsive to many of the more localized public interests in the community. The costs of maintaining control in gargantua's public service may be so great that its production of public goods becomes grossly inefficient.

Gargantua, as a result, may become insensitive and clumsy in meeting the demands of local citizens for the public goods required in their daily life. Two to three years may be required to secure street or sidewalk improvements, for example, even where local residents bear the cost of the improvement. Modifications in traffic control at a local intersection may take an unconscionable amount of time. Some decision-makers will be more successful in pursuing their interests than others. The lack of effective organization for these others may result in policies with highly predictable biases. Bureaucratic unresponsiveness in gargantua may produce frustration and cynicism on the part of the local citizen who finds no point of access for remedying local problems of a public character. Municipal reform may become simply a matter of "throwing the rascals out." The citizen may not have access to sufficient information to render an informed judgment at the polls. Lack of effective communication in the large public organization may indeed lead to the eclipse of the public and to the blight of the community.

The problem of gargantua, then, is to recognize the variety of smaller sets of publics that may exist within its boundaries. Many of the interests of smaller publics might be properly negotiated within the confines of a smaller political community without requiring the attention of centralized decision-makers concerned with the big system. This task of recognizing the smaller publics is a problem of "field" or "area" organization. The persistence of bureaucratic unresponsiveness in the big system, however, indicates it is not easily resolved. Large-scale, metropolitan-wide organization is unquestionably appropriate for a limited number of public services, but it is not the most appropriate scale of organization for the provision of all public services required in a metropolis.

IV. PUBLIC ORGANIZATION IN A POLYCENTRIC POLITICAL SYSTEM

No *a priori* judgment can be made about the adequacy of a polycentric system of government as against the single jurisdiction. The multiplicity of interests in various public goods sought by people in a metropolitan region can only be handled in the context of many different levels of organization. The polycentric system is confronted with the problem of realizing the needs of wider community interests or publics beyond the functional or territorial bounds of each of the formal entities within the broader metropolitan region. The single jurisdiction, in turn, confronts the problem of recognizing and organizing the various subsidiary sets of interests within the big system. It is doubtful that sub-optimization in gargantua is any easier to accomplish than supra-optimization in a polycentric political system.

The performance of a polycentric political system can only be understood and evaluated by reference to the patterns of cooperation, competition and conflict that may exist among its various units. Cooperative arrangements pose no difficulty when joint activities produce a greater return to all parties concerned, if the appropriate set of public interests are adequately represented among the negotiators. A contractual arrangement will suffice. As a result, this discussion of the behavior of a polycentric political system will focus upon the more difficult problems of competition, of conflict and its resolution. If a polycentric political system can resolve conflict and maintain competition within appropriate bounds it can be a viable arrangement for dealing with a variety of public problems in a metropolitan area.

Competition.[14] Where the provision of public goods and services has been successfully internalized within a public jurisdiction, there are no substantial spill-over effects, by definition. In such circumstances there need be no detrimental consequences from competition in the municipal services economy. Patterns of competition among producers of public services in a metropolitan area, just as among firms in the market, may produce substantial benefits by inducing self-regulating tendencies with pressure for the more efficient solution in the operation of the whole system.

Variety in service levels among various independent local government agencies within a larger metropolitan community may give rise to a quasi-market choice for local residents in permitting them to select the particular community in the metropolitan area that most closely approximates the public service levels they desire. Public service agencies then may be forced to compete over the service levels offered in relation to the taxes charged. Such competition, however, would only be appropriate for those public goods which are adequately internalized within the boundaries of a given political jurisdiction.

Conditions amenable to competition normally exist among local units of government where a number of units are located in close proximity to each other and where information about each other's performance is publicly available. Information can lead to comparison and comparison can lead to pressure for performances to approximate the operations of the more efficient units. Where more than one public jurisdiction is capable of rendering service in a single area, further competitive tendencies may develop. Contractual arrangements among public jurisdictions for the provision of specific public services have long provided a competitive alternative to each jurisdiction which might otherwise produce its own services.

The separation of the *provision* of public goods and services from their *production* opens up the greatest possibility of redefining economic functions in a public service economy. Public control can be maintained in relation to performance criteria in the provision of services, while allowing an increasing amount of competition to develop among the agencies that produce them.

With the incorporation of the City of Lake-

[14] This analysis is confined to competition between units of government and makes no reference to competitive forces within a unit of government. Competition among pressure groups, factions and political parties is a fundamental feature of the democratic political process, but is not within the primary focus of this paper and its concern with the polycentric system.

wood in 1954, Los Angeles County, for example, expanded its system of contracting for the production of municipal services to a point approaching quasi-market conditions. Newly incorporated cities, operating under the so-called Lakewood Plan, contract with the county or other appropriate agencies to produce the general range of municipal services needed in the local community.

Each city contracts for municipal services for the city as a whole. Services beyond the general level of performance by county administration in unincorporated areas are subject to negotiation for most service functions. Each city also has the option of producing municipal services for itself. Private contractors too have undertaken such services as street sweeping, engineering, street maintenance and repair, and related public works. Some contracts have been negotiated with neighboring cities. As the number of vendors increases, competition brings pressures toward greater responsiveness and efficiency.

By separating the production from the provision of public goods it may be possible to differentiate, unitize and measure the production while continuing to provide undifferentiated public goods to the citizen-consumer. Thus Los Angeles County has, under the Lakewood Plan, unitized the production of police services into packages, each consisting of a police-car-on-continuous-patrol with associated auxiliary services. A price is placed on this police-car-on-continuous-patrol package, and a municipality may contract for police service on that basis. Within the local community, police service is still provided as a public good for the community as a whole.

Problems of scale arising from possible conflicts between criteria of production and criteria of political representation may be effectively resolved in this way. Efficient scales of organization for the production of different public goods may be quite independent of the scales required to recognize appropriate publics for their consumption of public goods and services. But competition among vendors may allow the most efficient organization to be utilized in the production, while an entirely different community of interest and scale of organization controls the provision of services in a local community.

The separation of production from provision may also have the consequence of turning local governments into the equivalents of associations of consumers. While Sidney and Beatrice Webb viewed local governments as associations of consumers, the dominance of production criteria in American municipal administration has largely led to the subordination of consumer interests.[15] However, cities organized to provide the local citizenry with public services produced by other agencies may be expected to give stronger representation to consumer interests. Among the so-called Lakewood Plan cities in Los Angeles County, for example, the local chief administrative officer has increasingly become a spokesman or bargainer for local consumer interests.

In this role, the chief administrative officer is similar to a buyer in a large corporation. Recognizing that the greater the number of vendors of public services, the greater the competition, the local chief administrative officer may seek to expand the number of his potential suppliers. As competition increases, vendors become more sensitive to the consumer demands he negotiates.

The production of public goods under the contract system in Los Angeles County has also placed considerable pressure upon the county administration to become more responsive to demands of the public service clientele organized through their local cities. Important changes in operating procedures and organizational arrangements have been introduced into the county's administration of police protection, fire protection, library services, street maintenance, building inspection and engineering services in order to increase efficiency and responsiveness.

Under these circumstances, a polycentric political system can be viable in supplying a variety of public goods with many different scales of organization and in providing optimal arrangements for the production and consumption of public goods. With the development of quasi-market conditions in production, much of the flexibility and responsiveness of market organization can be realized in the public service economy.

Several difficulties in the regulation of a competitive public service economy can be anticipated. Economic pricing and cost allocation are dependent upon the development of effective measurement of municipal services. Since the preferred states of affairs in a community cannot be converted to a single scale of values such as dollar profits in a private enterprise, it may be more difficult to sustain an objective competitive relationship in a public service economy. Although costs of contract services from different vendors of a public

[15] Sidney and Beatrice Webb, *English Local Government: Statutory Authorities for Special Purposes* (London: Longmans, Green and Co., 1922), p. 437 ff.

good may be the same, objective standards for determining the value of the benefits are needed, and may be hard to come by; otherwise the latitude of discretion available to the negotiators may limit the competitive vitality of the system and shift the competition to side-payoffs.

Without careful control of cost allocations and pricing arrangements, funds from non-competitive welfare functions might be used to subsidize the more competitive service areas. In Los Angeles County, close scrutiny of cost accounting practices and pricing policies by the grand jury has helped to prevent funds from being so transferred.

Any long-term reliance upon quasi-market mechanisms in the production of public goods and services no doubt will require more of such careful scrutiny, control and regulation than has been applied toward maintaining the competitive structure of the private market economy. The measurement of cost and output performance may become an essential public function of the state in the administration of metropolitan affairs if continued reliance is placed primarily upon a polycentric system in the government of metropolitan areas.

Reliance upon outside vendors to produce public services may also reduce the degree of local political control exercised. The employee is subject to the control of the vendor and not directly to the control of the municipality. In contrast to the more immediate lines of responsibility and communication between local municipal employees and city officials, reliance upon vendors to provide municipal services may also restrict the quality and quantity of information about community affairs that are provided to the city's decision-makers. This constraint on information might reduce the degree of their control over public affairs.

This discussion merely indicates some of the considerations to be examined in an analysis of the effects of competitive arrangements in providing public services. As long as the particular contracting agencies encompass the appropriate sets of public interests no absolute impediment to their use need exist. With appropriate public control, competitive arrangements may afford great flexibility in taking advantage of some of the economies of scale for the production of public services in a metropolitan area, while, at the same time, allowing substantial diversity in their provision for the more immediate communities, based upon political responsibility within local patterns of community identification.

Conflict and Conflict Resolution. More difficult problems for a polycentric political system are created when the provision of public goods cannot be confined to the boundaries of the existing units of government. These situations involving serious spill-over effects are apt to provoke conflict between the various units in the system. Arrangements must be available for the resolution of such conflicts if a polycentric political system is to solve its problems. Otherwise, competition and conflict are apt to become acute.

No community, on its own initiative, has much incentive to assume the full costs of controlling adverse consequences which are shared by a wider public. The competitive disadvantage of enforcing pollution abatement regulations, for example, against individuals and firms within a single community, when competitors in neighboring communities are not required to bear such costs, leads each community to excuse its failure to act by the failure of other similarly situated communities to act. In a polycentric system this is especially serious where many of the public "goods" involve the costly abatement of public nuisances.

Concerted action by the various units of government in a metropolitan area is easier to organize when costs and benefits are fairly uniformly distributed throughout the area. By way of example, this has been done under contractual agreements for mutual aid to assure the mobilization of greater fire-fighting capability in case of serious conflagrations. The random and unpredictable nature of such fires causes them to be treated as a uniform risk that might occur to any community in the larger metropolitan area.

Similar considerations apply to efforts to control mosquito infestations or air pollution. Leagues of cities, chambers of commerce and other civic associations have frequently become the agencies for negotiating legislative proposals for the creation of mosquito abatement districts, air pollution control districts and the like.

More difficult problems for the polycentric political system arise when the benefits and the costs are not uniformly distributed. Communities may differ in their perception of the benefits they receive from the provision of a common public good. In turn, a community may be unwilling to "pay its fair share" for providing that good simply because its demands for provision are less than in neighboring communities. These situations call for effective governmental mechanisms which can internalize the problem. If necessary, sanctions must be available for the enforcement of decisions.

The conflicting claims of municipal water supply systems pumping water from the same underground basins in Southern California, for example, have uniformly been resolved by recourse to legal actions in the state courts. The courts have thereby become the primary authorities for resolving conflicts among water supply agencies in Southern California; and their decisions have come to provide many of the basic policies of water administration in the Southern California metropolitan region. The state's judiciary has played a comparable role in conflicts among other local government agencies in such diverse fields as public health, incorporation and annexation proceedings, law enforcement, and urban planning.

The heavy reliance upon courts for the resolution of conflicts among local units of government unquestionably reflects an effort to minimize the risks of external control by a superior decision-maker. Court decisions are taken on a case-by-case basis. The adversaries usually define the issues and consequently limit the areas of judicial discretion. This method also minimizes the degree of control exercised following a judgment. California courts, in particular, have accepted the basic doctrines of home rule and are thus favorably disposed to the interests of local units of government in dealing with problems of municipal affairs.

The example of municipal water administration may be pursued further to illustrate other decision-making arrangements and their consequences which bear upon the resolution of conflict in a polycentric political system.[16]

While litigation may be an appropriate means for resolving conflicts over a given supply of water, local water administrators in Southern California have long recognized that law suits never produced any additional water. Organization for the importation of new water supplies was recognized as the only means for solving the long-term problem.

Los Angeles built the first major aqueduct to import water into the area on its own initiative. This water supply was used to force adjoining areas to annex or consolidate to the City of Los Angeles if they wished to gain access to the new supply. The condition for the provision of water required adjoining areas to sacrifice their identities as separate political communities. To get that one public good they were forced to give up other public goods. This provoked sufficient opposition to block any new developments which were not based upon consent and cooperation. The mechanisms for the resolution of subsequent conflicts were required to take on new forms.

The importation of Colorado River water was later undertaken by a coalition of communities in Southern California formed through the agency of the southern section of the League of California Cities. The League afforded a neutral ground for the negotiation of the common interests of the City of Los Angeles and the other cities in the metropolitan area which shared common water problems. After satisfactory arrangements had been negotiated, including provision for the formation of a new metropolitan water district and endorsement of the Boulder Canyon project, a Boulder Dam Association was formed to realize these objectives. In due course a new agency, the Metropolitan Water District of Southern California, was formed; and the Colorado River aqueduct was constructed and put into operation by this new district.

More recently, the Southern California Water Coordinating Conference, meeting under the auspices of the Los Angeles Chamber of Commerce, has been the agency for negotiating regional interests in the development of the California Water Program. The Metropolitan Water District was not able to represent areas in Southern California which did not belong to that district; and the rise of a variety of special municipal water districts precluded the League of California Cities, which represents cities only, from again serving as the agency for the negotiation of metropolitan interests in municipal water supply.

These illustrations suggest that a variety of informal arrangements may be available for negotiating basic policies among local government agencies in a metropolitan area. Such arrangements are vital in negotiating common interests among them. The larger public is taken into account in an informally constituted political community. These arrangements work effectively only so long as substantial unanimity can be reached, for formal implementation of such decisions must be ratified by each of the appropriate official agencies, including the state government when changes in state law or administrative policies are involved.

Higher levels of government may also be invoked in seeking the resolution of conflict among local governments in metropolitan areas. Again recourse is sought to a more inclusive political community. Under these circumstances, conflict tends to centralize decision-making and control. The danger is that the more inclusive political community will not give appropriate recognition to the particular

[16] For further detail see: Vincent Ostrom, *Water and Politics* (Los Angeles, Haynes Foundation, 1953), esp. chs. 3, 6 and 7.

public interests at issue and tend to inject a variety of other interests into settlements of local controversies.

Appeal to central authorities runs the risk of placing greater control over local metropolitan affairs in agencies such as the state legislature, while at the same time reducing the capability of local governments for dealing with their problems in the local context. Sensitivity over the maintenance of local control may produce great pressure for the subordination of differences while conflicting parties seek a common position approximating unanimity. A substantial investment in informal negotiating and decision-making arrangements can be justified from the perspective of the local authorities if such arrangements can prevent the loss of local autonomy to higher levels of government.

Ironically but logically, this effort to avoid recourse to conflict and the consequent centralization of decision-making tends also to reduce the local autonomy or degree of independence exercised by the local governing boards. Pressure for agreement on a common approach to some metropolitan problem limits the choices available to any particular local government. However, this range of choice may still be greater than that which would result from a settlement by a central authority. Negotiation among independent agencies allows the use of a veto against any unacceptable position. Agreement must be negotiated within the limits of the various veto positions if the alternative of recourse to an external authority at a higher level of political jurisdiction is to be avoided.

To minimize the costs of conflict to their power positions, administrators of local government agencies in metropolitan areas have tended to develop an extensive system of communication about each other's experience and to negotiate standards of performance applicable to various types of public services. Professional administrative standards may, thus, operate to constrain the variety of experience in local government agencies. Information about areas of difference and of potential conflict tend to be repressed under these circumstances. The negotiations about common problems through informal agencies are apt to be conducted in secrecy, and careful control may be developed over sensitive information.

These pressures to avoid the costs of conflict and seek agreement about metropolitan problems reflect the importance to local governments of resolving general public problems by negotiation at the local level in a metropolitan community. To the extent that these pressures are effective, the patterns of local government in a metropolitan area can only be understood by attention to the variety of formal and informal arrangements that may exist for settling area-wide problems.

Contrary to the frequent assertion about the lack of a "metropolitan framework" for dealing with metropolitan problems, most metropolitan areas have a very rich and intricate "framework" for negotiating, adjudicating and deciding questions that affect their diverse public interests. Much more careful attention needs to be given to the study of this framework.

28. The Valley Authority and Its Alternatives*

CHARLES MCKINLEY

In examining the Valley Authority as an administrative device for Federal water resource management this paper will assume that its essential characteristics are those exemplified by the Tennessee Valley Authority, with such additional complications as might be necessitated by the irrigation functions performed in the western states by the Bureau of Reclamation.[1] We may legitimately brush aside the allegations of communism and dictatorship as unwarranted propaganda exaggerations devoid of genuine reality. We may similarly discount many of the "new heaven and new earth" asseverations of those social idealists most susceptible to verbal inebriation who have stood out as the most ardent and vocal advocates of the new mode of organizing Federal resource administration.

I. QUESTIONS NOT OF THE ESSENCE

The functional activities of the Tennessee Valley Authority add little that is

[1] There has been a spate of Valley Authority proposals incorporated in bills presented for congressional consideration in which many variants on the TVA pattern have been made. It will be impossible to consider them here, but most of their features have been digested (down to the end of 1946) in two articles: (1) by Wesley Clark in this REVIEW, Vol. 40, pp. 62 ff. (February, 1946), and (2) by Robert Greenleaf in the *Iowa Law Review*, Vol. 32, pp. 339 ff. (January, 1947).

* Reprinted from the *American Political Science Review*, Vol. 44 (Sept. 1950).

wholly new to the gamut of Federal activities found scattered among several of our orthodox administrative agencies. The fact that it prosecuted its construction activities by force account rather than by contract necessitated that it do the things that the private contractor would have to do. These have given the private enterprise alarmists their propaganda illustrations for the cries of communism. Its great reservoir projects located in rural and often remote areas required construction camp facilities for hundreds of workmen and their families, together with the essential community facilities. That TVA showed a more wholesome concern for the quality of housing, restaurant services, schools, recreation and health facilities of its employees than has been manifest by the typical private contractor is to its great credit. Its policies in these respects have helpfully influenced the construction camp planning of the Corps of Engineers and the Bureau of Reclamation, some of whose recent projects are providing much more adequate camp plans and facilities than was their wont.[2]

It should also be recognized that in the early thirties, when TVA was being launched, the national climate of opinion at first encouraged its Board to take a wide and generous view of the many welfare by-products that its construction program permitted. Its immediate task in 1933 was not only to create dams and reservoirs for harnessing the waters of the Tennessee River, but to put people to work. The folk affected were largely rural people living in substandard rural conditions. The generosity shown by TVA toward educational activities, its relocation program for the owners of bottom lands drowned by its reservoirs, its conception of ways to increase the utilization of hydroelectric energy in such a region, its need to keep its workmen and their families in good health—all of these interests when given concrete expression in a regional situation like that in the Tennessee Valley in 1933 seemed new, startling and radical to the *laissez-faire* engineers who directed the policies of the old river construction agencies.

The TVA was of course given a broader grant of legal right to pursue such by-product objectives than were its orthodox competitors. Toward the close of the War, the Bureau of Reclamation, in anticipation of the renewal of the irrigation phase of its Grand Coulee-Columbia Basin project, tried to obtain legislation to permit its District Engineer to provide better housing and other facilities for the expanded construction force. But the congressional climate had changed, and the real estate boys and other high cost purveyors of cheap facilities in Coulee City blocked the authorization.

TVA's right to buy watershed lands for watershed protection and conservation could not have been matched by the Bureau or the Corps, even had they

[2] We need not take the town of Norris as the typical TVA contribution. It was an expensive, permanent town, whose cost was not repeated elsewhere. More characteristic was the construction town for Fontana Dam, where acceptable, portable, temporary houses were used for that portion of the town that would shrink when construction was finished. The amenities furnished there give the kind of example which has beneficially influenced the Corps and the Bureau.

been interested. Until recently they had no right to buy watershed land not needed for flowage and water storage purposes. Consequently when these agencies were finally given the authority to consider the recreational by-products of projects already constructed—such as the great Franklin D. Roosevelt Lake behind Grand Coulee Dam—an expensive purchase program of land acquisition, due to appreciated values gratuitously handed to private owners by federal enterprise, became necessary. But we should note that in this matter the TVA policy in recent years has moved, under the influence of the conservatism alleged by Selznick to stem from the Division of Agricultural Relations-State College-Farm Bureau forces, toward the former position of the Corps of Engineers and the Bureau of Reclamation.

In clearing away the underbrush about the Valley Authority issue we may also dismiss the allegation of encroachment on states rights. With the single exception of the control of resale rates charged for electric energy by its distributors (an exception amply warranted by the ineffectiveness of state utility regulation) TVA has not tangled with the legal jurisdiction of the states. Were valley authorities to be transplanted to the West, they would have the additional issue of private water rights which are controlled by the states. While some of the earlier MVA and CVA bills blundered into a position which gave some legitimacy to the hue and cry that arose on this question, care has been exercised since the second Mitchell bill of 1945 to subordinate the proposed authority's irrigation development functions to the traditional state sovereignty over water rights.

To eyes not blinded by unreasoning prejudice it should be fairly easy to see that TVA has been of great help to towns, school districts, counties and states in the valley in the exercise of latent powers which formerly they had either neglected or had performed inadequately. By its policy of delegating many of its tasks to state and local institutions, on a contractual and compensatory basis, and by its proffer of free technical assistance, it has constituted a major source of the yeast that during the past fifteen years has greatly raised the level of state and local services in that part of the South, and strengthened rather than impaired the vigor of established local institutions. The concern for the virility of the orthodox local and state agencies under the impact of TVA when valley authorities are proposed elsewhere is certainly not matched within the Tennessee Valley. As a matter of fact precisely the opposite criticism is made by Selznick in his recently published study of the TVA.[3] He asserts that its support of the State College-Extension Service agencies has inhibited the growth of the new local institutions (Soil Conservation Districts) which would have competed with the former. His evidence seems also to point to undue self-restraint on TVA's part in supervising and auditing the expenditure of its grant-in-aid funds to the State Colleges which were its agents in the land-use program. Whether these criticisms are fully warranted we do not at present know; nor do we know whether the other grants which TVA as a reappropriat-

[3] Philip Selznick, *TVA and the Grass Roots* (Berkeley, 1949).

ing agency has disbursed to many state and local governments have been handled with too little control. (Had controls been irksome Congress would undoubtedly have aired the grievances.) It is most unfortunate that the Hoover Commission felt unable, or unwilling, to provide a systematic and thorough staff analysis of the TVA as a Federal operating entity, for until a competent and comprehensive study of its administrative experience is available we will not be able to evaluate for application elsewhere many of the techniques it has used.

The battle over the allegations of "communism," "dictatorship" and "states rights" has tended to obscure from our attention the real problems imbedded in the Valley Authority question. The debate ought to turn on the more narrow and semi-technical issues of how the field administration of Federal resource development and management functions can best be performed. What are the shortcomings of the present traditional administrative structure used by the Federal Government for the job of harnessing the waters of our river valleys so as to minimize their destructive aberrations and to expand their human usefulness? What are the deficiencies, if any, in the Federal management of its own wild land resources, including the forests, and in speeding up the acceptance of conservation practices by state, local and private land owners? What obstacles to fuller development and more complete utilization of our mineral, timber and agricultural resources inhere in the traditional bureau, departmental and field structure? What now obscures the comprehensive, all-regional view which should guide the mosaic of Federal resource programs and policies in whole water-shed regions, and which should subordinate bureaucratic jealousy and foster an integrated administrative product shared not only by Federal agency partners but by the states and local government as well? Will the Valley Authority device offer the best administrative cure for the defects that exist? These are the relevant questions we should ask and for which we should seek answers.

II. DECENTRALIZATION BY FEDERAL AGENCIES

There are deficiencies, and serious ones, in the present Federal field structure on the whole resource front. Let us briefly describe some of the more outstanding items in this indictment. First, powers of bureau field officers differ greatly among Federal agencies. Program correlation is impeded by these differences. While each agency is represented by a field establishment, the degree of delegation to deal with its own functions as well as with interagency problems varies from that of Bonneville Power Administration—in effect a full fledged bureau located in a single region and reporting directly to the Secretary of the Interior—to the numerous scattered Geological Survey field offices with almost no discretion to make decisions on interagency matters and no common regional superior responsible for the total field effort of the Survey. Such a structure is like the 19th century battle fleet whose speed was determined by its slowest collier. Interagency cooperation and the making of integrated resource plans and programs are slowed down and hindered because some field officials have no discretion to commit their agencies or no power to command a region-wide field staff. This handicap of uneven delegation of field authority, of variation in the degree of regional integration of agency structure and of differing regional boundaries for field administration applies to water, land and mineral agencies.

Yet we must note that during the last few years improvement, real though slow, has been made in bureau-field patterns of structure and powers. The Department of the Interior, which had remained the most highly centralized of the major resource departments, awoke in the early forties to the need to overcome some of these administrative lags. Thus the Bureau of Reclamation has been changed, since 1943, from a highly centralized, Denver-directed agency, to a fairly decentralized and regionally oriented structure. The old General Land Office has at last been pulled out of its hard cocoon of centralized, inert, legalistic red tape and is in process of metamorphosis into an active, on-the-ground resource management agency with a new name—the Bureau of Land Management—and with new leadership. The National Park Service, during the last decade, has regionalized and to some extent decentralized. Within the past six months the Bureau of Mines has reconsidered its structure and redistributed its powers in the light of a decentralized conception of field needs. The Corps of Engineers has long given its District and Division Engineers large initiative and responsibility in the design and construction of river structures. In the Department of Agriculture the Forest Service under Gifford Pinchot's leadership pioneered the movement for efficient, decentralized, on-the-ground resource management. That lead has been followed by the Soil Conservation Service, which shares with it the major burden of active land and watershed resource work within the Department of Agriculture.

III. DEVELOPMENT AND MANAGEMENT OF WATER-IN-THE-CHANNEL

A second defect in the current situation is the friction and disjointedness of the structure that deals with the water-in-the-channel problems. This is well illustrated by the situation in the Pacific Northwest where there are three major construction and operating agencies: The Corps of Engineers, the Bureau of Reclamation and the Bonneville Power Administration. A fourth, the Federal Power Commission, shares in river planning, though its actual interest has been principally concentrated on the hydroelectric phases of water planning. But sound river plans and operations also depend on the hydrologic and stream data developed by the Geological Survey which installs and operates stream gages, studies ground water supplies, makes topographic maps, locates dam sites, etc. This is a creaky, friction-producing structure.

There is plenty of evidence that in the seventeen western states, where the Bureau and the Army operate on the same river systems, duplication in river planning and friction over jurisdictional matters develop. Years ago, when the Army kept to the lower parts of the rivers and concerned itself chiefly with harbor and channel work and the Bureau stayed in the semi-arid hinterland on the upper basins, they got along amicably because they did not compete. Each was then chiefly concerned with special water purposes. Today they are both multiple-purpose oriented and system-wide conscious. This laudable departure from single purpose, single project obsession nevertheless multiplies the jurisdictional problems in planning, timing and operations. The Corps of Engineers has moved upstream while the Bureau moves toward the sea, each seeking to stake out its claim for construction and operation of major multiple purpose works. The result has been a state of latent warfare which, despite the pressure for harmony induced by the threat of an Authority, sometimes breaks out into the open as it did in the Missouri and the Central Vallies and, more recently, over Foster Creek and Hells Canyon Dams on the Columbia. Although during the past year a truce has been signed between the Departments of the Interior and the Army which amicably divides the potential construction jobs in the Columbia River basin, comparable pacification has not been attained in the Central Valley or the Southwest. Peace on this front, even if it may be assumed to last, will not solve the conflict issues that are bound to arise in the operation of an hydraulically and electrically interlocked system of river structures. The planning and operation of a system of river structures is the job of a single administrative organization, as the Hoover Commission concluded a year ago. Voluntary cooperation on the technical level—of which there has been a great deal—is not enough. The flowing channel waters of any river system constitute a great single force which demands unified human manipulation for its best utilization.

Where there have been created special hydroelectric transmission agencies for wheeling energy from the Bureau- and Army-operated generators to the market load centers, as is true in the Columbia River valley and in one part of the Southwest, there is a third party to this vital interest in the manipulation of the "water-in-the-channel." An agency such as the Bonneville Power Administration builds the transmission lines and sub-stations, finds the customers to buy the power and collects the revenue that makes possible the repayment of a large proportion of the reimbursable features of the Federal river structures. It must "pay out" but it has no control over the costs of the water-in-the-channel structures or of the operation of the generator facilities, and no final right to fix the rates for electric energy developed at Army-built structures.[4]

The design of generating facilities has an integral functional relation to the technical characteristics of the transmission system. Faults on the transmission system will have a vital effect on the switch-yards through which the generating plant and transmission system are connected and on the generator installations. There is a reciprocal relationship when trouble occurs in the generating plants, that may disrupt service to the customers of the transmission agency. Space does not permit other illustrations of the organic-like nexus that binds electric

[4] The Federal Power Commission determines the rates, as it also allocates the joint costs among the several purposes on the Army built dams, and approves the power facilities to be installed in structures built by the latter agency. It has no comparable rate making or cost allocating functions for river projects built by the Bureau of Reclamation. This difference in jurisdiction is an accident of history and makes no sense in river system planning and control.

transmission interests with those of design, construction, and operation of the dams and reservoirs.

If in contrast we look again at the Tennessee Valley Authority, we will find that its most signal contributions to Federal administrative experience lie, first, in the manner in which it has handled water resources, and second, in its intermeshing in over-all regional terms of all of its resource development and utilization programs.

Let us first examine its work as a water agency. There are a few limitations on its water functions. It is not generally realized that it still shares with the Corps of Engineers and the Coast Guard some of the water-in-the-channel duties. The Corps designs, operates and maintains the locks in the navigation structures on the main Tennessee; it builds the levees that are necessary for supplementary flood control protection at Chattanooga; it still makes studies and local flood control plans for the tributaries where the works required do not involve dam construction; it must give its consent to the building of structures affecting navigation along or across the streams while the TVA gives a second review for all the purposes within its jurisdiction; and the Army continues to regulate the clearances of bridges and the operation of draw spans. These duplications of navigation and flood control functions are wasteful and irritating, but the Army shows no sign of voluntary retreat on the Tennessee front and Congress has not yet compelled it.

A second minor duplication results from the transfer from the Army to the Coast Guard in 1937 of the mapping of sailing lines and the placing of channel markers on the main Tennessee. Though TVA's maintenance staff constantly patrol the river, and its engineers collect the data essential to the marking of channels and the mapping of sailing lines, the Coast Guard maintains three depots and a small staff on the Tennessee for these navigation functions.

The rest of the water-in-the-channel functions on the Tennessee system have been wholly under TVA jurisdiction. It has been charged with the construction of a system of dams and reservoirs on the main river and its tributaries which would provide a nine-foot channel with appropriate water supply to maintain it from the mouth near Paducah to Knoxville, and would aid in controlling destructive floods on the Tennessee and in the Mississippi drainage. The original TVA authorized not separate projects but a system of river structures based upon a unified plan of development for the whole basin. Out of this has come an integrated system of nine main river dams and reservoirs, fifteen storage reservoirs on the tributaries, and five smaller tributary dams owned by Alcoa which, under agreement with TVA, are operated as integral parts of the Federal river structures.[5] Some minor additions to the system are anticipated, but the major river structures needed for its water management job have been built.

To obtain maximum multiple-purpose benefits from this system requires the accurate conceptualization at the time it is designed of the part that each completed structure is to play. This would be a matter requiring great care were

[5] Four of the TVA owned tributary dams and one of the main river dams were acquired by purchase from the Tennessee Electric Co., when that system was purchased.

flood control or navigation the sole objectives, but when to these purposes are added hydroelectricity, malaria control and fisheries, forethought is especially demanded. (If the Tennessee were a western stream, irrigation would have to be added and malaria might be subtracted.) In the calculation of design characteristics as well as in planning reservoir operating rule curves TVA has not been under the kind of special loyalty to one or a few purposes that the older water agencies so often have shown. To be sure the statute on which it rests gives specific priorities to navigation and flood control, but there is no traditional allegiance to blinker the process of adjustment so as also to prevent the maximum reconciliation with other purposes.

We can perhaps see the significance of integrated management of all the water-in-the-channel functions if we briefly indicate the administrative structure and operating practices TVA has developed for this purpose. First, notice that, in its organization under the General Manager, the Chief Engineer has been entrusted with carrying out the water use priorities established by the Board. It is to him, and his Water Control Planning unit, that the Board looks for advice in setting the rule curves for each reservoir based upon the allocations made therein for each of the several water purposes. The Water Control Planning Division has been detached from any operating connection with any special water use. The power function is administered by a Power Manager who stands apart from the organization under the Chief Engineer and thus removes from him any temptation to distort plans for water use in favor of the revenue producing hydro-electric utilization. The head of the Water Planning Division chairs a continuing water policy committee of three (one member from Power and the other from Health) which strives to resolve any conflicts between the several water purposes. The chairman circularizes all TVA departments in advance of any meeting to invite their representatives if their interests are affected by the agenda before the Committee. Recommendations on use policies go to the Chief Engineer, who, in the absence of unanimity, makes the decision.

Next, TVA's day-to-day operating arrangements further exemplify how administrative structure may be directed toward unbiased adjustment of purposes. When reservoir operations confront problems not covered by rule curves or by specific instructions, the issues are resolved by the head of the River Control Section in the Water Planning Department, who is connected by leased wire with the operator of each reservoir.[6] He makes the decision when some unforeseen mosquito control, navigation or other problem requires a quick change in the level of a reservoir.

During the flood season, when a major storm is on its way, it is the Chief Engineer's organization that takes command. By confining heavy precipitation in this valley to the period between mid-December and April 1st and by routing storms over a definite pathway, Nature has made possible reasonably accurate forecasts, of both long and short range. These forecasts are made by a meteorological unit maintained at Knoxville by the Weather Bureau. During a flood

[6] The operating crews at the dams are in respect to other matters under the direction of the Power Manager.

period it works closely with the engineers of the Water Planning Division, making possible three daily changes of water control program in any or all of the reservoirs if forecasts and rain and stream gauge reports so indicate. The whole watershed is dotted with gauges from which reports pour into the Water Planning Division each day (some at two hour intervals), making it possible to watch carefully the actual run-off conditions confronting each reservoir in the system. Experimental studies of rates of water flow in the channels and the reservoirs between significant points in the whole river system, together with the quantitative forecasts and the reports of run-off on each segment of the watershed, make possible the development of operating plans to get the flood past the critical points in the valley with least damage. As the heavy rains sweep up from the Gulf of Mexico and begin falling upon the flat lower valley, the down-stream reservoirs are opened for rapid evacuation. Because it requires an interval of from two to three days for the storm to reach the high slopes of the up-stream tributaries, the reservoirs on the latter can be lowered so that when the rains hit the upper country these reservoirs will have maximum storage space to catch the run-off and ease the demand on the main stem reservoirs down in the lower valley.

It is impossible here to describe the intricate sequences in the manipulation of the system of reservoirs that may be involved in mastering a single flood-menacing storm, or to trace the seasonal schedules and interrelationships among the units of the system for electric power production, malaria control and the spawning of fish. It is clear enough to any one who has examined TVA's water-in-the-channel operations that a great river system of control structures cannot be satisfactorily operated on the basis of inter-agency agreements, written or oral. Written guides and instructions are important for "normal" non-emergency operating conditions, but when the unexpected happens or the crisis conditions (which are the essence of great floods) must be met, a single center of decision which will evaluate the current facts and give the orders for manipulating each affected part of the entire river system is essential. Even for reconciling the non-emergency conflicts between competing, or partly competing uses, a single integrating, operating judgment is the best arrangement for water-in-the-channel functions. This will smooth out frictions and delays and minimize wastes in many of the processes of administration, including the construction-design phases.

I am convinced that the best development and management of the water-in-the-channel functions (including the hydroelectric transmission job) requires a single operating agency. Whatever happens to the Valley Authority proposal, a nationwide unified River Development Administration which absorbs the civilian functions of the Corps of Engineers, the Bureau of Reclamation, the Bonneville Power Administration, the Southwest Power Authority, and the water planning tasks of the Federal Power Commission should be constituted.

IV. MANAGEMENT OF WATERSHED LAND

Granting the significance of TVA in demonstrating the above proposition, does it also follow that the function of water-shed conservation must be joined in the same administrative organization? It may be answered that it does not, provided planning and program budgeting phases of land and water functions are integrated.

Watershed management does affect in a number of particulars the volume, timing and quality of the run-off which must be handled by the water-in-the-channel structures. Sometimes land management practices are of importance, but often they are of minor or no consequence for the design and operation of these engineering structures. The situation differs markedly from river basin to river basin, and even within the same river system. Within the Tennessee system (as in other river basins in this country) the greatest floods for which the large river structures must be planned would occur regardless of the completeness with which the watershed lands were clothed with vegetation.[7] The coupling of land management functions, including the farm soil conservation programs, along with river development powers under the TVA was based largely on the assumption that only by this combination could the reservoirs be protected from rapid siltation. Strangely enough the danger of silt damage, except to structures on one of the small tributaries, seems to have been greatly exaggerated. TVA's own silt studies indicate a very low rate of silt accretion.[8]

But even assuming the existence of siltation menace, it would still not be necessary to place the land use management tasks within the same operating organization. There is no evidence that either in the Tennessee Valley or elsewhere the watershed management of National Forest wild lands by the Forest Service is any less efficient for water conservation purposes than is that of TVA over those parts of its watershed estate which it has retained for direct control. TVA has not hesitated to turn over large tracts of wild land adjacent to National Forests or National Parks to the Forest Service or the National Park Service for independent management. Evidence is not available to prove the superiority of the TVA financed (but State Extension Service administered) farm land conservation programs over the Soil Conservation Service's work through local Soil Conservation Districts which it services. TVA has not been able to furnish accurate statistics showing the results that have been attained

[7] In the arid West there are some small streams or tributaries where the principal source of flood waters is snow melt and where the soil texture is such that good watershed management could probably greatly reduce or, in some cases, might eliminate spring floods.

Soil permeability in these arid regions, increased by good vegetal cover, might care for all or part of a local flood menace. Similarly, restoration of vegetal cover on the mountain meadows of the inter-mountain region, and the brush covered slopes of the mountains in Southern California would prevent the mud-rock flows that have cursed the towns and villages along the Wasatch front, in Southern Utah, and some of the Southern California cities, when heavy rainstorms descend in fury on these localized areas.

[8] On the Columbia River system no recent or adequate siltation studies exist, but such evidence as is available (as assembled by Consulting Engineer John Stevens for the Corps of Engineers at the time of the construction of Bonneville Dam) indicates no siltation danger to the main river structures. On the other hand, there can be no doubt that in the inter-mountain basins, in the southwest river systems and on some of the streams of the southeast, siltation is a very real menace to the longevity of river projects and the perpetuation of irreplaceable dam sites.

in its farm land conservation program. If we may credit Philip Selznick's recently published study, the operation of this farm land conservation program has received very loose supervision from TVA and has in effect been the program of seven independent State Extension Services.[9]

There are some fundamental differences in essential administrative arrangements as between managing land resources, especially those of the "wild lands," and handling "water-in-the-channel." The latter is a liquid substance moving more or less rapidly in a constricted pathway and varying in volume and force with seasonal changes of climate. Confined to this common pathway is the energy it creates (except for the released hydroelectric energy transmitted from the generators), the freight it bears on its surface, the fish it nourishes in its depths. It requires a common master to organize and direct the intimate relationships thus physically existing among its several uses. Nothing like this complexity or intimacy of physical relationships ties one part of the land surface of a whole river watershed to all other parts. Timber on a local watershed can be liquidated without interfering with the practice of sustained yield on a neighboring tributary. It is usually possible to exercise good grazing control and maintain good ground cover in one pasture, even though across the fence ill management has destroyed the grass and produced a sage brush waste. To be sure there are some problems of land management, such as fire control, pest or insect control, and some erosion situations that necessitate cooperation between the managers of adjacent land units. But even these situations requiring joint administrative effort are local and do not embrace whole river basin watersheds. The essential administrative unit for direct wild land management is the grazing district, the ranger district, or a minor tributary watershed. Each has its peculiarities of topography, soil composition, forest and ground cover, temperature and precipitation. Infinite variability in the land resource requires great variation in direct local management practices even while general social goals are pursued in common.

The regional headquarters of a land management agency should only rarely be called upon to "direct" operations. It should be a coordinating, facilitating, advising and occasionally a checking unit for the field managers. In contrast to a river administration it does not need to order an action at some location high on the water-shed which will be felt in a physical management sense at every other point throughout the region. Its plans for physical structures are intended for localized management purposes, not as parts in an integrated service tied together in prospective daily operations for a whole watershed.

The predominant body of knowledge and skills needed for land management differs markedly from those essential for the water-in-the-channel tasks. It is from the biological sciences that the fundamental facts and ideas are chiefly drawn for giving increased control over land resource use. The immediate users of the land resources are the farmers for the "tame lands," the live-stock ranchers for the grazing and range lands and for the extensive forage resources in the timber of the National Forests, the loggers and saw-mill operators who

[9] See Selznick, *op. cit.*, pp. 124 ff.

buy and get out the timber, the hikers, campers, skiers, the hunters and fishermen who tramp the woods and mountains and whip the streams for recreation. While there is some overlap, on the whole the clientele and the economic and social considerations of Federal land resource management differ markedly from those of the water-in-the-channel functions. As to the latter the shipping and water transport interests are concerned with navigation, the private co-operative and public electric distribution systems and the industrial consumers of large blocks of power are the immediate beneficiaries of hydroelectric energy, whereas the owners of land and structures on the flood plain, particularly concentrated in the industrial sections of the larger urban centers, are the most substantial beneficiaries of flood control. Irrigation projects find ardent support from the railways, from town businessmen expecting increased trade, from the contractors who build the dams and canals, and from some of the agricultural interests.

Operating consolidation of Federal land resource management tasks with water resources, whether under a Valley Authority or under a single national Resources Department is not essential, so long as provision is made for *integrating the planning and capital budget phases of land and water programs.* The concept of an organic unity in nature which compels a single administrative entity for both aspects of resources is only partly true and may be overworked. This is the exaggeration into which the eloquent minority of the Hoover Commission falls. Messrs. Acheson, Pollock and Rowe play tunes with the notion that the unity of nature constitutes a kind of "natural law" to which public administration must structurally conform.[10] This grossly over-simplifies both the facts of nature and the nature of administration.

Unity and diversity coexist in the relationships among physical resources as among many other subjects of governmental function. What is important to note is the degree, the frequency and the character of the unification needed, and the varying administrative structures and methods most appropriate for the particular administrative objectives. If a group of differing but interrelated activities has constant need of joint attention in its day-to-day functioning, then clearly the administrative structure required is one which will permit day-to-day direction with day-to-day communication up and down the line of command. If, however, the activities are on the whole capable of efficient daily conduct with only occasional consultation about the joint relationships or "unity" matters, lesser organizational closeness of control is indicated. There are many differing degrees of administrative coordination required for these differing but occasionally related tasks of management. There are moreover "pulsating" changes in the need for relatedness—sometimes much joint attention is required, sometimes slight. The concept of "planning" coordination as distinguished from "operating" coordination assumes that effective joint attention shall be given to interrelationships (unities) when basic policies and principal programs to implement them are being decided. My criticism, therefore, of

[10] See Commission on Organization of the Executive Branch of the Government, *Department of the Interior* (Washington, 1949), pp. 69 ff.

both the Valley Authority advocates and the Hoover Commission minority thesis is that neither sufficiently distinguishes those "unities" that require an identical "operating" structure with the same directing superior from other "unities" that can be well satisfied by a common planning or other coordinating mechanism.

Yet it is true that the Valley Authority is the only Federal device that has as yet satisfactorily filled that common regional planning need for water and land resource development. It has not only done a good job in this matter, but it has had unique success in communicating to the staff in its several divisions a remarkable understanding of the total situation in the Valley and much sensitive perception of the interrelated interests among the many facets of the whole Authority program. However, it does not appear, on the basis of Selznick's data, to have broken through the Farm Bureau myopia and the Extension Service orientation of its Agricultural Relations Department, in the handling of its land use programs on Valley farms, its care of reservoir-displaced persons, and its water-shed purchase and management policies. If there is to be a serious search for alternative modes of organizing Federal resource administration, as there ought to be, the regional planning function which TVA has provided must be recognized.

V. NATIONAL AND INTER-REGIONAL INTERESTS

I am reluctant to approve the transplantation of Valley Authorities to all the major river watersheds because of the difficulties I believe such a blanketing of authorities would bring to the adjustment of *inter-regional* problems and the pursuit of *national* interests. A river system watershed region, or any other regional area, is not adequate for a self-contained unit of government. We must not lose sight of the inter-regional interests and conflicts which will certainly arise when we split the job of resource development among these valley entities. There would then be required a national administrative organization divorced from particular Valley Authority allegiance which could make the administrative adjustments required and could effectively spearhead the changes in congressional policy which would inevitably be needed from time to time. Behind the several Valley Authorities will develop tremendous political "oomph"; particular interests adhering to each of the many programs will build alliances with the local congressional delegations. An Authority will be constantly tempted to use these alliances to break presidential restraint exercised in the interest of inter-regional adjustment or national objectives. The localist ethos which determines congressional behavior under our check and balance system makes peculiarly likely this union of local interest groups under the Authority aegis. We may thus get a new and uncontrollable sectionalism, pulling us apart at a time when from the standpoint of both our domestic and international interests we must be increasingly guided in public administration by national policies and goals. If the Valley Authority mechanism becomes standard, then certainly we must drastically revamp the national executive structure on the domestic front to equip the President with the administrative arrangements for mastering his own establishment. I find it very difficult to reconceive an executive organization in which this would have reasonable assurance of attainment.

With few exceptions the advocates of the Authority plan have ignored this basic issue. Because of national and inter-regional interests which I shall presently illustrate as part of my case against the Authority schemes, the least change required would involve the creation of a super-cabinet department able to command the headquarters staff services of all the resource bureaus in the Department of the Interior, at least the similar facilities of the Forest Service, the Soil Conservation Service, the Farmers Home Administration, the old AAA unit of the Production and Marketing Administration, the Bureau of Plant Industry and Soils, the Bureau of Entomology and Plant Quarantine and probably other scientific and credit functional units of the present Department of Agriculture, and part of the staff facilities of the Department of Commerce recently pointed toward area development and furnishing technical assistance to small business. These bureaus in these departments would have to be reduced to a functional staff relationship for servicing the Valley Authority units through the super-cabinet chief exercising line control over the latter. This may not be an impossible task, but I am very doubtful about its accomplishment, and therefore I should prefer to try an alternative scheme built on the essential principles of our existing executive organization and on incipient changes already under way.

We should remind ourselves that, regardless of the administrative need of regionalized units of executive agencies so important for the planning and execution of resource objectives, our basic cultural tendencies are in the direction of national uniformity of social needs. The national and international interest in the location, extraction, use and ownership of physical resources is strikingly illustrated by the part which fissionable materials are destined to play in human welfare. All of us acknowledge that national and international interests must have right of way over regional considerations in deciding how and by whom these materials shall be taken from the earth, processed and used. The whole conservation "problem" in this material so transcends all regional interests that no one, least of all David Lilienthal, is suggesting that development and management of these resources be delegated to a Valley Authority.

This is not a typical case, yet there are aspects of resource management in every material which call for national action, not only by Congress but by the national executive officers who serve the President. Our mineral resources, for example, are not renewable and many of them exist in limited quantities. There is clearly a national concern with reference to their exploitation and utilization, which, however well expressed in congressional statutes, will require for its administrative fulfillment and control some kind of national executive entity to furnish supervision and to inaugurate the research in extraction techniques, processing and use so as to maximize and prolong the life of these exhaustible and ofttimes irreplaceable resources. No matter how ingenious we may be in decentralizing operating authority so that it will improve management by making the jobs more "manageable" and by giving attention to diversities, there is still a clear case for an administrative center at the national level to act for the President and the Congress in the interest of national policy. To do this it must have ultimate power to curb, to advise, to give technical aid, and if necessary to withdraw administrative power from the regional establishment through which we should seek to accomplish the bulk of the operating jobs.

The case for centralized administrative supervision may be illustrated from the renewable resource group. The Forest Service maintains its great Forest Products Laboratory at Madison. It is expensively staffed with a large corps of chemists, physicists, research engineers and others. It is equipped with machines, contrivances and space costing millions of dollars. To duplicate that staff and plant in every regional area to serve the several Valley Authorities would be economically indefensible. Even though certain wood laboratory problems may well be handled in smaller specialized regional laboratories there are obvious economies in the use of central laboratory and research facilities for a great deal of the research which is so essential to good and progressively improved resource management of every sort. The Forest Service in other research needs, the Soil Conservation Service, the Bureau of Reclamation and the Corps of Engineers use both centralized and field research units to solve their research problems. Sometimes it is found that one regional laboratory can do the chief research for a number of regions—as illustrated by the heavy equipment laboratory in Portland which services all the Forest Service regions. The magnificent Denver laboratory does both the basic and most of the applied research that has made possible the success of such stupendous structures as Boulder and Grand Coulee Dams and it is being used to work out many difficult engineering problems of the Central Valley Project in California.

These research facilities must be closely tied by administrative allegiance to all the regional engineering organizations that do the building and the resource managing. This would be very difficult if not impossible with a series of independent Valley Authorities.

But there are other administrative needs also which, regardless of the way we organize for resource management in the field, ought to be performed by national centers of administration. Within the limits of congressional policy these centers must devise the functional standards of quality, quantity, variety and cost for similar programs performed in all the river basins of the land. Such standards must be based in part upon national interests. Look, for example, at the case of timber resources. Soil and climate differ greatly from region to region in their relation to timber production. More rapid growth can be obtained with less effort and cost in the southeastern part of the United States than in Idaho or in most other parts of the Rocky Mountain area. Decisions concerning the intensiveness of forest management made by a regional agency might be thoroughly unjustified in the light of comparative facts in all regions and in terms of over-all national costs and policy. It is likely to be good public policy to spend most heavily for intensive timber management where forest production per unit of investment will be high. It may even be wise to manage some low-producing timber areas primarily for watershed protection, grazing or recreation.

Congress cannot develop the measurement of the many variable factors relating to resources which is necessary for building management standards. This task cannot be safely performed by isolated or competing regional administrative agencies, whether of the Authority or the traditional pattern. It must be the job of a central administrative organization which utilizes the data and insight developed throughout the entire national experience.

The hydroelectric resource illustrates another kind of inter-regional interest. It is to the regional interest to obtain the benefit of low power rates which reflect the low cost at which power can be developed in a particular region, such as the Pacific Northwest, as compared with other regions. There is, however, a national interest in preventing undue inter-regional price competition in power rates. The reconciliation of these conflicting interests requires an over-all national executive view which is absent even today. Space does not permit exploration of the inter-regional problems raised by the diversion, actual and potential, of water from one river system like the Columbia which possesses a surplus, to a water deficient region; of the complications increasingly to be anticipated as the economic transmission distance for electricity—already 500 miles—increases. But these are important questions transcending single river basins.

VI. RECASTING OF THE TRADITIONAL ADMINISTRATIVE STRUCTURE

In searching for alternatives to the Valley Authority we ought not to abandon but should improve the functional principles on which our national executive structure rests. We should be guided by a goal which will include the attainment of comprehensive and regionally-integrated resource programs while simultaneously affording balanced development as between regions. The goal must include the attainment of minimum national standards of resource conservation and use in all the river basins (or other regional areas) of the United States. Our problem is to find ways of remolding and completing our traditional functional pattern so as to repeat in all parts of the country those significant advances achieved by the TVA, while forestalling or adjusting inter-regional conflicts and inequities.

As suggested above there are many values implicit in the traditional vertical bureau and departmental mode of organizing national administration. By way of summary these may be said to include: (1) greater assurance that similar treatment will be accorded similar problems throughout the nation; (2) the utilization of central staff services and research or laboratory facilities that cannot be afforded in each regional area; and (3) the restraint of sectionalist or provincialist tendencies which in this and other countries have often injured administrative efficiency and prejudicially distorted the fulfillment of policies in the national and international interest.

Four inter-locked steps in structural change are essential: (1) A regrouping of departmental services so as to give more coherent and unified operating agencies for the several major resource clusters; (2) the more general use of decentralized regional field services; (3) completion of the intra-departmental coordinating arrangements in the field and in Washington now incipiently but too slowly developing within the Departments of Agriculture and the Interior; and (4) the location in each regional area of a representative of the Office of the President reporting to a Resource Field Service Division who will lead the interdepartmental planning and capital budget programming of resource development on a region-wide basis.

The Hoover Commission has already charted the outlines for revamping the departmental clusters to secure better management. On the water phase, which is our chief interest, its plan for the creation of a new Water Development Service is a major contribution toward a desirable alternative. This would group civilian functions now performed by the Corps of Engineers with those of the Bureau of Reclamation, the Bonneville Power Administration, the Southwest Power Authority, and the Power Division of the Department of the Interior. It would give the major water-in-the-channel activities a fitting administrative vehicle for coordinated performance. The majority ought to have accepted the minority view that the river planning and Federal project rate-making functions of the Federal Power Commission should also be transferred to this new agency, for these are duties involving unnecessary duplication.

Two other minor amalgamations would have been beneficial, namely (1) the Coast Guard channel-marking and mapping on the rivers, and (2) the water data-collecting duties of the Geological Survey. Elimination of the Coast Guard on the rivers would cut out unnecessary duplication, because the river maintenance forces of the Water Development Service will have to perform some of these services and could handle all of them with no appreciable increase in cost.

The proposal to transfer the Geological Survey functions will meet with more legitimate objection. It will be said that the business of collecting and evaluating stream flow and other water data should be performed by an agency not biased by construction functions. This position would be sound if the Geological Survey had really been used for this purpose with any completeness. But the sad fact is that the Geological Survey, through no fault of its own, has never had enough money to gather the essential information required for a large proportion of river projects when these were authorized by Congress. Congress and the river construction agencies have barged ahead with their construction plans. The Corps and the Bureau of Reclamation have thrown small sums to the Survey to scramble together, after the fact, such supplementary data as could be obtained in the short periods before structure designs have had to be frozen. Ever since the National Resources Committee's Water Resources Committee published its report on "Deficiencies in Hydrologic Data," Congress has been repeatedly told of the urgency of more complete hydrologic information to prevent the wastes of over- or under-building on the streams. But the Survey still weeps in vain for funds with which to meet its responsibilities. It seems time to try another tack, and give to the unified construction organization, which will fall heir to the influence over Congress of its several predecessors, the full responsibility of getting the funds so as to obtain the water facts on which it should base its plans.

The other major departmental regrouping of resource tasks that will vitally affect the case of needed field coordination with water resource activities relates to the wild public lands. Again the Hoover Commission report offers a way (or two ways—if we include the vigorous minority recommendation) of doing this by amalgamating the Forest Service with the Bureau of Land Management into a new operating agency in the Department of Agriculture. Small doubt exists that an amalgamation of the land management functions of these services is essential (whatever department gets them) both for operating the land functions and for making easier the correlation, through an interdepartmental planning structure, of water with land programs where such correlation is indicated.

VII. INTRADEPARTMENTAL REGIONAL COORDINATION

Given the rationalization of the Departments of Agriculture and of the Interior and the withdrawal of civilian engineering jobs from the Army, efficient regional resource management will be much easier to attain. So far as water resource operations are concerned, if the Hoover Commission plan is accepted, the major tasks will be correlated within a single Water Development Service. With a generously decentralized field organization for each major river basin there is no good reason why the TVA mode of developing and of operating water facilities cannot be universalized.

But the matching of TVA's contributions of greatly heightened awareness of the total regional situation among Federal resource field officers and the timing of land and mineral programs to the mutual advantage of all resources Federally controlled or influenced call for two permanent new centers of regional field coordination. The first of these is an extension of departmental structure to the field.

At this point two subordinate alternatives are possible. The simplest schematic plan would be to abolish in the Departments of the Interior and of Agriculture the present line-authority bureaus, and to create regional departmental administrators to take charge within their several areas of all the programs of all the resource bureaus having field operations. The traditional bureaus, under this arrangement, would retreat to a strictly staff status. The regional departmental administrator would then be fully responsible for planning, programming, budgeting, controlling and operating. Assuming the further functional rationalization of these two departments along the lines proposed by the Hoover Commission report, such a plan would present two major administrative structures for resource management in each region as against the single Valley Authority or as contrasted with the present eight separate bureaus in Interior plus the four principal action agencies in Agriculture.[11] The problem of mastering the federal programs in the region would be enormously simplified for there would be left, so far as field correlation is concerned, simply the correlation of the work of the two Departments. This alternative would retain Washington administrative controls in the hands of the two respective Secretaries, who,

[11] Of course one of the eight Interior agencies, Indian Affairs, would be transferred out of the resource Departments.

buttressed by their revamped headquarters functional staff offices, would set the national standards, perform the central research services, provide the inspectorates for performance, audit, etc., and keep the interregional resource issues in hand.

The regional departmental administrators would perforce require large field staff establishments to develop and operate their many programs. Special organizational devices and self-denying practices would be required to prevent the administrators from the typical absorption in the day-to-day problems at the expense of long range, integrated region-wide planning and programming functions which are so urgently needed.

This design, like that of the Valley Authority, should include as many vocational, consumer and state official advisory boards as may be useful in sensitizing the administrator of the Department to the impact of Federal programs on those vitally affected by them. Advisory participation in the administrative process was invented long before the Valley Authority, though its full and proper utilization has been very imperfectly practiced.

Attractive as is this alternative to the Authority plan, obstacles to its political and administrative feasibility seem tremendous. It would arouse on a nation-wide scale the opposition of every client interest of the extant operating bureaus in the two Departments. For this plan would have to be adopted simultaneously on a nation-wide basis and would call for drastic reconstruction of the whole current departmental scheme. The Valley Authority has the political feasibility that it can be created in one basin at a time, and thus shear off power from established bureaus piecemeal. Until it has blanketed a large part of the country it leaves existing bureaus functioning elsewhere as before.

To concentrate so much regional authority in a single departmental Administrator would also invite the demand that this job be made a political one, with a political Assistant Secretary to fill it. So to staff it would greatly endanger its administrative success. It is very probable, for example, that a regional Administrator for the Department of the Interior would be named by the President (or the National Party Committee Chairman) and that a region like the Pacific Northwest would be administered by a lame duck Governor, Senator or Congressman. (A similar danger undoubtedly exists for new Valley Authorities. The unique circumstances attending the birth of the TVA in 1933 are not likely to be repeated.)

The administrative difficulties in perfecting such a drastic reconstruction of operating machinery and practice would be great, though probably not insuperable. To pick apart and reassemble the functional divisions of the present (and transferred-in) bureaus of each of the Departments into effective and manageable regional operating entities, and to give them proper functional staff relationships with a reconstituted departmental galaxy of Washington functional program staff offices will be no easy task. Yet it may be assumed that in time it could be successfully accomplished. While the complexities of developing the appropriate adjustments of functional and line relationships for this monolithic operating department plan would be much greater than for even the largest existing bureau, the basic principles developed heretofore could probably be successfully applied after some cost in trial and error.

Assuming the successful replacement of the traditional bureau structure by this new area departmental operating agency, would the regional administrator be so connected with the client group pressures adhering to the water development-construction programs that he could respond adequately to the ofttimes complementary or conflicting interests of the land, mineral and (in regions like the Pacific Northwest) anadromous fish resources? A monolithic operating structure inhibits the presentation of internal conflict issues for secretarial readjustment. These will have been decided within the regional administration and will usually not rise to the surface for secretarial decision. If they are resolved in response to the major social forces which adhere to the regional departmental administration, the "minority" interests—land, fisheries and minerals—deprived of separate organizational status cannot so effectively pose issues for mediation and adjustment which run counter to the water development constellation.

These considerations make for a preference for the second alternative to give departmental unity of resource policy and program in the field, namely, the completion and perfection of the field integrating devices already taking shape for the two major resource departments.

Four years ago the Secretaries of Agriculture and of the Interior located in the Missouri and the Columbia River Basins their own departmental spokesmen.[12] Each secretarial representative is assisted by a committee of field officers of the several operating bureaus of their respective Departments. Roughly, their assignments have been to prepare long-term department-wide programs for the two regions, and in the process to bring into harmony and synchronization the regional programs of the several bureaus in each Department.

The Interior representative is clothed with less authority than his counterpart in the Department of Agriculture, and his status, which limits his program correlation function, is officially merely that of the chairman of a field committee composed of operating agency representatives.[13] Yet despite this fact and despite the inability of the Secretary of the Interior to swing his

[12] Interior created six field committees—plus one for Alaska—in August, 1948, and named a secretarial representative as chairman for each. Information on which this discussion is based is drawn from the experience of the structure for the Pacific Northwest. Secretary Brannan has also recently selected a third regional representative to cover the Southwest, with headquarters at Salt Lake City.

[13] During the first two years of the oldest of these regional coordination efforts, that in the Pacific Northwest, the Secretary had no representative. It was the committee alone which was charged with coordinating responsibility, but it leaned heavily upon the suggestions and staff assistance of an Executive Director. The latter's position was highly anomalous because of his staff tie to the Secretary's Washington office and his subordinate status to the Field Committee as its employee. This situation was cleared late in 1948 when the Executive Director was appointed permanent chairman of the committee and as the Secretary's representative reported to Washington through the Departmental Program Committee Chairman.

Washington bureau headquarters people into hearty support of this field correlation program (especially before the presidential election of 1948) a significant beginning has been made. A number of minor successes in the way of intradepartmental interagency adjustment of conflicting programs have been achieved. A regional departmental six-year program has been drafted and approved and is now undergoing its second annual revision. In the fall of 1949 a department-wide budget for the region, drafted by the field committee under the chairman's guidance, was presented by Assistant Secretary Davidson to the Bureau of the Budget. True, it followed the review of the several bureau budget presentations and thus came too late to be most effective. Nevertheless it was an unprecedented event in the history of our traditional Federal departments. It is confidently expected that the second regional Department of the Interior budget, now undergoing preparation, will be heard both by the departmental budget-reviewing officials in Washington and by the Bureau of the Budget in advance of the separate bureau requests for field programs in the Pacific Northwest.

Before this effort at intradepartmental integration of plans and programs for resource management will fully succeed in its mission, there must be many changes in bureau structure and practice.[14] A more even delegation of field authority to the several regional bureau chiefs must take place, and the delegations must be broad enough to permit field decisions in making adjustments in plans and programs without constant resort to Washington. Since programs are fully crystallized in periods of budget preparation it is of special importance that the regional representatives of each bureau have genuine initiatory discretion and responsibility for field budget proposals. It is also of great importance that the required periods for budget estimating be synchronized among the several agencies so that they may be reviewed together, as to proposed major program additions or modifications, first by the departmental regional representatives and their field committees and then by the presidential field representative and staff, presently to be discussed. A second annual simultaneous field review will be essential because when Congress completes its appropriations and headquarters allocations have been changed to meet the reductions (or, rarely, the additions) made by the Congress, anticipated programs will have to be modified. Such changes may have important interagency repercussions, which will need adjustment.

The Hoover Commission recommendations for enhancing the Secretary's

[14] In Interior bureaus have responded, albeit reluctantly, in a number of important instances during the past four years. The highly centralized and nonregionalized Bureau of Mines has at last regionalized and clothed its regional chiefs with real power. The Office of Indian Affairs has been moving in the same direction since late in 1946 and is making genuine headway toward a responsible, decentralized field structure. The Bureau of Land Management, through new leadership in Washington and in the field, has in the past two years rapidly pushed forward into an active decentralized land management organization. The Bureau of Reclamation burst the bonds of the Chief Engineer at Denver during the War, and it has continued to feed to the regional and district Engineers more and more power to plan and carry through their irrigation functions.

power over his operating bureaus, particularly by making the Secretary instead of a particular bureau legally responsible for programs, would greatly facilitate the above listed changes. This would be of special importance in the Department of the Interior which could then shed its "holding company" status and become a genuine agency for integrated management.[15]

Experience also points to a few essential changes in the status and powers of the departmental regional representative. While there doubtless remain many problems of discovery and invention in the development of these new area co-ordinators for whole departments, we may set down a few essentials that must soon be forthcoming. Thus far, in both the Departments of the Interior and of Agriculture, the Secretary's representative has in no sense been "the boss." He has moved with great circumspection. He has been most meagerly staffed for purposes of bringing to him a free and full flow of information from the operating agencies and for watching the "follow through" on agreed activities. The system of reporting, save for the Missouri Basin Interior office at Billings, is almost undeveloped. To provide an accurate, prompt, and frequent appraisal of program progress from every operating agency is indispensable to any correlation function. It takes not only agency willingness to do this but staff facilities both for it and for the secretarial representative, together with well designed reporting techniques. The secretarial representative needs specific authority to work this out, together with funds for the agencies and his office to make it work.

It is no disparagement of Interior's regional programming and budgeting in the Pacific Northwest noted above to observe that the Chairman, as the Secretary's representative, has been in no position to exercise effective criticism in reviewing the program and budgetary proposals of the several agencies. When a clash between two or more agencies arises, he has been able to suggest compromises and adjustments. But on program budget estimates he has had no authority to question items and inadequate means of knowing when to offer either constructive or negative criticism. Undoubtedly the wide acquaintance of the Secretary's representative with the programs of all the Federal resource agencies in the region, his extraordinary knowledge of the region, and his persuasive competence have influenced the content of the regional program in ways difficult to measure. But something more is certainly needed. The least that should be given him is technical staff qualified to aid in furnishing effective criticism.

It is also clear that where conflicts of agency programs exist or impend, the factual studies and field surveys essential to their resolution and to the building

[15] Reorganization Plans Numbers 3 and 4, submitted to Congress on March 13, 1950, incorporate the Hoover Commission policy for giving the Secretaries of the Interior and Agriculture responsibility for all programs, with minor exceptions, in their respective departments. The Congress permitted the Interior plan to become law, but the Senate vetoed the plan for Agriculture. It can only be a matter of time before the latter Department will be accorded the same treatment as Interior.

of a really comprehensive departmental plan either for a sub-basin or for the region should be launched on a departmental basis. The conflict on the Rogue River basin makes this clear. There the Bureau of Reclamation was arrayed on certain features against the Fish and Wild Life Service, the National Park Service, and, in a minor respect, the Bureau of Land Management. The factual studies essential to coping with the issues were undertaken separately by the several agencies without any advance comprehensive plan for the studies and without agreement of the factual areas to be explored. Data collection has dragged unevenly for several years because funds have been deficient in some agencies and adequate in others. The Secretary's regional representative should be clothed with responsibility and funds to see that the surveys and studies are so mapped and prosecuted as to afford a completed factual analysis free of significant omissions, ample in coverage, authentic in quality, and finished on schedule.

Ample facts will not always melt the obstacles to agreement. This too the Rogue River basin study clearly illustrates. But they are indispensable to the quest for adjustments and compromises that afford the greatest total utility to a multiple purpose river development program. Here again, Interior's experience might argue that the Secretary's representative, the Chairman of the Field Committee, should be expected and even required to break the deadlock of bureau intransigence by recommending to the Secretary the resolution of those aspects of a program which could not win full agency consensus.

VIII. REGIONAL REPRESENTATIVES OF THE PRESIDENT

This alternative to a Valley Authority will still be incomplete until the whole Federal resource interest in each region is given a focus higher than departmental management affords. There is only one executive center which can give this focus and that is the office of the President. Just as it has been necessary to find staff facilities within his immediate office to help him manage the executive departments at Washington so will it be an essential for regional integration of Federal plans and activities that some of his staff facilities be appropriately amplified on a regional basis.

The River Basin Committees, now operating in the Missouri and Columbia Valley Regions, clearly do not meet this requirement. Stemming as they do from the central Federal Inter-Agency River Basin Committee (a voluntary interdepartmental committee) they, like their parent, have been impotent to resolve interdepartmental jurisdictional disputes, or to build truly comprehensive, balanced regional plans. They have performed chiefly informational services and have been of some value in formulating a few technical recommendations. Their rotating chairmen give their respective departments the edge on publicity during their brief tenure of office.[16] During the past two years the Columbia Basin Inter-Agency Committee has widened the range of its interest to

[16] See also Henry Hart's evaluation of the Missouri River Basin Committee in *Public Administration Review*, Vol. 8, pp. 1–11 (Winter, 1948).

give initial attention to watershed problems. But the relative impotence of this body was clearly signalized by the manner in which it was ignored when the great 1948 flood was bringing disaster to people in the Columbia Valley. The job of Federal disaster assistance, reconstruction and planning was thrown to the Federal Works Agency, the Corps of Engineers, the Department of the Interior and the Housing and Home Finance Agency. The departmental representative of Agriculture participated in minor ways during the flood and in the collection of data on the damages as the waters receded.

A field service unit at Washington in the Executive Office of the President will be required as the central focus for a group of regional presidential representatives whose assignment should provide the capstone for correlating in each region the total Federal interest in resource administration. It would be the job of the presidential field officers to bring into proper adjustment the plans and programs for water, land, mineral and energy resources of all the Federal departments and agencies, and to assist the departmental field representatives in articulating Federal with state and local policies. The latter task is inescapable if resource problems are to be met, because so much of the legal jurisdiction over all natural resources lies in state hands.

There are of course no blueprints for such a new area management job, for reconciling it with departmental and agency operating functions, or for enlisting the participating cooperation of the state. But the need is urgent. Administrative invention will have to write a new set of job descriptions, relationships and procedures to distinguish this new level of area coordination from those with which we are familiar in the well-managed operating agency. But they will probably resemble, albeit on a distinctly interdepartmental basis, the arrangements now taking shape for the departmental field representatives. The success of the latter experiment will greatly smooth the way toward gearing into proper mesh the total Federal resource responsibility. It is at this point that the water and all the land and mineral resource functions must be made to complement one another, wherever a genuine interdependence exists. The basic tools for so doing exist in the planning and capital budgeting processes and in the occasional plugging of a gap in a research need when essential missing data must be found for which no agency or department has responsibility. The administrative devices needed will also probably parallel those now developing for the Departments of Agriculture and the Interior. A Federal interdepartmental field committee and subcommittees, a small but broad-gauged staff to share in technical leadership in planning and budgeting, liaison arrangements with the department field units and the appropriate state agencies (with representation of the latter where state and Federal interests join)—all these kinds of administrative mechanisms will be essential. The limits of their activity will have to be discovered in the process of working through the problems to be met.[17]

[17] Some of these complexities might be avoided under a more revolutionary revision of the departmental system than has been suggested in any of the official reorganizations thus far proposed. Were the national executive departments regrouped into a handful of super-

If this kind of alternative seems complex when compared with the apparent simplicity of the Valley Authority, it may be answered (1) that complexity will soon displace simplicity when Valley Authorities are multiplied and (2) only by some such mode of extending the logic of our traditional Federal structure is it possible to assure executive responsibility. The resource tasks are many and the relationships are complex. When we face them squarely in every part of the country we shall learn to complete the minimum structure of organization, field and center, which responsible administrative mastery requires.

departmental units, similar to that modelled for Defense, the whole range of resource functions now scattered in three departments might be combined into another super-cabinet unit—perhaps called by some such title as Agriculture and Natural Resources. As in the case of the military model, such a department would need three or four sub-departments charged with management of clusters of operating bureaus or Services. (Dean Samuel T. Dana, of the Hoover Commission Task Force on Natural Resources, was in favor of uniting Agriculture and Interior under a new title of "Department of Conservation.") This idea has some resemblance to the Departments of Conservation adopted in a number of states for unifying resource work, but the states have not usually included the agricultural duties, which remain with the land grant colleges and the state Departments of Agriculture.

Were a new design adopted, embodying the larger aggregation notion suggested above, it might be justified on the ground that it would reduce the "span of control" strain upon the President and his management staff. It would, however, raise questions of presidential control because of the increased political power centering around such huge departments. Certainly the use of such a principle should be applied throughout the whole executive establishment, if it is applied at all, or difficult "imbalances" would result to the detriment of presidential influence. Unless and until a plan is adopted which would subsume all the Federal resource functions under a single great department, we shall have to rely upon a field representative from the President's office for bringing all resource programs into proper focus within the several regions.

Objectives and Evaluation

29. Establishing Goals for Regional Economic Development

CHARLES L. LEVEN

In formulating regional development programs, explicit consideration must be given to goals. The frequently used objective of maximizing regional employment is critically evaluated and its relation to other possible goals considered. A model for assessing the effects of development policy on several goals is then presented. But unless development goals are specified independently, the model cannot by itself indicate an optimum policy.

In recent years, there has been a very rapid increase in the use of systems analysis techniques in the study of regional economies. We have seen the construction of income and product accounts, interindustry tables, and micro-analytic models for specific regions.[1] It is not the purpose of the present paper to describe or evaluate such model-building efforts. Rather, it is to attempt assessing the role of these forms of analysis in the determination of regional economic development policy.

All these models attempt to represent the economy of a region, or of some aspects of it, by a set of mathematical relationships, generally containing three kinds of variables: *one,* dependent variables, *two,* independent non-controllable variables, and *three,* independent controllable variables. In the case of a simple interindustry model of a regional economy, an example of a dependent variable would be the amount of coal used in the production of steel within the region. It is dependent since the amount of steel produced in the region appears explicitly in the system, and the amount of coal needed for its production would thus be fully explained by the system itself.[2]

An independent non-controllable variable would be the demand of the rest of the world for steel produced in the region. This demand could not be explained as a function of other variables within the region. Nor is it subject to control by policy within the region to an important extent, at least in the short run and probably in the long run as well. Finally, an example of an independent but controllable variable would be the funds devoted to public highway construction or to financing the current costs of public education. In part, of course, these expenditures would be affected by the other variables in the system; that is, they are to some extent dependent variables. But public authorities have a good deal of discretion with regard to service levels, so that the total outlays for these purposes can ultimately be regarded as both independent and controllable.

The interest planners have in the development of analytical systems is the hope that such models will enable them to make more accurate forecasts and more intelligent decisions on the use of resources for regional economic development. In this regard, it is important to recognize that analytical systems *by themselves* can perform neither of these functions. Insofar as making predictions is concerned, it is necessary to provide estimates of the independent variables, both controllable and non-controllable, before the model can provide numerical estimates for the dependent variables in the future. It is, of course, true that systems are currently being developed in which more and more of the variables can be treated as dependent, whereby they explain more of what is going on. This is a result both of more articulate theorizing and of advances in computer technology. Even so, it seems fair to ask whether it is easier to predict the independent variables in the system than to predict directly those dependent variables in which one is specifically interested. It is not clear that the independent variables can be predicted more easily. And if not, the moral should be clear: there is a legitimate basis for skepticism about the use of sophisticated analytical systems simply for the purpose of obtaining more accurate predictions of such major regional economic aggregates as employment, population, or income.

The use of a more sophisticated system is more clearly justified when we wish either to predict in relatively fine detail or even in a general way, the results of some fairly specific events. For example, in answering the simple question, "How many people will be employed in the region in 1980?" it is not at all clear that a complicated analytical model will necessarily produce a more accurate estimate than mechanical extrapolation techniques, tempered perhaps by qualitative judgment. A structural model becomes useful only in answering such questions as "What will be the level of employment in 1980 in the paperboard container industry?" or "What will be the effect on total employment by 1980 of the construction in 1965 of a new hydroelectric generating plant of specified capacity?" And even in these cases, though an analytical system may provide the means for making more specific estimates, it does not necessarily make them more "accurate."[3] In short, then, a good deal of misunderstanding can be avoided if the users of analytical systems can learn to regard them not as question-answering devices but as means of achieving increased understanding of the processes relevant to policy decisions.

But if these systems are to be used as aids to policy-making, an additional ingredient must be supplied in the specification of development goals for the region. An empirically operational model is capable of producing estimates of income, population, or employment, in great detail if desired and for *any specified level of the controllable independent variables*. The policy determination problem can be thought of as selecting that set of values for the controllable independent variables that will result in the most favorable outcome. Where the most favorable outcome is one-dimensional, such as maximizing the number of jobs regardless of other consequences, the problem is a fairly simple one.

However, where development officials are simultaneously concerned with several objectives, such as employment, per capita income, and the amenity value of public services, the problem is much more difficult. This paper will not be concerned with the question of what the most worthwhile goals of a program are in substance or how they should be weighted in importance; that is essentially the job of the planner. Rather, the concern will be with the consequences likely to arise from an oversimplified goal specification, and with the kind of analytical and judgmental exercise the planner must perform to avoid these consequences and to develop a concept of development goals sufficiently articulate to be used in the systems analysis of a regional economy.

In the first part of this paper, the kinds of goals associated with regional development, usually those of maximizing total output or employment, will be evaluated critically and a more comprehensive set of development goals outlined. In the main, the discussion will consist of a systematic consideration of the kinds of issues that need to be considered in framing a development policy, without attempting specifically to establish any ordering of substantive ends. For the most part, the discussion will be confined to the *economic* development of regions. The second part of the paper will be concerned with the implications of a more extended specification of development goals (that is, a multidimensional view) than is typical of the kinds of analytical models ordinarily used to depict regional economic structure and change.

I. A MODEL TO MAXIMIZE REGIONAL OUTPUT

In general, economic development policy and economic structure can be represented by a set of behavioral relationships between dependent and independent variables, together with some function, to be maximized, of one or more of the dependent variables, subject to the limitation that the behavioral relationships cannot be violated and that at least one of the independent variables cannot exceed some specified value. Stated in typical linear programming notation, a system aimed simply at maximizing regional product[4] could be represented by

Maximize:

$$V_p = \sum_{i=1}^{n} P_1 X_1 \qquad (1)$$

Subject to:

$$X_i = \sum_{j=1}^{n} a_{ij} X_j + a_{i0} X_0 \qquad (i = 1, \ldots, n) \qquad (2)$$

$$X_i \geqslant 0 \qquad (i = 0, 1, \ldots, n) \qquad (3)$$

and

$$X_0 \leqslant K \qquad (4)$$

where V_p is net output, or value added in production in the region, X_i is the output of the ith industry, or activity, P_i is value added per unit of output of the ith industry, a_{ij} is the quantity of the ith industry's output needed for the production of one unit of output of industry j, X_0 is the total input of labor, and K is the available labor supply.

Aside from the question of whether the simple economic policy implied by this model is appropriate, certain technical aspects of the model may also be questioned. Objections can properly be made to the linear production functions used in the model, which are not always realistic. Moreover, even where a linear approximation seems valid, the stability of the coefficients may be questioned. This issue is particularly important in a regional context where input coefficients depend not only on technological but also on trading relationships, that is, the proportion of each input requirement obtained from within the region rather than from outside sources. As a region's dependence on interregional trade increases, the appropriateness of assuming stable input coefficients becomes even more questionable.

All the foregoing comments, however, refer to technical imperfections of the model, which, at least theoretically, can be handled by relaxing the assumptions.[5] Important as these problems might be from an analytical point of view, they are not directly relevant to policy considerations and will not be considered here further. The specific form of the model is not central to this discussion. For expositional ease it is posed in terms of a linear program of interindustry activities. Alternatively, it could have been expressed as a set of income and product relationships, but this too is not critical in the present discussion.[6] What is significant is whether maximizing the value of product is a sufficiently articulate goal for development policy, and this, basically, is the question to be examined.

Migration and Employment Goals

In part, the answer will depend on whether the input of labor operates as a constraint. Population could, for instance, be regarded as a totally independent variable. In that event, the economy's full employment production level would be a function of the region's natural rate of increase plus net migration. Alternatively, net migration and hence total population could be regarded as dependent on the level of economic activity in the region. Though it will be useful to discuss the issue in terms of these extreme assumptions, it is important to note that actual situations would necessarily fall somewhere between them. Despite this fact, the desired economic end embodied in most community and regional development programs is a simple one-dimensional goal: to secure the largest possible increase in the number of available jobs in the region. In many instances, the expansion of the region's employment base is accepted virtually without question as an expression of development policy. A major purpose of this paper is an evaluation of this thesis.

Even in an area where in- and outmigration are completely restricted, economic objectives other than maximizing the number of available jobs would be relevant. The level of earned income per gainfully employed individual, the rate of compensation per hour of productive effort, the stability of employment and income over time, the growth of employment and income in subsequent periods, the ratio of wage rates to commodity prices, and the size distribution of income all would have an effect on the region's economic welfare. And in the usual case where migration is *not* subject to restriction, maximum growth of employment is even more subject to qualification as a single development goal.

Some examples may help to make this clear. Growth in employment opportunities could, for instance, be achieved by substituting jobs having low productivity for those with high productivity. The employment growth objective would accordingly conflict with a goal of maximum earning power per worker. Similarly, once a given level of employment is reached, it might be impossible to increase it further without reducing the stability of employment. Even more likely, perhaps, is the possibility of a conflict between the size of average earnings and their stability, since higher wage rates are typical of durable goods and the construction industries, both of which are subject to larger than average cyclical instability. Another possible source of conflict is between immediate and longer-term considerations. An area could be faced with a choice between a sizable immediate expansion in an industry having little prospect for growth in subsequent periods, or another industry offering a smaller increment to the industrial base currently but promising more than compensating growth over a decade or so. In addition to the foregoing conflicts, the more traditional difficulties of welfare economics, such as changes in relative prices and income distribution, would be involved.

If the assumption of no in- or outmigration is dropped, all the foregoing complications would exist in addition to several new ones. Where people are relatively free to move, it is not clear that increasing the value of production in a region would increase economic welfare, even if stability, future growth potential, and all the other interacting factors listed above remain unchanged. There are two ways in which the increased value added in the region could be dissipated. First, part or all of it could accrue to workers commuting from other areas or to nonresident owners of capital in the region. Second, there is the possibility of higher per capita costs of public services, if these are subject to diseconomies of scale.

Finally, considering interregional effects, it is not logically necessary for the pursuit of optimal programs for each region to result in an optimal development for the nation as a whole. In a world of perfect competition, such an inconsistency could not, of course, arise. But in a world where capital markets are imperfect, capital facilities are durable and immovable, and personal relocation is resisted on social and psychological grounds, the problem is a genuine one.

The Preoccupation with Regional Growth

How can the rather complex view of development goals outlined above be reconciled with the typical view of development officials and civic leaders that an increase in employment is, by itself, both a necessary and sufficient condition for increased community welfare? In part, this view can be attributed to a simple lack of understanding of the development process. In part, it may result from the morbid fascination of Americans with growth for its own sake. If these were the primary reasons for the myopic view of regional development, the problem of activating a more coherent policy would not seem too difficult. However, other explanations of the inconsistency pose a greater challenge.

The fixation on economic growth as a development goal for regions is perhaps simply an extension of its acceptance as a national goal. But this ignores the very significant differences which exist between the regional and the national economic environments. First, the increased cyclical instability which may result from national economic growth can be counteracted by monetary and fiscal measures. For an individual region acting unilaterally this is not feasible. Second, while the problem of short- vs. long-run growth maximization exists for the nation as well as the region, it exists for the former at an entirely different level. The nation does not have the problem of committing a limited supply of land to large increments of slow-growing industries. For a bounded metropolitan region, however, this limitation may be critical. Third, if economic expansion is accompanied by adverse changes in the distribution of income, the federal government has vastly greater powers for making offsetting adjustments than do state or local governments.

A preoccupation with community growth may also stem from what appears at times to be a rather frantic concern with the problem of human relocation. Communities do worry about having enough jobs available to absorb at least their natural increase in population. For the nation, of course, this is not a problem over and above that of maintaining full employment. The pattern of national growth may force workers to change jobs, industries, or even location, but it does not force them to leave the United States. Moreover, where transitional problems become acute, remedial powers exist: witness the legislation for agricultural support, aid to depressed areas, and manpower retraining. For an individual community the problem may be a real one. And the fact that people move does not demonstrate that they are happy doing so. On the other hand, maximizing national productivity, and hence average regional productivity, depends on the mobility of resources, both occupationally and geographically. This relationship may produce a real conflict in objectives, and it would consequently not be irrational for a community to trade some economic efficiency for greater locational stability. But before this proposition is accepted too readily, it is necessary to investigate whether the regret over induced migration is mainly expressed by individuals who have had to move to realize an improved economic position, or by individuals who are confronted with declining markets for local goods and services. In a capitalistic economy, the losses of the latter are ordinarily regarded as having been taken into account in the original investment decision in the same way as potential technological obsolescence.

A third possible explanation of the fixation on a simple growth goal is that growth may result in substantial economic benefits to certain segments of the population, even where there is no increase in the community's aggregate economic welfare. And many people who are likely to gain in such a situation may also be in positions of substantial influence in their communities. This should not be taken to mean, however, that individuals or groups necessarily want to profit at the expense of the community. It should be recognized, however, that firms in decreasing-cost industries are likely to gain from a simple expansion of regional population with no increase, and perhaps even a decrease, in per capita income. In their planning, such firms do not ordinarily take into account cyclical instability, the potential growth of other firms, or the distribution of income in the region, except as they are affected by them. And here again there is potential conflict.

The issue essentially involves political vs. economic sovereignty and will not be commented upon further, except to point out that where a group with an economic self-interest in growth does exist, it has at hand a number of arguments that may be difficult to oppose politically: "Growth will provide jobs for our young people," "Growth will increase our tax base," "Growth will bring new people and businesses to our town," "Growth will add to our nation's productivity and hence contribute to fighting the cold war," and finally, "Growth will make us the biggest city in the state." In short, while growth usually and perhaps always contributes to economic welfare, it must be recognized that the deck is stacked rather badly against the possible case of growth that would not add or might even detract from the aggregate economic welfare of a region.

Finally, the last explanation of adherence to an expanding economic base as an exclusive development goal is simply that it is part of a process of interregional competition. But if all regions followed a rational economic policy, why should any region try to inhibit the outmigration of one of its production establishments? There are three possible reasons: *one,* it may be cheaper to move labor than industrial plants; *two,* even where it is not cheaper, the region's share in the gains of relocation may be smaller than its costs; and *three,* the costs of providing public services may increase with relocation and exceed the possible gains in efficiency. In addition, where other regions pursue a policy of growth for its own sake, they may well force an inefficient relocation to occur. Every region would then be forced into a purely promotional effort simply to offset the deviations from an efficient locational pattern resulting from the "imperialistic" policies of its neighbors.

How can more articulate development policies be formulated? In part this is a problem of education. But it also involves philosophical issues such as: *one,* the relationship between population mobility and economic efficiency; *two,* the comparison of economic well-being for different individuals; *three,* the priority of national over regional goals; and *four,* the extent to which an individual's well-being depends on the economic well-being of his region or community independently of his own situation. Rather than dwell on these issues further, however, I shall turn to the question of the analytical feasibility of a more extended system of development goals than simply maximization of output.

II. A MODEL FOR MULTIPLE DEVELOPMENT GOALS

Assuming for the moment that development officials did typically adopt policies based on a more articulate concept of goals, is there any way of determining an optimum development policy with respect to all the considerations raised above? Dose an optimum policy solution necessarily exist? Is it a unique solution? Clearly, if the answer to all of these questions is "no," this could provide an additional and rather convincing explanation of why maximizing growth is all that is sought. The rest of this paper will be concerned with examining the conditions under which answers to these questions could be obtained.

So far as the first question is concerned, it should be obvious that not all the factors potentially relevant to economic welfare can be taken into account. To do so would require an operational dynamic general equilibrium model extended for n regions which would also have to incorporate the size distribution of income. Nevertheless, while presently available analytical techniques can hardly be extended that far, they can take explicitly into account at least several goals in addition to growth of output or employment.

It will be convenient to express a development model with a more extended concept of goals in the form of a linear program. In linear programming, the interaction of growth and economies of scale cannot be considered. This approach is a matter of expositional ease so far as this paper is concerned, and a matter of computational economy so far as the model is concerned. Non-linear models could account for scale effects. And in the special case of public services, it may be possible to allow for scale effects even in a linear model.

A more serious problem is posed by external economies and diseconomies. Economic development certainly does affect input-output relations even in firms and industries which are not undergoing shifts in scale. But, aside from the possible use of industrial complex analysis in certain closely related manufacturing industries, it would be extremely difficult even to identify, much less to measure such effects. Especially difficult to estimate are the external effects of expanded transportation, communication, and business services, on the one hand, and of increased congestion, smoke and noise levels, and water pollution, on the other.

To weigh the effects of price changes and changes in the distribution of income would require some kind of general welfare model. This approach would require separating households of the region into an unrealistic number of groupings, and an equally difficult comparison of personal preferences or utility schedules. Consequently, these considerations will be excluded from the model as it is formulated here. Finally, it is necessary to omit from consideration possible conflicts between the level of aggregate income and the average number of hours worked per week, or the work vs. leisure issue. This omission is probably not very serious, since working hours are largely determined institutionally and are fairly standard in our economy. Also, at least for the moment, a model will be posited for a fully-employed economy with no in- or out-migration. These last two assumptions will subsequently be relaxed.

The omission of all of the factors discussed in the preceding paragraph means that the development model outlined below cannot legitimately be regarded as a general purpose model relevant to all development decisions. It does represent one format within which it is technically possible to consider more than one goal at a time. With greater understanding of planning principles, the objective function to be maximized can be made more explicit. With greater knowledge of the underlying economic and social process, the constraints can be expanded to take a wider range of phenomena into account. With more sophisticated systems analysis techniques, experimentation with non-linear forms would be possible. Thus, the model illustrated here represents not so much a specific model to be used uncritically in regional development policy formulation as it does an example of what may be an improved way of looking at the development planning process.

With these limitations in mind, a model of regional development could be formulated as:

Maximize

$$a(V_p - \Delta G) - \beta Cv_p + \gamma \dot{V}_p \tag{5}$$

where as before

$$V_p = \sum_{i=1}^{n} P_i X_i \tag{1}$$

and where

$$Cv_p = \delta Cx \tag{6}$$

and

$$\dot{V}_p = \epsilon \dot{X} \tag{7}$$

Subject to:
as before,

$$X_i = \sum_{j=1}^{n} a_{ij} X_j + a_{i0} X_0 \qquad (i = 1, \ldots, n) \tag{2}$$

and also,

$$C_x = \sum_{i=1}^{n} \frac{Cx_i X_i}{X_i} \tag{8}$$

and

$$\dot{X} = \sum_{i=1}^{n} \frac{\dot{X}_i X_i}{X_i} \tag{9}$$

and again, as before,

$$X_i \geqslant 0 \qquad (i = 0, 1, \ldots, n) \tag{3}$$

$$X_0 \leqslant K \tag{4}$$

where V_p, P_i, X_i, X_0, a_{ij}, a_{i0}, and K are as defined previously, ΔG is the increase in the cost of providing a constant level of government services, Cv_p and C_x are the coefficients of variation around their trend values of value added and total production, and $\dot{V}_p$ and $\dot{X}$ are the first derivatives of value added and output with respect to time.

The inclusion of ΔG in (5) is to take account of scale effects in the provision of public goods. The production of public goods would, of course, still be included in the vector X_i, but since the model has been framed in linear terms, adjustment for scale effects must be on an ad hoc basis. Because of the central importance of governmental activity in development programs, some such adjustment is both necessary and possible, since most local government services enter as inputs directly only to households. In some cases, of course, ΔG could be negative.

As an example of how ΔG would be calculated, let it be supposed that an increase in export demand leads to a gain in V_p equivalent to 1000 workers. This change would include some increase in local government employment, say 50 workers, derived from an assumption that employment in local government would increase in direct proportion to total employment. In fact, however, this assumption may be invalid, and perhaps 75 additional government workers would be needed to provide *the same level of services*. In that case ΔG would be equal to 25. It could be argued, of course, that this kind of *ex post* adjustment could be made for every industry. But this could be done more appropriately through a non-linear programming model. Even in that case, however, a special adjustment for government would still be needed. In the absence of a market valuation of its output, there is no way to test the shape of its production function, at least as such functions are usually regarded.

Two questions are of more critical importance in evaluating the extended objective function, (5): Are the welfare impacts of income level, income stability, and income growth independent and additive? And how can estimates be obtained for the parameters α, β, and γ? Before discussing possible answers, some aspects of the other relationships in the model will be mentioned.

Refinements of the Model

Equations (6) and (7) simply state that stability and growth of value-added are proportional to stability and growth of total output. Where a change in the level of output results in a change in the proportion of input requirements obtained from domestic sources, the model could be adjusted by stipulating further conditions, perhaps disaggregating Cv_p and $\dot{V}_p$ and estimating them separately for each industry group. Generally, however, the simpler procedure implied by equations (6) and (7) would probably provide a reasonable first approximation.

The equations represented by (2) provide for ordinary linear homogeneous production function constraints, and equations (8) and (9) express aggregate stability and growth as weighted averages of individual industry stability and growth. In order to take account of locational shifts the technical coefficients a_{ij} in (2) could be replaced by t_{ij} which indicate not the amount of industry i's output needed to produce a unit of industry j's output, but the amount of industry i's output purchased domestically per unit of output of industry j.[7]

It could be argued that the informational requirements of (8) and (9) are rather severe, calling essentially for an estimate of future stability and growth prospects for every existing and prospective industry in the region. But if these are relevant development considerations, even very rough estimates would seem to be preferable to ignoring them. As a basis for these estimates, it would perhaps be tempting to use historical data for the United States as a whole, or for some major subregion. While this approximation would certainly be better than no information at all, use of such data would involve not only the ordinary problems of any extrapolation but also rather difficult disaggregation problems; for example, every subregion within a region could easily be more unstable cyclically than the region as a whole.

The objective function itself, equation (5), contains what are probably the most critical elements of all in determining the analytical feasibility of a welfare model of regional economic development: these are the questions of its form and the values of the parameters. So far as form is concerned, the presumption that level, stability, and growth of income are independent in their influence on welfare seems reasonably valid; it is difficult to think of exceptions. The assumption of linearity is subject to more question, but in this case it is difficult to think of an alternative formulation that could be defended a priori. Moreover, even in its simplest form, as in (5), the problem of obtaining estimates for the parameters is a formidable one.

Nevertheless, if development programs are to be formulated with respect to economic welfare, some concept of a region's economic goals must be made reasonably explicit, either through social-psychological research, through the political process, or through invoking an organismic concept of the region as having ends of its own. Although this paper is not the place to pursue the subject of how to find out what people want, it is in order to point out that there are two levels of problems in determining community preferences. Individual preferences with respect to income level, stability, and growth must be evaluated, and the individual preference functions must be aggregated. With regard to individual preferences, more than one solution may be optimal for a given individual, but at least one optimal solution would have to exist. For the community as a whole, however, even the existence of a solution is by no means assured. Such objectives as a higher level of income, greater stability, or more rapid growth of income essentially must be considered jointly, at least as they would be viewed from the vantage point of an economic development program. And there may well be irreconcilable views with respect to these three factors among different individuals or groups.[8] Moreover, given the complexity of the ends involved, there is no assurance that such conflicts could necessarily be resolved by a majority decision. However, even where an impasse is reached and a unique policy decision can be reached only by some kind of authoritarian imposition, it would seem important to know what the points of conflict are and the identity of the opposing groups.

If the assumption of full employment is dropped, the model could be extended without becoming much more complex, perhaps in the form

$$\alpha(V_p - \Delta G) - \beta C v_p + \gamma \dot{V}_p - \lambda(K - X_0) \tag{10}$$

where the last term, $(K - X_0)$, is simply the existing level of unemployment. The values of the parameters would, of course, be different than in (5). Note that unemployment enters in a non-dynamic way; as formulated, λ is constant and not dependent on $(K - X_0)$ over time. However, since development programs are typically highly discontinuous this does not seem to be too unrealistic.

Relaxing the assumption of no in- or outmigration would also seem to cause relatively little difficulty in the model. The variables V_p and $\dot{V}_p$ would have to be converted to a per capita basis, but this would cause no special problem. The unemployment term should probably stay unchanged as it seems implausible to assume that a region would be concerned about providing jobs for non-residents (that is, for *future* immigrants) where this goal would make no contribution to the economic welfare of existing residents. Here, too, the parameters and ΔG are likely to have very different values from what they had in the closed region case. Also, the basic assumption of no external economies underlying the whole model becomes somewhat more strained. The only other change occasioned by permitting migration is with respect to (4), the constraint on labor input. If this constraint were completely dropped, serious problems would result with respect to the existence of a unique solution. Fortunately this possibility could not reasonably be regarded as a relevant case since any region is areally bounded so that there would be some maximum population and associated labor force which could be regarded as desirable, supportable, or at the very least conceivable.

The model developed to this point certainly represents a considerable compromise with reality. Only some of the factors which were discussed at the beginning, other than growth itself, have been accounted for, and some of these only imperfectly. There are other economic goals which have not been mentioned, such as minimizing seasonal variations in employment. And nothing at all has been said about possible interactions between purely economic and other types of goals which may form part of a development program. On the other hand, the model proposed here represents an improvement over the uncritical acceptance of maximum growth as the sole criterion of economic development. While it would be desirable to develop a comprehensive welfare function, this is not very likely to happen. First of all, the empirical problems of regional analysis are substantial. Second, there is no reason to assume that the same general analytical model can be applied successfully to all regions, even allowing for differences in the values of its parameters.

On the other hand, the preceding discussion is meant to emphasize the importance of considering goal formulation explicitly, independent of structural analysis, and to suggest some ways of approaching this task. Formidable problems remain in estimating community preferences for economic goals. However, the question of values cannot be avoided in policy decisions. If values are hard to identify and measure, this is hardly the fault of the model as such.

III. NATIONAL AND REGIONAL GOALS

Up to this point little has been said about the possible inconsistencies between adopting policies for optimizing economic development in every region and a single optimum policy for the set of regions as a whole. There are several reasons why optimal regional development may be inconsistent with optimal national development. Since development goals are typically for a number of key variables, it may be as difficult to arrive at a common denominator between regions as between individuals in the same region. But even if maximum productive growth is the only goal of regions and the nation alike, it may be impossible to achieve both because of a certain lumpiness and immobility of capital investments. Moreover, where interregional population movements are unencumbered, the relocation of population necessitated by regional differentials in growth rates is not accomplished without some cost. Although the cost may be less than the resulting gains in efficiency, the direct and indirect costs of relocation are not necessarily borne in any easily discernible or fixed proportions between regions with net out- and inmigration. Finally, even with complete and costless human and real capital transfer possible, maximum output for the sum of all regions would equal the sum of the maximum outputs for each region only under conditions of perfect competition in the spatial assignment of activities and population. Formally, the conditions for efficient spatial allocation would be analogous to efficient allocation among industries in a spaceless economy.

In sum, there are at least three major reasons why optimization at a national level may be inconsistent with optimization at the level of the region. First, where there are multi-dimensional economic goals, the preference patterns of regions may be such that there will not be a consistent ordering of these goals at the national level. Second, even if maximum output were the only goal, each region's share in the relocation costs needed to achieve it may not be equal to their share in the resultant gains. Third, in either case, external economies or diseconomies in production extending across regional boundaries have not been taken into account.

Even an individual region acting unilaterally and concerned only with its own welfare would have to take into account at least the third of these possible inconsistencies—the effects on its own production functions of developments in other regions. Similarly, it is conceivable that some measures it might take to enhance its own productivity could have beneficial effects on other regions equal to or even greater than would accrue to itself. But for a single region, these external effects are likely to be small, diffused, and uncertain.

The second kind of inconsistency is more likely to be considered explicitly by individual regions. It takes the form of a concern with expenditures for education or retraining of people who are likely to migrate elsewhere. While there may be serious and legitimate sociological and political objections, it is clear that a more rational economic policy would be served by financing such activities on a multi-regional (frequently a national) basis.

Finally, there is a greater basis for concern about inconsistent goals or marginal rates of substitution between goals among regions. Responsibility in this case cannot be assigned to the individual regions, but to policymakers concerned with the nation's economic welfare as a primary objective. An individual region would probably concern itself with this problem only to the extent that it maintained an oligopolistic relationship with a limited number of very closely competing regions. In that event, it might try to take its competitors' preferences into account as a way of formulating a defensive development strategy designed to offset development policies of its neighbors. This prospect of mutually antagonistic regional policies is, of course, the reason why those concerned with the national welfare must consider the possibility of inconsistent regional goals. To moderate the effects of interregional competition, economic welfare at the national level would probably have to be optimized, subject not only to the kinds of constraints already indicated, but subject to the additional constraint that the performance of any region with respect to any particular goal must not fall below some arbitrarily specified levels.

This paper does not suggest how these levels should be set. Hopefully, it points to the kinds of issues which must be faced in establishing any kind of development policy; it is meant to suggest some ways of attacking them. Finally, it has attempted to demonstrate that, however difficult they may be to resolve, these issues cannot be avoided. The discussion is meant to leave the reader with the view that coherent policies can and should be constructed on the basis of multiple objectives if planners are to make serious headway in approaching an optimum development strategy for regions.

NOTES

[1] See, for example, Charles M. Tiebout, *Markets for California Products* (Sacramento: California Development Agency, 1962); Charles L. Leven, "Regional Income and Product Accounts; Construction and Application," in *Design of Regional Accounts,* ed. Werner Hochwald (Baltimore: Johns Hopkins University Press, 1961). The use of micro-analytical systems, i.e., systems which take into account the behavior of individual decision-making units, have mainly been developed in connection with urban renewal problems. Examples are the work currently underway in the CRP program in Pittsburgh and that being planned under CRP programs elsewhere. Another substantial effort at building micro-analytic models is the current work on Philadelphia within the Penn-Jersey Transportation Study.

[2] How accurately it would be explained is, of course, open to question. If, as in the typical case, it were determined from the amount of steel output on the assumption that the production function for steel is linear homogeneous (i.e., that the amount of coal needed would vary in direct proportion to the amount of steel produced), the estimate of coal needed might be inaccurate to the extent that this assumption were unwarranted. In principle, though, an accurate production function relationship could be determined.

[3] However, unlike the case of simple extrapolations, standard errors generally can be computed more readily for estimates made within a structural system.

[4] Ordinarily this would be equivalent to maximizing employment.

[5] For example, see C. L. Leven, *op. cit.,* for a discussion of the problem of variable trade coefficients.

[6] For a discussion of the relationships of inter-industry to income and product models see Leven, *op cit.*

[7] For an extended discussion of this point see Leven, *op cit.*

[8] See Kenneth Arrow, *Social Choice and the Theory of Value* (New York: John Wiley & Sons, 1956), chaps. i–iii.

30. Criteria for Evaluating Regional Development Programs*

JOHN V. KRUTILLA[1]

I

A regional development program will suggest different things to different individuals, and to all it is likely to suggest not a single program but a number of related programs focusing on a common objective. To a staff member of a development agency, a regional development program implies literally scores of individual programs ranging from those involving engineering projects to those basically educational in nature carried out co-operatively with educational and other regional institutions. Since these programs are neither comparable nor amenable to uniform methods of analysis, a complete discussion of criteria for their evaluation cannot be attempted in a paper such as this. This paper will discuss the problem only in general terms, therefore, to sketch out at least the nature of the problem and to inquire into some general lines of approach in handling it.

To indicate the scope of the paper and to begin with a common understanding as to terminology, let us start by defining what will be meant by various terms employed.

This paper will skirt the controversy as to what constitutes a region, since opinions among economists vary from a belief that the concept of a region has little value,[2] to the opposite position that there can be demarcated "but one best set of regions."[3] For the purpose of this discussion it will be adequate to define a region simply as an identifiable geographical area, whether a river basin, an administrative unit, or a combination of administrative units, depending on the specific problem at hand. Regions to be considered will be subareas of the United States and thus will represent open economics engaging in interregional trade. The paper will confine itself, also, largely to the problem of relatively underdeveloped regions.

[1] The author is indebted to Pierre Crosson, Henry Erlanger, John Peterson, and Vernon Ruttan, of the TVA, and Otto Eckstein for their comments and suggestions on an earlier draft of the paper.

[2] Rutledge Vining, "The Study of the Spatial Structure of an Economic System." Paper presented at the December, 1951, meetings of the American Economic Association.

[3] Walter Isard, "Some Emerging Concepts and Techniques for Regional Analysis" (*Proceedings* of the Western Exploratory Group of the Social Science Research Council on Regional Economic Analysis, Berkeley, 1952).

* Reprinted from the *American Economic Review*, Vol. 45 (May 1955).

Regional development, for our purposes, will be defined as a process resulting in a secular growth of regional output or real income. (This, of course, is less than a comprehensive definition of regional development, as many intangible aspects of development are not susceptible of measurement by a monetary yardstick.) This growth can occur autonomously. It may be influenced, also, by the impact of national economic expansion imparted through the private sector of the economy. A regional development program, therefore, must be distinguished as an influence exogenous to the normal functioning of the private economy. For the purpose of this discussion, a regional development program will be defined as a public undertaking, most likely a governmental undertaking, one of whose primary objectives is to influence the underlying factors affecting regional output.

II

Attempts at evaluating regional development programs in the past have frequently used an aggregate economic indicator, such as total personal income, to compare relative changes for a region in which a development program exists with relative changes for another region. This comparison between two regions over an appropriate time period is assumed to reveal the extent to which development efforts have been economically justified.[4] This procedure is dubious at best for it implies that the development efforts being evaluated, to be effective, must have exercised a dominant influence on regional income—and in the relatively short run. The fact that statistical data which have been compiled in such attempts to evaluate the TVA, for example, have not appreciably influenced the area of agreement regarding the value of TVA programs suggests that this approach falls short of providing evaluative results. An examination of the implicit assumptions underlying this approach will afford some excellent reasons why this may be the case.

First, an evaluation by this method implicitly assumes that the comparison being made is between a region which has a development program and one in which such a program is lacking. But if relative changes in total income are used to measure regional development, the influence of other governmental programs which affect regional income, regardless of the administrative device employed, must be eliminated from both regions to provide the *ceteris paribus* conditions essential for a valid comparison. It is seldom recognized, for example, that the

[4] See, for examples, B. U. Ratchford, "Government Action or Private Enterprise in River Basin Development: An Economist's View," and discussant Joseph Ransmeier's remarks, AEA *Papers and Proceedings,* May, 1951, pp. 304-306, 311-312. Also, "Study of Agricultural and Economic Problems of the Cotton Belt," *Hearings before Special Subcommittee on Cotton of the Committee on Agriculture* (House of Representatives, 80th Congress), p. 687.

activities of the TVA to a considerable extent supplant activities which are carried out by a number of other federal agencies in other regions. The relative magnitude of governmental expenditures for programs other than resource development is likewise almost never taken into account. Federal expenditures for military procurement in California and New York during a five-year period (1950-54), for example, were roughly seven times as large as federal expenditures associated with the TVA over a twenty-one year period. In many other states, although not as large, they were multiples of the twenty-one year total of TVA expenditures. These expenditures, along with grants-in-aid to states, federal construction, and various other direct governmental activities throughout the nation, suggest that the absence of valley authorities does not preclude the possibility that federal expenditures in regions other than the Tennessee Valley account directly for a larger portion of their growth in income.

Second, regional comparisons of income relatives as a method of evaluation implicitly assumes that the activities of development agencies are encompassed within a relatively well-defined geographical area. In reality, since development agencies usually have responsibility for a number of resource problems rather than the economy of a well-defined region, development activities may radiate into adjacent regions observing no common boundary for the entire "package" of resource development programs. For example, the water control program of the TVA is confined to the 125 watershed counties in parts of seven Valley states. The power program relates to a somewhat different area of about 170 counties in these states. TVA's activities in regard to tributary watershed development involve relations with the seven Valley states and its national responsibilities for fertilizer research and development involve co-operative relations with institutions in 35 states. The incidence of benefits stemming from these programs, moreover, is not confined to the areas in which the programs are centered. It is not meaningful, therefore, to take one area influenced by a development program for comparison with another area in which the program's influence has also been felt, in evaluating program results.

Third, such attempts at evaluation involve hidden assumptions that, despite differences in the variety and quality of resources which exist among regions, all regions have a uniform development potential. Stated differently, an assumption is implied that regardless of the differences which may exist among regions in all other determining variables, every region can be expected to develop economically as rapidly as another except for the presence or absence of a development program.

To sum up, then, past attempts to evaluate regional development programs by comparisons of income relatives have not examined critically what constitutes a regional development program apart from the administrative machinery used to implement it, what constitutes a region for the purpose at hand, and how realistic are other assumptions which are implied to hold.

However, quite apart from these critical observations, there remains another question of importance which seemingly has escaped attention. The degree to which a program can be expected to stimulate regional development depends largely upon the magnitude of the program relative to the total of other factors affecting the region's development. A comprehensive regional development program might conceivably involve responsibilities for monetary and fiscal policy, welfare programs, regulation of transportation rates, interregional trade and migration, and other governmental activities which vary with political philosophies and the contingencies of a particular time and place. Such programs would involve all of the measures with which government can influence the level of income. By contrast, regional development efforts in the United States, such as resource development programs, represent efforts of rather limited scope when viewed in relation to the aggregate of economic activities which engage the productive factors of a region. Given the margin of error in our economic data, is the influence which such limited development programs can be expected to have on regional income capable of being accurately indicated by comparisons of relative changes?

It has been observed by Morgenstern that a probable error of 10 per cent attaches to our estimates of national income. (*On the Accuracy of Economic Observations,* page 84.) There is little reason to believe that estimates of income on the regional level are more accurate. If these estimates are used to provide measures of relative change, a regional development program would have to contribute a third to the income of a region in a given year before its influence would be equal to the range of possible error in an index whose base (prior to program introduction) and given year estimates are subject to a 10 per cent error. To illustrate: The index of estimated income payments from manufacturing for the year 1953 (1929 = 100) was 543 for the 11 southeastern states and 602 for the 201 counties representing the Tennessee Valley and TVA power service area—a difference of 59 percentage points. If we assume that the true income was underestimated for the Tennessee Valley while overestimated for the Southeast in the base year, and overestimated in the given year for the Tennessee Valley while underestimated for the Southeast (all by as little as 10 per cent), the true index would be 664 for the Southeast and but 493 for the Tennessee Valley. If estimating errors of opposite sign but equivalent magnitude for the base and given years are assumed, the true index for the Southeast would be 445 and 735 for the Tennessee Valley. With a range of possible error exceeding 200 percentage points in the index, we cannot feel secure that the indicated difference of 59 percentage points has not been influenced more by errors of estimation than by the development program. Since errors in estimating can produce a wider range of differences in our income relatives than can be realistically anticipated from the influence of limited development programs, one can legitimately question the validity of using comparative data on income (and other) relatives to evaluate development program results.

III

If relative changes in our economic data are not likely to provide a sufficiently accurate basis for evaluating development programs, what alternatives remain? The most fruitful approach, it seems, is one which examines each program activity individually for its impact on the sector of the economy toward which it is directed. One method of this type seeks to provide approximations of real income produced (or losses averted) by such programs which can then be compared quantitatively with costs. This procedure is used to indicate whether the criterion of efficient resourse allocation has been met.

This approach presents several problems. It is desirable to recognize a specific limitation at the outset. Taking the TVA as an example, again, there are programs such as flood control, navigation, and power for which the development agency has exclusive responsibility and from which direct benefits are largely tangible. On the other hand, there are programs, such as tributary watersheds, stream sanitation, forestry, agriculture, and scores of others, which are co-operative ventures involving agencies of state and local government in addition to TVA. These programs involve research, development, and demonstration, in the main, and are fundamentally educational in orientation. Given the state of our research methods and knowledge, developmental results of some of these programs are scarcely less difficult to assay than results of research and public education generally, nor can quantitative valuation be placed on them more easily. With limitations on estimating the benefits of this type of program and shared responsibility for the results, a precise quantitative comparison of benefits and costs from the agency viewpoint does not seem feasible.

This type of program, however, has accounted for only about 10-15 per cent of total expenditures in the case of TVA. The major portion of this relatively small share, moreover, is accounted for by TVA's national responsibilities for fertilizer research and development and defense chemicals. Costs of the fertilizer and munitions program, while not found in other regions, are largely recovered by sale of munitions to defense establishments and receipts from fertilizers distributed in agricultural programs. Resource development expenditures, apart from the chemical, power, navigation, and flood control programs, therefore, have accounted for only about 3-4 per cent of total program expenditures. The remaining and preponderant portion of expenditures is more readily amenable to quantitative analysis.

Accordingly, an evaluation might proceed by analysis of each program activity which provides opportunity for quantitative evaluation. This will permit judgment as to how efficient an allocation of resources the major portion of program activities represents. In the private sector, of course, the pricing system is assumed to provide a reasonably efficient method of allocation. In the public sector, on the other hand, investment decisions must often be made to provide services which are not available through conventional markets. Public revenues from taxation can be used for these purposes without reference to costs in the capital market, while valuation of the services provided also frequently cannot be obtained directly from the operation of product markets.

This poses a difficult problem of establishing procedures for estimating costs and "returns" to which a good deal of attention has been given and to which a satisfactory solution may emerge. The continuing work of the Subcommittee on Benefits and Costs of the Federal Interagency River Basin Committee[5] is developing a conceptual framework for estimating benefits and costs of river basin projects. Briefly, the method of estimating costs recommended includes imputation of a rate of interest to cover real costs of project capital as well as other costs incurred through conventional factor markets. Valuation of services provided is made by estimating actual or imputed market value of these services, usually measured by the cost of the most economical alternate method of providing similar services. A ratio of benefits to costs is then computed and, assuming that project capital (and other factors) would otherwise be employed at the margin where returns would be just equal to costs, opportunity costs will be met for the total of factors employed in the project if the benefit-cost ratio exceeds unity.

This *ex ante* approach to investment decisions in the public sector can be extended with appropriate modification to evaluation of such

[5] *Proposed Practices for Economic Analysis of River Basin Projects;* see also John M. Clark, Eugene L. Grant, Maurice W. Kelso, *Report of the Panel of Consultants on Secondary or Indirect Benefits of Water-Use Projects,* to Michael W. Straus, Commissioner, Bureau of Reclamation.

programs after they have been in operation. Established operating programs, moreover, provide known construction and operating costs and experience on which to base estimates of benefits. In this connection one consideration bears stressing. Facilities employed in such programs have useful lives which are limited, in the main, only by technological obsolescence. Related development which such programs induce will doubtless require some time to gain momentum. Evaluation of existing programs, therefore, should avoid judgment based on the first year's or an average of early years' results. Cumulative costs over the life of the program should be considered in relation to cumulative benefits expected to accrue over the entire life of the facilities as is done in conventional benefit-cost analyses. Projections based on experience with costs and benefits to date should facilitate estimating realistic cumulative totals. The problem posed by the difference in time distribution of outlays and benefits must be taken into account, of course, and can be handled by use of the interest rate or discount factor.

While this procedure provides criteria for evaluting development programs, it has a national rather than a regional focus; i.e., it is addressed to the problem of allocating resources efficiently within the total economy. Without supplementary analysis to determine the spatial distribution of benefits from program activities, it fails to provide much insight into the effect such programs have had on the development of the region itself. To answer this question, a somewhat different approach may be preferred for analysis and evaluation from a regional viewpoint.

IV

Regional development has been defined as a process resulting in a secular rise in regional output or real income. Increasing regional output and income implies both expansion of the region's productive capacity and growth of effective demand for the region's output. Both conditions are necessary and combined will represent a sufficient condition for regional development. Attention has often been sharply focused on increasing output through stimulating increased participation of underutilized resources and/or increasing the productivity of resources being employed. Perhaps not enough attention has been directed to the process by which effective demand may be increased; namely, through retaining an adequate share of the resulting increased factor receipts in the region to increase the region's effective demand for its own output and ensuring that the increased output include goods and services for which there is a highly elastic demand both from within and outside the region.

The demand aspect in regional development becomes particularly important when viewed in the light of a rising secular trend in national income. In fact, resource development programs derive their justification largely from the implicit assumption that long-run economic growth will require the factors or services provided by such programs. This assumption must be examined carefully, however, in connection with each program activity. But within the context of an expanding national economy, the degree to which development efforts will make a contribution to underdeveloped regions will depend on how effectively they assist the regions to supply, over time, a greater share of the total economy's expanding demand for goods and services.

Development programs may be evaluated from the regional viewpoint, accordingly, in terms of their aid in increasing the productive capacity of the region and in stimulating effective demand for the region's output.

To promote these dual objectives, resource development programs of the kind undertaken by the federal government should focus attention (within the limitation of their statutory authority) on influencing the supply functions of factors for which demand is highly responsive to secularly rising income nationally. These factors may be referred to as "strategic" factors. They will consist of productive factors for which demand will be relatively elastic both with respect to price and income, and favorably influenced by changing technology and tastes. Development programs which alter favorably the supply functions of strategic resources will improve the region's competitive position in the national market. Cross-elasticity of the derived demand for localized resources will increase the probability that location advantages thus provided will attract external capital to the region. Branch plants of national concerns represent a typical form of such capital movements in a nationally expanding economy. If the strategic factors, furthermore, are required by "growth" industries, i.e., those industries for which product demand is income elastic and influenced positively by the trend in changing consumer preferences, the rate at which capital formation will occur in response to shifts in regional supply functions and the extent to which these and complementary resources will be employed can be expected to increase.

Criteria for evaluating the developmental effects of regional development programs might then be: how effective were the development programs in shifting the supply function of factors on which their efforts were focused and how strategic, as indicated by their demand characteristics, were the factors whose supply functions were thus affected?

As an illustration, we know that multiple-purpose development of the Tennessee River, by altering the production function for the region's power, produced a substantial shift in the supply schedule. Development of an inland waterway increased the supply of low-cost transport services. The water control program, by regularizing stream flows and permitting settling to occur in the reservoirs, lowered the cost and increased the dependable supply of high-quality processing and cooling water.

We know that these factors, i.e., power, water, and in some cases water transport, are basic inputs in the chemical industry, which incidentally has experienced a half-century of sustained vigorous growth. With respect to product demand, as an example, we know that changing technology, rising income, and changing consumer preferences have altered the derived demand for industrial fibers. There has been a spectacular substitution of synthetic for natural fibers. This in turn has fostered a vigorous demand for factors employed in the production of synthetics. In response to this growing national demand and the procurement advantages in the Tennessee Valley for basic inputs, investment in facilities along the Tennessee River for the production of synthetic fibers has exceeded 50 million dollars during the past several years alone.

Stimulating capital formation is not limited to providing procurement, processing, and distribution advantages directly for new industrial enterprise. Such advantages provided originally may be reinforced by triggered developments. The most spectacular illustration of this in the Tennessee Valley is the developing chemical complex at Calvert City, Kentucky, near the base of Kentucky Dam. The initial development at Calvert City took place in 1948 when Pennsylvania Salt Manufacturing Company erected a hydrofluoric acid plant. In addition to fluorspar, the basic requirements of the firm were relatively low-cost electric energy, large quantities of processing and cooling water, and water transportation for shipment of sulphur and salt. Concurrently, the Pittsburgh Metallurgical Company built facilities for producing ferroalloys to realize savings through joint development of docking and rail facilities. Pennsalt added a chlorine plant which, along with B. F. Goodrich's plans to locate vinyl chloride facilities in the area, prompted construction of a calcium carbide and acetylene plant by Air Reduction. The latter's location decision was influenced by the favorable source of intermediate products supplied jointly by Pennsalt and Goodrich, along with other favorable location characteristics of the area. These three firms now have two plants each at Calvert City which, along with Pittsburgh Metallurgical Company and the recent addition of General Aniline and Film Corporation, represent an investment of approximately 70 million dollars—only slightly short of the total investment in flood control, navigation, and power facilities of the Kentucky Dam project. This capacity has been built within a period of ten years after completion of the dam. The favorable opportunities for realizing agglomeration economies provided by the developing industrial complex, moreover, suggest a triggered development which in the long run will dwarf the resource development expenditures necessary, although not sufficient, to spark it initially.

Analyses of the industrial demand for power, use of the navigation channel for movement of bulk materials, and use of industrial water supplies in the Tennessee Valley suggest that the water resource development programs have attracted the light metals industries, additive metals using electrometallurgy, synthetic fibers, and other chemical industries. Investment since the beginning of TVA's resource development activities in plant and facilities along the Tennessee River (exclusive of TVA's installations) for which industrial water supplies, water transportation, and/or relatively inexpensive electrial energy are significant location factors, totals approximately 2 billion dollars. Data and conceptual limitations preclude our measuring how much the rate of investment has been increased. We know, however, by computing the location quotients for these industries, that a larger proportion of the rapidly growing new capacity nationally has been built in the Tennessee Valley since the advent of the resource development programs than was being built prior to it.

Although the rate at which capital is formed will affect the rate at which regional income will increase, there may exist a sufficient difference in the ratio of the increment in income to the increment in investment, over time, to merit comment. Investment expenditures of a development program in an underdeveloped region, as well as triggered investment in the early phases of development, will produce something less than the full multiplier effect on that region's income. In the first place, the region will be unable to supply from domestic production a large part of the investment goods required for the program. In the second place, as indicated by family budget studies and the economic structure of underdeveloped regions, the marginal propensity to import from the rest of the economy associated with the second as well as the first round of new expenditures is likely to be very great in relation to the marginal propensity to import from the region by the rest of the national economy. This results from the low income elasticity of demand for a large portion of the region's output (agricultural products, textiles, etc.). The net effect of the regional multiplier will be restricted largely to that produced by expenditures for investment goods and services which can be supplied from regional production. Only a small additional export multiplier can be anticipated from the national economy's imports from the region resulting from its exports of investment goods to the region.[6] Accordingly, despite the high marginal propensity to consume among low income underdeveloped regions, the region's inelastic supply of investment goods and the low income elasticity of demand for the region's output, in the short run, will limit the multiplier effect of capital formation on the region itself.

If the regional development programs have focused on development of strategic resources, increased factor receipts from the employment of these resources in the region by material-oriented industries will provide, in time, the increment to total income necessary and sufficient to attract market-oriented consumer goods industries for which final demand is income elastic. This process of development reflects a change in the composition as well as level of regional output. If the region thus increases its capacity to supply from home production its demand for income-elastic goods as well as supply a larger part of the expansion in demand originating nationally, *ceteris paribus,* the regional multiplier effect of capital formation both regionally (investment multiplier) and nationally (export multiplier) will tend to increase.[7]

The effects on capital formation and the income multiplier of development programs which improve the region's capacity to supply strategic factors can be contrasted with results to be anticipated from

[6] The regional multiplier in this case will be similar to an investment multiplier involving two countries (cf. Fritz Machlup, *International Trade and the Foreign Trade Multiplier,* pp. 175-176) where the fraction of investment goods and services provided by domestic production is equivalent to "home investment" in the Machlup formulation and the fraction of investment items provided from outside the region is akin to investment in the "second country."

The regional multiplier can be expressed as follows:

$$y = \frac{ai\ (s' + m') + m'a'i}{(s' + m')\ (s + m) - m'm} \quad \text{and} \quad k = \frac{a(s' + m') + m'a'}{(s' + m')\ (s + m) - m'm}$$

Where:

y = change in regional income associated with new investment; i = total amount of new investment; a = fraction of investment goods and services provided by regional capacity; a' = fraction of investment items provided by remainder of the economy; m = marginal propensity to import by the region; m' = marginal propensity to import from the region by remainder of the economy; s = marginal propensity to save in the region; s' = marginal propensity to save of the remainder of the economy; k = the regional multiplier.

[7] The increase in regional income accompanying new capital formation can be obtained from the following expression:

$$y = \frac{ai(s' + m') + m'(a'i + i')}{(s' + m')\ (s + m) - m'm}$$

Where all symbols remain as previously defined while i' represents new investment nationally outside the region. The numerator will be increased by larger values of a and m' in the first term and the increased value of m' which applies to i' as well as the decreased value of a' in the second term. The denominator will be decreased by opposite changes in values of m and m'. The latter follows because of the different order of magnitude in the change in import propensities governed by the relative magnitude of the trading areas.

programs which focus on resources for which demand is relatively inelastic. The agricultural sector is useful as an illustration in this case because final demand for agricultural products generally is characterized by both price and income inelasticity. Growth in demand for agricultural output and hence for total factor input will not be proportional to growth of national income. Although substitution of factors, e.g., fertilizers and capital for land and labor, may result in a derived demand for some factors employed in agriculture to grow more than proportionally with demand for agricultural output, aggregate factor demand in agriculture will be subject to relative decline. Given an absence of production controls and price supports, resource development programs which contribute to increasing the aggregate factor employment in agriculture would tend to affect adversely the terms of trade between agriculture and other sectors of the economy. Because of inelastic demand, income from agriculture may decline by virtue of the increase in output. For a region which is predominantly agricultural and seeks to achieve development through these means, the development effort will produce an extraregional consumers' surplus with regional benefits being eroded away by adverse changes in the terms of interregional trade.

V

In summary, one may conclude that any meaningful evaluation of a regional development program requires intimate knowledge of the many activities which it represents. Furthermore, an approach which attempts to evaluate each program activity individually for its impact on the sector of the economy toward which it is directed is more promising than one which attempts to determine justification for the entire package of development programs by analyses conducted at levels several stages removed from the area of direct program impact. Moreover, it is probable that development programs which are financed nationally have essentially a national rather than a regional focus and that benefits from such programs are not confined within the region in which the program is centered. Regional comparisons of relative change in so-called "economic indicators," therefore, are not appropriate to the problem being posed. Moreover, because of the wide margin of possible error in indexes using such data, they provide a specious measure of the success of regional development programs, even should other conditions required for their use be fulfilled.

Benefit-cost analysis, while approaching the problem at the appropriate level, is designed to provide an investment criterion rather than criteria for evaluating developmental effects on the region in which the program is centered. Perhaps more useful for this latter purpose is an analysis of the process of development and how regional development programs may influence that process. This requires an examination of the effects such programs have on the parameters of the region's production and consumption functions over time and the trend in the structure of markets. Although precise quantitative criteria may be more difficult to formulate in this case, an approach along these lines is likely to be more relevant, more informative, and more suited for analysis of the dynamic aspects inherent in problems of economic development.

31. The Role of Accounts in the Economic Study of Regions*

EDGAR M. HOOVER AND BENJAMIN CHINITZ

THIS PAPER aims to help clarify the part that systematic regional accounts can appropriately play in basic economic studies of metropolitan regions. Our views have been shaped largely by experience in the design and early phases of execution of the Pittsburgh Regional Planning Association's three-year study of the Pittsburgh region, and in the latter part of this paper we shall refer specifically to that design. We hope, however, that this methodological discussion will be of wider interest and applicability.

I. GENERAL FUNCTIONS OF ACCOUNTS IN THE ECONOMIC ANALYSIS OF A REGION

It is well at the start to set up our notion of what comes under the term "accounts" in the context of this paper. Accounts mean, to us, systematic and quantitative cross-tabulations of economic transactions and claims, primarily in money units and primarily

* Reprinted from Werner Hochwald, ed., *Design of Regional Accounts.*

cross-sectional in nature. Basic to this notion of accounts is the feature of double-entry: every transaction and every claim involves two parties, and in principle each item in a set of accounts is cross-checkable because it occurs twice. The "parties" in a set of regional accounts are not individual households or firms, but appropriate groupings thereof, which we shall call "sectors." Finally we propose to confine our attention in this paper to transactions (debits/credits) accounts only, ignoring the whole area of "balance-sheet" or asset/liability accounting.

Accounts, as just defined, are useful at two different stages of regional analysis. Though the distinction is perhaps not so clear-cut as we here (for simplicity's sake) make it appear, we can separate two major roles of accounts under the heads of "consistency-checking" and "impact evaluation."

Consistency-Checking

It is clearly important that any analysis avoid internal contradictions so far as possible. Double-entry bookkeeping is an eminently logical way in which to impose that constraint upon our educated guesswork.

Three types of consistency-checking suggest themselves, though perhaps only one of these really involves accounting in a legitimate full-fledged sense:

a) Identity of the two sides of a single intersector transaction flow; i.e., *A*'s payments to *B* are the same as *B*'s receipts from *A*. Symbolically we might write this as:

$$\underset{A \quad B}{Cr} = \underset{B \quad A}{Dr},$$

or

$$\underset{A \quad B}{Dr} = \underset{B \quad A}{Cr}.$$

Example: expenditures by residents at regional drug stores are identical with sales of regional drug stores to residents. This is of course tautological; such identities may be useful reminders but in themselves are merely building blocks for full-fledged accounts.

b) Summation of one side of a sector's accounts; i.e., *A*'s total payments are the sum of *A*'s payments to all specific sectors. Symbolically,

$$\Sigma_A Cr = {}_A Cr_B + {}_A Cr_C \ldots . + {}_A Cr_N.$$

Example: a synthesis or breakdown of the region's personal income. This is also tautological if the total is arrived at simply by measuring all the components and adding them up. The summation-type equation is really useful only if there is some independent way of estimating the total, and if some components (but not too many) are impossible to measure directly with accuracy. In this case, the hazy component(s) can be derived as a residual—or rough independent estimates of its size can be checked for consistency.

c) Balancing the books of a specific sector. Symbolically,

$$\Sigma_A Cr = \Sigma_A Dr,$$

or [cf. (a) above]:

$$\Sigma Cr_A = \Sigma Dr_A.$$

Here we have a full-fledged sector-accounting constraint, capable of making a major consistency contribution and of being built into an over-all system of accounts describing the intersector transactions of the economy.

Example: the regional balance of payments.

It has already been suggested that a real consistency check requires some direct estimation of all components in an aggregate—unless a residual is moderately small and subject to some appraisal of its plausibility, the account of which it forms a part cannot be used to impose consistency in any real sense.

The essential point here is that as we depart substantially from exhaustive accounts, the usefulness of the accounting procedure very rapidly dissipates, so far as consistency-checking is concerned. This sharpens the question a regional economic study design has to face. The effort devoted to filling out accounts must be of at least critical minimum size, or reliance on accounts *per se* to impose a consistency check must be foregone.

Impact Evaluation

This includes the identification and measurement of relationships among the various sectors of the regional economy, in such fashion that the results of any expected or supposed change upon the economy can be traced through the series of direct and indirect repercussions.

We have two points to make here regarding the potential usefulness of comprehensive regional economic accounts. First, their usefulness can be minimal if they are done on a one-shot basis. Second, even full and current accounts would not provide an adequate apparatus to generate the results a regional economic study should provide. Let us examine these two points separately.

Need for Continuous Accounting. Before a regional analysis can be of substantial real use to planners and policy-makers it must take on some dynamic character. A one-time cross-sectional description of the "economic base" or of the trade flows and other connections among sectors of the regional economy is only a first step (albeit an essential one) *toward* a useful analytical apparatus.

It is clear in this context that if accounts are to play an effective part, they must be kept more or less current, and must cumulate as time series. The national income accounts would lose most of their manifold utility if they were not compiled as continuing time series. Regional accounts, too, will have to be put on a continuing basis if they are to serve as the basis for evaluation of changes over time. Most of the payoff comes not when the first balancing of books is achieved, but at a much later stage.

The preparation of a comprehensive regional accounts system is therefore an appropriate task for a continuing statistical agency, and not for an *ad hoc* project with limited life span.

Adequacy of Accounts for Tracing Impacts. Perhaps the most frequently suggested operational *application* of regional accounts (as distinct from their direct consistency-checking role) is in the evaluation of "multiplier" effects. The question here addressed is, "What changes in total regional business activity and income will result from a specific change in the region's earnings from export of goods and services?" Coefficients derived from interindustry and intersector transactions accounts are used in tracing repercussions of the initial change. The additional receipts from exports are distributed to businesses (for materials, supplies, and services), to government (as taxes), and to households (for labor services or as proprietary income). Out of such parts of these payments as are received within the region, further payments for goods and services are made by the recipients; and so on. At each round, a part of the new flow of payments leaks out of the region, and the ultimate total increment to regional activity and income is derived as a function of those leakages.

The attempt to derive a useful multiplier along such lines is, of course, beset by special difficulties when we deal with an open regional economy. The interindustry and intersector coefficients are not only difficult to determine, but may well be even less stable than the corresponding relations for the national economy. The most serious difficulty, however, is with the "leakages." The input side of each technical coefficient has to be broken down into inputs from internal versus outside sources, and that breakdown, even if once determined on a cross-sectional basis, is certainly in most instances highly unstable.

One may question how useful such a multiplier calculation would be even if it were based on precise and complete accounts of all the transactions involved. It is important to note that only a quite limited range of repercussion effects (in terms of locational analysis, only those linkages involving "market orientation") is actually subject to evaluation in this way. Our impression is that the importance of the multiplier effect for real policy and planning guidance has been oversold. In practice, only very occasionally does a major decision in private or public planning rest on a question like, "If we get (or lose) this export establishment, by how much will total local employment and payrolls ultimately be raised (or lowered)?" Instead, we are faced with questions like the following:

1) What industrial and population size and structure should we assume five, ten, or twenty years ahead as a basis for investment or other decisions that have to be made now?

2) Where in the region will changes occur? (This geographical aspect is almost always crucial.)

3) What effects on growth or internal patterns are foreseeable if (for example) we:

a) put through a renewal project,
b) change the tax structure,
c) improve the skills of the labor supply,
d) redistribute the costs of internal passenger movement,
e) impose stricter pollution controls,
f) negotiate lower freight rates,
g) attract the headquarters of a big national corporation,
h) build convention facilities, or
i) increase the stature of our universities?

The "multiplier" effect and transactions-accounting play a quite minor role in an analysis adequately responsive to such questions as the above regarding repercussions of an assumed exogenous event. They play no role at all in the explanation or prediction of the exogenous event itself.

Alternative Emphases in Regional Economic Analyses

The discussion above has shown (1) that development and maintenance of a comprehensive system of accounts for a regional economy is an even more formidable task than might at first appear, if the system is to be sufficiently complete, current, and historically grounded to function adequately; (2) that regional economic studies have to provide answers on a great many questions in which accounts could at best play a minor role; and (3) that the time and resources available to such studies and their responsibilities, as distinct from those of continuing statistical agencies, limit the extent to which they can appropriately commit effort to development of accounts as such.

All these considerations bear on the way in which the research effort of such a study can best be focused. Later in this paper we shall set forth the approach charted for the Pittsburgh Study. But first it will be helpful here to consider a more general dichotomy of approaches. The two approaches we shall characterize in terms of "vertical" vs. "horizontal" emphasis.

By "vertical" we mean an approach that seeks to probe as deep as possible into the workings of the economy of the region under study, while the outside world as such is not studied or even observed directly. Only transactions with the outside world are recognized, as items in the accounts of the region in question.

What we call here the "horizontal" approach leans heavily on (1) interregionally comparative structural analysis, and (2) locational analysis in terms of interregional competition and complementarity.

The vertical approach addresses itself to a much narrower range of questions than the horizontal, since it takes all events or influences emanating from the outside world as exogenous, and merely seeks to provide a mechanism for evaluating the internal impacts of certain types of events that may be assumed to occur, such as an increase in exports. The "multiplier" type of question already cited is illustrative of the range of inquiry appropriate to this approach. The horizontal approach, by contrast, pays a great deal of attention to the "outside world," and seeks to exploit another dimension of the mass of available data: namely, data for other regions either (1) similar to, or (2) economically tied to, the region under study.

Groups of *similar* areas are studied in order to discover empirically some useful trends, regressions, and other statistical relationships that form parts of the explanation of past or prospective behavior of the region we are studying. For example, in seeking to understand the levels and patterns of consumer and business service activities in the Pittsburgh Region, we have found it helpful to examine statistically the ways in which such activities are associated with total employment, population, income, retail sales, age structure, and industrial specialization, etc., among the medium sized and larger metropolitan areas of the United States in years for which data are readily available. This is quite different from the "vertical" approach, which would measure the receipts and outpayments of each of these types of service establishments in the Pittsburgh area and try to develop from such accounts some rules about how levels of local service activities would react to, say, changes in total Pittsburgh income, or Pittsburgh exports.

Secondly, the "horizontal" approach considers specific regions other than, but *economically related to,* the region under study. This is in connection with interregional locational analysis, which is aimed at explaining and projecting the region's activity levels in what are often called "basic" industries. All this is exogenous to the "vertical" approach *per se*—accounts for a region are not generally designed to *explain* the levels of the basic activities. The outside regions to which analysis is extended in the "horizontal" approach include primarily regions related to ours either as markets or as competitors. For example, the Pittsburgh level of output of one of our specialties, oil-country goods, depends largely on (1) the growth of demand of certain oil and gas producing areas, particularly in the Gulf region, and (2) changes in Pittsburgh's cost position relative to two or three areas that offer its principal competition in serving those markets.

As suggested earlier, the development and use of comprehensive regional accounts go with the "vertical" approach. Accounts are de-emphasized in the horizontal approach. Partly this is because many regions, rather than one, are involved, and no one has yet seriously suggested that it is feasible to carry out an operationally adequate metropolitan economic study in the framework of a multi-region interindustry model of the Leontief, Isard, Moses or other types. But also, accounts play a minor role in the horizontal approach partly because the use of that approach implies, as a rule, a strong interest in evaluating economic links and relationships on which accounts themselves throw little or no light, and which are outside the scope of a vertical-type investigation. Also, the horizontal approach dispenses with a great deal of accounts effort because it provides acceptable (and often easier) ways of accomplishing some of the same purposes.

This last point brings us back to the fact that the two approaches (one in effect maximizing the use of accounts and one minimizing it) are, to an important degree, alternatives. We have heard of no instance in which a metropolitan economic study had the resources to push both approaches simultaneously to the limits of their productiveness. The typical if not inevitable situation is one calling for a major choice between "vertical" or "horizontal" emphasis in the allocation of relatively limited resources.

The choice will depend on many factors, not excluding the analytical predilections of the study designers. One important consideration is the necessary commitment of resources for those study objectives (e.g., analysis of the interregional location factors affecting the levels of basic industries in the region) which must in any event use a "horizontal" approach. If enough resources then remain to develop also the vertical approach through an adequate set of regional accounts, and if there is a prospect that such accounts can be kept current, that effort may be advisable—though the possibilities for either supporting or shortcutting the accounts task by horizontal analysis of comparative economic structures in similar areas may still be considerable.

Regional Development Strategies

32. Interregional and International Transmission of Economic Growth*

ALBERT O. HIRSCHMAN

"Growing Points" and Lagging Regions

TO COMPLETE our survey of inducement mechanisms, we shall examine in this chapter how growth can be communicated from one region or one country to another. In this inquiry we may take it for granted that economic progress does not appear everywhere at the same time and that once it has appeared powerful forces make for a spatial concentration of economic growth around the initial starting points. Why substantial gains may be reaped from overcoming the "friction of space" [1] through agglomeration has been analyzed in detail by the economic theory of location. In addition to the locational advantages offered by *existing* settlements others come from nearness to a *growing* center where an "industrial atmosphere" has come into being with its special receptivity to innovations and enterprise. It was largely the observation of the latter connections that suggested to Marshall the concept of external economies.[2]

Whatever the reason, there can be little doubt that an economy, to lift itself to higher income levels, must and will first develop within itself one or several regional centers of economic strength. This need for the emergence of "growing points" or "growth poles" [3] in the course

1. This term was used by Robert M. Haig in "Toward an Understanding of the Metropolis," *Quarterly Journal of Economics, 40* (1926), 184–5.

2. A good survey of Marshall's views and of other contributions to this subject is in Eric A. Lampard, "The History of Cities in the Economically Advanced Areas," *Economic Development and Cultural Change,* 3 (Jan. 1955), 81–137, particularly 92–101.

3. "Pôle de croissance" is the term used for both regional and sectoral growth leadership in the expanding and instructive French literature on the subject. See, e.g., Perroux, "Note sur la notion de 'pôle de croissance'"; *Matériaux pour une analyse de la croissance économique,* Cahiers de l'Institut de Science Eco-

* Reprinted from Albert O. Hirschman, *The Strategy of Economic Development.*

of the development process means that international and interregional inequality of growth is an inevitable concomitant and condition of growth itself.

Thus, in the geographical sense, growth is necessarily unbalanced. However, while the regional setting reveals unbalanced growth at its most obvious, it perhaps does not show it at its best. In analyzing the process of unbalanced growth, we could always show that an advance at one point sets up pressures, tensions, and compulsions toward growth at subsequent points. But if all of these points fall within the same privileged growth space, the forces that make for transmission of growth from one country, one region, or one group of persons to another will be singularly weak.

The ability and tendency of growth to round itself out for a long time within some subgroup, region, or country while backwardness retains its hold elsewhere has often been noted. If the tendency manifests itself along clearly marked geographic lines, the result is the division of the world into developed and underdeveloped countries and the split of a country into progressive and backward regions. On the other hand, progress and tradition may dwell in close spatial proximity by simply fastening on different human groups and economic activities that exist side by side; this state of affairs, often encountered in developing countries, has been aptly termed "dualism" and has already been examined in our analysis of the industrialization process (Chapter 7).

With respect to different social or income groups a similar phenomenon may be noted: once one group has shown its readiness to acquire new wants and its ability to afford the products satisfying them, it will be catered to by a multitude of firms all tailoring their output to the type of per capita buying power and to the size of the market that have been revealed. It takes innovators like Ford and Giannini to strike out beyond this charmed circle, just as it seems to take a special kind of boldness to establish a new basic industry or to perceive the development potentials of the more backward regions of a developing country.

Thus investors spend a long time mopping up all the opportunities around some "growth pole" and neglect those that may have arisen or

nomique Appliquée, Série D, No. 8, 1955; J. R. Boudeville, "Contribution a l'étude des pôles de croissance brésiliens," Cahiers, Série F, No. 10, 1957.

could be made to arise elsewhere. What appears to happen is that *the external economies due to the poles, though real, are consistently overestimated by the economic operators.*

The reason for this tendency—perhaps implicit in the phrase "nothing succeeds like success"—must be sought in the realm of social psychology. The progressive sectors and regions of an underdeveloped economy are easily overimpressed with their own rate of development. At the same time, they set themselves apart from the less progressive operators by creating a picture of the latter as lazy, bungling, intriguing, and generally hopeless. There seems to be a cliquishness about progress when it first appears that recalls the same phenomenon among adolescents: the girls who menstruate and the boys who shave have an acute sense of their superiority over those who cannot yet claim such achievements. The tendency to magnify the distance that separates one group or region from another shows up in the derogatory use of the term "indio" in some Latin American countries to designate whoever is economically or socially one's inferior. Similarly, the average Italian, in whose country economic progress has long been closely associated with latitude, is always ready to declare that Africa begins just south of his own province.

Thus the successful groups and regions will widely and extravagantly proclaim their superiority over the rest of their country and their countrymen. It is interesting to note that to some extent these claims are self-enforcing. Even though the initial success of these groups may often be due to sheer luck or to environmental factors such as resource endowment, matters will not be left there. Those who have been caught by progress will always maintain that they were the ones who did the catching; they will easily convince themselves, and attempt to convince others, that their accomplishments are primarily owed to their superior moral qualities and conduct. It is precisely this self-righteousness that will tend to produce its own evidence: once these groups have spread the word that their success was due to hard work and virtuous living, they must willy-nilly live up to their own story, or at the least will make their children do so.[4] In other words, there is reason to think that the "protestant ethic," instead of being

4. Observation would seem to confirm that the behavior of second generation businessmen is far more compulsively "businesslike" than that of the pioneer generation.

the prime mover, is often implanted *ex post* as though to sanctify and consolidate whatever accumulation of economic power and wealth has been achieved. To the extent that this happens, a climate particularly favorable to further growth will actually come into existence in the sectors or regions that have pulled ahead, and this will confirm the economic operators in their preference for these regions and make it somewhat less irrational.

The less developed groups and regions also make unwittingly a contribution to the process which we can only sketch here. Faced with the sudden improvement in the fortunes of some of their own compatriots, they will frequently retort to the claims of superiority of these *nouveaux riches* by accusing them of crass materialism, sharp practices, and disregard for the country's traditional cultural and spiritual values. While such charges are directed with particular relish at minorities, whose importance in the process of development is well recognized, purely indigenous entrepreneurial groups are by no means exempt from them. In this way these groups are, as it were, converted into minorities in their own country,[5] often estranged from the rest of their compatriots, and ostracized by the traditional elites. Such a development is particularly likely when the first stages of commercial and industrial progress are localized in a center other than the capital city. In this case, the rift between this center and the capital may well widen cumulatively over a long period of time. The very fact that the leading families of such cities as Barcelona, São Paulo, Medellín, and Guayaquil lived far away from, and often in conflict with, the centers of politics, public administration, and education made for a dogged concentration of succeeding generations on business pursuits rather than for absorption of the most talented by other careers that carry more prestige in a traditional society. This situation may again lead

5. A good example is supplied by the inhabitants of Antioquia, a province of Colombia. The Antioqueños have been outstandingly enterprising in bringing virgin lands under coffee cultivation and in establishing industries, mostly in their capital of Medellín. Their racial, religious, and cultural characteristics do not differentiate the Antioqueños from the other Colombians; but having taken such a prominent part in the country's development, they are *now* considered practically as a separate group; and even though it is unsupported by any evidence (see J. J. Parsons, *Antioqueño Colonization in Western Colombia* [Berkeley, 1949], p. 62), the conviction is widespread that they are really of Jewish, or at least of Basque, origin!

to a clustering of investment around the initial growing point, which is healthy for the consolidation of economic growth at its beginning but may represent irrational prejudice and clannishness at a later stage.

Trickling-Down and Polarization Effects[5a]

No matter how strong and exaggerated the space preference of the economic operators, once growth takes a firm hold in one part of the national territory, it obviously sets in motion certain forces that act on the remaining parts. In examining these direct interactions, we shall call "North" the region which has been experiencing growth and "South" the one that has remained behind. This terminology is suggested by the fact that a large number of lagging areas, at least in the Northern Hemisphere, appear to be located in the southern parts of the countries to which they belong. The term "South" as used here does not include *undeveloped*—i.e., largely unsettled—areas.

The growth of the North will have a number of direct economic repercussions on the South, some favorable, others adverse. The favor-

5a. Footnote added in proof: The argument of the following sections was outlined originally in my article "Investment Policies and 'Dualism' in Underdeveloped Countries," *American Economic Review, 47* (Sept. 1957), 550–70. I now find that Gunnar Myrdal has addressed himself to similar problems in *Economic Theory and Under-Developed Regions* (London, 1957), particularly in chapters 3 to 5, and has had recourse to the same conceptual tools that are employed here: his "backwash" and "spread" effects correspond exactly to my "polarization" and "trickling down" effects. Nevertheless, there are considerable differences in emphasis and conclusions. Myrdal's analysis strikes me as excessively dismal. In the first place, he fails to recognize that the emergence of growing points and therefore of differences in development between regions and between nations is inevitable and is a condition of further growth anywhere. Secondly, his preoccupation with the mechanism of cumulative causation hides from him the emergence of the strong forces making for a turning point once the movement toward North-South polarization within a country has proceeded for some time. Finally, the picture he paints of international transmission of growth is also too bleak in my opinion as he overlooks that the polarization (backwash) effects are much weaker between nations than between regions within the same country. However, I fully agree with Myrdal on the importance of political forces in effecting a North-South rapprochement within a country and on the need for the emergence of such forces on the international level to help narrow the gap between the developed and the underdeveloped countries. I have anticipated here the discussion contained in the remainder of this chapter.

able effects consist of the *trickling down* of Northern progress: by far the most important of these effects is the increase of Northern purchases and investments in the South, an increase that is sure to take place if the economies of the two regions are at all complementary. In addition, the North may absorb some of the disguised unemployed of the South and thereby raise the marginal productivity of labor and per capita consumption levels in the South.

On the other hand, several unfavorable or *polarization* effects are also likely to be at work. Comparatively inefficient, yet income-creating, Southern activities in manufacturing and exports may become depressed as a result of Northern competition. To the extent that the North industrializes along lines in which there is no Southern production, the South is also likely to make a bad bargain since it will now have to buy Northern manufactures, produced behind newly erected tariff walls, instead of similar goods previously imported from abroad at lower prices.

A most serious, and frequently observed, polarization effect consists in the kind of internal migration that may follow upon the economic advances of the North. Instead of absorbing the disguised unemployed, Northern progress may denude the South of its key technicians and managers as well as of the more enterprising young men. This type of migration may actually be undesirable not only from the point of view of the South but also from that of the country as a whole, for the loss to the South due to the departure of these men may be higher than the gain to the North. This possibility is inherent in the contact between the expanding North and the stagnant South: in the North new jobs must be manned and, at least in the skilled grades, the wage and salary scale will reflect relative scarcities and productivities; whereas in the South skilled work and better-than-average performance will often be poorly remunerated either because they are simply not recognized or because they are not valued very highly [6] or because they carry nonmonetary rewards. Thus actual pay differentials between North and South are likely to overstate considerably the real productivity differentials in the most productive and skilled grades. In addition, of course, mobility is highest in these same lines so that it becomes almost a certainty that the South will lose to the North first

6. Even societies that actively discourage better-than-average performance (see p. 12) are unable to abolish it altogether simply because of innate differences.

and foremost its more highly qualified people. And, along with skill and enterprise, what little capital the South generates is also likely to migrate northward.

In spite of this bleak picture, we would still feel confident that in the end the trickling-down effects would gain the upper hand over the polarization effects if the North had to rely to an important degree on Southern products for its own expansion. For instance, if the North specializes in manufactures and the South in primary production, the expanding demand of the North ought to stimulate Southern growth. But things may go less smoothly. It is likely, in particular, that the short-run supply elasticity is low in the South so that the terms of trade will move against the North.[7]

In this case, three possibilities arise. In the best of worlds, the rise in Southern prices would fairly soon prove effective in raising production. Another possible, though far less satisfactory, outcome would consist in the slowing down of Northern progress resulting from rising labor and material costs. But such a development is unlikely as long as the North is not entirely dependent on the South. The third possibility is therefore for the North to alter its method of procuring needed primary products. Faced with the upward trend in Southern prices and exasperated by the unreliability of Southern production, Northern operators may draw on imports from foreign areas or may replace Southern products by developing their own primary production. In this way, *checks to the trickling-down effects* may well come into play, and as a result the South could be left in a far worse backwater than before. For once the North possesses within itself a large and productive agricultural area or is able to supply its needs in primary products from abroad and through domestic synthetic production, the South will be largely cut off from beneficial contact with Northern development, while remaining exposed to the adverse polarization effects. Under these conditions—which are or were fairly typical of such backward regions as Brazil's Nordeste, Colombia's Oriente, and Italy's Mezzogiorno—the stage would be set for a prolonged split of the country into a progressive and a depressed area.

7. This situation has been fully analyzed by H. G. Johnson for the case in which a developing industrial country trades with a stagnant agricultural country; see his "Economic Expansion and International Trade," *Manchester School of Economic and Social Studies,* 23 (May 1955), 96–101.

Eventually, economic pressures to remedy such a situation are likely to assert themselves again. Industry will become congested in Northern cities and its expansion will be hampered by the insufficient size of the home market resulting from the depressed income levels in the South. Also, economic policy makers will be impelled to take a close look at Southern development potentials whenever balance-of-payments or other supply difficulties make it clear that the country is harming itself by its failure to utilize fully its Southern resources.

In other words, if the market forces that express themselves through the trickling-down and polarization effects result in a temporary victory of the latter, deliberate economic policy will come into play to correct the situation. Actually, of course, economic policy will be an important influence throughout the process. The nature of this influence will be analyzed presently.

The Regional Distribution of Public Investment

The most obvious manner in which economic policy affects the rates of growth of different parts of a country is through the regional allocation of public investments. Three principal patterns of allocation can be distinguished: dispersal, concentration on growing areas, and attempts to promote the development of backward areas.

In contrast to widespread impressions, the most pervasive tendency of governments of underdeveloped countries in making their investment decisions is not so much the obsession with one showpiece as the dispersal of funds among a large number of small projects scattered widely over the national territory.

While this pattern is *dominant* only in countries where dynamic economic growth has not yet taken hold, it can be said to exert a steady pull in practically all underdeveloped countries. The most obvious reason is that public investment decisions are easily the most political ones among the economic policy decisions taken by governments. Whether to build a road here rather than there, whether to construct a power plant that is to supply towns *A*, *B*, and *C*, rather than *D*, *E*, and *F*—these are questions that have decisive local political impact.

Thus, as all governments regardless of their democratic character desire and need support from all sections of the country, the temptation is strong to scatter the investment effort far and wide. Disconnected roads are built at many points; small Diesel power plants and aqueducts are installed in many towns; even low-cost housing programs which should obviously concentrate on relieving critical shortages and on slum clearance in the big cities are often similarly dispersed.

More fundamentally, the tendency toward wide dispersal of investment funds may be due to what was called in Chapter 1 the group-focused image of change, i.e., to the fact that economic progress is conceived as a force which ought to affect equally all members and sections of the community. Wherever this idea prevails, governments are unprepared and unwilling to make the choices about priorities and sequences that are the essence of development programs. When the feeling is widespread that something is wrong with even temporarily preferred treatment for some regions, the government may find it politically dangerous not to take this factor into account.

Finally, the dispersal pattern can be explained by certain shortages usually affecting underdeveloped countries. The elaboration of the many small projects into which public investment is typically split up when this pattern is dominant requires comparatively little engineering and planning talent, whereas the larger projects in electric power, transportation, or basic industry require far more such talent than is usually available to the government. This is why entirely too much has been made of the argument that development is held back not by the scarcity of funds, but by a scarcity of "bankable," i.e., well-conceived and engineered, projects. The question which should come first, the project or the funds, is really of the chicken-egg variety. Obviously funds can be spent only on clearly defined projects. But without definite expectations that funds—from domestic or foreign sources—will be forthcoming, the considerable cost of engineering and economic studies and the administrative effort required to gather the necessary staff and to obtain the assistance of foreign consultants will most likely not be undertaken. The promise of foreign funds—provided the studies prove the project feasible and worth while—is particularly important if this effort is to be made, as a large project usually results in one region's obtaining for the time being a substantial advantage over all others. This is an investment decision which a national government may find it difficult and imprudent to make unless it has the feeling—and the excuse vis-à-vis the other regions—that international development capital is not to be had at all on other terms.

Moreover, the study and preparation of a large-scale project implies in itself—especially in countries where there is the rhetorical tradition of confusing the word with the deed, and the announcement of plans with their realization—a commitment to the region which is going to be principally benefited. Governments are therefore reluctant to start such studies unless they feel reasonably sure that they will be able to "deliver." Unless they have assurances in this regard, they would be politically much better off to let sleeping projects lie.

The International Bank for Reconstruction and Development has often defended itself against charges of insufficient lending by the argument that there were not enough "bankable" projects available.[8] But in fact the Bank has frequently acted in accordance with the point of view just outlined—i.e., it has helped in the preparation of such projects by virtually committing itself in advance to the financing of their foreign exchange costs, including even the cost of the preliminary engineering surveys.

In this way the availability of international development capital may make for a shift from dispersal of public investment toward concentration on a few key projects. The "demonstration effect" of similar projects undertaken in other countries also works in this direction. But the most important force opposing the tendency toward excessive dispersal of public investment is the growth pattern characteristic of rapidly developing countries. Development often begins with the sudden, vigorous, and nearly spontaneous growth of one or a few regions or urban centers, resulting in serious shortages of electric power and water supply, as well as in housing and transportation bottlenecks. Thus, urgent demands for several types of capital-intensive public investment appear and must be given the highest priority whether or not

8. Statements to this effect can be found in several of the Bank's annual reports; e.g.: "Perhaps the most striking single lesson which the Bank has learned in the course of its operations is how limited is the capacity of the underdeveloped countries to absorb capital quickly for really productive purposes. . . . The Bank's experience to date indicates that the Bank now has or can readily acquire sufficient resources to help finance all the sound productive projects in its member countries that will be ready for financing in the next few years, that can appropriately be financed through repayable foreign loans and that cannot attract private capital." *Fourth Annual Report* (Washington, 1948–49), pp. 8, 13.

they correspond to the government's sense of distributive justice and to its pattern of regional political preference. The public investment in overhead capital in turn makes possible further growth of industry and trade in the favored areas and this growth requires further large allocations of public investment to them.

Determined as it is by the volume of private investment and the general rise in income in the developing areas, public investment clearly plays here an "induced" role, and investment choices are often remarkably and unexpectedly obvious. It is not always easy, however, to have these obvious choices adopted, partly because of the continuing desire of governments to revert to the policy of scatter, and partly because a new pressure soon makes itself felt—namely, to accelerate development in the areas that have fallen behind.

A situation in which the bulk of public investment is continuously being sucked into the comparatively developed portions of the national territory cannot in the long run be considered satisfactory by governments because of compelling considerations of equity and national cohesion. In fact, the attempt to change drastically the distribution of public investment in favor of the country's poorer sections often comes at a point that seems premature to the foreign observer or adviser for the simple reason that the more rapidly advancing sections do not strike *him* as so outstandingly prosperous. It is, however, quite understandable that the attempt should be made long before these sections have come anywhere near fully developing their potential. Moreover, the poorer sections of the country, where careers in industry and trade are not promising, often produce, for this very reason, a majority of the country's successful politicians and thereby acquire influential spokesmen in the councils of government.

It is possible that the transition from the second pattern—concentration of public investment on spontaneously growing areas—to the third—attempt to ignite development in the heretofore stagnant areas through "autonomous" public investment—is facilitated by certain peculiar properties of public investment. Usually the second phase results not in a mere shift from scatter to concentration of a given investment total, but in a considerable enlargement of the total amount of funds required for public investment. These funds are secured through the introduction of new and higher taxes or through other *permanent* revenue-raising devices.

On the other hand, it is probably reasonable to assume that the need for the investment of public funds in the country's spontaneously growing areas is particularly great in the initial stages of development, as basic utilities are created and rapidly expanded. After development has proceeded for some time, the need for public investment in relation to private investment tends to decline and in any event an increased portion of public investment can be financed out of earnings of previous investments. This kind of change in the composition of investment is implicit in the term "social *overhead* capital."

As the taxation and other measures which have financed the original spurt in public investment continue to yield revenue, some funds may thus become, if not unemployed, at least less compellingly employed than previously. This is likely to be immediately sensed by the officials responsible for apportioning public investment and provides an excellent opportunity to those among them who want to change its geographic composition in favor of the less developed sections.

Thus, while public investment policy may accentuate at one stage the North-South split, it can be counted upon to stage at least an attempt to heal the split should it turn out to be prolonged. For this reason governmental intervention is particularly prevalent in the development of the backward areas within underdeveloped countries. In fact, the government will, to the best of its ability, attempt to counteract in part the polarization effects that result from the operation of market forces: to counterbalance the northward emigration of capital and talent, an even larger flow in the opposite direction will be organized; to offset the locational advantages of the North, governments may offer special tax advantages or create similar external economies in the South through public investments.

Naturally, the channeling of large-scale expenditures toward the underprivileged areas of a country contains the danger of misguided investment to a much higher degree than where spontaneous growth has already staked out fairly well the areas in which public investments are urgently required. The most obvious and least "risky" course [9] is to endow the South with just as good a system of transportation, electric power stations, and other social overhead capital facilities as are available in the North. But we have already explained that this may not be the most efficient method of inducing growth in

9. See pp. 165–6.

the South because of the weakness of its entrepreneurship and the purely "permissive" character of the inducement mechanisms set in motion by these investments. Although some investment in public utilities may be indispensable, the essential task is to endow the South with some ongoing and actively inducing economic activity of its own, in industry, agriculture, or services. For this reason, the building of a steel mill in Colombia's Oriente and the founding of the new Brazilian capital in the long neglected "interior" will probably turn out to be effective governmental development moves in spite of initial mistakes, difficulties, and setbacks.

Interregional and International Transmission Compared

Our discussion has made it clear that the interregional transmission of growth cannot be expected to proceed smoothly. Obstructionist forces have been seen to be at work alongside those that make for integration, in the economic and political fields. It is tempting then to apply an a fortiori argument to the *international* transmission of growth: if interregional transmission is beset with obstacles, is it not natural to conclude that international transmission will be even more difficult?

While the disparity in the development levels of different countries would seem to support such a conclusion, it is not at all justified by the arguments we have used in demonstrating the difficulties of interregional transmission of growth. Some of these arguments rather point to the somewhat unsettling thought that the various "Souths" might be better off if they were sovereign political units, i.e., that in some respects growth may be more easily transmitted from one nation to another than from one region to another within the same country. We will first explore these "economic arguments for separatism" and then show in what respects transmission mechanisms are after all more effective between regions than between sovereign countries.

The case for separatism. In general it may be expected that because of the closer contact and more intensive interaction that exist among regions of the same country than among sovereign nations, both trickling-down *and* polarization effects will be found to be stronger in interregional than in international economic relations.

The case for separatism will therefore consist largely in showing that the polarization effects will be far less damaging to a country than to a region. This is certainly the case for the mobility of factors of production. We have seen that within a country this mobility can be highly prejudicial for the South, and conceivably even uneconomic from the point of view of the country as a whole. If the South were an independent country, mobility would certainly be far lower and the Southern development potential would be less impaired.

Another polarization effect consisted in the debilitating influence of Northern competition on Southern economic activities satisfying domestic or export demands. Again, this effect would be virtually absent between independent countries. With respect to the latter, countries compete in international markets on the basis of comparative advantage, regions within a country on the basis of absolute advantage. Suppose that North and South, considered independently, both have a comparative advantage in cane sugar, but that production is more efficient in the North. Then, if each were an independent country, they would both specialize in sugar, with real factor returns being lower in the South. But if North and South are united in one country, sugar production would be expanded in the North and may be abandoned in the South even though the maintenance and expansion of sugar exports could represent the valuable beginning of a "growth pole" for the South.

The same reasoning holds for industrialization. It has frequently been pointed out that, if there is any substance to the various arguments for protection, they must apply just as much to a region as to a country; but the region cannot ordinarily protect its industries except through exemption from minor local taxes. Also, within a country (or in relations between a country and its colonies) Northern industrialists may often effectively prevent or delay the development of industry in the South; in relations between sovereign countries, attempts in this direction have sometimes been made, but obviously have far smaller chances of success.

Finally—and related to the previous points—the absence of economic sovereignty with respect to such matters as currency issue and exchange rate determination may be a considerable handicap for the development of a region.

The preceding argument is reminiscent of Viner's celebrated thesis that a customs union between two countries may lead to a less, rather than more, efficient allocation of resources.[10] To prove this proposition, Viner invoked only the "trade-diverting effects," i.e., the possibility that the partners of a customs union will now buy from each other what they could previously obtain more cheaply—and what can be more efficiently produced—in third markets. This argument is also applicable to our problem, but the polarization effects relating to factor mobility and North-South competition in exports and industry are perhaps more important in a developmental situation.

The case for surrender of sovereignty. We must now come to the other half of our story. As the polarization effects will be stronger when there are no frontiers to cross, so will the trickling-down effects. The advance of the North is bound to lead to purchases and investments in the South. All complementarities that exist within a country will be readily exploited. Regional specialization patterns will emerge and are not likely to be tampered with even when they are based more on historical accident than on comparative resource endowments. Not so between sovereign countries. Here potential complementarities are likely to be taken advantage of in a far more selective and spotty fashion, not only because of the "friction of space" but because of the many other frictions that are encountered as soon as frontiers are crossed. Protectionist movements and reactions to balance-of-payments difficulties will set up strong obstacles to the emergence of a finely articulated division of labor and will always threaten it if it should arise.

The trickling-down effects will still be powerfully effective in promoting development of countries with resources that are highly prized by the industrial countries. But if a country has nothing particularly essential or attractive to offer, it may remain excluded for a long time from any important participation in world trade when, as a region integrated into a larger country, it might have contributed quite nicely to interregional trade.

In our treatment of interregional transmission of growth we saw the principal danger of an emergence of a North-South problem in

10. Viner, *The Customs Union Issue* (New York, 1950), ch. 4. For a systematic discussion of the issues raised by Viner, see J. E. Meade, *The Theory of Customs Unions,* Amsterdam, 1955.

the low supply elasticity characteristic of the South and in the consequent loss of interdependence as the North extricated itself from dependence on Southern products in a variety of ways. In international relations these checks to the trickling-down effects are stronger, just as the trickling-down effects themselves are weaker, than in interregional relations. Within a country, the loss by the South of its markets in the North will be resisted: not entirely unselfish efforts will be made by Northern interests to help the South overcome its supply difficulties which, if unresolved, will make it necessary for the North to look elsewhere. And, as has already been pointed out, even if a temporary lapse in North-South trade occurs, such efforts are likely to be resumed whenever balance-of-payments or other supply difficulties press upon the country.

In relations between advanced and underdeveloped nations, one of the major forces making for the growth of the latter is the need of the advanced nations for certain, usually primary, products of the underdeveloped areas. But if the foreign producers for one reason or another are unable to fulfill the rapidly growing requirements of the industrial centers, they cannot expect to be treated with the same patience and periodic consideration that they would receive if they were part of the industrial countries themselves. Domestic or other foreign sources of supply will be tapped or synthetic production will be undertaken largely on the basis of economic calculations, whereas political and social considerations will importantly affect similar decisions in North-South relations and are likely to help the South retain its role as a supplier of the North.

In this fashion we are brought back to the political forces making for the transmission of growth. These forces help definitively to redress the balance of our argument away from separatism. Within a country, as we have seen, there will come a point when a determined effort will be made to pull the underdeveloped regions within that country out of their stagnation. The ultimate reason for the confidence one may have in the emergence of such an effort is the solidarity that binds different parts of a nation together and the ability of each part to make itself heard and to bring pressures to bear on the central government. In spite of much progress in recent years, international solidarity of this kind is unfortunately still in its infancy.

We conclude that, on balance, the forces making for interregional transmission of growth are likely to be more powerful than those making for international transmission.

Optimal Institutional Arrangements

The reader may wonder why we examined in so much detail whether it is better for an underdeveloped area to be a region or a nation. Few areas can choose. Nevertheless, the realization that growth is transmitted more easily between nations than between regions from the point of view of some of the mechanisms we have analyzed, while the opposite holds for others, makes it tempting to think about the possibility of optimal institutional arrangements. If only we could in some respects *treat a region as though it were a country* and in some others *treat a country as though it were a region,* we would indeed get the best of both worlds and be able to create situations particularly favorable to development.[11]

Let us look first at the regions. Their advantage consisted largely in their greater exposure to the trickling-down effects and in their ability to call for help from the larger unit to which they belong. Their disadvantage seemed to lie principally in their exposure to polarization effects, in their inability to develop production for exports along lines of *comparative* advantage, and in the absence of certain potentially development-promoting policy instruments that usually come with sovereignty. A nation attempting to develop its own backward regions should therefore provide certain "equivalents of sovereignty" for these regions. The most important of such equivalents is a reaction against the feelings of despondency and self-denigration so often encountered in the South, and the mobilization of its energies through regional institutions and programs. The need for this approach has been felt in several countries where regional development corporations and banks have been set up. Effective aid to the establishment of industries in the South may call also for national income tax deductions (equivalent to tariff protection) and some autonomy in bank credit policy. To permit production to proceed on the basis of com-

11. We assume that the areas we are talking about have a substantial untapped development potential. There are of course many regions and perhaps even some countries whose natural resources are so poor or depleted that their best hope lies in becoming empty spaces—or at least far emptier than they are now.

parative advantage, Southern exports could be—and have at times been—stimulated through preferential exchange rates. Under such conditions, it might be held that imports into the South should be subject to compensating surtaxes, but this complication can be avoided on the ground that the South could satisfy many of its needs more cheaply in world markets if it were not prevented from doing so by the protection of Northern industries.

It is in line with our analysis that a policy of closing the gap between the South and the North requires the use of instruments that would ordinarily be thought to be disruptive of the very integration they are designed to achieve. While it is the purpose of these instruments to cut down the strength of the polarization effects, great care must be taken, of course, not to interfere with the efficacy of the trickling-down effects. Thus, the economic policies just outlined are designed to insulate the South sufficiently so that it may undertake certain industrial and export activities in competition with the North; but, at the same time, the complementary relationships that make the South a supplier of the North must be preserved and intensified.

For *international* transmission of growth, the optimal institutional arrangements would be of the opposite kind. The task here is to keep the polarization effects as weak as they normally are among independent nations, but to increase the strength of the trickling-down effects. In other words, the underdeveloped countries ought to retain the developmental advantages of sovereignty: obstacles to the emigration of skills and capital and a measure of independence in tariff, monetary, and foreign exchange policy. At the same time, they must be more closely integrated into the world economy through arrangements that make for more rapid growth and greater stability in their export markets. In addition, their development could of course be greatly accelerated if the community of nations disposed of a political mechanism similar to the one that within a nation makes eventually for a redistribution of public investment funds in favor of the South.

The world is already groping for formulas that would combine in this way the advantages of sovereignty with those of integration.[12] For the time being, these efforts are largely the incidental results of

12. Attempts of sovereign countries to assess themselves for costs incurred in joint programs are reviewed in Thomas C. Schelling, *International Cost-Sharing Arrangements*, Essays in International Finance No. 24, Princeton, 1955.

a struggle for power. Yet it is obvious that they would be intensified rather than abandoned if this struggle were to cease tomorrow. It seems a pity, therefore, that we in the United States insist so loudly that the bold and pioneering steps we are taking to help the underdeveloped countries are dictated by military necessity or are "straightforward business transactions." [13] Must we thus pave with apologies the road to what can be one of mankind's highest achievements? But perhaps it is inevitable that progress along this road should be reluctant. For, as Bergson has said, "the moral, original and fundamental structure of man is made for simple and closed societies . . . man outwits nature when from the solidarity of these societies he steps into human fraternity." [14]

13. Gunnar Myrdal makes some interesting observations on this point in *An International Economy* (New York, 1956), ch. 9.

14. *Les deux sources de la morale et de la religion* (Paris, 1934), pp. 53–4.

33. Regional Allocation of Resources in India[1*]

Louis Lefeber

1. Efficiency of regional resource allocation is crucial for increasing the capacity for investment and economic growth.

2. It is a paradoxical but inevitable fact that in order to accelerate the future development of retarded regions the growth of industrially more advanced areas must be encouraged. If the latter is stifled by insufficient investment the over-all capacity to save will be diminished and the advancement of retarded areas will be delayed even longer.

3. At the same time, retarded areas need not be neglected. On the one hand, a somewhat greater national effort than the current one would provide resources for regional advancement over and above the requirements for maintaining a 5 per cent rate of national growth. On the other hand, rational pricing and transportation policies and certain other methods would efficiently allocate industrial investments in agricultural producing regions.

4. State and local governments must be persuaded that greater concentration of industrial resources in certain limited areas works out to their long-run advantage. However, this can be done only if rational and explicit long-run planning is introduced.

5. In the meantime improvement of pricing policies and consideration of the viability of individual projects in particular areas would result in rapid improvement in the efficiency of allocation.

I. INTRODUCTION

The purpose of economic development is to increase the standard of living of the masses of people in low-income groups. To attain

[1] This essay is essentially identical to the Occasional Paper of similar title written by the author for the consideration of the Indian Planning Commission in February 1961. The ideas expressed here benefited from discussions with Professor Thomas Balogh of Oxford and Professor P. N. Rosenstein-Rodan of MIT. However, the responsibility for the ideas and errors contained here lies entirely with the author.

* Reprinted from Paul Rosenstein-Rodan, *Pricing and Fiscal Policies: A Study in Method.*

this goal national income must grow at a faster rate than the increase in population, and the benefits of income growth must be distributed equitably.

Increase in living standards and redistribution can be attained by alternative patterns. Which one to select depends on many not always clearly specified and frequently contradictory social goals.

To specify all social goals in India and to attach relative weights to each might be exceedingly difficult. However, there seems to be clear and overwhelming national consensus about the desirability of ending unemployment 'as soon as possible'. Also, national consensus would support the notion that all unemployed without regard of racial, religious, or regional affiliation have equal rights to the feasible opportunities for future employment. If these two very general principles are accepted, then it follows that those new employment patterns are desirable which minimize the time needed to achieve meaningful full employment for the nation as a whole. Furthermore, equitable distribution of income in the context of India requires first and foremost the creation of regular employment opportunities at a faster rate than the increase in the potential labour force. In other words, when unemployment exists on a broad scale, income redistribution in favour of the unemployed must take precedence over redistribution among those who enjoy a regular income at or above a level which is just sufficient to maintain a minimum socially acceptable standard of living.

In order to provide a sufficient increase in employment opportunities to keep abreast of unemployment in the future, capital formation would have to take place at a rate faster than it did during the Second Plan or foreseen in the Third Plan. Increased capital formation must be matched, however, with corresponding increases in saving.

There are at least two major weapons to be used for achieving suitable increases in savings: fiscal policy and rigorous observation of the rules of efficient resource use. For effectiveness both have to be supported with moral suasion by the highest political authority.

Fiscal policy is needed to ensure that those who enjoy regular incomes, including earners at the minimum acceptable level, should not appropriate further benefits from development as long as large-scale unemployment exists. Hence, in addition to the upper classes, the increasing numbers of employed urban and rural labour must also be reached by taxation.

Efficiency in resource use as a method for increasing savings is not traditionally discussed in economic analysis since it is assumed to be assured by the working of competitive markets.[1] This is at best a questionable assumption in developed market economies and certainly untenable in underdeveloped countries where regular competitive market checks may not exist at all.

Inefficiency in resource use implies that one or several outputs could be produced in greater amounts with the same amount of inputs. For any level of effort efficient resource use will increase investment potential in the short run because more projects can be realized with the same amount of resources; increase savings in the intermediate run because returns on investments will be larger; accelerate the rate of growth and employment in the long run because of the above beneficial effects.

In the context of a planned economy conscious policies to maintain efficient resource allocation are crucial. They must be based on pricing policies that properly reflect changes in the demand and supply conditions prevailing in diverse markets; and investment policies must be responsive to the signalling of the price system.[2]

II. REGIONAL ALLOCATION OF RESOURCES

Regional distribution of resources is an important aspect of over-all efficiency in allocation. It determines the rate of growth of each particular region; hence the growth of the entire nation is also determined. The question is: What are the principles on which regional allocation should be based?

It is quite clear that regional distribution of resources cannot be considered entirely as a non-political decision. Here national and regional social goals are in conflict: On the one hand there is the understandable desire of each state to develop its own resources and increase the standard of living of its own population as fast as possible; on the other hand rapid national growth may require the concentration of larger resources in particular areas.

[1] Efficiency in this context implies that the production of no output can be increased without sacrificing some other output. Under such conditions scarce productive inputs are fully employed and in the light of technological feasibilities optimally used; i.e. the economy operates on its production possibility surface.

[2] In this respect current price policy in India is entirely deficient; the term is used to denote a type of anti-inflationary policy which is not only inefficient but also may itself be inflationary in the long run.

This unfortunate conflict arises from the very nature of the growth process. Some areas are better endowed with natural resources than others. The exploitation of certain resources has greater urgency than others for phasing development. Investment is lumpy: many projects must be undertaken in large chunks in order to attain a minimum efficient scale in production. Furthermore, there is a powerful motivation to agglomerate industrial investment at selected areas because of external economies consisting of sharing the same social overhead facilities, service industries, skilled labour pools, and expert management. Then again, markets are also unevenly distributed, requiring uneven development in transportation and market-oriented activities. And in addition to all these influences there is a natural tendency for agglomeration because the proportion of resources used in diverse branches of production can be more economically adjusted if larger pools of the different resources are pulled together.

Regions which have existing advantages can grow at a faster rate than others. In the process of growth, employment opportunities increase and a flow of labour from other regions is attracted, which should have beneficial effects both on the industrializing areas and on the more stagnant regions. Furthermore, the rapidly growing areas can yield surpluses for future investment. Such surpluses arise from the profits of the expanding private and state enterprises and from increasing private incomes which in turn yield larger savings and taxes. Initially a good part of these savings must be used to maintain growth in the vigorous centres. But as savings continue to increase and new investment outlets are needed, more and more resources can be channelled to the development of other areas, which in turn will raise the living standard of the local population and create new surpluses and resources for continued development. The latter will manifest itself in the creation of new 'growing points' in other previously stagnant or slowly moving areas. In good time the number of growing areas should increase to a density which is adequate to provide a satisfactory regional balance. It is a paradoxical conclusion that for developing the retarded areas the growth of the more advanced regions must be encouraged. If the latter is stifled because of insufficient investment on an uneconomical scale, surpluses will be insufficient and stagnant regions which are unable to raise their own savings must be doomed to an even longer period of waiting and poverty.

The implication is not that some areas should receive all the attention and others none. It is a matter of social decision to what degree the benefits from realized progress should be used to bring immediate relief to those who are not only underprivileged but also tied by immobility to their retarded regions. The question is how to realize such an object in a way which is compatible with the goal of maintaining a high rate of national economic growth and rapid elimination of unemployment.

Barring some special and obvious cases, most industrial investments, if located in retarded areas, would have very low current yields, if any at all, and only questionable higher returns in the distant future. Similarly, many government sponsored rural programmes would be of the low-yield type. It might be argued that either approach to increase 'regional balance', i.e. low-yield type rural programmes or arbitrary location of industrial investment, is more in the nature of a transfer payment to improve income distribution than a contribution to economic development. In effect, it uses resources which otherwise would be available to increase national economic growth. It follows that expenditures budgeted for retarded areas must be such as to minimize per rupee spent their adverse effects on savings and growth.

Resources needed for the creation of 'economic' investments, i.e. industrial and agricultural capacity that directly or indirectly can yield immediate high returns, should be allocated with the strictest regard for economic efficiency. The surpluses from these projects are essential to maintain future investment and growth. Investments undertaken with the purpose of bringing relief to retarded areas should be based on low-cost rural labour and locally available materials. They should be oriented to prepare the ground for national integration and future development. In addition to local irrigation, land reclamation, reforestation, and other projects some of which can have high immediate returns, public works which increase communication and mobility should be emphasized. Among these, road building and rural school construction programmes are of primary importance.

Since low-yield investment in retarded regions competes for resources with investment needed to maintain the rate of economic growth, the amount of effort which can be devoted to regional balance is determined by, first, the minimum level of politically acceptable national growth rate and, second, the over-all savings effort the nation is willing to undertake over and above the one needed to maintain the desired national growth.

According to the Third Plan five per cent compound growth is the goal. However, given the existing level of effort, resources available to attain and maintain this rate even with most efficient utilization seem to be barely sufficient. The implication is that extensive efforts to increase 'regional balance' would interfere with the desired rate of development.

Nevertheless, approaches could be explored for large-scale rural labour mobilization for labour intensive projects of the type discussed above. Even if five million people would benefit on a rupee-a-day basis, the total annual cost over two hundred days a year, including organizational and capital expenditures, should not exceed say 1·5 billion rupees. Whereas this is still a considerable monetary commitment, the real resource equivalent is very low because a very large part of the total expenditure would have to be matched by food grain provisions which in turn could be covered by P.L. 480 supplies.

While it is true that only large-scale rural labour mobilization of the type mentioned above could bring immediate relief to retarded areas, it is also clear that it is necessarily a short-run measure. Long-run relief can come only from the gradual accumulation of viable, economically efficient industrial and agricultural investments. For this reason it is important to note that many projects, if allocated with strict economic rationality, would benefit industrially retarded areas if efficiency in price policy and allocation were given greater consideration. For instance, railway rates for carrying grain discourage milling in the producing areas where it logically should take place since the commodity loses weight and bulk in processing. Furthermore, there are many small-scale industrial projects in either local consumer oriented industries or in agricultural processing which logically belong to the agricultural producing areas. To promote these types of industries the Plan should give greater attention both to their requirements and to improvements in transportation and pricing policy.

Agricultural development encouraged by suitable regional price stabilization based on crop shortage and crop insurance schemes both in grain and in cash-crop farming are also crucial for growth. Farmers must be protected against the short-run vagaries of free markets and the vagaries of nature if they are to adopt costlier but more efficient production methods. Such protection would have immediate beneficial employment effects. The example of the US farming policies shows that industrial investment is not the only way to increase regional betterment of living standards. Encouragement given to agricultural export and to import-substituting output would also be efficient in the Indian context and conducive to wider regional distribution of resources.

Another neglected project is the broadening of the social and regional base of middle and higher education, another area where national and regional interests coincide. In addition to increasing future skill requirements for national development, a broadened educational base would have a most desirable effect on income distribution, and on improving equality of opportunity. Furthermore, the lack of elementary technical skills in the countryside is an obstacle to a meaningful rural labour mobilization.

Unfortunately state governments frequently compete for certain types of industrial investments not on economic grounds but out of political necessity or misguided eagerness. In effect, regional self-sufficiency in fertilizer production or in petroleum refining is almost a status symbol and the sign of an active state government. Rational economic evaluation of regional production patterns and real cost-benefit calculations would demonstrate that many of these projects are wasteful from the point of view of both the nation and the state. The national interest is to make use of the economies of large-scale production, standardization, and other advantages in order to achieve efficient resource utilization for any desired level of output. The states' interest is to obtain the largest return on whatever funds for investment is available to them. Frequently fewer resources than needed for 'conspicuous investments', if skilfully employed, can accomplish more for the welfare of the local population than badly located larger investments. The latter are usually capital intensive and hence do not provide great employment opportunities; since they cannot be competitive, instead of providing surpluses, they must be subsidized.

A nationally integrated economy implies, of course, anything but regional self-sufficiency in major industrial activities; and the less industrialized states must be persuaded that faster industrial growth in some other areas will in turn enhance their own economic development. However, they can be persuaded only if a comprehensive long-run plan is provided for the entire country which develops goals, phasing, and resource development by their geographical and time patterns.

Without such a master plan, the logic of which is open to inspection and can be continuously reworked and improved over time, democratic planning cannot take place. Without it regional governments cannot be expected to sacrifice or to wait patiently for the advancement of their own areas, which, as far as they know, may never come.

At present a long-term plan does not exist. However, even before such a plan is brought into existence there are a number of measures which could immediately improve the efficiency of resource allocation, regionally and otherwise. These consist of the reworking of the price mechanism for planning purposes and the application of basic criteria to project evaluation.

III. CRITERIA FOR EFFICIENT RESOURCE ALLOCATION

Correct allocation of industrial investment involves the application of competitive principles, particularly when government ownership is prevalent. Efficient allocation can take place only if there is a suitable norm to channel resources into activities that will maximize the real value of national income for given supply-and-demand relationships. Such a norm is provided by an efficiently working pricing mechanism.

Since free-market determination of prices may not be desired by India because of the distortions that might be caused by the prevailing income distribution and certain shortcomings of free markets, the price system must be adjusted suitably to reflect desirable conditions of production and marketing either in a real or in a 'shadow' price mechanism. Actually, with markets of diverse characters and income-distribution problems, a combination of the two might be desirable.

In the context of regional allocation of resources the following pricing rules should be followed:[1]

1. Prices of commodities and rates for services should reflect real costs (including real interest and foreign exchange rates) at the place of production and at the place of consumption.

2. Prices of homogeneous goods should be the same at a given location without regard of origin and should differ from location to location by the marginal cost of transportation *if* the commodity is transported and at most by that cost if not transported between two separate locations.

[1] A detailed analysis is contained in my monograph *Allocation in Space*, The North Holland Publishing Company, Amsterdam, 1958.

3. The present discounted value of the investment at the optimal location should be larger than or equal to the present discounted value of the same project computed for any other location (basing the computation on real costs and interest).[1]

The violation of these principles results in wasting resources and in diminishing future savings and growth potential. A few examples will illustrate this.

Example 1: Railway rates of certain commodities are below cost of hauling, and total revenues barely cover total railway expenditures. The rate for coal is illustrative. Since the railways are unable to make adequate profits from the existing rate, they cannot finance badly needed improvements and new railway investment to keep up with demand. New locational decisions by investors (private or public) are made in terms of the money cost of transportation rather than the real costs; hence they have no motivation to seek out the most economical location, and production costs must increase. Other modes of transportation (particularly coastal shipping) cannot move coal at the same monetary rates even though on long-distance movement their real costs are less than those of the railway; hence there cannot be rational distribution of cargo among alternative modes. Furthermore, discriminatory rates in favour of low-value bulk commodities result in larger flows of goods than needed to sustain a given level of national income at a time of a transportation bottleneck.[2] The remedy is to undertake, say, a five-year programme to 'rationalize' the rate system.

Example 2: Pithead prices of approximately equal quality coal from mines in Madhya Pradesh and Bihar-West Bengal are fixed at levels close to each other. Monetary transportation costs from the pitheads to Bombay differ by, say, six rupees (which is less than the real cost difference). The consequence is that either the Bombay buyers pay differential prices for comparable fuel, the most 'influential' ones taking the benefit, or an intermediary such as a dealer or a mining or transportation official reaps the transport difference for his private gain. With rational pricing policies the pithead price of M.P. coal should be higher than the Bihar-West Bengal price by the real transport cost, and this differential should

[1] The present discounted value of the project at the optimal location must be, of course, at least as great as its cost.

[2] Arguments which claim that such rates are needed to encourage economic growth and/or to avoid inflation are of doubtful validity. See L. Lefeber and Datta Chaudhuri, *op. cit.*

be maintained as long as both areas are needed to supply the Western Seaboard. Thus the price of coal in Bombay should be FOB West Bengal plus transport cost without regard of origin.[1] The increased revenues of M.P. mines should be used for intensified exploitation of M.P. mines, or, alternatively, for other investments of possibly higher priority. Thus funds from illegitimate private gains would be channelled to saving and investment, and the burden on the railways would decrease. Also, in the long run coal prices would be favourably affected.[2]

Example 3: Here the need to consider the present discounted value of investments in locational decisions will be shown. The present discounted value of a project is the sum total of the yearly net revenues over its lifetime discounted by the market rate of interest in a free enterprise, or by a shadow rate of interest in a controlled economy. In general, for industrial investments with marketable outputs the present discounted value must exceed or be at least equal to its cost if the project is to be undertaken. If this condition cannot be met, the indication is that the investment is not worth undertaking as its output would have to be subsidized.

The discounting must be done with a rate that adequately reflects the market forces that determine investment; in the case of India 10 per cent can be considered as a minimum.[3] The larger the rate, the greater weight will be given by the discounting process to returns

[1] Actually, one should determine prices by simultaneous consideration of the demands for and supplies of coal in all areas. This can be readily done by programming techniques.

[2] Many other examples of detrimental pricing policies can be provided. The 'equalization funds' in steel and fertilizer industries must lead to the overutilization of the inefficient and the underutilization of the efficient producers. The decision to sell steel at equal prices at any geographical point without regard to transportation cost is reminiscent of the very detrimental 'basing point' system of the American steel industry, which caused irreversible distortions not only in the development of the latter but also in the locational choices of steel using industries. The harmful effects in all these policies can be demonstrated by simply reasoning.

[3] The relationships which lead to the estimation of the real rate of interest cannot be readily discussed in the context of this paper. It is sufficient to point out that the smaller the initial saving effort, the larger the interest rate must be to accumulate a desired feasible level of capital stock. Conversely, given any level of initial savings, the larger capital stock we want to accumulate, the larger the interest rate must be. Either proposition would imply that in a country like India the interest rate should be on the high side. In effect, there is much empirical evidence to support this contention. In addition, my own statistical measurements indicated that the real rate of interest computed after taxes is about 10 per cent for the economy as a whole.

accruing in the near future, and distant ones will barely be registered. This has, of course, important implications for phasing of projects and choice of industrial location. It suggests that industrial projects which bring their fruits only in the distant future are wasteful and hence not to be undertaken. Also, projects which are desirable may have a net discounted surplus value in some locations and may be unprofitable in other locations.

A good example is the Assam refinery project. First, it is well recognized that refineries are best located in the proximity of markets since the transport of diverse outputs is more expensive than that of crude. At this point there is no market which warrants an efficient-scale refinery in Assam. Second, the capacity of the refinery is below optimal whereas the economies of scale in refining are very large. The implication is that the bulk of the output will have to be transported away at excessive transport cost which will further augment the already prohibitive unit cost of production. The output in the market areas will not be competitive with the output of the Bihar refinery or the product imported by way of Calcutta. Hence production will have to be subsidized. The counter argument says that, while it is true that for the time being there is insufficient market in Assam, this capacity will be needed at a later date when development begins. This argument, of course, completely neglects the question of economies of scale. But even more important is the fact that prospects distant in time cannot justify the tying up of capital when alternative investments or choices of location would provide positive immediate returns. Had the present discounted value of the Assam refinery investment been considered relative to its cost, the decision could not have been in favour of constructing it.[1]

IV. CONCLUSION

The process of economic development in its geographical setting requires growth at different rates in different areas. Attempts to

[1] Assam provides particularly good opportunities in rational and bold planning. In addition to its under-populated fertile soil it has vast unutilized natural resources. For instance, a large-scale project of land clearing would provide agricultural opportunities for great numbers of landless families. Large-scale paper pulp production and its transportation to other states for processing could be offset by opposite flows of commodities needed in Assam. Such plans would result in efficient production patterns according to comparative advantage and in optimal utilization of transportation facilities. Assam, as other states, must be encouraged to integrate gradually with the national economy rather than to strive toward regional self-sufficiency.

industrialize retarded regions ahead of time and at the cost of slowing down the growth of more vigorous areas must necessarily put off the date of bringing relief to the former. Inefficient regional allocation of investments results in wasting of scarce resources and in unnecessary burdening of the transport system. Losses in the saving and investment potential go hand in hand with higher costs of production. Inefficient plants operating in unsuitable locations require subsidies which are frequently hidden in complex administered pricing formulas. Such pricing policies lead to further wastes along with increases in the price level.

The short-run solution is to apply more vigorous criteria to regional investment choices in accordance with a rationally adjusted pricing mechanism. In the long run, however, the states cannot be expected to co-operate unless the distant benefits of current patience and sacrifice are spelled out in the form of explicit long-term plans. Without such plans the democratic approach to development will have to be replaced by fiat.

34. Regional Allocation of Investment*†

M. A. Rahman

Introduction

The aim of this paper is to analyze, in aggregative terms, the logic of regional allocation of investment in a two-region economy where the following conditions hold:

(1) central control and planning of investment are aimed at maximizing the rate of growth of total national income over a certain planning period (in other words, to maximize national income at the end of the planning period);

(2) regional sentiments demand that the process of economic growth should not bring about any wide disparity in regional living standards; and

(3) the productivity of investment (increase in income flow resulting from a given amount of investment) and the rate of saving both differ in the two regions.

The analysis runs in terms of an explicit planning model for a closed economy,[1] with linear and homogeneous consumption and investment functions, and with a certain political tolerance limit to regional income disparity in either direction. It is assumed that planned saving[2] equals planned investment through central direction.

* This paper is part of a doctoral thesis written at Harvard University during 1961–62. The author wishes to acknowledge the guidance of Professors H. S. Houthakker, W. Leontief, and E. S. Mason, and opportunities of discussion with Dr. R. Gangolly (M.I.T.), and Dr. G. Papanek (Harvard). A Ford Foundation doctoral dissertation grant made the work financially possible. The author alone, however, is responsible for any faults or inadequacies of the paper.

1. The formal reasoning applies also to an open economy where external accounts are always kept balanced (with the help of an exchange control system if necessary). Foreign aid could be explicitly introduced without any change in the qualitative properties of the solution.

2. In a controlled economy the concept of "planned saving" diverges from the Keynesian "propensity concept" insofar as the central authority consciously attempts to force (by means of taxation, inflation, control of foreign exchange, and whatever other instruments are available) an amount of saving that would differ from, and presumably exceed, what the community left to itself would "desire" in an aggregative market-mechanism sense.

† Reprinted from the *Quarterly Journal of Economics*, Vol. 77 (Feb. 1963).

The main finding of the analysis is that, in the presence of differential regional rates of saving, the rate of growth of total national income is not necessarily maximized by concentrating[3] investment in the more productive region throughout the planning period. If the more productive region also has the higher rate of saving, then of course the less productive region has no economic claim to turn investment allocation policy in its favor. But if the *less* productive region has the *higher* rate of saving, then it may pay under certain conditions to concentrate investment in a number of *initial* years of the plan in this region, *if* the planning period is long enough so that the initial loss of income resulting from such a policy may be repaid eventually with the help of the higher saving rate offered by this region. Under the assumptions of an instantaneous consumption function and an investment function having a gestation lag of one year (period) in each region, the precise technical condition for the above is that the "internal rate of growth" of income, defined below, in the less productive region should be higher than that in the more productive region. This "internal rate of growth" of income in a region is the rate at which its income would grow if it were a closed region so that its income grew out of its own saving only. It can also be called the "increment to saving resulting from unit investment"[4] in the region, and is given by the *ratio of the region's saving rate to its capital/output ratio.* If the less productive region has a higher internal rate of growth, then optimality would require investment to be concentrated in this region for a number of initial years of the plan, after which the policy should switch in favor of the more productive region. How many initial years would comprise the first phase of such a "switching" program depends, given the length of the planning period, on how high the "internal rate of growth" in the less productive region is in relation to that in the other region, and on how narrow are the political tolerance limits to regional income disparity.

Analysis of an n-region extension of the model (without assuming any political tolerance limits), would show that the optimum program may "switch" more than once; the maximum number of

3. Insofar as possible short of violating the political tolerance limits to regional income disparity.

4. Analogous to Galenson and Leibenstein's "reinvestment quotient." Walter Galenson and Harvey Leibenstein, "Investment Criteria, Productivity, and Economic Development," this *Journal*, LXIX (Aug. 1955), 343–70. The difference between the two studies lies in the nature of the respective problems presented: in the choice of technology problem studied by the above authors it is a once-for-all choice between different technologies, while in the present study the choice is confronted repeatedly every year, and a "switch" of choice is possible.

switches that may occur equals the number of regions, if any, whose "internal rates of growth" exceed the internal rate of growth of the most productive region.

These results may be compared with the solution of a simple programming problem of the von Neumann type[5] with two productive processes (or sectors) producing one homogeneous output. The rate of saving in a von Neumann model is the same whichever process is used, and the optimum program is determined by technical coefficients alone. A single "von Neumann path" in such a case becomes the optimal one, depending on which of the two processes is the more productive. In the present study the rate of saving is assumed to differ according as production is located in one region or the other. This, as is seen, opens up the possibility of the optimum program switching from one path to another in the course of its temporal movement.

The Problem Defined

Imagine a closed economy with two regions, A and B. National income of the country in any year t equals the sum of the two regional incomes, and may be written as:

$$z_t = x_t + y_t,$$

where z, x, and y stand for national income, income of region A and that of region B respectively.

Assume consumption to depend on current income and investment to have a gestation lag of one year in each region, so that

$$(C_A)_t = c_1 x_t,$$
$$(C_B)_t = c_2 y_t,$$
$$k_1(x_{t+1} - x_t) = (I_A)_t,$$
$$k_2(y_{t+1} - y_t) = (I_B)_t,$$

where C_A, C_B, I_A, and I_B stand for consumption and investment in the respective regions; c_1 and c_2 the rates of consumption in regions A and B respectively; and k_1 and k_2 the familiar incremental capital/output ratios for regions A and B respectively.

Now $z_t = x_t + y_t = (C_A)_t + (I_A)_t + (C_B)_t + (I_B)_t$. Combining this with the above equations, we get

$$z_t = c_1 x_t + c_2 y_t + k_1(x_{t+1} - x_t) + k_2(y_{t+1} - y_t).$$

Let $s_1 = 1 - c_1$ and $s_2 = 1 - c_2$, so that s_1 and s_2 represent the rates of saving in the respective regions. Then we have, by substitution,

5. Robert Dorfman, *et al.*, *Linear Programming and Economic Analysis* (New York: McGraw-Hill, 1958), Chap. 11. John von Neumann, "A Model of General Economic Equilibrium," *Review of Economic Studies*, XIII (1945–46), 1–9.

$$z_t = (1 - s_1)x_t + (1 - s_2)y_t + k_1(x_{t+1} - x_t) + k_2(y_{t+1} - y_t)$$

or

$$k_1(x_{t+1} - x_t) + k_2(y_{t+1} - y_t) = s_1x_t + s_2y_t, \quad (1)$$

the left-hand side representing total investment and the right-hand side representing total saving in the whole country in year t.

We shall assume that all the coefficients s_1, s_2, k_1, and k_2 are positive.[6] Further, without loss of generality we assume region A to be the more productive of the two, so that to get a given increase of income less investment is required in region A than in B. In other words, $k_1 < k_2$.

Two types of constraints are imposed on equation (1):

(a) Total investment equals, and is therefore limited to, total saving available in the economy in the year concerned. In other words, there cannot be any net consumption of capital or disinvestment in any region.[7] Such *non-disinvestment constraints* may be expressed as:

$$\text{(i) } x_{t+1} \geqslant x_t, \text{ and (ii) } y_{t+1} \geqslant y_t. \quad (2)$$

(b) Regional income disparity, measured by the ratio of two regional incomes, cannot exceed a certain political tolerance limit in either direction. These *political constraints* are expressed in the following form:

$$\text{(i) } \frac{y_{t+1}}{x_{t+1}} \geqslant r_1, \text{ and (ii) } \frac{x_{t+1}}{y_{t+1}} \geqslant r_2;\ 0 < r_1, r_2 < 1. \quad (3)$$

To illustrate, let $r_1 = .75$. Then income of region B cannot be allowed to fall below 75 per cent of income of region A.[8]

The problem is to maximize $z_T = x_T + y_T$, subject to conditions (1), (2), and (3), where t ranges from 0 to $T - 1$, and x_0, y_0 are given as initial conditions.

A graphic representation of the problem is given below:

Let x and y be represented by the two axes. Regional incomes

6. In practice s_1 and s_2 are likely to lie between 0 and 1, k_1 and k_2 are each likely to be greater than unity. These arguments are not needed for the analysis.

7. This implies that "capital stock" has to be maintained in each region (depreciation of capital may be incorporated in the consumption functions so that saving and investment become "net" concepts), so that income of no region can fall.

8. Such limits to regional income disparity may be derived from analogous limits to disparity in *per capita* regional incomes (or consumptions). In the event of unequal regional rates of population growth, limits to regional income disparity derived from *given* limits to per capita income disparity would change every year. For simplifying the exposition we shall keep r_1 and r_2 unchanged; it will be apparent as the analysis proceeds that this is not necessary for the qualitative conclusions about the structure of the optimum program arrived at in this study.

in year 0 are represented by the point (x_0, y_0). Regional incomes in year 1 will be given by a position (x_1, y_1) lying on a straight line F_1 (to be called the *frontier* for year 1) which is given by equation (1) with $t = 0$. The range of attainable points on F_1 depends on which of the four constraints — (2i), (2ii), (3i), and (3ii) — happen to be binding for this particular year.

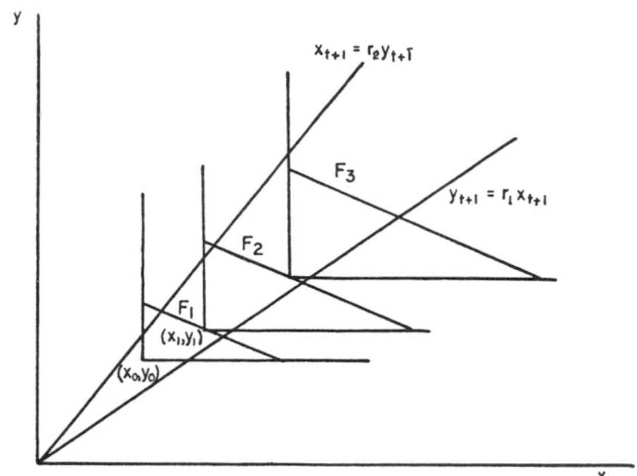

A similar frontier F_2 is defined for year 2 when a specific position (x_1, y_1) is chosen on F_1. And so on for all other years; a frontier F_m is defined when a specific position (x_{m-1}, y_{m-1}) is chosen on frontier F_{m-1}.

A position (x_m, y_m) may be chosen at either extreme of the attainable range of frontier F_m, or somewhere in between. In the former case we shall call the chosen position to lie *at an extreme*, "favoring" that region whose income for year m is maximized at that extreme.

The problem is to choose (x_{t+1}, y_{t+1}) and hence $(I_A)_t$ and $(I_B)_t$, for all t ranging from 0 to $T - 1$, so as to maximize, $z_T = x_T + y_T$.

The Solution

We shall give a complete qualitative solution of the problem in the form of a series of propositions. The method of proof will consist of an application of *Bellman's Principle of Optimality*,[9] which states that if certain initial decisions are taken, whatever they are, the remaining decisions must be optimal with respect to

9. Richard Bellman, *Dynamic Programming* (Princeton: Princeton University Press, 1959).

the state resulting from the initial decisions in order for the whole set of decisions to be optimal.

Proposition 1: In general the optimum income combination (henceforth called the "optimum position") lies at an extreme every year.

Proof:

Suppose investment decisions for all years up to year $T-2$ have already been taken, so that x_{T-1} and y_{T-1} are given. It remains to take investment decision for year $T-1$, or in other words to find x_T and y_T, so as to maximize z_T. We have

$$z_T = x_T + y_T;$$

and

$$k_1(x_T - x_{T-1}) + k_2(y_T - y_{T-1}) = s_1x_{T-1} + s_2y_{T-1}$$

or

$$k_1x_T + k_2y_T = (s_1 + k_1)x_{T-1} + (s_2 + k_2)y_{T-1} = \lambda_{T-1},$$

where λ_t stands for $(s_1 + k_1)x_t + (s_2 + k_2)y_t$ when x_t and y_t are given.

Solving z_T in terms of x_T, we have

$$Z_T = \frac{\lambda_{T-1}}{k_2} + \left(1 - \frac{k_1}{k_2}\right)x_T.$$

As x_T increases, z_T also increases, since $k_2 > k_1$, so that for optimization x_T should be maximized. In other words investment should be concentrated as far as possible in region A in year $T-1$, and the optimum position for year T will lie at the extreme that favors region A.

Suppose now that investment decisions have been taken for the first $t-2$ years, so that x_{t-1} and y_{t-1} are given. It remains to take optimal decisions for the remaining years from year $t-1$ onwards. Suppose also that optimum positions for all years from T down to $t+1$ (looking backwards) are known to lie at one or other extreme every year. This would turn $T-t$ of the constraints (2) and (3) into equalities. We have accordingly the following three sets of equations:

		number of equations	
(a)	$z_T = x_T + y_T$	1	(4)
(b)	$k_1(x_\tau - x_{\tau-1}) + k_2(y_\tau - y_{\tau-1}) = s_1x_{\tau-1} + s_2y_{\tau-1};$ $[\tau = t, t+1, \ldots\ldots, T-1, T]$	$T - t + 1$	
(c)	The equalities that replace constraints (2) and (3).	$T - t$	

A total of $2(T-t)+2$ equations with $2(T-t)+3$ variables, viz., z_T; $x_t, x_{t+1}, \ldots\ldots, x_T$; $y_t, y_{t+1}, \ldots\ldots, y_T$.

The number of variables being greater than the number of equations by 1, we can give an arbitrary value to x_t and solve z_t in terms of x_t. This would yield a relation of the form $z_T = p.x_t + q$, where p and q are constants.

Define $\Delta_t = dz_T/dx_t = p$ as obtained above. z_T will be maximized by maximizing or minimizing x_t according as Δ_t is positive or negative. In either case optimization requires that in year t also the program should lie at one of the extremes.[1]

We have earlier seen that in year T the optimum position does in fact lie at an extreme. Proof of proposition 1 by induction is now immediate.

Proposition 2: If $s_2/k_2 < s_1/k_1$, then the optimum program favors the more productive region, A, throughout the entire plan-period.

Proof:

Suppose Δ_t, as defined above, is positive for $t = m \leqslant T$.

z_T, the maximand, can be expressed as a weighted sum of x_m and y_m as follows:

$$z_T = x_T + y_T;$$

but

$$x_T = x_{T-1} + \frac{\sigma_1}{k_1}(s_1 x_{T-1} + s_2 y_{T-1}),$$

and

$$y_T = y_{T-1} + \frac{\sigma_2}{k_2}(s_1 x_{T-1} + s_2 y_{T-1}); \; [0 \leqslant \sigma_1, \sigma_2 \leqslant 1; \; \sigma_1 + \sigma_2 = 1]$$

where σ_1 and σ_2 are the proportions of total saving of year $T - 1$ that are invested in regions A and B respectively. Therefore z_T can be expressed as a weighted sum of x_{T-1} and y_{T-1}, the weights being positive.

By repetition of the same argument while working backwards through time, it can be finally shown that $z_T = w_1 x_m + w_2 y_m$, where w_1 and w_2 are two positive weights whose values do not interest us.

We now have

$$z_T = w_1 x_m + w_2 y_m,$$

and

$$k_1 x_m + k_2 y_m = \lambda_{m-1},$$

x_{m-1} and y_{m-1} being given by decisions already taken. From this we get

$$\Delta_m = dz_T/dx_m = w_1 - w_2 \cdot \frac{k_1}{k_2}.$$

1. In the exceptional case when $\Delta_t = 0$ for some t, an infinite number of solutions become optimal, which however still includes an optimum in terms of extreme positions.

Since Δ_m is positive (by assumption), the optimum position in year m favors region A. There are two possibilities:

(a) $y_m = r_1 x_m$, if the relevant political constraint is binding. In this case we can calculate Δ_{m-1} as follows:

Assume investment decisions have been taken for all initial years up to year $m - 3$, but not for year $m - 2$. Then regional incomes up to year $m - 2$ only are given. Hence we have

$$z_T = w_1 x_m + w_2 y_m = (w_1 + w_2 r_1) x_m; \text{ [since } y_m = r_1 x_m]$$

$$k_1(x_m - x_{m-1}) + k_2(y_m - y_{m-1}) = s_1 x_{m-1} + s_2 y_{m-1},$$

or

$$(k_1 + k_2 r_1) x_m - (s_2 + k_2) y_{m-1} = (s_1 + k_1) x_{m-1};$$

and

$$k_1 x_{m-1} + k_2 y_{m-1} = \lambda_{m-2}.$$

Or, writing in matrix form, we have

$$\begin{pmatrix} 1 & -(w_1 + w_2 r_1) & 0 \\ 0 & k_1 + k_2 r_1 & -(s_2 + k_2) \\ 0 & 0 & k_2 \end{pmatrix} \begin{pmatrix} z_T \\ x_m \\ y_{m-1} \end{pmatrix} = \begin{pmatrix} 0 \\ s_1 + k_1 \\ -k_1 \end{pmatrix} x_{m-1} + \begin{pmatrix} 0 \\ 0 \\ \lambda_{m-2} \end{pmatrix}$$

Solving z_T in terms of x_{m-1}, and calculating Δ_{m-1}, we have $\Delta_{m-1} = dz_T/dx_{m-1}$

$$= \frac{1}{(k_1 + k_2 r_1) k_2} \begin{vmatrix} 0 & -(w_1 + w_2 r_1) & 0 \\ s_1 + k_1 & k_1 + k_2 r_1 & -(s_2 + k_2) \\ -k_1 & 0 & k_2 \end{vmatrix}$$

$$= \frac{w_1 + w_2 r_1}{(k_1 + k_2 r_1) k_2} \cdot (s_1 k_2 - s_2 k_1) > 0, \text{ if } s_1 k_2 > s_2 k_1, \text{ or if } s_2/k_2 < s_1/k_1.$$

(b) Alternatively, $y_m = y_{m-1}$, if the relevant nondisinvestment constraint is binding. In this case Δ_{m-1} can be calculated as follows:

$$z_T = w_1 x_m + w_2 y_m = w_1 x_m + w_2 y_{m-1};$$

$$k_1(x_m - x_{m-1}) + k_2(y_m - y_{m-1}) = s_1 x_{m-1} + s_2 y_{m-1};$$

or

$$k_1 x_m - s_2 y_{m-1} = (s_1 + k_1) x_{m-1};$$

and

$$k_1 x_{m-1} + k_2 y_{m-1} = \lambda_{m-2}.$$

Or

$$\begin{pmatrix} 1 & -w_1 & -w_2 \\ 0 & k_1 & -s_2 \\ 0 & 0 & k_2 \end{pmatrix} \begin{pmatrix} z_T \\ x_m \\ y_{m-1} \end{pmatrix} = \begin{pmatrix} 0 \\ s_1 + k_1 \\ -k_1 \end{pmatrix} x_{m-1} + \begin{pmatrix} 0 \\ 0 \\ \lambda_{m-2} \end{pmatrix}$$

whence $\Delta_{m-1} = dz_T/dx_{m-1}$

$$= \frac{1}{k_1 k_2} \begin{vmatrix} 0 & -w_1 & -w_2 \\ s_1 + k_2 & k_1 & -s_2 \\ -k_1 & 0 & k_2 \end{vmatrix}$$

$$= w_1 - w_2 \cdot \frac{k_1}{k_2} + \frac{w_1}{k_1 k_2} (s_1 k_2 - s_2 k_1)$$

$$= \Delta_m + \frac{w_1}{k_1 k_2} (s_1 k_2 - s_2 k_1).$$

Since $\Delta_m > 0$, we must have $\Delta_{m-1} > 0$ if $s_1 k_2 > s_2 k_1$, or if $s_2/k_2 < s_1/k_1$.

Thus in both cases (a) and (b), Δ_{m-1} is positive if $s_2/k_2 < s_1/k_1$. Since $\Delta_T > 0$, proof of proposition 2 by induction is complete.

Proposition 3: In order that the optimum program may favor the less productive region, B, in any year at all, s_2/k_2 *must exceed* s_1/k_1.

This is a corollary of proposition 2. In the event that s_2/k_2 happens to equal s_1/k_1, Δ_{m-1} remains positive in case (b); in case (a) Δ_{m-1} becomes zero, so that the case of multiple optima [2] occurs. In neither case is an extreme position *favoring* region *B* required. Hence the optimum program would favor the less productive region, if at all, only if s_2/k_2 exceeds s_1/k_1.

Proposition 4: If in any particular year the optimum position favors the less productive region, then in all earlier years, if any, the same region must be favored.

Proof:

Proof is very much similar to proof of proposition 2 and need not be elaborated. Let $\Delta_m < 0$, so that region *B* is favored in year *m*. There are again two possibilities:

(a) $x_m = r_2 y_m$. In this case Δ_{m-1} is derived from the following system:

$$\begin{pmatrix} 1 - (w_1 r_2 + w_2) & 0 & \\ 0 & k_1 r_2 + k_2 & -(s_2 + k_2) \\ 0 & 0 & k_2 \end{pmatrix} \begin{pmatrix} z_T \\ y_m \\ y_{m-1} \end{pmatrix} = \begin{pmatrix} 0 \\ s_1 + k_1 \\ -k_1 \end{pmatrix} x_{m-1} + \begin{pmatrix} 0 \\ 0 \\ \lambda_{m-2} \end{pmatrix}$$

whence $\Delta_{m-1} = dz_T/dx_{m-1} = \dfrac{w_1 r_2 + w_2}{(k_1 r_2 + k_2) k_2} \cdot (s_1 k_2 - s_2 k_1) < 0,$

since $s_2/k_2 > s_1/k_1$ by proposition 3.

(b) $x_m = x_{m-1}$. In this case we shall have

$$\begin{pmatrix} 1 - w_2 & 0 & \\ 0 & k_2 & -(s_2 + k_2) \\ 0 & 0 & k_2 \end{pmatrix} \begin{pmatrix} z_T \\ y_m \\ y_{m-1} \end{pmatrix} = \begin{pmatrix} w_1 \\ s_1 \\ -k_1 \end{pmatrix} x_{m-1} + \begin{pmatrix} 0 \\ 0 \\ \lambda_{m-2} \end{pmatrix}$$

2. See footnote 1, p. 32.

whence $\triangle_{m-1} = dz_T/dx_{m-1}$

$$= \frac{1}{k_2^2} \cdot \begin{vmatrix} w_1 - w_2 & & 0 \\ s_1 & k_2 - & (s_2 + k_2) \\ -k_1 & 0 & k_2 \end{vmatrix}$$

$$= \frac{w_1 + w_2 \cdot k_1}{k_2} + \frac{w_2}{k_2^2}(s_1 k_2 - s_2 k_1)$$

$$= \triangle_m + \frac{w_2 (s_1 k_2 - s_2 k_1)}{k_2^2} < 0,$$

since $\triangle_m < 0$ and $s_2/k_2 > s_1/k_1$.

In either case $\triangle_{m-1} < 0$ if $\triangle_m < 0$. This proves proposition 4.

Proposition 5: Given $s_2/k_2 > s_1/k_1$, and a plan-period sufficiently large, the optimum program must favor the less productive region in a number of initial years.

Proof:

In the last year, T, there are two possibilities:

(a) $y_T = r_1 x_T$. In this case $\triangle_{T-1}$ is given by analysis (a) for proposition 2 if we put $w_1 = w_2 = 1$. Hence

$$\triangle_{T-1} = \frac{1 + r_1}{(k_1 + k_2 r_1) k_2} \cdot (s_1 k_2 - s_2 k_1) < 0, \text{ if } s_2/k_2 > s_1/k_1,$$

so that the optimum program favors region B in year $T - 1$ and hence in all initial years up to $T - 1$: the program switches in favor of region A only in the last year T.

(b) $y_T = y_{T-1}$. In this case $\triangle_{T-1}$ is given by analysis (b) for proposition 2, putting $w_1 = w_2 = 1$ again. Hence

$$\triangle_{T-1} = \frac{1}{k_1 k_2} \cdot \begin{vmatrix} 0 & -1 & -1 \\ s_1 + k_1 & k_1 - s_2 & \\ -k_1 & 0 & k_2 \end{vmatrix} = \frac{1}{k_1 k_2} \cdot \begin{vmatrix} s_1 + k_1 - s_2 & \\ -k_1 & k_2 \end{vmatrix} - \frac{k_1}{k_2}$$

$$= \frac{k_2 - k_1}{k_2} + \frac{s_1 k_2 - s_2 k_1}{k_1 k_2}.$$

$\triangle_{T-1}$ thus obtained may be negative or positive, depending on how high s_2 is in relation to the other parameters.

Suppose $\triangle_{T-1} > 0$. Then optimality requires region A to be favored in year $T - 1$ also, and we must have $y_{T-1} = y_{T-2}$. The other possibility, viz., $y_{T-1} = r_1 x_{T-1}$ cannot occur, because:

(i) $y_T > r_1 x_T$ (since the political constraint is not binding in year T),

(ii) $y_{T-1} = y_T$, and

(iii) $x_{T-1} < x_T$ (since income of region A has grown), so that $y_{T-1} > r_1 x_{T-1}$.

We shall now proceed to derive $\triangle_{T-2}$. We have:

$z_T = x_T + y_T = x_T + y_{T-2}$ (since $y_T = y_{T-1} = y_{T-2}$),

$k_1 x_T = (s_1 + k_1) x_{T-1} + s_2 y_{T-2}$,

$k_1 x_{T-1} = (s_1 + k_1) x_{T-2} + s_2 y_{T-2}$, and

$k_1 x_{T-2} + k_2 y_{T-2} = \lambda_{T-3}$,

assuming x_{T-3} and y_{T-3} are given by decisions already taken.

Writing in matrix form, we have

$$\begin{pmatrix} 1 & -1 & 0 & -1 \\ 0 & k_1 & -(s_1 + k_1) & -s_1 \\ 0 & 0 & k_1 & -s_2 \\ 0 & 0 & 0 & k_2 \end{pmatrix} \begin{pmatrix} z_T \\ x_T \\ x_{T-1} \\ y_{T-2} \end{pmatrix} = \begin{pmatrix} 0 \\ 0 \\ s_1 + k_1 \\ -k_1 \end{pmatrix} x_{T-2} + \begin{pmatrix} 0 \\ 0 \\ 0 \\ \lambda_{T-3} \end{pmatrix}$$

whence

$$\triangle_{T-2} = dz_T/dx_{T-2} = \frac{1}{k_1^2 k_2} \cdot \begin{vmatrix} 0 & -1 & 0 & -1 \\ 0 & k_1 & -(s_1 + k_1) & -s_2 \\ s_1 + k_1 & 0 & k_1 & -s_2 \\ -k_1 & 0 & 0 & k_2 \end{vmatrix}$$

$$= \frac{s_1 + k_1}{k_1^2 k_2} \cdot \begin{vmatrix} s_1 + k_1 & -s_2 \\ -k_1 & k_2 \end{vmatrix} - \frac{s_2}{k_2} - \frac{k_1}{k_2}$$

$$= \frac{s_1 + k_1}{k_1} \cdot \left[\frac{1}{k_1 k_2} \cdot \begin{vmatrix} s_1 + k_1 & -s_2 \\ -k_1 & k_2 \end{vmatrix} - \frac{k_1}{k_2} \right] + \frac{s_1 + k_1}{k_2} - \frac{s_2 + k_1}{k_2}$$

$$= \frac{s_1 + k_1}{k_1} \cdot \triangle_{T-1} + \frac{s_1 - s_2}{k_2}.$$

The sign of $\triangle_{T-2}$ can again be either negative or positive. Suppose $\triangle_{T-2}$ is positive, so that for optimization

$y_T = y_{T-1} = y_{T-2} = y_{T-3}$.

We can similarly derive $\triangle_{T-3}$, and it can be shown that

$$T - 3 = \frac{s_1 + k_1}{k_1} \cdot \triangle_{T-2} + \frac{s_1 - s_2}{k_2}.$$

By repeating the argument it can be shown that if $\Delta_{T-(r<\tau)}$ is positive for all r, then

$$\Delta_{T-\tau} = \frac{s_1 + k_1}{k_1} \cdot \Delta_{T-(\tau-1)} + \frac{s_1 - s_2}{k_2}, \text{ for any } \tau > 1.$$

This gives a nonhomogeneous first order difference equation with initial condition

$$\Delta_{T-1} = \frac{k_2 - k_1}{k_2} + \frac{s_1k_2 - s_2k_1}{k_1k_2}.$$

The solution of the difference equation is given by

$$\Delta_{T-\tau} = P \cdot \left(\frac{s_1 + k_1}{k_1}\right)^{\tau-1} + Q,$$

where $Q = \dfrac{k_1(s_2 - s_1)}{s_1k_2} > 0$, since $s_2 > s_1$,

and $P = \dfrac{s_1k_2 - s_2k_1}{k_2}\left(\dfrac{1}{k_1} + \dfrac{1}{s_1}\right) < 0$, since $s_2/k_2 > s_1/k_1$.

Since the root $\left(\dfrac{s_1 + k_1}{k_1}\right) = \left(1 + \dfrac{s_1}{k_1}\right)$ is greater than unity, and the sign of its coefficient P is negative, $\Delta_{T-\tau}$ must eventually become negative as we work backwards from Δ_{T-1} (i.e., as τ increases), provided the plan-period T is sufficiently large to make it possible. The optimum program will therefore favor region B in at least one initial year; and if T is larger, in a number of initial years.

This completes proof of proposition 5 and also the qualitative solution we are seeking to the problem.

Summary

The solution as outlined by propositions 1–5 can be summarized as follows:

The optimum program can be of two general types: [3]

Type A: The more productive region is favored throughout the entire planning period. This occurs when $s_2/k_2 < s_1/k_1$. In this case the less productive region is unable to offer a rate of saving high enough to offset higher productivity of the other region. Optimality requires that investment be concentrated in the more productive region every year, subject of course to the constraints of the model.

Type B: The less productive region is favored in a number of initial years, after which the program switches to the other extreme in favor of the more productive region for the remaining years. This occurs when $s_2/k_2 > s_1/k_1$, and the planning period is large enough so that the initial loss of income resulting from concentrating investment in the less productive region can be recovered, within

3. Leaving out the exceptional case when $\Delta_t = 0$ for some t so that multiple optima occur.

the planning horizon, with the help of the higher saving rate of this region. In this sense we can talk of a "period of recovery" such that, given the condition $s_2/k_2 > s_1/k_1$, a *Type B* program emerges if the plan-period T is greater than the period of recovery. To illustrate, if the political constraints are narrow enough to be binding every year, then according to analysis (a) under proposition 5 the period of recovery is 1 year: with a planning period greater than that a *Type B* program emerges, favoring the less productive region for the first $T - 1$ years. In the event the planning period does not exceed the period of recovery, the optimum program retains a *Type A* character; failure of *Type B* program to emerge may then be attributed to what may be called "shortsightedness."

The n-region case

An n-region extension of the above analysis is possible and is rather easily made if one abstracts from any political constraints. One could follow the same line of reasoning as above to demonstrate certain interesting properties of the structure of the optimum program in this case as well.[4] An alternative approach that arrives at the same conclusions but is more elegant and, in some respects, superior is presented by Professor Dorfman in a note to this paper. The main conclusions obtainable from an analysis of the n-region case may be briefly summarized as follows:

Looking at its backward course, the optimum program starts with the most productive region, and stays with it if this also offers the highest "internal rate of growth," s/k. If there are regions which, though less productive than the former, have higher internal rates of growth, the program must eventually switch to one of them, depending on whose contribution to the ultimate objective from the standpoint of the year in question is the greatest (see Dorfman's note). As long as there are regions which have still higher internal rates of growth, the program must eventually switch again, and so on. At no time will a switch be made from a region with a higher internal rate of growth to one with a lower rate. Nor will a switch be made except to one higher in the order. As a corollary, once the program switches away from a region, it never comes back to it. In any case the regions, if any, whose internal rates of growth are lower than that of the most productive region, will never be favored; hence the maximum number of switches that can occur equals the number of regions whose internal rates of growth are

4. See the author's Ph.D. thesis, "The Logic of Regional Investment Allocation," Harvard University, 1962, Appendix 1, pp. 61–70.

higher than that of the most productive region. Further, since there will be no further switch once the highest-internal-rate-of-growth region is reached, the last phase of the program's backward course will always favor the region with the highest internal rate of growth.

Conclusion

As a general conclusion we may say that the rate of growth of national income is not necessarily maximized by concentrating investment in the most productive region of a country if regional rates of saving are not identical. Whether a less productive region can offer significantly higher rates of saving (more specifically, higher internal rate of growth) than the most productive region so as to turn the program in its "favor" in a number of initial years, is a matter of specific enquiry for the country concerned. A priori the rate of saving in a region does not have any direct connection with its productivity. Saving is a function not only of income, but also of social habits, institutions, and, in a controlled economy, of the administrative and political ability of the central authority to squeeze saving out of the region. It is quite conceivable that in a particular country a less productive region may happen to offer a higher rate of saving.[5] In this case the possibility of a switching program cannot be ruled out.

5. Pakistan seems to be a case in point: available evidence suggests that East Pakistan, widely believed to be the less productive region, has had a significantly higher rate of saving than that of West Pakistan over the last decade. Mahbubul Haq, *The Strategy of Economic Planning* (Oxford: Clarendon Press, forthcoming).

35. Development Policies for Southern Italy*†

Hollis B. Chenery

Despite the current popularity of policies for promoting development, there has been little systematic study of the effects of such policies on the actual course of economic growth. This situation is due in large part to the relatively short period over which most development programs have been in operation. Only a handful of countries has followed a fairly consistent policy for a period of as long as ten years, which is perhaps the minimum required for even a preliminary judgment of the effectiveness of a particular approach.

Within this small group, Southern Italy is of considerable interest because there the Italian government has attempted to carry out the theoretically attractive procedure of developing external economies by a massive dose of public works while leaving the direct investment in commodity production to private individuals. In this policy it has received substantial support from the U.S. government, the World Bank, and other international agencies. Since the program got under way in 1951, Southern Italy has had an import surplus equal to 25 per cent of its regional income, indicating one of the highest levels of external assistance in the world.

* Research for this paper was done at the Associazione per lo Sviluppo dell'Industria nel Mezzogiorno (SVIMEZ), Rome, with the assistance of Mrs. M. I. Salvemini. Financial support was provided by the American Commission for Cultural Exchange with Italy (Fulbright Commission). I am indebted to Vera Cao Pinna, G. G. Dell'Angelo, Veniero Marsan, Claudio Napoleoni, Nino Novacco, Franco Pilloton, Camillo Righi, Paul Rosenstein-Rodan, and Pasquale Saraceno for helpful comments. The analysis does not take account of developments since the summer of 1961.

† Reprinted from the *Quarterly Journal of Economics,* Vol. 76 (Nov. 1962).

With a population of eighteen million and a separate historical tradition, Southern Italy is a distinct economic entity having a per capita income somewhat below that of the average for Latin America. In cultural heritage, social structure, and resistance to institutional change, it has many other parallels to Latin American countries.[1] In particular, the conflict between left- and right-wing elements of the Italian government over the lines of Southern development policy has led to a compromise that might be called "intervention without planning," which finds its counterpart in many Latin American countries.[2] Certain objectives of Southern development were set out in the Vanoni "Plan" of 1954,[3] but the measures necessary to achieve them were not specified and the scheme has had little practical effect. Despite the fact that it has authority to spend three billion dollars over a fifteen year period, the Southern development agency (the Cassa per il Mezzogiorno) makes no overall economic analysis against which to judge its past accomplishments and current program. In general, the government has preferred to follow a policy of unplanned growth and of influencing resource allocation in industry and agriculture by fiscal instruments rather than by more direct measures.

A considerable debate is now in progress over the success of Southern development policies to date and the direction that they should take in the future.[4] Although the rate of growth of regional income has been substantial (4 per cent per year), it has been somewhat less than that of the rest of Italy and no higher than the average for other Mediterranean countries that receive much less

1. It will be recalled that Southern Italy was also under Spanish rule until 1861.

2. Current American efforts to use economic aid to achieve specific social objectives in Latin America encounter many of the same political and institutional obstacles that similar efforts met with in Southern Italy ten years ago. The analysis of current aid policy may therefore benefit from a study of the effects of U.S. policies in Italy in a period when it was receiving very large amounts of American aid.

3. Comitato dei Ministri per il Mezzogiorno, *Relazione al Parlamento Presentata dal Presidente del Comitato dei Ministri per il Mezzogiorno* (Rome, 1961).

4. For a range of views see: *ibid*; A. Buffa, *Tre Italie* (Palermo, 1961); G. M. Di Simone, "Integrazione Economica e Sviluppi Comparativi Nord-Sud," *Mondo Economico*, No. 16 (April 1960); V. Lutz, "Italy as a Study in Development," *Lloyds Bank Review*, No. 58 (Oct. 1960); G. Pescatore, *Dieci Anni di Esperienze della Cassa per il Mezzogiorno* (Rome, 1961); P. Saraceno, "Dopo un Decennio di Intervento nel Mezzogiorno," *Nord e Sud*, No. 15 (Mar. 1961); S. Wellisz, "Economic Planning in the Netherlands, France, and Italy," *Journal of Political Economy*, LXVIII (June 1960).

outside assistance. The stated objective of Southern policy — to develop as fast as or faster than the North — has not yet been met, and in fact per capita income in the South has fallen from 63 per cent to 56 per cent of the national average in the past decade. It is not clear whether it is the direction of policy that has been wrong, or whether the time period of ten years is just too short for a proper test.

The present paper will be concerned with three aspects of development policy in Southern Italy: (i) the significance of the differences between Southern Italy and the typical economy of its income level; (ii) the explanation of the lower rate of growth in output in the South, and the extent to which it results from the policies followed in the past decade; (iii) the nature of the structural changes needed for more successful development in the future. A simple interregional growth model will be used as a basis for the analysis of development policy.

I. Southern Italy as an Underdeveloped Economy

An underdeveloped region of a more advanced national economy has important differences from as well as similarities to a country of the same income level. Before trying to explain the pattern of Southern growth, I shall therefore make a statistical comparison of Southern Italy with low-income countries and try to show how its economic structure is influenced by being part of a more advanced national economy. Further differences will be brought out by comparing Italian development policies with those of other countries.

The Structure of the Southern Economy

Although there has been much discussion of the economic structure of Southern Italy, it is only in the past year that the Central Institute of Statistics (ISTAT) has published a detailed study of regional income and its components for 1951–59.[5] Since 1951 is also the year in which the Southern development program got under way, I shall take it as the starting point for the present analysis.[6]

In 1951, the region traditionally defined as the South ("Mez-

5. Instituto Centrale di Statistica (ISTAT), *Primi Studi sui Conti Economici Territoriali* (Rome, 1960).

6. The Cassa per il Mezzogiorno was established in 1950, but expenditures on a significant scale began only in 1951.

zogiorno") had a per capita income of 125,000 lire, or about $200.[7] This income level was in contrast with $500 per capita in the industrial Northwest and $320 per capita for the country as a whole.[8] The difference in the available resources is substantially less, however, because there has been a continuing transfer of income from North to South by means of taxes and public expenditure. In 1951 this transfer reduced the regional resources per capita (i.e., the total of regional consumption and investment) to $415 in the North and raised regional resources to $235 per capita in the South. In subsequent years (as shown in Table III below), the interregional income transfer has become considerably larger as the programs for developing the South have gotten under way.

Since one of the main problems of the South is lack of industry, it is interesting to compare the industrial output of the region with that of countries having similar income levels. This can be done most accurately by utilizing the results of a statistical comparison of production by sector in fifty countries,[9] which gives regression equations relating value added by sector to the income level and population of the country. The actual levels of total demand (regional income plus import surplus) and population in Southern Italy can be substituted in these equations to estimate the "normal" productive structure of a country having these characteristics. The results of these calculations for 1951 and 1959, along with the actual values for Southern Italy, are given in Table I.[1] The ratios of actual to normal in the main branches of production — 1.12 for primary production and .84 for industry in 1951 — show somewhat less industrial development than would be found in the typical country,

7. *Primi Studi sui Conti Economici Territoriali, op. cit.*, p. 138.

8. One important innovation in the ISTAT study is the division of the nation into three regions — Northwest, Center-Northeast, and South — instead of the North-South division that has been used up to now. The North (Piemonte, Lombardia, Liguria, Valle d'Aosta) contains the highly industrialized "industrial triangle" of Milan, Turin, Genoa. The South (Abruzzi, Campania, Puglie, Lucania, Calabria, Sicilia, Sardegna) is the area traditionally called the "Mezzogiorno," for which there is a separate development agency and policy. The Center comprises the remaining provinces (Tre Venezie, Emilia, Romagna, Marche, Toscana, Umbria, Lazio).

9. H. B. Chenery, "Patterns of Industrial Growth," *American Economic Review*, L (Sept. 1960).

1. Since the level of total demand (consumption plus investment) is the main factor influencing sector output, I have used this variable instead of the regional product (income) in the regression equations. The international comparison is based on per capita income, but on the average there is little difference between the two. If income is used, however, the South had a ratio of 1.06 to the normal for all industry in 1951 and 1.29 in 1959.

TABLE I

ACTUAL AND NORMAL VALUE ADDED BY SECTOR IN SOUTHERN ITALY, 1951 AND 1959
(In dollars per capita)

Sector	1951			1959		
	Actual Value Added [1]	Normal Value Added [2]	Actual / Normal	Actual Value Added [1]	Normal Value Added [2]	Actual / Normal
	(1)	(2)	(3)	(4)	(5)	(6)
Primary Sectors						
1. Agriculture	80.70	70.90	1.14	94.19	83.22	1.13
2. Mining	2.93	3.99	.73	6.10	5.41	1.13
Total primary	83.67	74.89	1.12	100.29	88.63	1.13
Industry						
3. Food and tobacco	17.07	11.21	1.52	22.90	16.11	1.42
4. Textiles	.93	4.33	.21	0.93	7.10	.13
5. Clothing and leather	2.10	2.55	.82	3.15	4.44	.71
6. Wood products	2.58	1.66	1.55	3.78	2.97	1.27
7. Metals	1.11	2.69	.41	2.42	5.59	.43
8. Metal products	4.48	2.72	1.65	9.12	6.37	1.44
9. Nonmetallic mineral products	1.21	1.72	.70	2.85	2.94	.97
10. Chemicals, rubber and petroleum refining	3.16	3.18	.99	6.15	5.63	1.09
11. Paper	.29	.54	.54	.56	1.33	.42
12. Other manufacturing	.60	1.82		1.19	3.17	. .
Unclassified small industry		6.13			6.36	
Total (3–12)	33.93	38.55	.88	53.06	61.96	.86
13. Construction	7.69	10.75	.72	17.65	15.64	1.12
14. Electricity, gas and water	4.48	(5.00)		7.65	(8.00)	
Total industry (3–14)	45.73	54.30	.84	78.36	85.60	.92
15. Transportation	13.70	14.00	.98	19.30	21.34	.90
16–20. Services	65.01	81.50	.80	80.29	115.10	.70
Total [3]	209.24	224.69		278.21	310.67	

1. Cols. (1) and (4) are based on *Primi Studi Sui Conti Economici Territoriali, op cit.* Total value added in each sector was converted to 1953 dollars at the exchange rate of 625 lire per dollar and divided by the population of 17.65 million in 1951 and 18.99 in 1959.

2. Cols. (2) and (5) are computed by substituting values of $235 per capita income and 17.65 population for 1951, and $326 and 18.99 for 1959, in the regression equations given in Tables 2 and 3 of Chenery, *op. cit.*

3. The differences in the totals are due to the fact that the total of the regression estimates is some 10 per cent less than the corresponding level of total value added, plus the fact that there is an import surplus of $35 in 1951 and $70 in 1959.

but the deviations are no greater than those in many other countries in the original sample.[2]

2. Chenery, *op. cit.*, Table 6.

The effect on Southern Italy of being part of a more advanced national economy is more noticeable in the composition of industrial output. In 1951 regional specialization within the Southern Italian economy is shown by the relatively high values of agriculture and food processing, reflecting exports from the South to the North, and low values of textiles, metals, paper, and nonmetallic mineral products, reflecting relatively high imports of these products into the South from the rest of the country. By 1959 the deviation in nonmetallic mineral products was eliminated, but the pattern of specialization in the remaining sectors showed little change.[3]

It will be shown in the subsequent analysis that this pattern of specialization is a distinct handicap to Southern growth, and in this respect belonging to a national economy will be a liability if it inhibits future changes in the economic structure. However, two other features of economic integration are definite assets, which should in the future outweigh any handicap resulting from the existing structure of production. The first, of which mention has already been made, is the income transfer to the South from the North,[4] which has contributed 20 per cent of the total resources available in the South for the period 1951–60. As shown in Table III below, a substantial part of this income transfer goes to finance consumption, which is somewhat larger than the total income produced in the region. Even so, since 1954 gross investment has averaged 20 per cent of total resources or 25 per cent of regional income, which is much higher than the level achieved in the typical country of this income level.

The second difference from other underdeveloped countries is the higher emigration rate that is made possible for the South by being part of a larger political unit. The rate of natural increase in the South of about 1.4 per cent in recent years is close to the median population growth for Mediterranean countries of its income level,[5] although much lower than the rates of over 2.5 per cent that now prevail in the Near East and Latin America. However, the rate of population increase in the South over the past decade was lowered to 0.5 per cent by emigration (to the North and abroad), as shown

3. Construction increased very markedly in this period, but this reflects an increase in local demand rather than a change in specialization.

4. There is no detailed analysis of the financing of this import surplus, but the principal elements are social insurance payments and public works expenditures.

5. For the period 1953–57, percentage rates of population increase in the Mediterranean were: Spain, 0.8; Portugal, 0.8; Greece, 0.9; Jugoslavia, 1.4; Algeria, 2.0; Egypt, 2.4; Turkey, 2.8; and Lebanon, 3.0.

TABLE II

DEMOGRAPHIC MOVEMENTS, 1951–1959
(In thousands)

	North		Center	South	Italy
Population Physically Present[1]					
Total 1951		29,766		17,459	47,225
Natural increase		1,136		2,092	3,228
External migration		−470		−743	−1,213
Internal migration	(+790)	610	(−180)	−610	..
Total 1959		31,042		18,198	49,240
Index $\frac{1959}{1951}$:		104.3		104.2	104.3
Annual rate of:					
Natural increase		0.49		1.42	0.83
External migration		−0.19		−0.51	−0.33
Internal migration		+0.25		−0.48	..
Net increase		0.54		0.52	0.54
Resident Population[2]					
1951	11,720		18,040	17,651	47,411
1959	12,650		18,839	18,991	50,480
Index	107.9		104.4	107.6	106.5
Rate of increase	0.96		0.54	0.92	0.79

1. Source: SVIMEZ
2. Source: ISTAT, *Primi Studi sui Conti Economici Territoriali*, *op. cit.*, Table 17.

in Table II. This rate is much lower than the normal for an underdeveloped country. Internal migration has thus had the effect of equalizing population growth in the different regions of the country, and in the short run at least it makes the problem of raising per capita income in the South easier.

Southern and National Growth, 1951–60

When we turn from the productive structure to the rate of growth in the past decade, the effect on the South of belonging to a national economy is even more noticeable. The growth of the Mezzogiorno has been stimulated by the fact that gross national product in Italy as a whole has been increasing at 5.6 per cent per year, as shown in Table III. The factors producing this high rate affect the South differently from the North, however, and on balance cause it to lag behind.

The rapid growth of the Italian economy since 1950 has been due to a number of factors: a relatively high rate of savings and investment, the initial existence of unused capacity in a number of sectors,

TABLE III

SOURCES AND USES OF REGIONAL RESOURCES, 1951–1960

(In billions of lire)

	Northern and Central Italy					Southern Italy					Italy				
	Gross Product [3]	Net Exports	Net Resources	Consumption	Gross Investment	Gross Product [3]	Net Imports	Net Resources	Consumption	Gross Investment	Gross Product [3]	Net Imports	Net Resources	Consumption	Gross Investment
1951[1]	8,020	283	7,737	6,086	1,651	2,366	382	2,748	2,297	451	10,386	99	10,485	8,383	2,102
1960	13,630	1174	12,456	9,099	3,357	3,351	1,203	4,555	3,476	1,079	16,982	29	17,011	12,575	4,436
Per capta[2] 1960	426		389	284	105	175	63	238	182	56	332		333	246	87
Increase 1951–60	5,611	890	4,719	3,013	1,706	985	821	1,807	1,179	628	6,596	−70	6,526	4,192	2,334
% of increase in net resources			100%	63.8%	36.2%			100%	65.3%	34.7%			100%	64.2%	35.8%
Annual rate of growth	6.07%	17.3%	5.44%	4.58%	8.21%	3.95%	13.6%	5.77%	4.70%	10.19%	5.62%		5.51%	4.60%	8.65%

1. Source: ISTAT, *Primi Studi sui Conti Economici Territoriali, op. cit.*

2. Resident population in 1960 was 32,013 thousand in the North and Center, 19,138 in the South, and 51,151 in all Italy. See *Relazione al Parlamento Presentata dal Presidente del Comitato dei Ministri per il Mezzogiorno, op. cit.*

3. Total consumption has been recalculated by correcting the income from housing where statistical criteria have changed on the basis of the ratio of 1959 noncorrected figures to corrected figures; this brought about a corresponding change in gross product.

unemployed labor, trade liberalization, and an unexpectedly rapid growth of exports of goods and services.[6] From 1950 to 1956, one of the main factors that set a limit to growth was the balance of payments, which prevented a more rapid absorption of the excess labor supply because of the danger that import requirements would outrun exports.[7] The rapid growth of exports removed this limitation after 1957 and also provided the stimulus for continued growth of output.[8]

The factors determining the growth of the Mezzogiorno are quite different. It has a relatively small share of national production in the sectors that have contributed the bulk of the increase in exports — metals and metal products, chemicals, tourism. Although it benefits indirectly from the income growth in the North and Center, its exports to the rest of the country and abroad have not grown so fast as its imports, since it produces commodities having lower income elasticities of demand. In this respect the South resembles the typical underdeveloped country. Local demand in the South has however been stimulated by the investment program of the Cassa per il Mezzogiorno and by increases in other types of government expenditure.[9] The nature of this relationship between the South and the rest of the country will be analyzed more fully in Section II.

The differences between the South and the rest of the country are shown very clearly in the pattern of investment over the period 1951–59 and its effects on output, which are summarized in Table IV. In the distribution of investment by sector, the South has a higher than average proportion in overhead facilities (34 per cent

6. Presidenza del Consiglio dei Ministri, *Documenti sulla Programma di Sviluppo Economico* (2d ed., Rome, 1957), and P. Saraceno, "Linee di Sviluppo dell'Economia Italiana e Ruolo dell'Agricoltura e della Bonifica," to be published in *Proceedings of the Naples Conference on La Bonifica nello Sviluppo del Mezzogiorno*, May 1961.

7. This was one of the main conclusions of the analysis of development prospects by the U.S. government in 1952 (see H. B. Chenery, P. G. Clark and V. Cao Pinna, *The Structure and Growth of the Italian Economy*, U. S. Mutual Security Agency, Special Mission to Italy for Economic Cooperation, Rome, 1953) and of the Vanoni Plan in 1954 (see *Documenti sulla Programma di Sviluppo Economico, op. cit.*).

8. Presidenza del Consiglio dei Ministri, *Riconsiderazione dello Schema Vanoni nel Quinto Anno dalla sua Presentazione*, Rapporto del Presidente del Comitato per lo Sviluppo dell'Occupazione e del Reddito (Rome, 1960).

9. The mechanism by which expenditure in the South is translated into production and income in both North and South is analyzed in detail by F. Pilloton, *Effetti Moltiplicativi degli Investimenti della Cassa per il Mezzogiorno* (Rome: Giuffrè 1960).

TABLE IV

GROSS FIXED INVESTMENT AND INCREASES IN OUTPUT (1951–59)[1]

	Commodity Production		Overhead Facilities				
	Agriculture 1	Industry 2	Transportation and Trade 3	Public Works 4	Housing 5	Other 6	Total 7
			a) *Gross Fixed Investment* (In billions of lire)				
North	534	3,653	1,425	446	2,319	553	8,929
Center	1,248	2,745	1,362	830	2,709	572	9,467
South	1,284	1,242	1,026	988	1,041	310	5,891
Italy	3,065	7,640	3,813	2,264	6,069	1,435	24,286
			b) *Percentage of Total Investment by Regions*				
North	5.97	40.91	15.96	4.99	25.97	6.20	100.00
Center	13.18	29.00	14.38	8.77	28.62	6.05	100.00
South	21.80	21.08	17.42	16.77	17.67	5.26	100.00
Italy	12.62	31.46	15.70	9.32	24.99	5.91	100.00
			c) *Ratio of Increase in Value Added to Gross Fixed Investment*				
North	.233	.340			.141		.228
Center	.319	.314			.150		.220
South	.176	.241			.139		.169
Italy	.244	.315			.144		.211
Ratio of South to Italy	0.722	0.765			0.964		0.801

1. Source: ISTAT, *Primi Studi sui Conti Economici Territoriali, op. cit.*

vs. 25 per cent). In large measure, this difference stems from the lack of transportation, communications, and other public facilities in the South and the need to improve them before commodity production can be increased. Within the sectors of commodity production, a much higher proportion goes to agriculture and a lower proportion to industry in the South than in the rest of the country. The increase in value added per unit of investment is significantly lower in the South, both in agriculture and in industry. The average profitability of this investment was probably lower as well, since differences in wage rates can hardly have made up for the substantial difference in value added.[1]

All three of these factors — the large share of overhead facilities, the lower proportion of industry, and the lower return on investment in both agriculture and industry — combine to give a lower increase in output per unit of investment in the South than in the rest of Italy. The marginal capital-output ratio for this period (measured as gross investment/increase in gross product) is about 6 for the Southern economy as a whole and 4.8 for commodity production, both of which are high in comparison with most other underdeveloped countries.

Regional Development Policy

It is in the field of policy rather than in its economic structure that Southern Italy differs most significantly from the typical underdeveloped country. In principle, the objective of raising regional income as rapidly as possible is common to both. In Southern Italy, however, this objective must be reconciled with the interests of the rest of the country, and the instruments by which it is pursued are therefore limited by the type of policy chosen for the nation as a whole. The result is quite a different approach to development from that which is currently popular in Asia and Latin America.

The principal postwar objective of government policy in the South, stated most clearly in the Vanoni Plan,[2] has been to reduce the difference in consumption and income levels between the South and the rest of the country. The Cassa per il Mezzogiorno was set up for this purpose in 1950.[3] At that time, it was assumed

1. The social profitability of the investment in the South was not necessarily lower, particularly in the field of industry, because there was probably a substantial difference between the opportunity cost of labor and its wage rate in the South and little or none in the North.

2. *Documenti sulla Programma di Sviluppo Economico, op. cit.*

3. The Cassa was strongly supported by the U.S. Government at its inception, and half of its financing in its first two years came from the counter-

that substantial progress could be made toward this objective within a period of ten years, and this assumption was incorporated in the projections of regional income that were made for the Vanoni Plan in 1954. These showed income in the South increasing by 8 per cent over the period 1954–64 as compared with 4 per cent in the Center and North and 5 per cent for the country as a whole.

As the years have passed without any gain in the growth rate of the South over the rest of the country, official statements on development policy have tended to shift this goal to an indefinite time in the future and to stress the establishment of a self-sustaining process of growth as the main objective.[4] The integration of the South into the national economy remains the ultimate goal, however, and this implies that income levels cannot be allowed to get too far out of line between the two regions.

The means by which the goal of Southern development is pursued are limited by the general principles guiding national economic policy. Italy's notable economic success over the past fifteen years has been based on orthodox economic policies of fiscal restraint, price stability, and the freeing of trade in accord with other members of the O.E.E.C. and the Common Market. These national policies imply the lessening of protection and reliance on subsidies and tax incentives in sectors where it is desired to promote production and investment. The most common instrument of development policy, the protection of local industry, has therefore not been used in the South. The alternative (and theoretically more desirable) means of stimulating industry have not been applied very vigorously, however.

One reason for not actively promoting industry in the South has been the difficulty for private entrepreneurs in setting up new plants to compete with the established firms in the North. The initial program of the Cassa per il Mezzogiorno made no provision for industrial investment, and measures to promote industry are still limited to tax incentives and loans at low interest rates.[5] The

part funds generated by U.S. aid (see Chenery, Clark, and Cao Pinna, *op. cit.*, p. 97).

4. See Pescatore, *op. cit.* and Saraceno "Dopo un Decennio di Intervento nel Mezzogiornia." *op. cit.*, for example.

5. In 1953 special regional institutions (IRFIS, CIS and ISVEIMER) were set up to provide industrial credit at favorable terms to industry in Sicily, Sardenia, and the rest of the South respectively. These and other measures to favor industrial development are summarized in Associazione per lo Svilluppo dell'Industria nel Mezzogiornia (SVIMEZ), *Measures to Promote Industrialization in Southern Italy* (Rome, 1954) and Wellisz, *op. cit.*

principal exception to this general policy has been the provision that the state-owned industrial holding companies (I.R.I. and E. N. I.) should make 40 per cent of their total industrial investments in the South.[6]

These factors have combined to produce a regional development policy that is devoted primarily to improving the economic environment. Over the past ten years the principal expenditures under the Cassa per il Mezzogiorno have been as follows (in billions of lire): [7]

Land reclamation	305	(31.6%)
Land reform	280	(29.0%)
Water supply and sewage disposal	127	(13.1%)
Roads	118	(12.2%)
Railways and shipping	72	(7.5%)
Mountain basins	42	(4.3%)
Tourism	22	(2.3%)
Total	966	billion
	($1,516	million)

It is estimated that only about 25 per cent of these expenditures has a direct effect on commodity production.[8] The remainder will have an indirect impact over an extended period.

As shown in Table IV, this program has been successful in reducing somewhat the gap in public facilities between the South and the rest of the country. The distribution of these facilities within the South has, however, been guided to a large extent by the political necessity of providing some immediate improvement in public services in all areas. The further contribution which overhead facilities make to increasing output must be judged by the increase in commodity production that has taken place in the South and will take place in the next decade.

Although the Cassa per il Mezzogiorno administers the bulk of the government's programs for Southern development, its policy-making functions are limited to the sectors of the economy covered by its appropriations. The general scope of Southern development policy is established by an interministerial committee (the Comitato dei Ministri per il Mezzogiorno). Since there is no over-all program for Southern development, the committee tends to formulate policy on an *ad hoc* basis without being able to judge the total impact of

6. According to Law No. 634, July, 1959.

7. Summarized in Pescatore, *op. cit.*, p. 23 through Dec. 1960 and given in detail in Cassa per Opere Straordinarie di Publico Interesse nell'Italia Meridionale (Cassa per il Mezzogiorno), *Bilancio 1959–60* (Rome, 1961).

8. G. M. Di Simone, "Sviluppo Economico del Mezzogiorno e Sviluppo Economico Italiano," *L'Industria,* No. 3, 1960.

various measures on the regional economy.[9] This procedure may partially explain the very high proportion of government expenditures that is devoted to public works and welfare expenditures in comparison with the development programs of other underdeveloped countries. Few countries having active development policies place such heavy reliance on the market mechanism to bring about the changes in the economic structure that are needed to promote growth.

In summary, the past decade has been characterized by a substantial transfer of resources to Southern Italy, devoted very largely to making up the deficit in public facilities of all sorts and to increasing private consumption. It had been hoped that the increase in local demand resulting from these expenditures would lead to the development of local industry without the need for more direct intervention. At the end of the decade, this policy had not yet produced much change in the structure of the Southern economy, and there has recently been a tendency to use more direct measures to promote industrialization.

II. A Model of Regional Development

One of the lessons of the past decade is that the development policies followed have so far proved to be inconsistent with the objective of reducing the regional gap in income. The principal reason for this result has been the failure to take account of the development of the rest of the economy in planning for Southern Italy. The relation between the two can best be established by means of a simple model of regional growth.

The first requirement of a regional model is to show the way in which an increase in national income is translated into increases in production in each region. Once this structural pattern has been established, actual and potential government policies can be analyzed in terms of the changes that they bring about in the existing structure of supply and demand.

Design of a Regional Policy Model

The discussion of Section I shows that it is more realistic to regard regional development policy in Italy as a modification of national policy than as an effort to maximize the growth of Southern Italy. In this respect, the model to be suggested is basically dif-

9. The need for a more comprehensive program to guide the Cassa has recently been stressed by its director. See Pescatore, *op. cit.*

ferent from that which I used in 1954 to investigate the optimum allocation of resources in Southern Italy.[1] The earlier study determined the pattern of investment and production that would lead to a given growth in Southern income with a minimum of investment from the North, but it did not take account of the difficulty of changing existing supply patterns. The present model focuses on the stability of established supply patterns rather than on the availability of investment resources as being the main limit to growth. The results of the previous analysis will, however, be used to give an indication of the different investment patterns that might result from different policies.

Existing and potential regional development policies are reflected in the model in the following ways:

(i) in the total growth of national income in Italy and its effects on commodity demand in each region;

(ii) in the transfer of resources from the rest of Italy to the South to increase consumption or investment;

(iii) in increases in the production of specific commodities in the South resulting from investment incentives or direct government investment;

(iv) in the rate of migration from Southern Italy to the rest of the country and abroad.

These elements will be described by "policy variables." The latter are chosen to reflect the main alternatives available to the government, such as migration versus increased local production, even though a phenomenon such as migration is susceptible to only limited and indirect government influence. Although the concept of a policy variable is less specific than the "instrument variable" used by Tinbergen,[2] which the government is supposed to control directly, the policy variable performs a similar function in the model, that of specifying a given government action. The value given to the policy variable may be the predicted outcome of a laissez-faire policy (e.g., the emigration rate), or the result of specific intervention by the government (e.g., state investment in steel production in the South).

The form of the structural relations to be assumed is limited by the data available in the ISTAT breakdown of production and in-

1. H. Chenery, "The Role of Industrialization in Development Programs," *American Economic Review, Papers and Proceedings,* XLV (May 1955).

2. J. Tinbergen, *Economic Policy: Principles and Design* (Amsterdam: North Holland Publishing Co., 1956).

come by region.[3] Commodity supply can be divided among the three regions, but demand can be calculated only for the country as a whole. The extent to which demand is localized must be estimated mainly from the nature of the commodity, and sectors will be assumed to have either a regional or a national market. The more realistic assumption of varying proportions of the two is ruled out by lack of data. Since differences in the rate of growth of total demand in the three regions have not been large, however, this simplification is not very important to the analysis of regional growth over the past decade.

In analyzing past developments, the values of the policy variables are given. The equations comprising the model show how they have determined the growth of income in each region. In analyzing future possibilities, alternative values for the policy variables, representing different directions of policy, will be assumed.

Formal Statement of the Model

The regional model determines levels of output in twenty sectors and three regions of Italy, but its form is quite general. Sectors 1–12 have national markets; the others are regional. The following variables will be used in the analysis (the subscripts i and R denote commodity and region;[4] the superscript t denotes time):

X_i Total national production in sector i ($i = 1 \ldots\ldots\ldots 20$).
X_{iR} Production of commodity i in region R ($R = N, C. S$).
M_i Imports of commodity i from abroad.
Z_i Total supply of commodity i in the nation (sectors 1–12).
Z_{iR} Total supply of commodity i in region R (sectors 13–20).
D_i Domestic final demand for commodity i in the nation.
E_i Exports of commodity i.
W_i Intermediate demand for commodity i in the nation.
V_{iR} Value added in sector i in region R.
V_R Total value added in region R (gross regional product).
Y_R Total regional resources (gross regional product plus transfers).
T_R Net transfer of resources to region R (excess of regional imports over regional exports).
V Total value added in the nation (approximately gross national product).

For the regional analysis, gross national product (V), (na-

3. *Primi Studi sui Conti Economici Territoriali, op. cit.*

4. The regions are designated North (N), Center (C), South (S), and are defined in footnote 8, p. 518.

tional) exports (E_i) and regional transfers (T_r) are taken as given. For convenience, I assume a constant growth rate in GNP and exports, so that their values in any year can be expressed as a function of their initial values and their rates of growth:

Gross national product

(1) $$V^t = (1+g)^t V^o$$

where g is the annual growth in GNP.

Exports of commodity i

(2) $$E^t_i = (1+e_i)^t E^o_i$$

where e_i is the annual growth in exports of i.

The structural relations and equilibrium conditions comprising the model are as follows:

Total demand and supply for commodity i (national sectors)

(3) $$Z_i = D_i + W_i + E_i = X_{iN} + X_{iC} + X_{iS} + M_i \qquad (i = 1 \ldots\ldots 12).$$

Total demand and supply for commodity i (regional sectors)

(4) $$Z_{iR} = D_{iR} + W_{iR} = X_{iR} \qquad (i = 13 \ldots\ldots 20).$$

Regional production of commodity i (national sectors)

(5) $$X^t_{iR} = s^o_{iR}\, Z^t_i + \Delta s^t_{iR}\, Z^t_i,$$

or

(5a) $$\Delta X^t_{iR} = X^t_{iR} - X^o_{iR} = s^o_{iR}\, \Delta Z^t_i + \Delta s^t_{iR}\, Z^t_i \qquad (i = 1 \ldots\ldots\ldots 12),$$

where s^t_{iR} is the supply coefficient[5] (fraction of total supply of commodity i that is furnished by region R in period t) and Δs^t_{iR} is the change in this fraction from time o to time t. The change in the supply coefficient will be treated as a policy variable. This procedure implies that growth in regional output proportional to total demand ($s^o_{iR}\, \Delta Z^t_i$) is the normal pattern and that policy is concerned with changes in this pattern. (There is no implication that changes in the supply pattern result only from deliberate policy, however).

Domestic demand (national sectors)

(6a) $$D^t_i = D^o_i \left(\frac{V^t}{V^o}\right)^{\eta_i} \qquad (i = 1 \ldots\ldots 12).$$

(6b) $$W^t_i = \sum_j a_{ij} X^t_j \qquad (i = 1 \ldots\ldots 12).$$

The first of these equations assumes for each commodity i a constant average income elasticity (γ_i) of total final demand (private con-

5. An alternative definition that would be equally plausible in some sectors would take the supply coefficient as the share of *national* supply, which would not be affected by a change in import proportions. The concept chosen has some significance in the analysis of agriculture, in which the share of imports has increased in Italy, but it makes little difference in other sectors.

sumption, government consumption, and investment).[6] The second, for intermediate demand, is the standard form of input-output equation in which the input coefficient, a_{ij}, measures the amount of commodity i required per unit of output of j. In the absence of inter-industry estimates in Italy for the whole period, it will be necessary to use a cruder estimate of intermediate demand. I shall therefore assume a constant income elasticity for total demand as a first approximation and shall replace equations (6a) and 6b) by:

$$(6) \qquad (D^t_i + W^t_i) = (D^o_i + W^o_i)\left(\frac{V^t}{V^o}\right)^{\eta_i},$$

where η_i is the average income elasticity of total demand in sector i. So long as the weights of the different demand components do not change greatly, the average income elasticity (which is a weighted average of the income elasticities γ_i of all sectors using the commodity) will be reasonably constant.

Domestic demand (local sectors)

$$(7) \qquad (D^t_{iR} + W^t_{iR}) = (D^o_{ir} + W^o_{iR})\left(\frac{Y^t_R}{Y^o_R}\right)^{\eta_{iR}},$$

where the total regional resources Y_R replaces the gross national product as the explanatory variable.

Sector value added

$$(8) \qquad V_{iR} = v_{iR}\, X_{iR},$$

where v_{iR} will be assumed constant among regions in all sectors except agriculture in the Italian application of the model.

Regional value added

$$(9) \qquad V_R = \Sigma\, V_{iR}.$$

Total regional resources

$$(10) \qquad Y_R = V_R + T_R,$$

where T_R, the net resource transfer to region R, is a policy variable.

These ten equations comprise a policy-oriented version of the type of regional input-output model used by Leontief and others to explain regional production levels in different sectors.[7] The model serves to allocate a given growth in gross national product among sectors and regions according to the value of the parameters e_i, η_i, η_{iR}, s^o_{iR} and s^t_{iR} and the regional transfers, T_R. Alternatively, targets can be set for the relative growth of GNP by region and solutions made for feasible values of the policy variables. This approach is followed in Section IV.

6. No allowance is made for changes in the rate of population growth, so that total income can be used in place of per capita income.

7. See Chenery, Clark, and Cao Pinna, *op. cit.*, Chap. 12.

The simplicity of this regional model derives from the fact that it omits the analysis of factor use and of changes in prices. The increase in regional income is measured in constant prices, which precludes any effect of changes in the terms of trade between regions.

III. The Pattern of Regional Growth

This model will now be applied to the Italian economy for the period 1951–59 to determine its usefulness in explaining past regional growth and hence in judging future policy. The basic assumption of the model is that regional supply patterns change very slowly in the absence of deliberate measures to alter them. To test the validity of this assumption, it will be useful to maintain the division of Italy into the three regions that are given in the ISTAT study even though my primary concern is with Southern Italy.

The analysis is based on data for the three regions and twenty sectors of the Italian economy in the years 1951 and 1959. After a study of the values of the variables and the supply patterns in the intervening years, I decided that estimates based on the terminal years only would be sufficiently accurate.[8] The results of the analysis are aggregated into nine sectors in the present paper. The values of the parameters pertaining to the South and the national economy are shown in Table V.[9]

Equation (5a) breaks down the growth in sector output into two parts. The first term, $s^o_{iR}\Delta Z_i$, may be called the *demand effect*, since it assumes no change in the regional supply coefficients; output in each sector is therefore assumed to increase at the same rate in all regions. The second term, $\Delta s_{iR} Z^t_i$, measures the change in regional output at a constant level of total demand due to the change in the regional supply coefficient. It will therefore be called the *supply effect*.[1]

8. This assumption was tested further by breaking the period into two parts, 1951–56 and 1956–59, but the breakdown added little to the one-period analysis and was subsequently dropped.

9. An appendix to this paper, giving the data and calculations for twenty sectors and all three regions, is available on request to the Secretary, Research Center in Economic Growth, Stanford University, Stanford, California. The more complete analysis is published in Italian (H. B. Chenery, "Politiche di Sviluppo per l'Italia Meridionale," Giuffrè, Rome, 1962).

1. In "The Role of Industrialization in Development Programs," *op. cit.*, I defined "import substitution" for a national economy in a similar way. "Import substitution" refers to the change in the fraction of the local market that is supplied from regional sources; the "supply effect" measures the change in the share of the national market. It thus includes increased exports as well

TABLE V

SELECTED PARAMETERS FOR THE SOUTH AND ITALY[1]

Sector	Export Growth e_i %	Demand Elasticities η_i	η_{is}	Southern Supply Coefficients 1951 s^{51}_{is}	1959 s^{59}_{is}	Change Δs_{is}
National Sectors						
1. Agriculture	7.1	.67		.309	.284	−.025
2. Mining	1.5	2.00		.155	.152	−.003
3. Food and tobacco	4.1	1.05		.319	.294	−.025
4. Textiles	3.2	.37		.026	.023	−.003
5. Clothing and leather	17.7	.99		.198	.193	−.005
6. Wood products	3.4			.194	.191	−.003
7. Metals	16.8	1.89		.049	.055	+.006
8. Metal products	12.8	1.68		.062	.074	+.012
9. Nonmetallic Mineral products	7.2	1.90		.115	.132	+.017
10. Chemicals, rubber, petroleum refining	12.4	1.98		.079	.070	−.009
11. Paper		1.70		.068	.074	+.006
12. Other manufactures	9.6	2.16		.052	.043	−.009
Regional Sectors						
13. Construction			2.09	.241	.223	
14. Electricity, gas, water			1.41	.183	.214	
15. Transportation			.96	.252	.251	
16. Trade			.84	.207	.203	
17–19. Other services			.26	.221	.214	
20. Public administration			.71	.313	.321	

1. Estimated from *Primi Studi sui Conti Economici Territoriali*, *op. cit.*

The Effects of Demand on Regional Growth

Since the usefulness of this regional model depends on supply coefficients being relatively stable, I shall first compare the rates of regional growth that would be predicted from the observed growth

as reduced imports. A similar distinction is made by H. Perloff, E. Dunn, F. Lampard, and R. Muth in *Regions, Resources, and Economic Growth* (Baltimore: The Johns Hopkins Press, 1960), p. 71, in analyzing shifts in regional employment. Their "net differential shift in employment" corresponds to my supply effect, while their "proportionality shift" is the difference between my total demand effect and proportional regional growth. They do not utilize these concepts in the framework of a specific regional model, however.

of sector demand alone, with no change in the supply pattern, with the actual rates. This is done in Table VI.

TABLE VI

PREDICTED AND ACTUAL REGIONAL GROWTH RATES, 1951–1959
(In percentages)

	North	Center	South	ITALY
Predicted Growth Rates with No Supply Effects				
1. National sectors[1]	6.6	5.9	5.1 (4.95)[3]	
2. Total output[2]	6.1	5.5	5.0 (4.9)[3]	
Actual Growth Rates				
3. National sectors	6.3	6.6	4.3	5.9
4. Total output	5.8	5.8	4.6	5.5
Differences from National Growth of Total Output				
5. Predicted[4]	+0.6	0	−0.5 (−0.6)[3]	
6. Actual[5]	+0.3	+0.3	−0.9	

1. Predicted output in national sectors derived from demand effects in Table V.
2. Predicted total output is based on average relations of local to national sectors except in the South, where allowance is made for the increase in the income transfer.
3. Predicted values if agriculture is treated as a local sector.
4. Differences between values in line 2 and 5.5 per cent.
5. Differences between values in line 4 and 5.5 per cent.

The "demand prediction" is that total output in the South will grow at 89 per cent of the national average (4.9 per cent) whereas the actual rate was 83 per cent of the national average (4.6 per cent). (Since constant income elasticities are assumed, the actual rate of growth is irrelevant to this prediction, which would be the same proportion of any national rate.) For the North the demand prediction is also too optimistic, whereas for the Center it is overly pessimistic. Over half of the total variation in the regional rates from the national average is explained by the change in demand and the existing supply pattern, however, and for the South in particular the demand prediction provides a useful point of departure.

The reason why the South lags behind the North and Center on the basis of demand factors alone is readily seen from Tables VII and VIII. The South provides only 9 per cent of the national supply of manufactured goods (apart from food) and 16 per cent of the supply of minerals. These are the only sectors in which the elasticity of total demand is substantially greater than 1. Conversely, the weight of agriculture, for which the elasticity of total demand has been .70 in the past decade, is much higher in the South than in the rest of the country. For the national sectors, the ratio of "normal" Southern growth to national growth of .87 can be interpreted as a weighted average of the demand elasticities in the South in sectors 1–12 compared with the national average for the same sectors. Since the same elasticities are used, the difference is entirely due to the difference in weights. The income transfer to the South, which affects only the local sectors in this model, raises the "normal" (i.e., the relative growth rate without change in the supply pattern) somewhat, but not enough to offset the existing supply structure.

Effects of Supply Changes on Regional Growth

The way in which supply effects modify this basic pattern is shown in Table VII. For Italy as a whole, the supply effects can be interpreted as the change in the proportion of imports in the total supply of each commodity. This proportion has increased for agriculture and consumer goods and diminished for minerals and basic industrial goods, with a net rise of less than 0.8 per cent for all the national sectors. The rising ratio of imports to GNP (from .125 to .148) therefore represents primarily a demand effect rather than a change in import proportions of individual commodities. The most significant increase is in agriculture, in which imports have risen from 11.5 per cent to 12.9 per cent of total supply.

The principal result of changes in the regional supply pattern has been to increase the share of the Center in both primary production and manufacturing. In primary production, the gain of the Center has been at the expense of the South, while in manufacturing it has been at the expense of the North. In the latter case, it is only the producer goods industries that are becoming more evenly distributed, with the share of the North dropping from 62 to 59.5 per cent and the other two regions making gains in proportion to their initial shares. In the consumer goods industries (including food) there has been on balance almost no change in the supply pattern, with a slight fall in the share of the South and a rise in imports.

As a result of these supply changes, it is the Center rather than the South that has achieved the objective of closing the gap in the growth rate between itself and the traditional industrial area of the North. Some of the main elements in this process have been the discovery of natural gas in the Po valley, the development of a petrochemical industry in the Center, and the decentralization of the metal-working industries. Since population has increased some-

TABLE VII

CAUSES OF INCREASE IN REGIONAL OUTPUT, 1951–1959[1]

(In billions of lire)

Sectors	NORTH			CENTER			SOUTH			ITALY		
	Demand Effect	Supply Effect	Total	Demand Effect	Supply Effect	Total	Demand Effect	Supply Effect	Total	Demand Effect	Supply Effect	Total
I. Primary Production												
1. Agriculture	155	−31	124	323	74	397	327	−101	226	805	−58	747
2. Mining	19	22	41	44	47	91	41	− 1	40	104	68	172
Subtotal	174	−9	165	367	121	488	368	−102	266	909	10	919
II. Manufacturing[2]												
3. Food	114	22	136	97	−4	93	106	− 23	83	317	− 5	312
4, 5, 6, 12. Other consumer goods	230	−32	198	150	7	157	45	− 6	39	425	−31	394
7–11. Producer goods	930	−61	869	478	47	525	121	16	137	1,529	2	1,531
Subtotal	1,274	−71	1,203	725	50	775	272	− 13	259	2,271	−34	2,237
III. Local Sectors												
13. Construction	230	0	230	231	0	231	125	0	125	586	0	586
10–15. Utilities	135	0	135	216	0	216	119	0	119	470	0	470
16–19. Service	234	0	234	224	0	224	106	0	106	564	0	564
20. Government	71	0	71	152	0	152	119	0	119	342	0	342
Subtotal	670	0	670	823	0	823	469	0	469	1,962	0	1,962
Total	2,118	−80	2,038	1,915	171	2,086	1,109	−115	994	5,142	−24	5,118

1. Derived from equation (5a) applied to data for 20 sectors.
2. Other consumer goods include textiles, clothing, wood products, "other"; producer goods include metals, metal products, nonmetallic mineral products, chemicals and petroleum refining, and paper.

what less rapidly in the Center than in the other two regions, the gain in per capita income is even higher here than in the North.

In the South, the supply effects shown in Tables V and VII were exactly the opposite of the pattern of development that the Cassa was expected to induce. Ten years after the start of the regional development program, the production of agricultural products and consumer goods has not kept up with the growth of either regional or national demand.[2] Without exception, the supply effects in these sectors are negative, and together they account for the difference between the demand prediction and the actual rate of growth of total income. It is only in the field of producer goods, for which the market is a national one, that the growth rate in the South has more than kept up with the national average. Since this group of industries starts from a small base, their contribution to the growth of regional income in this period is relatively small, but it promises to increase in the future. Even though in consumer goods production, local demand is more important, plants are typically smaller, and entry is generally easier, these sectors have not responded adequately to the rise in local demand and the fiscal concessions made by the government. Therefore the policy of induced development by means of demand increases cannot yet be counted a success.

Effects of Other Factors

Several factors that are omitted from the regional model must be added in order to round out the picture of regional income growth. As shown in Table II the rate of population increase has been nearly equal in all regions, and therefor there is little difference between relative rates of growth by region and relative rates of per capita growth. A second omitted factor, changes in the "terms of trade" among regions, has also been relatively small in this period.[3] Productivity rises have been more rapid in industry than in agriculture, but this difference has been offset to some extent by the greater price rise in agriculture.

In one respect, the evaluation of the development of the South in terms of current output has a substantial downward bias. Since

2. In analyzing the period 1951–59 in the South, it makes little difference whether sectors are assumed to be regional or national because the regional growth in total demand is about the same as the national growth, due to the increase in transfers.

3. Saraceno, "Linee di Sviluppo dell'Economia Italiana e Ruolo dell'-Agricoltura e della Bonifica," *op. cit.*, and C. Segrè, *Produttivitá e Prezzi nel Processo di Sviluppo — L'Esperienza Italiana 1950–1957*. SVIMEZ (Rome: Giuffrè, 1959).

many of the overhead investments require a long period before they become fully productive, the presently unused capacity in these facilities should be given a value. A start has been made toward providing the housing and public services needed to move the population away from the overcrowded hilltop towns to which they were once driven by the prevalence of malaria in the lowlands. A much better base for future agricultural and industrial development therefore existed in the South by 1960 than in 1950.

IV. Implications For Development Policy

The experience of Southern Italy in the past decade shows the seriousness of the obstacles that must be overcome to change the economic structure of a country or region. Despite the large transfer of resources to the region, the investment in overhead facilities, the rapid growth of consumption and investment, the considerable incentives given to private investors, and substantial use of Northern technicians, the composition of output has changed relatively little since 1950. If the large income transfer were to be cut off next year, it is probable that the South would revert to a considerably lower growth rate than its present 4 per cent because of the limited demand for the commodities which it produces. Whatever judgment may be passed on the program of the Cassa per il Mezzogiorno when more complete information becomes available, it is clear that in its first decade it has not really come to grips with one of the most basic Southern economic problems: the concentration of production in sectors that do not offer the possibility of rapid growth.

As Saraceno has recently pointed out,[4] the main objective of development policy in the South should be to achieve an economic structure capable of sustained growth rather than a particular ratio between the growth rate in the South and in the North. The first requirement of a viable economic structure in Southern Italy is that the normal increase in export demand plus internal demand should generate a satisfactory rate of growth in production and income without excessive reliance on income transfers. The growth rate that is considered "satisfactory" cannot be much lower than that in the rest of the country, however, if it can be shown that parity can be achieved with a different allocation of given resources. The present economic structure is deficient in this respect because if an income growth of say 5 per cent per year is initiated (by whatever means), the growth of regional exports will be inadequate to cover

4. Saraceno, "Dopo un Decennio di Intervento nel Mezzogiorno," *op. cit.*

the growth of demand for commodities that are now imported, and the growth in total expenditure can only be sustained by continued external financing of a large import surplus.

To judge from official statements on the subject, the magnitude of the structural changes required to produce self-sustaining growth in the South has not been appreciated by the government. The extent of those changes and the direction that future policy should take can be ascertained only from a comprehensive analysis of the economic structure. Aggregate projections of the type used in the Vanoni Plan tend to conceal some of the difficulties involved and do not provide an adequate guide to the execution of policy.

A second requirement of a viable economy is that local savings plus "normal" income transfers should cover investment needs. Although it is impossible to estimate the level of local savings that would be forthcoming with a smaller import surplus in relation to regional income, this requirement seems to be easier to meet in Southern Italy than the structural problem. The following analysis therefore concentrates on the need for structural change.

The Principal Lines of Policy

There are three principal policies of structural change to be considered, which may for simplicity be identified as:

(1) agricultural development,
(2) industrial development,
(3) increased emigration.

Although the best development policy probably consists of a combination of all three, it is useful to consider them first in isolation.

In terms of the model presented in Section II, these policies of structural change may be defined as follows:

(1) Growth of agricultural production in an amount and composition that will permit the South to supply a larger share of total Italian internal and external demand.

(2) Growth of industrial production sufficient to permit the South to supply a larger fraction of the total Italian market (which in most sectors implies supplying a larger proportion of the regional market also).

(3) Increasing emigration in an amount sufficient to make up for any shortfall in the growth of production.

Although other possible development policies might be advanced, such as price support for Southern agriculture, they are of a palliative nature and conflict with the national policy of freer trade and economic integration with the rest of Europe.

The policy of the past decade was primarily one of agricultural development, with increasing attention to industrial development by the end of the decade. The analysis in Section III showed that the results fell short of maintaining the 1951 share of the South in the national output of both agriculture and industry. One way to indicate the magnitude of the problem is to calculate how much additional output (or reduced population) would have been required under each policy to achieve a growth rate of per capita output in the South equal to the national average.

Under policies (1) and (2), this objective would have required an additional value added of 260 billion lire in the South in 1959. In each case it may be assumed that 45 per cent will be produced in local sectors, as indicated by the elasticity of demand for their products (Table V). Under policy (1), the remaining 140 billion lire of value added is assumed to be produced in agriculture and food processing, while under policy (2) it would be produced in the remaining sectors of manufacturing industry. The results of successfully carrying out these policies in the period 1951–59 would have been as follows, compared with the actual results:

		Actual		Required	
		Growth Rate	Δs	Growth Rate	Δs
Policy (1)	Growth of agriculture	2.9%	−.025	4.0%	0
	Growth of food processing	4.7%	−.025	6.5%	+.017
Policy (2)	Growth of other manufacturing	8.8%	+.005	13.5%	+.039

Adequate agricultural development would have required a growth rate of 4 per cent and maintenance of the Southern share in total agricultural supply. Adequate industrial growth would have involved an over-all growth rate of 13.5 per cent outside of food processing, and an increase of nearly 4 per cent in the share of Southern manufacturing in the national supply. Achieving equal growth in per capita output by means of emigration alone would have necessitated an increase in the rate of per capita growth of 3.6 per cent to the national average of 4.7 per cent. To achieve this result, population would have had to remain constant in the South, with a total emigration of 2,100,000 instead of the 750,000 recorded.[5]

Although it is unlikely that any one of these three results could have been achieved by itself within the existing institutional framework, a combination of the three would probably have been feasible

5. This calculation is based on the "resident" population in Table II, which underestimates the emigration that has taken place. On the basis of population physically present the total emigration would have to have been 2,500,000 instead of the observed 1,400,000.

within the resources available. It is more useful, however, to turn our attention to future development policies than to speculate on what might have been.

The Role of Industrialization in Future Policy

Since only demand limitations are taken into account in the present regional model, additional information on supply is needed to narrow down the range of policies to be considered. A recent study by Saraceno[6] gives some idea of the possibilities for future agricultural development in the South, taking into account the investments already made by the Cassa. A comprehensive study of energy demand and supply[7] also indicates some of the possibilities for mineral expansion.

If an economic limit is set to the growth of primary production, based on demand factors, natural resources and costs of production in the South, the main policy alternatives for achieving a given per capita income in the South are industrial development and emigration. Since the output of the local sectors is limited by the growth of local income, they cannot be considered as a separate alternative, but must be assumed to vary with the level of value added in sectors 1–12.

To indicate the rates of growth required of the industrial sectors under various assumptions, I shall repeat the analysis of Table VII for the period 1959–70, aggregating the regional model into five sectors. Greater detail would, of course, be needed in making an actual development program, but the more aggregated model is adequate to indicate the quantitative significance of different lines of policy.

The basic assumptions common to all the projections are:

(i) a national growth rate of GNP of 5 per cent per year (or of 4.2 per cent in per capita income) for 1959–70;

(ii) roughly the same patterns of demand increase in the next decade as in the past (as shown in the demand elasticities in Table VIII);

(iii) a target for regional growth in per capita income of 5 per cent per year.

(iv) increase in transfers to the South in proportion to the growth in income.

6. Saraceno, "Linee di Sviluppo dell'Economia Italiana e Ruolo dell'-Agricoltura e della Bonifica," *op. cit.*

7. V. Paretti, V. Cao Pinna, L. Cugia and C. Righi, *Struttura e Prospettive dell'Economia Energetica Italiana*, (Turin, 1960).

TABLE VIII

ALTERNATIVE REGIONAL PROJECTIONS FOR 1970

(In billions of lire)

		ITALY				SOUTHERN ITALY											
		Value Added					Program A[1]			Program B				Program C			
Sector	Income Elasticity	1959	Index	1970	Growth rate %	1959	s_S	V_S	Growth rate %	Δs_S	ΔV_S	V_S	Growth rate %	Δs_S	ΔV_S	V_S	Growth rate %
Primary Production																	
1. Agriculture		3250	1.31	4280	2.5	1120	.3	1470	2.5	.013	60	1530	2.9	.013	60	1530	2.9
2. Mining		250	2.28	580	7.8	70	.29	160	7.8	0		160	7.8	0		160	7.8
Total primary		3500	1.33	4860	3.0	1190	.34	1630	2.6	.012	60	1690	3.2	.012	60	1690	3.2
Manufacturing																	
3. Food processing	1.03	880	1.74	1530	5.2	270	.31	470	5.2	.013	20	490	5.6	.013	20	490	5.6
4–12. Other manufacturing	1.33	4160	2.04	8510	6.7	360	.09	740	6.7	.030	260	1000	9.8	.074	630	1370	13.0
Total manufacturing	1.29	5040	2.00	10040	6.5	630	.12	1210	6.1	.028	280	1490	8.1	.065	650	1860	10.4
Local Sectors																	
13–20.	.95	6090	1.665	10,120	4.7	1480		2230	3.8		230	2460	4.7		490	2720	5.7
TOTAL		14,630	1.71	25,020	5.0	3300		5070	4.0		570	5640	5.0		1200	6270	6.0
Migration rate[2]									−2.4%				−1.4%				−0.5%

1. Under Program A, the ratio of Southern production to national production in 1970 is the same as that in 1959 in all sectors ($\Delta s_s = 0$).
2. Based on resident population and the past rate of natural increase of 1.4 per cent.

The national growth rate assumed in GNP is lower than the 5.5 per cent of the past decade, but is still rather optimistic. The regional target for per capita income is 20 per cent above the national rate, but it falls short of the rate of 6 per cent that would be needed to stop the widening of the regional gap in per capita income by 1970.

The three Southern development programs illustrated in Table VIII are based on the following hypotheses as to technical possibilities and policy direction:

Program A represents a continuation of past policies and may be labeled a "demand projection." It assumes that output will be determined by the growth of demand and the existing productive structure, maintaining fixed supply coefficients.[8] (The forecast growth rate of 2.5 per cent in agriculture in both regions is somewhat more optimistic than Saraceno's estimate of 2.3 per cent).

Program B is intended to establish the minimum structural change that will suffice to produce a growth of 5 per cent in GNP over the period. It therefore makes an optimistic assumption as to the growth of Southern agriculture, which is assumed to be higher than that in the rest of the country. The growth of manufacturing and of local production are determined from the model, taking total growth as given.

Program C determines the minimum structural change ($\triangle s_S$) required to achieve the income objective with no increase in the emigration rate. The same assumptions about primary production are made as in Program B.

The growth of the South under Program A[9] lags more behind the national growth rate than has the actual development of the past decade because there is less projected increase in income transfers. The emigration rate required to achieve the target of per capita income growth is more than three times the present rate and would probably result in a very unfavorable population structure in the South, since people of working age constitute the bulk of the migrants. It would also reduce investment incentives in the South because of the lower growth rate.

Program B requires an increase of 2.8 per cent in the share of total industry located in the South, which would raise the growth

8. For simplicity, the supply coefficient is redefined as the ratio of output in the South to total output, thereby ignoring further changes in the proportion of imports.

9. This type of program is implied by Mrs. Lutz's (*op. cit.*) recommendations to develop the North instead of the South.

rate in sectors 4–12 to 9.8 per cent, slightly above its recent level. In Program C, on the other hand, the share of industry in the South must be increased by 6.5 per cent of the national total, which is equivalent to producing 25 per cent of the increase in industrial output in this region. Under the last assumption, the growth rate in sectors 4–12 would rise to 13 per cent and the supply effect would nearly equal the demand effect in causing the growth of industry.

To select the "best" development program requires an analysis of the social costs in both North and South and of the institutional implications of the alternatives being considered. In my previous analysis of development possibilities in Southern Italy,[1] I calculated the pattern of production that would lead to a 5 per cent growth in output with a minimum investment cost. On the assumptions of that study, the increase in output under the optimum program was divided between agriculture and industry in the ratio of 30:70. This is very close to the proportion that results from Program C, and in contrast with the 50:50 ratio that has characterized the past decade. Both analyses therefore support the idea that a much higher share of industry in the Southern development program would be consistent both with the demands of the country and the supply conditions in the South. This shift in emphasis seems to be essential if the South is going to become a viable economy without really massive emigration.

Conclusions

Southern Italy provides one of the first cases in which we can see the results of a deliberate policy of giving heavy emphasis to overhead facilities and relying on them to stimulate commodity production. Although the government's expectations as to the outcome of this program were never formulated in precise terms, it is clear that this approach to development has serious weaknesses when it is carried to such extremes as it has been in Southern Italy. In the first place, the capital required per unit of increase in regional output has proven to be very high, yielding a gross capital-output ratio of between 5 and 6 in comparison with the ratio of between 3 and 4 obtaining in the rest of Italy and the even lower values in most underdeveloped countries. Secondly, the high proportion invested in sectors in which there is a long interval before the investment reaches full utilization (agriculture and overhead facilities) means that domestic production and saving increase more slowly

1. "The Role of Industrialization in Development Programs," *op. cit.*

under this approach, and a greater reliance on outside assistance is necessary to maintain a given growth in income. Finally, the "overhead approach" either ignores the other structural changes that are needed in the rest of the economy or assumes that they will take place automatically. In Southern Italy the failure of the increase in local demand to stimulate import substitution is very clear in the first decade, although one may hope that it will begin to take place in the second. Since investment has been limited mainly to commodities that the South already produces, for which demand is growing slowly, there is considerable evidence that actual investment has fallen short of utilizing fully the available resources, which have therefore been invested elsewhere.

The drawbacks to the approach that has been followed in Southern Italy stem largely from the fact that the area is not an administrative unit and that there is no over-all plan for its development. An over-all plan would enable judgments to be made as to the comparative advantage of different types of production, based on the opportunity costs of labor, capital, and the available natural resources. To the extent that this analysis indicated the desirability of developing types of production that are not profitable at current market prices — as it almost certainly would in Southern Italy — an independent government would have a much wider choice of instruments (subsidies, tariffs, wage policy, devaluation, etc.) than does the region at present. Although there has been ample political support for increasing the total resource transfer to the South, there has been considerable resistance to developing the industries that would be rational for the South, which might increase competition with the established plants in the North. Because of this reluctance to plan realistically for the South, much of the overhead investment has gone for facilities that would not be of high priority in an integrated approach.

The central government is now challenged to provide some of these advantages within the framework of an integrated national economy. So far it has not devised a substitute for the protection of infant industries that is an effective stimulus to development, and the working of comparative advantage is further hindered by the national wage policy.[2] The channeling of investment resources into

2. The great importance of wage differentials and induced changes in supply patterns of low-wage industries in the recent development of the southeastern United States is shown in V. R. Fuchs, "The Determinants of the Redistribution of Manufacturing in the United States since 1929," *Review of Economics and Statistics,* XLIV (May 1962).

less productive uses has therefore offset to a considerable degree the large capital inflow from the rest of the country.

In more general terms, the experience of Southern Italy over the past decade shows that a change in the productive structure must be put on a par with an increase in total investment as an immediate objective of development policy. The development of overhead facilities is only one aspect of the total change that is needed.

PART V

A Guide to the Literature

A Guide to the Literature

The readings listed here are a selection. Just as this volume is, they are concerned more with the results of analysis than with the techniques by which these were obtained. The purpose of this bibliography is to lead the student to a comprehension and mastery of the diverse theories that contribute to an understanding of regional development processes. Though not any less important, writings on methodology as such have been excluded. They are expertly reviewed in a compendium by Walter Isard (5) which will serve regional scientists as a major reference work for years to come. In addition, there are brilliant review articles by John Meyer (7) on recent work in regional economics and Brian J. L. Berry (59) on geographers' contributions to the study of spatial systems. The annotated bibliography of central place studies by Berry and Pred (54) is a further indispensible reference. The categories used are of necessity arbitrary, and many selections might have been differently classified.

Starred items in the following list are included in the present volume.

I. REGIONAL SCIENCE AND PLANNING

Regional science is the awkward name under which scholars from many disciplines have rallied. The name itself was invented some ten years ago by Walter Isard, and the publications of the Regional Science Association as well as a number of books have become the principal source of technical material for scholars interested in the spatial aspects of human activities. Its unifying concern, as in the case of geography, is space as a variable determining human behavior, but its style is strongly analytical and abstract, including advanced forms of quantitative analysis. Regional planning, on the other hand, derives its basic orientation from regional science and is concerned with the normative ordering of activities in space. Since regional scientists might want to claim most of the writings in this bibliography as belonging to their own field, only key contributions have been included in this category, in particular those of Walter Isard (5, 6, 22).

1. Boudeville, J. R., "Frontiers and Interrelations of Regional Planning," paper given at *International Congress on Economic Development,* Vienna, August–September 1962.

*2. Friedmann, John R. P., "Regional Planning as a Field of Study," *Journal of the American Institute of Planners,* Vol. 29, No. 3 (August 1963), pp. 168–175.

3. Friedmann, John R. P., "Regional Planning in Post-Industrial Society," *Journal of the American Institute of Planners,* Vol. 30, No. 2 (May 1964), pp. 84–90.

4. Harris, Britton, "Plan or Projection: An Examination of the Use of Models in Planning," *Journal of the American Institute of Planners,* Vol. 26, No. 4 (November 1960), pp. 265–272.

5. Isard, Walter, *Methods of Regional Analysis: An Introduction to Regional Science,* New York, The Technology Press of the Massachusetts Institute of Technology and John Wiley & Sons, Inc., 1960.

6. Isard, Walter and John H. Cumberland, eds., *Regional Economic Planning: Techniques and Analysis for Less Developed Areas,* Paris, European Productivity Agency of the Organization for European Economic Cooperation, 1961.

7. Meyer, John R., "Regional Economics: A Survey," *American Economic Review,* Vol. 53, No. 1 (March 1963), pp. 19–54.

*8. Perroux, François, "Economic Space: Theory and Applications," *Quarterly Journal of Economics,* Vol. 64, No. 1 (February 1950), pp. 89–104.

II. LOCATION THEORY

Location analysis is one of the most fruitful approaches to the study of regional economic development. Economic concepts and techniques provide practical tools for the selection of project locations and the regional allocation of investments. Two approaches may be distinguished. Classical location theory primarily concerns the location decision of the firm. Other, generally later, work has dealt with location as a system of spatial relations. Both approaches are of concern to regional development planning: the first by providing a basis for individual project and program location; the second, by providing the analytical framework for a normative ordering of the space economy. In addition to the theoretical literature, there are a number of empirical studies of industrial location which supplement more abstract writings on the subject.

A. Theory of the Firm

*9. Alonso, William, "Classical Location Theory: a Summary," this volume.

10. Chinitz, Benjamin, "Contrasts in Agglomeration: New York and Pittsburgh," *Papers and Proceedings, American Economic Review,* Vol. 51, No. 2 (May 1961), pp. 279–289.

11. Friedrich, Carl Joachim, ed., *Alfred Weber's Theory of the Location of Industries,* Chicago, The University of Chicago Press, 1929.

12. Greenhut, Melvin L., *Plant Location in Theory and in Practice: The Economics of Space,* Chapel Hill, North Carolina University Press, 1956.

13. Hoover, Edgar M., *The Location of Economic Activity,* New York, McGraw-Hill Book Co., Inc., 1948.

B. LOCATION AS A SYSTEM OF SPATIAL RELATIONS

14. Alonso, William, *Location and Land Use,* Cambridge, Massachusetts, Harvard University Press, 1964.

15. Beckmann, Martin, "Some Reflections on Lösch's Theory of Location," *Papers and Proceedings of the Regional Science Association,* Vol. 1 (1955), pp. N1–N9.

16. Beckmann, Martin, and Thomas Marschak, "An Activity Analysis Approach to Location Theory," *Kyklos,* Vol. 8 (1955), pp. 125–143.

17. Böventer, Edwin von, "Die Struktur der Landschaft. Versuch einer Weiterentwicklung der Modells Johann Heinrich von Thünens, Walter Christallers, und August Löschs," *Schriften des Vereins für Sozialpolitik,* Neue Folge, Vol. 27 (1962), pp. 77–133.

18. Böventer, Edwin von, "Spatial Organization Theory as a Basis for Regional Planning," *Journal of the American Institute of Planners,* Vol. 30, No. 2 (May 1964), pp. 90–100.

19. Dunn, Edgar S., Jr., *The Location of Agricultural Production,* Gainsville, Florida, University of Florida Press, 1954.

20. Fox, Karl A., "A Spatial Equilibrium Model of the Livestock Feed Economy in the United States," *Econometrica* Vol. 21, No. 4 (October 1953), pp. 547–566.

21. Grotewold, Andreas, "Von Thunen in Retrospect," *Economic Geography,* Vol. 35 (October 1959), pp. 346–355.

22. Isard, Walter, *Location and Space Economy,* New York, The Technology Press of the Massachusetts Institute of Technology and John Wiley & Sons, Inc., 1956.

23. Koopmans, Tjalling C., and Martin Beckmann, "Assignment Problems and the Location of Economic Activities," *Econometrica,* Vol. 25, No. 1 (January 1957), pp. 53–76.

24. Lefeber, Louis, *Allocation in Space: Production, Transport, and Industrial Location,* Amsterdam, North-Holland Publishing Company, 1958.

25. Lösch, August, *The Economics of Location,* New Haven, Connecticut, Yale University Press, 1954.

*26. Lösch, August, "The Nature of Economic Regions," *Southern Economic Journal,* Vol. 5, No. 1 (July 1938), pp. 71–78.

27. Moses, Leon, "A General Equilibrium Model of Production, Interregional Trade, and Location of Industry," *Review of Economics and Statistics,* Vol. 42, No. 4 (November 1960), pp. 373–399.

28. Thünen, Johann Heinrich von, *Der isolierte Staat in Beziehung auf Landwirtschaft und Nationalökonomie.* Rostock, 1826. Summarized in Michael Chisholm, *Rural Settlement and Land Use: An Essay in Location,* London, Hutchinson University Library, 1962, Chapter 2.

C. Empirical Studies

29. Fuchs, Victor R., *Changes in the Location of Manufacturing in the United States Since 1929,* New Haven, London, Yale University Press, 1962.

30. Florence, P. Sargant, *Investment, Location, and Size of Plant,* Cambridge, Cambridge University Press, 1948.

31. McLaughlin, Glenn E., and Stefan Robock, *Why Industry Moves South: A Study of Factors Influencing the Recent Location of Manufacturing Plants in the South,* Washington, D. C., National Planning Association, 1949.

32. Prociuk, S. G., "The Territorial Pattern of Industrialization in the USSR: A Case Study in Location of Industry," *Soviet Studies,* Vol. 13 (July 1961), pp. 69–95.

33. Wallace, L. T., and Vernon W. Ruttan, "The Role of the Community as a Factor in Industrial Location," *Papers of the Regional Science Association,* Vol. 7 (1961), pp. 133–142.

34. Wonnacott, Ronald J., *Manufacturing Costs and the Comparative Advantage of United States Regions,* University of Minnesota, Upper Midwest Economic Study, Study Paper No. 9, April 1963.

III. MEASURES OF REGIONAL ECONOMIC CHANGE

Any discussion of regional economic development implies the existence of measures by which progress or retrogression can be objectively determined. This requirement has led a number of economists to explore the possibilities of regional income accounting. (41) The problem has been made more difficult by the fact that national income concepts do not apply directly and by the relative scarcity of appropriate data for local areas. It is still being explored from a variety of viewpoints, and no single method has prevailed. The situation is likely to remain in flux for as long as the main policy purposes for which regional accounting data will be used remain relatively uncrystalized.

35. Artle, Roland, *Studies in the Structure of the Stockholm Economy: Towards a Framework for Projecting Metropolitan Community Development,* Stockholm, Stockholm School of Economics, 1959.
36. Berman, Barbara R., Benjamin Chinitz, and Edgar M. Hoover, *Projection of a Metropolis: Technical Supplement to the New York Metropolitan Region Study,* Cambridge, Massachusetts, Harvard University Press, 1961.
37. Chipman, John S., *The Theory of Inter-sectoral Money Flows and Income Formation,* Baltimore, The Johns Hopkins Press, 1951.
38. Duncan, Otis D., Ray P. Cuzzort, and Beverly Duncan, *Statistical Geography: Problems in Analyzing Areal Data,* New York, The Free Press of Glencoe, 1961.
39. Hirsch, Werner Z., "Interindustry Relations of a Metropolitan Area," *Review of Economics and Statistics,* Vol. 41, No. 3 (August 1959), pp. 360–369.
40. Hirsch, Werner Z., "Design and Use of Regional Accounts," *Papers and Proceedings, American Economic Review,* Vol. 52, No. 2 (May 1962), pp. 365–373.
41. Hochwald, Werner, ed., *The Design of Regional Accounts,* Published for Resources for the Future, Inc., Baltimore, The Johns Hopkins Press, 1961.
*42. Hoover, Edgar M., and Benjamin Chinitz, "The Role of Accounts in the Economic Study of the Pittsburgh Metropolitan Region," in Werner Hochwald, ed., *Design of Regional Accounts,* Published for Resources for the Future, Inc., Baltimore, The Johns Hopkins Press, 1961, pp. 253–270.
*43. Krutilla, John V., "Criteria for Evaluating Regional Development Programs," *Papers and Proceedings, American Economic Review,* Vol. 45, No. 2 (May 1955), pp. 120–132.
44. Leontief, W. W., and A. Strout, *Multiregional Input-Output*

Analysis, Paper presented at the International Conference on Input-output Techniques, Geneva, September 1961.

45. Moore, F. T., "Regional Economic Reaction Paths," *Papers and Proceedings,* Vol. 45, No. 2 (May 1955), pp. 133–148.

46. *Regional Income,* Princeton, New Jersey, National Bureau of Economic Research Studies in Income and Wealth, Vol. 21 (1957). See especially "Problems of Assessing Regional Economic Progress" by Harvey S. Perloff, pp. 35–62.

47. Stevens, Benjamin H., "An Interregional Linear Programming Model," *Journal of Regional Science,* Vol. 1, No. 1 (Summer 1958), pp. 60–98.

48. Stone, Richard, "Social Accounts at the Regional Level: A Survey," in Walter Isard and John H. Cumberland, eds., *Regional Economic Planning: Techniques of Analysis for Less Developed Areas,* Paris, European Productivity Agency of the Organization for European Economic Cooperation, 1961.

49. Tiebout, Charles M., *The Community Economic Base Study,* New York, Committee for Economic Development, Supplementary Paper No. 16, December 1962.

IV. THE ROLE OF CITIES IN ECONOMIC DEVELOPMENT

A concern with the role of cities, particularly as the nodes that structure the networks of communication and commodity flows and the distribution of population, has attracted scholars from many fields. A 1954 symposium on the subject (75) stimulated a good deal of subsequent research. Geographers have been concerned with the problem of city location and urban functions chiefly within the framework of central place theory. (50–52). Economists and regional scientists have attempted to reinterpret statistics on urban growth and structure using concepts derived from statistical systems theory (Vining, 63, 64 and Berry, 57, 58). Geographers and some sociologists have studied the effects of distance from urban centers on the distribution and interaction of activities. Much of the relevant literature on this subject has been critically evaluated by Otis Duncan and associates (69). The name of Bert Hoselitz (80) is associated with the renewed interest in the relation of urban sociology and economic development. A number of studies inspired by his work have pointed to the critical importance of urbanization in the process of regional development (Friedmann, 76). The growing concentration of economic activities has been noted and fashioned into a major tool for analysis and explanation by François Perroux's concept of "growth pole" and "development axis" (88). Finally, a number of careful studies have been made by William Nicholls (94) and others of the influence of urbanization on agricultural productivity. In general, the distance to urban nodes was found to be a significant variable explaining differences in per capita rural productivity. This is one of the most significant discoveries in regional theory. It is substantiated on a larger scale by studies carried out by the United Nations Economic Commission for Europe (96).

A. Location and Function of Cities

50. Baskin, C. W., *A Critique and Translation of Water Christaller's Die Zentralen Orte in Süddeutschland,* Unpublished Ph.D. Thesis, University of Virginia, 1957. Abstracted in Brian J. L. Berry and Allen Pred, *Central Place Studies: A Bibliography of Theory and Applications,* Philadelphia, Regional Science Research Institute, 1961, pp. 15–18.

51. Berry, Brian J. L., and Willian L. Garrison, "The Functional Bases of the Central Place Hierarchy," in Harold M. Mayer and Clyde F. Kohn, eds., *Readings in Urban Geography,* Chicago, The University of Chicago Press, 1959, pp. 218–228.

52. Berry, Brian J. L., and William L. Garrison, "Recent Developments in Central Place Theory," *Papers and Proceedings of the Regional Science Association,* Vol. 4 (1958), pp. 107–121.

53. Berry, Brian J. L., and Allen Pred, *Central Place Studies: A Bibliography of Theory and Applications,* Philadelphia, Regional Science Research Institute, 1961.

54. Borchert, John, *The Urbanization of the Upper Midwest: 1930–1960,* University of Minnesota, Upper Midwest Economic Study, Urban Report No. 2, February 1963.

55. Norborg, Knut, ed., *Proceedings of the IGU Symposium in Urban Geography Lund 1960,* Lund Studies in Geography, Series B, Human Geography No. 24, The Royal University of Lund, Sweden, Department of Geography, 1962.

56. Philbrick, Allen K., "Principles of Areal Functional Organization in Regional Human Geography," *Economic Geography,* Vol. 33, No. 4 (October 1957), pp. 299–336.

B. Statistical Conceptions of Urban Systems

57. Beckmann, Martin, "City Hierarchies and the Distribution of City Size," *Economic Development and Cultural Change,* Vol. 6, No. 3 (April 1958), pp. 243–248.

*58. Berry, Brian J. L., "Cities as Systems Within Systems of Cities," *Papers of the Regional Science Association,* Vol. 10 (1964), forthcoming.

*59. Berry, Brian J. L., "City Size Distributions and Economic Development," *Economic Development and Cultural Change,* Vol. 9, No. 4 (July 1961), Part 1, pp. 573–587.

*60. Morrill, Richard L., "The Development of Spatial Distribution of Towns in Sweden: an Historical-Predictive Approach," *Annals of the Association of American Geographers,* Vol. 53, No. 1 (March 1963), pp. 1–14.

61. Stewart, Charles T., Jr., *The Size and Spacing of Cities,* in Harold M. Mayer and Clyde F. Kohn, eds., *Readings in Urban Geography,* Chicago, The University of Chicago Press, 1959, pp. 240–256.

62. Stewart, John Q., "Empirical Mathematical Rules Concerning the Distribution and Equilibrium of Population," *Geographical Review,* Vol. 37, No. 3 (July 1947), pp. 461–485.

63. Vining, Rutledge, "Delimitation of Economic Areas: Statistical Conceptions in the Study of the Spatial Structure of an American Economic System," *Journal of the American Statistical Association,* Vol. 48, No. 261 (March 1953), pp. 44–64.

64. Vining, Rutledge, "On Describing the Structure and Development of a Human Population System," *Journal of Farm Economics,* Vol. 41, No. 5 (December 1959), pp. 922–942.

C. Spatial Patterns of Urban Influence

65. Anderson, A. H., "Space as a Social Cost," *Journal of Farm Economics,* August 1950, pp. 411–430.

66. Borchert, John R., and Russell B. Adams, *Trade Centers and Trade Areas of the Upper Midwest,* University of Minnesota, Upper Midwest Economic Study, Urban Report No. 3, September 1963.

67. Carrothers, Gerald, A. P., "An Historical Review of the Gravity and Potential Concepts of Human Interaction," *Journal of the American Institute of Planners,* Vol. 22, No. 2 (Spring 1956), pp. 94–102.

68. Harris, Chauncey D., "The Market as a Factor in the Localization of Industry in the United States," *Annals of the Association of American Geographers,* Vol. 44, No. 3 (September 1954), pp. 315–348.

69. Duncan, Otis Dudley, W. Richard Scott, Stanley Lieberson,

Beverly Duncan, and Hal H. Winsborough, *Metropolis and Region,* Published for Resources for the Future, Inc., Baltimore, The Johns Hopkins Press, 1960.

70. Pitts, Forrest R., ed., *Urban Systems and Economic Development,* Papers and Proceedings of the Conference on Urban Systems Research in Underdeveloped and Advanced Economies, University of Oregon, School of Business Administration, 1962.

71. Pred, Allen, *The External Relations of Cities During Industrial Revolution,* The University of Chicago, Department of Geography, Research Paper No. 76, 1962.

*72. Thompson, John H., et al., "Toward a Geography of Economic Health: the Case of New York State," *Annals of the Association of American Geographers,* Vol. 52, No. 1 (March 1962), pp. 1–20.

73. Warntz, William, *Towards a Geography of Price,* Philadelphia, University of Pennsylvania Press, 1959.

D. Urbanization as a Social Process

74. Benet, Francisco, "Sociology Uncertain: the Ideology of the Rural-Urban Continuum," *Comparative Studies in Society and History,* Vol. 6, No. 1 (October 1963), pp. 1–23.

75. *Economic Development and Cultural Change,* Special Issues on the Role of Cities in Economic Development and Cultural Change, Vol. 3, No. 1 (October 1954), and Vol. 3, No. 2 (January 1955).

*76. Friedmann, John R. P., "Cities in Social Transformation," *Comparative Studies in Society and History,* Vol. 4, No. 1 (November 1961), pp. 86–103.

77. Harden, Warren R., "Social and Economic Effects of Community Size," *Rural Sociology,* Vol. 25 (June 1960), pp. 204–211.

78. Hauser, Philip M., ed., *Urbanization in Asia and the Far East,* Calcutta, UNESCO Research Center on the Social Implications of Industrialization in Southern Asia, 1957.

79. Hauser, Philip M., ed., *Urbanization in Latin America,* New York, International Documents Service, 1961.

80. Hoselitz, Bert F., *Sociological Aspects of Economic Growth,* Glencoe, Illinois, The Free Press of Glencoe, Inc., 1960, Chapter 7: "The Role of Cities in the Economic Development of Underdeveloped Countries"; Chapter 8: "Generative and Parasitic Cities"; and Chapter 9: "Urbanization and Economic Growth in Asia."

*81. Lampard, Eric E., "The History of Cities in Economically Advanced Areas," *Economic Development and Cultural Change,* Vol. 3, No. 2 (January 1955), pp. 81–136.

*82. Morse, Richard M., "Latin American Cities: Aspects of Function and Structure," *Comparative Studies in Society and History,* Vol. 4, No. 4 (July 1962), pp. 473–493.

83. Sovani, N. V., "The Analysis of Over-Urbanization," *Economic Development and Cultural Change,* Vol. 12, No. 2 (January 1964), pp. 113–122.

84. Sjoberg, Gideon, *The Preindustrial City, Past and Present,* Glencoe, Illinois, The Free Press of Glencoe, Inc., 1960.

*85. Tangri, Shanti, "Urbanization, Political Stability, and Economic Growth," in Roy Turner, ed., *India's Urban Future,* Berkeley, University of California Press, 1962, pp. 192–212.

86. Turner, Roy M., ed., *India's Urban Future,* Berkeley, University of California Press, 1962.

E. Growth Poles and Related Concepts

87. Baillargeon, Jean-Paul, "Le Rôle des Pôles dans le Développement: Exposé introductif," *Développement et Civilisations,* No. 5 (January–March 1961), pp. 31–37.

88. Perroux, François, *L'économie du XXe siécle,* Paris, Presses Universitaires de France, 1961, Part II, "Les Pôles de croissance."

89. Perroux, François, "Une distinction utile à la politique des pays à croissance retardée: Points de développement et foyers de progrès," *Cahiers de l'Institute de Science Économique Appliquée,* Série F, No. 12 (November 1959), pp. 3–41.

90. Pottier, P., "Axes de communication et développement économique," *Revue Économique,* Vol. 14, No. 1 (January 1963), pp. 58–132.

*91. Ullman, Edward L., "Regional Development and the Geography of Concentration," *Papers and Proceedings of the Regional Science Association,* Vol. 4 (1958), pp. 179–198.

F. Agricultural Adjustments to Urbanization

92. Fox, Karl A., "The Study of Interactions Between Agriculture and the Non-Farm Economy: Local, Regional and National," *Journal of Farm Economics,* Vol. 44, No. 1 (February 1962), pp. 1–34.

93. Morgan, Theodore, "The Long-Run Terms of Trade Between

Agriculture and Manufacturing," *Economic Development and Cultural Change,* Vol. 8, No. 1 (October 1959), pp. 1–23.

*94. Nicholls, William B., "Industrialization, Factor Markets, and Agricultural Development," *Journal of Political Economy,* Vol. 69, No. 4 (August 1961), pp. 319–340.

95. Ruttan, Vernon W., "The Impact of Urban-Industrial Development on Agriculture in the Tennessee Valley and the Southeast," *Journal of Farm Economics,* Vol. 37, No. 1 (February 1955), pp. 38–56.

*96. United Nations, Economic Commission for Europe, *Economic Survey of Europe, 1954,* Geneva, 1955, Chapter 6: "Problems of Regional Development and Industrial Location in Europe."

V. REGIONAL ECONOMIC DEVELOPMENT

The economics of development has generally skirted regional issues. Nevertheless, there has been a recent flurry of interest in the subject. Possibly the best single study to date has been that of Harvey S. Perloff and his associates (102), a study not only rich in empirical detail but also full of insight into basic processes of regional economic change. As sources of explanation for the facts of diverging regional growth patterns, natural resource advantages, interregional trade patterns, and internal migration have received close attention, and special sections are devoted below to these topics. Economists have also devoted some attention to rational decision rules for the spatial allocation of investment. This discussion has been mainly focused on the apparent dilemmas between "growth" and "welfare," "concentration" and "dispersion." Major theoretical contributions have been made here by Albert O. Hirschman (126) and Gunnar Myrdal (100). Finally, a number of rigorous case studies of regional development are now available. Among the best of these are the books by George W. Rogers (151 and 152) on Alaska, Bowman and Haynes (132) on East Kentucky, Hollis B. Chenery on Italy's Mezzogiorno (135), and Stefan Robock (149) on Brazil's Northeastern Region.

A. General

97. Balassa, Bela, *The Theory of Economic Integration,* Homewood, Ill., Richard D. Irwin, Inc., 1961, Chapter 9: "Regional Problems in a Common Market."

98. Broude, Henry W., "The Significance of Regional Studies for

the Elaboration of National Economic History," *The Journal of Economic History,* Vol. 20 (December 1960), pp. 588–596.

99. Juillard, E., "L'aménagement régional," in *Colloque National de Géographic Appliquée,* Strasbourg, April 20–22, 1961. Paris, 1962, pp. 118–125.

100. Myrdal, Gunnar, *Rich Lands and Poor: The Road to World Prosperity,* New York, Harper and Brothers, Publishers, Inc., 1957, Chapter 3: "The Drift Toward Regional Economic Inequalities in a Country."

101. Perloff, Harvey S., and Vera W. Dodds, *How a Region Grows: Area Development in the U. S. Economy,* New York, Committee for Economic Development, Supplementary Paper No. 17, 1963.

102. Perloff, Harvey S., Edgar S. Dunn, Jr., Eric E. Lampard, and Richard F. Muth, *Regions, Resources, and Economic Growth,* Published for Resources for the Future, Inc., Baltimore, The Johns Hopkins Press, 1960.

B. Resource Immobilities and External Relations

103. Andrews, R. B., "Mechanics of the Urban Economic Base: Historical Development of the Base Concept," *Land Economics,* Vol. 29, (May 1953), pp. 161–167 and subsequent issues to February 1956.

*104. Baldwin, Robert E., "Development Patterns in Newly Settled Areas," *Manchester School of Economics and Social Studies,* Vol. 24, No. 2 (May 1956), pp. 161–179.

105. Friedmann, John R. P., "Locational Aspects of Economic Development," *Land Economics,* Vol. 32, No. 3 (August 1956), pp. 213–227.

106. Keirstead, B. S., *The Theory of Economic Change,* Toronto, Macmillan of Canada, Ltd., 1948, Part V.

107. North, Douglass C., *"Agriculture in Regional Economic* Growth," *Journal of Farm Economics,* Vol. 41, No. 5 (December 1959), pp. 943–954.

*108. North, Douglass C., "Location Theory and Regional Economic Growth," *Journal of Political Economy,* Vol. 63, No. 3 (June 1955), pp. 243–258; also comments and reply, *Journal of Political Economy,* Vol. 64, No. 2 (April 1956), pp. 160–169.

109. North, Douglass C., "The Spatial and Interregional Framework of the United States Economy: an Historical Perspective,"

Papers and Proceedings of the Regional Science Association, Vol. 2 (1956), pp. 201–209.

*110. Perloff, Harvey S., and Lowdon Wingo, Jr., "Natural Resource Endowment and Regional Economic Growth," in Joseph J. Spengler, ed., *Natural Resources and Economic Growth,* Washington, D. C., Resources for the Future, Inc., 1961, pp. 191–212.

111. Robinson, E. A. G., ed., *Economic Consequences of the Size of Nations,* New York, St. Martin's Press, 1960.

112. Spengler, Joseph J., ed., *Natural Resources and Economic Growth,* Washington, D. C.: Resources for the Future, Inc., 1961.

C. INTERNAL MIGRATION

113. Bachmura, Frank T., "Man-Land Equalization Through Migration," *American Economic Review,* Vol. 49, No. 5 (December 1959), pp. 1004–1017.

114. Borts, George H., "The Equalization of Returns and Regional Economic Growth," *American Economic Review,* Vol. 50, No. 3 (June 1960), pp. 319–347.

*115. Hathaway, Dale E., "Migration from Agriculture: the Historical Record and its Meaning," *Papers and Proceedings, American Economic Review,* Vol. 49, No. 2 (May 1960), pp. 379–396.

116. Kuznets, Simon, and Dorothy S. Thomas, "Internal Migration and Economic Growth," in Milbank Memorial Fund, *Selected Studies of Migration Since World War II,* New York, 1958, pp. 196–211.

*117. Okun, Bernard, and Richard W. Richardson, "Regional Income Inequality and Internal Migration," *Economic Development and Cultural Change,* Vol. 9, No. 2 (January 1961), pp. 128–143.

118. Stouffer, Samuel A., "Intervening Opportunities: A Theory Relating to Mobility and Distance," *American Sociological Review,* Vol. 5, No. 6 (December 1940), pp. 845–867.

D. INVESTMENT CRITERIA

119. Chenery, Hollis B., "Comparative Advantage and Development Policy," *American Economic Review,* Vol. 51, No. 1 (March 1961), pp. 18–51.

*120. Lefeber, Louis, *Regional Allocation of Resources in India,* Massachusetts Institute of Technology, Center for International Studies, Mimeographed, December 1961.

*121. Leven, Charles, "Establishing Goals for Regional Economic Development," *Journal of the American Institute of Planners,* Vol. 30, No. 2 (May 1964), pp. 100–110.

122. Rahman, Md. Anisur, "Regional Allocation of Investment," *Quarterly Journal of Economics,* Vol. 77, No. 1 (February 1963), pp. 26–39.

123. Reiner, Thomas, "Regional Investment Allocation Criteria," *Cuardernos de la Sociedad Venezolana de Plantificación,* Special Issue, September 1963, pp. 179–214.

124. Scitovsky, Tibor, "Growth—Balanced or Unbalanced," in M. Abramovitz, ed., *Allocation of Economic Resources,* Stanford, California, Stanford University Press, 1959, pp. 207–217.

125. Wiles, Peter J. D., *The Political Economy of Communism,* Cambridge, Massachusetts, Harvard University Press, 1962, Chapter 8: "Spatial Rationality and the Territorial Principle."

E. Investment Strategies

*126. Hirschman, Albert O., *The Strategy of Economic Development,* New Haven, Connecticut, Yale University Press, 1958, Chapter 10: "Interregional and International Transmission of Growth."

*127. Rodwin, Lloyd, "Choosing Regions for Development," in Carl J. Friedrich and Seymour E. Harris, eds., *Public Policy,* A Yearbook of the Harvard University Graduate School of Public Administration, Vol. 12 (1963), pp. 141–162.

128. Rodwin, Lloyd, "Metropolitan Policy for Developing Areas," *Daedalus,* (Winter 1961), pp. 132–146.

129. Streeten, Paul, *Economic Integration,* Leyden, A. W. Sythoff, 1961, pp. 53–67.

130. Tinbergen, Jan, *Regional-Economische Planning,* University of Gent, January 26, 1961.

F. Case Studies

131. Bourguinat, Henri, *Espace économique Européene,* Paris, Société d'Edition d'Enseignment Supérieur, 1962.

132. Bowman, Mary Jean, and W. Warren Haynes, *Resources and People in East Kentucky,* Published for Resources for the Future, Inc., Baltimore, The Johns Hopkins Press, 1963.

133. Caudill, Harry M., *Night Comes to the Cumberland,* Boston, Little Brown and Co., 1962.

134. Chapin, F. Stuart, Jr., and Shirley F. Weiss, eds., *Urban*

Growth Dynamics in a Regional Cluster of Cities, New York, John Wiley & Sons, Inc., 1962.

*135. Chenery, Hollis B., "Development Policies for Southern Italy," *Quarterly Journal of Economics,* Vol. 76, No. 4 (November 1962), pp. 515–548.

136. *Entwicklungsprogramm Mühlviertel, Vorschläge für den Wirtschaftsausbau,* Wien: Institute für Raumplanung, 1961.

137. Ford, Thomas R., ed., *The Southern Appalachian Region: A Survey,* Lexington, University of Kentucky Press, 1962.

138. Friedmann, John, *Regional Policy for Developing Areas: A Case Study of Venezuela,* Cambridge, Massachusetts, M.I.T.-Harvard Joint Center for Urban Studies, 1963, mimeographed.

139. Friedmann, John, *The Spatial Structure of Economic Development in the Tennessee Valley,* The University of Chicago, Program of Education and Research in Planning, Research Paper No. 1; and Department of Geography, Research Paper No. 39, March 1955.

140. Hirschman, Albert O., *Journeys Toward Progress: Studies of Economic Policy-Making in Latin America,* New York, The Twentieth Century Fund, 1963, Chapter 1: "Brazil's Northeast."

141. Holzman, F. D., "The Soviet Ural-Kuznetsk Combine: A Study of Investment Criteria and Industrialization Policies," *Quarterly Journal of Economics,* Vol. 71, No. 3 (August 1957), pp. 368–405.

142. Lasuen, José Raymon, "Regional Income Inequalities and the Problems of Regional Growth in Spain," *Papers of the Regional Science Association,* Vol. 8 (1962), pp. 169–188.

143. Martin, Roscoe C., ed., *TVA: The First Twenty Years: A Staff Report,* Knoxville, University of Tennessee Press, 1956.

144. Nicholls, William H., *Southern Tradition and Regional Progress,* Chapel Hill, University of North Carolina Press, 1960.

*145. Nicholls, William H., "Southern Tradition and Regional Economic Progress," *Southern Economic Journal,* Vol. 26, No. 3 (January 1960), pp. 187–198.

*146. Pfister, Richard L., "External Trade and Regional Growth, A Case Study of the Pacific Northwest," *Economic Development and Cultural Change,* Vol. 11, No. 2 (January 1963), Part I, pp. 134–151.

147. *Regional Development in the European Economic Community, London: Political and Economic Planning, London,* George Allen and Unwin, 1962.

148. "Regional Planning," Seminar on Regional Planning, Tokyo, July 28 to August 8, 1958, Special Issue of *Housing, Building and Planning,* Nos. 12 and 13 (1959).
149. Robock, Stefan H., *Northeast Brazil: A Developing Economy,* Washington, D. C., The Brookings Institute, 1963.
150. Rodwin, Lloyd, *The British New Towns Policy,* Cambridge, Massachusetts, Harvard University Press, 1956.
151. Rogers, George W., *Alaska in Transition: The Southeast Region,* Published for Resources for the Future, Inc., Baltimore, The Johns Hopkins Press, 1960.
152. Romus, Paul, *Expansion économique régionale et Comunauté Européene,* Leyden, A. W. Sythoff, 1958.
153. Stevens, Rayfred L., and Paulo R. Brandão, "Diversification of the Economy of the Cacao Coast of Bahia, Brazil," *Economic Geography,* Vol. 37, No. 3 (July 1961), pp. 231–253.
154. Tang, Anthony M., *Economic Development in the Southern Piedmont, 1860–1950: Its Impact on Agriculture,* Chapel Hill, University of North Carolina Press, 1960.
155. United Nations, Department of Economic and Social Affairs, *Economic Survey of Europe for 1953,* Geneva, Economic Commission for Europe, 1954.
156. Ward, Benjamin, *Problems of Greek Regional Development,* Research Monograph Series, No. 4, Athens, Center of Economic Research, n.d.

VI. ORGANIZATION FOR REGIONAL PLANNING AND DEVELOPMENT

Practical problems of regional planning include the definition and delimitation in space of suitable planning regions and organizational arrangements providing for coordination of public programs for area development. The first of these problems has been intensively debated by geographers. There are those, especially Russian geographers such as P. Alampiev (157), who believe in the physical reality of regions and who consequently regard regional boundaries as relatively fixed and stable. Others, like K. Dziewonski (159), recognize that regions undergo historical change and admit to a regional concept that includes the dimension of time in its definition. Still others, such as Norton Ginsburg (162), regard planning regions from an essentially pragmatic viewpoint; according to them, the definition of the region is largely a matter of convenience in serving the public purpose. Part of this discussion is also the question of whether river basins, city regions, or regions defined by industrial complexes should serve as the basic units for the administration of development programs. One of the best general discussions of the regional concept, although without reference to planning, will be found in Derwent Whittlesey's comprehensive review of the literature (169).

The second, organizational, problem has many ramifications, only some of which have been studied. Cultural regionalism as a political force is discussed in a series of excellent essays in the volume edited by Merrill Jensen (176). Problems in relating regional to national planning are treated from various viewpoints and historical contexts, as in the volume on French planning by the Hacketts (174) and in Charles McKinley's perceptive piece on the Valley Authority as an administrative device (178). Theoretical studies are still a rarity on the subject of the areal organization of planning and administration. In addition to the items reprinted in this volume, the work of Philip Selznick (182) deserves to be mentioned.

A. Concept and Definition of Region

157. Alampiyev, P., "The Objective Basis of Economic Regionalization and Its Long-Range Prospects," *Soviet Geography,* Vol. 2 (October 1961), pp. 64–74.

158. Berry, Brian J. L., Review of Donald J. Bogue and Calvin L. Beale, *Economic Areas of the United States,* in *Journal of the American Institute of Planners,* Vol. 28 (August 1962), pp. 198–200.

159. Dziewonski, Kazimierz, "Theoretical Problems in the Development of Economic Regions," *Papers of the Regional Science Association,* Vol. 8 (1962), pp. 43–54.

160. Fisher, Joseph L., "Concepts in Regional Economic Development Programs," *Papers and Proceedings of the Regional Science Association,* Vol. 1 (1955), pp. W1–W20.

*161. Friedmann, John, *The Concept of a Planning Region: The Evolution of an Idea in the United States,* United Nations Working Paper No. 12, June 25, 1958.

162. Ginsburg, Norton S., "The Regional Concept and Planning Regions," in *Housing, Building, and Planning,* Nos. 12 and 13, Special issue on Regional Planning (1959), pp. 31–44.

163. Isard, Walter, "Regional Science, the Concept of Region, and Regional Structure," *Papers and Proceedings of the Regional Science Association,* Vol. 2 (1956), pp. 13–26.

164. Juillard, E., "La Région: Essai de Définition," *Annales de Géographie,* Vol. 71, No. 387 (September–October 1962), pp. 483–499.

165. Knetsch, Jack L., and William J. Hart, "The Watershed as an Entity in Development Planning," *Journal of Farm Economics,* Vol. 43, No. 4, Part I (1961), pp. 749–760.

166. Kolosovskiy, N. N., "The Territorial Production Combination (Complex) in Soviet Economic Geography," *Journal of Regional Science,* Vol. 3 (Summer 1961), pp. 1–26.

167. Saushkin, Julian G., "Large Areal Complexes of Productive Forces of the Soviet Union," *Papers of the Regional Science Association,* Vol. 8 (1962), pp. 93–104 (European Congress, The Hague, 1961).

168. Saushkin, Julian G., "On the Objective and Subjective Character of Economic Regionalization," *Soviet Geography,* Vol. 2 (June 1960), pp. 75–81.

169. Whittlesey, Derwent, "The Regional Concept and the Regional Method," in Preston James and Clarence F. Jones, eds., *American Geography: Inventory and Prospect,* Published for the Association of American Geographers, Syracuse, New York, Syracuse University Press, 1954.

B. POLITICAL AND ADMINISTRATIVE CONSIDERATIONS

170. Abrams, Charles, "Regional Planning Legislation in Underdeveloped Areas," *Land Economics,* Vol. 35, No. 2 (May 1954), pp. 85–103.

171. *Die Raumordnung in der Bundesrepublik Deutschland,* Gutachten des Sachverständigenausschusses für Raumordnung, Stuttgart, Kohlhammer, 1961.

172. Finer, Herman, *The TVA: Lessons for International Application,* Montreal, International Labor Office, 1944.

173. Fox, Irving K., and Lyle E. Craine, "Organizational Arrangements for Water Development," *Natural Resources Journal,* Vol. 2 (1962), pp. 1–44.

174. Hackett, John, and Anne-Marie Hackett, *Economic Planning in France,* Cambridge, Massachusetts, Harvard University Press, 1963.

175. Hare, F. Kenneth, "Regionalism and Administration: North American Experiments," *Canadian Journal of Economy and Political Science,* Vol. 13 (November 1947), pp. 563–571.

176. Jensen, Merrill, ed., *Regionalism in America,* Madison, Wisconsin, University of Wisconsin Press, 1951.
177. Maass, Arthur, ed., *Area and Power: A Theory of Local Government,* Glencoe, Illinois, The Free Press of Glencoe, Inc., 1959.
*178. McKinley, Charles, "The Valley Authority and Its Alternatives," *American Political Science Review,* Vol. 44, No. 3 (September 1950), pp. 607–630.
179. McKinley, Charles, *Uncle Sam in the Pacific Northwest,* Berkeley, University of California Press, 1952.
180. Martin, Roscoe C., ed., *River Basin Administration and the Delaware,* Syracuse, New York: University of Syracuse Press, 1960.
*181. Ostrom, Vincent, Charles Tiebout, and Robert Warren, "The Organization of Government in Metropolitan Government: a Theoretical Inquiry," *American Political Science Review,* Vol. 55, No. 4 (December 1961), pp. 831–842.
182. Selznick, Philip, *TVA and the Grass Roots,* Berkeley, University of California Press, 1949.
183. Touretski, C., "Regional Planning of the National Economy in the U.S.S.R. and Its Bearings on Regionalism," *International Social Science Journal,* Vol. 11 (1959), pp. 380–392.
*184. Ylvisaker, Paul, "Some Criteria for 'Proper' Areal Division of Governmental Powers," in Arthur Maass, ed., *Area and Power: A Theory of Local Government,* Glencoe, Illinois, The Free Press of Glencoe, Inc., 1959, pp. 27–49.

VII. JOURNALS

Certain academic journals are especially useful to students of regional development and planning. The great majority of articles germane to the subject will be found in them.

A. North American

Journal of Regional Science
Papers and Proceedings of the Regional Science Association
American Economic Review
Quarterly Journal of Economics
Journal of Farm Economics
Southern Economic Journal

Economic Development and Cultural Change
Natural Resources Journal
Annals of the Association of American Geographers
Economic Geography
Geographical Review
Land Economics
Journal of the American Institute of Planners
American Journal of Sociology
American Sociological Review
Traffic Quarterly

B. West European

Raumforschung und Raumordnung (Hannover)
Berichte zur Landesforschung und Landesplanung (Wien)
Mitteilungen des Institutes für Raumplanung (Wien)
Économie Appliquée (Paris)
Problèmes Économiques (Paris)
Lund Studies in Geography, Series B, Human Geography
Urbanistica (Turin)
Urbanisme (Paris)
Schweizerische Zeitschrift für Volkswirtschaft und Statistik

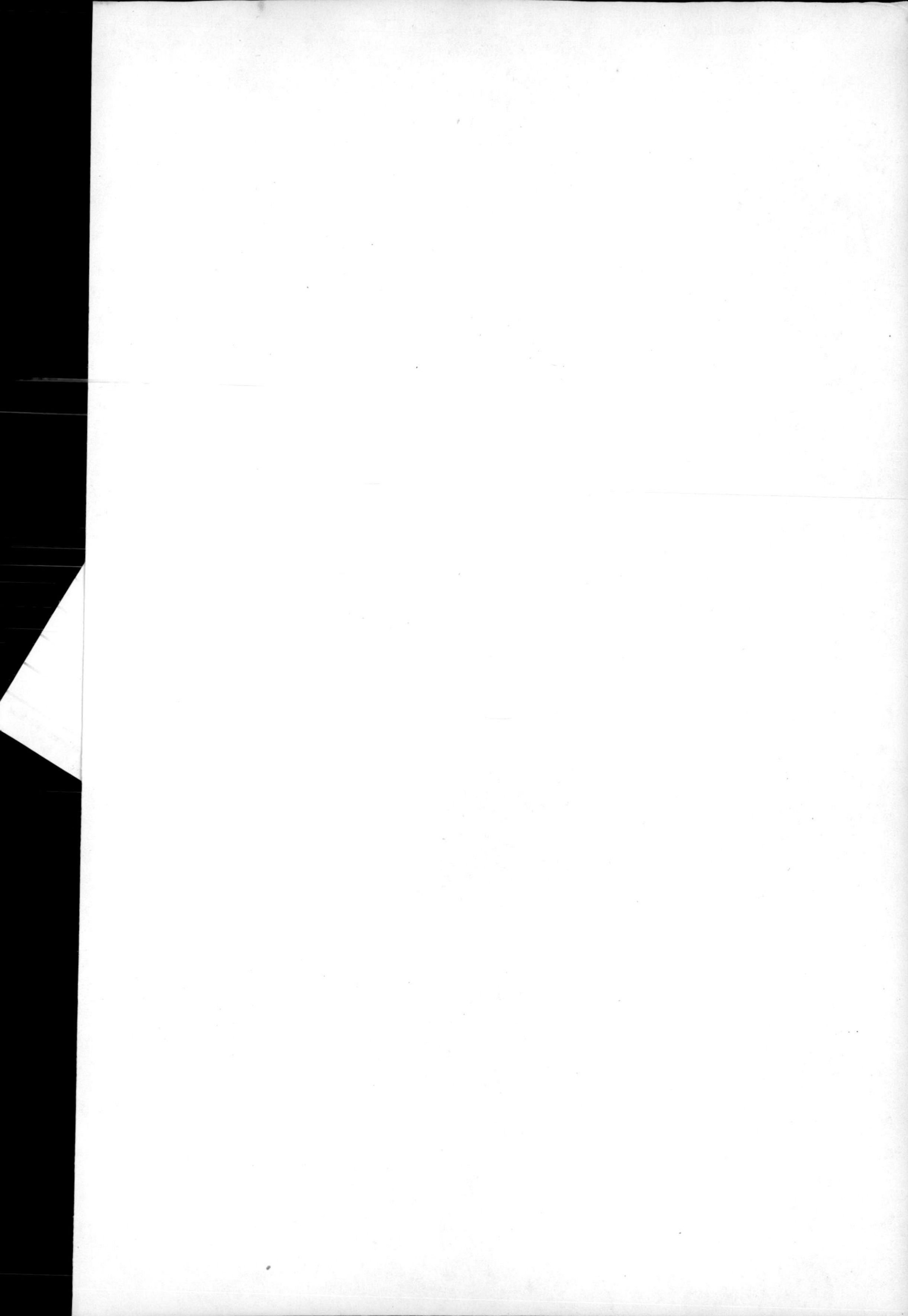